$12.00

THE
ATLAS OF
CANADA
AND THE
WORLD

ACKNOWLEDGEMENTS

· ·

Text by Norman Hillmer
Designed by Philip D Clucas, MSIAD
Edited by Joseph F Ryan

Author's Acknowledgements

I am grateful to my close friend, Professor Robert Bothwell of the University of Toronto, for his indispensable assistance with this project.

Nothing that I do, or could be done in this field, can escape the influence of James H Marsh and his monumental *Canadian Encyclopedia,* which is available in a CD-ROM version revised and updated yearly under the imprint of McClelland and Stewart Publishers of Toronto, Ontario.

Statistics Canada publishes the *Canada Year Book,* which has had as long a life as Canada itself. The 1999 edition was particularly helpful in preparing this atlas. I also profited from the *Historical Atlas of Canada* (3 volumes; University of Toronto Press, 1987-1993), *The National Atlas of Canada* (Macmillan, 1974), *A Dictionary of Canadianisms on Historical Principles* (Gage, 1967) and *Colombo's Canadian Quotations* (Hurtig, 1974), all works of considerable scholarship.

Dr Joseph Ryan was the resourceful editor and coordinator of the atlas, and I am happy to report that a friendship of long standing appears to have survived the ordeal unimpaired.

I thank the University of Toronto Press for the two short quotations from their books. The material from *The Arctic Traveller* appears with the permission of Nunavut Tourism.

My wife, Anne Hillmer, was as always a supporter and adviser on all fronts. The atlas is dedicated to her father, Frederick William Trowell of Saltcoats, Saskatchewan and Ottawa, Ontario, 1912-1998, and to my father, George Powell Hillmer of Southampton, Ontario and Toronto, Ontario, 1906-1998.

Photographic Credits

The majority of photographic illustrations in this book are courtesy of Whitecap Books (picture location in brackets): page 4 Michael E Burch (R, FR); 5 Brian Milne/First Light (FL); 20 Michael E Burch (A); 21 Michael E Burch (BL, A), John Sylvester/First Light (B); 22 Michael E Burch (AR); 23 (TR), Michael E Burch (AL); 24 (AR); 25 (L, A); 28 (A); 29 (A), Michael E Burch (BL, B); 30 Jürgen Vogt (A), Michael E Burch (R, BR); 31 Michael E Burch (B, BR); 32 Jürgen Vogt (A, R); 33 Jürgen Vogt (FL, L, A); 34 Jürgen Vogt (A, AR); 35 Irwin Barrett/First Light (BL), Jürgen Vogt (L, B); 36 John Sylvester/First Light (A), Jürgen Vogt (AR); 37 Irwin Barrett/First Light (B), John Sylvester/First Light (A), Jürgen Vogt (L); 38 Jürgen Vogt (A); 39 Jürgen Vogt (L), Darwin Wiggett/First Light (B); 40 Jürgen Vogt (A); 41 Michael E Burch (TR), John Sylvester/First Light (AL), Jürgen Vogt (TL, A); 42 Ron Watts/First Light (A); and 44 Robert Lankinen/First Light (TR). Thanks are also due to the following for their kind permission to reproduce the remaining photographs in this atlas: Digital Vision pages 1 and 6; and the Visit Canada Centre of the Canadian Tourism Commission, London, pages 3 Tourism Vancouver; 5 (A, AR), Lyn Hancock (L); 21 Alberta Economic Development & Tourism (L); 22 Alan Zenuk (A); 23 (A); 24 (A); 25 (B); 26 (A, R); 27 (A), Drie/Meir (L), Jim Merrithew (BL); 29 (L); 38 Camera Art (T), John Sylvester (AR); 39 John Sylvester (FL); 42 (T); 43 (A), Dan Heringa (BL), David McNicoll (TL); and 44 (A, AR).

5150 Atlas of Canada and the World
Published in 1999 by Whitecap Books
Copyright © 1999 Quadrillion Publishing Ltd
Godalming, Surrey, GU7 1XW, UK
ISBN 1-55110-901-8
Printed in Spain

Canadian Cataloguing in Publication Data
Main entry under title:
The atlas of Canada and the world

Includes index.
ISBN 1-55110-901-8

1. Atlases, Canadian. 2. Canada—Maps. I. Hillmer, Norman, 1942-
II. Ryan, Joseph F.
G1021.A832 1999   912   C99-910716-X

THE
ATLAS OF
CANADA
AND THE
WORLD

WHITECAP BOOKS
VANCOUVER/TORONTO/NEW YORK

CONTENTS

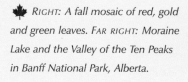

RIGHT: A fall mosaic of red, gold and green leaves. FAR RIGHT: Moraine Lake and the Valley of the Ten Peaks in Banff National Park, Alberta.

FAR LEFT: The Dempster Highway, Yukon Territory. LEFT: Hiking at Auyuittuq, Baffin Island, Nunavut. ABOVE: Taking a well-earned break in Saskatchewan.

ABOVE RIGHT: Fishing against the magnificent backdrop of British Columbia's rugged mountains.

🍁 *ABOVE: Satellite image of part of the Northwest Territories, showing Buffalo Lake. This lies to the south of the massive Great Slave Lake, which is the fifth largest in North America.*

INTRODUCTION

The country's longest serving prime minister once wondered aloud whether Canada had too much geography. Its 10,000,000 square kilometre rectangle, bigger than Europe, extends from the Pacific Ocean to the Atlantic west to east, and from the polar icecap in the north all the way to the 42nd parallel of latitude, near Detroit, Michigan. "Who can know our loneliness, on the immensity of prairie, in the dark forest and on the windy sea rock?", the celebrated journalist Bruce Hutchinson wrote in 1942, "All about us lies Canada, forever untouched, unknown, beyond our grasp". The national anthem trumpets the "true north strong and free" and Canadians cling to their self-portrait as, in Rudyard Kipling's phrase, the "young, fair and stalwart maiden of the north", but few of them travel very far beyond the cities and towns of the extreme south. In a line running from Quebec City to Montreal, Toronto and Windsor, and then around the Great Lakes to Sault Ste Marie not halfway west across Ontario, 60 per cent of the population is concentrated on a little over two per cent of the landmass of Canada.

Vastness contributes to fragility. National unity is always precarious, and a national consciousness elusive. Canada is all too easily divisible into regions, with their persistent loyalties; Quebec is not the only area of Canada which insists upon its distinctiveness. With its great expanses of permafrost, boreal forests and mountains, and the hard ancient Canadian Shield rock that dominates the central core, much of the country is uninhabitable, or uninhabited. Ecosystems in the colder northern tracts are tenuous at best and vulnerable to even slight environmental changes, putting subsistence livelihoods at risk.

Economic impulses track from north to south, rather than east to west. Development and commerce on a pan-Canadian scale are difficult and expensive, and made more so by natural and interprovincial barriers. Most Canadians, almost 90 per cent of them, live within a short drive of the United States. They admire what Hutchinson called "the raging energy of America", but are particularly exposed to its cultural, political and economic influences. As one historian put it, "Canada has been called 'America's problem', but the United States has many problems which loom as large or larger; for Canada the United States is *the* problem". Few would question today that Canada's orientation is primarily to America, or that its destiny lies with the continent and the western hemisphere. Canada's long British and European history is largely forgotten, as is the traditional search for alternatives to the power of the United States. Independence was a long time coming. In the era of free trade and American dominance, it will be more difficult to keep.

EAST SIBERIAN
SEA

ARCTIC OCEAN

CHUKCHI
SEA

International Date Line

BEAUFORT SEA

4100m

2300m

Point Barrow
Barrow
Wainwright

Banks Island

Sachs Harbour

Victoria Islan

Mys
Shelagskiy
Pevek

Wrangel Island

Arctic Circle

Toygunen

Cape Lisburne

55m

Prince Pat

Prudhoe Bay

Chukot
Peninsula

Point Hope

20m

Colville

Cape
Bathurst

Aklavik

Inuvik

Tuktoyaktuk

Amundsen Gulf

550m

Holman

Umingmaktok

Uelen
Shishmaret

Noatak

Kotzebue

Selawik
Shungnak

BROOKS RANGE

Arctic Village

Old Crow

Fort McPherson

NORTHWEST
TERRITORIES

Kugluktuk

Coronation
Gulf

Cambridge
Bay

Gulf of
Anadyr
Providen* iya

80m

Cape
Prince of Wales

Bering Strait

Seward
Peninsula

ALASKA

Allakaket

Yukon

Porcupine

Fort Yukon

Fort Good Hope

Norman Wells

Déline

Great Bear
Lake

Echo Bay

Bathurst
Inlet

Gambell

St. Lawrence
Island

40m

Nome

Norton
Sound

Unalakleet
St. Michael

(USA)

Tanana

Nenana
Fairbanks

Circle

Dawson

YUKON

Mackenzie Mountains

Rae

Reliance

Nunivak
Island

60m

Hooper Bay

Holy Cross

Yukon

Delta Junction

Klondike

TERRITORY

Carmacks

Wrigley

Lac la
Marte

Yellowknife

The Ion

Bethel

20m

Dillingham

Kuskokwim

ALASKA RANGE

Willow

Mt Foraker
5304m

Mt McKinley
6194m

Talkeetna

Gulkana

Chitina

Snag

Yukon

Ross River

Liard

Great
Slave
Lake

Mackenzie

Back

Nakhek

Anchorage
Palmer

Mt Bona
5005m

Mt Lucania
5226m

Whitehorse

Teslin

Fort Providence

Hay River

Slave

Fort Smith

CANADA

65m

Bristol
Bay

Kenai
Peninsula

Valdez

Seward

Homer

Mt Logan
5951m

Haines
Junction

Haines

Watson Lake

Fort Nelson

Fort
Chipewyan

Uranium City

Lake
Athabasca

Churchill

95m

Afognak

Kodiak

Kodiak

GULF OF
ALASKA

3300m

Skagway

Coast Mountains

Telegraph Creek

Dawson
Creek

Peace

Mount St. Elias
5489m

Juneau

Peace River

Athabasca

McMurray

Reindeer
Lake

Sherridon

Lynn Lake

Nelson

Alaska Peninsula

Chignik

250m

Trinity Islands 2200m

3800m

Hoonah

Chichagof
Island

ALBERTA

Fort

Unimak

165m

6700m

4700m

Alexander
Archipelago

Sitka
Petersburg

Wrangell

BRITISH

Hazelton

Prince
George

Grande Prairie

Athabasca

Edmonton

Red
Deer

North
Battleford

Prince Albert

SASKATCHEWAN

MANITOBA

The Pas

Norway House

Pickle
Lake

Red Lake

1005m

Klawock

Ketchikan

COLUMBIA

Quesnel

Mt Robson
3954m

Leduc

Saskatoon

Lake
Winnipegosis

Prince of Wales
Island

Graham Island
900m

Prince
Rupert

Kitimat

Bella
Coola

Fraser

Calgary

South Saskatchewan

Regina

Lake
Manitoba

Lake
Winnipeg

Selkirk

Kenora

Sioux
Lookout

3716m

Queen
Charlotte
Islands

Moresby
Island

3300m

Queen
Charlotte
Sound

Columbia Mountains

Kamloops

Banff

Lethbridge

Medicine Hat

Moose Jaw

Brandon

Winnipeg

Lake of the
Woods

Thunder

3826m

Vancouver Island

Courtenay

Squamish

Nelson

ROCKY MOUNTAINS

International
Falls

45m

5257m

Nanaimo

Vancouver

Victoria

Cape Flattery

Bellingham

Everett

WASHINGTON

Coeur d'Alene

Glasgow

Williston

Minot

Grand
Forks

Fargo

Duluth

Superior

Seattle

Olympia

Tacoma

Spokane

Missoula

Great Falls

Fort Peck
Lake

Missouri

NORTH
DAKOTA

MINNESOTA

Eau Cla

St. Cloud

St. Paul

Mt Rainier
4392m

Yakima

Helena

MONTANA

Bismarck

WISCONS

2700m

Portland

Oregon City
Pendleton

Columbia

Walla Walla

Butte

Billings

Miles City

SOUTH
DAKOTA

Aberdeen

Madison

PACIFIC

3000m

Salem

Bend

Snake

IDAHO

Idaho Falls

Sheridan

Rapid
City

Pierre

Sioux Falls

Rochester

Minneapolis

Milwaukee

Chicago

OCEAN

Coos Bay

OREGON

Boise

WYOMING

North
Platte

Sioux City

Des
Moines

ILLINOIS

Roseburg

Klamath
Falls

Great Salt
Lake

Ogden

Rock
Springs

Cheyenne

IOWA

Eureka

Redding

Elko

Salt Lake
City

Provo

Grand
Island

Lincoln

Omaha

NEBRASKA

St.
Joseph

Peoria

Indianapo

Cape Mendocino

CALIFORNIA

UNITED STATES

Colorado

Grand
Junction

Denver

Rawlins

Rock

Topeka

Kansas City

KANSAS

Jefferson City

St. Louis

Sacramento

Carson City

NEVADA

Cedar
City

UTAH

Colorado Springs

COLORADO

Pueblo

Springfield

MISSOURI

Louisville

San Francisco

Oakland

Mt Whitney
4418m

Las
Vegas

Sierra Nevada

Arkansas

Dodge City

Wichita

Springfield

Indi

San Jose

Monterey

Fresno

1300m

Grand
Canyon

Colorado
Plateau

Woodward

Ohio

1 : 30,000,000

0   250   500   750   1000   1250   1500 KILOMETRES

0   250   500   750   1000 STATUTE MILES

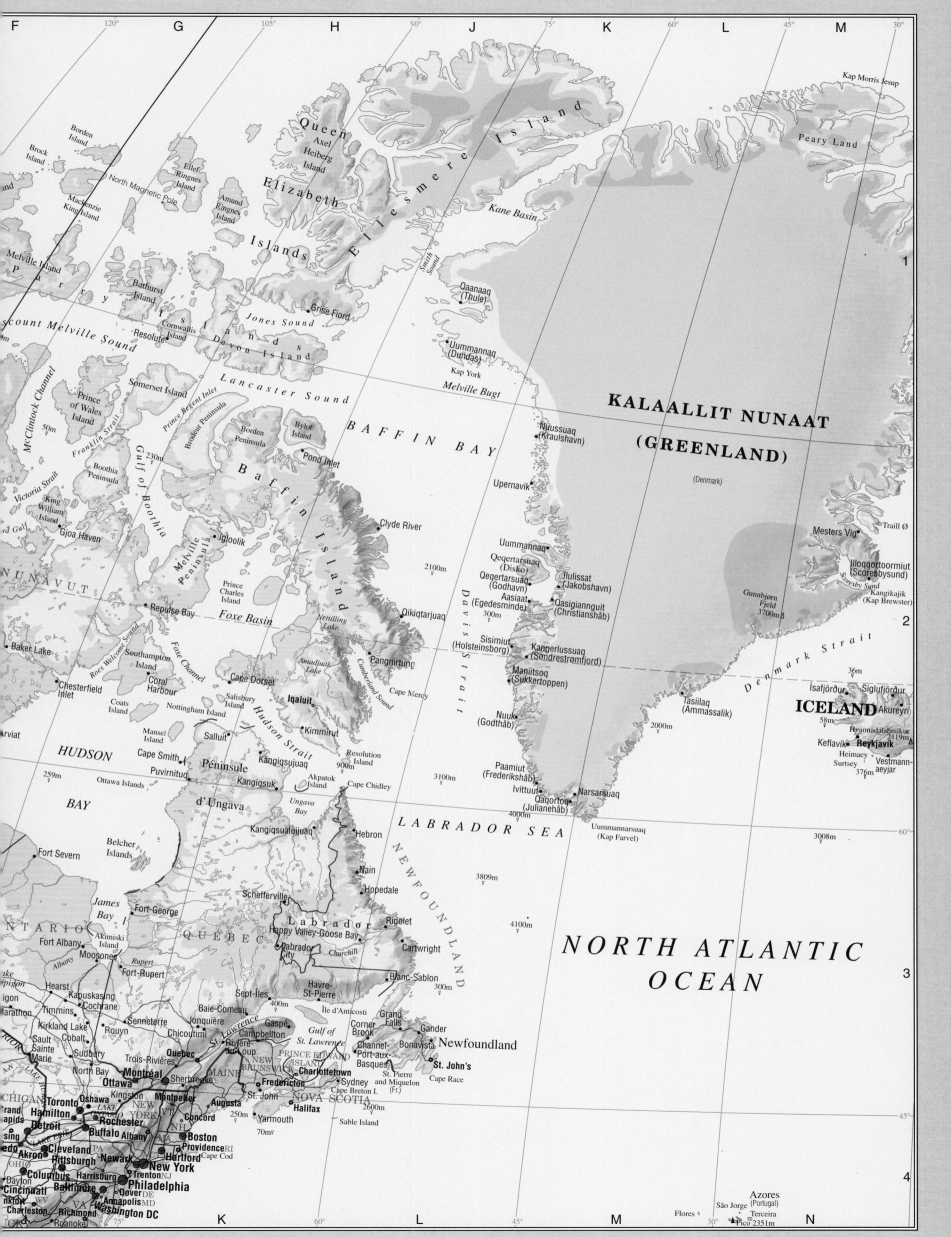

F | G | H | J | K | L | M

120° · 105° · 90° · 75° · 60° · 45° · 30°

Kap Morris Jesup

Queen Axel Heiberg Island

Peary Land

North Magnetic Pole

Borden Island

Brock Island

Mackenzie King Island

Ellef Ringnes Island

Amund Ringnes Island

Elizabeth

Ellesmere Island

Islands

Kane Basin

1

Melville Island

Parry Island

Bathurst Island

Cornwallis Island

Resolute

Grise Fiord

Jones Sound

Devon Island

Qaanaaq (Thule)

scount Melville Sound

McClintock Channel

Somerset Island

Prince of Wales Island

Franklin Strait

50m

230m

Gulf of Boothia

Prince Regent Inlet

Brodeur Peninsula

Borden Peninsula

Bylot Island

Lancaster Sound

BAFFIN BAY

Uummannaq (Dundas)

Kap York

Melville Bugt

KALAALLIT NUNAAT

(GREENLAND)

(Denmark)

Boothia Peninsula

Victoria Strait

King William Island

Gjoa Haven

a Gulf

NUNAVUT

Melville Peninsula

Igloolik

Pond Inlet

Clyde River

Baffin Island

2100m

Uummannaq

Qeqertarsuaq (Disko)

Qeqertarsuaq (Godhavn)

Ilulissat (Jakobshavn)

Aasiaat (Egedesminde)

Qasigiannguit (Christianshåb)

Nuussuaq (Kraulshavn)

Upernavik

Mesters Vig

Traill Ø

Illoqqortoormiut (Scoresbysund)

Scoresby Sund

Kangikajik (Kap Brewster)

2

Repulse Bay

Foxe Basin

Prince Charles Island

Netilling Lake

Qikiqtarjuaq

300m

Davis Strait

Sisimiut (Holsteinsborg)

Kangerlussuaq (Søndrestrømfjord)

Maniitsoq (Sukkertoppen)

Gunnbjørn Fjeld 3700m

Denmark Strait

36m

Baker Lake

Chesterfield Inlet

Southampton Island

Roes Welcome Sound

Foxe Channel

Coral Harbour

Amadjuak Lake

Cape Dorset

Salisbury Island

Pangnirtung

Cumberland Sound

Cape Mercy

2351m

2000m

Tasiilaq (Ammassalik)

ICELAND

Ísafjörður

Siglufjörður

Akureyri

rviat

Coats Island

Nottingham Island

Iqaluit

Kimmirut

58m

Hvannadalshnúkur 2119m

Keflavík

Reykjavik

HUDSON

Chesterfield Inlet

Mansel Island

Salluit

Kangiqsujuaq

Resolution Island

900m

Nuuk (Godthåb)

Heimaey

Surtsey

Vestmann-aeyjar

376m

Cape Smith

Puvirnituq

Péninsule

Kangiqsuk

Akpatok Island

Cape Chidley

3100m

Paamiut (Frederikshåb)

259m

Ottawa Islands

d'Ungava

Ungava Bay

4000m

Ivittuut

Qaqortoq (Julianehåb)

Narsarsuaq

BAY

Belcher Islands

Kangiqsualujjuaq

Hebron

LABRADOR SEA

Uummannarsuaq (Kap Farvel)

3008m

60°

Fort Severn

Nain

Hopedale

3809m

James Bay

Fort-George

Schefferville

Rigolet

4100m

Fort Albany

Akimiski Island

Moosonee

Albany

QUEBEC

Labrador

Happy Valley-Goose Bay

Labrador City

Churchill

Cartwright

NORTH ATLANTIC

OCEAN

3

NTARIO

Hearst

Kapuskasing

Cochrane

Rupert

Fort-Rupert

Blanc-Sablon

300m

igon

pigon

arathon

Timmins

Kirkland Lake

Cobalt

Rouyn

Senneterre

Jonquière

Chicoutimi

Baie-Comeau

Sept-Îles

Île d'Anticosti

Corner Brook

Grand Falls

Gander

400m

Newfoundland

Sault Sainte Marie

Sudbury

North Bay

Quebec

Trois-Rivières

Campbellton

St. Lawrence

Gaspé

Gulf of St. Lawrence

Channel-Port-aux-Basques

Bonavista

CHIGAN

Toronto

Oshawa

Kingston

Ottawa

Montréal

Sherbrooke

Rivière-du-Loup

MAINE

PRINCE EDWARD ISLAND

St. Pierre and Miquelon (Fr.)

St. John's

Cape Race

rand apids

Hamilton

Buffalo

Rochester

Albany

NEW YORK

VT

Montpelier

NH

Concord

Augusta

NEW BRUNSWICK

Fredericton

St. John

Sydney

Cape Breton I.

Charlottetown

NOVA SCOTIA

Halifax

2600m

sing

Detroit

Cleveland

Akron

Pittsburgh

PA

Buffalo

Newark

New York

Hartford

RI

Providence

Boston

Cape Cod

250m

Yarmouth

70m

Sable Island

45°

edo

OHIO

Dayton

Columbus

Cincinnati

nkton

WV

Charleston

Roanoke

VA

Harrisburg

Baltimore

Dover

DE

Annapolis

MD

Washington DC

Richmond

Trenton

NJ

Philadelphia

4

75°

60°

45°

30°

Flores

Azores (Portugal)

São Jorge

Terceira

Pico 2351m

© 1999 Lovell Johns Ltd/Quadrillion Publishing

9

K | L | M | N

1 : 5,000,000

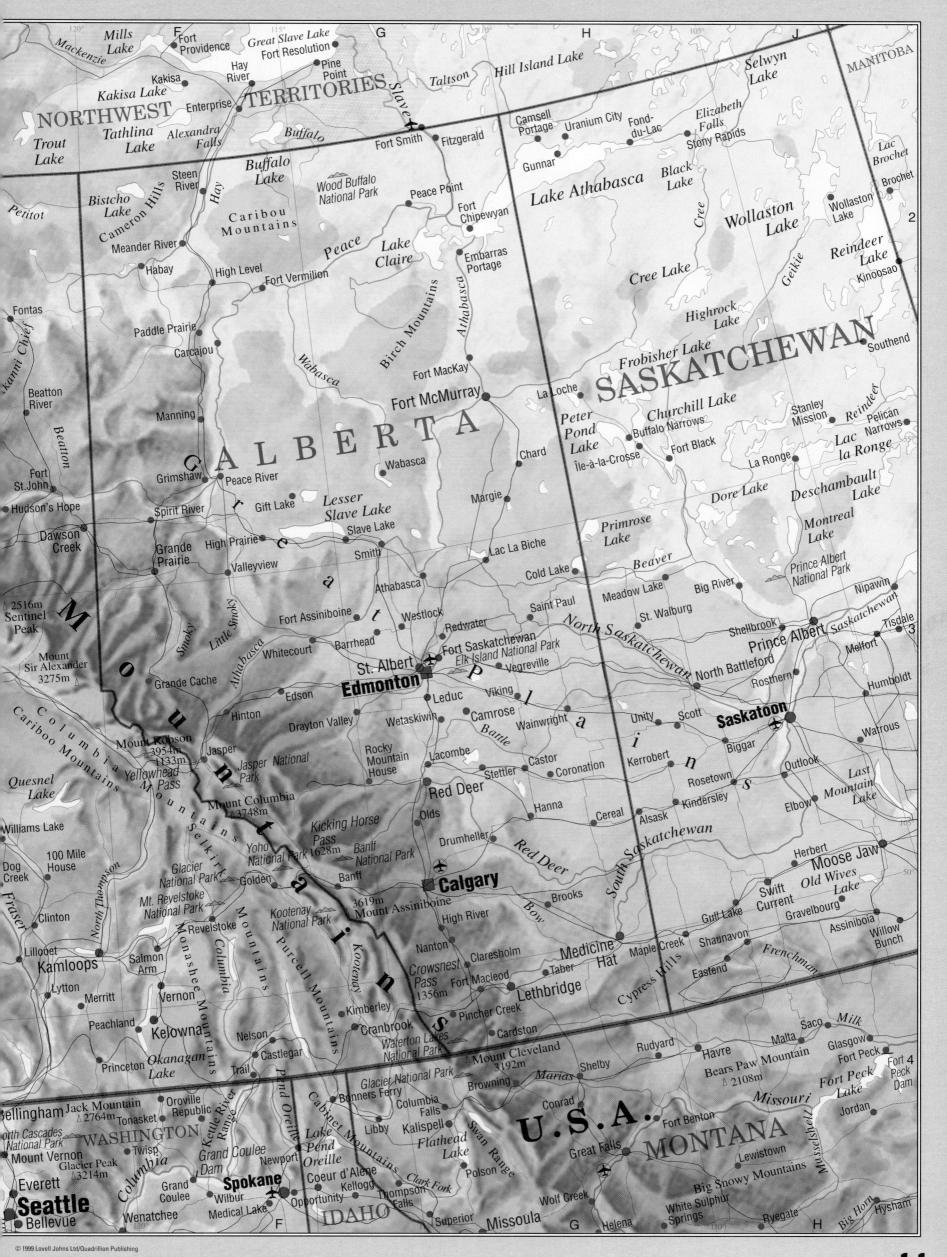

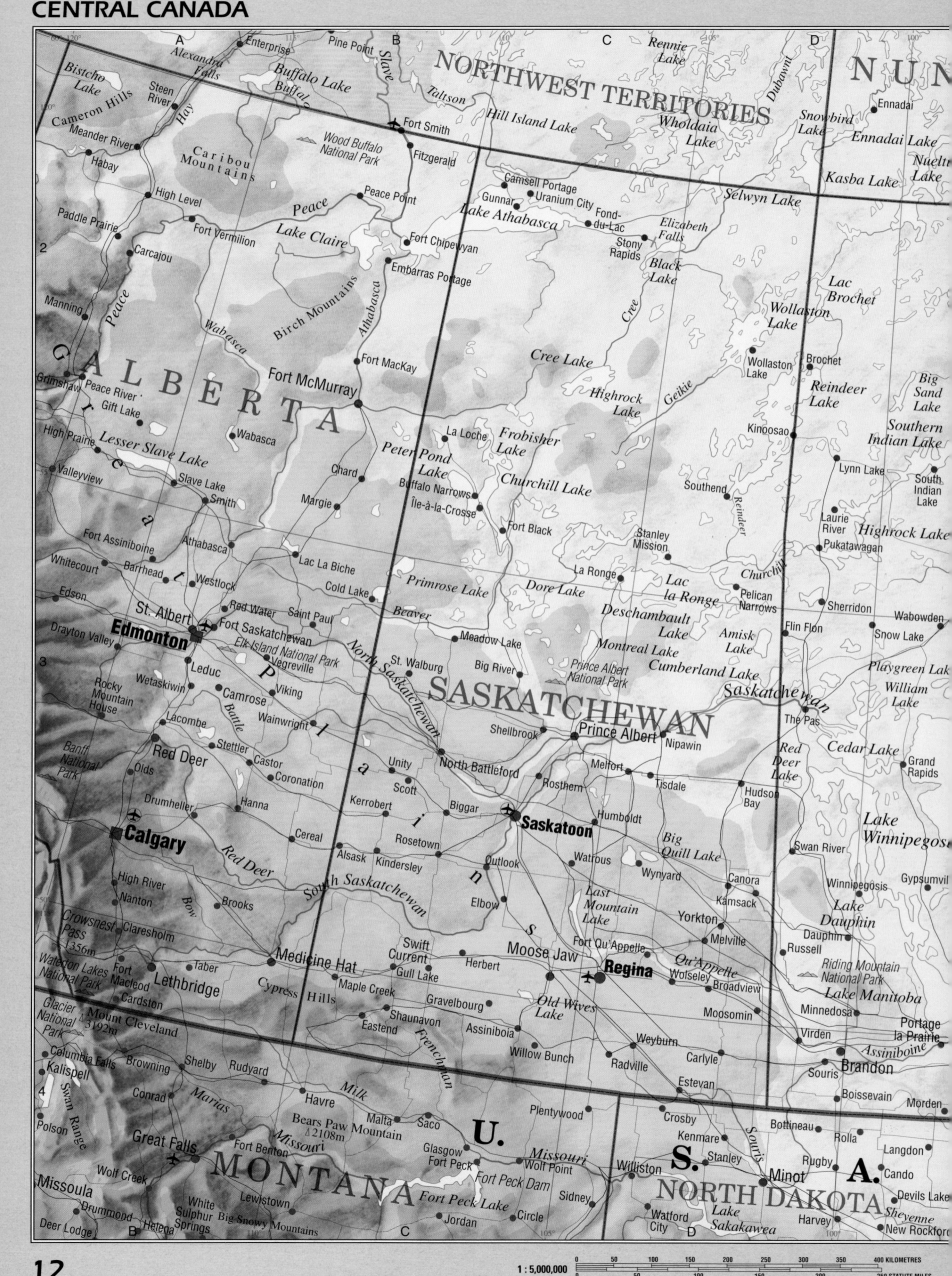

1 : 5,000,000

| 0 | 50 | 100 | 150 | 200 | 250 | 300 | 350 | 400 KILOMETRES |

| 0 | 50 | 100 | 150 | 200 | 250 STATUTE MILES |

E | F | G | H | J

AVUT

Henik Lakes

Tha-anne

Thlewiaza

Dawson Inlet

Arviat

Cape Smith
Mosquito Bay

Puvirnituq

Pointe aux Écueils

H u d s o n   B a y

Ottawa Islands

259m

Promontoire Portland

Hopewell Islands

Nejanilini Lake

Seal

Hubbart Point

Button Bay

Churchill Cape Churchill

McClintock

Port Nelson

Port Nelson

York Factory

Cape Tatnam

Fort Severn

Winisk

Sleeper Islands

King George Islands

North Belcher Islands

Sanikiluaq

Belcher Islands

Cape Henrietta Maria

Long Island

Pointe Loius-XIV

Tadoule Lake

Northern Indian Lake

Granville Lake

Burntwood

Kelsey

Thompson

Sipiwesk

Split Lake

Bird

Gillam

Ilford

Nelson

Hayes

Shamattawa

Gods

M A N I T O B A

Severn

Winisk

Lake River

James Bay

Akimiski Island

Twin Islands

Sipiwesk Lake

Cross Lake

Oxford Lake

Norway House

Island Lake

Island Lake

Gods Lake

Gods Lake

Severn Lake

Bearskin Lake

Big Trout Lake

Big Trout Lake

Shibogama Lake

Winisk Lake

Ekwan

Attawapiskat

Missisa Lake

Attawapiskat

Kapiskau

Fort Albany

60m

Lake Winnipeg

Berens River

Berens

Little Grand Rapids

Popar Hill

Pikangikum

Sandy Lake

Sandy Lake

Deer Lake

Weagamow Lake

North Caribou Lake

Wunnummin Lake

Attawapiskat Lake

Otoskwin

Lansdowne House

Fort Hope

Ogoki

O N T A R I O

Albany

Moose

Moosonee

Missinaibi

Abitibi

verton

Bissett

Gimli

Selkirk

Beausejour

Morris

Steinbach

Pembina

Red

rafton

rand orks

McKenzie Island

Red Lake

Red Lake

Ear Falls

Cat Lake

Trout Lake

Lake St Joseph

Lac Seul

Savant Lake

Sioux Lookout

Pickle Lake

Armstrong

Cavell

Nakina

Ogoki

Mammamattawe

Smoky Falls

Winnipeg

Lake of the Woods

Keewatin Kenora

Dryden

Vermilion Bay

Eagle Lake

Gold Rock

Crow Lake

Ignace

Savanne

Graham

Sturgeon Lake

Lake Nipigon

Longlac

Geraldton

Nipigon

Long Lake

Hornepayne

Terrace Bay

Kabinakagami Lake

Marathon

White River

Hearst

Opasatika

Boon

Oba

Dunrankin

Franz

Fraserdale

Kapuskasing

Smooth Rock Falls

Cochrane

Timmins

Foleyet

Pine Falls

Winnipeg

Thief River Falls

Crookston

MINNESOTA

Baudette

Fort Frances

International Falls

Rainy Lake

Atikokan

Thunder Bay

St. Ignace Island

Grand Marais

Grand Portage

Isle Royale

Michipicoten Island

Wawa

Michipicoten Bay

Agawa Bay

Chapleau

Ramsey

Westree

Upper Red Lake

Lower Red Lake

Lake Superior

1

2

3

4

© 1999 Lovell Johns Ltd/Quadrillion Publishing

13

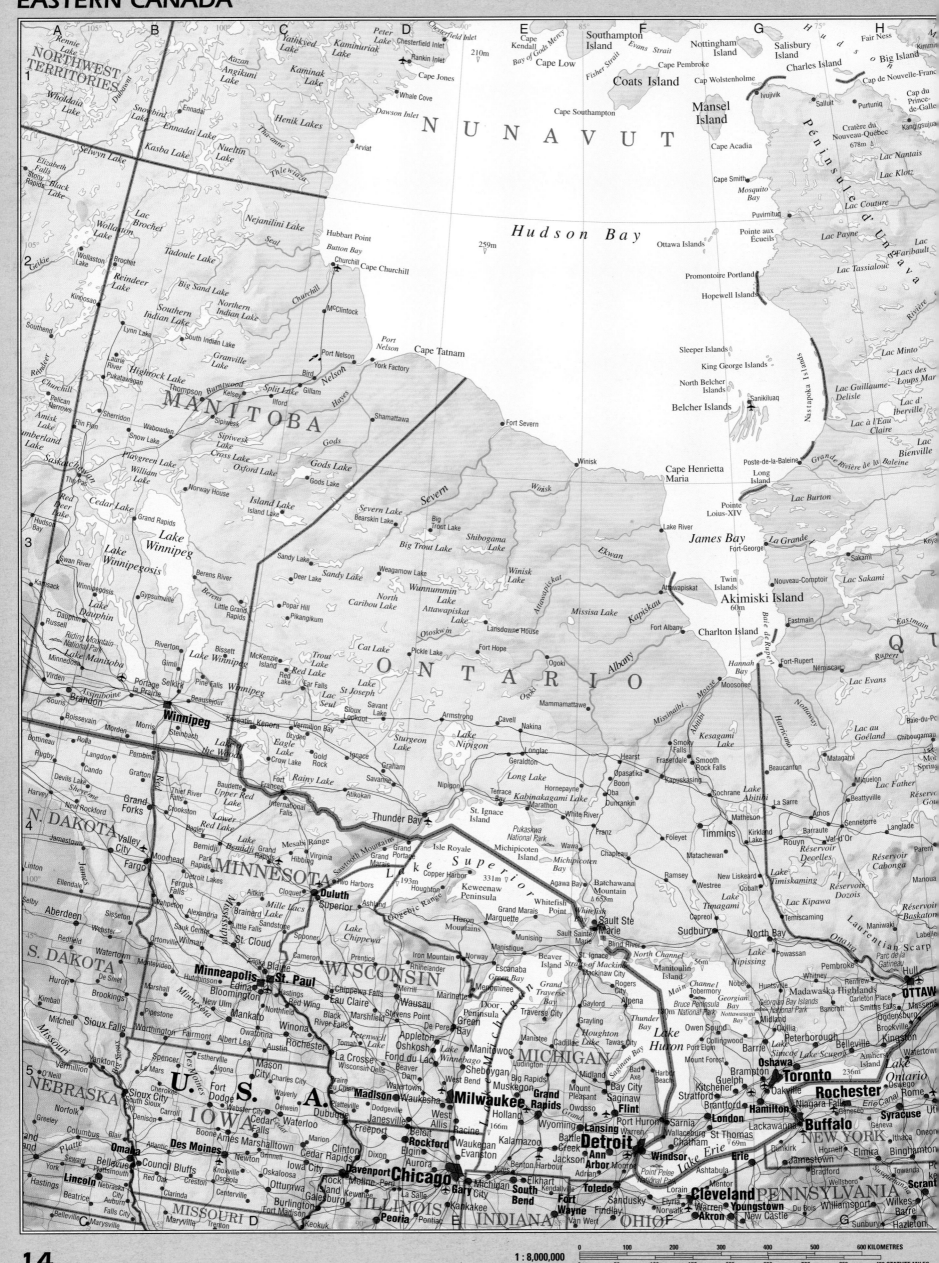

1 : 8,000,000

| 0 | 100 | 200 | 300 | 400 | 500 | 600 KILOMETRES |

| 0 | 50 | 100 | 150 | 200 | 250 | 300 | 350 | 400 STATUTE MILES |

CLIMATE, VEGETATION AND GEOLOGY

* Northwest Territories statistics include Nunavut

Climate

Annual Average Snowfall in cms

Whitehorse · Victoria · Vancouver · Yellowknife · Calgary · Edmonton · Regina · Winnipeg · Toronto · Ottawa · Montréal · Québec City · Fredericton · Halifax · Charlottetown · St. John's

Annual Average Total Precipitation in mms

Whitehorse · Victoria · Vancouver · Yellowknife · Calgary · Edmonton · Regina · Winnipeg · Toronto · Ottawa · Montréal · Québec City · Fredericton · Halifax · Charlottetown · St. John's

Whitehorse
Yellowknife
Iqaluit
Edmonton
Calgary
Victoria · Vancouver
Regina
Winnipeg
St. John's
Charlottetown
Québec City · Fredericton
Montréal · Halifax
Ottawa
Toronto

Climate Zones
(based on the standard Köppen system which classifies the seasonal variations caused by temperature, precipitation and vegetation)

- Polar: tundra
- High Elevations: highlands
- Continental: subarctic
- Continental: cool
- Continental: warm
- Mild: marine west coast
- Dry: semi arid

Vegetation

Geology

Geological Classes

- Igneous Effusive (Lavas)
- Igneous Intrusive (Schists & Granites)
- Archæan Schists & Old Massive Crystalline
- Primary or Palæozoic
- Secondary or Mesozoic
- Tertiary or Cainozoic
- Post-Tertiary or Quaternary
- Uncertain

Types of Natural Vegetation

- Ice Cap & Ice Shelf
- Mountain Vegetation
- Tundra (Moss & Lichens)
- Boreal Forest ("Taiga")
- Conifer Forest (Pine, Spruce & Larch)
- Mixed Forest (Broadleaf & Conifer)
- Prairie (Long Grass)

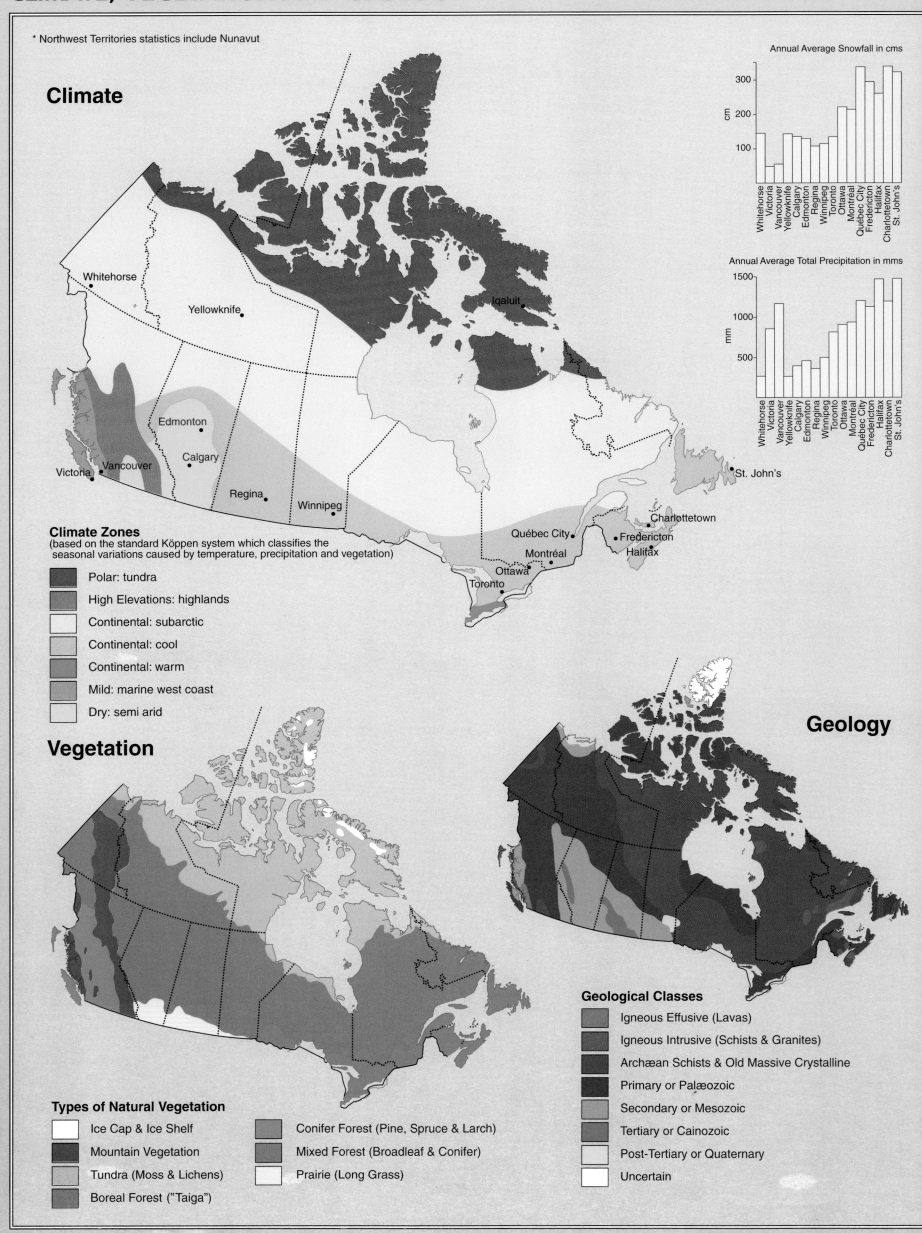

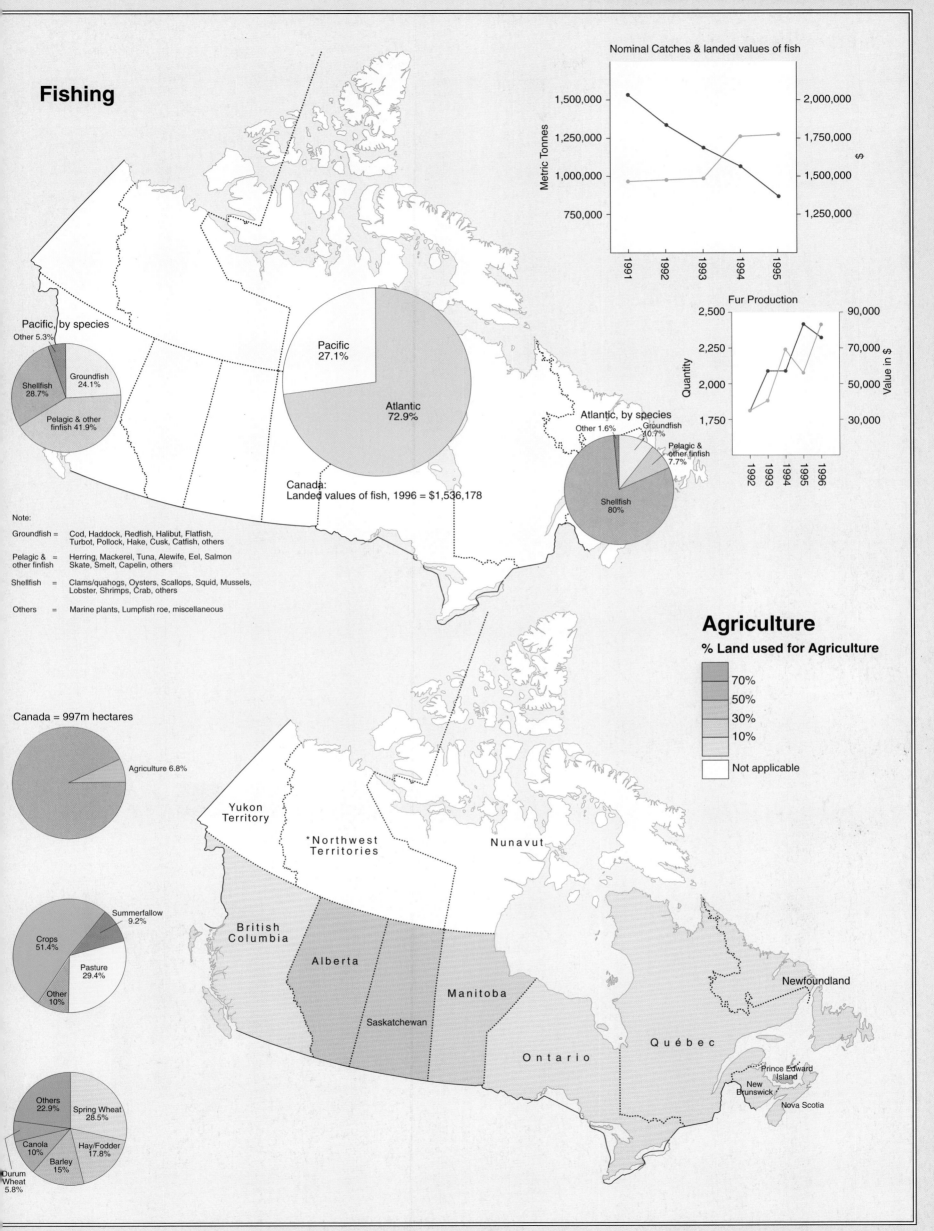

Fishing

Nominal Catches & landed values of fish

Metric Tonnes / $

1,500,000 · 1,250,000 · 1,000,000 · 750,000

2,000,000 · 1,750,000 · 1,500,000 · 1,250,000

1991 · 1992 · 1993 · 1994 · 1995

Fur Production

Quantity / Value in $

2,500 · 2,250 · 2,000 · 1,750

90,000 · 70,000 · 50,000 · 30,000

1992 · 1993 · 1994 · 1995 · 1996

Pacific, by species

Other 5.3%
Shellfish 28.7%
Groundfish 24.1%
Pelagic & other finfish 41.9%

Pacific 27.1%

Atlantic 72.9%

Canada:
Landed values of fish, 1996 = $1,536,178

Atlantic, by species

Other 1.6%
Groundfish 10.7%
Pelagic & other finfish 7.7%
Shellfish 80%

Note:

Groundfish = Cod, Haddock, Redfish, Halibut, Flatfish, Turbot, Pollock, Hake, Cusk, Catfish, others

Pelagic & other finfish = Herring, Mackerel, Tuna, Alewife, Eel, Salmon Skate, Smelt, Capelin, others

Shellfish = Clams/quahogs, Oysters, Scallops, Squid, Mussels, Lobster, Shrimps, Crab, others

Others = Marine plants, Lumpfish roe, miscellaneous

Agriculture

% Land used for Agriculture

70%
50%
30%
10%

Not applicable

Canada = 997m hectares

Agriculture 6.8%

Summerfallow 9.2%
Crops 51.4%
Pasture 29.4%
Other 10%

Others 22.9%
Spring Wheat 28.5%
Canola 10%
Barley 15%
Durum Wheat 5.8%
Hay/Fodder 17.8%

Yukon Territory

*Northwest Territories

Nunavut

British Columbia

Alberta

Saskatchewan

Manitoba

Ontario

Québec

Newfoundland

Prince Edward Island

New Brunswick

Nova Scotia

Mineral Wealth

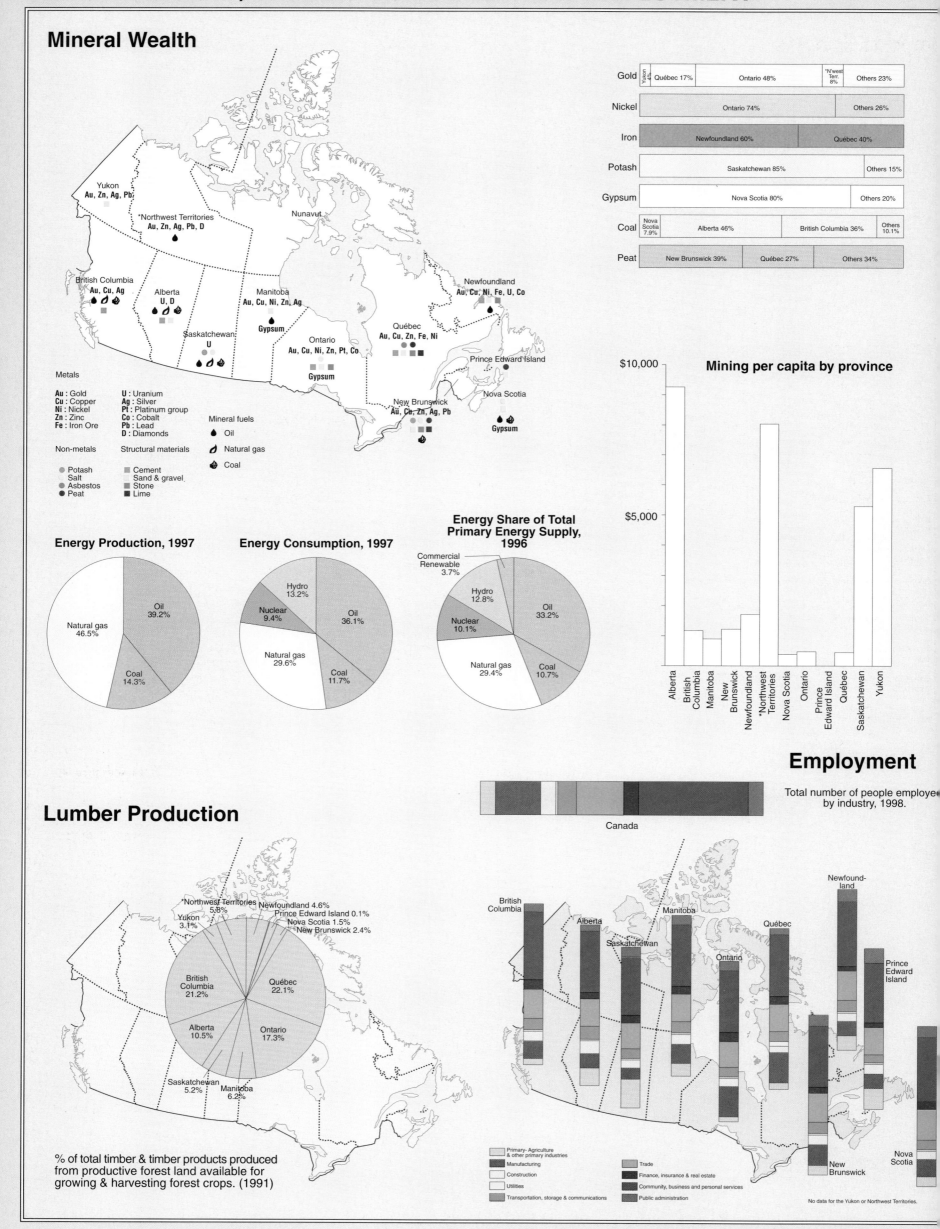

Gold: Yukon | Québec 17% | Ontario 48% | *'N'west Terr. 8% | Others 23%
Nickel: Ontario 74% | Others 26%
Iron: Newfoundland 60% | Québec 40%
Potash: Saskatchewan 85% | Others 15%
Gypsum: Nova Scotia 80% | Others 20%
Coal: Nova Scotia 7.9% | Alberta 46% | British Columbia 36% | Others 10.1%
Peat: New Brunswick 39% | Québec 27% | Others 34%

Metals
Au : Gold
Cu : Copper
Ni : Nickel
Zn : Zinc
Fe : Iron Ore
U : Uranium
Ag : Silver
Pt : Platinum group
Co : Cobalt
Pb : Lead
D : Diamonds

Mineral fuels
Oil
Natural gas
Coal

Non-metals
Potash
Salt
Asbestos
Peat

Structural materials
Cement
Sand & gravel
Stone
Lime

Mining per capita by province

$10,000

$5,000

Alberta · British Columbia · Manitoba · New Brunswick · Newfoundland · *Northwest Territories · Nova Scotia · Ontario · Prince Edward Island · Québec · Saskatchewan · Yukon

Energy Production, 1997
Oil 39.2%
Natural gas 46.5%
Coal 14.3%

Energy Consumption, 1997
Hydro 13.2%
Nuclear 9.4%
Oil 36.1%
Natural gas 29.6%
Coal 11.7%

Energy Share of Total Primary Energy Supply, 1996
Commercial Renewable 3.7%
Hydro 12.8%
Nuclear 10.1%
Oil 33.2%
Natural gas 29.4%
Coal 10.7%

Employment

Total number of people employed by industry, 1998.

Canada

Lumber Production

*Northwest Territories 5.8%
Yukon 3.1%
Newfoundland 4.6%
Prince Edward Island 0.1%
Nova Scotia 1.5%
New Brunswick 2.4%
British Columbia 21.2%
Québec 22.1%
Alberta 10.5%
Ontario 17.3%
Saskatchewan 5.2%
Manitoba 6.2%

% of total timber & timber products produced from productive forest land available for growing & harvesting forest crops. (1991)

British Columbia · Alberta · Saskatchewan · Manitoba · Ontario · Québec · Newfoundland · Prince Edward Island · New Brunswick · Nova Scotia

Primary- Agriculture & other primary industries
Manufacturing
Construction
Utilities
Transportation, storage & communications
Trade
Finance, insurance & real estate
Community, business and personal services
Public administration

No data for the Yukon or Northwest Territories

Imports/Exports

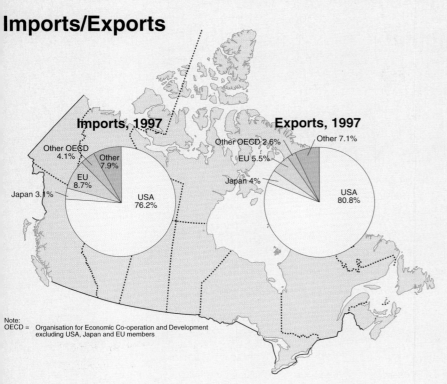

Imports, 1997

- Other OECD 4.1%
- Other 7.9%
- EU 8.7%
- Japan 3.1%
- USA 76.2%

Exports, 1997

- Other OECD 2.6%
- Other 7.1%
- EU 5.5%
- Japan 4%
- USA 80.8%

Note:
OECD = Organisation for Economic Co-operation and Development excluding USA, Japan and EU members

Top 10 Imports of goods on a balance-of-payments basis, 1997	$ Millions	Top 10 Exports of goods on a balance-of-payments basis, 1997	$ Millions
Machinery & equipment	$91,202.6	Other machinery & equipment	$40,344.2
Automotive products	$60,630.1	Passenger autos & chassis	$36,561.3
Industrial goods & materials	$54,369.6	Metals & alloys	$19,970.6
Other machinery & equipment	$39,673.2	Other agricultural & fishing products	$19,618.1
Motor vehicle parts	$34,383.9	Motor vehicle parts	$18,967.4
Other consumer goods	$29,588.1	Chemicals, plastics & fertilizers	$17,037.2
Industrial & agricultural machinery	$25,494.1	Lumber & sawmill products	$16,724.5
Miscellaneous consumer goods	$23,814.8	Industrial & agricultural machinery	$14,716.4
Other Industrial goods & materials	$20,471.3	Trucks & other motor vehicles	$14,528.1
Chemicals & plastics	$19,535.0	Aircraft & other transportation equipment	$12,922.0

* Northwest Territories statistics include Nunavut

GDP per province/territory, 1997

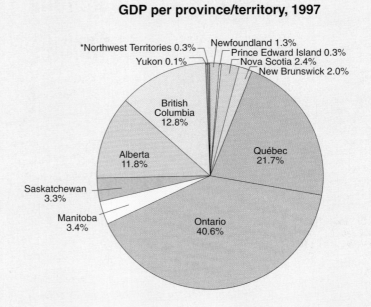

- *Northwest Territories 0.3%
- Newfoundland 1.3%
- Yukon 0.1%
- Prince Edward Island 0.3%
- Nova Scotia 2.4%
- New Brunswick 2.0%
- British Columbia 12.8%
- Québec 21.7%
- Alberta 11.8%
- Saskatchewan 3.3%
- Manitoba 3.4%
- Ontario 40.6%

Full-time university enrolment, 1997-98
Canada 573,099

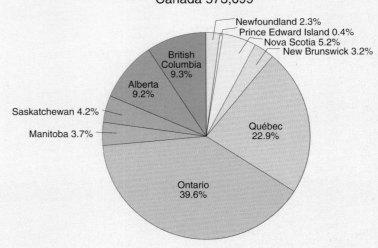

- Newfoundland 2.3%
- Prince Edward Island 0.4%
- Nova Scotia 5.2%
- New Brunswick 3.2%
- British Columbia 9.3%
- Alberta 9.2%
- Saskatchewan 4.2%
- Manitoba 3.7%
- Québec 22.9%
- Ontario 39.6%

Population

Population Profile

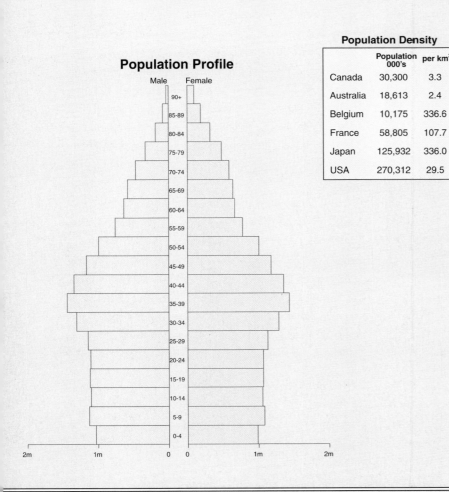

Male / Female

90+, 85-89, 80-84, 75-79, 70-74, 65-69, 60-64, 55-59, 50-54, 45-49, 40-44, 35-39, 30-34, 25-29, 20-24, 15-19, 10-14, 5-9, 0-4

2m 1m 0 0 1m 2m

Population Density

	Population 000's	per km²
Canada	30,300	3.3
Australia	18,613	2.4
Belgium	10,175	336.6
France	58,805	107.7
Japan	125,932	336.0
USA	270,312	29.5

Population, 1998
% of Total

- 40%
- 25%
- 15%
- 5%
- 0%

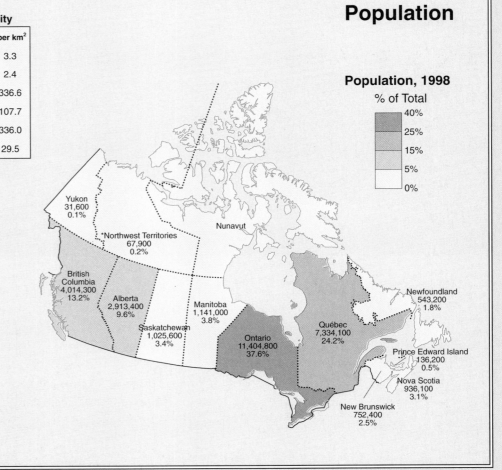

- Yukon 31,600 0.1%
- Nunavut
- *Northwest Territories 67,900 0.2%
- British Columbia 4,014,300 13.2%
- Alberta 2,913,400 9.6%
- Saskatchewan 1,025,600 3.4%
- Manitoba 1,141,000 3.8%
- Ontario 11,404,800 37.6%
- Québec 7,334,100 24.2%
- Newfoundland 543,200 1.8%
- Prince Edward Island 136,200 0.5%
- Nova Scotia 936,100 3.1%
- New Brunswick 752,400 2.5%

CANADA

The evolution of Canada has been a gigantic struggle against nature because the natural sea and land communications of North America run in a general north and south direction. When man drew an arbitrary line separating Canada and the United States, he defied nature. Canada has been bucking nature ever since.

(LIEUTENANT COLONEL KENNETH STUART, CANADIAN ARMY, 1932)

POPULATION
30,300,600 (1998)

AREA
9,970,610 square kilometres

(3,849,675 square miles)

CAPITAL
Ottawa

MOTTO
A Mari usque ad Mare
("From Sea to Sea")

FLORAL EMBLEM
Maple Leaf

The Land At almost seven per cent of the Earth's surface, Canada is the second largest country in the world, after Russia and ahead of China and the United States. It is bounded by three oceans, the Arctic, the Atlantic and the Pacific, and stretches from the North Pole to the 42nd parallel, roughly the latitude of Corsica, Istanbul or northern California. Only 10 per cent of the land is populated.

Eighty per cent of Canada, centred on Hudson's Bay, consists of lowlands. The fringes of the country, in the Arctic, along the Pacific coast, and in the southeast, are mountainous. Almost 50 per cent of the landmass is the rocky and mineral-rich Canadian Shield. The best

warmer winters along with cool summers. Central Canada has a "continental" climate, with hot summers and cold winters. Rainfall is heaviest along the coasts, while the Prairies and the North have less. In fact, much of the North is a semidesert in terms of precipitation. Fifteen per cent of the world's coastline is Canadian.

History The word "Canada", adopted by the early explorers, derives from the Huron-Iroquois word *kanata*, meaning "village" or "settlement". By the 19th century, it was generally accepted to mean northern North America.

The ancestors of Canada's aboriginal population are estimated to have arrived in North America about 12,000 to 15,000 years ago, across a land bridge between Alaska and Siberia, or by sea from northeast Asia. Their descendants were mistaken by European explorers to be "Indians"; that is, inhabitants of India. Europeans, after a brief foray in AD 1000, colonized North America in the 17th and 18th centuries. The French were first to settle what is now Canada, but were conquered by the British in 1760, and Canada became part of the British Empire. Canadians thereafter were divided into French- and English-speaking communities. The American Revolution severed the United States and Canada in 1776, and American refugees loyal to Great Britain emigrated to Canada as a result. The British colonies in North America were federated between 1867 and 1873 into a single country, Canada, with the exception of Newfoundland, which joined Canada only in 1949.

Canada grew slowly in population between 1867 and 1900, but thereafter attracted large numbers of immigrants from Europe, especially between 1900 and 1914, 1921 to 1929, and after 1945. Canada participated in the First and Second World Wars as a part of the British Empire, and after 1945 was a close ally of the United States. During and after the Second World War the Canadian economy grew enormously, financing a generous national health and welfare system.

The People Canadians for the most part live in close proximity to the United States border, and the population density is among the lowest in the world, at

ABOVE: *The indented coastlines of Canada's eastern provinces provide safe harbour for countless fishing and pleasure craft.*

agricultural lands lie around the Great Lakes and in the Prairie provinces of Alberta, Saskatchewan and Manitoba, although there are fertile pockets in British Columbia and the Maritime provinces as well.

On the Atlantic coast, summers are cool, while winter temperatures hover at, or just below, freezing. The West or Pacific coast, by contrast, has slightly three people for every square kilometre. Fertility rates are low and the population is aging. Immigration drives population increases; new Canadians from Asia and the Caribbean are changing the Anglo-French face of the country. Approximately 75 per cent of Canadians ordinarily use English, while 25 per cent speak French; 16 per cent can speak both languages. Forty-five per cent of the population is Catholic, 36 per cent Protestant. Canadians of aboriginal origin constitute roughly three per cent of the total population. According to the United Nations, Canada ranked first in quality of life in the 1990s.

LEFT: Trailriding near Canmore, which lies to the west of Calgary, Alberta. BELOW LEFT: A "nodding donkey" – ubiquitous outward symbol of the wealth of natural gas and oil that lies beneath the fertile agricultural soil. BELOW: Placid winter scene by the Wheatley River, Prince Edward Island.

The Economy Canada is often seen in terms of its natural resources or primary products: agriculture, minerals, timber, pulp and paper. These are important parts of the economy, to be sure: Canada is the world's sixth-largest wheat producer, third in copper, first in lead and second in nickel production, among other important products. But industry is important as well – Canada, for example, is the world's fourth-largest exporter of automobiles and automotive products, ahead of France, Great Britain and Italy – and a very large number of Canadians work in the service sector. Canada is a trading nation, ranking ninth in terms of its percentage of world exports, and the economy is usually rated eighth or ninth in size in the world.

Government and Politics Canada is a democratic constitutional monarchy, parliamentary in form, with the national Parliament consisting of an elected House of Commons and a Senate whose members are appointed by the government. The British monarch, taking the form of Queen or King of Canada, is the head of state, represented in Canada by a governor-general. The country is a federal state, with a central government in

Ottawa, 10 provincial governments, and three territories under federal jurisdiction. The central government handles foreign policy, trade and most communications, and possesses important economic powers. The provinces manage education, natural resources, highways and municipal affairs. Health care, welfare, agriculture and labour policy are shared, sometimes uncomfortably, between Ottawa and the provinces. The 1969 Official Languages Act guarantees Canadians public service at the federal level in French or English as they choose.

National and provincial parliaments or legislatures are chosen by election, usually every four or five years, and the largest party in each parliament typically forms the government. Governments are headed by a prime minister or premier, directing a Cabinet of ministers, who are responsible to their respective parliaments or legislatures. The Conservatives and Liberals are the only political parties who have formed governments at the federal level, although there are now members of several parties in the House of Commons. In power for most of the 20th century, the Liberals are often called the "Government Party", and regard themselves as such.

ABOVE: The coastline of Canada comprises fifteen per cent of the world's total. Dotted along the country's shores, therefore, numerous lighthouses – some of them centuries old – flash out their rhythmic warnings of the rocks that lurk for unwary seafarers.

BRITISH COLUMBIA

... an immense land of mountain, forest, and flood, the Alpine ranges soaring in some of their peaks to the height of Mont Blanc – a land in the main so deeply and wonderfully forested that you may, on its seacoast, cut timber thirty and forty inches square of a uniform size for one hundred feet – a country where the rivers rush impetuously through tremendous gorges to run in shorter navigable reaches into harbours which are defended by a gigantic natural breakwater formed by the long rocky island of Vancouver. Here, on this island, we have a climate like that of the south of England.

(*THE MARQUIS OF LORNE, GOVERNOR-GENERAL OF CANADA, 1878-1883*)

The Land "B. C." fronts on the Pacific between the American states of Alaska and Washington, and is divided from the rest of the country by towering mountain ranges, characterized by spectacular scenery and, in popular myth, by a kinder climate.

The coast consists of deep, mountainous inlets or fjords, protected from the ocean by a screen of offshore islands, from the Queen Charlottes in the north to the very large Vancouver Island in the south. The Coastal Range of mountains is penetrated by a number of rivers, of which the most important is the Fraser, which reaches the ocean at Vancouver, and stretches far into the interior. The Fraser River delta is an important

a mild climate, with the warmest winters in Canada. The coastal mountains block much of the rainfall, as well as moderating winds from the ocean. The interior, as a result, has extreme variations in temperature – bitterly cold winters and sweltering summers, as well as much less rainfall. Some parts of the interior are arid and require intensive irrigation for crops.

History There has been settlement in British Columbia for at least 8,000 years. It was originally populated by Indians, divided into coastal and interior tribes. Coastal Indians, such as the Haida and Kwakiutl, lived off the sea and from trading, and were noted for their wooden

🍁 *ABOVE: The maritime tradition of Canada's west coast is evident in this picture of a huge anchor at Victoria, provincial capital of British Columbia. ABOVE RIGHT: The Empress Hotel is one of the landmarks of Victoria.*

agricultural region, especially for market gardening. The mountains and the interior are heavily forested, though there are also large areas of grasslands which allow for ranching. In the east, the Rocky Mountains extend from the United States border some 1,200 kilometres to the Liard River Basin in northern British Columbia.

The coast and the islands receive more rain than any other place in Canada. Coastal British Columbia enjoys

villages and totem poles. Interior Indians, like the Kootenay, lived more typically from hunting.

Spanish and British explorers arrived in British Columbia by sea and land in the late 18th century, closely followed by fur traders. Permanent settlements sprang up around fur trading posts and then around mines in the interior in the 1850s. British Columbia was first organized as a colony in 1858 and subsequently joined Canada in 1871. A transcontinental railway linked British Columbia to eastern Canada after 1885; a continuous and convenient highway to the East did not appear until the 1950s. British Columbia was originally heavily dependent on its natural resources, especially forestry and fishing, but by the 1940s an industrial base developed around its great port city, Vancouver.

The People British Columbia, Canada's third-largest province in population and up half a million people in the first five years of the 1990s alone, is growing at a startling rate. Indeed, it is the only province which has outperformed the national average population increase in every census since 1871. It is Canada's most urbanized province, with the population heavily centred around Vancouver (the third largest Canadian city, at just short of two million, where house prices are the highest in the country), and also the most diverse, with

substantial groups of Europeans and Asians, especially British, Chinese and South Asians. Along with St-Catherines-Niagara in Ontario, Victoria (313,000 people; the country's 14th ranking city) has the greatest proportion of seniors in Canada's urban centres.

The Economy British Columbia has one of Canada's most vibrant economies. More than half of the area is forested, and the province is the principal producer of wood products in the country. The interior is mineral-rich, producing silver, gold, lead, zinc, molybdenum and copper, among other ores. Fishing has always been an important industry along the coast, although by the 1990s stocks of salmon in particular were heavily depleted. There is a solid industrial sector grounded in forestry and mining, with one-third of manufacturing

concentrated in wood products. The economy is geared towards international trade, and the export profile favours the United States, Japan and the Pacific.

Government and Politics British Columbia, like other Canadian provinces, has a lieutenant-governor who holds at the provincial level the limited powers which the governor-general has for Canada as a whole. The leader of the largest party in the unicameral, popularly elected legislature becomes premier of the province and chooses a Cabinet from supporters in the assembly. There are three major parties in the province on the federal level, Reform, New Democratic and Liberal, and two on the provincial, Liberal and New Democratic. The Social Credit party, in power at Victoria from 1952 to 1991, is recently much diminished in stature. The province is a long way from central Canada and Ottawa, and there is often political advantage to be gained in provincial politics by vociferously criticizing the federal government. W A C Bennett, the fiery premier from 1952 to 1972, was a master of the art.

🍁 *ABOVE LEFT: The forests of British Columbia teem with wildlife, including magnificent wapiti or elk, black and grizzly bears, wolves and a variety of big cats. TOP RIGHT: Spring wild flowers in the mountains. ABOVE: Marker to honour the opening of the Trans-Canada Highway at Rogers Pass in the Selkirk Mountains.*

ALBERTA

POPULATION
2,913,400 (1998)

AREA
661,185 square kilometres

(257,862 square miles)

MOTTO
Fortis et Liber
("Strong and Free")

FLORAL EMBLEM
Wild Rose

CAPITAL
Edmonton

Alberta, although in its southern part a prairie province, contains within its borders part of the eastern side of the Rockies, with its abrupt slopes and irregular surface deeply cut by canyons and ravines. This part of Alberta is famous for its mountain scenery and Banff, Lake Louise, and Jasper Park are visited by thousands of tourists. North of the prairies is a belt of parkland, where open prairie alternates with clumps of woodland. The innumerable coppices of birch and poplar provide fuel for the settler and also serve to shelter his house and stock from the cutting winter winds. The rainfall is heavier than farther south, and the country is dotted with lakes and intersected by countless creeks and streams. These make it particularly well-suited for stock-raising. The soil is even better than that of the open prairies. North of the Saskatchewan River, the land is more heavily timbered, although there is much open land even there.

("ONTARIO PUBLIC SCHOOL GEOGRAPHY", ONTARIO DEPARTMENT OF EDUCATION, 1935)

The Land Early Alberta was a product of geography. The Great Plains of North America are in the south of the province, once dominated by the Blackfoot nation which depended on the buffalo hunt, on horseback after the 18th century. In the north, Alberta is forested and woodland tribes such as the Cree prevailed there. European fur traders from Hudson's Bay or from Montreal came there, linking what is now Alberta with the east.

The Rocky Mountains run along the southern edge of the Alberta-British Columbia frontier. Chinook winds coming through the mountains eastwards can produce amazing increases in temperature; however, cold winters and short summers are the provincial norm. Hugging the border with the Northwest Territories, Wood Buffalo National Park, one of 37 national parks and reserves across the country, is larger than Switzerland.

History Alberta was added to Canada in 1870 by purchase from the Hudson's Bay Company, and shortly thereafter Canada sent out a mounted police force to occupy the region. Alberta became a district of the Canadian Northwest Territories in 1882 and a province of Canada in 1905. Large numbers of immigrants arrived in the province between 1900 and 1914; from that time until 1945, Alberta depended on agriculture – wheat farming and cattle ranching, with a small timber products and mining sector. The economy of Alberta was transformed after the Second World War by the discovery of large quantities of oil at Leduc in 1947, the foundation of the province's economy ever since. Largely because of Alberta's production, Canada is petroleum self-sufficient, as well as the world's 11th-largest oil-producing nation.

The People The population of Alberta skyrocketed in the first decade of the 20th century, growing by 300,000 to reach 374,000 by 1911. Inhabitants are mostly of European descent (British, German, Ukrainian and French), but with a large element of recent arrivals from East and South Asia. The aboriginal population is estimated at 64,000, and the province has the largest number of Métis in the country. Alberta is centred around its two largest population concentrations in Edmonton (900,000 people; fifth largest city in Canada) and Calgary (850,000 people; sixth biggest), which both

divide and dominate the province. Like British Columbia, the province is fast growing. The two have increased their combined share of Canada's people from 15 per cent in 1951 to 22 per cent in 1991.

The Economy Much of the land is suitable for agriculture, from wheat growing in the Peace River plain in the north to the semiarid cattle ranches of the south. Farming is more varied but less crucial to the economy than that of the other two prairie provinces, Manitoba and Saskatchewan. Alberta's principal natural resources are oil and natural gas, which are exported to the rest of

ABOVE: People of the First Nations make a unique and colourful contribution to Alberta's heritage.
ABOVE RIGHT: Castle Mountain, in legend home of the Chinook wind that melts the prairie snow in spring.

Left: Strikingly coloured Peyto Lake in the centre of Banff National Park. Below: Over the course of time, the effects of wind erosion, searing summer heat and winter frosts have sculpted the mysterious rock structures that form such a distinctive feature of Alberta's badlands.

Canada and the United States. Eighty per cent of Canadian production of these commodities comes from Alberta.

Though Alberta's reserves of light crude oil have been depleted over time, the province contains immense reserves of heavy oil which are expected to sustain the provincial as well as the national economy in decades to come. Projections are that new oil projects will bring up to $25 billion in investment, substantial construction employment and 44,000 permanent jobs in the period to the year 2030. Most of the reserves of Canada's natural gas are in Alberta as well.

The provincial economy has been considerably diversified, particularly into forestry, foods and chemicals; the refinement of oil is only a fraction of the province's manufacturing. Alberta ranks third in per capita personal income among the provinces, after Ontario and British Columbia.

Government and Politics Alberta has a single legislative assembly, elected every four or five years. The leader of the largest group in the assembly is appointed provincial premier and chooses a Cabinet, usually made up of party members, from the legislature. A federally-chosen lieutenant-governor is the nominal head of government.

Alberta's politics are the most unusual of any Canadian province. Although there have always been two or more parties functioning in the province, historically Alberta has been dominated by a single party: the Liberals from 1905 to 1921, the United Farmers of Alberta from 1921 to 1935, Social Credit from 1935 to 1971, and the Progressive Conservatives from 1971. More recently, the diversification of the provincial economy, the growth in population and the distinction, if not rivalry, between Edmonton and Calgary have resulted in a slightly more balanced party system. In 1999, there were three parties represented in the provincial legislature: the Progressive Conservatives, the Liberals and the New Democratic Party. Generally speaking, southern Alberta has been more conservative in politics, and northern Alberta (especially Edmonton) more centrist or liberal in outlook.

Above: The skyscrapers of downtown Calgary, situated on the Bow River, are compressed between the river and the main line of the Canadian Pacific Railway. The city's name is believed to derive from a Gaelic word which means clear, running water.

SASKATCHEWAN

There is a greatness here – even in the unpainted small towns. It is a greatness not easy to define or describe, yet one feels it deeply. It has something to do with the strength that comes from the soil. Something to do with the domination of land and sky, the sweep of fields, the high cloud formations. And in the inescapable preoccupation of the people with the weather, and change of season, and growing things ...

(ELIZABETH TROTT, A VISITOR TO SASKATCHEWAN FROM ONTARIO, 1946)

The Land Saskatchewan's boundaries are a geometric construct – straight lines on all sides. There are no natural boundaries, and the province stretches across a number of distinct regions. In the north, the Canadian Shield, with its rocks and lakes, cuts across the province; in the northwest there is Lake Athabaska, one of the northern great lakes. Further south there is a belt of coniferous forest and, south again, the broad lands of the Canadian prairie. The southwest corner of the province is exceptionally dry, and some commentators have questioned whether it should have been opened to farming and settlement.

The two branches of the Saskatchewan River traverse the province from west to east. These were the paths along which the fur trade travelled in the 18th and 19th centuries. The province's name derives from a word meaning "swiftly flowing river" in the language of the Cree, the dominant Indian nation of original Saskatchewan.

History Saskatchewan was annexed to Canada in 1870, as part of the Canadian purchase of the Hudson's Bay Company lands in the west. Settlers gradually drifted into the area, which was generally neglected by the central government in Ottawa. Partly as a consequence of that neglect, and partly because of the activities of a part-Indian and part-French firebrand, Louis Riel, there was a brief rebellion in central Saskatchewan in 1885, suppressed by troops sent from the John A Macdonald government in Ottawa.

Saskatchewan did not become attractive to large-scale settlement until around 1900; thereafter settlement was so rapid (it multiplied 500 per cent between 1900 and 1910) that the area was made a province in 1905. Saskatchewan's economy, and its politics, centred on the production of wheat on its broad prairie. When the international price of wheat soared, so did Saskatchewan; when it fell, so did the province's prospects. In the First World War and the

ABOVE: A Canadian canoe on the Clearwater River in the northwest of Saskatchewan. RIGHT: A typical scene, marked by the colourful profiles of grain elevators, that is repeated across the Prairie provinces.

1920s, when demand and prices were high, times were good. When prices fell, as they did in 1929 and throughout the Depression of the 1930s, the result was misery. Low wheat prices, combined with a devastating drought, forced farmers off the land.

 LEFT: The exciting sport of ice sailing at the Waskimo Winter Festival, Regina. BELOW LEFT: Pumpjacks at Gull Lake, in the southwest of Saskatchewan, nod in silent testimony to the presence of a significant oil and gas industry.

The People Saskatchewan's population multiplied five times to 400,000 from 1901 to 1911, and Regina grew from 7,700 to 70,000 in the same decade. Most inhabitants are of European origin and, within that category, British, German, Ukrainian, Polish and Scandinavian. There is a good-sized aboriginal population of 76,000 that is increasingly important in the towns and cities of central and northern Saskatchewan. There has been a steady outflow of mostly younger people since 1930, so that the population in 1996 was still not much larger than it was in 1931. The average age is perceptibly higher than elsewhere in Canada: over 17 per cent of the population is over the age of 65. The main population concentrations are the cities of Regina (195,000) and Saskatoon (212,000).

The Economy Saskatchewan was developed as an agricultural province, and agriculture continues to play an important role in its economy. The province accounts for a third of Canada's agricultural land, which produces an abundance of grains and oilseeds. Recently, Saskatchewan has become a centre of potash and uranium production; indeed, some estimates predict that Saskatchewan may have the richest uranium deposits in the world. There is also an oil and gas industry, yielding 16 per cent of Canadian production in the case of oil, and four per cent of the nation's natural gas. The manufacturing sector is small, unemployment relatively low and exports crucial.

Government and Politics Saskatchewan has a lieutenant-governor, and also a legislative assembly, the latter elected by universal suffrage every four or five years The leader with majority support is the premier, who appoints a Cabinet from among party followers in the assembly. Saskatchewan politics are much more varied than those of neighbouring Alberta. The province's precarious economic experience encouraged voters to experiment with socialism, electing what was for many years Canada's only democratic socialist government. Under the banner of the Co-operative Commonwealth Federation (now the New Democratic Party), it implemented a variety of social programmes, most importantly a government health care system inaugurated in 1961.

There is a provincial reputation for radicalism in politics, but one close observer of the Saskatchewan political scene, Evelyn Eager, suggests otherwise: "the electorate of the province has shown the traditional conservatism of a farming population. Electors have not tended to radical behaviour in the sense either of favouring extreme change or of casting their votes mainly for basic principle."

 ABOVE: The Legislative Building in Regina, capital of Saskatchewan, overlooks Wascana Lake across fine gardens. Built in 1908-1912 in the shape of a cross, and topped by a dome, the Tyndall limestone structure is a graceful addition to the city.

MANITOBA

The province of the fur trade, the grain trade, the long freights thundering to the Lakehead, of the city clustered by the Forks like teepees on the plain, of the long, low, brooding mountains of its west, of the lake-set Shield and the coursing Nelson ...

(W L MORTON, "MANITOBA: A HISTORY", UNIVERSITY OF TORONTO PRESS, 1967)

POPULATION
1,141,000 (1998)

AREA
650,087 square kilometres
(253,533 square miles)

CAPITAL
Winnipeg

MOTTO
Unofficially, "Home of the [Hudson's] Bay" or "The Prairie Province"

FLORAL EMBLEM
Prairie Crocus

The Land Most of the province is formed from the Canadian Shield, through which a number of large rivers (the Hayes, Nelson and Churchill) flow to Hudson Bay. Along Hudson Bay there is a stretch of barren land, succeeded inland by coniferous forest. Along the fringes of the Shield lie three very large lakes (Winnipeg, Winnipegosis and Manitoba), with some marginal agricultural land in the region between them. Almost one-sixth of the province is inland water. At the southern end of the province lie fertile agricultural lands, the easternmost portion of the Canadian Prairies. The dry and clear Prairie climate of warm summers and cold winters is in evidence.

History Manitoba (its name apparently derived from an Algonquian word) was originally inhabited by a variety of aboriginal nations, divided, as is the province, between woodland and plains cultures. Europeans

 ABOVE: "The Prairie Province" offers endless vistas of wide sky and open road cutting across mile after mile of rich farmland.

penetrated first to the province's extreme northeast, along the coast of Hudson Bay, early in the 17th century. The Hudson's Bay Company established its North American headquarters at York Factory on Hudson Bay, and slowly in the 17th and 18th centuries sent explorers and traders inland. At the same time, southern

Manitoba became a crucial trading route for the Hudson's Bay Company's principal rivals, traders from Montreal, organized in the North-West Company.

Lord Selkirk, one of the shareholders in the Hudson's Bay Company, founded a colony along the Red River, athwart the North-West Company's trade route, and in consequence a small war broke out there between 1814 and 1816. Red River became an established settlement in the mid-19th century, well enough entrenched to object when it was purchased by Canada from the Hudson's Bay Company in 1870. A brief rebellion erupted, which was appeased only by the creation of a new Canadian province of Manitoba in that same year.

Manitoba was originally more or less equally populated by English- and French-speakers. Over time, however, settlers from Ontario flooded in, changing the character of the population and the politics of the province so that by 1890 it closely resembled Ontario. Fierce disputes broke out over the language of government and schooling; they ended with the relegation of French, by then the language of a small minority, to inferior status.

The Red River colony meanwhile developed into the city of Winnipeg, built around the Forks where the Red and Assiniboine rivers come together. Winnipeg developed into the provincial capital, a major transportation and manufacturing centre, and the conduit through which all of Canada's transcontinental railways passed. Winnipeg also became the focus of a number of labour movements, and was the scene of a General Strike in 1919. The boundaries of the province, which was at the very beginning restricted to a small tract of land around the Red River, were extended to include the north in 1912.

The People Like the other Prairie provinces, Manitoba attracted many immigrants early in the century, growing from 255,000 to 461,000 persons between 1901 and 1911. British, German, Ukrainian and French origins predominate among an ethnically diverse provincial population. There is also a substantial number of aboriginal people. Although French is spoken by less than five per cent of Manitobans, they are heavily concentrated in the city of St Boniface, across the Red

the heart of Canada's grain trade, as well as a railway hub, but it failed to develop into an air transport attraction of the first rank.

With its varied agriculture and manufacturing of products such as food, machinery and chemicals, Manitoba's current economy rests on a broader base than that of the other Prairie provinces. Wheat is the staple crop, but other grains are grown. There is also dairy farming, and feedlots for cattle. Copper, nickel, zinc, tantalum and gold are mined in the north, and there is a small oil industry. The Churchill-Nelson hydroelectric development, based on the northern rivers, makes Manitoba a major producer of electricity.

LEFT: The end of a glorious day's fishing at Gunisao Lake, which lies to the east of Lake Winnipeg.

BELOW LEFT: Spring sunshine helps to melt the remaining blanket of snow, which traditional sharp-angled roofs have shed long ago. BELOW: A field of sunflowers. The oil from their seeds is used in the making of food, the leaves are used as fodder and the flowers produce a yellow dye.

River from Winnipeg. St Boniface is the largest French-speaking community outside of Quebec. The bulk of the population lies in the south of the province, and Winnipeg is overwhelmingly the largest city, and Canada's eighth largest, at 850,000 persons. Other cities include second-largest Brandon, as well as Thompson, Portage la Prairie, Flin Flon and Selkirk.

The Economy After the First World War, Manitoba and Winnipeg tended to lag behind in population and economic growth relative to the rest of Canada. A government railway connecting the south with the port of Churchill on Hudson Bay failed to attract sufficient traffic to be economically viable. Winnipeg remained

Winnipeg is the large industrial concentration, drawing on the province's hydroelectric capacity, and both Brandon and Portage la Prairie have a manufacturing and distribution role for their regions.

Government and Politics Manitoba has a single chamber legislative assembly, elected every four or five years. The chief of the largest party is the premier, who chooses a Cabinet from among party advocates in the legislature. Three main parties vie for support: the Progressive Conservatives, the New Democratic Party and the Liberals. The compulsory ceremonial leader, the lieutenant-governor, is at the apex of the political structure.

ABOVE: The barn owl and its numerous sub-species are widespread throughout the world. On the Prairies, however, crop-spraying has introduced deadly pesticides into its food, and elsewhere in Canada reduction in forest land threatens to limit its current range.

ONTARIO

POPULATION
11,404,800 (1998)

AREA
1,068,582 million
square kilometres

(416,747 square miles)

CAPITAL
Toronto

MOTTO
*Ut Incepit Fidelis Sic
Permanent* ("Loyal It
Began, Loyal It Remains")

FLORAL EMBLEM
White Trillium

*RIGHT: The Rideau Canal,
Ottawa, and the Peace Tower of the
Parliament Buildings. BELOW RIGHT:
Queen Street, Toronto.*

Beyond the flat farmland near the lower lakes – or what is left of it – lies the gently rolling and fertile country ... Then come the lower reaches of the Canadian Shield revealed by Champlain, the tireless explorer. Beyond that again is Northern Ontario where ... mines and mills invade the stillness of the forest but have not conquered it.

(G P DE T GLAZEBROOK, "LIFE IN ONTARIO", UNIVERSITY OF TORONTO PRESS, 1968)

The Land Ontario is Canada's second largest province in size. It is really two geographical regions: northern Ontario, starting north of Georgian Bay, rocky, rugged with thick forests and spotted with lakes, and southern Ontario, rolling agricultural lands spattered with hardwood forests. Two geographical features – the Canadian Shield, rocky, treed and dense with lakes, and the Hudson Bay lowlands, sparsely forested and characterized by bogs and swamps – dominate Northern Ontario. The southern Ontario peninsula, nestled between Lakes Erie, Ontario and Huron, on the west, is fertile and densely populated. Slightly to the east, around Kingston, the Canadian Shield divides the rest of the province from a flat plain around Ottawa in the valleys of the Ottawa and St Lawrence rivers. One-sixth of the province's surface consists of lakes and rivers.

History In historic times, Ontario was settled by Algonquian-speaking Indians to the north, and Iroquoian speakers to the south. When in 1615 the French penetrated what is now Ontario, they formed an

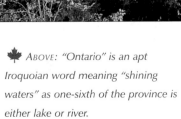

ABOVE: "Ontario" is an apt Iroquoian word meaning "shining waters" as one-sixth of the province is either lake or river.

association with a local Iroquoian nation, the Huron, who lived just south of Georgian Bay. The Huron and their French allies were decimated by another Iroquoian people, the Six Nations, in a cycle of war and disease that depopulated southern Ontario. During the 18th

century, the war between the French and the British for the possession of North America touched the fringes of Ontario. The region passed into British hands in 1758-1759 and remained in their possession during and after the American Revolution of the 1770s.

Refugees loyal to the British crown (Loyalists, referred to in the province's motto) settled much of southern Ontario in the 1780s. The British government created a separate colony, Upper Canada, to accommodate them. Though underpopulated and remote, it survived an American invasion in the War of 1812. Following that war, large numbers of immigrants arrived from Great Britain, reinforcing Upper Canada's attachment to Great Britain, which even a local rebellion (easily put down) in 1837-1838 failed to shake. In 1840, Upper Canada was temporarily merged with Lower Canada (now Quebec) in a single colony, Canada, but it was separated out again (and finally given the name of Ontario, an Iroquoian word probably meaning "beautiful water" or "lake") when the new federal union of Canada was created in 1867. Since then, Ontario has consistently had the largest population in the country, and along with Quebec has dominated Canadian federal politics.

The People Ontario is home to 37 per cent of the Canadian people. The province's population more than doubled between 1950 and 1996, outstripping that of the next largest province, Quebec, by an increasingly large margin. Roughly half of Ontario lives in the "Golden Horseshoe" around the western end of Lake Ontario, centred on the provincial capital of Toronto. More than 80 per cent of Ontarians live in cities, including Ottawa, the national capital, and Hamilton, Kitchener, St Catherines-Niagara, London, Windsor, Oshawa, Thunder Bay and Sudbury.

Ontario once had an overwhelmingly British-derived population, but since 1945 other groups have become increasingly important, transforming the province. Greater Toronto, the country's largest city, attracts some 70,000 immigrants a year. In 1999, it was estimated that the city comprised people from 169 countries, speaking 100 different languages, with one in five inhabitants having arrived since 1981. Toronto is also home to 42 per cent of Canada's visible minority population. French, once a significant language in Ontario, has tended to diminish over time, and in the 1990s was spoken by between four and five per cent of the provincial population. These numbers are dwarfed by more than a million Ontarians of South or East Asian origins. Ontario has more aboriginal people than any other Canadian jurisdiction.

The Economy Ontario is the heartland of the national economy, producing 50 per cent of total manufactures. It is also the country's chief mining province, and headquarters to the Canadian mining industry. Though agriculture was once the foundation of the province's economy, it has long since been surpassed, first by industry and then by the service sector. In

manufacturing, the automobile industry, founded as early as the 1900s but exponentially increased since a free trade "Autopact" with the United States in 1965, is far and away the most important component. Traditionally, Ontario's economic leaders have been protective of their province's position against competition from the United States, but since the Free Trade Agreement between Canada and the United States, implemented after 1989, Ontario's exports to that country have consistently grown, even in industries like wine or furniture that free trade was expected to

extinguish. In the 1990s, Ontario was a major factor not only in the Canadian economy, as it had traditionally been, but in a larger North American economy as well. The people of Ontario lead the country in individual income.

Government and Politics Ontario has a single-chamber legislative assembly elected in most cases every four or five years by universal suffrage. The leader of the largest party in the legislature is appointed premier, and chooses a Cabinet from supporters in the assembly. The principal parties provincially are the Progressive Conservatives, the Liberals and the New Democrats. For four decades, from 1942 to 1985, the Conservatives held power exclusively, governing from the centre. Since the mid-1980s, all three parties have had terms in government.

BELOW: Watson's Mill, Manotick, south of Ottawa. Constructed in 1860 from river limestone, this substantial Victorian building had a sad beginning. The very day that the mill was opened, the wife of the newly married mill owner died. BOTTOM RIGHT: Toronto's City Hall, which was completed in 1965, and fountains in Nathan Phillips Square.

QUEBEC

This province is a country within a country. Quebec the original heart. The hardest and deepest kernel. The core of first time. All around, nine other provinces form the flesh of this still-bitter fruit called Canada.

(ANNE HÉBERT, QUEBEC NOVELIST AND AUTHOR, 1967)

POPULATION
7,334,100 (1998)

AREA
1,540,680 square
kilometres

(600,865 square miles)

CAPITAL
Quebec City

MOTTO
Je me souviens
("I Remember")

FLORAL EMBLEM
Fleur-de-lis
(Madonna Lily)

The Land The word Quebec comes from an Algonquian word meaning "where the river narrows", the location on the St Lawrence River of the capital city of Quebec. More than one-sixth of the total area of Canada, over twice the size of Texas, the province stretches from the American border to Hudson Strait, bounded on the east by Newfoundland, on the south by New Brunswick, Maine, Vermont, New Hampshire and New York, and on the west by Ontario. The Canadian Shield, with its characteristic rocks and lakes, sweeps across Quebec. Combined with cool summers and cold winters, it makes most of the province unsuitable for agriculture. Only the St Lawrence Valley and the adjacent Appalachian region along the province's southern fringe, where the climate is less forbidding, are suitable for large-scale agriculture. The great rivers of northern and central Quebec drive hydroelectric development.

History Present-day Quebec was originally the French colony of New France, discovered by the explorer Jacques Cartier in 1534 and first settled by Samuel de Champlain in 1608. New France grew slowly under French rule. Limited in population (about 60,000 in 1750) and beset by enemies, New France succumbed to British attacks in 1760 and was formally transferred to Great Britain in 1763. The British government organized the territory as the Province of Quebec, granted its inhabitants the right to use the French language and French civil laws, and to practice the Roman Catholic religion.

In 1791, Quebec's name was changed to Lower Canada, and an elected assembly was created. British governors and French-speaking politicians found many occasions to quarrel, culminating in a rebellion in 1837-1838, which was suppressed by the British army. Lower Canada was merged with English-speaking Upper Canada as a consequence, and in 1848 this united province ("Canada") received control over its own government. Quebec became a province of the newly created country of Canada in 1867, with its own system of laws and majority French language intact.

For many years it was an inward-looking province, its French-speaking inhabitants content to resist encroachments by English-speakers, who formed a significant minority in parts of the province and dominated the economic life of Quebec. The Catholic Church throughout this period was a major force in daily life, especially in education and social policy.

ABOVE: North America's largest gannet colony is on Bonaventure Island. RIGHT: Visitors to the Basilica of Notre Dame, Montreal, are frequently struck both by its size and the richness of its interior decoration.

FAR LEFT: High-rise buildings tower to the sky in modern Montreal. LEFT: The Old City of Quebec as seen from Champlain Boulevard. A lighthouse looks out over the Saint Lawrence River and, on the heights, Château Frontenac dominates the skyline. This palatial hotel was built in 1892 on the original site of Samuel de Champlain's Fort St Louis.

Quebec's largest city, Montreal, became Canada's financial, industrial and transportation centre. Politicians from Quebec played a major role in the affairs of Canada, but periodic disagreements with the English-speaking majority in Canada occurred, especially around the issue of participation in the First and Second World Wars, French-speaking Quebeckers preferring to abstain.

The People Historically, Quebec has been about 80 per cent French-speaking, mainly the descendants of the original French settlers of colonial times, and 20 per cent speaking some other language, mainly English. English-speakers have been concentrated in and around the great cosmopolitan city of Montreal, which like other North American cities received many immigrants in the 19th and 20th centuries. Worried by their small numbers relative to the very large numbers of English-speakers in North America, Quebec's French-speaking majority in the 1970s and 1980s passed laws restricting the use of English and promoting the use of French. These actions have tended to diminish the number of English-speakers in Quebec, as well as the number of immigrants. Moreover, the birth rate in Quebec has been relatively low. Quebec's population as a proportion of the Canadian total fell from 29 to 25 per cent between 1951 and 1996.

The Economy Quebec has an abundance of natural resources. Its northern rivers, flowing into Hudson and James Bays, have been developed by huge hydroelectric projects at James Bay and Manicouagan. The Canadian Shield is a storehouse of lumber and minerals, and

Quebec is a major producer of lumber and primary minerals such as iron ore. Agriculture has always been of significance to the province, and farmers are an important political pressure group. The province has Canada's most varied manufacturing sector, from wood products and chemicals to foods and transportation equipment.

Government and Politics The atmosphere of Quebec politics changed considerably in the 1950s and 1960s. French-speakers turned away from the Catholic Church and toward the provincial government. The role of the church diminished, therefore, while that of the local state increased. Confrontations with the national government in Ottawa followed, and helped give rise to a substantial separatist movement in Quebec, which sought the province's independence as a French-speaking state distinct from the majority English-speaking state of Canada.

One of Quebec's two major parties, the Liberals, supports in general the federal system, and their position has been sustained in two provincial referendums on the independence question, in 1980 and 1995. The other main party, the Parti Québécois, stands for separation from Canada by democratic means. Non-French-speaking Quebeckers overwhelmingly wish to remain in Canada, while about 60 per cent of French-speakers favour the independence option in a diluted form, involving a continuing economic association with the other nine provinces. The cleavage between the province and the "rest of Canada" has dominated Quebec and national politics since the 1960s.

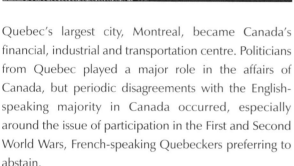

ABOVE: Montreal is an amazing mélange of cultures, as can be seen in its diverse architectural styles. When explorer Jacques Cartier was taken, in 1535, to admire the view from the island's high ground, overlooking where the city stands today, he remarked that it was "un mont réal" (a royal mountain), and the name stuck.

33

NEW BRUNSWICK

POPULATION
752,400 (1998)

AREA
73,436 square kilometres

(28,640 square miles)

CAPITAL
Fredericton

MOTTO
Spem Reduxit
("Hope Was Restored")

FLORAL EMBLEM
Purple Violet

We are going to begin our study of Geography with an imaginary journey across our own country ... We have chosen the aeroplane for our trip because it is so fast and because we can see much more of the country from high in the air ... Leaving Nova Scotia behind, we sweep across the Bay of Fundy and begin our flight over New Brunswick. It seems to be a province of trees. For mile after mile we see almost unbroken forest. Through the woods run many rivers, some of them of great size. Here and there on the river banks are little villages, each clustered about a saw-mill. There are farms, too, and occasionally we see a town or a city. But we shall always remember New Brunswick as a forest province.

(*CHILDREN'S SCHOOLBOOK OF THE 1930S*)

The Land New Brunswick's surface, a square of land measuring about 500 kilometres or 200 miles from north to south and east to west, is surprisingly varied. There is sea on three sides, moderating the temperatures in the coastal areas. Central and western New Brunswick, dominated by the fertile St John River valley, are important for agriculture. In the north there are rolling hills, and to the southeast salt marshes and a coastal plain. The province was once heavily forested, and the harvest of wood is still important for the local economy.

the area. At first the British included the whole Maritime region in their colony of Nova Scotia, but after the American Revolution, and with the arrival of 14,000 Loyalist refugees along the St John River, New Brunswick was made a separate colony in 1784. This was named after the German duchy of Brunswick-Lauenberg, to which the British royal family were connected. New Brunswick joined the movement for Canadian Confederation in the 1860s, though hesitantly, and became one of the four original provinces of Canada in 1867.

 ABOVE: This Dutch colonial-style cottage on Campobello Island belonged to United States President Franklin D Roosevelt. When young, he was brought here every summer. In later life, he would spend time there with his wife, Eleanor, and children. ABOVE RIGHT: A glorious display of red maple near Goshen.

History New Brunswick was first settled by the Micmac, whose communities spread across all of what are today Canada's Maritime Provinces. The Micmac at first welcomed and assisted the French, who explored the Bay of Fundy coast early in the 17th century. French settlement (called *Acadie*, or Acadia) was concentrated across the Bay, but spread into coastal New Brunswick. The Chignecto Isthmus, adjacent to Nova Scotia, developed a unique agricultural community, dependent on dikes. The French settlers were caught up in the wars between France and Britain, and in 1755 the British expelled most of them in order to secure their control of

The People The Loyalists who arrived in the 1780s were supplemented by substantial immigration from Ireland and Scotland in the 19th century. Some Acadians never left, while others drifted back; many French-speakers arrived from adjacent parts of Quebec. This migration gave New Brunswick a substantial French minority.

The population of New Brunswick remained remarkably stable in numbers through the 1990s. There are no large cities in the province (Fredericton, the capital and biggest city, has roughly 80,000 inhabitants), and the population is about 50 per cent urban.

34

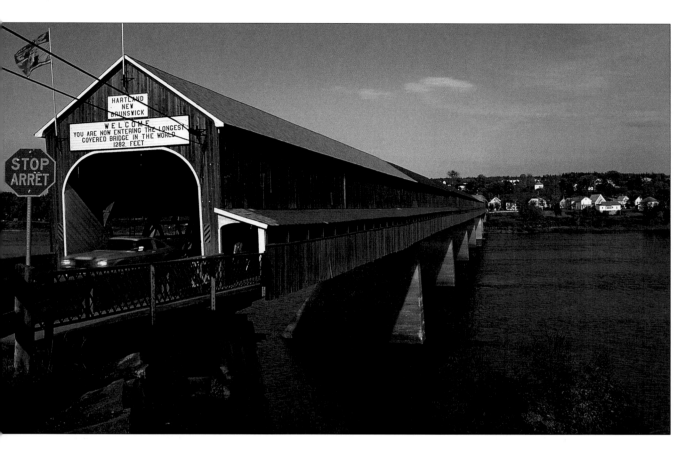

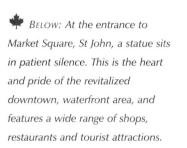

improved considerably after 1960, and New Brunswick is the strongest and most diversified of the Atlantic province economies, with a good manufacturing component, a burgeoning telecommunications sector and the United States market for its exports.

Wood is New Brunswick's most important natural resource and lumbering, pulp and paper have been crucial throughout the 20th century to the provincial economy. Second in importance is the mining of base metals, potash, coal and even some gold deposits; there is also a good deal of resource-related manufacturing. Farming is important in the south, and along the St John River, where potatoes have formed the basis for a small agricultural empire. Moncton has traditionally been a rail transport centre, though its importance as such has declined. Saint John has an oil refinery and a container port, as well as some shipbuilding. New Brunswick is home to two great commercial empires, the Irving interests (organized around oil refining) and the McCain food processing conglomerate.

Nevertheless, there is a rivalry and a considerable difference among the three largest cities: Fredericton, Saint John, a port city at the mouth of the St John River, and Moncton, where French is a common language. Approximately two-thirds of the province speak English and one-third French. French speakers are concentrated in the northern part of the province and the eastern shore, clustering around Moncton.

The Economy Agriculture in the St John valley, lumbering and the timber trade, fishing and shipbuilding dominated the economy of colonial New Brunswick. New Brunswick-built clipper ships were famous around the world for their quality and speed, but shipbuilding declined, as in Nova Scotia, with the advent of iron ships in the 1860s. In the years after 1867, New Brunswick tended to be less prosperous than the rest of Canada, and provincial politics concentrated on ways and means of improving the provincial economy, while seeking assistance from the national government. The situation

Government and Politics New Brunswick is governed by a unicameral legislative assembly, elected every four or five years. The leader of the majority party in the assembly is appointed premier and in turn appoints a Cabinet from the legislature. The Liberals and the Progressive Conservatives are the dominant parties; one or the other has been in power since 1867. In recognition of its substantial French-speaking minority, New Brunswick is an officially bilingual province, the only jurisdiction in Canada apart from the federal government to enjoy this formal status.

NOVA SCOTIA

Boys, brag of your country. When I'm abroad, I brag of everything that Nova Scotia is, has, or can produce; and when they beat me at everything else, I turn round on them and say, "How high does your tide rise?"
(JOSEPH HOWE, NOVA SCOTIAN POLITICIAN AND JOURNALIST, 1804-1873)

The Land Nova Scotia's coastline, heavily indented, is almost 7,600 kilometres long. Only 10 per cent of the land can be used for agriculture, mainly in the Annapolis Valley off the Bay of Fundy, and along the Northumberland Strait that divides the province from Prince Edward Island. The rest of the province is hilly and rocky, replete with lakes.

History Nova Scotia was originally settled by the Micmac nation, a branch of the Algonquian language group. Norse voyagers may have visited Nova Scotia around AD 1000, but the first certain landfall by a European was by John Cabot in 1497. Cabot sailed on behalf of the English crown, but it was the French in 1605 who established the first European settlement in Nova Scotia, at Port Royal in the fertile Annapolis Valley. James VI of Scotland (James I of England) laid claim to the region shortly after, calling it Nova Scotia (Latin for New Scotland), but no settlers arrived to enforce his claim. Instead, Nova Scotia became part of the French colony of Acadia, whose settlement was concentrated around Port Royal.

The colony was seized by the British in 1710, and Port Royal renamed Annapolis Royal, in honour of Queen Anne. The name of the colony changed at this time, from Acadia to Nova Scotia. Although France ceded Acadia (except for Cape Breton Island) to Great Britain in 1713, the British hold was feeble until reinforced by the foundation of Halifax, in 1749, as a garrison and naval base. In 1755, the British expelled most of the French-speaking Acadians and invited settlers from New England to replace them. This made Nova Scotia a predominantly English-speaking province, and it has remained so ever since. In 1758, the British granted an elected assembly to the settlers; that same year the British took the French fortress of Louisbourg on Cape Breton Island, completing the conquest of what is now Nova Scotia.

During the American Revolution, the British managed to retain Nova Scotia, which became a centre for Loyalist refugees from the newly independent United States. New Brunswick was detached from Nova Scotia in 1784 and, for a time (until 1820), Cape Breton was governed as a separate colony. In the 1860s, Premier Charles Tupper brought Nova Scotia into

Confederation with Canada. This was briefly unpopular with Nova Scotians, but they eventually adjusted to a system that brought them railway connections to the heart of the continent, and profited the port and industries of Halifax. Nevertheless, Nova Scotia's restricted size and remote location eventually produced a steady exodus of people to the rest of Canada, and to the United States, in search of better opportunities.

The People Nova Scotia's population grew slowly but steadily over the last years of the 20th century. Most of the population is of British descent; six per cent claim purely French ancestry. Of that number, roughly four per cent spoke French, and 93 per cent English. Immigration is low, and there is a small net outflow of people to other provinces. Halifax, the capital, is by far the largest city (347,000 in its metropolitan area in 1996).

The Economy In the early 19th century, Nova Scotia prospered. Lumbering, shipbuilding, agriculture and fishery made the province an attractive destination for thousands of immigrants. Coal mining began on Cape Breton Island. The wars of the 20th century benefited Halifax, as a naval and shipping port, as well as the coal and steel industries of Cape Breton. Halifax and Sydney were two of the main Allied convoy staging ports for the protection of transatlantic shipping in both world wars.

With one of the biggest natural harbours in the world, Halifax remains the home of the Canadian

🍁 *ABOVE: Sea stacks at Cape Breton Highlands National Park. The Atlantic waters that crash around this rock-fringed nature reserve are among the most treacherous in North America.*
ABOVE RIGHT: Safe harbour for vessels at Blue Rocks, near Lunenburg.

navy's Atlantic fleet and the country's most complex military base. The biggest city in the region east of Montreal, the Nova Scotian capital is also the principal legal, financial and transportation centre for Atlantic Canada, as well as a hub of university research and culture.

Agriculture, small manufacturing, mining, tourism and services have been important components of a many-sided provincial economy, with tourism markedly on the rise in the 1990s, and services a bigger part of the mix than the national norm. The formerly important coal-mining industry of Cape Breton has been in steady decline since the 1950s, and attempts to modernize it or to diversify the island's output have not been successful. The federal and provincial governments have poured billions of dollars into resuscitating Nova Scotia's, and especially Cape Breton's, ailing economy, which generally performs under the Canadian average in areas such as employment and growth.

Government and Politics Nineteenth-century politics were lively as appointed governor and elected assembly contended for power. Eventually, as a result of the efforts of the editor-politician Joseph Howe, the assembly prevailed in 1848, and Nova Scotia became the first colony in the British Empire to achieve responsible government in which governments were no longer appointed from London, but rather as the result of local elections.

Nova Scotia has a unicameral elected assembly, with elections usually every four or five years. The leader of the largest party becomes premier and chooses a

Cabinet from among that party's supporters in the assembly. Provincial politics in Nova Scotia have been dominated by the two traditional Canadian parties, the Liberals and the Conservatives, which have alternated in government ever since 1867.

The procurement of money from the federal treasury to support the troubled economy has been crucial. As a result, questions of social welfare and industrial subsidy have been extremely important in Nova Scotia politics, and attempts to reduce such programmes have met with disfavour at the polls. Discontent with federal subsidies contributed in the 1990s to the rise of the New Democratic Party, both provincially and federally.

ABOVE: Sandstone cliffs tower above a deserted inlet near Blomidon.

PRINCE EDWARD ISLAND

The scene of the play is an island, south of Newfoundland and northwest of Nova Scotia, jutting out into the mystery of the Atlantic, and known among the Maritime Provinces of Canada as the garden spot of the Gulf.

(ELMER HARRIS, AMERICAN PLAYWRIGHT, STAGE DIRECTIONS FOR "JOHNNY BELINDA", 1940)

The Land   Visitors to Canada's smallest province immediately notice its red soil, made up of sand and clay. The island itself was a deposit from freshwater streams at the end of the Ice Age, and originally was not an island at all. Rising water levels that accompanied the melting of the glaciers severed it from the mainland about 5,000 years ago. The climate is mild, fog relatively rare and rainfall abundant.

History   Known to its early settlers, the Micmacs, as *Abegweit* or "cradled on the waves", "the Island" was Isle St-Jean to the French, and finally (in 1799) Prince Edward Island after Edward, Duke of Kent and father to Queen Victoria.

The first aboriginal settlement on the island dates back 10,000 years; the Micmacs arrived at least 2,000 years ago. The French began to settle the land in the 1720s, and it became a refuge for French-speaking Acadians under pressure from the British on the mainland. The British deported all but a few hundred of the island's inhabitants during the Seven Years' War (1756-1763), and the island was formally ceded to the British in 1763.

Originally called the Island of St John, a simple translation of its French name, the island was at first governed as part of Nova Scotia. More important than its government, however, was its ownership. In 1767, the British government parcelled it out in large tracts to landlords or proprietors, most of whom refused to settle there. Settlers who did come to the island had to buy their land from the proprietors, or pay heavy rents. Although the proprietors were supposed to pay taxes to maintain a government, many refused.

Despite these adverse conditions, the island was settled, largely by Scots, in the 1770s, and by Loyalist refugees in the 1780s. The population eventually grew to over 60,000 by the mid-19th century, attracted by the natural beauty and fertile soil. Nineteenth-century immigrants, unlike those of the 18th century, were largely Irish and Catholic, and their arrival gave a religious and cultural edge to island politics, and a greater urgency to the question of the ownership of

land. Relations between proprietors and tenants dominated the economy and politics for this whole period. Eventually, but very gradually, the proprietors were bought out – "compensated" for land that few of them had done anything to develop – and a burden on the province was removed.

The Island of St John received a separate administration in 1769, including a lieutenant-governor and an elected assembly. Eventually, in 1851, Prince

Edward Island obtained local control over government ("responsible government"). The geographical and cultural isolation of the island made it initially resist absorption into newly founded Canada, but by 1873 economic difficulties made union with the mainland inevitable, and the province joined Confederation in that year.

The People   Although it has more people than ever before, Prince Edward Island has the smallest provincial population in Canada. Given the physical size of the island, however, it is the most densely populated. The province is unusually ethnically homogeneous, mostly of British origin, though a small group derive from the early French Acadian settlers. There is also a small Micmac community. Island couples marry more often than other

TOP: A colourful autumnal vista.
ABOVE: Cavendish Beach. The town of Cavendish is at the centre of the beloved Anne of Green Gables story.
ABOVE RIGHT: Lighthouse and harvested field at Cape Tryon.

on lobsters, crabs, scallops and oysters, the Malpeque oyster being especially well known. Tourism and service industries are also vital cogs in the provincial economy.

Government and Politics Prince Edward Island has a single chamber, elected assembly, with elections every four or five years. The leader of the majority party becomes premier, and appoints a Cabinet from among supporters in the assembly. Island politics have been dominated since the 1850s by two parties, Liberals and Conservatives, though there are signs that this two-party tradition may be breaking down.

Canadians and the divorce rate is the lowest: 24 out of every 100 marriages end in divorce, compared with 48 in Quebec and 56 in the Yukon Territory.

Prince Edward Island is technically Canada's least urban province and its only city, the provincial capital, Charlottetown, has a population of about 16,000. However, if Charlottetown's suburbs are counted, over half the island's population lives in or around the capital.

The Economy The island maintained a farming and fishing economy after 1873. It also produced a surplus of inhabitants who, given the restricted size of the province, found themselves obliged to move, either to other parts of Canada or to the United States. As a result, the island's population gradually declined, and did not again reach the levels of the late 19th century until after about 1950, when urbanization and greater economic diversity made it possible to expand again.

As part of the Confederation bargain with Canada in 1873, the federal government maintained ferry services across the 15 kilometres of the Northumberland Strait, but distance, water and weather made the island relatively isolated, a condition that some inhabitants cherished as a unique and even essential part of its identity and culture. After a referendum, Islanders approved a bridge to the mainland, and it was duly built in the late 1990s. For the first time it became possible to drive on or off the island.

Originally forested, Prince Edward Island now only has scattered clumps of trees. Its main resource is its soil, and its main occupation agriculture, with fishing an important secondary industry. Called "Spud Island" because of its suitability for growing potatoes, the island has a small beef industry as well. Fishery concentrates

FAR LEFT: Opened in 1997, Confederation Bridge provides a permanent link between Prince Edward Island and the mainland of Canada. An amazing feat of engineering, it is the longest continuous marine span bridge in the Western Hemisphere. BELOW: The delightful fishing village of French River on Prince Edward Island's northern shore.

LEFT: Province House in Queen's Square, Charlottetown, was built in 1843-1847 and houses the Provincial Legislature. Within the three-storey sandstone structure is the famous room where representatives of Canada, New Brunswick, Nova Scotia and Prince Edward Island met in 1864 to discuss political union. This led to Confederation three years later.

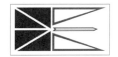

NEWFOUNDLAND AND LABRADOR

Look, sir, at the map of the continent of America, and mark that island commanding the mouth of the noble river that almost cuts our continent in twain. Well, sir, that island is equal in extent to the kingdom of Portugal.

(GEORGE BROWN, LEGISLATIVE ASSEMBLY, PROVINCE OF CANADA, 1865)

The Land   The island is a continuation of the Appalachian system, while Labrador is a part of the Canadian Shield, with rocky terrain and lakes, and traversed by rivers. There is little arable land, and the climate does not encourage agriculture. Nevertheless, there is some farming for local consumption. Labrador accounts for three-quarters of the landmass of the province.

History   An aboriginal people, the Beothuk, settled the island of Newfoundland, while mainland Labrador was inhabited, along the coast, by Inuit. Norse explorers came early to Newfoundland and briefly established a settlement at Anse-aux-Meadows around AD 1000. The

 ABOVE: Bay de Verde lies directly north of the capital of St John's, across Conception Bay, on the far northern extremity of the Avalon Peninsula.

next visitor to what is now Newfoundland was the explorer John Cabot, who named the place the "new isle" or New Land, *Terra Nova* in Latin. The Portuguese under Gaspar Corte-Real further explored Newfoundland in 1500, and Jacques Cartier demonstrated that it was an island in 1534-1535.

The real attraction of Newfoundland for Europeans was the ocean of fish that surrounded it, and by the mid-16th century a regular fishery was established along the coasts by the English, French, Spanish (Basque) and Portuguese. Cod was king in Newfoundland from the 16th century to the 20th; salted and cured along the coast, it was the staple diet of the poor in Western Europe. Fish merchants from the English West Country dominated the trade and tried to discourage permanent settlement. Nevertheless, Sir Humphrey Gilbert, with Queen Elizabeth I's authority, attempted just that in 1583, and by 1610 small colonies were established on the Avalon Peninsula.

Life was harsh in 17th-century Newfoundland, embittered by the clashing interests of the permanent settlers and the fishers from England. The French further complicated matters by asserting their own claims to the island, so that Newfoundland became a scene of war, centring on the French fort at Plaisance (Placentia). By the Treaty of Utrecht of 1713, the French abandoned their claim to land, but received instead privileges to cure fish along part of the coast ("the French Shore"), which guaranteed further trouble with local settlers.

Newfoundland grew steadily in population through the 18th century, and conditions of life eased after the establishment of an organized government. Wars and diplomacy still complicated matters: a treaty in 1763 confirmed French fishing rights and gave France two small islands off the south coast, St Pierre and Miquelon, while after the American Revolution the United States received privileges in the fishery. By the late 18th century, St John's on the Avalon Peninsula had become the centre of government and trade, dividing the island between the interests of the St John's merchants and the fishing folk of the remote settlements, the "outports". For reasons of convenience, the British government attached the "coast of Labrador" to Newfoundland.

Like other British colonies, Newfoundland eventually received an elected assembly, but not until 1832. Local autonomy ("responsible government") came even later (1855), and much complicated by ethnic and religious rivalries among the population, especially between Irish

Catholics and West Country English Protestants. The fishery continued to attract immigrants, but in the 19th century pulp and paper, lumber and mining began to contribute to the economy. Newfoundlanders were confident enough to resist joining Canada in the 1860s, and repeated their refusal in the 1890s and 1910s. In 1934, Newfoundland gave up its elected government and became a British dependency again, paid for by the British taxpayer and run by British officials. Newfoundland voted, narrowly, to join Canada in 1949.

The People Newfoundland is the only place in Canada which is losing population. Almost 200,000 native

Newfoundlanders are believed to reside elsewhere in Canada, and this number does not account for those who may have moved to the United States. Most Newfoundlanders live on the island rather than in Labrador, and are of European descent. Inuit and Naskapi-Montagnais live almost entirely in Labrador, although the majority of the population there is of European origin. St John's is the largest city at 178,000.

The Economy The island of Newfoundland sits in the middle of its principal natural resource, the fishing grounds of the northwest Atlantic. Politicians balanced the demands of economic development against the existing interests of the fishery, but Newfoundland's fortunes rose and fell with the price of cod. When, in the

1930s, the price plummeted, and the prices of other Newfoundland-produced commodities fell as well, the colony had to declare bankruptcy. The Newfoundland economy revived with the Second World War and in its aftermath.

Joining Canada brought Canadian social services and subsidies from the central government in Ottawa. The economy diversified, but at the same time emigration increased. In the 1980s and 1990s, the cod fishery saw serious difficulties. Groundfish stocks have declined catastrophically and it is difficult to know when, and how, they can be restored, although there has been some success in shell and other types of fishing.

The island is mostly forested and supports a pulp and paper industry, while offshore discoveries of oil have raised hopes of an energy bonanza. The water resources of Labrador have been developed for electricity, but much of that is sold at a low price to adjacent Quebec. Iron-ore mining is also a significant factor in the Labrador economy. Tourism and especially government services are vital to the economy. Traditionally, the Newfoundland economy lags behind that of other provinces.

Politics and Government Newfoundland is governed by a single chamber assembly, elected usually every four or five years by universal suffrage. Since 1949 two parties, the Liberals and the Progressive Conservatives, have dominated politics and formed governments, though the New Democratic Party has made inroads from time to time.

 TOP LEFT: Typical wooden clapboard buildings in St John's. ABOVE LEFT: Rugged Atlantic coastline at Tor Bay. TOP RIGHT: Gros Morne National Park, on the western coast, contains some of Canada's most geologically interesting and spectacular land forms. ABOVE: The lighthouse at Cape Bonavista, built in 1841-1843.

POPULATION
31,600 (1998)

AREA
482,515 square kilometres

(188,181 square miles)

CAPITAL
Whitehorse

MOTTO
Unofficially,
"Home of the Klondike"

FLORAL EMBLEM
Purple Fireweed

TOP: *Snowmobiles offer the fastest means of transport across the frozen land when winter blankets the Yukon in snow.* ABOVE: *Autumnal colours tint the forest.*

YUKON TERRITORY

This is the Law of the Yukon, that only the Strong shall thrive;
That surely the Weak shall perish, and only the Fit survive.
(ROBERT SERVICE, "THE SPELL OF THE YUKON AND OTHER VERSES", 1907)

The Land Yukon Territory takes its name from a Loucheux Indian word, *Yu-kun-ah*, meaning "great river", the Yukon River which drains most of the region and flows through Alaska to the sea. One of the oldest known sites of human habitation in North America lies in the Yukon, which many archaeologists believe was a main thoroughfare for immigrants to the North American continent from northeast Asia.

Three-quarters of the land surface is drained by the Yukon River and its tributaries. Most of the territory is part of the western cordillera, forested in the south and tundra to the north. In the extreme north, there is the Arctic coastal plain, while to the east there is a small plain around the Peel River.

History The Yukon country was remote and inaccessible to early travellers. The British explorer, Sir John Franklin, investigated the Arctic coast in 1825, but used the Mackenzie River, rather than the Yukon, as his main route. Hudson's Bay Company fur traders made their way into the Yukon region in the 1840s, followed by gold-seekers mostly from British Columbia later in the 19th century. On 17 August 1896, one prospector, George Carmack, struck gold on a claim on Bonanza Creek, in the Klondike basin in central Yukon. A new settlement, Dawson Creek, at the junction of the Klondike and Yukon rivers, was founded to serve the anticipated rush of people eager to make their fortunes. In 1898, the Canadian government hastily organized the Yukon into a separate territory, and dispatched administrators and the North West Mounted Police (today's Royal Canadian Mounted Police) to keep order.

The People According to the 1901 census, the population of the Yukon was 27,000 but most people slipped away when the gold was gone, until only 4,000 were left in the territory. The south and central Yukon were inhabited by members of the Dene language group, including the Tagish, Nahanni and Kutchin. To the north, along the coast, the Inuit prevailed. Approximately 20 per cent belong to one or another of the aboriginal nations, living in the northern or central regions of the territory. Over half of the Yukon's population lives in the capital, Whitehorse; Dawson, the

previous capital, accounts for many of the rest. With a high birth rate and diminishing mortalities, the Yukon Territory grew faster in the 1990s than any place in Canada except British Columbia. Yukoners are more apt to marry than other Canadians, and more apt to divorce.

The Economy The Yukon gold rush began in earnest in 1897. By 1898, Dawson had 40,000 people – larger at the time than Vancouver. Whitehorse sprang into existence as a transshipment point on the way to Dawson. After 1904, the mines began to decline, most people left and the Yukon reverted to being a remote frontier, dependent on mining, but on a much reduced scale, and not only of gold but of silver and lead. Fur trapping resumed its importance.

During World War II, the United States government constructed a highway from northern British Columbia through the Yukon to Alaska, as well as airfields to sustain an aerial supply operation across the Bering Strait. The Alaska Highway did three things: it injected money into the Yukon economy, it brought immigrants into the Yukon, and it shifted the economic centre of gravity south. Recognizing the population shift, the capital was moved from Dawson to Whitehorse in 1952.

In the postwar period, transportation and tourism remained important, while large-scale mining from time to time injected money into the territorial economy. Mining, for example in the Faro lead-zinc mine, dominates the present-day Yukon economy, with tourism and services as important adjuncts.

Government and Politics As a territory, the Yukon does not have the same autonomy as Canadian provinces. The federal government in Ottawa controls important government powers and, in return, is ultimately responsible for the territory's budget. Naturally, the Yukon tries to be as self-sufficient as it can, but its geography, climate, small population base and vulnerability to the boom-and-bust cycle of the crucial mining sector make it almost impossible to sustain normal government activities without outside help. One interesting feature is native self-government, with agreements signed between the Ottawa government and various aboriginal groups within the territory.

NORTHWEST TERRITORIES

No one who has flown over the North West Territories has been able to do so without marvelling at the courage and inspiration of the men who fought their way to the Arctic practically foot by foot.
(C H "PUNCH" DICKENS, CANADIAN BUSH PILOT, 1929)

The Land The Northwest Territories is the name originally applied to the land purchased from the Hudson's Bay Company by Canada in 1870 and stretching from the Rockies to Hudson Strait. Organized and administered by the federal government, the Territories were tacitly defined to be those regions of Canada that could not be self-supporting, and hence were not eligible for provincial status. In 1870, Manitoba was carved out of part of the Territories, as were Alberta and Saskatchewan in 1905. Ontario, Quebec and Manitoba all expanded northwards into the Territories, which after 1912 were confined to the area east of the Yukon and north of 60 degrees in the west, and north of Hudson Bay and Hudson Strait in the east.

The Mackenzie Valley is the most important river and transportation corridor, flanked on the west by an extension of the western cordillera and on the east by the Canadian Shield. The Mackenzie River, at the heart of the inhospitable Taiga Plains, is the largest in the country. Great Bear Lake is vast: the greatest lake wholly within Canada and ranking eighth in size globally at 31,000 square kilometres. Yellowknife, the biggest community, is colder in winter and has more sun in summer than any city in Canada.

History European explorers came early to the eastern Arctic, in search of the Northwest Passage from the Atlantic to the Pacific, and Asia. The explorers were doomed to disappointment, finding only impassable ice and impenetrable tundra. Although a Northwest Passage of a kind was proved to exist in the 1850s, and actually navigated in 1903, sea travel in the north has never been an especially fruitful quest.

Fur traders penetrated the Northwest Territories via the Mackenzie River in the west, named after its discoverer, Sir Alexander Mackenzie, who travelled its length to the Arctic in 1789. Fur-trading posts were established in the Mackenzie Valley and, somewhat later, missionary stations. Eventually, the Canadian government sent the North West Mounted Police north to assert its presence.

The People Though sparsely settled throughout their history, the Northwest Territories have supported indigenous peoples for thousands of years, Dene below the tree line, and Inuit to the north. It was only with the advent of large-scale mining around Great Slave Lake, and the development of service centres for the indigenous population, that any significant numbers of people moved in from the south.

The Economy The Northwest Territories were founded on the fur trade, but mining has come to be dominant in the local economy. There is gold mining around Yellowknife and lead and zinc at Pine Point, but silver, uranium and other metals have been discovered and exploited. The Norman Wells field is Canada's fourth largest oil producer.

Government and Politics The Northwest Territories are under the jurisdiction of the national government, and are administered by a popularly-elected legislative assembly under a commissioner.

POPULATION
42,900
(estimate, 1999)

AREA
1,479,000 square
kilometres

(576,810 square miles)

CAPITAL
Yellowknife

MOTTO
Unofficially,
"The New North"

FLORAL EMBLEM
Mountain Avens

TOP LEFT: Nahanni National Park lies in the southwest of the Northwest Territories. It is not a place for the faint-hearted, but its spectacular wilderness is a compelling lure for the adventurous. BOTTOM LEFT: Boathouses at Yellowknife, the capital of the Northwest Territories. ABOVE: The eery, but beautiful, Northern Lights shimmer in the night sky.

NUNAVUT

Most of Nunavut shows the effects of glaciation, from the u-shaped valleys and hanging glaciers of Baffin Island to the eskers of the central barrenlands. Icecaps still adorn Baffin, Ellesmere, Devon, and Bylot Islands ... In other places, the ice sheets are gone, but have left their mark. In places the land is carved, lakes are precisely aligned, and the very bedrock is deeply grooved, cut by the abrasive effects of rocks embedded in ice more than a mile thick grinding across the land – sandpaper beyond imagination.
("THE ARCTIC TRAVELLER", 1999)

The Land Nunavut stands for "Our Land" in Inukitut, the language of the Inuit people. Cut out of the Northwest Territories at the cap of Canada in 1999, the territory is the country's largest jurisdiction, almost one-fourth of the national landmass, more than five times the size of Germany and four times that of Sweden. Winter persists in Nunavut for longer than six months, and the ground is permanently frozen to a great depth all year round. The capital of Iqaluit has a mean temperature in January of -30 degrees Celsius and in July of 15 degrees; there are 24 hours of daylight each day in June and six hours in December.

 ABOVE: The use of the snowmobile and the rifle have revolutionized hunting methods. ABOVE RIGHT: Many Inuit still rely on hunting to obtain their meat and fish. TOP RIGHT: A majestic polar bear.

The Canadian Shield dominates the central mainland. Major rivers run to Hudson Bay in one direction and the Arctic Ocean in another. The territory reaches the Arctic Circle at the longitude of Repulse Bay, goes almost to the North Pole and takes in a large number of islands, the most striking being the enormous Baffin Island (507,451 square kilometres), where polar bears, narwhals, belugas, seals, walruses and a multiplicity of seabirds reside.

History The government of Canada declared its support for a separate territory of Nunavut in 1990 and agreed to its creation by 1999 as an ingredient of the 1993 Nunavut Land Claim Agreement, which promised the Inuit people "a form of self-government" and title to 350,000 square kilometres of land in the eastern Arctic.

The commission charged with giving advice on the establishment of the territory wanted innovative two-member ridings for the legislature, with one woman and one man representing each constituency, but this was decisively rejected by a plebiscite in 1997.

The People The Inuit, meaning in Inukitut "the people, those who are living today", claim an ancestry going back 5,000 years to a time when their forebears travelled across the Bering land bridge from Asia and, more recently, to the Thule people, who came from Alaska 1,000 years ago. Seventy-five per cent of the inhabitants are Inuit. The population density per square kilometre is 0.01, but the growth rate in the population is high. Iqaluit is the largest community at 3,600 people.

The Economy The bulk of employment is with government, and there are some mining, trapping and tourism jobs. Most products have to be brought in at considerable cost; bread and milk, for example, cost three times more than they do in southern Canada.

Government and Politics A federal territory, Nunavut is governed by a commissioner and an Inuit-controlled legislative assembly, first elected in 1999.

MAP LEGEND

SETTLEMENT

For scales larger than 1 inch : 30 miles   Population

	BIRMINGHAM	>1,000,000
	GLASGOW	500,000–1,000,000
	CARDIFF	250,000–500,000
	LIMERICK	50,000–250,000
•	**Dover**	10,000–50,000
•	Lossiemouth	5,000–10,000
○	Church Stretton	<5,000
	CROYDON	London Borough

For scales between 1 inch : 30 miles and 1 inch : 190 miles

	NEW YORK	>5,000,000
	MONTRÉAL	2,500,000–5,000,000
▪	**SAN DIEGO**	1,000,000–2,500,000
•	**Hyderabad**	500,000–1,000,000
•	Adelaide	100,000–500,000
○	Key West	<100,000

For scales smaller than 1 inch : 190 miles

▪	**LOS ANGELES**	>1,000,000
•	**Maracaibo**	500,000–1,000,000
•	Santa Fe	<500,000

Washington National capital   **Winnipeg** State, provincial capital

COMMUNICATIONS

═══════	Highway
╌╌╌╌╌╌	Highway under construction
──────	Principal road
--------	Principal road under construction
──────	Other main road
─ ─ ─ ─	Track, seasonal road
⟶ ⟵	Road tunnel
──────	Principal railroad
─ ─ ─ ─	Principal railroad under construction
⊢ ⊣	Railroad tunnel
✈	International, main airport

BOUNDARIES

▬▬▬▬	International
▬ ▬ ▬	Undefined, disputed
──────	Internal, state, provincial
─ ─ ─ ─	Armistice, ceasefire line

The representation of a boundary in this atlas does not denote its international recognition and therefore the de facto situation has been depicted.

HYDROGRAPHIC FEATURES

〜〜	River, stream
- - -	Intermittent watercourse
〜〜	Waterfall, rapids
〜〜	Dam, barrage
⟋⟋⟋	Irrigation, drainage channel
⟋⟋⟋	Canal
〜〜	Lake, reservoir
〜〜	Intermittent, seasonal lake
〜〜	Salt pan, mud flat
⋅	Oasis
▦	Marsh, swamp
⌣⌣⌣	Reef

Depth of sea in meters

Scales larger than 1 inch : 190 miles

0
200
3000

Scales smaller than 1 inch : 190 miles

0
1000
5000

OTHER FEATURES

▲ 3798	Elevation above sea level (meters)
▼ -133	Depression below sea level (meters)
≂	Pass
•⟋\⟍•	Oil, gas pipeline with field

ENVIRONMENTAL TYPES

	Permanent ice and snow
	Mountain and moorland
	Tundra
	Coniferous forest
	Deciduous forest
	Tropical forest
	Prairie
	Temperate agriculture
	Mediterranean scrub
	Savannah
	Desert

This representation of the environment and its associated vegetation gives an overview of the landscape. It is not intended to be definitive.

CONVERSION SCALES

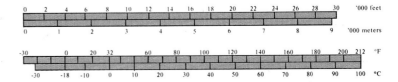

West of Greenwich

ARCTIC OCEAN

Queen
Elizabeth
Islands

Ellesmere
Island

Lincoln
Sea

Kane
Basin

Baffin Bay

GREENLAND
(Denmark)

Jan Mayen
(Norway)

Banks
Island

Viscount Melville
Sound

Beaufort Sea

Ostrov Vrangelya

Pt. Barrow

Chucki
Sea

Amundsen
Gulf

Victoria Island

Oikiqtaluk

Davis Str.

Norwegia
Sea

Brooks Range

ALASKA
(U.S.A.)

Great Bear Lake

Foxe
Basin

ICELAND

Reykjavik

Føroyar
(Denmark)

McKINLEY
6194

Mackenzie Mts.

Great Slave Lake

Hudson Str.

Shetland Is.
(U.K.)

Alaska Range

Gulf of Alaska

Reindeer Lake

Hudson Bay

Labrador Sea

Kap Farvel

UNITED
KINGDOM

Bering
Sea

Kodiak I.

CANADA

L. Winnipeg

Labrador

Dublin
IRELAND

Amste
s'Graven
LONDON
Bru
PARIS

Aleutian Islands

Aleutian Trench

Vancouver I.

Great
Lakes

Ottawa

Newfoundland

NORTH

FRA

NORTH
PACIFIC
OCEAN

Great
Plains

UNITED STATES
OF
AMERICA

CHICAGO

Appalachian Mts.

NEW YORK
PHILADELPHIA
Washington

ATLANTIC
OCEAN

PORTUGAL

Açores
(Port.)

Lisboa

Madrid
SPAIN

SAN FRANCISCO

Gt. Salt Lake

LOS ANGELES

Madeira
(Port.)

Bermuda
(U.K.)

MOROCCO

Rabat
El D

Atlas Mountains

Hawaiian

Isla de
Guadalupe
(Mex.)

Ilas Canarias
(Sp.)

ALGE

Tropic of Cancer

Islands

BAHAMAS
Nassau

WESTERN
SAHARA

Al Aaiun

MEXICO
CIUDAD DE
MÉXICO

La Habana

CUBA

West Indies

MAURITANIA

Nouakchott

MALI

HAWAII
(U.S.A.)

Islas de Revillagigedo
(Mex.)

Belmopan
BELIZE Kingston
GUATEMALA HAITI
Guatemala JAMAICA
HONDURAS
Tegucigalpa
EL SALVADOR
San Salvador
Managua
NICARAGUA
San José
COSTA RICA
PANAMA

Port au Prince
DOMINICAN REP.
Puerto Rico (U.S.A.)
Santo Domingo

Leeward Is.

Caribbean Sea

Windward Is.

BARBADOS

TRINIDAD
AND TOBAGO

CAPE
VERDE
IS.
Praia

Dakar SEN
THE
GAMBIA Banjul
GUINEA Bissau
BISSAU
Conakry
SIERRA LEONE
Monrovia
LIBERIA

Bamako

BUR
FASO
Ouagadougou
GH
Yamoussoukro Lome
Freetown Accra
IVORY
COAST

Polynesia

Christmas I.

Panamá

Caracas
VENEZUELA

Georgetown
Paramaribo
Cayenne
FRENCH GUIANA

SÃO TO
AND PRIN

Equator

Phoenix Is.

KIRIBATI

Line Islands

Bogotá
COLOMBIA

Orinoco

GUY
SUR

Islas Galápagos
(Ecuador)

Quito
ECUADOR

Isla Fernando
de Noronha
(Brazil)

Ascension
(U.K.)

Iles Marquises
(Fr.)

French Polynesia
(Fr.)

PERU

LIMA

BRAZIL
Planalto do
Mato Grosso

Cordillera

St. Helena
(U.K.)

SOUTH

SAMOA
Apia
Samoa
(U.S.A.)

Iles Tuamotu

SOUTH
PACIFIC
OCEAN

La Paz
BOLIVIA

Brasília

Ilha da Trindade
(Brazil)

SOUTH

Tahiti
Iles de la
Société

TONGA
Nuku'alofa

PARAGUAY
SÃO PAULO
Asunción
RÍO DE JANEIRO

ATLANTIC

Tropic of Capricorn

Iles Gambier

Pitcairn I.
(U.K.) Ducie I.
(U.K.)

Isla de Pascua
(Easter I.)
(Chile)

ACONCAGUA
6960

URUGUAY
Montevideo

OCEAN

Islas Juan
Fernández
(Chile)

Santiago
ARGENTINA

BUENOS AIRES

Tristan da Cunha
(U.K.)

Gough I.
(U.K.)

Chatham Is.
(N.Z.)

Patagonia

Andes

Falkland Is.
(U.K.)

South Georgia
(U.K.)

Cabo de Hornos

Scotia Sea

South
Sandwich
Is. (U.K.)

Cook Islands
(N.Z.)

Mercator Projection

1:85,000,000 (Scale at the Equator)

© COLOUR LIBRARY BOOKS

ARCTIC OCEAN

1

Zemlya Frantsa-Iosifa
(Russia)

Severnaya Zemlya

Novosibirskiye Ostrova

Karskoye More

Byrranga

More
Laptevykh

Lyakhovskiye
Ostrova

Vostochno
Sibirskoye
More

Novaya
Zemlya

Gory

Plato
Putorana

Kolmskaya
Nizmennost

Ostrov Vrangelya

2

Barentsevo
More

Nordkapp

Poluostrov
Yamal

Gydanskiy
Poluostrov

Sredne

Khrebet Cherskogo

Khrebet Kolymskiy

Anadyrskiy
Zaliv

Lappland

Sibirskoye

Ploskogor'ye

Zapadno

Ploskogor'ye

SWEDEN

FINLAND

Helsingfors

Sibirskaya

Ravnina

RUSSIA

Okhotskoye
More

Bering
Sea

Stockholm
Tallinn
ST. PETERSBURG

ESTONIA
Riga

Ozero Baykal

Aleutian   Islands

Sakhalin

København
LATVIA

MOSKVA

Ulaanbaatar

3

LITHUANIA
Vilnius
Minsk

Prikaspiyskaya
Nizmennost'

KAZAKHSTAN

MONGOLIA
Gobi

Kolmskaya

Kuril'skiye Ostrova

Berlin
Warszawa
BELARUS

Kirgiz
Step'

Tashkent
Alma-Ata

Tien Shan

Shikhote Alin'

POLAND
Kyyiv
(Kiev)

UKRAINE
MOLDOVA
Chisinau
(Kishinev)

Peski
Karakumy

Bishkek
KYRGYZSTAN

Tarim
Pendi

BEIJING

N. KOREA
Pyŏngyang

Sea of
Japan

Praha
CZECH
REP.

Bratislava

UZBEKISTAN
TAJIKISTAN

Taklimakan
Shamo

Kunlun Shan

TIANJIN

S. KOREA
SŎUL

JAPAN
TŌKYŌ

NORTH

GEORGIA
Ozero Balkhash

Xizang
Gaoyuan

Huang
Hai

PACIFIC

AZERBAIJAN

TURKMENISTAN
Ashgabat

Dushanbe

Hindu
Kush

CHINA

SHANGHAI

OCEAN

TURKEY

ARMENIA
Yerevan

Baku

Kabul

Islamabad

Himalaya

4

Tehran

IRAN

AFGHANISTAN

New
Delhi

Kathmandu

EVEREST

T'ai-pei
TAIWAN

Tropic of Cancer

SAUDI
ARABIA

PAKISTAN

INDIA

NEPAL

Thimphu

BANG.

CALCUTTA

Dhaka

Hanoi

HONG KONG

Karachi

MYANMAR

LAOS
Viangchan

THAI-
LAND
KRUNG THEP

VIETNAM

MANILA

Luzon

Marianas
Is.

Guam (U.S.A.)

Marshall Is.

EGYPT

MUMBAI
(Bombay)

Deccan

Bay of
Bengal

Yangon

CAM.
Phnom Penh

PHILIPPINES

Mindanao

Caroline Islands

Tarawa

Gilbert
Is.

ERITREA
SUDAN

YEMEN

Arabian
Sea

CHENNAI
(Madras)

Lakshadweep
(India)

Andaman
Islands
(India)

Bandar Seri
Begawan

BRU.

NAURU

Phoenix Is.

Colombo
SRI LANKA

MALAYSIA
Kuala Lumpur

Equator

SOMALIA

MALDIVES
Malé

SINGAPORE
Borneo

Sulawesi

Maluku

New
Guinea

PAPUA
NEW
GUINEA

SOLOMON ISLANDS

TUVALU
Fanafuti

UGANDA
KENYA
Nairobi

Victoria

SEYCHELLES

Sumatera
Jawa

JAKARTA

INDONESIA

Port Moresby

Honiara

Santa
Cruz
Is.

5

TANZANIA

INDIAN OCEAN

Timor

Laut Arafura

Coral
Sea

VANUATU

Nouvelle
Calédonie
(Fr.)

Vila

FIJI
Suva

6

C Horn (Nord Cap)

3 | A | B | C | D | E | F | G | H | J | K | L

ICELAND

Akureyri

Reykjavik

ÖRÆFAJÖKULL 2119

NORWEGIAN SEA

Tromsø

Lofoten Vesterålen

Narvik

Boda

KEBNEKAISE 2111

Kiruna

Gälliva

4

Mo i Rana

Namsos

Trondheim

Ålesund Åndalsnes

Østersund

Sundsvall

Umeå

Nor land

Lillehammer

Bergen

Haugesund

Drammen

Oslo

Ludvika

Gävle

Uppsala

Shetland Islands

Stavanger

Arendal

Kristiansand

Örebro

STOCKH

5

C. Wrath

Orkney Islands

Wick

Mallaig Inverness

Linköping

Götaland

Gotl (Sw

UNITED KINGDOM

BEN NEVIS Mts. 1344 Grampian

Aberdeen

Göteborg

Jönköping

REPUBLIC OF IRELAND

Malin Hd.

Glasgow Edinburgh

DENMARK KØBENHAVN

Ålborg

Kalmar

Bornholm (Den.)

BALTIC

Londonderry

Carlisle Newcastle upon Tyne

Odense

Malmö

Belfast

Isle of Man

The Pennines

Esbjerg

Flensburg

Kiel

Galway

Dublin

Holyhead Liverpool Leeds Manchester

Rostock

Schwerin

Koszalin

RUSS Kaliningrad

6

Cork

Mizen Hd.

Fishgard

SNOWDON 1085

Nottingham

BIRMINGHAM

Norwich

NETHERLANDS

Groningen

Wilhelmshaven

Bremen

HAMBURG

Gdańsk

Szczecin

Bydgoszcz

POLA

Cardiff Bristol

s'Gravenhage Amsterdam

Hannover

BERLIN

Poznań

WARSZAW

Land's End Penzance

LONDON ROTTERDAM

Utrecht

Braunschweig

Magdeburg

Cottbus

Łódź

Plymouth

Southampton

Dover Calais

Antwerpen Breda Bruxelles

Essen Duisburg Dortmund

Münster

GERMANY

Leipzig

Dresden

Wrocław

Rad

Brighton

BELGIUM

Lille Lens

Köln Düsseldorf

Karl-Marx-Stadt

Katowi

Channel Islands (U.K.)

Cherbourg

Le Havre

Amiens Charleroi Ardennes

Bonn

Weisbaden

Frankfurt am Main

PRAHA

Plzeň Bohemia

CZECH REP.

Olomouc Brno

Ostrava

7

Brest

Caen

Rouen

Reims

LUX Luxembourg

Mannheim

Nürnberg

České Budějovice

SLOVAK R

Rennes

Le Mans

PARIS

Orléans

Metz

Nancy

Karlsruhe

Stuttgart

Augsburg

Linz

WIEN

Bratislava

Nantes

Tours

FRANCE

Troyes

Dijon

Strasbourg

München

Salzburg

AUSTRIA

BUDAPEST

Poitiers

Bourges

Besançon

Basel

Zürich

Innsbruck

GROSSGLOCKNER

Graz

HUNGAR

La Rochelle

Limoges

Clermont-Ferrand

Massif

St.-Étienne

LYON

Bern

Lausanne

SWITZERLAND

LIECH

GROSSGLOCKNER 4049

Bolzano

Ljubljana

SLOV

8

Bordeaux

Brive-la-Gaillarde

Central

Valence

Genève

MtBLANC

Novara

Brescia

Verona

Trieste

ZAGREB

Novi Sad

La Coruña

C. Finisterre

Lugo

Cordillera Cantábrica

León

Santander

Bilbao

San

Grenoble

TORINO

MILANO

Venezia

Rijeka

CROATIA

VOJVO

Vigo

Gijón

Vitoria

Sebastian

Nîmes

Nice

Genova

Parma

Bologna

Ferrara

BOSNIA-HERZ.

BEOGRAD

Porto

Vila Real

Burgos

Pamplona

Pyrénées

Toulouse

Tarbes

Béziers

MARSEILLE

Aix-en-Provence

Cannes

MONACO

San Remo

La Spezia

SAN MARINO

Livorno

Rimini

Ancona

Sarajevo

YUGO

PORTUGAL

Coimbra

Valladolid

SPAIN

Salamanca

Zaragoza

Guadalajara

P. D'ANETO

ANDORRA

Lérida

Perpignan

Gerona

Toulon

Corse

Bastia

Firenze

Perugia

ITALY

Dubrovnik

Dalmatia

MONT.

Titograd

Lisboa

Cáceres

Toledo

MADRID

Tarragona

BARCELONA

Ajaccio

ROMA

Pescara

Foggia

Bari

Santarém

Badajoz

Ciudad Real

Albacete

Sassari

Ólbia

NÁPOLI

Brindisi

ALBANIA

Tirané

C. de São Vicente

Córdoba

Valencia

Palma

Mallorca

Menorca

Sardegna

Salerno

Taranto

Faro

Sevilla

Granada

Jaén

Murcia

Alicante

Ibiza

Islas Baleares (Spain)

Cágliari

TYRRHENIAN SEA

Cosenza

IONIAN SEA

Iónioi Nísoi

Cádiz

Málaga

Almería

Cartagena

C. Spartivento

Palermo

Messina

Reggio di Calabria

Igoumenítsa

Tanger

Gibraltar

Tétouan

Melilla

EL DJAZAÏR

MEDITERRANEAN

Bejaia

Bizerte

Annaba

C. Bon

Tunis

Trápani

Sicilia

Catania

C. Passero

9

DAR EL BEIDA

Rabat

Meknès Fès

Oujda

Oran

Saïda

ALGERIA

Constantine

TUNISIA

MALTA Valletta

MOROCCO

Hauts Plateaux

S fax

E | F | G | H | J | K | L

West of Greenwich

East of Greenwich

1:12,500,000

0 100 200 300 400 500 600 700 800 KILOMETRES

0 100 200 300 400 500 STATUTE MILES

© COLOUR LIBRARY BOOKS

Miller Oblated Stereographic Projection

Designed and produced by E.S.R.

Transverse Mercator Projection

1:1,175,000

© COLOUR LIBRARY BOOKS

| 0 | 10 | 20 | 30 | 40 | 50 | 60 | 70 | 80 KILOMETRES |

| 0 | 10 | 20 | 30 | 40 | 50 STATUTE MILES |

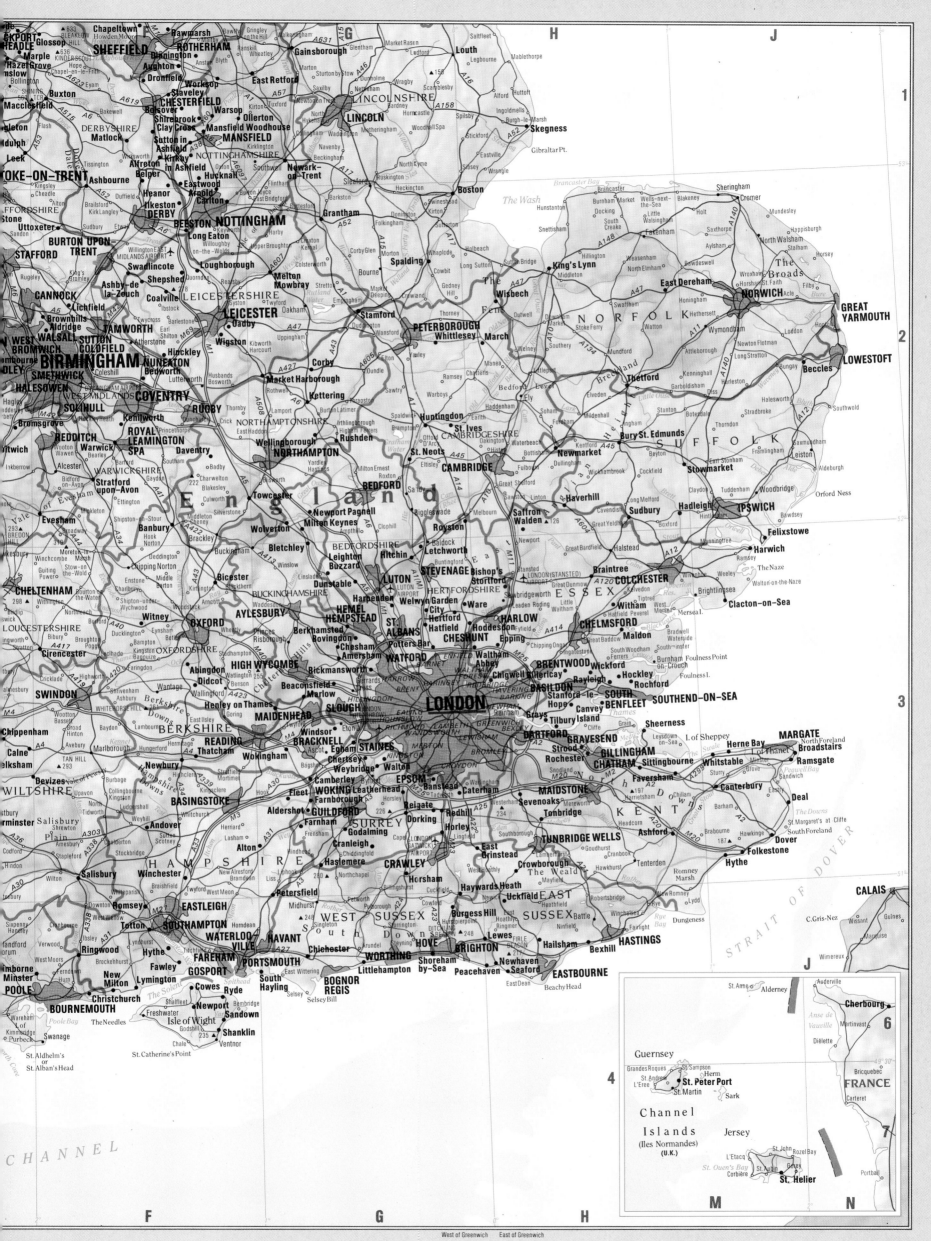

Transverse Mercator Projection

1:1,175,000

© COLOUR LIBRARY BOOKS

| 0 | 10 | 20 | 30 | 40 | 50 | 60 | 70 | 80 KILOMETRES |
| 0 | 10 | 20 | 30 | 40 | 50 STATUTE MILES |

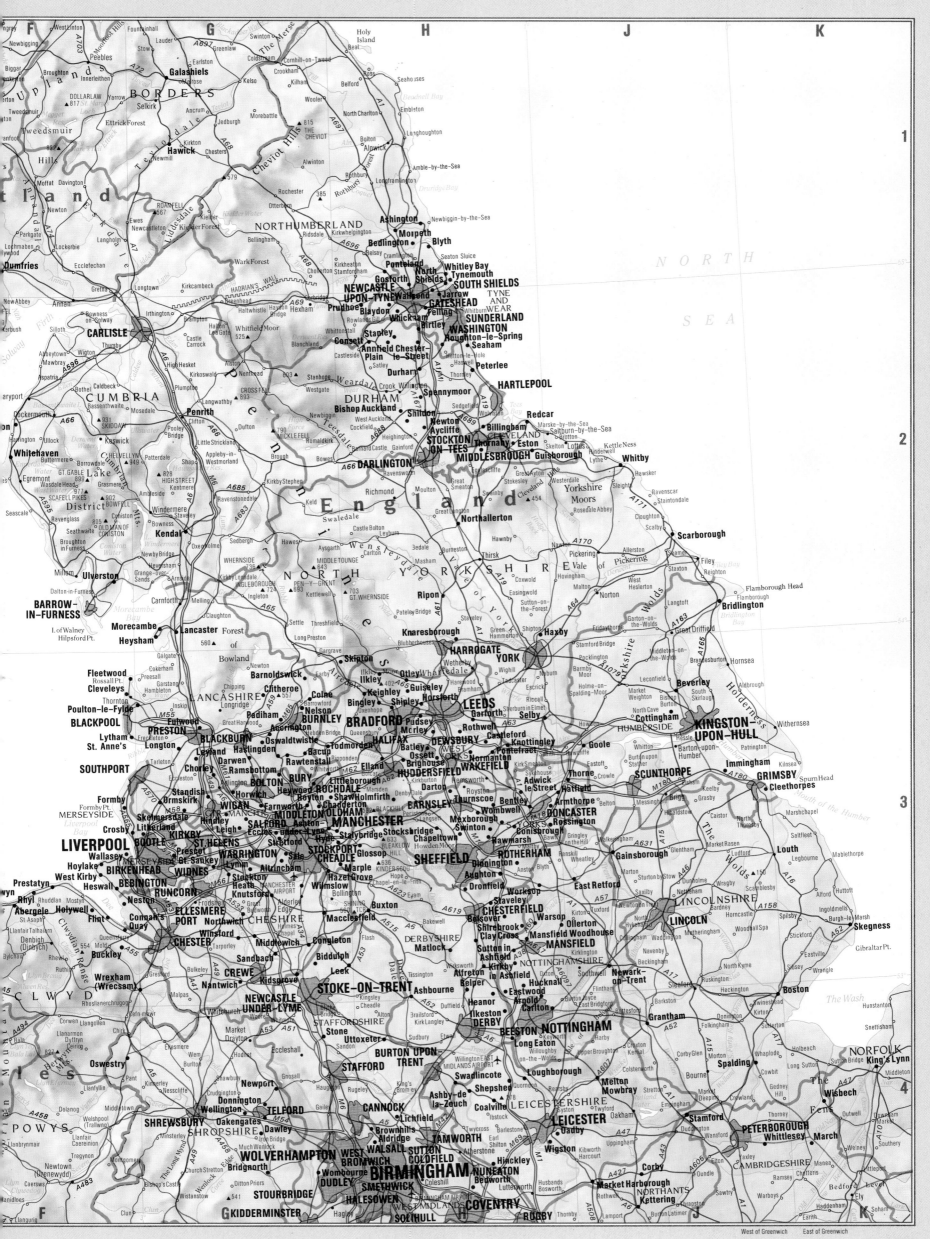

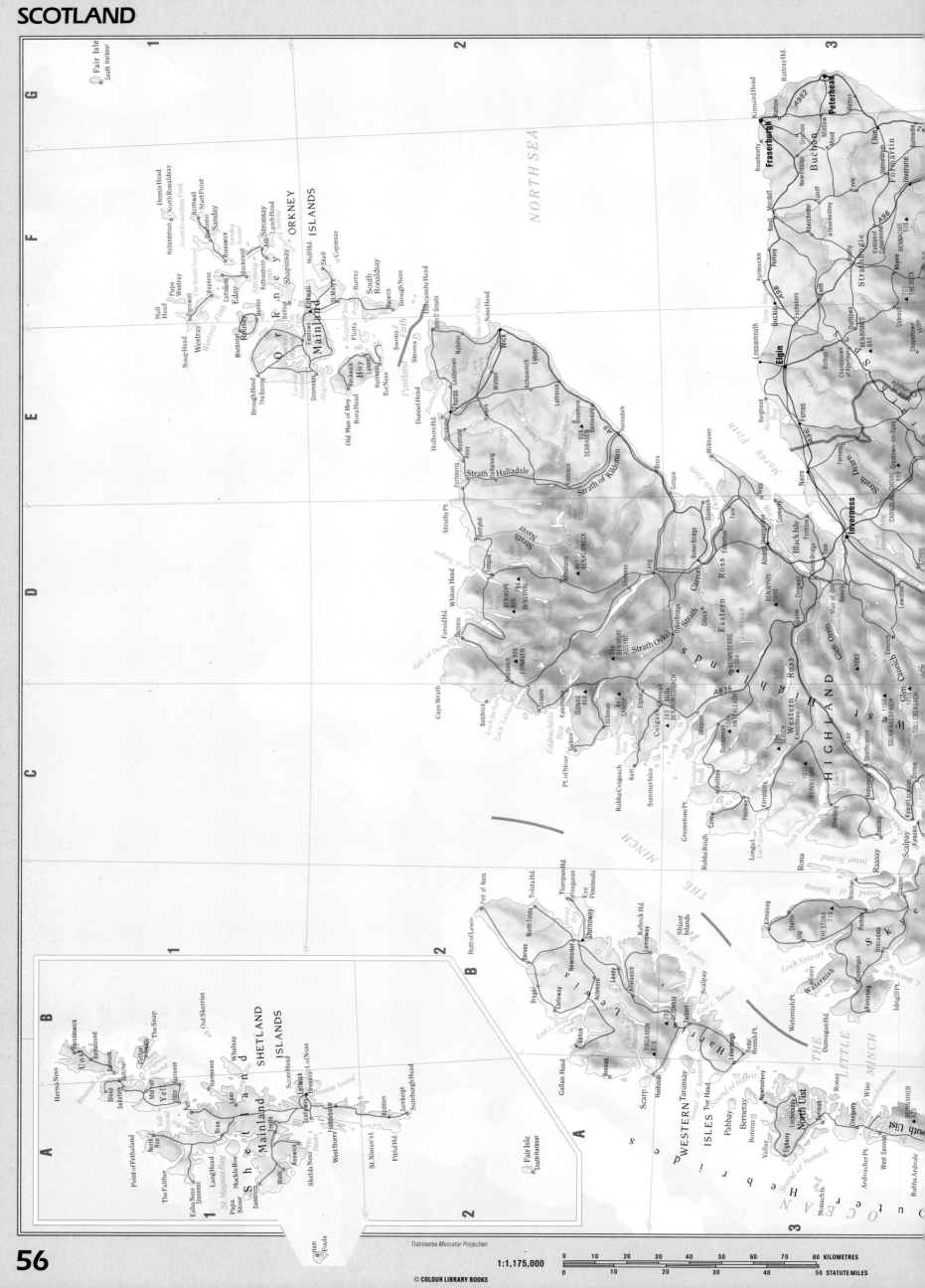

Transverse Mercator Projection

1:1,175,000

| 0 | 10 | 20 | 30 | 40 | 50 | 60 | 70 | 80 KILOMETRES |

| 0 | 10 | 20 | 30 | 40 | 50 STATUTE MILES |

© COLOUR LIBRARY BOOKS

West of Greenwich

Designed and produced by E.S.R.

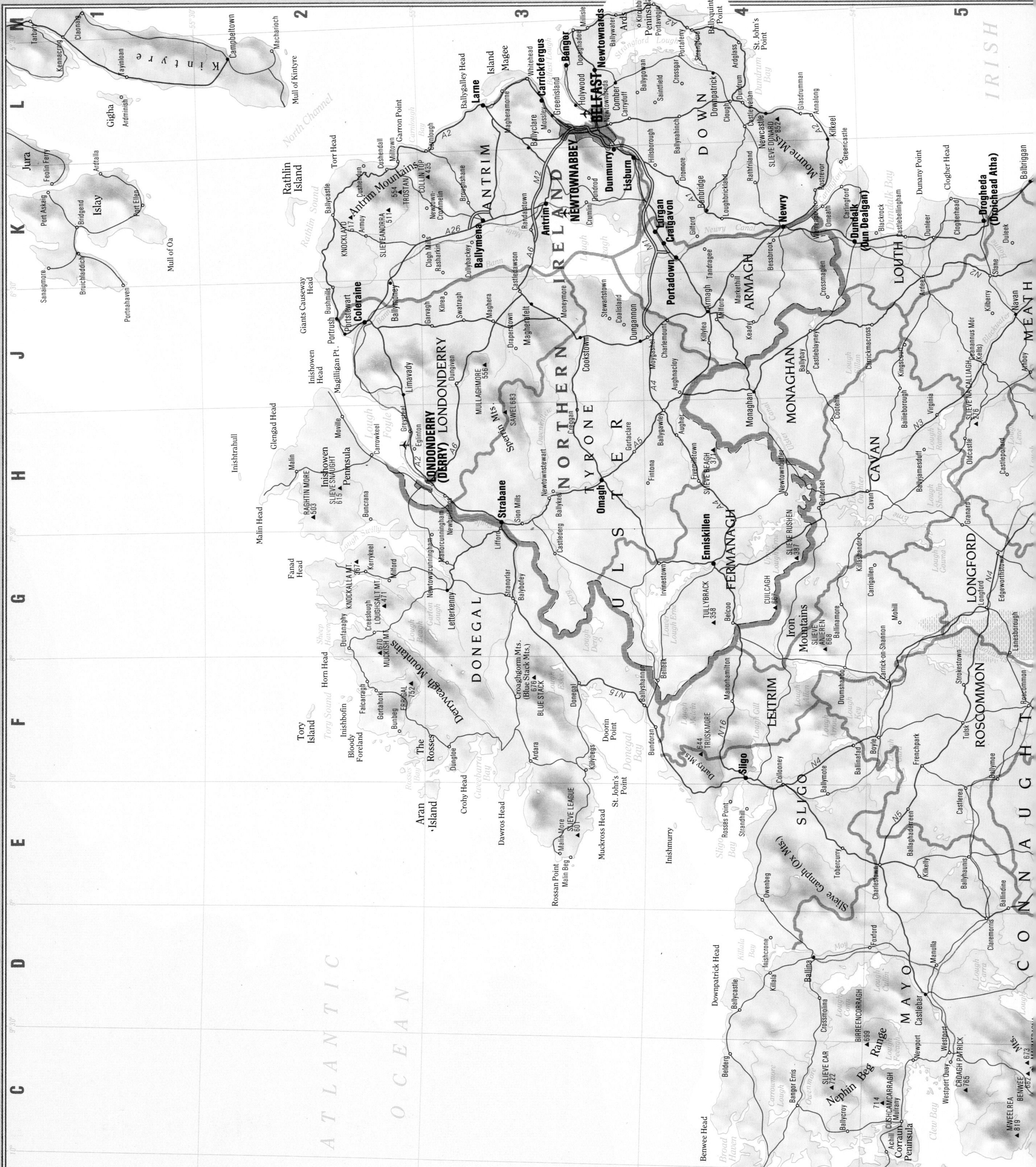

IRELAND

ATLANTIC OCEAN

IRISH SEA

North Channel

Kintyre
Mull of Kintyre
Campbeltown
Machrihanish
Tarbert
Claonaig
Kennacraig
Jura
Gigha
Islay
Port Askaig
Ardminish
Ardtalla
Bridgend
Port Ellen
Mull of Oa
Sanaigmore
Bruichladdich
Portnahaven

Rathlin Island
Rathlin Sound
Ballycastle
Torr Head
Cushendall
Cushendun
Garron Point
Giants Causeway
Portrush
Portstewart
Bushmills
Coleraine
Ballymoney
Ballygalley Head
Islandmagee
Larne
Magee Island
Whitehead
Carrickfergus
Bangor
Newtownards
Ards Peninsula
Kircubbin
Portaferry
Ballyquintin Point
Strangford Lough
BELFAST
Holywood
Greenisland
NEWTOWNABBEY
Dunmurry
Lisburn
Comber
Downpatrick
Killyleagh
Ardglass
St. John's Point
Killough
Clogher Head
Dundrum Bay
Newcastle
SLIEVE DONARD 852
Mourne Mts.
Kilkeel
Greencastle
Carlingford Lough
Warrenpoint
Rostrevor
Newry
Newry Canal
Portadown
Craigavon
Lurgan
Lough Neagh
Antrim
Ballymena
SLIEMISH 437
Ballyclare
Broughshane
Crumlin
Randalstown
Toome
Maghera
Magherafelt
Cookstown
Stewartstown
Dungannon
Coalisland
ANTRIM
SLIEVEANORRA 511
Armoy
KNOCKLAYD 517
COLLIN TOP 435
TROSTAN 554
Antrim Mountains
A26
Clogh Mills
Kilrea
Garvagh
Swatragh
Draperstown
Moneymore
LONDONDERRY (DERRY)
Eglinton
Limavady
Dungiven
MULLAGHMORE 550
Sperrin Mts.
SAWEL 683
NORTHERN IRELAND
TYRONE
ULSTER
Newtownstewart
Omagh
Strabane
Sion Mills
Liffording
Castlederg
Drumquin
Fintona
Ballygawley
Fivemiletown
SLIEVE BEAGH 374
Aughnacloy
Moy
Charlemont
Armagh
Tandragee
Markethill
ARMAGH
Keady
Castleblayney
MONAGHAN
Monaghan
Clones
Ballybay
DOWN
Dromore
Banbridge
Hillsborough
Dromara
Rathfriland
Loughbrickland
Gilford

LONDONDERRY
DONEGAL
Malin Head
Inishowen Head
Inishowen Peninsula
Malin
Carndonagh
Moville
Greencastle
Buncrana
RAGHTIN MORE 503
SLIEVE SNAGHT 615
Lough Swilly
Lough Foyle
Buncrana
Fahan
Newtoncunningham
Manorcunningham
Letterkenny
Ramelton
Rathmelton
Milford
Fanad Head
Mulroy Bay
KNOCKALLA MT. 361
Kerrykeel
Rathmullan
Horn Head
Dunfanaghy
Falcarragh
Gortahork
Bloody Foreland
Tory Island
Inishbofin
Bunbeg
Dungloe
The Rosses
Burtonport
Aran Island
Croaghbeg
Crohy Head
Dungloe
Gweebarra Bay
Glenties
Ardara
Dawros Head
Loughros More Bay
Killybegs
Rossan Point
Slieve League
Carrick
Kilcar
Teelin
St. John's Point
Donegal Bay
Donegal
Ballyshannon
Bundoran
Ballintra
Pettigo
Belleek
Kesh
Derrygonnelly
Enniskillen
FERMANAGH
Lough Erne
Lisnaskea
Lisbellaw
Maguiresbridge
Brookeborough
Newtownbutler
Derrylin
SLIEVE RUSHEN 387
CUILCAGH 666
TULLYBRACK 358
Belcoo
Blacklion
Manorhamilton
LEITRIM
Dowra
Drumkeeran

CAVAN
Cavan
Belturbet
Ballyconnell
Ballyhaise
Cootehill
Shercock
Bailieborough
Virginia
Kingscourt
Carrickmacross
Castleblayney
Crossmaglen
Newtownhamilton
LOUTH
Dundalk (Dún Dealgan)
Blackrock
Castlebellingham
Carlingford
Greenore
Clogherhead
Annagassan
Termonfeckin
Drogheda (Droichead Átha)
Baltray
Dunany Point
Clogher Head

MEATH
Slane
Navan
Kells (Ceanannus Mór)
Duleek
Nobber
Athboy
Trim

LONGFORD
Longford
Granard
Edgeworthstown
Ballymahon
Lanesborough

ROSCOMMON
Frenchpark
Castlerea
Tulsk
Strokestown
Elphin
Boyle
Ballaghaderreen
Ballinlough
Castlerea
Ballyhaunis
Ballindine

SLIGO
Sligo
Rosses Point
Strandhill
Ballysadare
Collooney
Coolaney
Ballymote
Tobercurry
Enniscrone
Inishmurry
TRUSKMORE 644
Slieve Camph (Ox Mts.)
Dartry Mts.

CONNAUGHT

MAYO
Castlebar
Westport
Newport
Foxford
Swinford
Charlestown
Kiltimagh
Claremorris
Ballinrobe
Ballina
Killala
Crossmolina
NEPHIN 806
NEPHIN BEG Range
Belmullet
The Mullet
Erris Head
Belderg
Benwee Head
Downpatrick Head
Ballycastle
Killala Bay
Killcummin
BIRREENCORRAGH 699
Bangor Erris
Corraun Peninsula
Achill Island
Achill Head
Keel
Dooagh
Achill Sound
SLIEVEMORE 672
CROAGH PATRICK 765
MWEELREA 819
CROAGHAUN
SLIEVE CAR 722
Louisburgh
Clew Bay
Clare Island
Inishturk
Inishbofin
Inishshark
Armagh Head
Clare Island
Blacksod Bay
Inishkea North
Inishkea South

N15 N16 N5 N4 N3 N2 N1

Lambert Conformal Conic Projection

58

1:1,000,000

0 10 20 30 40 50 60 70 80 KILOMETRES
0 10 20 30 40 50 STATUTE MILES

© COLOUR LIBRARY BOOKS

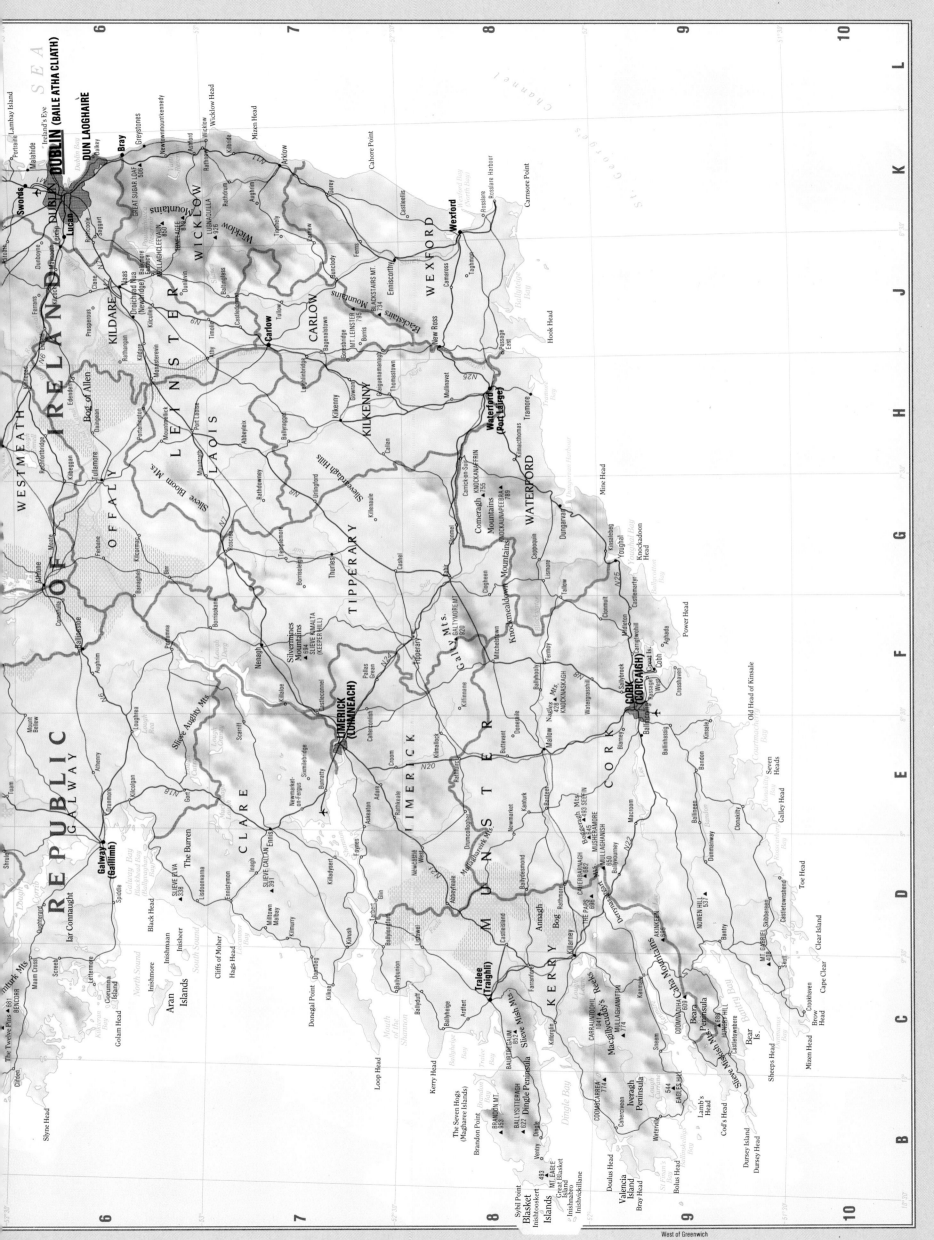

Designed and produced by E.S.R.

West of Greenwich

West of Greenwich

East of Greenwich

1:5,000,000

© COLOUR LIBRARY BOOKS

| 0 | 50 | 100 | 150 | 200 | 250 | 300 | 350 | 400 KILOMETRES |

| 0 | 50 | 100 | 150 | 200 | 250 STATUTE MILES |

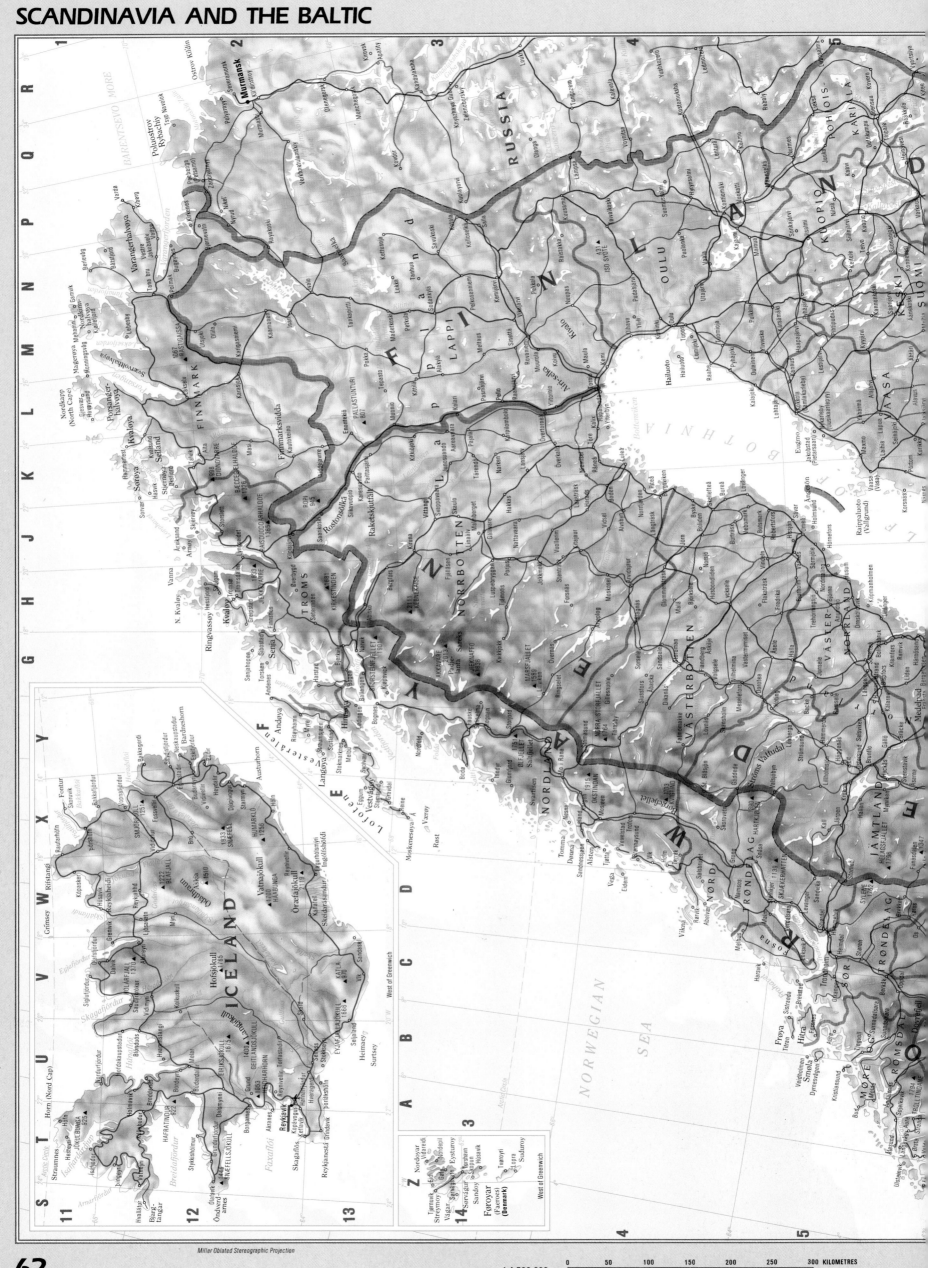

Miller Oblated Stereographic Projection

1:4,500,000

| 0 | 50 | 100 | 150 | 200 | 250 | 300 KILOMETRES |

| 0 | 50 | 100 | 150 | 200 STATUTE MILES |

© COLOUR LIBRARY BOOKS

East of Greenwich

Designed and produced by E.S.R.

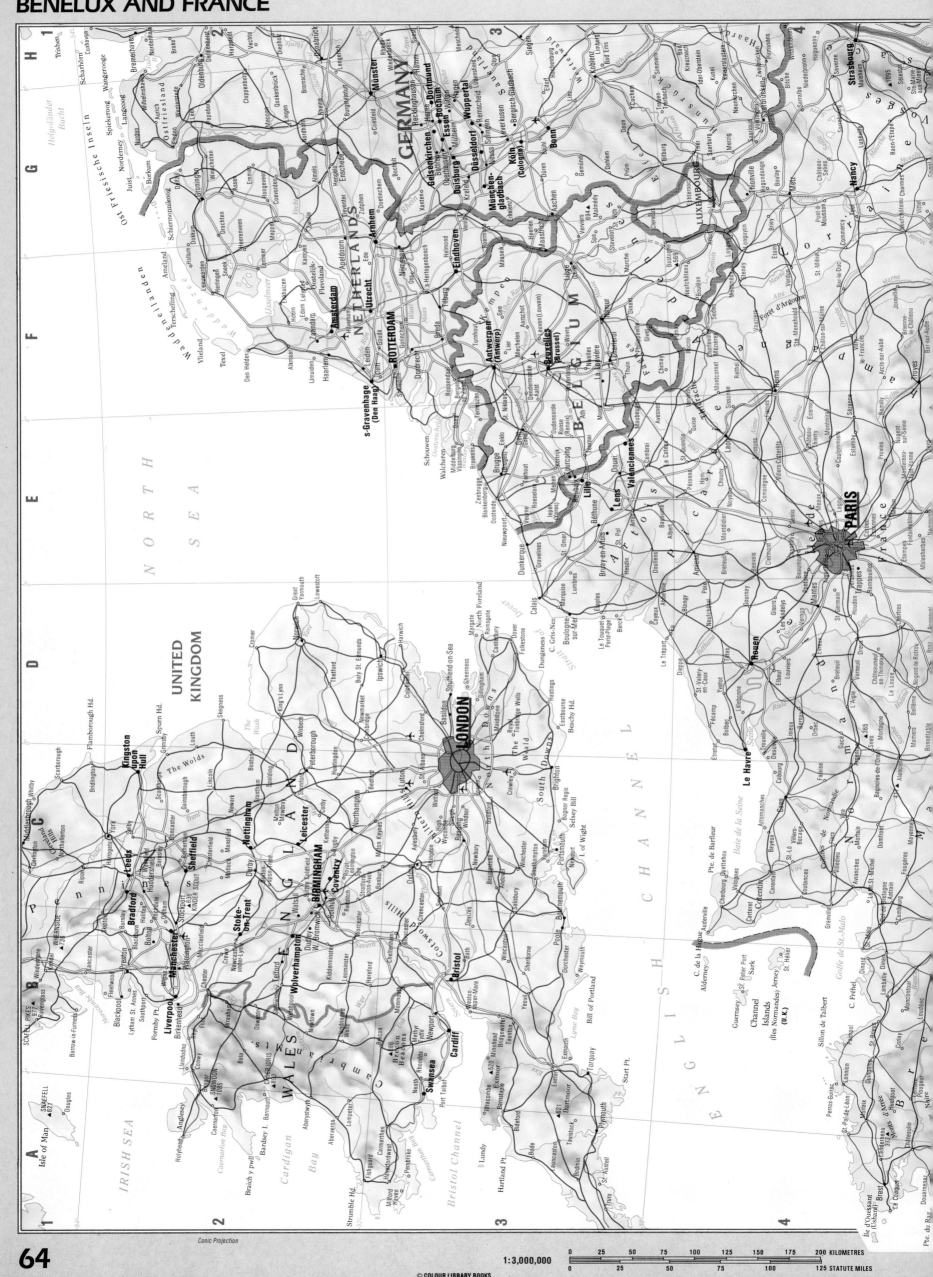

1:3,000,000

Conic Projection

| 0 | 25 | 50 | 75 | 100 | 125 | 150 | 175 | 200 KILOMETRES |

| 0 | 25 | 50 | 75 | 100 | 125 STATUTE MILES |

© COLOUR LIBRARY BOOKS

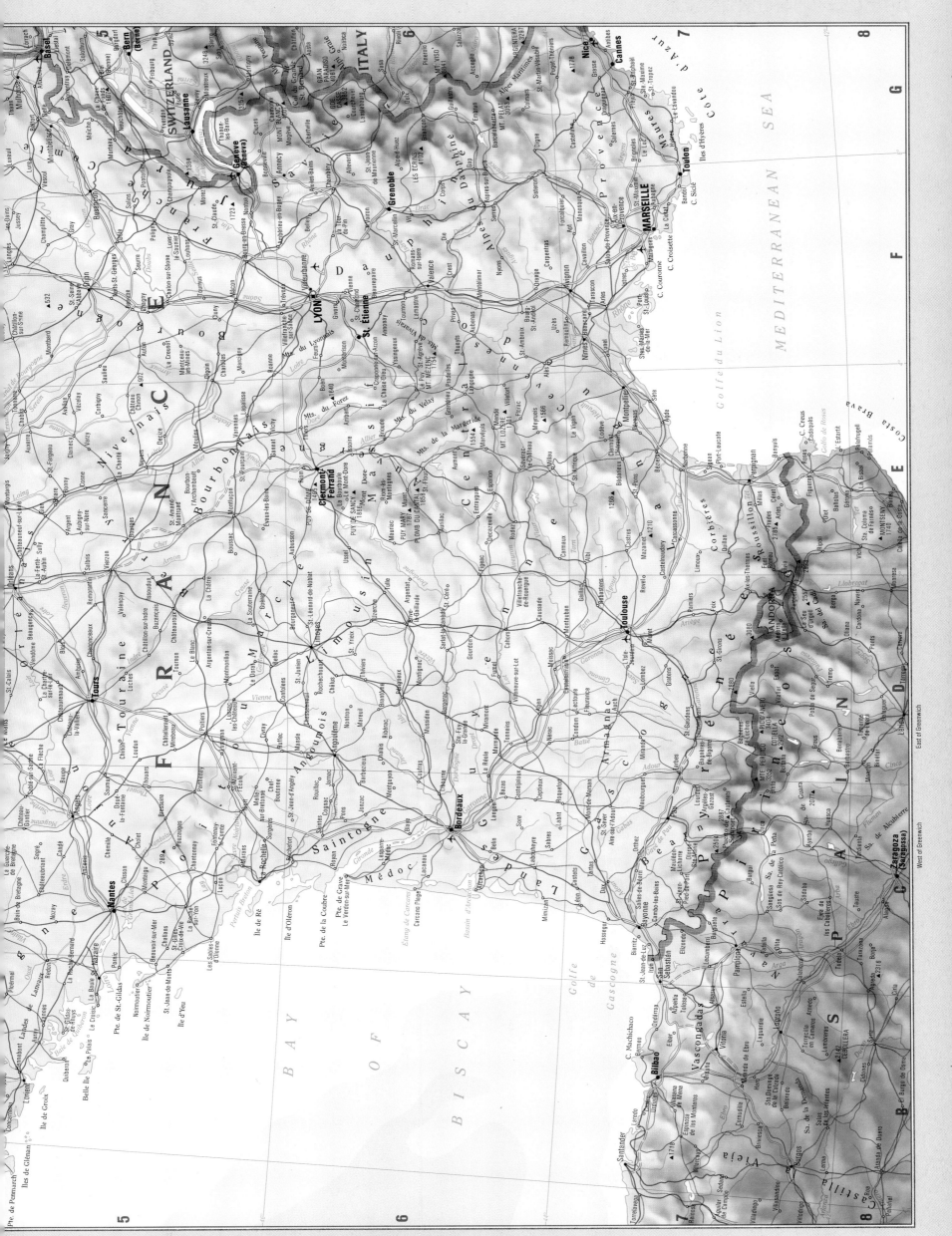

Designed and produced by E.S.R.

THE IBERIAN PENINSULA

Conic Projection

1:3,000,000

© COLOUR LIBRARY BOOKS

| 0 | 25 | 50 | 75 | 100 | 125 | 150 | 175 | 200 KILOMETRES |

| 0 | 25 | 50 | 75 | 100 | 125 STATUTE MILES |

Designed and produced by E.S.R.

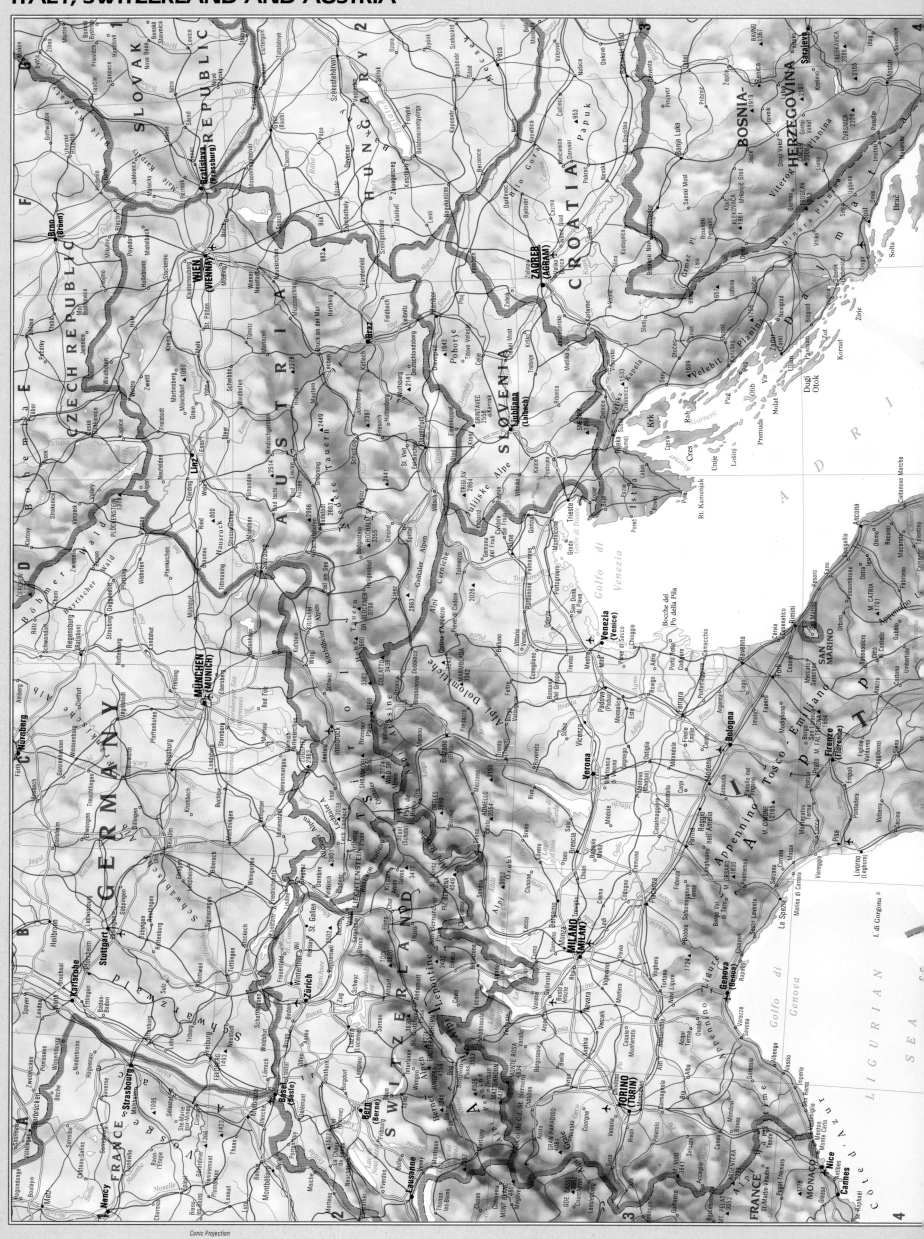

Conic Projection

1:3,000,000

0 25 50 75 100 125 150 175 200 KILOMETRES

0 25 50 75 100 125 STATUTE MILES

© COLOUR LIBRARY BOOKS

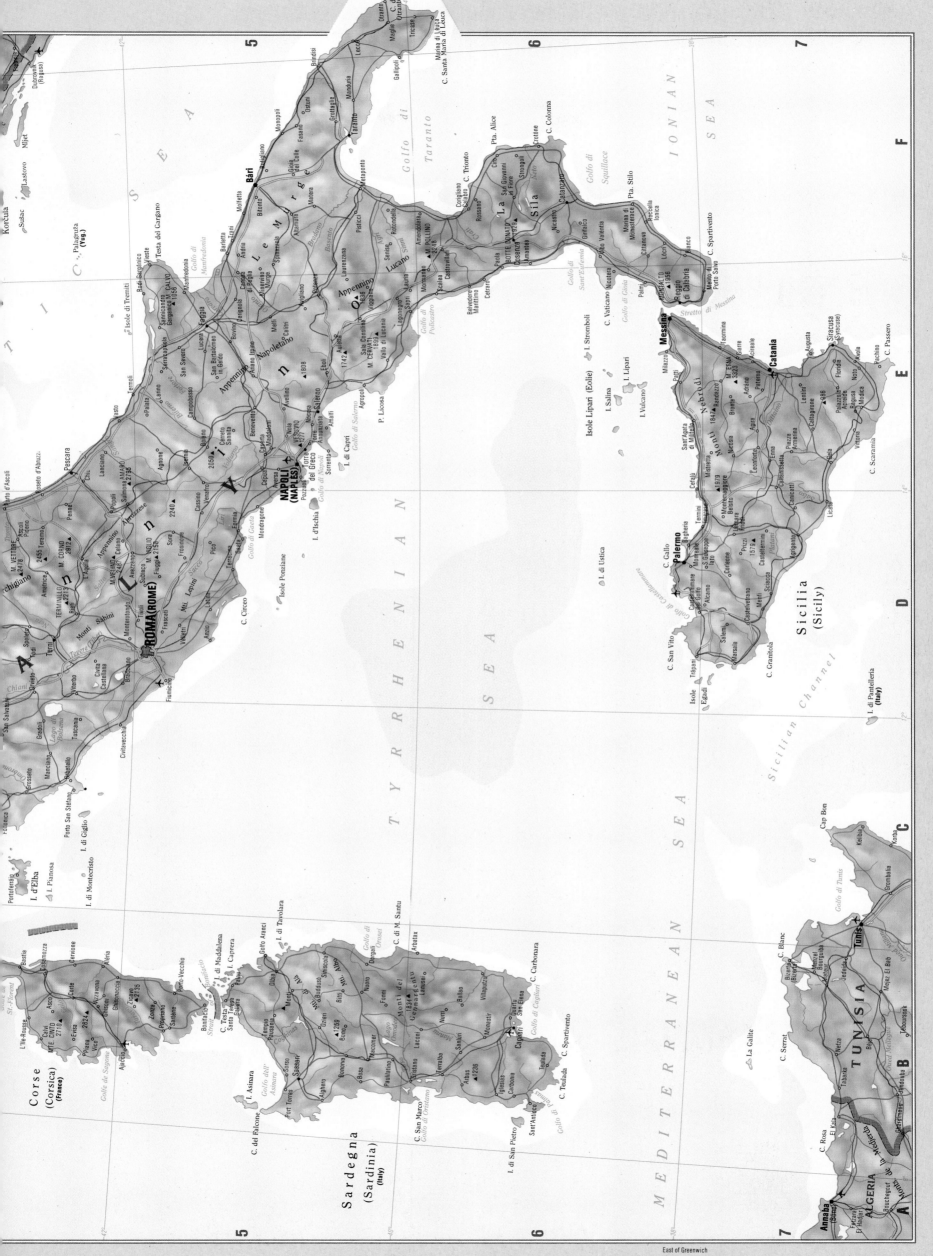

Designed and produced by E.S.R.

1:3,000,000

| 0 | 25 | 50 | 75 | 100 | 125 | 150 | 175 | 200 KILOMETRES |

| 0 | 25 | 50 | 75 | 100 | 125 STATUTE MILES |

Conic Projection

© COLOUR LIBRARY BOOKS

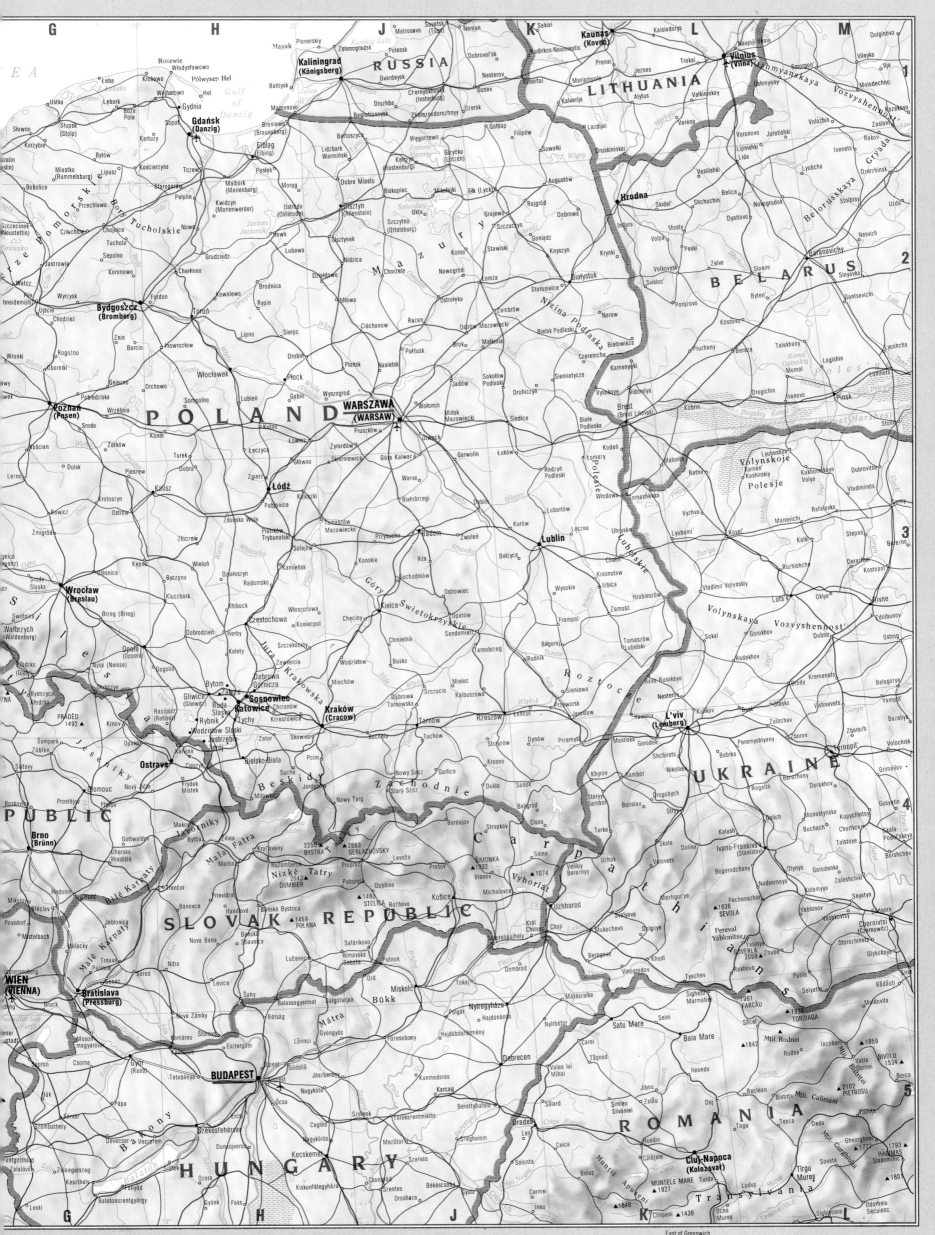

Designed and produced by E.S.R.

East of Greenwich

Conic Projection

1:3,000,000

© COLOUR LIBRARY BOOKS

0   25   50   75   100   125   150   175   200 KILOMETRES

0   25   50   75   100   125 STATUTE MILES

73

Conic Projection

1:3,000,000

| 0 | 25 | 50 | 75 | 100 | 125 | 150 | 175 | 200 KILOMETRES |

| 0 | 25 | 50 | 75 | 100 | 125 STATUTE MILES |

Lambert Conformal Conic Projection

© COLOUR LIBRARY BOOKS

1:3,500,000

| 0 | 50 | 100 | 150 | 200 | 250 KILOMETRES |

| 0 | 25 | 50 | 75 | 100 | 125 | 150 STATUTE MILES |

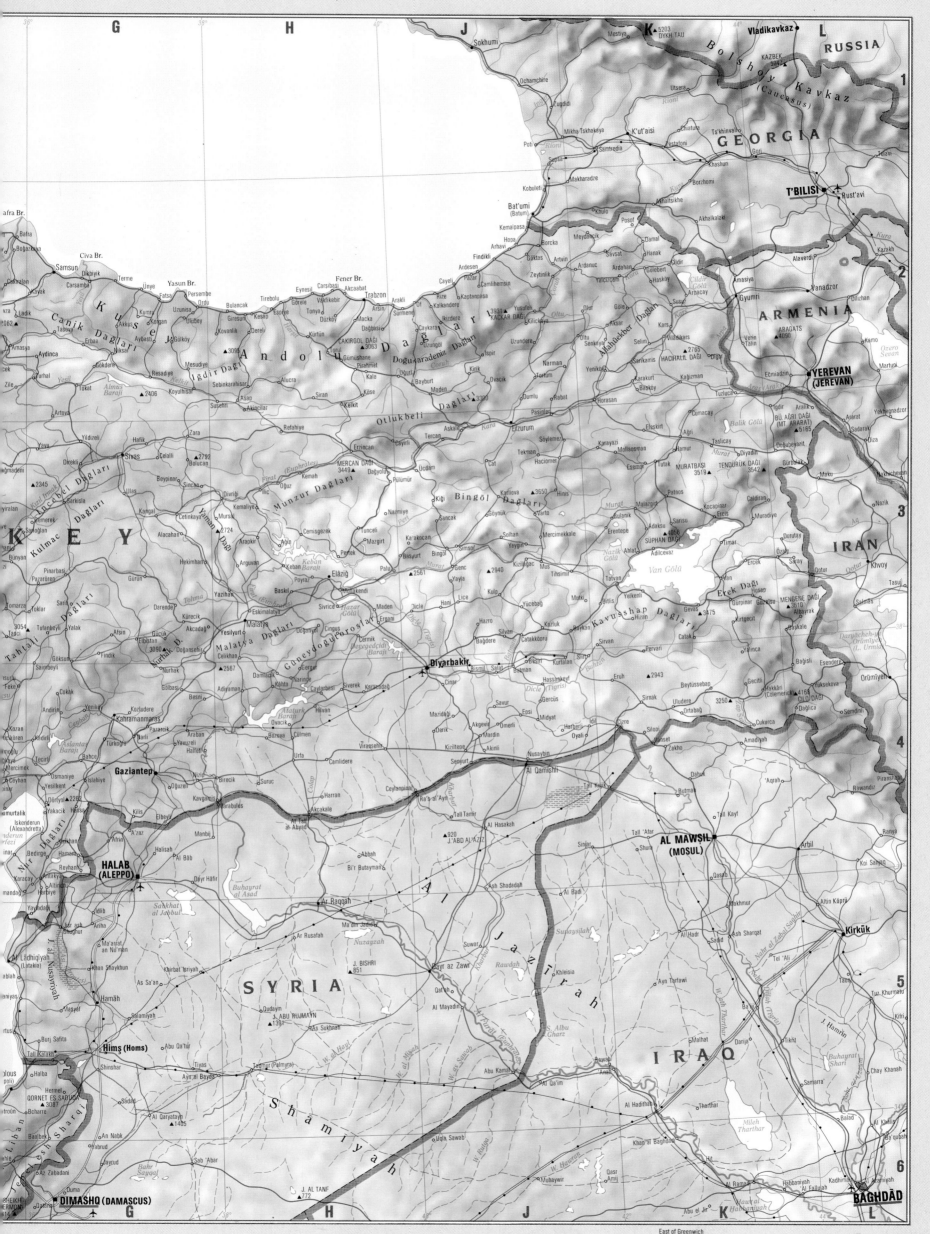

Miller Oblated Stereographic Projection

1:8,000,000

| 0 | 100 | 200 | 300 | 400 | 500 | 600 KILOMETRES |

| 0 | 50 | 100 | 150 | 200 | 250 | 300 | 350 | 400 STATUTE MILES |

© COLOUR LIBRARY BOOKS

East of Greenwich

Designed and produced by E.S.R.

Conic Projection

1:17,000,000

0 100 200 300 400 500 600 700 800 KILOMETRES

0 100 200 300 400 500 STATUTE MILES

© COLOUR LIBRARY BOOKS

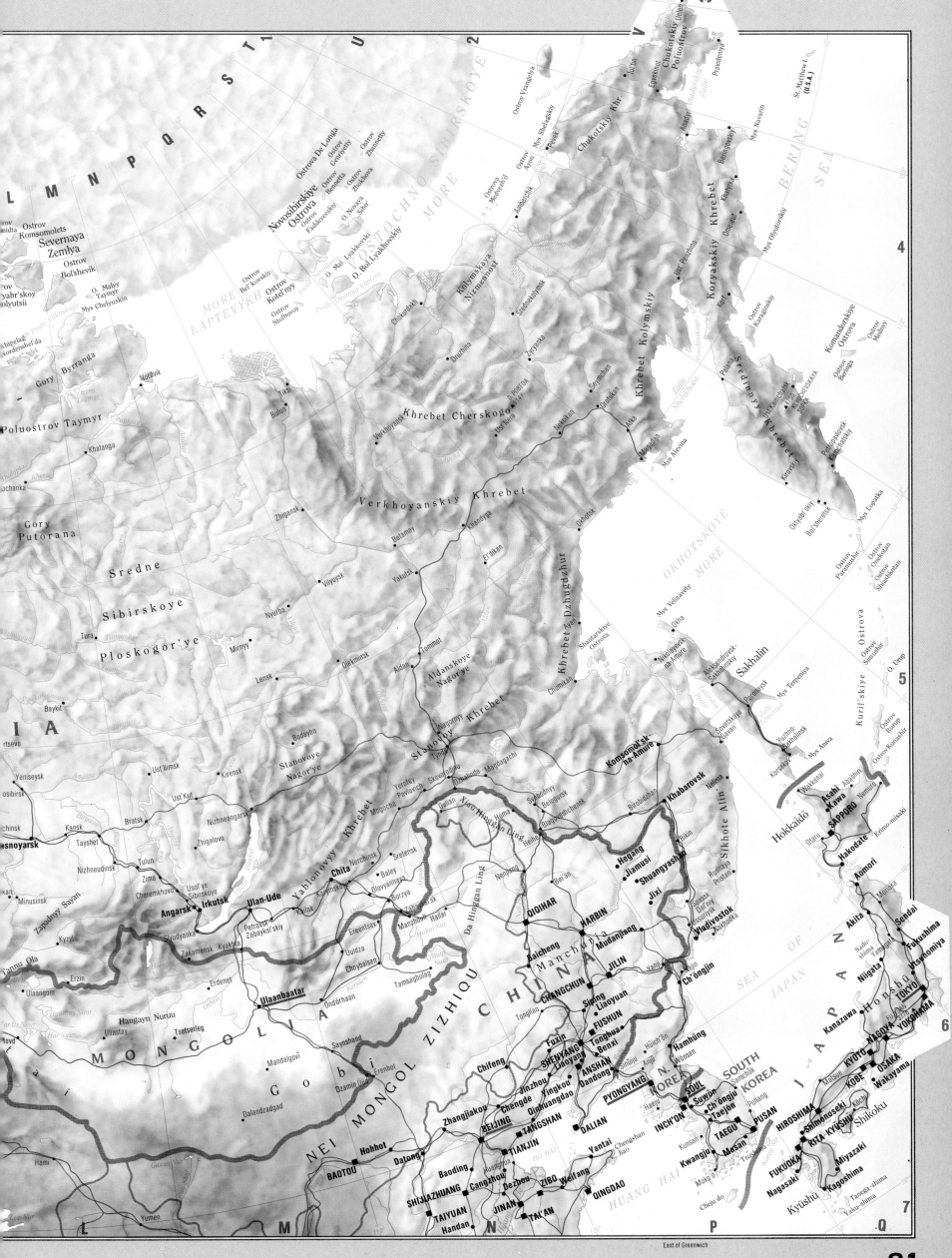

Designed and produced by E.S.R.

East of Greenwich

81

Lambert Azimuthal Equal Area Projection

© COLOUR LIBRARY BOOKS

1:25,000,000

| 0 | 200 | 400 | 600 | 800 | 1000 KILOMETRES |

| 0 | 100 | 200 | 300 | 400 | 500 | 600 STATUTE MILES |

Designed and produced by E.S.R.

East of Greenwich

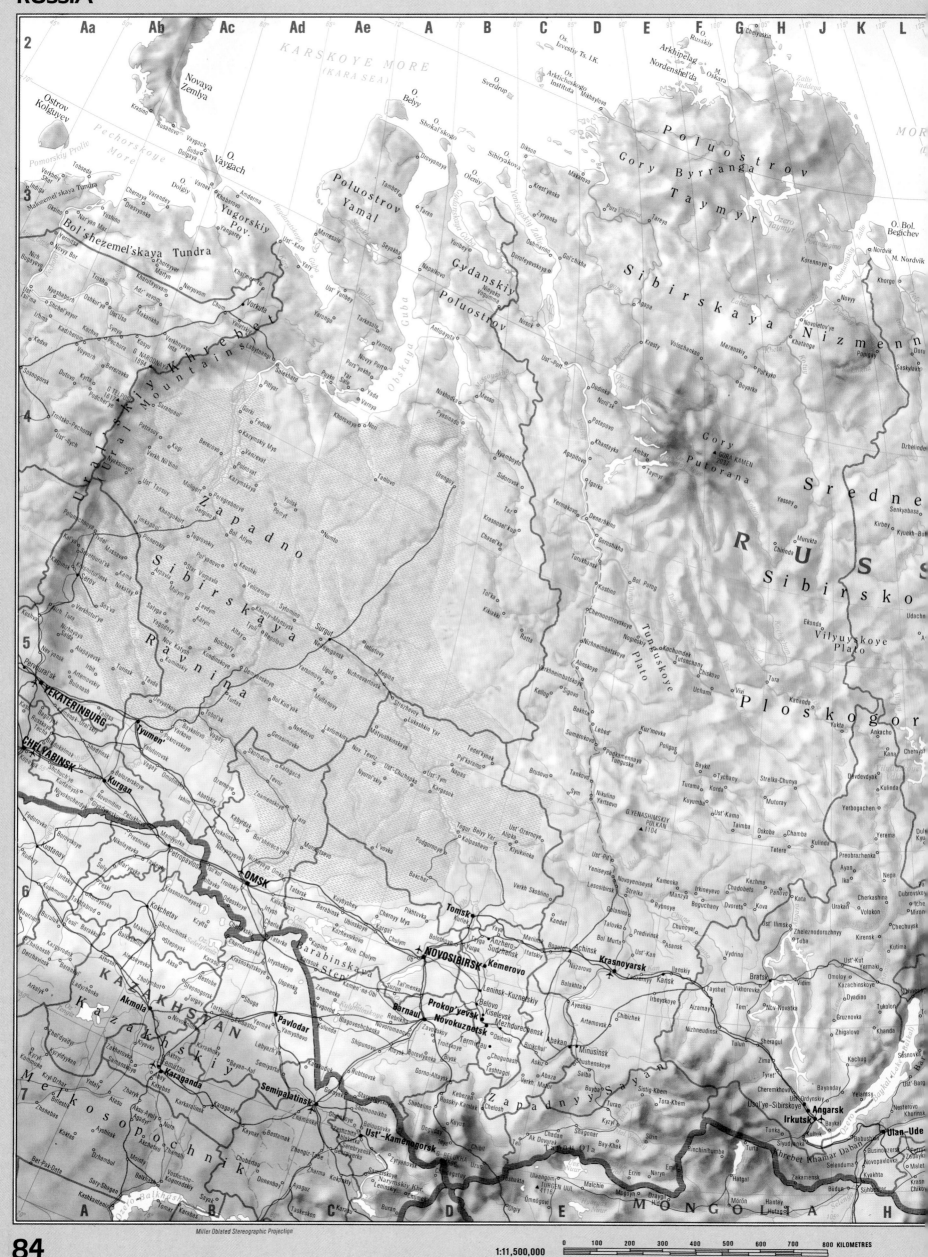

Miller Oblated Stereographic Projection

1:11,500,000

© COLOUR LIBRARY BOOKS

| 0 | 100 | 200 | 300 | 400 | 500 | 600 | 700 | 800 KILOMETRES |

| 0 | 50 | 100 | 150 | 200 | 250 | 300 | 350 | 400 | 450 | 500 STATUTE MILES |

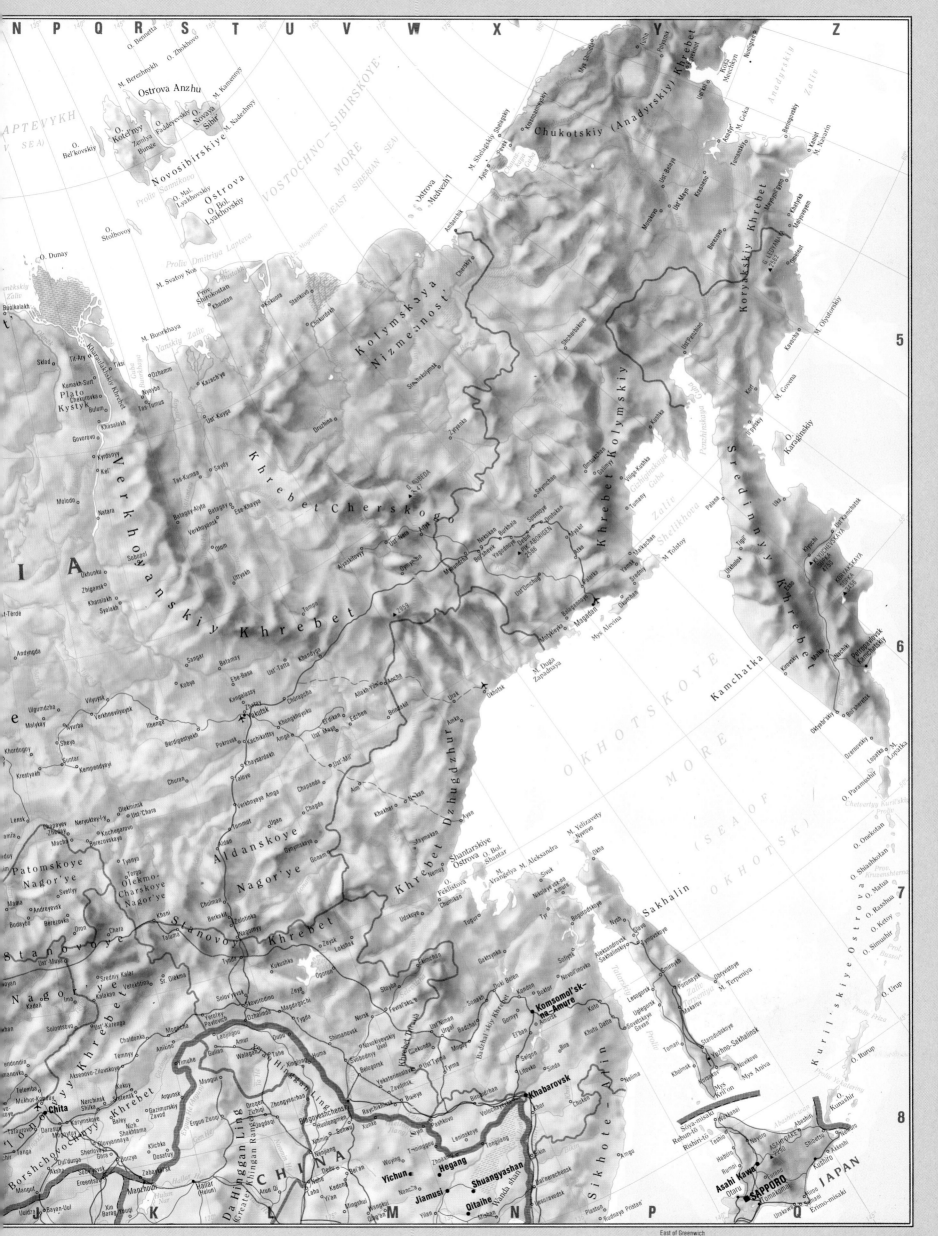

APTEVYKH
(V SEA)

Ostrova Anzhu

O. Bennetta
O. Zhokhova

M. Berezhnykh

O. Kotel'ny

Novaya
Sibir'

Ostrova
O. Bol.
Lyakhovskiy

Novosibirskiye

O. Stolbovoy

Proliv
Sannikova

O. Bel'kovskiy

Zemlya
Bunge

O. Mal.
Lyakhovskiy

Proliv Dmitriya Lapteva

VOSTOCHNO-SIBIRSKOYE

MORE

(EAST SIBERIAN SEA)

Chukotskiy (Anadyrskiy) Khrebet

Koryakskiy Khrebet

Sredinnyy Khrebet

Kamchatka

Kolymskaya
Nizmennost'

Khrebet Cherskogo

Khrebet Kolymskiy

Verkhoyanskiy Khrebet

Khrebet Dzhugdzhur

OKHOTSKOYE

MORE

(SEA OF OKHOTSK)

Aldanskoye
Nagor'ye

Patomskoye
Nagor'ye

Olekmo-
Charskoye
Nagor'ye

Stanovoye
Nagor'ye

Stanovoy Khrebet

Sakhalin

Kuril'skiye Ostrova

Shantarskiye
Ostrova

Chita

Komsomol'sk-
na-Amure

Khabarovsk

Sikhote-Alin

Da Hinggan Ling
(Greater Khingan Range)

CHINA

Yichun

Hegang

Jiamusi

Shuangyashan

Oitaihe

Asahi Kawa

SAPPORO

JAPAN

East of Greenwich

Designed and produced by E.S.R.

Miller Oblated Stereographic Projection

1:11,500,000

0	100	200	300	400	500	600	700	800 KILOMETRES
0	50	100	150	200	250	300	350	400	450	500 STATUTE MILES

© COLOUR LIBRARY BOOKS

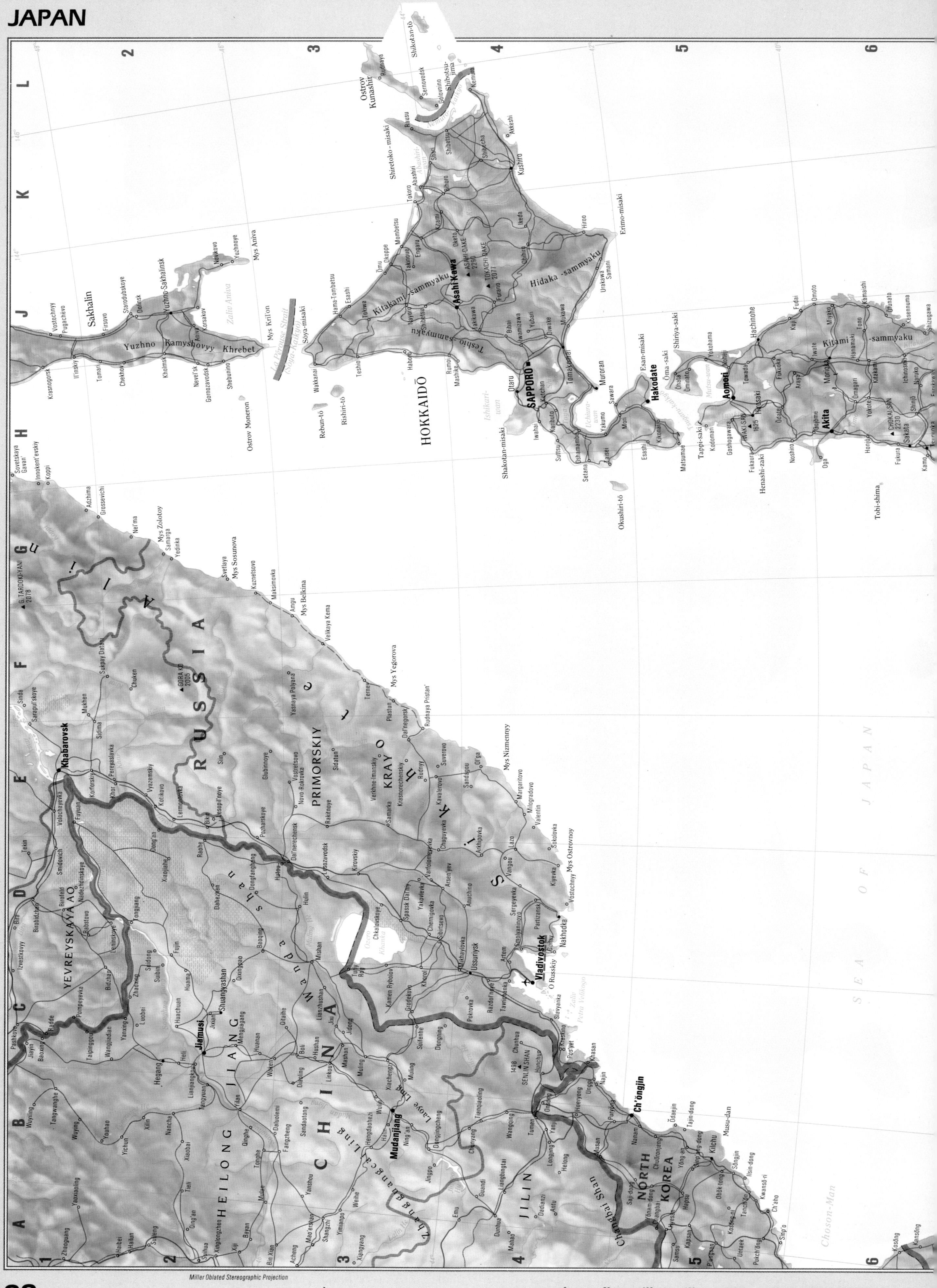

Shikotan-tō

Ostrov Kunashiri

Sakhalin

Yuzhno-Sakhalinsk

Mys Aniva

Mys Krilon

La Pérouse Strait (Soya-Kaikyō)

Yuzhno Kamyshovyy Khrebet

HOKKAIDŌ

Kitakami-sammyaku

Asahi Kawa

ASAHI-DAKE 2290

TOKACHI-DAKE 2077

Hidaka -sammyaku

Teshio-sammyaku

Wakkanai

Rebun-tō

Rishiri-tō

SAPPORO

Otaru

Tomakomai

Muroran

Hakodate

Esan-misaki

Shiriya-saki

Ōma-saki

Aomori

Mutsu-wan

Akita

CHŌKAISAN 2230

Kitakami -sammyaku

Okushiri-tō

Tobi-shima

Ostrov Moneron

Sovetskaya Gavan'

G. TARDOKI-ANI 2078

RUSSIA

GORA KO 2005

PRIMORSKIY KRAY

Mys Yegorova

Mys Nizmennyy

Mys Ostrovnoy

Mys Belkina

Velikaya Kema

Plastun

Khabarovsk

YEVREYSKAYA AO

HEILONGJIANG

CHINA

Changbai Shan

Jiamusi

Mudanjiang

Vladivostok

Nakhodka

Ussuriysk

Zaliv Petra Velikogo

JILIN

NORTH KOREA

Ch'ŏngjin

Musu-dan

Chosŏn-Man

SEA OF JAPAN

Miller Oblated Stereographic Projection

1:4,500,000

0 50 100 150 200 250 300 KILOMETRES

0 50 100 150 200 STATUTE MILES

© COLOUR LIBRARY BOOKS

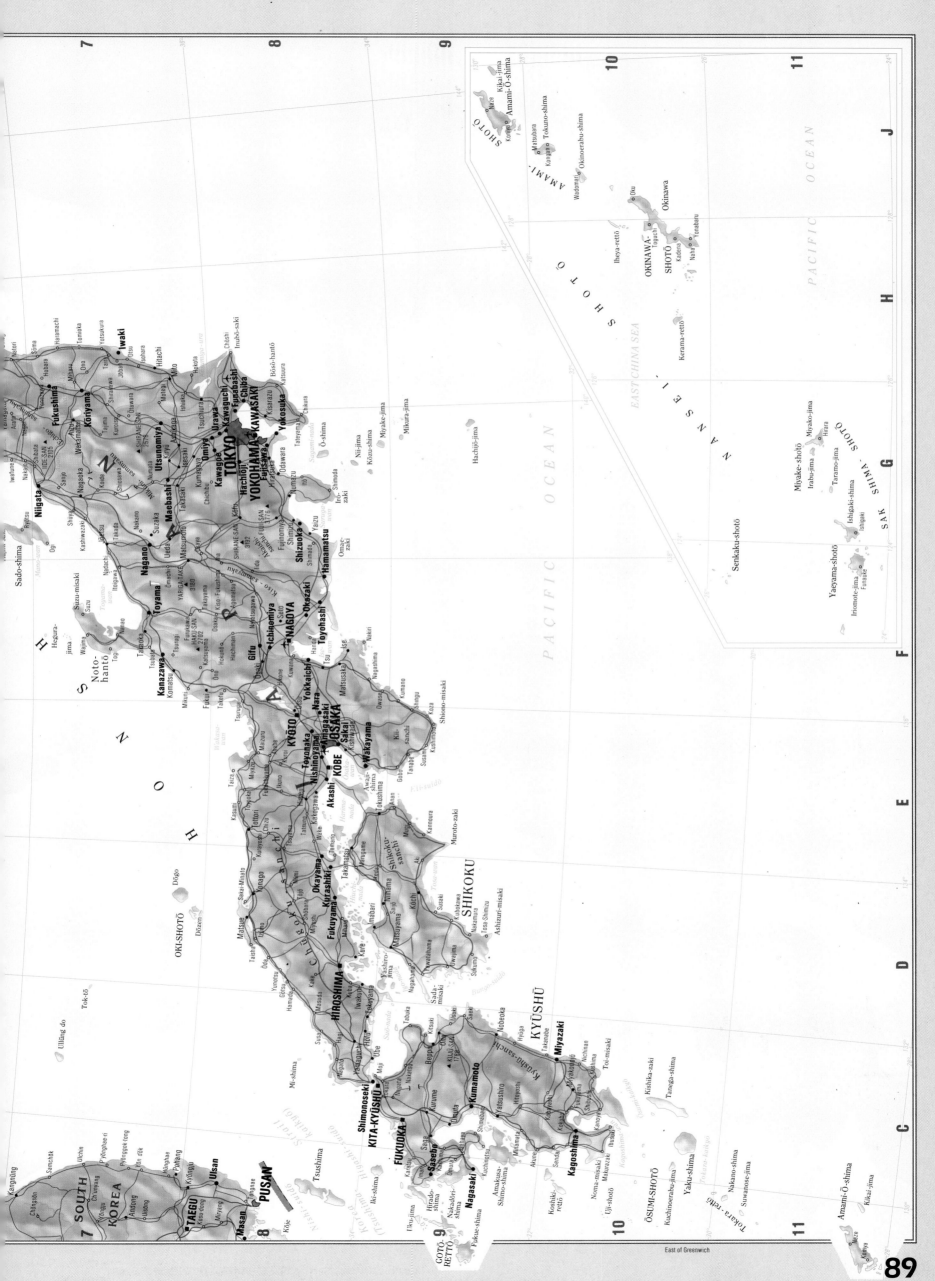

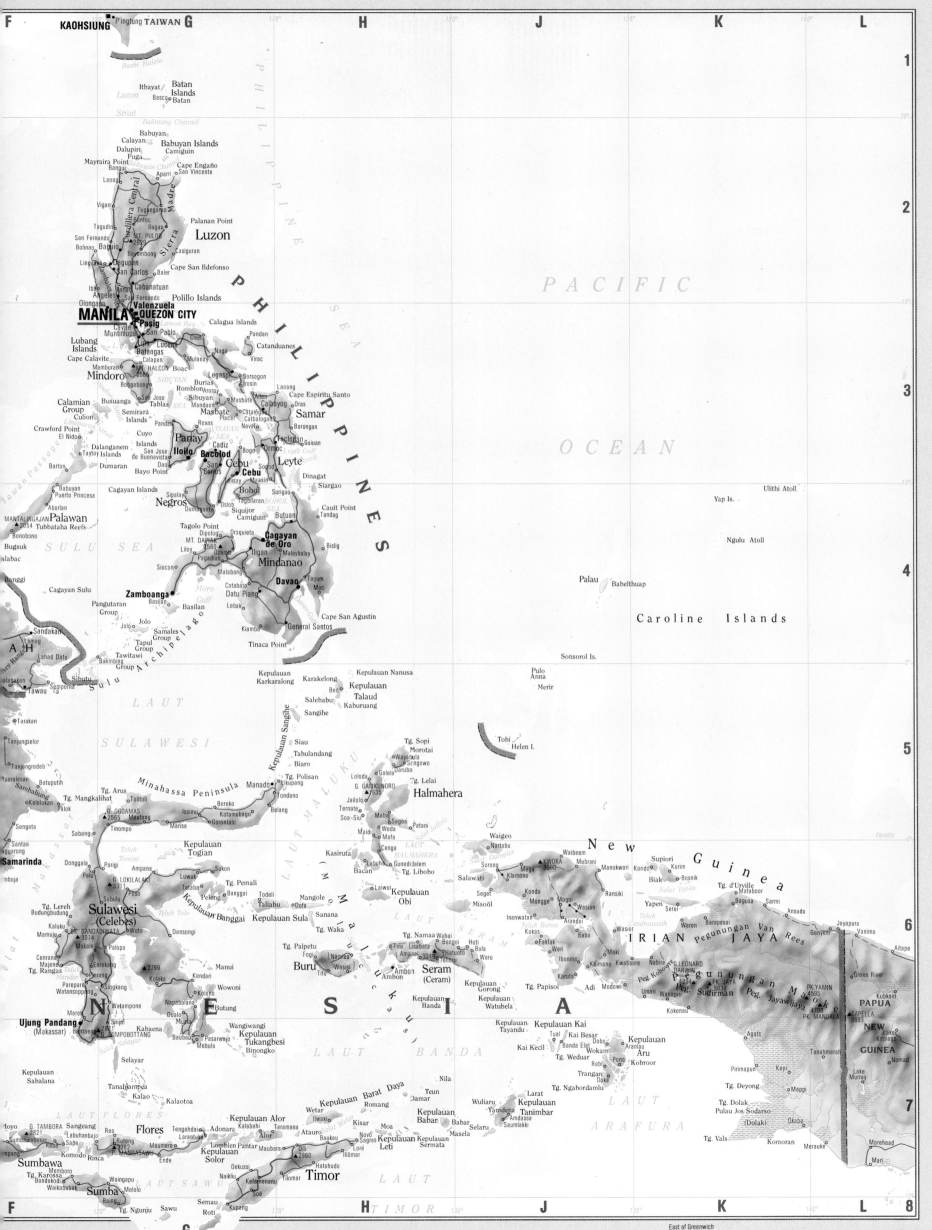

KAOHSIUNG ▪ P'ingtung TAIWAN H J K L

1

Bashi Hatxia

Itbayat • Batan
Basco • Islands
Batan

Luzon
Strait

Babuyan
Calayan • Babuyan Islands
Dalupiri • Fuga • Camiguin
Mayraira Point • Bangui
Laoag • Aparri • Cape Engaño
San Vincente

PACIFIC

Vigan • Tuguegarao
Tagudin • Bontoc • Ilagan
Baguio • MT. PULOG
2929 • Palanan Point
San Fernando • Cordillera Central
Bolinao • Bayombong • Sierra Madre
Lingayen • Baler
Ibo • Dagupan • Cape San Ildefonso
San Carlos • Cabanatuan

Luzon

2

OCEAN

Olongapo • Angeles • Cabanatuan
Iba • San Fernando
MANILA • Valenzuela
Cavite • QUEZON CITY
Muntinlupa • Pasig
San Pablo
Lubang • Lipa • Lucena
Islands • Batangas • Daet • Calagua Islands • Pandan • Catanduanes
Cape Calavite • Calapan • Mulanay • Naga • Virac
Mindoro • Mamburao • MT. HALCON • Boac • Legaspi • Sorsogon
2586 • Bongabong • Romblon • Burias • Irosin
San Jose • Tablas • Arroyo • Cape Espiritu Santo
Calamian • Busuanga • SIBUYAN • Masbate • Calbayog • Oras
Group • Culion • Semirara • SEA • Sibuyan • Mandaon • Catbalogan • Borongan
Islands • Pandan • Masbate • Placer • Samar
Crawford Point • El Nido • Cuyo • WISAYAN • Roxas • Navaa • Tacloban
Dalanganem • Islands • San Jose • SEA • Cadiz • Bogo • Guiuan
Taytay Islands • de Buenavista • Panay • Bacolod • Cebu • Leyte Gulf
Barton • Dumaran • Dao • Iloilo • San • Cebu • Maasin
Bayo Point • Carlos • Leyte

3

Babuyan • Cagayan Islands • Sipalay • Bohol • Surigao • Dinagat
Aborlan • Puerto Princesa • Negros • Dumaguete • Tagbilaran • Siargao
MANTALINGAJAN • Palawan • Siquijor • BOHOL • Butuan • Cauit Point
2054 • Tubbataha Reefs • Tagolo Point • Camiguin • Tandag
Bonobono • Dipolog • Oroquieta • Butuan
Bugsuk • SULU • SEA • MT. DAPIAK • Iligan • Bislig
alabac • 2560 • Malaybalay
Banggi • Liloy • Pagadian • Mindanao
Cagayan Sulu • Siocon • Cagayan de Oro
A H • Sandakan • Pangutaran • Malabang • Davao • Mati
Lahad Datu • Group • Jolo • Cotabato • Datu Piang • Tagum
Zamboanga • Basilan • Lebak • Demon Gulf
abakan • Basilan • Cape San Agustin
Tawau • Sempora • Samales • Kiamba • General Santos
Jolo • Group • Tinaca Point

4

Palau • Babelthuap

Ulithi Atoll
Yap Is.

Ngulu Atoll

Caroline Islands

Sonsorol Is.

Tg. Arus • Kepulauan • Kepulauan Nanusa
Karkaralong • Karakelong
Salebabu • Kepulauan • Pulo
Tapul • Balimbing • Sibutu • Beo • Talaud • Anna
Group • Group • Sangihe • Kaburuang • Merir

5

LAUT • Tarakan • Kepulauan Sangihe • Siau • Tahulandang • Biaro

SULAWESI • Tanjungselor • Tobi • Helen I.

Tanjungredeb • Tg. Mangkalihat • Tg. Polisan • Tg. Sopi • Morotai
Muaralesan • Minahassa Peninsula • Manado • Loloda • Wayabula • Daruba
Batuputih • Tolitoli • Boroko • Likupang • G. GAMKUNORO • Tg. Lelai
Sambaliung • Kelolokan • G. OGOAMAS • Moutong • Tondano • 1635 • Halmahera
Talok • 2565 • Issimu • Kotamobagu • Belang • Jailolo • Soa-Siu
Sengata • Sabang • Marisa • Gorontalo • Ternate • Patani
Santan • Tinompo • Maidi • Maba • Weda
nboja • Donggala • Kepulauan • Mafa • Segea
Samarinda • Parigi • Togian • Luwuk • Cenga • LAUT HALMAHERA
Palu • G. LOKILAKI • Ampana • Tg. Pemali • Kasiruta • Waigeo • Nartabu
Kaluku • 3331 • Poso • Todeli • Labuha • Gunedidjalem • Sorong • Doromena
Mamuju • Sabulu • Tataba • Peleng • Banggai • Dofa • Bacan • Salawati • Segel
Tg. Lereh • Makale • Wotu • Densongi • Taliabu • Sanana • Tg. Libobo • Konda • Waigeo

6

New Guinea

IRIAN JAYA

N E • Budungbudung • Sulawesi • Kolaka • Kepulauan Sula • Tg. Waka • Mangole • Kepulauan • Mongge • Wasian
Kaluku • (Celebes) • Enrekang • Manui • Tg. Namaa • Wahai • Bengoi • Obi • Faktak • Weri
Majene • GANDANGDEWATA • Pinrang • Kendari • Tg. Palpetu • Namlea • Piru • Lisabata • Hoti • Bula • Ibonma
Cenrana • 3074 • Parepare • Wowoni • Fogi • Namrea • Amaai • 3014 • Tehuru • Waru • Kaimana • Karufa
Tg. Rangas • 2799 • Watansoppeng • Kolaka • Buru • Wasisi • Seram • Kepulauan • Modowi
Mamuju • Sengkang • Napabalano • Butung • Ambon • (Ceram) • Gorong • Adi
Maros • Watampone • Dualo • Muna • Kepulauan • Umari • Wanapiri
S • Kabaena • Watubela • Kokenau
Ujung Pandang • LOMPOBATTANG • Wangiwangi • Kepulauan • Kepulauan
(Makassar) • Bantaeng • Kepulauan • Banda • Kai

7

Kepulauan • Tanahjampea • Kepulauan • Nila • Teun • Wuliaru • Larat • Kepulauan • Tg. Deyong
Sabalana • Kalao • Tukangbesi • Damar • Yamdena • Tanimbar • Tg. Dolak
Selayar • Binongko • Kepulauan Barat Daya • Romang • Kepulauan • Amdassa • Pulau Jos Sodarso
Kepulauan • Wetar • Kisar • Moa • Babar • Saumlakki • (Dolak) • Okaba
Sabalana • LAUT FLORES • Sangeang • Ilwaki • Selaru • Sermata • Komoran
G. TAMBORA • Tengahdai • Adonara • Tg. Vals
Flores • Labuanbajo • Larantuka • Kepulauan • LAUT • Morehead
Sumbawa • 2821 • Reo • Maumere • Alor • Baukau • Leti • ARAFURA
Ruteng • RANAKAH • Ende • Lomblen • Pantar • Dili • Mari
Komodo • Rinca • MANDASAWU • Kalabahi • Maubara • 2960
Rabo • Sape • Kepulauan • Kefamenanu • Tilomar
Memboro • Karossa • Solor • Naikliu • Hatuhudo • Soe
Bondokodi • Waingapu • Melolo • Dili
Waikabubak • Timor
Sumba • Bajui • LAUT SAWU • Semau • Kupang
Waitabula • Melolo • Roti • Sawu

East of Greenwich

Designed and produced by E.S.R.

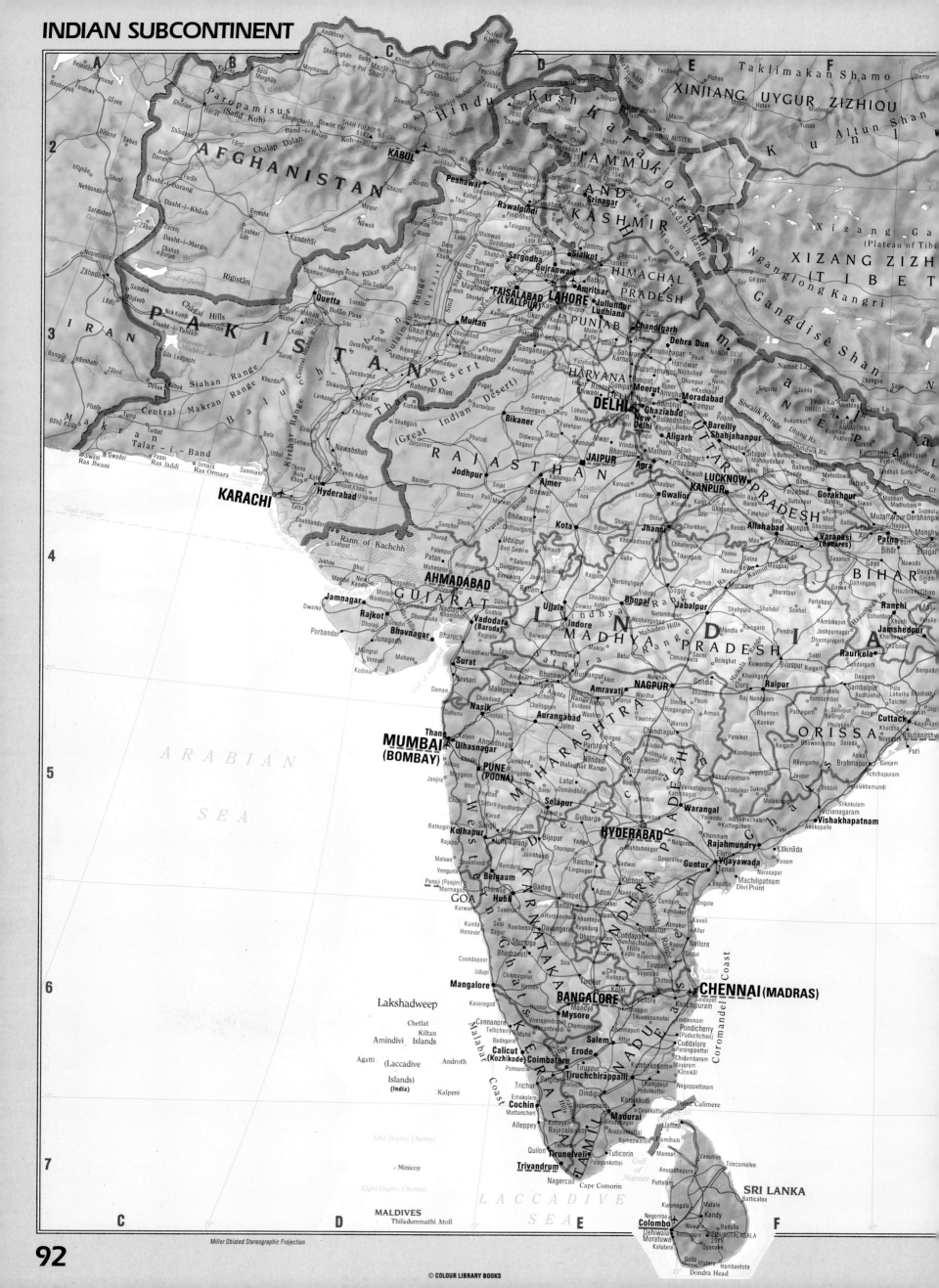

1:10,500,000

East of Greenwich

Designed and produced by E.S.R.

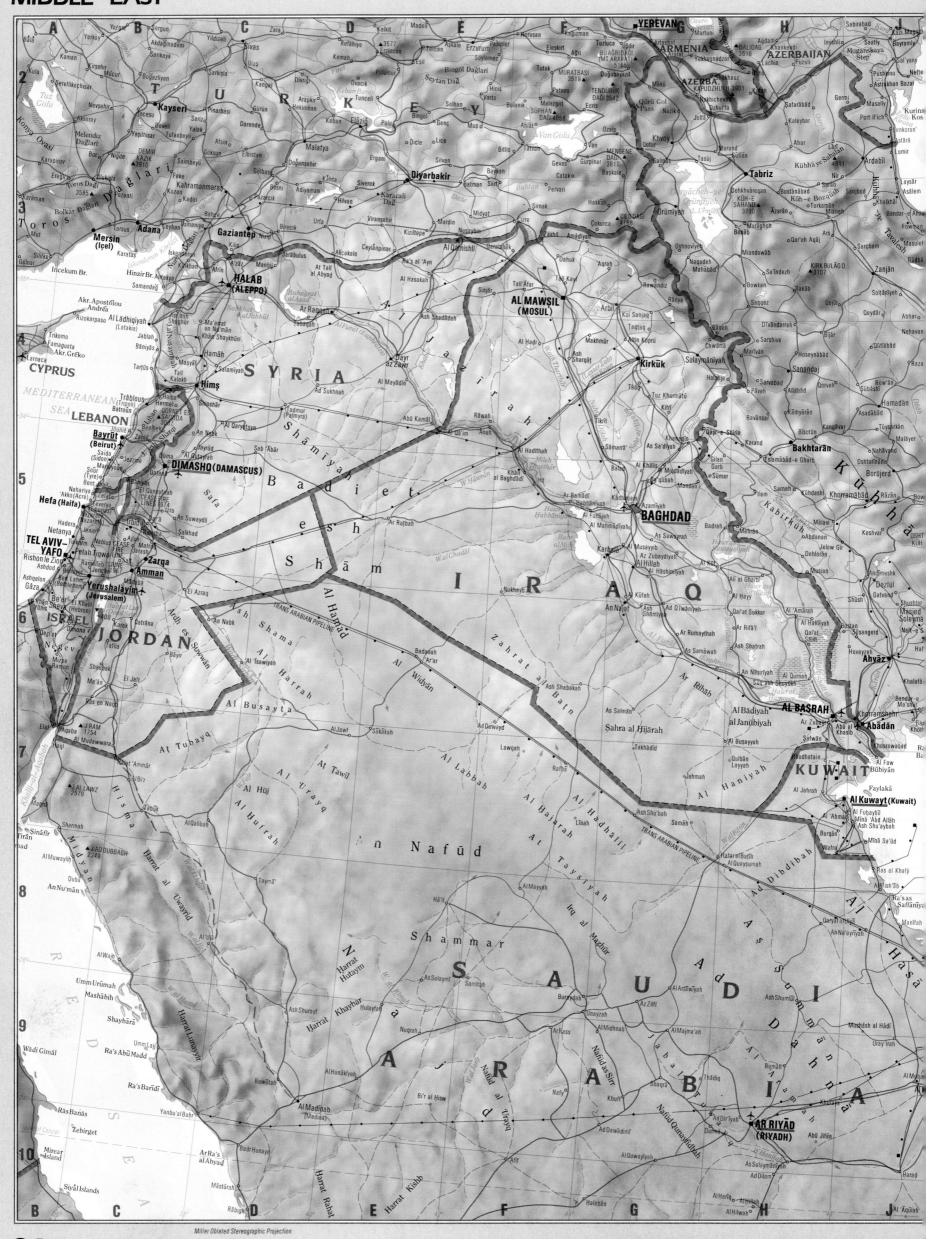

Miller Oblated Stereographic Projection

1:6,000,000

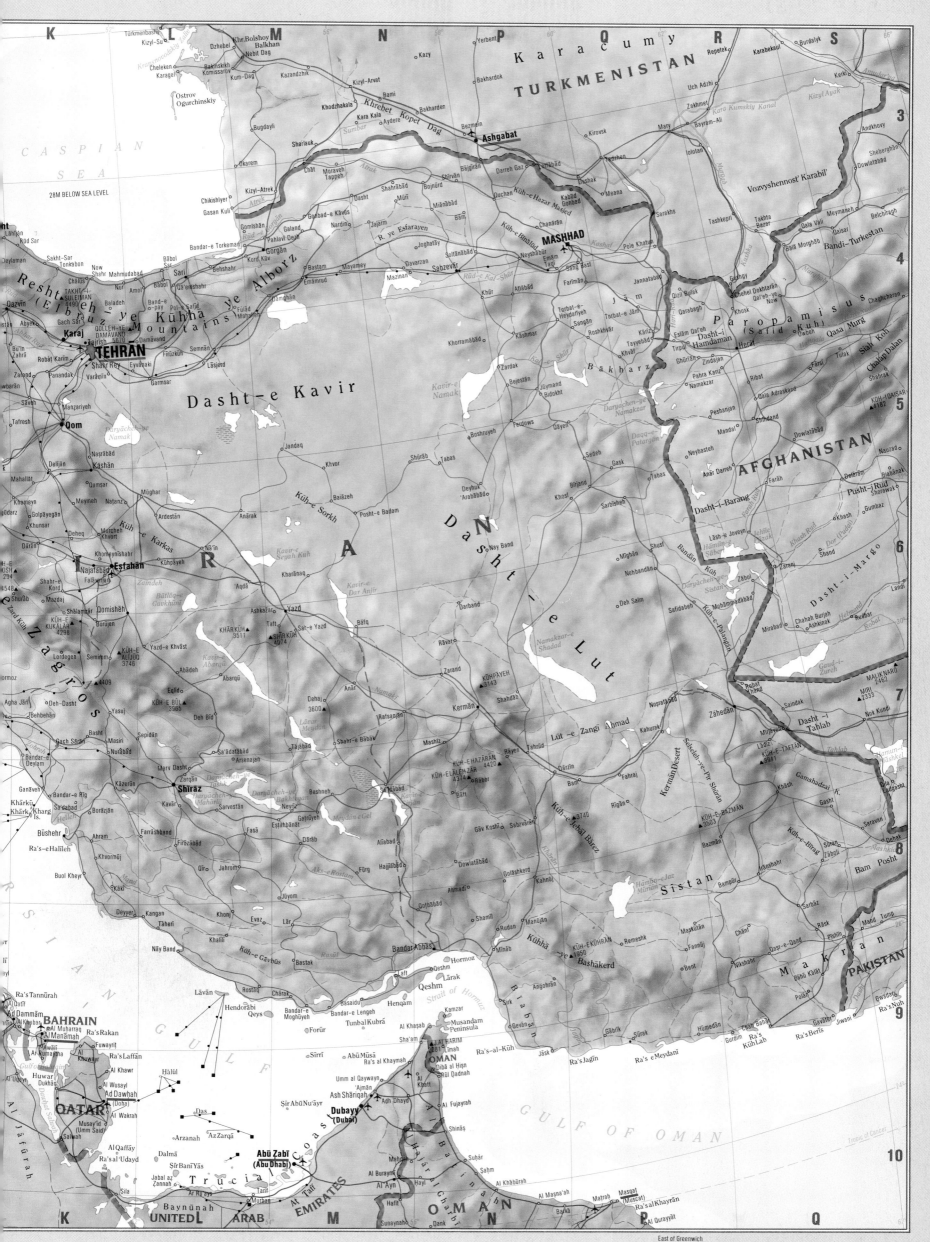

East of Greenwich

Designed and produced by E.S.R.

ARABIAN PENINSULA

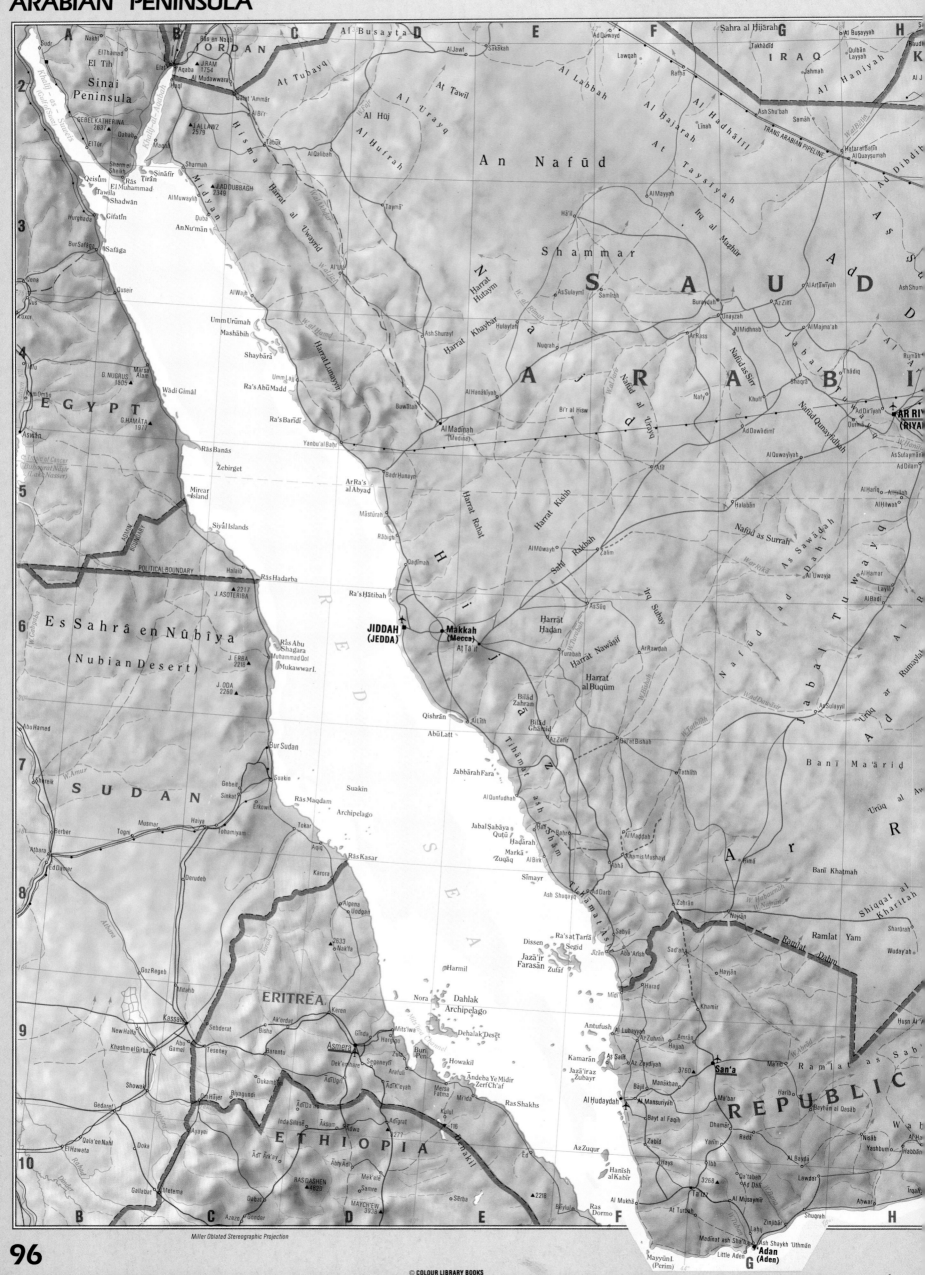

Miller Oblated Stereographic Projection

© COLOUR LIBRARY BOOKS

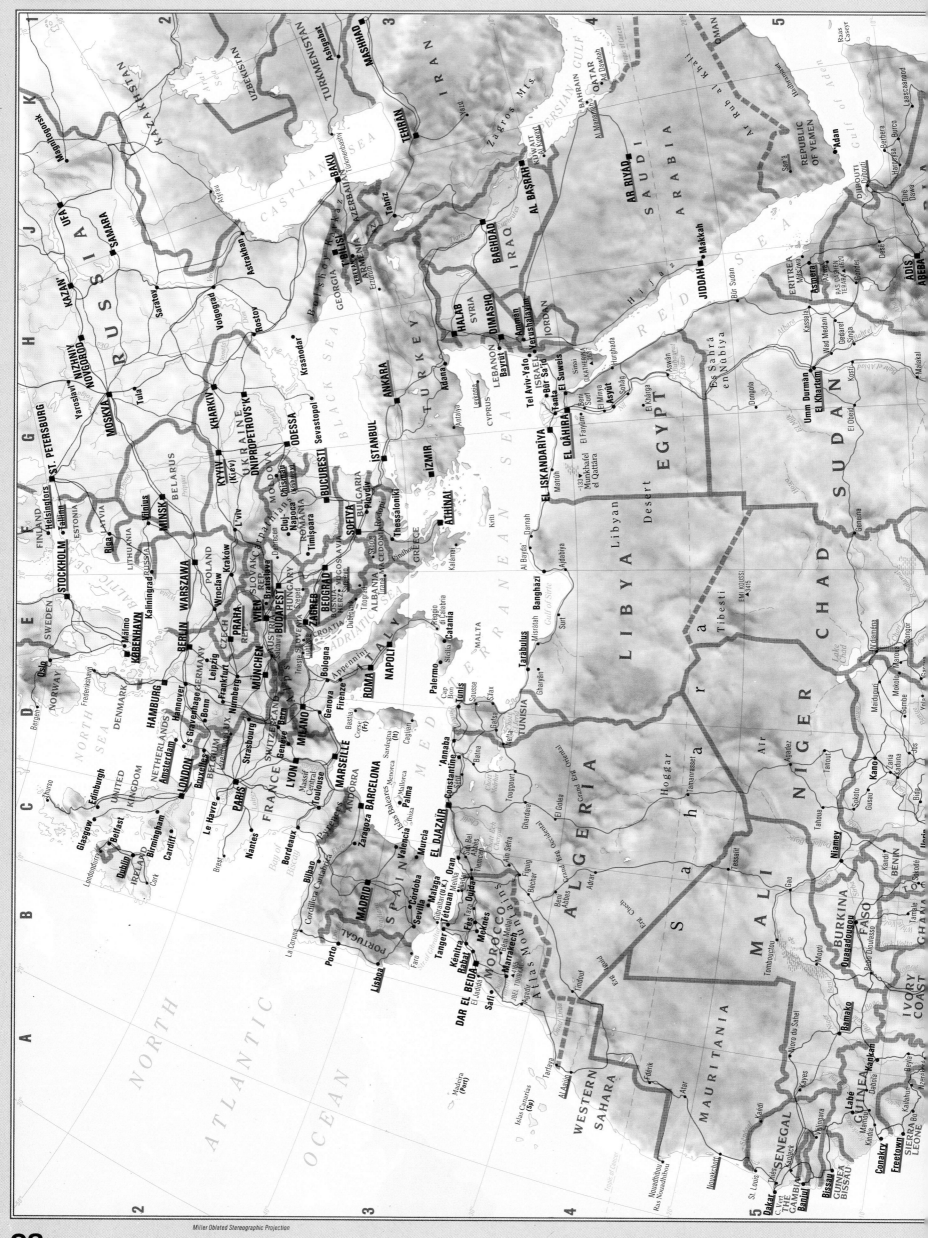

Miller Oblated Stereographic Projection

1:23,000,000

© COLOUR LIBRARY BOOKS

	250	500	750	1000	1250	1500 KILOMETRES
0	100	200	300	400 500 600	700 800	900 1000 STATUTE MILES

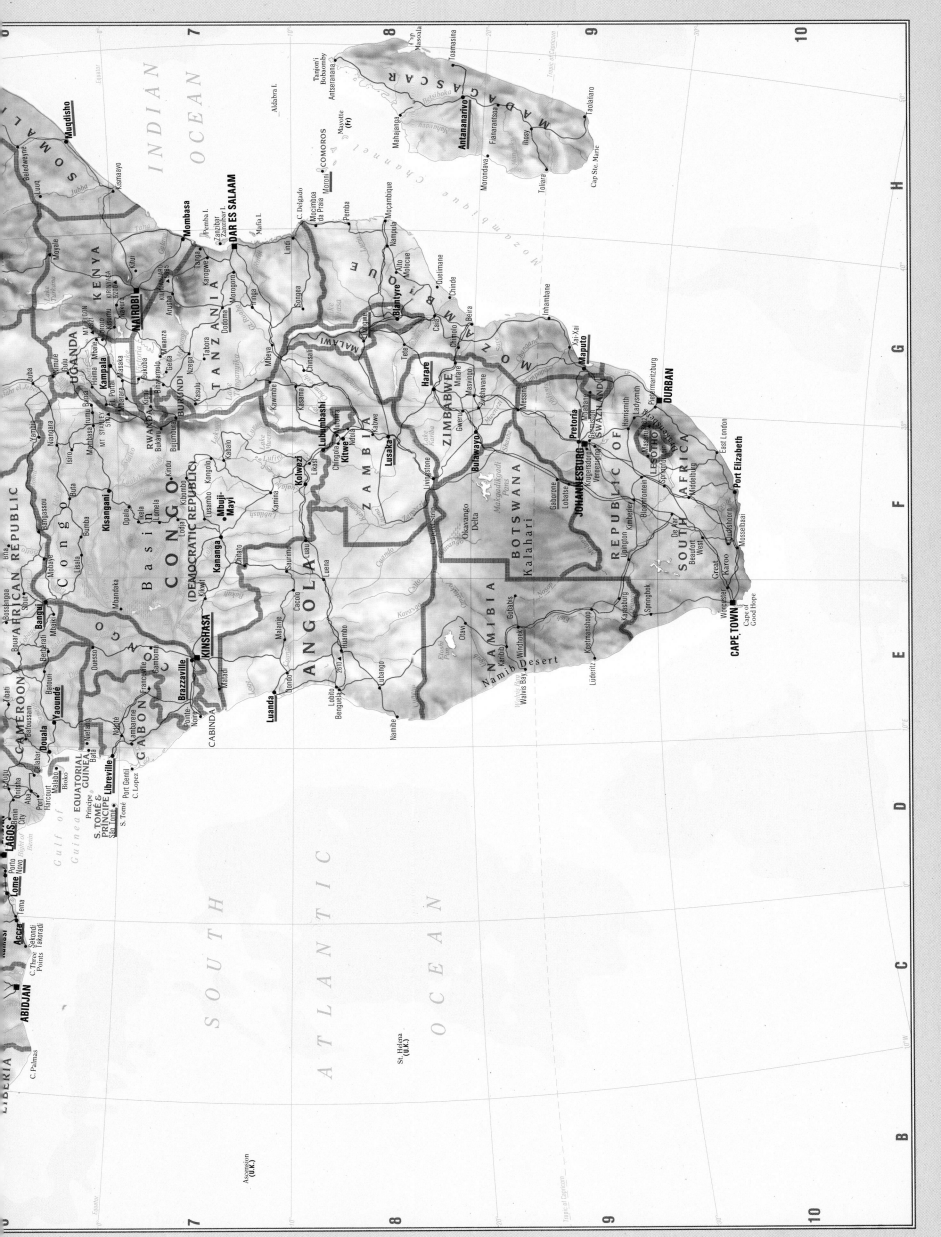

Designed and produced by E.S.R.

Miller Oblated Stereographic Projection

West of Greenwich

1:9,000,000

© COLOUR LIBRARY BOOKS

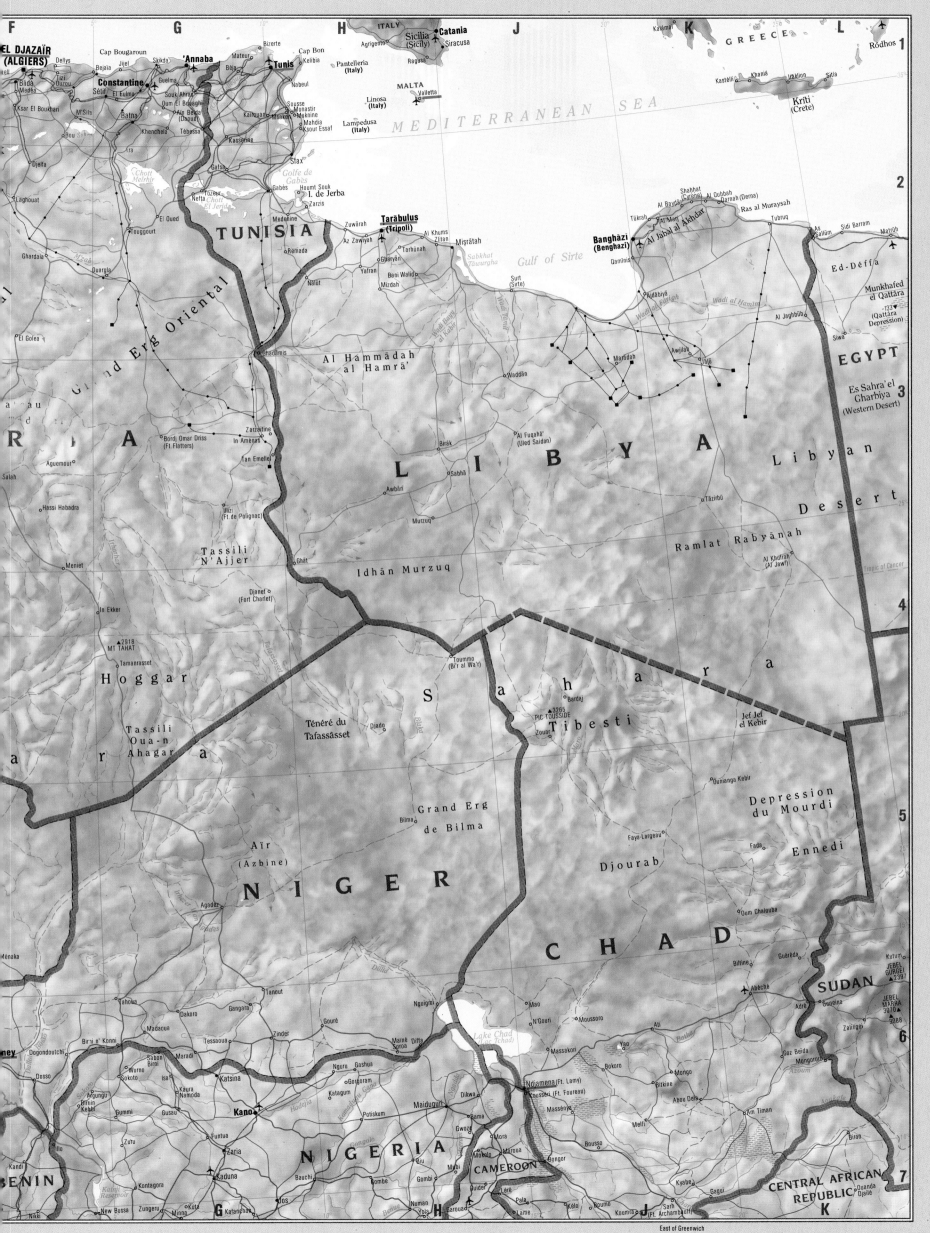

MEDITERRANEAN SEA

GREECE

ITALY
Sicilia (Sicily) · Catania
MALTA · Valletta

TUNISIA

LIBYA

EGYPT

Grand Erg Oriental

Hoggar

S a h a r a

Tibesti

NIGER

CHAD

SUDAN

NIGERIA

CAMEROON

CENTRAL AFRICAN REPUBLIC

East of Greenwich

Designed and produced by E.S.R.

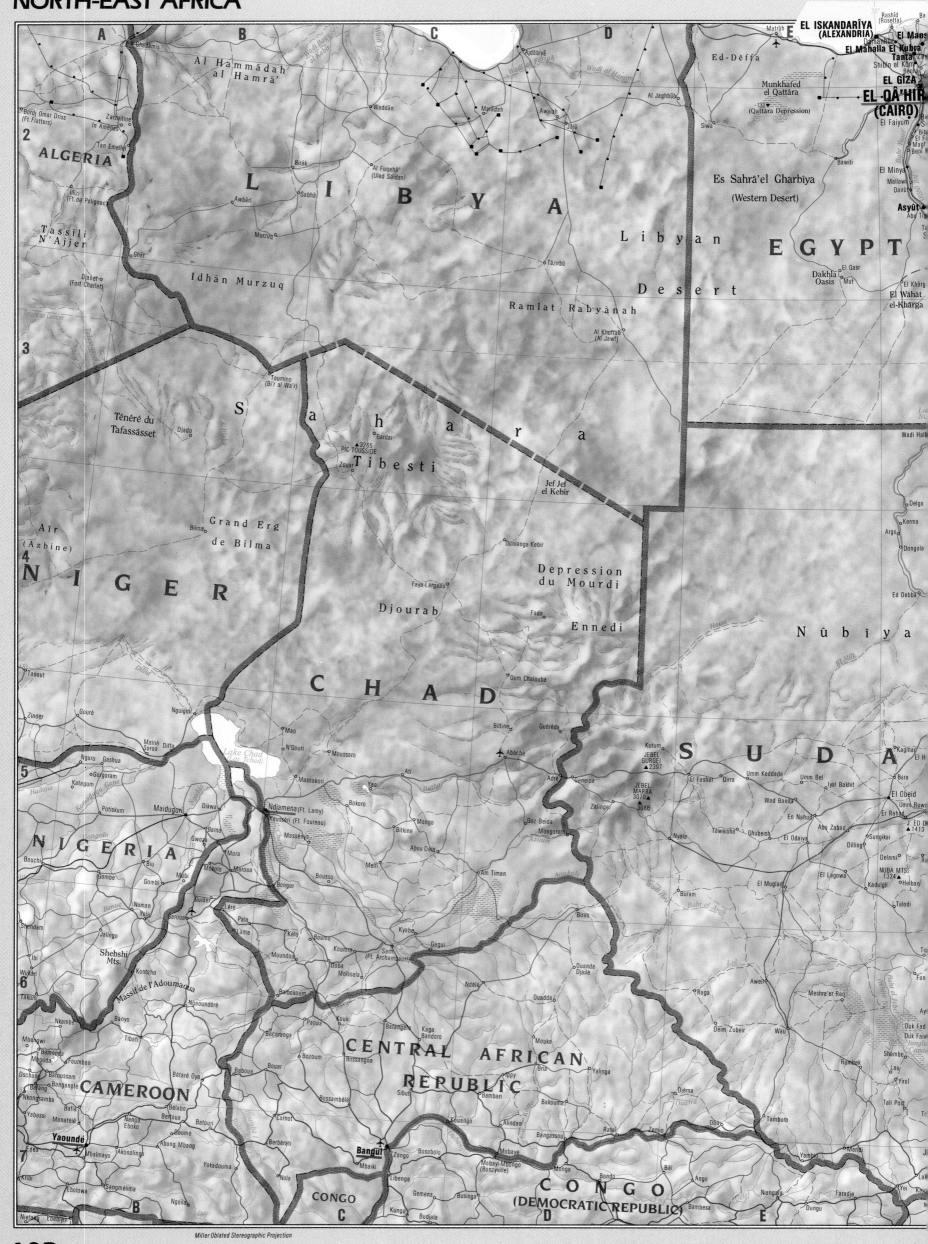

EL ISKANDARÎYA
(ALEXANDRIA)

ALGERIA

L I B Y A

EGYPT

EL GÎZA

EL QÂ'HIR
(CAIRO)

Es Sahrā'el Gharbiya
(Western Desert)

Munkhafed
el Qattâra
(Qattâra Depression)

Libyan

Desert

Al Hammādah
al' Hamrā'

Ramlat Rabyānah

Ténéré du
Tafassâsset

S a h a r a

PIC TOUSSIDE
Tibesti

Jef Jef
el Kebir

Nûbîya

Grand Erg
de Bilma

Aïr
(Āzbine)

Depression
du Mourdi

N I G E R

Djourab

Ennedi

C H A D

S U D A

Lake Chad
(Lac Tchad)

Ndjamena (Ft. Lamy)

NIGERIA

Shebshi
Mts.

Massif de l'Adoumaoua

CENTRAL AFRICAN

REPUBLIC

CAMEROON

Yaoundé

Bangui

CONGO

CONGO
(DEMOCRATIC REPUBLIC)

Miller Oblated Stereographic Projection

102

1:9,000,000

0 100 200 300 400 500 600 KILOMETRES
0 50 100 150 200 250 300 350 400 STATUTE MILES

© COLOUR LIBRARY BOOKS

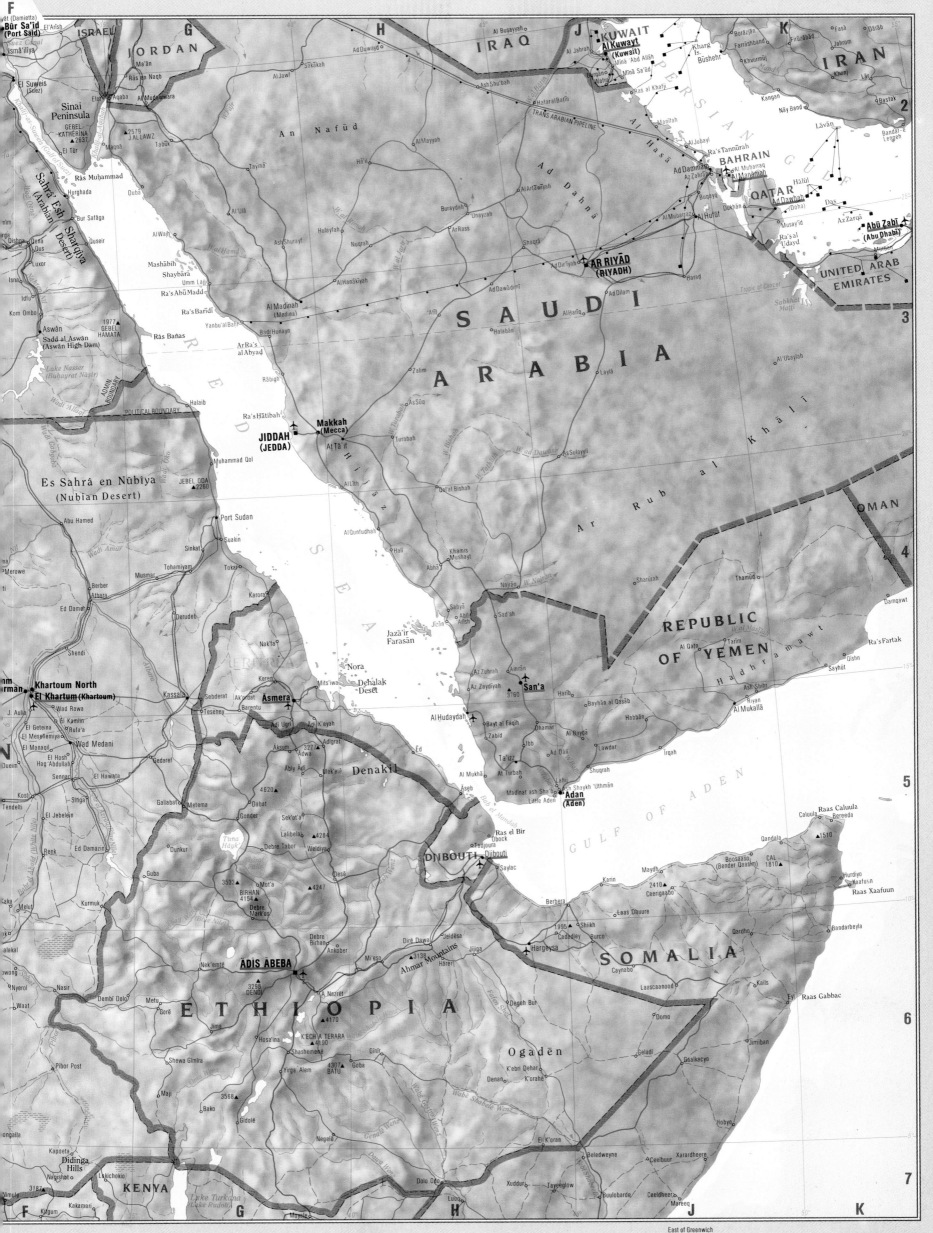

WESTERN SAHARA

C. Barbas

Nouadhibou
(Pt. Etienne)
Ras Nouadhibou
(C. Blanc)

C. Timiris

Fdérik Zouerate

Tropic of Cancer

Erg Chech

Tanezrouft

Taoudenni

MAURITANIA

Makteir

Ouarâne

Atar Chinguetti

Akjoujt

El Djouf

S a h

Tessa

Nouakchott Beila

Moudjéria

Tidjikdja

Tichitt

Araouane

M A L I

Boutilimit

Tamchaket

Oualata

Mederdra

Aleg

Aoun el Atrouss

Néma

Aguelho

St. Louis Dagana Podor Bogué Kaédi

Diorbivol

Mbout

Kiffa

L. Faguibine Tombouctou
(Timbuktu)

Gourma-
Rharous

Bamba

Bourem

Lougat Kébémer Linguère

Matam

Sélibabi

Ras el Ma

Goundam

Niger

Gao

Tivaouane Thiès

Bakel

Timbédra

Niafounké

Cape Vert
Dakar

SENEGAL

Kayes

Balié

Nioro du Sahel

Nara

Mopti

Douentza

Bandiagara

Mbour Fatick Foundiougne

Kaolack Kaffrine

Tambacounda

Bafoulabé

Sokolo

Djenné

San

Dori

BURKINA FASO

Banjul
(Bathurst) Brikama

Georgetown Maka Basse Santa Su

Niono

Ségou

Tougan

Yako

Ouahigouya

THE GAMBIA

Bioulloulou Kolda Velingara

Kédougou

Kita

Kati

Koutiala

Dédougou

Koudougou

Fada
N'Gourma

Ziguinchor

C. Roxo

Sinkounkoun

Satadougou

Bafing

Makana

Bamako

Bougou

Sikasso

Boromo

Ouagadougou

Houndé

Leo

Tenkodogo

**GUINEA
BISSAU**

Bafatá

Bissau Fulacunda

Bolama

Koundara

Foula Mori

Gaoual

Yamberlng

Siguiri

Massigui

Bobo
Dioulasso

Diébougou

Navrongo

Po

Bawku

Arquipelago
dos Bijagos

Boké

Telimélé

Pita **Labé**

Ditinn

Dalaba

Dinguiraye

Timbo Dabola

Kouroussa

GUINEA

Banfora

Tumu

Gaoua

Lawra

Bolgatanga

Dapango

Cap Verga

Boffa

Kindia

Mamou

Faranah

Kankan

Ferkessédougou

Kong

Wa

Daboya

White Volta

Tamale

Yendi

Dubréka

Conakry

Forécariah

Kabala

Kissidougou

1236

Odienné

Boundiali

Korhogo

Bouna

Bole

Damongo

Salaga

Kambia

Port Loko

Makeni

Sefadu

Guéckédou

Macenta

Beyla

Touba

Séguéla

Mankono

Katiola

Dabakala

Bondoukou

Kintampo

Kete

**SIERRA
LEONE**

Lunsar

Magburaka

Kailahun

Pendembu

Segbwema

Wologisi
Mts.

Nzérékoré

Lola

1752
MTS. NIMBA

Biankouma

Man

Zuénoula

Bouaflé

IVORY COAST

Bouaké

Sunyani

Mampong

GHANA

Freetown

Moyamba

Bo

Kenema

Gbarnga

Daloa

Yamoussoukro

Dimbokro

Abengourou

Aya-Yenéhino

Kumasi

Bekwai

Mampong

Akosombo
Dam

Ho

Yauri Bay

Shenge

Bonthe

Pujehun

Sherbro Island

Robertsport

LIBERIA

Tototua

Guiglo

Gagnoa

Sinfra

Toumodi

Agboville

Anyama

Obuasi

Awaso

Nsuta

Dunkwa

Asamankese

Koforidua

Winneba

Tema

Sherbro

Saint Paul

Buchanan

Timbo

Zwedru

Soubré

Bingerville

Aboisso

Enchi

Uda

Tarkwa

Sekondi Takoradi

Cape Coast

Saltpond

Accra

Monrovia

Greenville
(Sinoe)

Sasstown

San Pédro

Grand
Lahou

Sassandra

ABIDJAN

Axim

Dixcove

Cape Three Points

Harper

Tabou

C. Palmas

A T L A N T I C   O C E A N

CAPE VERDE inset:

B

Santo
Antão

Porto Novo

Mindelo

Sal

São Vicente

São Nicolau

**CAPE
VERDE**

Boa Vista

Fogo

São
Tiago

Maio

Brava

Praia

L

C

D

E

Miller Oblated Stereographic Projection

West of Greenwich

1:9,000,000

0 100 200 300 400 500 600 KILOMETRES

0 50 100 150 200 250 300 350 400 STATUTE MILES

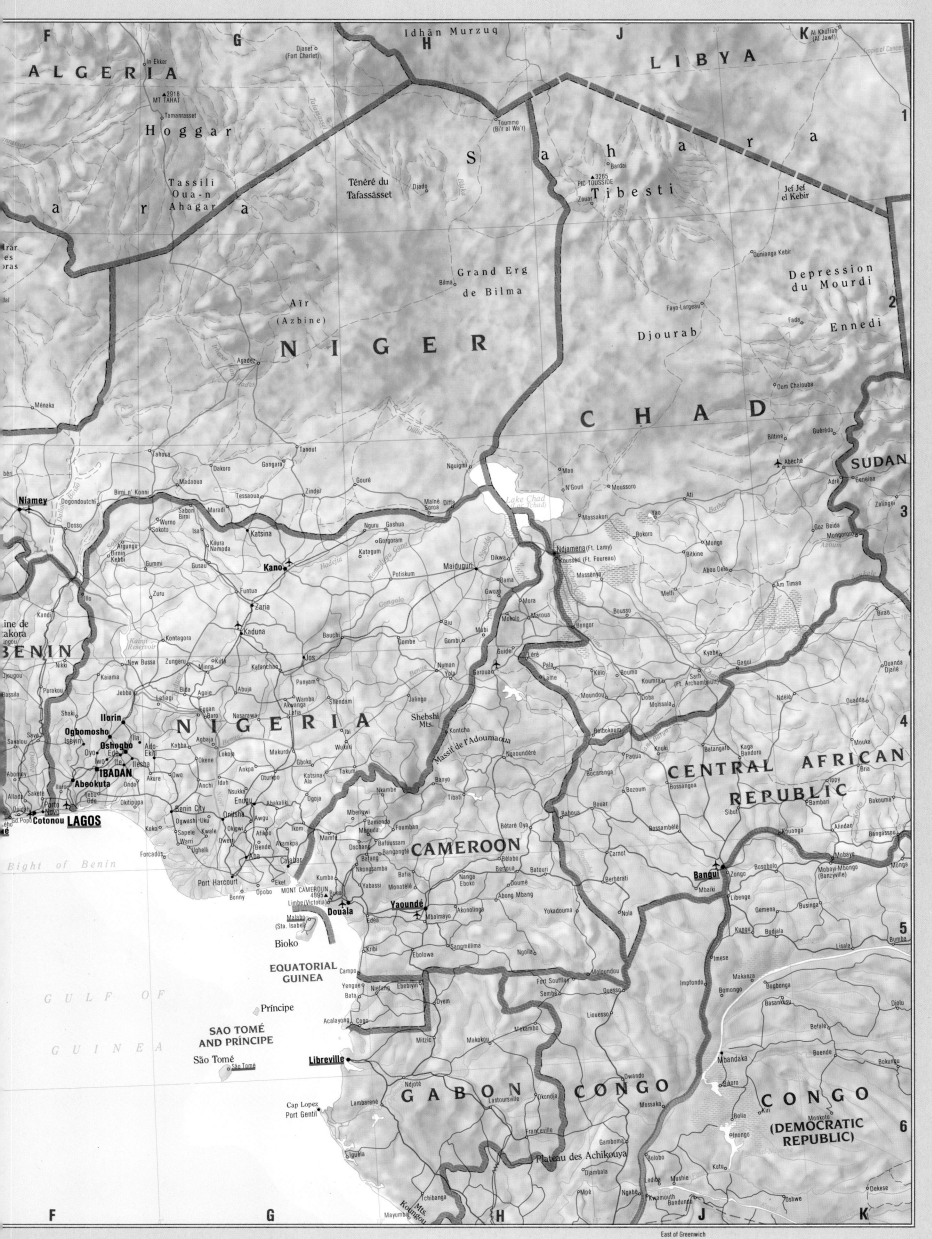

Designed and produced by E.S.R.

East of Greenwich

Miller Oblated Stereographic Projection

1:9,000,000

| 0 | 100 | 200 | 300 | 400 | 500 | 600 KILOMETRES |

| 0 | 50 | 100 | 150 | 200 | 250 | 300 | 350 | 400 STATUTE MILES |

© COLOUR LIBRARY BOOKS

Designed and produced by E.S.R.

East of Greenwich

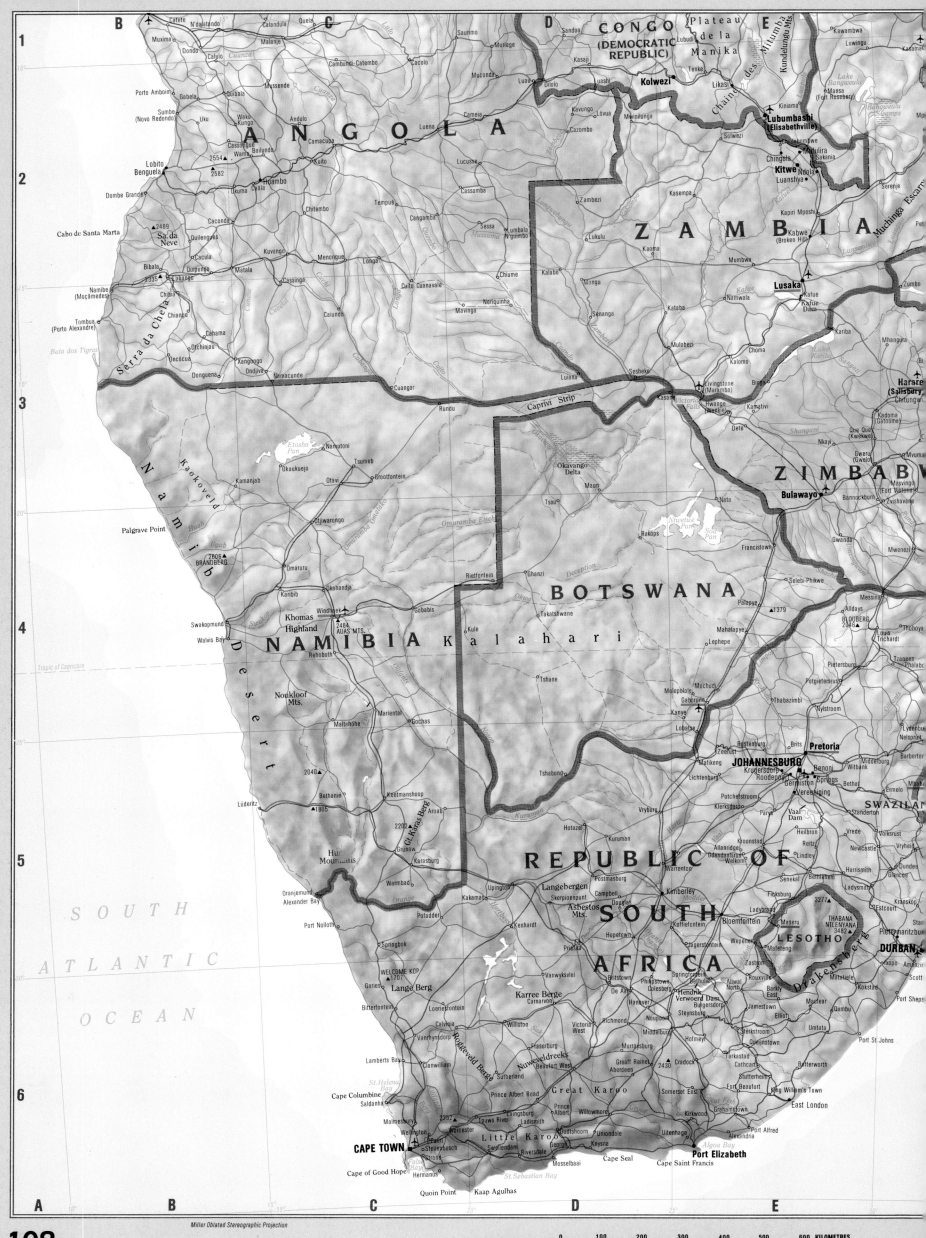

Miller Oblated Stereographic Projection

1:9,000,000

© COLOUR LIBRARY BOOKS

F

TANZANIA

MALAWI

MOZAMBIQUE

COMOROS

Grande
Comore
Moroni

Moheli   Anjouan

Dzaoudzi
Mayotte
(France)

Juan de Nova
(France)

Bassas
da India
(France)

I. de l'Europa
(France)

I N D I A N

O C E A N

MADAGASCAR

Tanjon'i Bobaomby

Antseranana
(Diego-Suarez)

Nosy
Mitsio

Nosy Bé
Hell-Ville

Vohimarina
(Vohémar)

Ambilobe

Massif du
Tsaratanana
▲2876

Sambava

Analalava

Antsohihy

Bealanana

Andapa

Antalaha

Betandriana

Maroantsetra

Mahajanga

Port-
Berga

Marovoay

C. Masoala

Mananara

C. St. André
Toraka Vestale

Soalala

Marovoay

Ambo-Boeny

Miarinarivo

Nosy Boraha
(Sainte-Marie)

Besalampy

Stampiky

Ambodifototra

Mahabe

Maevatanana

Tsaratanana

Fenoarivo Atsinanana

Vavatenina

Morafenobe

A'tomainty

Ankazobe

Anjozorobe

A'tondrazaka

Toamasina
(Tamatave)

Maintirano

Antsalova

Tsiroanomandidy

Miarinarivo

Moramanga

Bekopaka

Soavinandriana

Anivonimamo

Antananarivo
(Tananarive)

Andevoranto

Ambatolampy

Anosibe
an'Ala

Vatomandry

Belo-Tsiribihina

Betafo
Antsirabe

Morondava

Mahabo

Fandriana
Marolambo

Morombe

Manja
Bérora

A'tofinandrahana

Ambositra

Nosy-Varika

Ankilizao

Tsitondroina

Vohilava

Ifanadiana

Manakara

Fianarantsoa

Vohipeno

Ankazoabo

Ihosy

Ikongo

Fitsitika

Farafangana

Betroka

Toliara
(Tuléar)

Vangaindrano

Soalara

Betioky

Midongy
Atsimo

Itampolo

Ampanihy

Bekily

Mt. de l'Ivakoany
▲1956

Ambovombe

Taolañaro
(Fort Dauphin)

C. Sainte Marie Faux Cap

Plateau du Bemaraha

Massif du Makay

Andringitra

Beampingaratra

Tropic of Capricorn

J **K**

MAURITIUS

Port Louis
Beau Basin
Curepipe Mahébourg

Réunion
(France)
St. Denis
St. Benoit

St. Pierre

Mascarene
Islands

L

East of Greenwich

109

Designed and produced by E.S.R.

Bonne Projection

East of Greenwich

1:19,000,000

| 0 | 200 | 400 | 600 | 800 KILOMETRES |

| 0 | 100 | 200 | 300 | 400 | 500 STATUTE MILES |

© COLOUR LIBRARY BOOKS

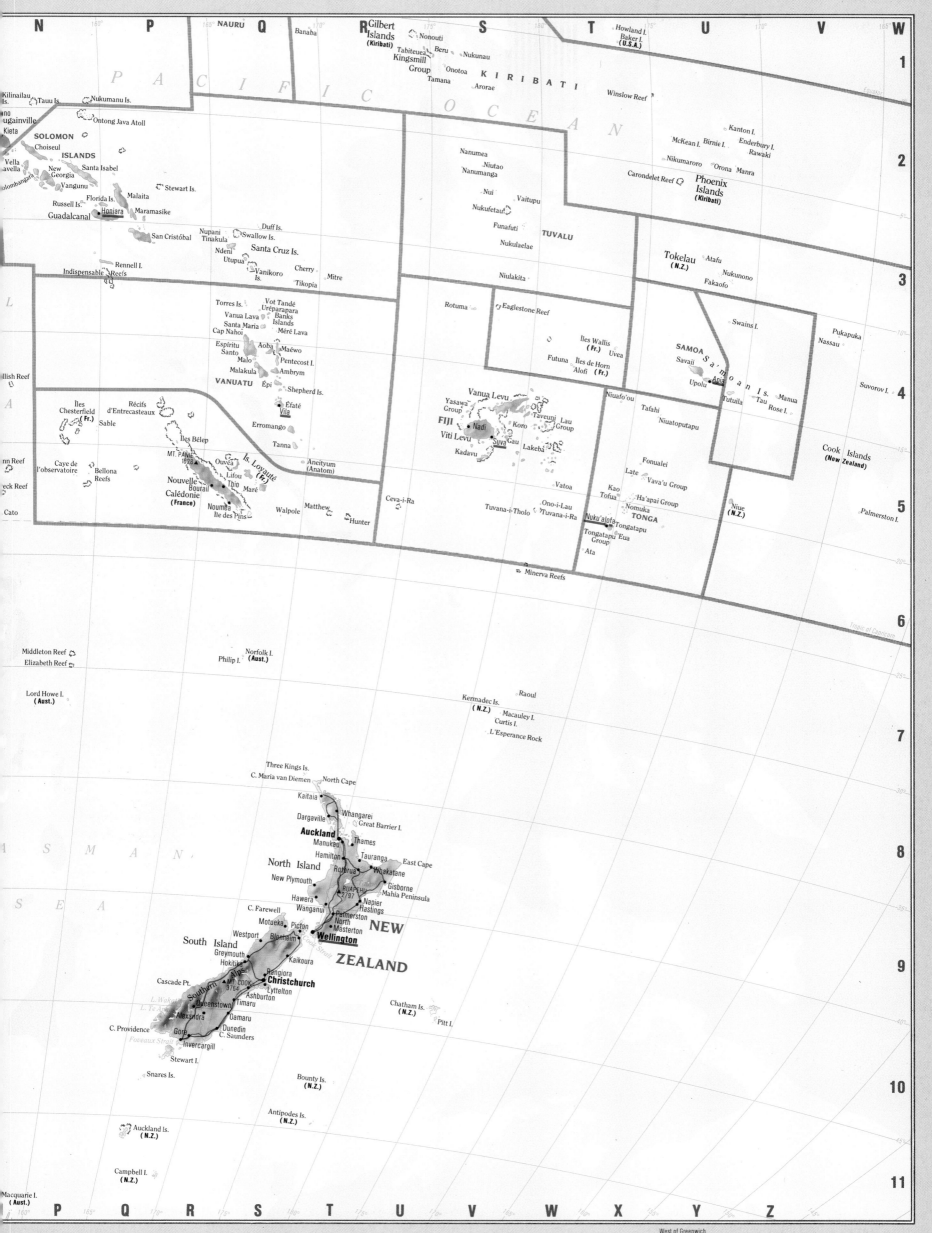

N P NAURU Q R Gilbert S T U V W
Islands
(Kiribati)
Banaba
Nonouti
Tabiteuea Beru Nukunau
Kingsmill Onotoa Tamana
Group Arorae

PACIFIC
Howell I.
Baker I.
(U.S.A.)
Winslow Reef

1

Kilmailau
Is. Tauu Is.
Nukumanu Is.
Ontong Java Atoll
Bougainville
Kieta
SOLOMON
Choiseul
ISLANDS
Vella
Lavella
New Santa Isabel
Georgia Vangunu
Russell Is. Florida Is. Honiara
Guadalcanal Maramasike Malaita

OCEAN

Nanumea
Niutao
Nanumanga

Nui
Vaitupu
Nukufetau
Funafuti TUVALU
Nukulaelae

Niulakita

Kanton I.
McKean I. Birnie I. Enderbury I.
Rawaki
Nikumaroro Orona Manra
Carondelet Reef Phoenix
Islands
(Kiribati)

Tokelau Atafu
(N.Z.)
Nukunono
Fakaofo

2

San Cristóbal
Nupani
Tinakula Duff Is.
Swallow Is.
Ndeni Santa Cruz Is.
Utupua
Rennell I. Vanikoro Cherry
Indispensable Reefs Is. Mitre
Tikopia

Rotuma
Eaglestone Reef

Swains I.

Pukapuka
Nassau

3

Torres Is. Vot Tandé
Uréparapara
Vanua Lava Banks
Santa Maria Islands
Cap Nahoi Méré Lava
Espíritu Aoba Maéwo
Santo Pentecost I.
Malo
Malakula Ambrym
VANUATU Épi
Shepherd Is.

Iles Wallis
(Fr.) Uvea
Futuna
Iles de Horn
Alofi (Fr.)

SAMOA Samoan Is.
Savaii
Upolu
Tutuila Tau Rose I. Manua
Apia Suvorov I.

4

Iles
Chesterfield (Fr.)
Sable
Récifs
d'Entrecasteaux
Caye de
l'observatoire
Bellona
Reefs
MT. PANIÉ
1628
Nouvelle
Bourail
Calédonie Thio
(France) Noumea
Ile des Pins
Ouvéa
Lifou
Maré
Is. Loyauté
(Fr.)
Walpole
Matthew
Hunter
Éfaté
Vila
Erromango
Tanna
Aneityum
(Anatom)

Vanua Levu
Yasawa
Group Taveuni
Viti Levu Koro Lau
FIJI Nadi Group
Suva Gau Lakeba
Kadavu
Ceva-i-Ra
Vatoa
Tuvana-i-Tholo
Tuvana-i-Ra
Ono-i-Lau

Niuafo'ou
Tafahi
Niuatoputapu
Fonualei
Late Vava'u Group
Kao
Tofua Ha'apai Group
Nomuka
Nomuka
Nuku'alofa Tongatapu
Tongatapu 'Eua
Group
Ata
Minerva Reefs
TONGA

Niue
(N.Z.)

Cook Islands
(New Zealand)

Palmerston I.

5

6

Middleton Reef
Elizabeth Reef

Lord Howe I.
(Aust.)

Philip I.
Norfolk I.
(Aust.)

Kermadec Is.
(N.Z.)
Raoul
Macauley I.
Curtis I.
L'Esperance Rock

7

TASMAN

SEA

Three Kings Is.
C. Maria van Diemen
North Cape
Kaitaia
Dargaville Whangarei
Great Barrier I.
Auckland Thames
Manukau
Hamilton Tauranga
North Island Rotorua East Cape
Whakatane
New Plymouth Gisborne
RUAPEHU Mahia Peninsula
2797
Hawera Napier
Wanganui Hastings
C. Farewell Palmerston
Motueka North
Picton Masterton
Westport Blenheim
South Island Wellington
Greymouth Kaikoura Cook Strait
Hokitika NEW
Alps Rangiora ZEALAND
Cascade Pt. MT. COOK Christchurch
3764 Lyttelton
Southern Ashburton
L. Wakatipu Timaru
Queenstown
Alexandra Oamaru
C. Providence Gore
Invercargill Dunedin
C. Saunders
Stewart I.
Snares Is.

Chatham Is.
(N.Z.)
Pitt I.

8

9

Bounty Is.
(N.Z.)

10

Antipodes Is.
(N.Z.)

Auckland Is.
(N.Z.)

Campbell I.
(N.Z.)

11

Macquarie I.
(Aust.)

N P Q R S T U V W X Y Z

West of Greenwich

Designed and produced by E.S.R.

Miller Oblated Stereographic Projection

1:10,500,000

© COLOUR LIBRARY BOOKS

| 0 | 100 | 200 | 300 | 400 | 500 | 600 | 700 | 800 KILOMETRES |

| 0 | 100 | 200 | 300 | 400 | 500 STATUTE MILES |

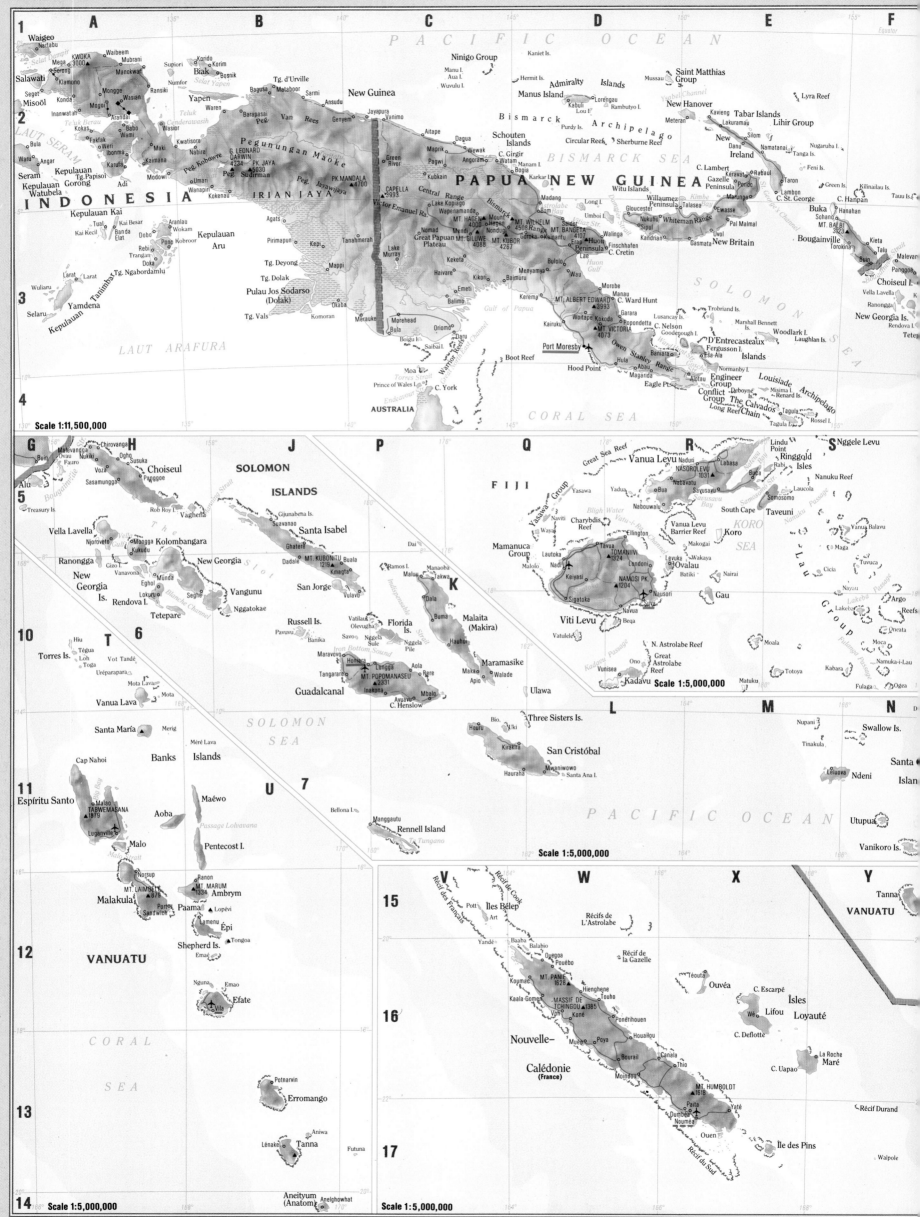

PACIFIC OCEAN

Equator

Waigeo
Nartabu
KWOKA
3000
Mega
Mubrani
Waibeem
Supiori
Korido
Korim
Kaniet Is.
Ninigo Group
Manu I.
Aua I.
Wuvulu I.
Hermit Is.
Mussau
Saint Matthias Group
Lyra Reef
Salawati
Seget
Klamono
Konda
Manokwari
Mangge
Wasian
Numfor
Biak
Bosnik
Yapen
Admiralty Islands
Manus Island
Kabuli
Lorengau
Lou I.
Rambutyo I.
Meteran
Kavieng
New Hanover
Lakuramau
Tabar Islands
Lihir Group
Misoöl
Mogoi
Arandal
Ransiki
Waren
Tg. d'Urville
Bagusa
Mataboor
Sarmi
Ansudu
New Guinea
Jayapura
Vanimo
Schouten Islands
Purdy Is.
Circular Reef
Sherburne Reef
New Ireland
Danu
Namatanai
Silom
Nugaruba I.
Tanga Is.
Seram
Bula
Waru
Angar
Fakfak
Weri
Rebi
Kokas
Babo
Wami
Maki
Kwatisora
Wasior
Barapasai
Van Rees
Peg.
Genyem
Walinga
Atape
Dagua
Maprik
Pagwi
Wewak
Angoram
Bogia
Watam
Manam I.
Karkar Is.
Madang
Bismarck
Bam
Long I.
Umboi I.
Gloucester
C. Lambert
Keravat
Rabaul
Taron
Feni Is.
Green Is.
Kilinailau Is.
Kepulauan Gorong
Tg. Papisoi
Adi
Modowi
Umari
Wanapin
Kokenau
Agats
G. LEONARD DARWIN
4234
Peg. Sudirman
PK. JAYA
5030
PK. MANDALA
4700
Peg. Jayawijaya
IRIAN JAYA
CAPELLA
3993
Central Range
Victor Emanuel Ra.
Lake Kopiago
Wapenamanda
MT. HAGEN
Mount
Hagen
4508
Nondugl
Nomad
Mendi
MT. BANGETA
4107
Walinga
Range
MT. WILHELM
4500
Saidor
Erap
Finschhafen
C. Cretin
Talasea
Nukuhu
Sipul
Kandrian
Gasmata
New Britain
Pal Malmal
Uvol
Whiteman Range
Gazelle Peninsula
Marunga
Willaumez Peninsula
Ewasse
Kimbe
Witu Islands
C. St. George
Lambom
Buka
Hanahan
MT. BALBI
3123
Bougainville
Kieta
Torokina
Buin
Talu
Panggoe
Choiseul I.
Malevavanga
Vella Lavella
INDONESIA
Kepulauan Kai
Tual
Kai Besar
Banda
Elat
Kai Kecil
Dobo
Aranlau
Wokam
Pono
Kobroor
Kepulauan Aru
Kepulauan Watubela
Pirimapun
Kepi
Tanahmerah
Mappi
Lake Murray
Great Papuan Plateau
MT. GILUWE
4088
MT. KUBOR
4267
Keketa
Bulolo
Lae
Menyamya
Wau
Huon Gulf
Huon Peninsula
PAPUA NEW GUINEA
BISMARCK SEA
Bismarck Archipelago
New Hanover
Larat
Wuliaru
Selaru
Yamdena
Kepulauan
Tanimbar
Tg. Ngabordamlu
Tg. Deyong
Tg. Dolak
Pulau Jos Sodarso
(Dolak)
Komoran
Merauke
Bula
Boigu I.
Morehead
Oriomo
Daru
Haivare
Kikori
Baimuru
Kerema
Emeti
Balimo
Keketa
MT. ALBERT EDWARD
3993
Woitape
Kokoda
MT. VICTORIA
4073
Owen Stanley Range
Garara
Popondetta
C. Nelson
Lusancay Is.
Trobriand Is.
Marshall Bennett Is.
Goodenough I.
Woodlark I.
Laughlan Is.
Kairuku
Port Moresby
Hood Point
Hula
Abau
Magarida
Aroma
Eagle Pt.
Alotau
Normanby I.
Fergusson I.
Esa-Ala
Baniara
D'Entrecasteaux Islands
Louisiade Archipelago
Misima I.
Renard Is.
Conflict Group
Deboyne
The Calvados Chain
Tagula
Rossel I.
Tagula
SOLOMON SEA
New Georgia Is.
Ranongga
New Georgia I.
Rendova Is.
Tetepare
CORAL SEA
Moa
Torres Strait
Prince of Wales I.
C. York
Saibai I.
Warrior Reef
Boot Reef
Endeavour Str.
AUSTRALIA

SOLOMON ISLANDS

Buin
Chirovanga
Ovau
Nukiki
Pauro
Ogho
Susuka
Choiseul
Alu
Treasury Is.
Voza
Samamungga
Panggoe
Vaghena
Rob Roy I.
Gijunabena Is.
Suavanao
Ghatere
Santa Isabel
MT. KUBONITU
1219
Buala
Dadale
Kmagta
Lindu Point
Ringgold Isles
Nggele Levu
Nanuku Reef
Vella Lavella
Njoroveto
Mongga
Kukudu
Kolombangara
New Georgia
Vanavona
Egholi
Munda
Seghe
Lokuru
Vangunu
Nggatokae
Dadale
Dai
San Jorge
Vulavu
Ramos I.
Malu
Takwa
Manaoba
Naduri
Vanua Levu
NASOROLEVU
1031
Labasa
Rabi
Bua
Nabavatu
Laucola
Nanuku Reef
FIJI
Yasawa Group
Yadua
Yasawa
Naviti
Waya
Mamanuca Group
Malolo
Lautoka
Nadi
Keiyasi
Sigatoka
Viti Levu
Navua
Beqa
Charybdis Reef
Bligh Water
Vata-i-Ra
Ellington
Tavua
TOMANIIVI
1324
Londoni
NAMOSI PK.
1204
Nausori
Levuka
Ovalau
Batiki
Nairai
Gau
Makogai
Vanua Levu Barrier Reef
Koro
South Cape
Somosomo
Taveuni
KORO SEA
Wakaya
Naitauba
Cicia
Nayau
Vanua Balavu
Mago
Tuvuca
Lau Group
Lakeba
Oneata
Moce
Argo Reefs
Russell Is.
Pavuvu
Banika
Vatilau
Olevugha
Florida Is.
Savo
Nggela Sule
Nggela Pile
Honiara
Lungga
Aola
Rere
Makai
Walade
Maramasike
Marovovo
Tangarare
MT. POPOMANASEU
2331
Inakona
Avuavu
Mbalo
C. Henslow
Guadalcanal
Malaita
(Makira)
Hauhoi
Apio
Ulawa
Moala
Totoya
N. Astrolabe Reef
Great Astrolabe Reef
Vunisea
Ono
Kadavu
Matuku
Fulaga
Ogea
Scale 1:5,000,000

Torres Is.
Hiu
Tégua
Loh
Toga
Uréparapara
Vot Tandé
Mota Lava
Mota
Vanua Lava
Santa María
Merig
Méré Lava
Banks
Cap Nahoi
Big Bay
Islands
Three Sisters Is.
Heuru
Uki
Kirakira
San Cristóbal
Mwaniwowo
Santa Ana I.
Hauraha
SOLOMON SEA
Nupani
Swallow Is.
Tinakula
Léluova
Ndeni
Santa Island
Espíritu Santo
Malao
TABWEMASANA
1879
Luganville
Malo
Bellona I.
Manggautu
Rennell Island
Te Tungano
PACIFIC OCEAN
Utupua
Vanikoro Is.
VANUATU
Norsup
Aoba
Maéwo
Ranon
MT. MARUM
1334
Ambrym
Tanna
Malakula
MT. LAIMBELE
879
Paama
Lopévi
Port Sandwich
Lamenu
Épi
Tongoa
Shepherd's I.
Emaé
Nguna
Emao
Efate
Vila
Ulei
Récif de Cook
Pott
Îles Bélep
Art
Récifs de L'Astrolabe
Yandé
Baaba
Balabio
Ouégoa
Pouébo
Oundou
Récif de la Gazelle
Téouta
Ouvéa
C. Escarpé
Koumac
Kaala-Gomen
MT. PANIE
1626
Hienghène
Touho
Wé
Lifou
Îles Loyauté
La Roche
Maré
Nouvelle-Calédonie
(France)
Kaala-Gomen
MASSIF DE TCHINGOU
1385
Voh
Koné
Ponérihouen
C. Deflotte
Mueo
Poya
Houaïlou
Bourail
Canala
Thio
C. Uapao
Moindou
MT. HUMBOLDT
1618
Paita
CORAL SEA
Potnarvin
Erromango
Aniwa
Tanna
Lénakel
Aneityum
(Anatom)
Anelghowhat
Futuna
Dumbéa
Nouméa
Yaté
Ouen
Île des Pins
Récif Durand
Récif du Sud
Walpole
VANUATU

Scale 1:5,000,000

Scale 1:5,000,000

Scale 1:5,000,000

Miller Oblated Stereographic Projection

114

© COLOUR LIBRARY BOOKS

North Island

South Island

NEW

ZEALAND

N E W   Z E A L A N D

TASMAN

SEA

PACIFIC

OCEAN

C. Young
Somes Pt.
Petre Bay
Waitangi
Te Whanga Lagoon
Hanson
Bay
Chatham
Chatham I.
Islands
Pitt Strait
Pitt I.

1:4,500,000

0   50   100   150   200   250   300 KILOMETRES

0   50   100   150   200 STATUTE MILES

East of Greenwich

Designed and produced by E.S.R.

Lambert Azimuthal Equal Area Projection

1:20,000,000

© COLOUR LIBRARY BOOKS

| 0 | 100 | 200 | 300 | 400 | 500 | 600 | 700 | 800 | 900 | 1000 KILOMETRES |

| 0 | 100 | 200 | 300 | 400 | 500 | 600 STATUTE MILES |

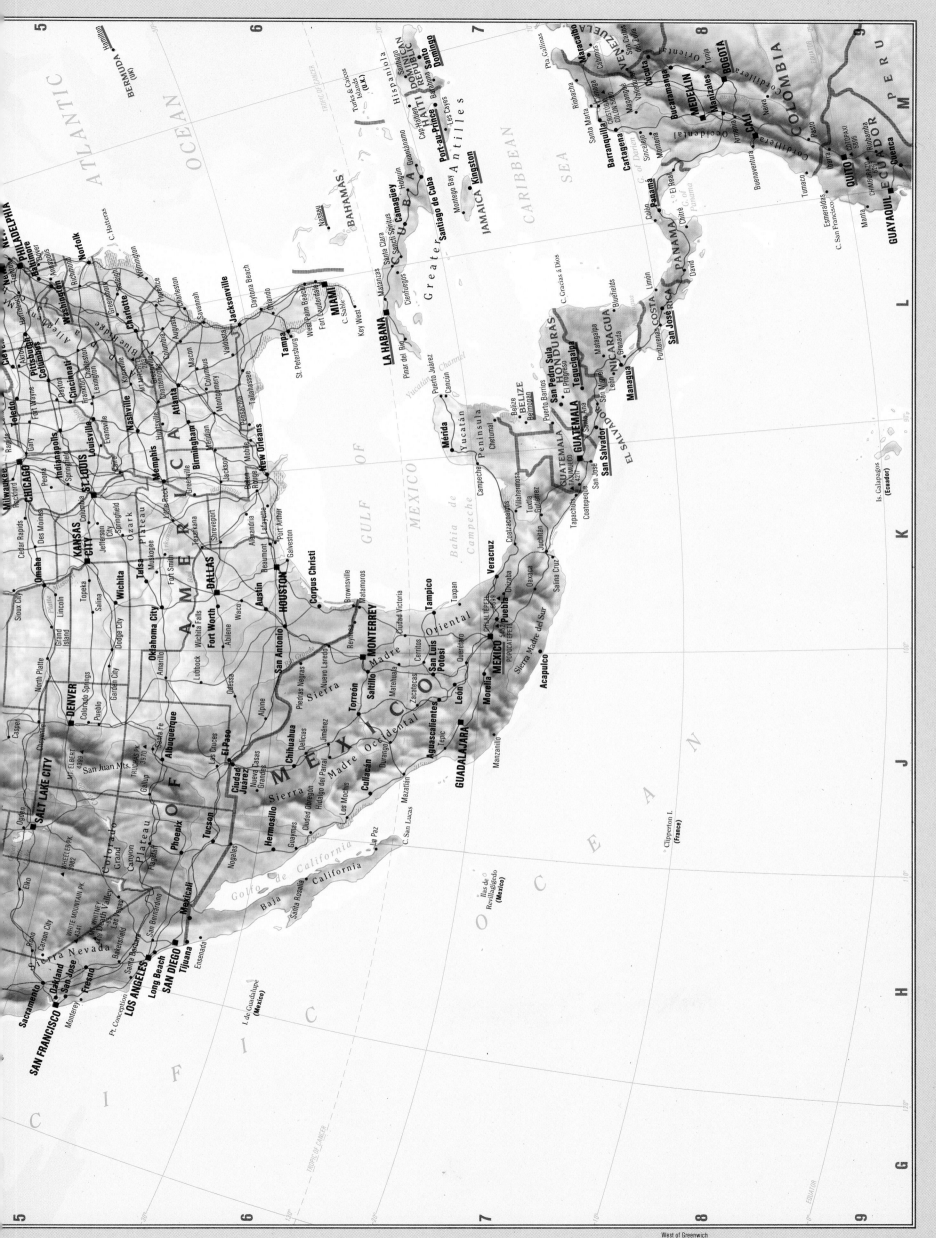

Designed and produced by E.S.R.

West of Greenwich

ALASKA

118

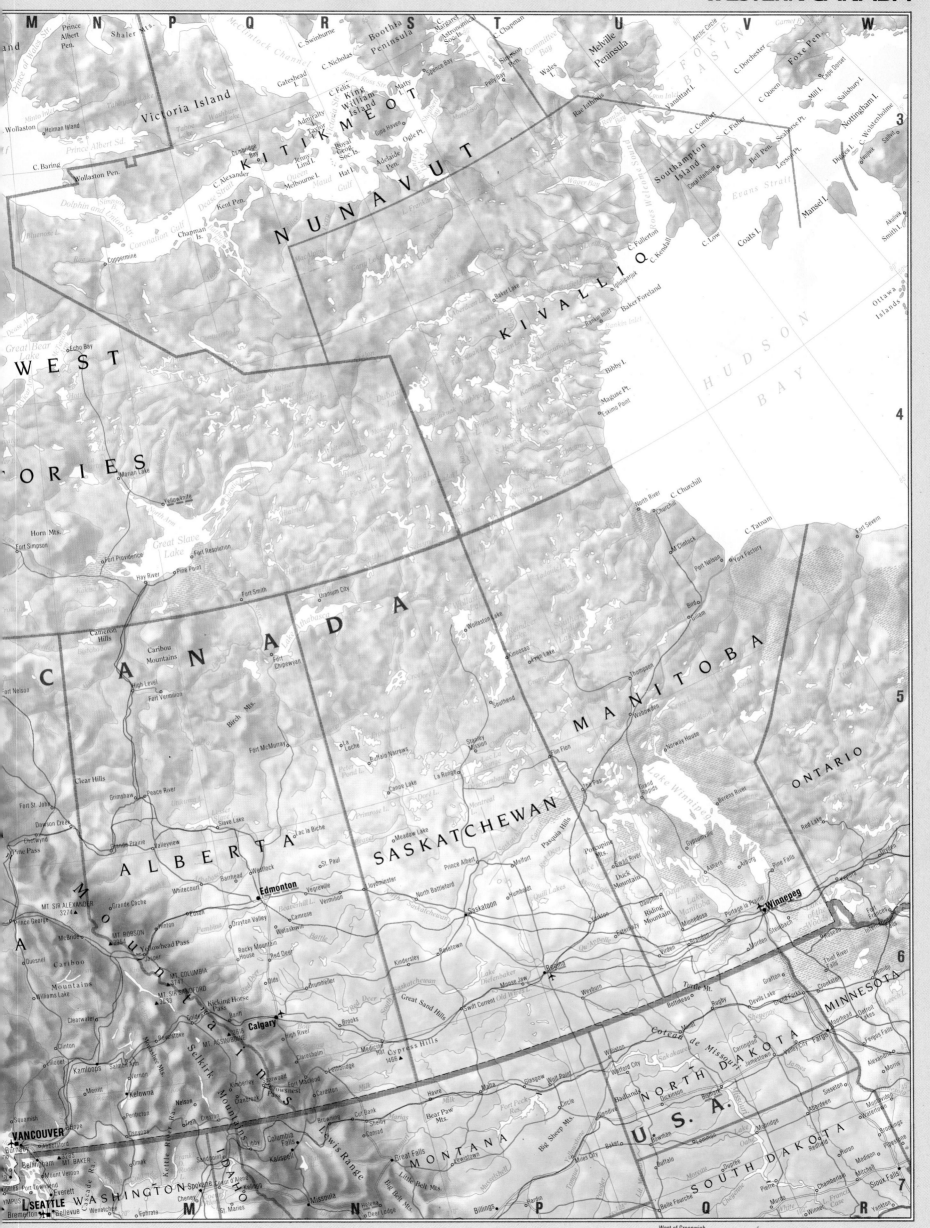

Designed and produced by E.S.R.

West of Greenwich

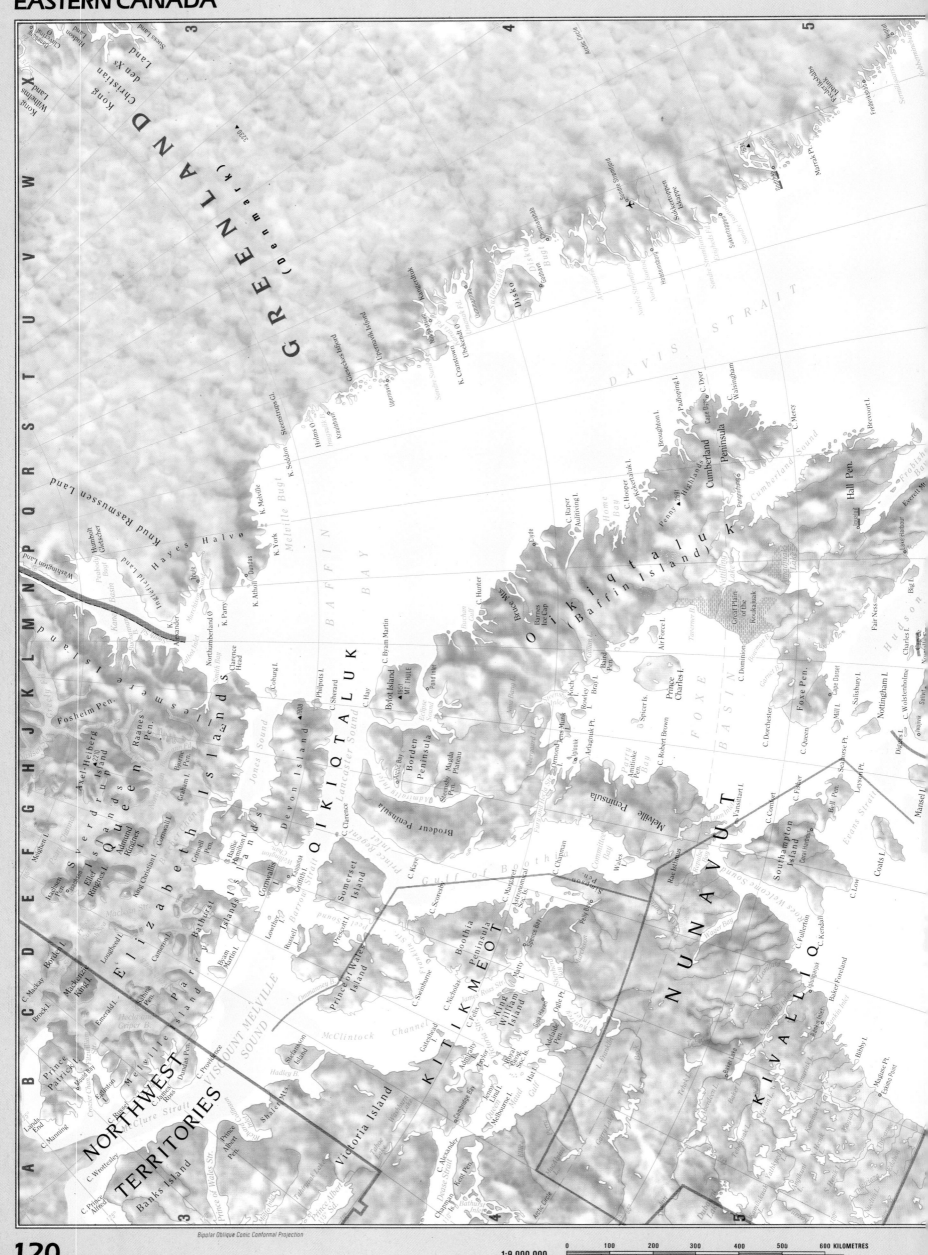

Bipolar Oblique Conic Conformal Projection

1:9,000,000

| 0 | 100 | 200 | 300 | 400 | 500 | 600 KILOMETRES |

| 0 | 50 | 100 | 150 | 200 | 250 | 300 | 350 | 400 STATUTE MILES |

© COLOUR LIBRARY BOOKS

Bipolar Oblique Conic Conformal Projection

1:5,000,000

| 0 | 50 | 100 | 150 | 200 | 250 | 300 | 350 | 400 KILOMETRES |

| 0 | 50 | 100 | 150 | 200 | 250 STATUTE MILES |

© COLOUR LIBRARY BOOKS

West of Greenwich

Designed and produced by E.S.R

Bipolar Oblique Conic Conformal Projection

1:5,000,000

| 0 | 50 | 100 | 150 | 200 | 250 | 300 | 350 | 400 KILOMETRES |

| 0 | 50 | 100 | 150 | 200 | 250 STATUTE MILES |

© COLOUR LIBRARY BOOKS

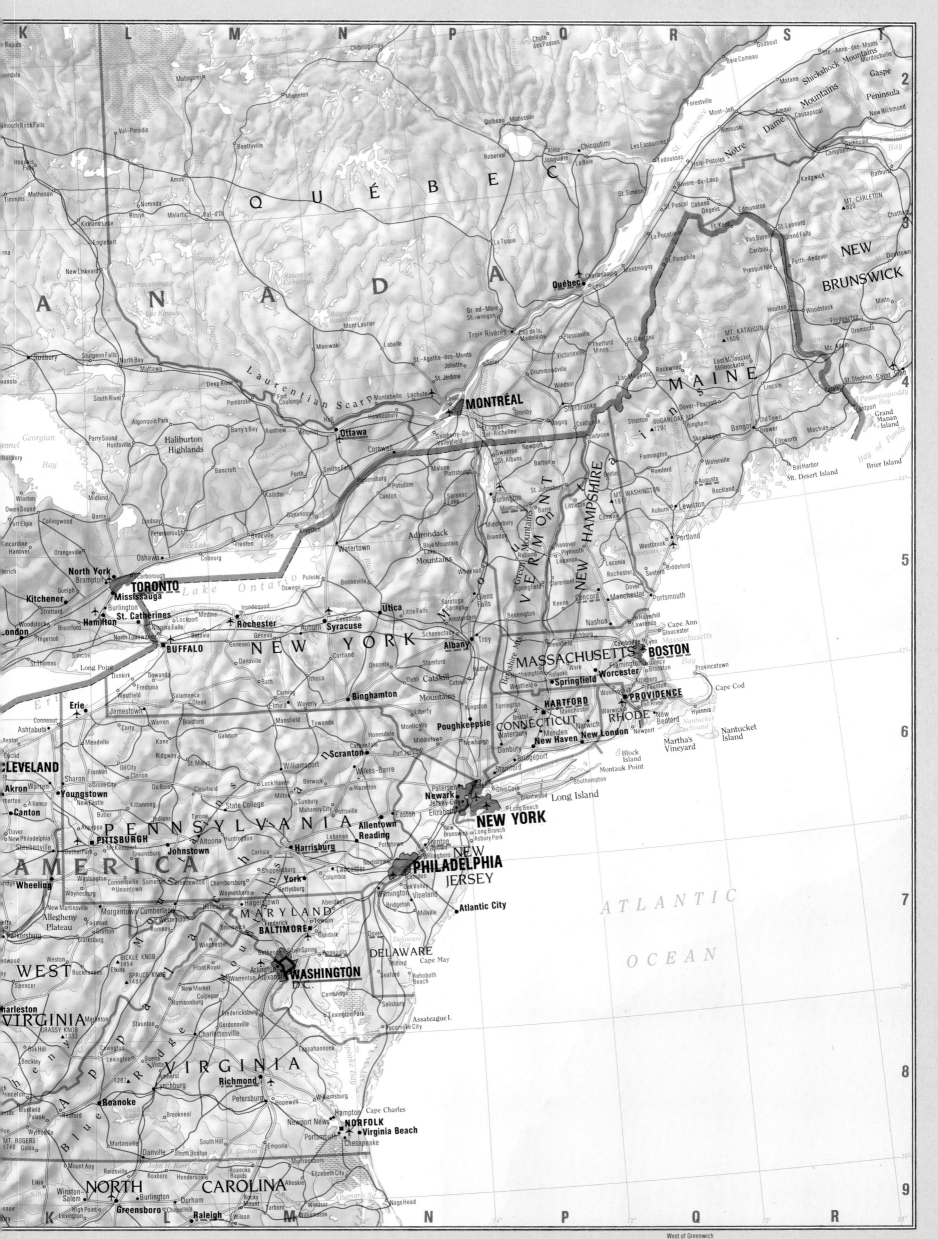

Designed and produced by E.S.R.

SOUTHWEST UNITED STATES

1:5,000,000

© COLOUR LIBRARY BOOKS

SOUTHEAST UNITED STATES

Bipolar Oblique Conic Conformal Projection

1:5,000,000

| 0 | 50 | 100 | 150 | 200 | 250 | 300 | 350 | 400 KILOMETRES |

| 0 | 50 | 100 | 150 | 200 | 250 STATUTE MILES |

© COLOUR LIBRARY BOOKS

MEXICO

Bipolar Oblique Conic Conformal Projection

1:6,500,000

© COLOUR LIBRARY BOOKS

| 0 | 50 | 100 | 150 | 200 | 250 | 300 | 350 | 400 KILOMETRES |

| 0 | 50 | 100 | 150 | 200 | 250 STATUTE MILES |

Bipolar Oblique Conic Conformal Projection

1:7,000,000

© COLOUR LIBRARY BOOKS

| 0 | 50 | 100 | 150 | 200 | 250 | 300 | 350 | 400 | KILOMETRES |

| 0 | 50 | 100 | 150 | 200 | 250 | STATUTE MILES |

ATLANTIC

OCEAN

Tropic of Cancer

Puerto Rico Trench

BAHAMAS

Arthur's Town
Cat I.
Hawknest Pt.
Conception I.
San Salvador
(Watling I.)
Rum Cay
Long I.
Clarence Town
Samana Cray
South Pt.
Crooked I.
Snug Corner
Abraham's Bay
Mayaguana I.
Acklins I.
Hogsty Reef
Little Inagua I.
Kew
Caicos Is. (U.K.)
Turks I. (U.K.)
Salt Cay
Great Inagua
Matthew Town

Cabo Maisí
Ile de la Tortue
Cap-Haitien
C. Isabela
Monte Cristi
Puerto Plata
Port-de-Paix
Gonaïves
Santiago
San Francisco de Macoris
La Vega
PICO DUARTE 3175
C. Samaná
Sabana de la Mar
Ba. de Escocesa
Ba. de Samaná

Santiago de Cuba
Guantánamo
Cabo de la Grecia

Golfe de la Gonâve
Ile de la Gonâve
St Marc
Hinche
Cordillera
Cibral

HAITI
PORT-AU-PRINCE
San Juan
Azua
Bani
SANTO DOMINGO
San Pedro de Macoris
Higüey
C. Engaño

C. Dame Marie
Dame Marie
Jérémie
Massif de la Hotte 2347
LA SELLE
2680
Lago Enriquillo
Barahona
Pedernales
DOMINICAN REPUBLIC
I. Saona
C. Rojo
I. Mona

Navassa I. (U.S.A.)
Pte.-à-Gravois
Les Cayes
Ile-à-Vache
Jacmel
Isla Beata
Cabo Beata

Windward Passage

Mona Passage

Aguadilla
Mayagüez
Arecibo
CERRO DE PUNTA 1338
Ponce
Bayamón
SAN JUAN
Caguas
Vieques
Puerto Rico (U.S.A.)
Frederiksted
St. Croix (U.S.A.)

Virgin Islands
St. Thomas (U.S.A.)
Charlotte Amalie
Road Town
Tortola (U.K.)
St. John (U.S.A.)
Anegada (U.K.)
Virgin Gorda (U.K.)
Anguilla (U.K.)
Saint Martin (Fr.)
Sint Maarten (Neth.)
Saba (Neth.)
St Eustatius (Neth.)
Basseterre
ST. KITTS-NEVIS (U.K.)
Montserrat (U.K.)
Plymouth

Leeward Islands

Barbuda
Antigua
St. John's
ANTIGUA AND BARBUDA

Guadeloupe (France)
La Désirade
Basse Terre
Pointe-à-Pitre
Marie Galante (France)
Iles des Saintes

I. de Aves (Bird I.) (Ven.)

DOMINICA
Roseau
Marigot

Martinique (France)
Fort-de-France

St. Lucia Channel
ST. LUCIA
Castries

Lesser Antilles

St. Vincent Passage
Kingstown
ST. VINCENT
The Grenadines
Carriacou
GRENADA
St. George's

Bridgetown
BARBADOS

Windward Islands

CARIBBEAN SEA

Lesser Antilles

Punta Gallinas
Oranjestad
Aruba (Neth.)
Curaçao (Neth.)
Willemstad
Bonaire (Neth.)
Kralendijk
Is. Las Aves (Ven.)
Is. Los Roques (Ven.)
I. Orchila (Ven.)
I. Blanquilla (Ven.)
Los Testigos (Ven.)
Tobago
Scarborough
TRINIDAD AND TOBAGO

Pto. Estrella
Peninsula de Guajira
Carrizal
Amuay
Penin. de Paraguaná
Pueblo Nuevo
Punto Fijo
Pto. Cumarebo
Bonaire Trench
Isla de Margarita (Ven.)
La Asunción
Porlamar
I. La Tortuga (Ven.)
Los Teques
Port of Spain
Toco
Trinidad
Serpent's Mouth

Santa Marta
Cabo de la Aguja
Ciénaga
Riohacha
Maicao
Castilletes
Golfo de Venezuela
Coro
San Rafael
Churuguara
Carora
San Felipe
CARACAS
Guarenas
Cabo Codera
Cumaná
Carúpano
Rio Caribe
Penín. de Paria
Güiria
Golfo de Paria
Arima
Rio Claro
San Fernando
Galeota Pt.

Barranquilla
Soledad
PICO CRISTÓBAL COLÓN 5775
Sierra de Perijá
Maracaibo
Cabimas
Attagracia
Sta. Rita
Capatárida
San Luis
Maiquetía
Pto. Cabello
Maracay
Villa de Cura
Barcelona
Maturín
Pedernales

Cartagena
Turbaco
Calamar
Valledupar
Robles La Paz
Machiques
Ciudad Ojeda
Lagunillas
Lago de Maracaibo
Trujillo
Tinaco
Cordillera de la Costa
2660
Anaco
San Mateo
Pariaguán
El Tigre
Mata Negra
Tucupita
Boca Grande

Sincelejo
Sincé
El Banco
Barranca
La Ceiba
Cordillera de Mérida
Valera
Güanare
Acarigua
San Carlos
Las Mercedes
Valle de la Pasqua
Zaraza
Barrancas
San José de Amacuro

Carmen
Majagual
Mompós
Boburés
Mérida
PICO BOLÍVAR 5007
Barinas
Nueva Florida
Calabozo
Zaraza
Orituco
Ciudad Bolívar
Pto. Ordaz
Ciudad Guayana
Upata
Serranía de Imataca
Port Kaituma

Planeta Rica
El Vigia
La Fría
El Sam'án de Apure
San Fernando de Apure
Cabruta
Boca del Pao
Mapire
Ciudad Piar
Guasipati

COLOMBIA
Ocaña
PICO BOLÍVAR
San Silvestra
Mantecal
VENEZUELA
CERRO MATO 1863
CERRO BOLÍVAR
San Pedro de las Bocas
El Callao
El Dorado
GUYANA

Caucasia
Zaragoza
ALTO DE TAMAR 2350
Cúcuta
EL VIEJO 4100
Pamplona
San Cristóbal
Rubio
San Antonio de Caparo
La Urbana
Tumeremo
Kartuni

Yarumal
Barrancabermeja
Bucaramanga
Piedecuesta
Cúbara
Arauca
Banadia
Guasdualito
La Paragua
Santa Maria

West of Greenwich

133

Designed and produced by E.S.R.

Bipolar Oblique Conic Conformal Projection

1:16,000,000

| 0 | 100 | 200 | 300 | 400 | 500 | 600 | 700 | 800 KILOMETRES |

| 0 | 100 | 200 | 300 | 400 | 500 STATUTE MILES |

© COLOUR LIBRARY BOOKS

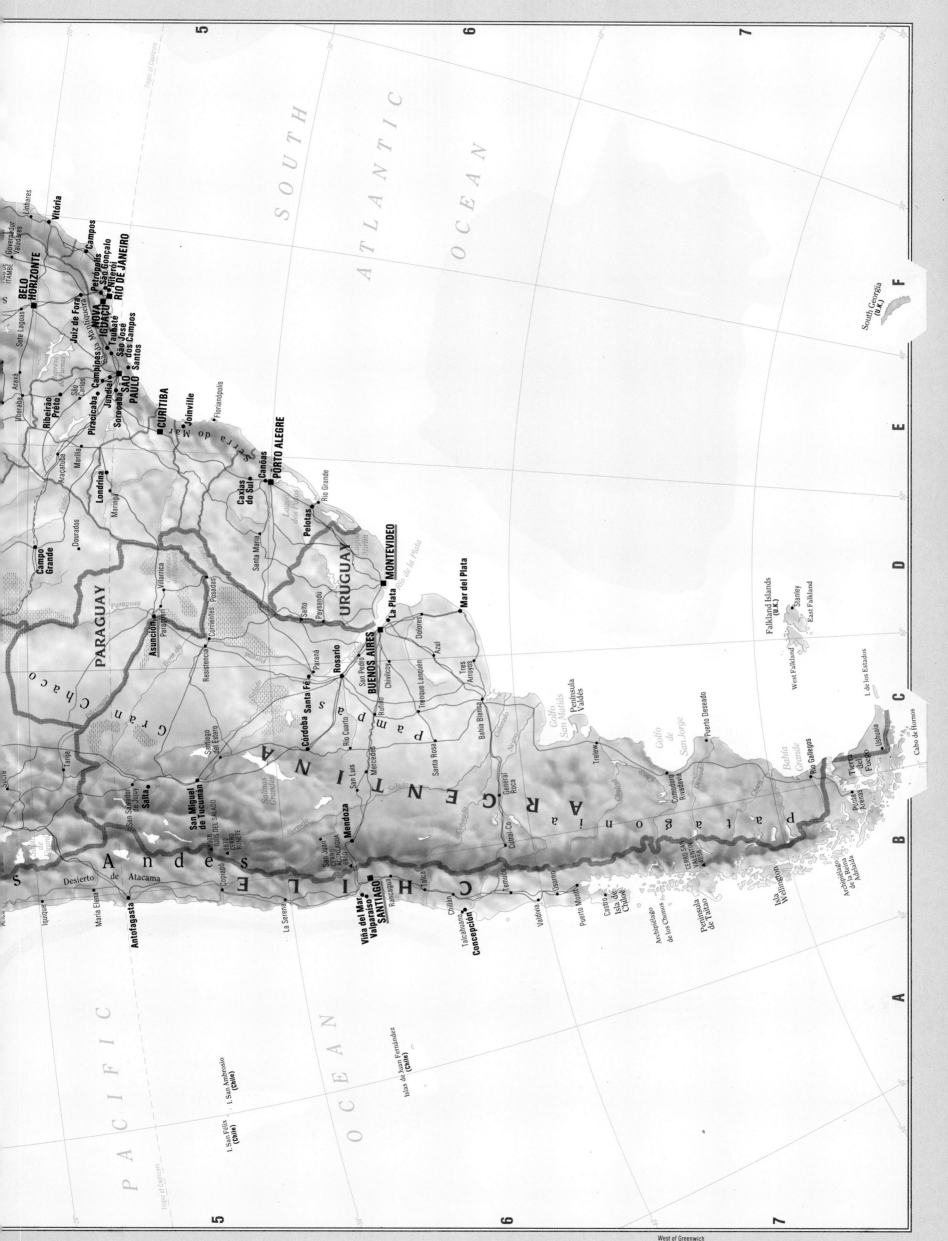

South Georgia (U.K.)

Falkland Islands (U.K.)
Stanley
West Falkland   East Falkland

I. de los Estados
Ushuaia
Cabo de Hornos

SOUTH   ATLANTIC   OCEAN

Tropic of Capricorn

Linhares
Governador Valadares
ITAMBE
Vitória
Campos
Sete Lagoas
Petrópolis São Gonçalo
BELO HORIZONTE   Niterói
Juiz de Fora   NOVA RIO DE JANEIRO
Araxá   IGUAÇU
Campinas Mantiqueira   Taubaté
Uberaba   São Carlos São José
Ribeirão   dos Campos
Prêto   Piracicaba Jundiaí   Santos
SÃO PAULO
Sorocaba
CURITIBA   Joinville
Marília
Londrina   Florianópolis
Maringá   Serra do Mar
Dourados
Campo   PÔRTO ALEGRE
Grande   Caxias Canoas
do Sul
Santa Maria   Rio Grande
PARAGUAY   Pelotas
Villarrica   Lagoa dos Patos
Asunción   Posadas   Salto   Lagoa Mirim
Paraguarí   Corrientes   Paysandú   MONTEVIDEO
Resistencia   URUGUAY
Gran Chaco   Paraná   Rosario   La Plata   Río de la Plata
Santa Fé   San Pedro   BUENOS AIRES
Córdoba   Paraná   Dolores
Santiago   Río Cuarto   Chivilcoy   Mar del Plata
del Estero   Azul
San Luis   Tres
Tarija   Salta   Mercedes   Trenque Lauquen   Arroyos
San Salvador   Rufino
Sucre   de Jujuy   ARGENTINA   Santa Rosa   Bahía Blanca
San Miguel   Salado
de Tucumán   CERRO DEL SALADO   Cutral-Có
CERRO   General
Salinas   BONETE   Negro   Roca   Península
Grandes   ACONCAGUA   Colorado   Valdés
San Juan   Bermejo   Golfo
Desierto   Mendoza   Neuquén   Trelew   San Matías
de Atacama   Conipto   Golfo
Andes   San Rafael   Temuco   de   Puerto Deseado
Rancagua   Talca   San Jorge
SANTIAGO   Osorno   Comodoro
Viña del Mar   Chillán   Rivadavia
Valparaíso   Talcahuano   Valdivia
Concepción   Puerto Montt   Deseado
CHILE   Castro   Isla de
Isla de   Chiloé   Bahía
Chonos   Grande   Río Gallegos
Archipiélago   Tierra
de los Chonos   Punta   del
Península   Arenas   Fuego
de Taitao   CERRO SAN
VALENTÍN   Puerto Natales
Isla   4058
Wellington   Archipiélago
de la Reina
Adelaida

S   A   n   d   e   s   Patagonia

PACIFIC   OCEAN

I. San Félix   I. San Ambrosio
(Chile)   (Chile)

Islas de Juan Fernández
(Chile)

Tropic of Capricorn

West of Greenwich

Designed and produced by E.S.R.

135

Bipolar Oblique Conic Conformal Projection

© COLOUR LIBRARY BOOKS

1:11,000,000

| 0 | 100 | 200 | 300 | 400 | 500 | 600 | 700 | 800 KILOMETRES |

| 0 | 100 | 200 | 300 | 400 | 500 STATUTE MILES |

SOUTHERN SOUTH AMERICA

Bipolar Oblique Conic Conformal Projection

1:11,000,000

| 0 | 100 | 200 | 300 | 400 | 500 | 600 | 700 | 800 KILOMETRES |

| 0 | 100 | 200 | 300 | 400 | 500 STATUTE MILES |

© COLOUR LIBRARY BOOKS

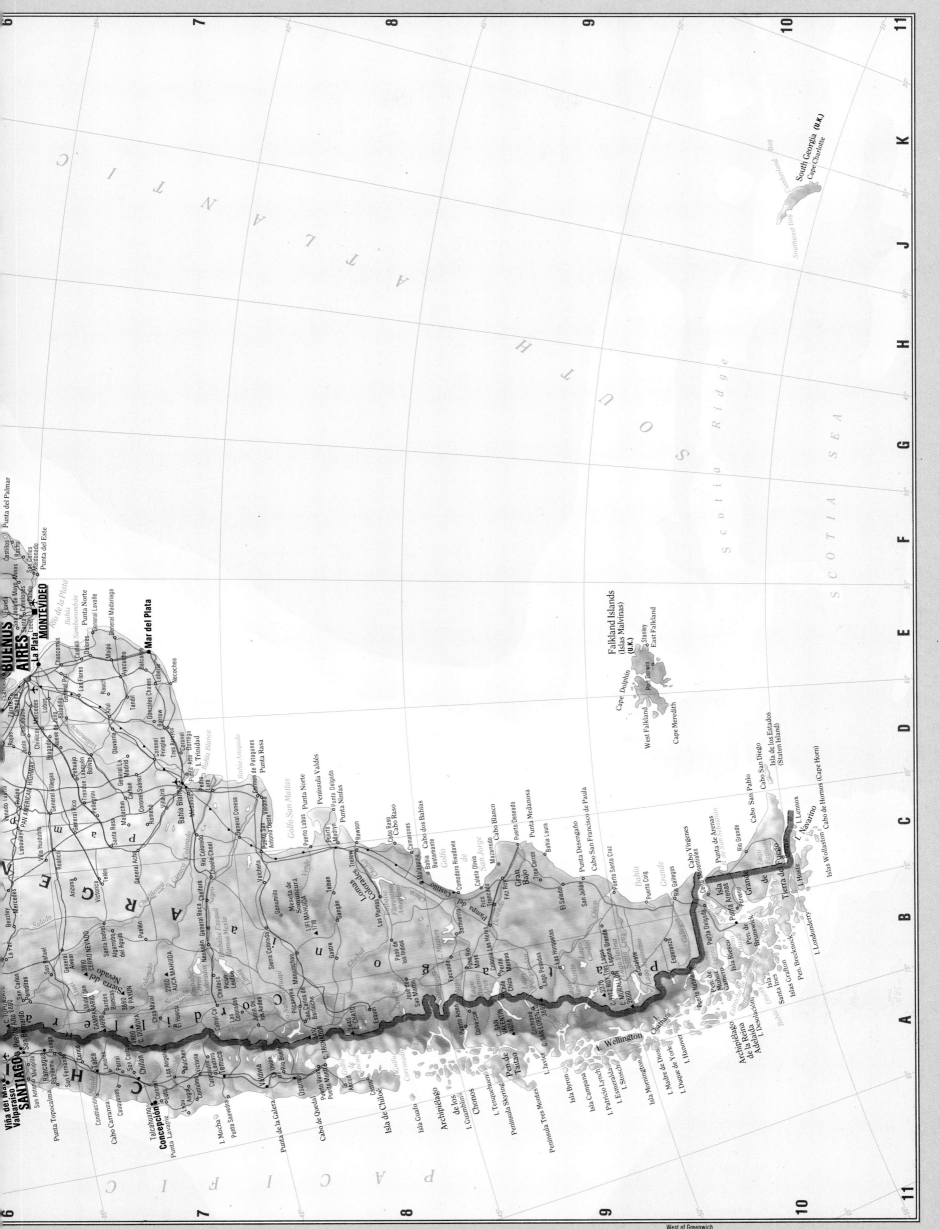

Designed and produced by E.S.R.

West of Greenwich

Polar Stereographic Projection

Scale 1:30,000,000 (Approx.)

© COLOUR LIBRARY BOOKS

| 0 | 250 | 500 | 750 | 1000 | 1250 | 1500 KILOMETRES |

| 0 | 250 | 500 | 750 | 1000 STATUTE MILES |

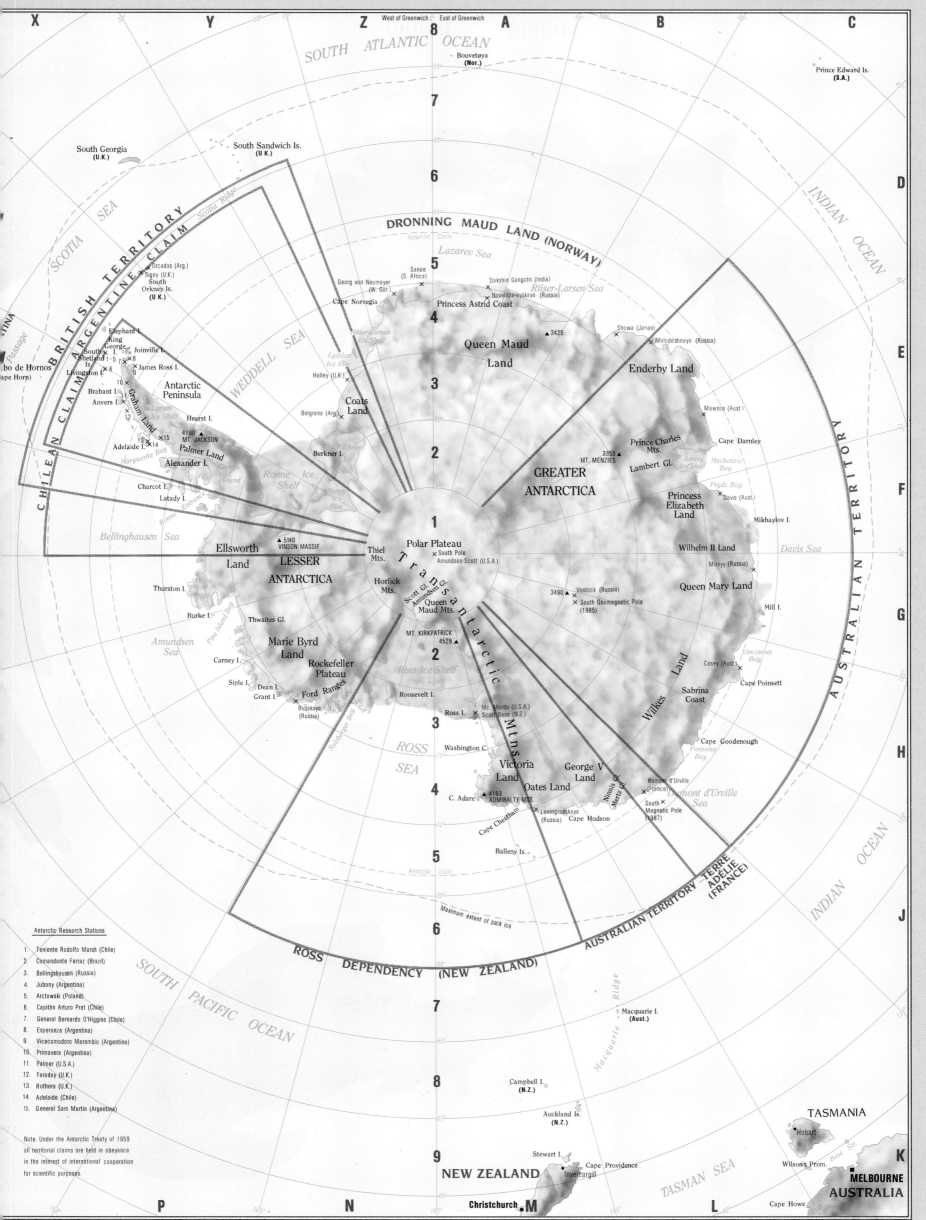

Antarctic Research Stations

1. Teniente Rodolfo Marsh (Chile)
2. Comandante Ferraz (Brazil)
3. Bellingshausen (Russia)
4. Jubany (Argentina)
5. Arctowski (Poland)
6. Capitán Arturo Prat (Chile)
7. General Bernardo O'Higgins (Chile)
8. Esperanza (Argentina)
9. Vicecomodoro Marambio (Argentina)
10. Primavera (Argentina)
11. Palmer (U.S.A.)
12. Faraday (U.K.)
13. Rothera (U.K.)
14. Adelaide (Chile)
15. General Sam Martin (Argentina)

Note. Under the Antarctic Treaty of 1959
all territorial claims are held in abeyance
in the interest of international cooperation
for scientific purposes.

Polar Stereographic Projection

Designed and produced by E.S.R.

Mercator Projection

1:85,000,000 (Scale at the Equator)

ARCTIC OCEAN

Vostochno
Sibirskoye
More

Ostrov Vrangelya

Khrebet Kolymskiy

Kamchatka

Bering
Sea

Aleutian Islands

Aleutian Trench

NORTH
PACIFIC
OCEAN

Hawaiian

Islands

HAWAII
(U.S.A.)

Marshall Is.

Micronesia

NAURU

Tarawa

Gilbert
Is.

Phoenix Is.

SOLOMON ISLANDS

Honiara

Santa
Cruz
Is.

TUVALU

Fanafuti

VANUATU

Vila

Nouvelle
Calédonie
(Fr.)

FIJI

Suva

Iles Wallis
(Fr.)

SAMOA

Apia

Samoa
(U.S.A.)

TONGA

Nuku'alofa

P o l y n e s i a

Line Islands

Christmas I.

KIRIBATI

Cook Islands
(N.Z.)

French Polynesia
(Fr.)

Iles Marquises
(Fr.)

Iles de la
Société

Tahiti

Iles Tuamotu

Iles Gambier

Pitcairn I.
(U.K.)

Ducie I.
(U.K.)

SOUTH
PACIFIC
OCEAN

Isla de Pascua
(Easter I.)
(Chile)

Islas Juan
Fernández
(Chile)

Tasman Sea

NEW ZEALAND

Wellington

Chatham Is.
(N.Z.)

Auckland Is.
(N.Z.)

Macquarie Is.
(Aus.)

Kermadec Trench

Tonga Trench

Pt. Barrow

Chucki
Sea

Anadyrskiy
Zaliv

Brooks Range

ALASKA
(U.S.A.)

McKINLEY
6194 ▲

Alaska Range

Kodiak I.

Gulf of Alaska

Vancouver I.

Banks
Island

Beaufort Sea

Amundsen
Gulf

Victoria Island

Mackenzie Mts

Great Bear Lake

Mackenzie

Great Slave Lake

L. Athabasca

Reindeer Lake

L. Winnipeg

Rocky Mountains

Gt. Salt Lake

Columbia

Missouri

Great
Plains

UNITED STATES
OF
AMERICA

SAN FRANCISCO

LOS ANGELES

Isla de
Guadalupe
(Mex.)

Islas de Revillagigedo
(Mex.)

MEXICO

CIUDAD DE
MÉXICO

Gulf of Mexico

Mississippi

CANADA

Great
Lakes

CHICAGO

Ottawa

Appalachian Mts

NEW YORK

PHILADELPHIA

Washington

Queen

Elizabeth

Islands

Viscount Melville
Sound

Ellesmere
Island

Kane
Basin

Lincoln
Sea

Oikiqtaluk

Foxe
Basin

Hudson Str.

Hudson Bay

Baffin Bay

Davis Str.

GREENLAND
(Denmark)

Denmark Strait

Arctic Circle

Reykjavik
ICELAND

Kap Farvel

Labrador Sea

Labrador

Newfoundland

NORTH
ATLANTIC
OCEAN

Açores
(Port.)

Bermuda
(U.K.)

Tropic of Cancer

BAHAMAS

Nassau

La Habana

CUBA

West Indies

Port au Prince

HAITI

Kingston

JAMAICA

DOMINICAN REP.

Santo Domingo

Puerto Rico (U.S.A.)

Leeward Is.

CAPE
VERDE

Praia

BELIZE

Belmopan

GUATEMALA

Guatemala

San Salvador

EL SALVADOR

HONDURAS

Tegucigalpa

Managua

NICARAGUA

San José

COSTA RICA

PANAMA

Panamá

Caribbean Sea

Caracas

VENEZUELA

Windward Is.

BARBADOS

TRINIDAD
AND TOBAGO

Georgetown

GUY

SUR

Paramaribo

Cayenne

FRENCH GUIANA

Bogotá

COLOMBIA

Orinoco

Quito

EQUADOR

Islas Galápagos
(Ecuador)

Equator

Isla Fernando
de Noronha
(Brazil)

PERU

LIMA

Cordillera

Peru-Chile Trench

La Paz

BOLIVIA

BRAZIL

Planalto do
Mato Grosso

Brasília

SÃO PAULO

RÍO DE JANEIRO

Ilha da Trindade
(Brazil)

PARAGUAY

Asunción

Tropic of Capricorn

ACONCAGUA
6960 ▲

Santiago

Chile

URUGUAY

Montevideo

BUENOS AIRES

ARGENTINA

Cordillera de los Andes

Patagonia

Falkland Is.
(U.K.)

South Georgia
(U.K.)

Cabo de Hornos

Scotia Sea

South
Sandwich
Is. (U.K.)

SOUTH
ATLANTIC
OCEAN

GLOSSARY AND ABBREVIATIONS

Language abbreviations in glossary

Afr	Afrikaans	*Dut*	Dutch	*I-C*	Indo-Chinese	*Mal*	Malay	*S-C*	Serbo-Croat
Alb	Albanian	*Fin*	Finnish	*Ice*	Icelandic	*Mlg*	Malagasy	*Som*	Somali
Ar	Arabic	*Fr*	French	*Ind*	Indonesian	*Mon*	Mongolian	*Sp*	Spanish
Ber	Berber	*Gae*	Gaelic	*It*	Italian	*Nor*	Norwegian	*Swe*	Swedish
Bul	Bulgarian	*Ger*	German	*Jap*	Japanese	*Per*	Persian	*Th*	Thai
Bur	Burmese	*Gr*	Greek	*Khm*	Khmer	*Pol*	Polish	*Tib*	Tibetan
Ch	Chinese	*Heb*	Hebrew	*Kor*	Korean	*Por*	Portuguese	*Tu*	Turkish
Cz	Czech	*Hin*	Hindi	*Lao*	Laotian	*Rom*	Romanian	*Vt*	Vietnamese
Dan	Danish	*Hun*	Hungarian	*Lat*	Latvian	*Rus*	Russian	*Wel*	Welsh

Glossary

A

Abar (*Ar*) – wells
Abyar (*Ar*) – wells
Adasi (*Tu*) – island
Adrar (*Ber*) – mountains
Ain (*Ar*) – spring, well
Akra (*Gr*) – cape, point
Alb (*Ger*) – mountains
Alpen (*Ger*) – mountains
Alpes (*Fr*) – mountains
Alpi (*It*) – mountains
Alto (*Por*) – high
-alv (*Swe*) – river
-alven (*Swe*) – river
Appenino (*It*) – mountain range
Aqabat (*Ar*) – pass
Archipielago (*Sp*) – archipelago
Arquipielago (*Por*) – archipelago
Arrecife (*Sp*) – reef
Ayia (*Gr*) – saint
Ayios (*Gr*) – saint
Ayn (*Ar*) – spring, well

B

Bab (*Ar*) – strait
Bad (*Ger*) – spa
Badiyah (*Ar*) – desert
Bælt (*Dan*) – strait
Baharu (*Mal*) – new
Bahia (*Sp*) – bay
Bahr (*Ar*) – bay, canal, lake, stream
Bahrat (*Ar*) – lake
Baia (*Por*) – bay
Baie (*Fr*) – bay
Baja (*Sp*) – lower
Ban (*Khm, Lao, Th*) – village
-bana (*Jap*) – cape, point
Banco (*Sp*) – bank
-bandao (*Ch*) – peninsula
Bandar (*Per*) – bay
Baraji (*Tu*) – reservoir
Barqa (*Ar*) – hill
Barragem (*Por*) – reservoir
Bassin (*Fr*) – basin, bay
Batin (*Ar*) – depression
Beinn (*Gae*) – mountain
Beloyy (*Rus*) – white
Ben (*Gae*) – mountain
Bereg (*Rus*) – bank, shore
Berg (*Ger*) – mountain
Berge (*Afr*) – mountains
Bheinn (*Gae*) – mountain
Biar (*Ar*) – wells
Bir (*Ar*) – well
Bi'r (*Ar*) – well
Birkat (*Ar*) – well
Birket (*Ar*) – well
Boca (*Sp*) – river mouth
Bocche (*It*) – mouths, estuary
Bodden (*Ger*) – bay
Bogazi (*Tu*) – strait
Boka (*S-C*) – gulf, inlet
Bol'shoy (*Rus*) – big
Bol'shoye (*Rus*) – big
Bory (*Pol*) – forest
Bratul (*Rom*) – river channel
Bucht (*Ger*) – bay
Bugt (*Dan*) – bay
Buhayrat (*Ar*) – lagoon, lake
Bukit (*Mal*) – hill, mountain
Bukt (*Nor*) – bay
Bulak (*Rus*) – spring
Burnu (*Tu*) – cape, point
Burun (*Tu*) – cape, point
Busen (*Ger*) – bay
Buyuk (*Tu*) – big

C

Cabo (*Por, Sp*) – cape, point
Cachoeira (*Sp*) – waterfall
Cap (*Fr*) – cape, point
Campos (*Sp*) – upland
Cao Nguyen (*Th*) – plateau, tableland
Cataratas (*Sp*) – waterfall
Cayi (*Tu*) – stream
Cayo (*Sp*) – islet, rock
Cerro (*Sp*) – hill
Chaco (*Sp*) – jungle
Chaine (*Fr*) – mountain chain
Chapada (*Por*) – hills
Ch'eng (*Ch*) – town
Chiang (*Ch*) – river
Chiang (*Th*) – town
Chott (*Ar*) – marsh, salt lake
Chute (*Fr*) – waterfall
Cienaga (*Sp*) – marshy lake
Ciudad (*Sp*) – city, town
Co (*Tib*) – lake
Col (*Fr*) – pass
Colinas (*Sp*) – hills
Cordillera (*Sp*) – mountain range
Costa (*Sp*) – coast, shore
Cote (*Fr*) – coast, slope
Coteau (*Fr*) – hill, slope
Coxilha (*Por*) – mountain pasture
Cuchillas (*Sp*) – hills

D

Dag (*Tu*) – mountain
Dagi (*Tu*) – mountain
Daglari (*Tu*) – mountains
-dake (*Jap*) – peak
-dal (*Nor*) – valley
Dao (*Ch*) – island
Darreh (*Per*) – valley
Daryacheh (*Per*) – lake
Dasht (*Per*) – desert
Denizi (*Tu*) – sea
Desierto (*Sp*) – desert
Djebel (*Ar*) – mountain
-djik (*Dut*) – dyke
Do (*Kor, Jap, Vt*) – island
Dolina (*Rus*) – valley
Dolok (*Ind*) – mountain
Dolna (*Bul*) – lower
Dolni (*Cz*) – lower
-dong (*Kor*) – village
-dorp (*Afr*) – village
Dur (*Ar*) – mountains

E

Eiland (*Dut*) – island
Eilanden (*Dut*) – islands
-elva (*Nor*) – river
Embalse (*Sp*) – reservoir
Erg (*Ar*) – sandy desert
Estero (*Sp*) – bay, estuary, inlet
Estrecho (*Sp*) – strait
Etang (*Fr*) – lagoon, pond
Ezers (*Lat*) – lake

F

Feng (*Ch*) – mountain, peak
Fels (*Ger*) – rock
Firth (*Gae*) – estuary
-fjall (*Swe*) – mountains
Fjeld (*Dan*) – mountain
-fjell (*Nor*) – mountain
-floi (*Ice*) – bay
-fjoraur (*Ice*) – fjord
Forde (*Ger*) – inlet
Foret (*Fr*) – forest
-foss (*Ice*) – waterfall

G

-gan (*Jap*) – rock
Gang (*Ch*) – harbour
Ganga (*Hin*) – river
Gata (*Jap*) – inlet, lagoon
Gave (*Fr*) – torrent
Gebel (*Ar*) – mountain
Gebirge (*Ger*) – mountains
Ghat (*Hin*) – range of hills
Ghubbat (*Ar*) – bay
Glen (*Gae*) – valley
Gletscher (*Ger*) – glacier
Gobi (*Mon*) – desert
Golfe (*Fr*) – bay, gulf
Golfo (*It, Sp*) – bay, gulf
Golu (*Tu*) – lake
Gora (*Bul*) – forest
Gora (*Pol, Rus*) – mountain
-gorod (*Rus*) – small town
Gory (*Pol, Rus*) – mountains
Grada (*Rus*) – mountain range
Grad (*Bul, Rus, S-C*) – city, town
Gross (*Ger*) – big
Gryada (*Rus*) – ridge
Guba (*Rus*) – bay
-gunto (*Jap*) – island group
Gunung (*Ind, Mal*) – mountain

H

Hadh (*Ar*) – sand dunes
Hafen (*Ger*) – harbour, port
Haff (*Ger*) – bay, lagoon
Hai (*Ch*) – sea
Haixia (*Ch*) – strait
-holm (*Dan*) – island
Halvo (*Dan*) – peninsula
-hama (*Jap*) – beach
Hamada (*Ar*) – plateau
-hamar (*Ice*) – mountain
Hammadah (*Ar*) – plain, stony desert
Hamun (*Per*) – marsh
-hanto (*Jap*) – peninsula
Harrat (*Ar*) – lava field
Hav (*Swe*) – gulf
Havet (*Nor*) – sea
-havn (*Dan, Nor*) – harbour
Hawr (*Ar*) – lake
He (*Ch*) – river
Heide (*Ger*) – heath, moor
-hisar (*Tu*) – castle
Ho (*Ch*) – river
Hohe (*Ger*) – hills
Horn (*Ger*) – peak, summit
Hu (*Ch*) – lake
-huk (*Swe*) – cape, point

I

Idd (*Ar*) – well
Idhan (*Ar*) – sand dunes
Ile (*Fr*) – island
Iles (*Fr*) – islands
Ilha (*Por*) – island
Ilhas (*Por*) – islands
Insel (*Ger*) – island
Inseln (*Ger*) – islands
Irq (*Ar*) – sand dunes
Irmak (*Tu*) – large river
Isfjord (*Dan*) – glacier
Iskappe (*Dan*) – icecap
Isla (*Sp*) – island
Islas (*Sp*) – islands
Isola (*It*) – island
Isole (*It*) – islands
Istmo (*Sp*) – isthmus

J

Jabal (*Ar*) – mountain
-jarvi (*Fin*) – lake
Jaza 'ir (*Ar*) – islands
Jazirat (*Ar*) – island
Jazovir (*Bul*) – reservoir
Jbel (*Ar*) – mountain
Jebel (*Ar*) – mountain
Jezero (*Alb, S-C*) – lake
Jezioro (*Pol*) – lagoon, lake
Jezirat (*Ar*) – island
-jiang (*Ch*) – river
Jibal (*Ar*) – mountain
Jiddat (*Ar*) – gravel plain
-jima (*Jap*) – island
-joki (*Fin*) – river
-jokull (*Ice*) – glacier

K

Kaap (*Afr*) – cape, point
-kai (*Jap*) – bay, sea
-kaikyo (*Jap*) – strait
Kanaal (*Dut*) – canal
Kap (*Ger*) – cape, point
-kapp (*Nor*) – cape, point
Kas (*Khm*) – island
Kavir (*Per*) – desert
-kawa (*Jap*) – river
Kenet (*Alb*) – inlet
Kep (*Alb*) – cape, point
Kepulauan (*Ind*) – archipelago, islands
Kereb (*Ar*) – hill, ridge
Khalij (*Ar*) – bay, gulf
Khawr (*Ar*) – wadi
Khrebet (*Ru*) – mountain range
Kiang (*Ch*) – river
Klein (*Afr, Ger*) – small
Ko (*Th*) – island
-ko (*Jap*) – inlet, lake
Koh (*Khm*) – island
Kolpos (*Gr*) – gulf
Kolymskoye (*Rus*) – mountain range
Korfezi (*Tu*) – bay, gulf
Kosa (*Rus*) – spit
Kotlina (*Cz, Pol*) – basin, depression
Kraj (*Cz, Pol, S-C*) – region
Krasnyy (*Rus*) – red
Kray (*Rus*) – region
Kreis (*Ger*) – district
Kryazh (*Rus*) – mountains
Kucuk (*Tu*) – small
Kuh (*Per*) – mountain
Kuhha (*Per*) – mountains
Kum (*Rus*) – sandy desert
Kyst (*Dan*) – coast
Kyun (*Bur*) – island
Kyunzu (*Bur*) – islands

L

La (*Tib*) – pass
Lac (*Fr*) – lake
Lacul (*Rom*) – lake
Laem (*Th*) – point
Lago (*It, Por, Sp*) – lake
Lagoa (*Por*) – lagoon
Laguna (*Sp*) – lagoon, lake
Lam (*Th*) – stream
Lande (*Fr*) – heath, sandy moor
Laut (*Ind*) – sea
Ling (*Ch*) – mountain range
Liman (*Rus*) – bay, gulf
Limni (*Gr*) – lagoon, lake
Llano (*Sp*) – plain, prairie
Llanos (*Sp*) – plains, prairies

Llyn

Llyn (*Wel*) – lake
Loch (*Gae*) – lake
Lough (*Gae*) – lake

M

Mae Nam (*Th*) – river
Mala (*S-C*) – small
Malaya (*Rus*) – small
Male (*Cz*) – small
Maloye (*Rus*) – small
Malyy (*Rus*) – small
Mar (*Por, Sp*) – sea
Mare (*It*) – sea
Masirah (*Ar*) – channel
Massif (*Fr*) – mountains
Mato (*Por*) – forest
Meer (*Afr, Dut, Ger*) – lake, sea
Menor (*Por, Sp*) – lesser, smaller
Mer (*Fr*) – sea
Mesa (*Sp*) – tableland
Minami (*Jap*) – south
-misaki (*Jap*) – cape, point
Mont (*Fr*) – mountain
Montagna (*It*) – mountain
Montagne (*Fr*) – mountain
Montagnes (*Fr*) – mountains
Montana (*Sp*) – mountain
Montanas (*Sp*) – mountains
Monte (*It, Por, Sp*) – mountain
Monti (*It*) – mountains
More (*Rus*) – sea
Mull (*Gae*) – cape, point, promontory
Munkhafad (*Ar*) – depression
Muntii (*Rom*) – mountains
Mynydd (*Wel*) – mountain
Mys (*Rus*) – cape, point

N

-nada (*Jap*) – gulf, sea
Nadrz (*Cz*) – reservoir
Nafud (*Ar*) – desert, dune
Nagor'ye (*Rus*) – highland, uplands
Nagy- (*Hun*) – great
Nahr (*Ar*) – river
Namakzar (*Per*) – desert, salt flat
Nei (*Ch*) – inner
Ness (*Gae*) – cape, promontory
Neu (*Ger*) – new
Nevada (*Sp*) – snow capped mountains
Nevado (*Sp*) – mountain
Ngoc (*Vt*) – mountain peak
-nisi (*Gr*) – island
Nisoi (*Gr*) – islands
Nisos (*Gr*) – island
Nizhnyaya (*Rus*) – lower
Nizina (*Pol*) – depression, lowland
Nizmennost' (*Rus*) – lowland
Noord (*Dut*) – north
Nord (*Dan, Fr, Ger*) – north
Norte (*Por, Sp*) – north
Nos (*Bul, Rus*) – point, spit
Nosy (*Mlg*) – island
Nova (*Bul*) – new
Nova (*Cz*) – new
Novaya (*Rus*) – new
Nove (*Cz*) – new
Novi (*Bul*) – new
Nudo (*Sp*) – mountain
Nuruu (*Mon*) – mountain range
Nuur (*Mon*) – lake

O

Ø (*Dan*) – island
Oblast' (*Rus*) – province

Occidental (*Fr, Rom, Sp*) – western
Oki (*Jap*) – bay
-oog (*Ger*) – island
Ojo (*Sp*) – spring
Orasul (*Rom*) – city
Ori (*Gr*) – mountains
Oriental (*Fr, Rom, Sp*) – eastern
Ormos (*Gr*) – bay
Oros (*Gr*) – island
Ort (*Ger*) – cape, point
Ostrov (*Rus*) – island
Ostrova (*Rus*) – islands
Otok (*S-C*) – island
Otoki (*S-C*) – islands
Ouadi (*Ar*) – wadi, dry watercourse
Oued (*Ar*) – dry river bed, wadi
Ovasi (*Tu*) – plain
Ozero (*Rus*) – lake

P

Pampa (*Sp*) – plain
Paniai (*Ind*) – lake
Paso (*Sp*) – pass
Passage (*Fr*) – pass
Passo (*It*) – pass
Pasul (*Rom*) – pass
Pelagos (*Gr*) – sea
Pendi (*Ch*) – basin
Pengunungnan (*Ind*) – mountain range
Peninsola (*It*) – peninsula
Peninsule (*Fr*) – peninsula
Pereval (*Rus*) – pass
Peski (*Rus*) – desert, sands
Phnom (*Khm*) – hill, mountain
Phu (*Vt*) – mountain
Pic (*Fr*) – peak
Picacho (*Sp*) – peak
Pico (*Sp*) – peak
Pik (*Rus*) – peak
Pingyuan (*Ch*) – plain
Pizzo (*It*) – peak
Planalto (*Por*) – plateau
Plana (*S-C, Sp*) – plain
Planina (*Bul, S-C*) – mountains
Plato (*Afr, Bul, Rus*) – plateau
Ploskogor'ye (*Rus*) – plateau
Ploskogorje (*Rus*) – plateau
Poco (*Ind*) – peak

Pohorie (*Cz*) – mountain range
Pointe (*Fr*) – cape, point
Pojezierze (*Pol*) – plateau
Poluostrov (*Rus*) – peninsula
Polwysep (*Pol*) – peninsula
Ponta (*Por*) – cape, point
Presa (*Sp*) – reservoir
Proliv (*Rus*) – strait
Pueblo (*Sp*) – village
Puerto (*Sp*) – harbour, pass
Pulau (*Ind, Mal*) – island
Puna (*Sp*) – desert plateau
Puncak (*Ind*) – peak
Punta (*It, Sp*) – cape, point
Puy (*Fr*) – peak

Q

Qalamat (*Ar*) – well
Qalib (*Ar*) – well
Qararat (*Ar*) – depression
Qolleh (*Per*) – mountain
Qornet (*Ar*) – peak
Qundao (*Ch*) – archipelago

R

Ramlat (*Ar*) – dunes
Ra's (*Ar, Per*) – cape, point
Ras (*Ar*) – cape, point
Rass (*Som*) – cape, point
Ravnina (*Rus*) – plain
Recife (*Por*) – reef
Represa (*Por*) – dam
Reshteh (*Per*) – mountain range
-retto (*Jap*) – island chain
Rijeka (*S-C*) – river
Rio (*Por, Sp*) – river
Riviere (*Fr*) – river
Rt (*S-C*) – cape, point
Rubha (*Gae*) – cape, point
Ruck (*Ger*) – mountain
Rucken (*Ger*) – ridge
Rud (*Per*) – river
Rudohorie (*Cz*) – mountains
Rzeka (*Pol*) – river

S

Sabkhat (*Ar*) – salt flat
Sagar (*Hin*) – lake
Sahara (*Ar*) – desert

Sahl (*Ar*) – plain
Sahra (*Ar*) – desert
Sa'id (*Ar*) – highland
-saki (*Jap*) – cape, point
Salar (*Sp*) – salt pan
Salina (*Sp*) – salt pan
San (*Sp*) – saint
-san (*Jap*) – mountain
-sanchi (*Jap*) – mountainous area
Sankt (*Ger, Swe*) – saint
-sanmyaku (*Jap*) – mountain range
Santa (*Sp*) – saint
Sao (*Por*) – saint
Sar (*Kur*) – mountain
Satu (*Rom*) – village
Sawqirah (*Ar*) – bay
Se (*I-C*) – river
See (*Ger*) – lake
-sehir (*Tu*) – town
Selat (*Ind*) – channel, strait
-selka (*Fin*) – bay
Selva (*Sp*) – forest
Serra (*Por*) – mountain range
Serrania (*Sp*) – mountains
-seto (*Jap*) – channel, strait
Severnaya (*Rus*) – southern
Sfintu (*Rom*) – saint
Shamo (*Ch*) – desert
Shan (*Ch*) – mountains
Shandi (*Ch*) – mountainous area
Shatt (*Ar*) – river mouth, river
-shima (*Jap*) – islands
Shiqqat (*Ar*) – interdune trough
-shoto (*Jap*) – group of islands
Sierra (*Sp*) – mountain range
Sint (*Afr, Dut*) – saint
Slieve (*Gae*) – range of hills
So (*Dan, Nor*) – lake
Soder- (*Swe*) – southern
Sondre (*Dan, Nor*) – southern
Song (*Vt*) – river
Spitze (*Ger*) – peak
Sredne (*Rus*) – middle
Stadt (*Ger*) – town
Stara (*Cz*) – old
Staraya (*Rus*) – old
Stenon (*Gr*) – strait, pass
Step' (*Rus*) – plain, steppe
Strelka (*Rus*) – spit
Stretto (*It*) – strait

-suido (*Jap*) – channel, strait
Sund (*Swe*) – sound, strait
Szent- (*Hun*) – saint

T

-take (*Jap*) – peak
Tall (*Ar*) – hill
Tallat (*Ar*) – hills
Tanggula (*Tib*) – pass
Tanjong (*Ind, Mal*) – cape, point
Tanjon'i (*Mlg*) – cape, point
Tanjung (*Ind, Mal*) – cape, point
Tao (*Ch*) – island
Taraq (*Ar*) – hills
Tassili (*Ber*) – rocky plateau
Tau (*Rus*) – mountains
Taung (*Bur*) – mountain, south
Tekojarvi (*Fin*) – reservoir
Tell (*Ar*) – hill
Teluk (*Ind*) – bay
Tenere (*Fr*) – desert
Terre (*Fr*) – land
Thale (*Th*) – lake
Thamad (*Ar*) – well
Tirat (*Ar*) – canal
Tjarn (*Swe*) – lake
Tso (*Tib*) – lake
Tonle (*Khm*) – lake
Tutul (*Ar*) – hills

U

Ujung (*Ind*) – cape, point
-ura (*Jap*) – inlet
Urayq (*Ar*) – sand ridge
Uruq (*Ar*) – dunes
Ust (*Rus*) – river mouth
Uul (*Mon*) – mountain

V

Valea (*Rom*) – valley
-varos (*Hun*) – town
-varre (*Nor*) – mountain
-vatten (*Swe*) – lake
Vaux (*Fr*) – valleys
Velika (*S-C*) – big
Velikaya (*Rus*) – big
Verkhne (*Rus*) – upper
-vesi (*Fin*) – lake, water
Ville (*Fr*) – town
Vinh (*Vt*) – bay

Virful (*Rom*) – peak
Vodokhranilishche (*Rus*) – reservoir
Volcan (*Sp*) – volcano
Vorota (*Rus*) – strait
Vostochnyy (*Rus*) – eastern
Vozvyshennost' (*Rus*) hills, upland
Vpadina (*Rus*) – depression

W

Wadi (*Ar*) – river, stream
Wahat (*Ar*) – oasis
Wai (*Ch*) – outer
Wald (*Ger*) – forest
Wan (*Ch*) – bay
Wasser (*Ger*) – lake, water
Wenz (*Ar*) – river
Wielka (*Pol*) – big

X

Xan (*Ch*) – strait
Xi (*Ch*) – stream, west
Xia (*Ch*) – gorge, lower
Xian (*Ch*) – county
Xiao (*Ch*) – small
Xu (*Ch*) – island

Y

Yam (*Heb*) – lake
-yama (*Jap*) – mountain
Yarimadasi (*Tu*) – peninsula
Yazovir (*Bul*) – reservoir
Ye (*Bur*) – island
Yoma (*Bur*) – mountain range
Yugo- (*Rus*) – southern
Yuzhnyy (*Rus*) – southern

Z

Zaki (*Jap*) – cape, point
Zalew (*Pol*) – bay, inlet
Zaliv (*Rus*) – bay
-zan (*Jap*) – mountain
Zapadno (*Rus*) – western
Zatoka (*Pol*) – bay
Zee (*Dut*) – sea
Zemiya (*Rus*) – island, land
-zhen (*Ch*) – town

Abbreviations

A

A. – Alp, Alpen, Alpi
Akr. – Akra
And. – Andorra
Arch. – Archipelago
Arr. – Arrecife
Aust. – Australia
Ay. – Ayios

B

B. – Bahia, Baia, Baie, Bay, Bucht, Bukt
Ba. – Bahia
Bang. – Bangladesh
Bah. – Bahrain
Bel. – Belgium
Ben. – Benin
Bg. – Berg
Bhu. – Bhutan
Bk. – Bukit
Bol. – Bol'shoy, Bol'shoye
Bos. – Bosnia-Herzegovina
Br. – Burnu, Burun
Bru. – Brunei
Bt. – Bukit
Bu. – Burundi
Bü. – Büyük
Bulg. – Bulgaria
Bur. Faso – Burkina Faso

C

C. – Cabo, Cap, Cape, Cerro
Cam. – Cambodia
Can. – Canal, Canale
Cga. – Cienaga
Chan. – Channel
Co. – Cerro
Col. – Columbia
Cord. – Cordillera
Cr. – Creek
Czech. – Czech Rep.

D

D. – Dag, Dagi, Daglari, Daryacheh
D.C. – District of Columbia
Den. – Denmark
Djib. – Djibouti

E

E. – East
Eq. – Equatorial
Est. – Estrecho

F

Fd. – Fjord
Fk. – Fork
Fr. – France
Ft. – Fort

G

G. – Golfe, Golfo, Guba, Gulf, Gora, Gunung
Gd. – Grand
Gde – Grande
Geb. – Gebirge
Gen. – General
Geog. – Geographical
Ger. – Germany
Gh. – Ghana
Gl. – Glacier
Gr. – Grande, Gross
Gt. – Great
Guy. – Guyana

H

Har. – Harbor
Hd. – Head
Hung. – Hungary

I

I. – Ile, Ilha, Insel, Isla, Island, Isle, Isola, Isole

Is. – Ilhas, Iles, Islands, Islas, Isles
Isth. – Isthmus

J

J. – Jabal, Jbel, Jebel, Jezioro, Jezero, Jazair
Jor. – Jordan

K

K. – Kap, Kuh, Kuhha, Koh, Kolpos
Kan. – Kanal, Kanaal
Kep. – Kepulauan
Khr. – Khrebet
Kör. – Körfezi
Kuw. – Kuwait

L

L. – Lac, Lacul, Lago, Lake, Limni, Llyn, Loch, Lough
Lag. – Lagoon, Laguna
Leb. – Lebanon
Liech. – Liechtenstein
Lit. – Little
Lux. – Luxembourg

M

M. – Mys
Mal. – Malawi
Mex. – Mexico
Mgne. – Montagne
Mt. – Mont, Mount, Mountain
Mti. – Monti
Mtii. – Muntii
Mts. – Monts, Mounts, Mountains

N

N. – Nord, North, Nos
Neb.– Nebraska
Neth. – Netherlands

Nev. – Nevado
N.H. – New Hampshire
Nizh. – Nizhnyaya
Nizm. – Nizmennost
Nor. – Norway
N.Z. – New Zealand

O

O. – Ost, Ostrov
Os. – Ostova
Oz. – Ozero

P

P. – Point
Pass. – Passage
Penn. – Pennsylvania
Peg. – Peganungan
Pen. – Peninsola, Peninsula, Peninsule
Pk. – Peak, Puncak
Pl. – Planina
Pol. – Poluostrov
Port. – Portugal
Prom. – Promontory
Pt. – Point
Pta. – Ponta, Punta
Pte. – Pointe
Pto. – Puerto, Punto

Q

Qat. – Qatar

R

R. – Reshteh
Ra. – Range
Rep. – Republic
Res. – Reservoir
Rés. – Réservoir
Rom. – Romania
Rw. – Rwanda

S

S. – Shatt, South
Sa. – Serra, Sierra
S.A. – South Africa
Sd. – Sound, Sund
Sp. – Spain
Sprs. – Springs
St. – Saint, Sint
Sta. – Santa
Ste. – Sainte
Str. – Strait
Sur. – Suriname
Switz. – Switzerland

T

Tg. – Tanjong, Tanjung
Tk. – Teluk

U

U.A.E. – United Arab Emirates
U.K. – United Kingdom
U.S.A. – United States of America

V

V. – Volcano
Vdkhr. – Vodokhranilishche
Ven. – Venezuela
Verkh. – Verkhne
Vn. – Volcan
Vol. – Volcan, Volcano

W

W. – Wadi, Wald, West

Y

Y. – Yarimadasi

Z

Zal. – Zaliv

INDEX

The index includes an alphabetical list of all names appearing in the map section of the atlas. Names on the maps and in the index are generally in the local language. For names in languages not written in the Roman alphabet, the officially accepted transliteration system has been used.

Most features are indexed to the largest scale map on which they appear. Extensive features are usually indexed to maps that show the features completely or show them in their relationship to surrounding areas. For extensive regional features, locations are given for the approximate center of the feature, those for linear features are given at the position of the name.

Each entry in the index is located by a page number and an alphanumeric grid reference on that particular page. The grid is defined by letters, positioned at the top and at the bottom of the map spread, and numbers, shown at the sides of the spread. For example, Bandung in Indonesia has the reference 90 D7. It can thus be found on page 90 in the grid square D7.

Where two identical names are referenced to the same page and grid square, it should be noted that they relate to different adjacent features. For example, the name Avon appears twice in the index and in both cases it is referenced to 52 E3. These two entries locate firstly the county of Avon and secondly the River Avon.

Name	Page	Grid
Adda	68	B2
Adda	68	B3
Ad Dakhla	100	B4
Ad Dali	96	G10
Ad Dammam	97	K3
Ad Darb	96	F8
Ad Dawadimi	96	G4
Ad Dawhah	97	K4
Ad Dila	97	K7
Ad Dilam	96	H5
Ad Diriyah	96	H4
Ad Duwaniyah	94	G6
Ad Duwayd	96	F1
Adel	124	C6
Adelaide *Antarctic*	141	V5
Adelaide *Australia*	113	H5
Adelaide *Bahamas*	129	P8
Adelaide Island	141	V5
Adelaide Peninsula	120	G4
Aden	96	G10
Aden, Gulf of	103	J5
Adh Dhayd	97	M4
Adi	114	A2
Adi Ark'ay	96	C10
Adi Dairo	96	D9
Adige	68	C3
Adigrat	96	D9
Adiguzel Baraji	76	C3
Adi Keyah	96	D9
Adilabad	92	E5
Adilcevaz	77	K3
Adin	122	D7
Adirondack Mountains	125	N4
Adis Abeba	103	G6
Adi Ugri	96	D9
Adiyaman	77	H4
Adjud	73	J2
Adjuntas, Presa de las	131	K6
Adka	118	Ac9
Adlington	55	G3
Admello	68	C2
Admiralty Gulf	112	F1
Admiralty Inlet	120	J3
Admiralty Island *Canada*	119	Q2
Admiralty Island *U.S.A.*	118	J4
Admiralty Islands	114	D2
Admund Ringnes Island	120	G2
Ado-Ekiti	105	G4
Adonara	91	G7
Adoni	92	E5
Adorf	70	E3
Adoumaoua, Massif de l'	105	H4
Adour	65	C7
Adra	66	E4
Adrano	69	E7
Adrar	100	E3
Adre	102	D5
Adria	68	D3
Adrian *Michigan*	124	J6
Adrian *Texas*	127	L3
Adriatic Sea	68	E4
Adwa	96	D9
Adwick le Street	55	H3
Adycha	85	P3
Adzhima	88	G1
Adzvavom	78	K2
Aegean Sea	75	H3
Afafura, Laut	91	K7
Afanasevo	78	J4
Affobakka	137	F3
Affric	56	C3
Afghanistan	92	B2
Afgooye	107	J2
Afif	96	F5
Afikpo	105	G4
Afmadow	107	H2
Afognak Island	118	E4
Afon Efyrnwy	52	D2
Afrin	77	G4
Afsin	77	G3
Afyon	76	D3
Agadez	101	G5
Agadir	100	D2
Agadyr	86	C2
Agaie	105	G4
Agalta, Sierra de	132	E7
Agano	89	G7
Agapa *Russia*	84	D2
Agapa *Russia*	84	D2
Agapitovo	84	D3
Agartala	93	H4
Agaruut	87	K3
Agats	114	B3
Agatti	92	D6
Agattu Island	118	Aa9
Agbaja	105	G4
Agboville	104	E4
Agdam	94	H2
Agde	65	E7
Agematsu	89	F8
Agen	65	D6
Aghada	59	F9
Agha Jari	95	J6
Agiabampo, Estero de	130	E4
Agin	77	H3
Agira	69	E7
Aglasun	76	D4
Agnanda	75	F4
Agno	68	C3
Agnone	69	E5
Agout	65	D7
Agra	92	E3
Agram	72	C3
Agreda	67	F2
Agri	69	F5
Agri	77	K3
Agrigento	69	D7
Agrinion	75	F3
Agropoli	69	E5
Agua Clara	138	F4
Aguadas	136	B2
Aguadilla	133	P5
Aguanaval	130	H5
Agua Prieta	127	H5
Aguascalientes	130	H7
Agua, Volcan de	132	B7
Aguelhok	100	F5
Aguemour	101	F3
Aguilar de Campoo	66	D1
Aguilas	67	F4
Aguja, Cabo de la	133	K9
Aguja, Punta	136	A5
Agulhas, Kaap	108	D6
Agusan	91	H4
Ahar	94	H2
Aheim	62	A5
Ahimahasoa	109	J4
Ahipara Bay	115	D1
Ahititi	115	E3
Ahlat	77	K3
Ahmadabad	92	D4
Ahmadi	95	N8
Ahmadnagar	92	D5
Ahmadpur	92	D3
Ahmar Mountains	103	H6
Ahoskie	129	P2
Ahram	95	K7
Ahtari	62	L5
Ahtarinjarvi	62	L5
Ahuachapan	132	C8
Ahvaz	94	J6
Ahvenanmaa	63	H6
Ahwar	96	H10
Aiddejavrre	62	K2
Aidhipsos	75	G3
Aigen	68	D1
Aigues	65	F6
Aiken	129	M4
Ailao Shan	93	K4
Ailsa Craig	57	C5
Aim	85	N5
Aimores, Serra dos	138	H3
Ain	65	F5
Ain Beida	101	G1
Ain Bessem	67	H4
Ain Defla	67	G4
Ain El Hadjel	67	H5
Ain Oulmene	67	J5
Ain Sefra	100	E2
Ainsworth	123	Q6
Aioun el Atrouss	100	D5
Aiquile	138	C3
Air	101	G5
Airbangis	90	B5
Airdrie	57	E5
Aire *France*	64	F4
Aire *U.K.*	55	J3
Airedale	55	H3
Aire-sur-l'Adour	65	C7
Air Force Island	120	M4
Airgin Sum	87	L3
Airi-selka	62	L3
Aisne	64	E4
Aitape	114	C2
Aith	56	F1
Aix-en-Provence	65	F7
Aix-les-Bains	65	F6
Aiyina	75	G4
Aiyinion	75	G2
Aiyion	75	G3
Aizawl	93	H4
Aizpute	63	J8
Aizu-Wakamatsu	89	G7
Ajaccio	69	B5
Ajana	112	C4
Ajanta Range	92	E4
Ajdabiya	101	K2
Ajlun	94	B5
Ajman	97	M4
Ajmer	92	D3
Akaishi-sanchi	89	G8
Akalkot	92	E5
Akamkpa	105	G4
Akaroa Head	115	D5
Akbou	67	J4
Akbulak	79	K5
Akcaabat	77	H2
Akcaakale	77	H4
Akcadag	77	G3
Akcakoca	76	D2
Akcaova	76	C4
Akcay	76	C4
Akchatau	86	C2
Ak Daglari	76	C4
Akdagmadeni	77	F3
Ak Dovurak	84	E6
Akershus	63	D6
Akeshir Golu	76	D3
Aketi	106	D2
Akgevir	77	J4
Akhalkalaki	77	K2
Akhaltsikhe	77	K2
Akhdar, Al Jabal al	101	K2
Akhdar, Jabal	97	N5
Akhdar, Wadi	96	C3
Akheloos	75	F3
Akhiok	118	E4
Akhisar	76	B3
Akhmim	103	F2
Akhtubinsk	79	H6
Akhtyrka	79	E5
Aki	89	D9
Akimiski Island	121	K7
Akincilar	77	H2
Akinkeen	59	D9
Akinli	77	J4
Akita	88	H6
Akjoujt	100	C5
Akkavare	62	J3
Akkeshi	88	K4
Akko	94	B5
Akkoy	76	B4
Akkus	77	G2
Aklavik	118	H2
Akmola	84	A6
Akniste	63	L8
Akola	92	E4
Akonolinga	105	H5
Akordat	96	C9
Akoren	76	E4
Akot	92	E4
Akpatok Island	121	N5
Akpinar	76	E3
Akqi	86	D3
Akranes	62	T12
Akron	125	K6
Aksar	77	K2
Aksaray	76	E3
Aksay *China*	86	G4
Aksay *Kazakhstan*	79	J5
Aksehir	76	D3
Akseki	76	D4
Aksenovo-Zilovskoye	85	K6
Aks-e Rostam	95	M7
Aksha	85	J6
Akshimrau	79	J7
Aksu *China*	86	E3
Aksu *Turkey*	76	D4
Aksu *Kazakhstan*	79	J5
Aksu-Ayuly	86	C2
Aksu Cayi	76	D4
Aksum	96	D9
Aksumbe	86	B3
Aktau *Kazakhstan*	84	A6
Aktau *Kazakhstan*	79	J7
Akti	75	H2
Aktogay	86	D2
Akulivik	120	L5
Akune	89	C9
Akun Island	118	Ae9
Akure	105	G4
Akureyri	62	V12
Akuse	104	F4
Akutan Island	118	Ae9
Akwanga	105	G4
Akyab	93	H4
Akyatan Golu	76	F4
Akyazi	76	D2
Akyurt	76	E2
Akzhar	86	C3
Al Aaiun	100	C3
Alabama *U.S.A.*	129	J4
Alabama *U.S.A.*	129	J4
Alaca	76	F2
Alacahan	77	G3
Alacam	77	F2
Alacam Daglari	76	C3
Alacran, Arrecife	131	Q6
Alagoas	137	K5
Alagoinhas	137	K6
Alagon *Spain*	66	C2
Alagon *Spain*	67	F2
Al Ahmadi	97	J2
Al Ajaiz	97	N7
Alajarvi	62	K5
Alajuela	132	E9
Alakanuk	118	C3
Alakol, Ozero	86	E2
Alakyla	62	L3
Al Amarah	94	H6
Alameda *California*	126	A2
Alameda *New Mexico*	127	J3
Alamicamba	132	E8
Alamo	126	E2
Alamogordo	127	K4
Ala, Monti di	69	B5
Alamos	127	H7
Alamosa	127	K2
Aland	63	H6
Alands hav	63	M6
Alanya	76	E4
Alaotra, Lake	109	J3
Alapayevsk	84	Ad5
Al Aqulah	97	J5
Alarcon, Embalse de	66	E3
Al Artawiyah	96	G3
Alasehir	76	C3
Al Ashkhirah	97	P6
Alaska	118	E3
Alaska, Gulf of	118	F4
Alaska Peninsula	118	Af8
Alaska Range	118	E3
Alassio	68	B4
Alatna	118	E2
Alatyr	78	H5
Alavus	62	K5
Al Ayn	97	M4
Alayor	67	J3
Alayskiy Khrebet	86	C4
Al Azamiyah	77	L6
Alazeya	85	S2
Alba	68	B3
Al Bab	77	G4
Albacete	67	F3
Alba de Tormes	66	D2
Al Badi	96	H5
Al Badi	77	J5
Alba Iulia	73	G2
Albak	63	D8
Alba, Mount	115	B6
Albanel, Lake	121	M7
Albania	74	E2
Albano	137	F4
Albany *Australia*	112	D5
Albany *Canada*	121	K7
Albany *Georgia*	129	K5
Albany *Kentucky*	124	H8
Albany *New York*	125	P5
Albany *Oregon*	122	C5
Albarracin	67	F2
Al Basrah	94	H6
Albatross Bay	113	J1
Albatross Point	115	E3
Al Bayda	96	G10
Albayrak	77	L3
Albemarle	129	M3
Albemarle Island	136	A7
Albemarle Sound	129	P2
Albenga	68	B3
Albentosa	67	F2
Alberche	66	D2
Alberga	113	G4
Albergaria-a-Velha	66	B2
Alberique	67	F3
Albert	64	E3
Alberta	119	M5
Albert Edward, Mount	114	D3
Albert Kanaal	64	F3
Albert, Lake	107	F2
Albert Lea	124	D5
Albert Nile	107	F2
Albertville *France*	65	G6
Albertville *Zaire*	107	E4
Albi	65	E7
Albina	137	G2
Al Bir	96	C2
Al Birk	96	E7
Albocacer	67	G2
Albo, Monti	69	B5
Alboran, Isla de	66	E5
Alborg	63	D8
Alborg Bugt	63	D8
Alborz, Reshteh-ye Kuhha ye	95	K3
Albro	113	K3
Albufeira	66	B4
Albu Gharz, Sabkhat	77	J5
Albuquerque	127	J3
Al Buraymi	97	M4
Albury	113	K6
Al Busayyah	94	H6
Al Buzun	97	K9
Alcacer do Sal	66	B3
Alcala de Henares	66	E2
Alcamo	69	D7
Alcanices	66	C2
Alcaniz	67	F2
Alcantara	137	J4
Alcantara, Embalse de	66	C3
Alcaraz	66	E3
Alcaraz, Sierra de	66	E3
Alcaudete	66	D4
Alcazar de San Juan	66	E3
Alcester	53	F2
Alchevsk	79	F6
Alcolea del Pinar	66	E2
Alcoutim	66	C4
Alcoy	67	F3
Alcubierre, Sierra de	67	F2
Alcublas	67	F3
Alcudia	67	H3
Aldabra Islands	82	C7
Aldama	131	K6
Aldan *Russia*	85	M5
Aldan *Russia*	85	N4
Aldanskoye Nagorye	85	M5
Alde	53	J2
Aldeburgh	53	J2
Aldeia Nova	66	C4
Alderley Edge	55	G3
Alderney	53	M6
Aldershot	53	G3
Aldridge	53	F2
Aleg	100	C5
Alegrete	138	E5
Aleksandra, Mys	85	P6
Aleksandriya	79	E6
Aleksandrov	78	F4
Aleksandrovac	73	F4
Aleksandrov Gay	79	H5
Aleksandrovsk	78	K4
Aleksandrovskoye	79	G7
Aleksandrovsk-Sakhalinskiy	85	Q6
Aleksandry, Ostrov	80	F1
Alekseyevka *Kazakhstan*	84	A4
Alekseyevka *Russia*	79	F5
Aleksin	78	F5
Alem Paraiba	138	H4
Alencon	64	D4
Alenquer	137	G3
Alentejo	66	C3
Alenuihaha Channel	126	S10
Aleppo	77	G4

Name	Page	Grid
Amuntai	90	F6
Amur *China*	87	N1
Amur *Russia*	85	Q6
Amuri Pass	115	D5
Amursk	85	P6
Amurskaya Oblast	85	M6
Amur, Wadi	103	F4
Amvrakikos Kolpos	75	F3
Amvrosiyevka	79	F6
Anabar	84	J2
Anaco	133	Q10
Anaconda	122	H4
Anadarko	128	C3
Anadyr *Russia*	85	W4
Anadyr *Russia*	85	X4
Anadyrskiy Khrebet	85	W3
Anafi *Greece*	75	H4
Anafi *Greece*	75	H4
Anafjallet	62	E5
Anah	77	J5
Anaheim	126	D4
Anahuac	128	B7
Anakapalle	92	F5
Anaktuvuk	118	E2
Analalava	109	J2
Anambas, Kepulauan	90	D5
Anamur	76	E4
Anamur Burun	76	E4
Anan	89	E9
Ananes	75	H4
Anantapur	92	E6
Anantnag	92	E2
Ananyev	73	K2
Ananyevo	86	D3
Anapolis	138	J3
Anapu	137	G4
Anar	95	M6
Anarak	95	L5
Anar Darreh	95	Q5
Anatuya	138	D5
Anaua	136	E3
Anavilhanas, Arquipielago das	136	E4
A Nazret	103	G6
Anbei	86	H3
Ancenis	65	C5
Ancha	85	P4
Anchi	105	G4
Anchorage	118	F3
Anchor Island	115	A6
Ancohuma, Nevado	138	C3
Ancona	68	D4
Ancrum	57	F4
Ancuabe	109	G2
Ancuaque	138	C3
Ancud	139	B8
Ancud, Golfo de	139	B8
Anda	87	P2
Andalgala	138	C5
Andalsnes	62	B5
Andalucia	66	D4
Andalusia	129	J5
Andaman Islands	93	H6
Andaman Sea	93	J6
Andamarca	136	C6
Andam, Wadi	97	P6
Andanga	78	H4
Andapa	109	J2
Andarai	137	J6
Andeba Ye Midir Zerf Chaf	96	E9
Andeg	78	J2
Andenes	62	G2
Andermatt	68	B2
Anderson *Canada*	118	K2
Anderson *Indiana*	124	H6
Anderson *Missouri*	124	C8
Anderson *S. Carolina*	129	L3
Anderson Bay	113	K7
Andes	136	B2
Andevoranto	109	J3
Andfjorden	62	G2
Andhra Pradesh	92	E5
Andikithira	75	G5
Andimeshk	94	J5
Andimilos	75	H4
Andiparos	75	H4
Andipaxoi	75	F3
Andirin	77	G4
Andizhan	86	C3
Andkhovy	95	S3
Andoas	136	B4
Andong	89	B7
Andongwei	87	M4
Andorra	66	G1
Andorra la Vella	67	G1
Andover	53	F3
Andoya	62	F2
Andraitx	67	H3
Andrascoggin	125	Q4
Andravidha	75	F4
Andreafsky	118	C3
Andreanof Islands	118	Ac9
Andrews	127	L4
Andreyevka	79	J5
Andreyevo Ivanovka	73	L2
Andreyevsk	85	J5
Andria	69	F5
Andrijevica	72	E4
Andringitra	109	J4
Andros	132	H2
Andros *Greece*	75	H4
Andros *Greece*	75	H4
Androth	92	D6
Andujar	66	D3
Andulo	106	C5
Andyngda	85	K3
Anegada	133	Q5
Anegada, Bahia	139	D8
Aneho	105	F4
Aneityum	114	U13
Anelghowhat	114	U14
Aneto, Pic D'	67	G1
Angamos, Punta	138	B4
Angar	114	A2
Angara	84	E5
Angara Basin	140	A1
Angarsk	84	G6
Ange	62	F5
Angel de la Guarda, Isla	126	F6
Angeles	91	G2
Angel Falls	136	E2
Angelholm	63	E8
Angelino	128	E5
Angellala	113	K4
Angermanalven	62	G5
Angermunde	70	F2
Angers	65	C5
Angeson	62	J5
Angical	138	J6
Angicos	137	K5
Angikuni Lake	119	R3
Anglesey	54	E4
Ango	106	E2
Angoche	109	G3
Angohran	95	N8
Angol	139	B7
Angola	106	C5
Angola *Indiana*	124	H6
Angoram	114	C2
Angostura, Presa de la	131	N9
Angouleme	65	D6
Angoumois	65	D6
Angren	86	B3
Anguila Islands	132	H3
Anguilla	133	R5
Angus, Braes of	57	E4
Anholt	63	D8
Anhua	93	M3
Anhui	93	N2
Anhumas	138	F3
Aniak	118	D3
Anidhros	75	H4
Animas, Punta de las	126	F6
Anina	73	F3
Aniva	88	J2
Aniva, Mys	88	J2
Aniva, Zaliv	88	J2
Aniwa	114	U13
Anjalankoski	63	M6
Anjou	65	C5
Anjouan	109	H2
Anjozorobe	109	J3
Anju	87	P4
Ankacho	84	H4
Ankang	93	L2
Ankara	76	E3
Ankazoabo	109	H4
Ankazobe	109	J3
Ankiliabo	109	H4
Anklam	70	E2
Ankleshwar	92	D4
Ankober	103	G6
Ankpa	105	G4
Anlong	93	L3
Anlu	93	M2
Anna	79	G5
Annaba	101	G1
Annaberg-Buchholz	70	E3
An Nabk *Saudi Arabia*	94	C6
An Nabk *Syria*	94	C4
Anna Creek	113	H4
Annagh Bog	59	D8
Annagh Head	58	B4
Annagh Island	59	C5
An Najaf	94	G6
Annalong	58	L4
Annan *U.K.*	57	E5
Annan *U.K.*	55	F2
Annandale	57	E5
Anna Plains	112	E2
Annapolis	125	M7
Annapurna	92	F3
Ann Arbor	124	J5
An Nasiriyah	94	H6
Ann, Cape	125	Q5
Annecy	65	G6
Annenskiy-Most	78	F3
Annfield Plain	55	H2
An Nhon	93	L6
Anniston	129	K4
Annonay	65	F6
An Nuayriyah	97	J3
An Numan	96	B3
Ano Arkhanai	75	H5
Anosibe an Ala	109	J3
Ano Viannos	75	H5
Anoyia	75	H5
Anqing	87	M5
Ansbach	70	D4
Anse de Vauville	53	N6
Anserma	136	B2
Anshan	87	N3
Anshun	93	L3
Ansley	123	Q7
Anson	127	N4
Anson Bay	112	G1
Ansongo	100	F5
Anston	55	H3
Anstruther	57	F4
Ansudu	114	B2
Antabamba	136	C6
Antakya	77	G4
Antalaha	109	K2
Antalya	76	D4
Antalya Korfezi	76	D4
Antananarivo	109	J3
Antarctic Peninsula	141	W5
An Teallach	56	C3
Antequera	66	D4
Anti-Atlas	100	D3
Antibes	65	G7
Anticosti Island	121	P8
Antigo	124	F4
Antigua	133	S6
Antigua and Barbuda	133	S6
Antigua Guatemala	132	B7
Antioch	126	B2
Antipayuta	84	B3
Antipodes Islands	111	S11
Antlers	128	E3
Antofagasta	138	B4
Antofagasta de la Sierra	138	C5
Antofalla, Salar de	138	C5
Antofalla, Volcan	138	C5
Antonio, Ponta Santo	137	K7
Antonovo	73	J4
Antrain	64	C4
Antrim *U.K.*	58	K3
Antrim *U.K.*	58	K3
Antrim Mountains	58	K2
Antrim Plateau	112	F2
Antsalova	109	H3
Antseranana	109	J2
Antsirabe	109	J3
Antsohihy	109	J2
Antu	88	B4
Antufush	96	F9
An-tung	87	N7
Antwerp	64	F3
Antwerpen	64	F3
Anuchino	88	D4
Anugul	92	F4
Anundsjo	62	H5
Anupgarh	92	D3
Anuradhapura	92	F7
Anvers Island	141	V6
Anxi	86	H3
Anxious Bay	113	G5
Anyama	104	E4
Anyang	87	L4
Anyemaqen Shan	93	J2
Anyudin	78	K3
Anzhero-Sudzhensk	84	D5
Anzhu, Ostrova	85	Q1
Anzio	69	D5
Aoba	114	T11
Aola	114	K6
Aomori	88	H5
Aosta	68	A3
Aoukale	102	D5
Aouker	100	D5
Apalachee Bay	129	K6
Apalachicola	129	K6
Apaporis	136	D4
Aparri	91	G2
Apatity	62	Q3
Apatzingan	130	H8
Apeldoorn	64	F2
Apia	111	U4
Apiacas, Serra dos	137	F5
Apin-Apin	90	F4
Apio	114	K6
Apizaco	131	K8
Apolda	70	D3
Apollonia	75	H4
Apopka, Lake	129	M6
Apostle Islands	124	E3
Apostolou Andrea, Akra	76	F5
Apostolovo	79	E6
Appennino	68	C4
Appleby-in-Westmorland	55	G2
Appleton	124	F4
Apsheronsk	79	F7
Apt	65	F7
Apucarana	138	F4
Apure	136	D2
Apurimac	136	C6
Apuseni, Muntii	73	G2
Aq	77	L3
Aqaba	94	B7
Aqaba, Gulf of	103	F2
Aqabah, Khalij-al-	96	B2
Aqal	86	D3
Aqda	95	L5
Aqiq	96	D7
Aqrah	77	K4
Aqueda	66	C2
Aquidauana	138	E4
Ara	92	F3
Arabab	95	N5
Araban	77	G4
Arabatskaya Strelkha, Kosa	79	F6
Araba, Wadi	94	B6
Arab, Bahr el	102	E5
Arabelo	136	E3
Arabian Desert	103	F2
Arabian Sea	97	N8
Arab, Shatt al	94	H6
Arac	76	E2
Aracaju	137	K6
Aracati	137	K4
Aracatuba	138	F4
Aracena	66	C4
Aracena, Sierra de	66	C4
Aracuai *Brazil*	138	H3
Aracuai *Brazil*	137	H3
Arad	73	F2
Aradah	97	L5
Arafuli	96	D9
Aragats	77	L2
Aragon	67	F1
Araguacema	137	H5
Aragua de Barcelona	136	E2
Araguaia	137	H5
Araguaine	137	H5
Araguari	137	G3
Araioses	137	J4
Arak	95	J4
Arakamchechen, Ostrov	118	A3
Arakan Yoma	93	H5
Arakhthos	75	F3
Arakli	77	J2
Araks	77	K2
Aral	86	E3
Aralik	77	L3
Aralqi	86	F4
Aral Sea	98	J2
Aralsk	86	A2
Aralskoye More	80	G5
Aramah, Al	96	H4
Aranda de Duero	66	E2
Arandai	114	A2
Aran Island	58	E3
Aran Islands	59	C6
Aranjuez	66	E2
Aranlau	114	A3
Araouane	100	E5
Arapahoe	123	Q7
Arapawa Island	115	E4
Arapiraca	137	K5
Arapkir	77	H3
Arapongas	138	F4
Ar'ar	94	E6
Araracuara	136	C4
Araraquara	138	G4
Araras, Serra das *Maranhao, Brazil*	137	H5
Araras, Serra das *Mato Grosso do Sul, Brazil*	138	F3
Ararat	77	L3
Araripe, Chapada do	137	K5
Arar, Wadi	94	E6
Aras	77	K2
Arato	89	H6
Arauca *Colombia*	136	C2
Arauca *Venezuela*	136	D2
Aravalli Range	92	D3
Araxa	138	G3
Araya	88	H5
Araya, Peninsula de	136	E1
Arba	67	F1
Arbatax	69	B6
Arbil	77	L4
Arboga	63	F7
Arboleda, Punta	127	H7
Arborg	119	R5
Arbra	63	G6
Arbroath	57	F4
Arbus	69	B6
Arcachon	65	C6
Arcachon, Bassin d	65	C6
Arcadia	129	M7
Arcata	122	B7
Arc Dome	122	F8
Archidona	66	D4
Arcis-sur-Aube	64	F4
Arco	122	H6
Arcos de la Frontera	66	D4
Arctic Bay	120	J3
Arctic Ocean	140	A1
Arctic Red	118	J2
Arctic Red River	118	J2
Arctowski	141	W6
Arda	73	H5
Ardabil	94	J2
Ardahan	77	K2
Ardalstangen	63	B6
Ardanuc	77	K2
Ardara	58	F3
Ardarroch	56	C3
Ardee	58	J5
Ardennes	64	F3
Ardentinny	57	D4
Ardesen	77	J2
Ardestan	95	L5
Ardfert	59	C8
Ardglass	58	L4
Ardgour	57	C4
Ardh es Suwwan	94	C6
Ardila	66	C3
Ardino	73	H5
Ardivacher Point	56	A3
Ardlussa	57	C4
Ardminish	57	C5
Ardmore	128	D3
Ardnacross Bay	57	C5
Ardnamurchan	57	B4
Ardnamurchan Point	57	B4
Ardnave Point	57	B5
Ardrossan	57	D5
Ardtalla	57	B5
Ardvasar	57	C3
Ardvule, Rubha	56	A3
Areao	137	H4
Arecibo	133	P5

Name	Page	Ref
Aube	64	F4
Aubenas	65	F6
Aubigny-sur-Nere	65	E5
Aubry Lake	118	K2
Auburn *Australia*	113	L4
Auburn *Alabama*	129	K4
Auburn *California*	126	B1
Auburn *Indiana*	124	H6
Auburn *Maine*	125	Q4
Auburn *Nebraska*	124	C6
Auburn *New York*	125	M5
Aubusson	65	E6
Auca Mahuida	139	C7
Auce	63	K8
Auch	65	D7
Auchavan	57	E4
Auchengray	57	E5
Auchterarder	57	E4
Auckland	115	E2
Auckland Islands	141	M8
Aude	65	E7
Auderville	64	C4
Audierne, Baie 'd	65	A5
Aue	70	E3
Augher	58	H4
Aughnacloy	58	J4
Aughrim *Galway, Ireland*	59	F6
Aughrim *Wicklow, Ireland*	59	K7
Aughton	55	H3
Augsburg	70	D4
Augusta *Australia*	112	D5
Augusta *Georgia*	129	M4
Augusta *Italy*	69	E7
Augusta *Kansas*	128	D2
Augusta *Maine*	125	R4
Augusta *Montana*	122	H4
Augustine Island	118	E4
Augustow	71	K2
Augustus, Mount	112	D3
Auletta	69	E5
Aulia	103	F4
Auliting Island	120	N4
Aulne	64	B4
Aultbea	56	C3
Aumont	65	E6
Aupalak	121	N6
Aurangabad	92	E5
Auray	65	B5
Aurdal	63	C6
Aure *Norway*	62	B5
Aure *Norway*	62	C5
Aurich	70	B2
Aurillac	65	E6
Aurkuning	90	E6
Aurora *Colorado*	123	M8
Aurora *Illinois*	124	F6
Aurora *Missouri*	124	D8
Aurora *Nebraska*	123	R7
Au Sable	124	J4
Auskerry Sound	56	F1
Aust-Agder	63	D7
Austin *Minnesota*	124	D5
Austin *Nevada*	126	D1
Austin *Texas*	128	D5
Austin, Lake	112	D4
Australia	110	F6
Australian Capital Territory	113	K6
Austria	68	D2
Austurhorn	62	X12
Autazes	136	F4
Authie	64	D3
Autlan	130	G8
Autun	65	F5
Auvergne *Australia*	112	G2
Auvergne *France*	65	E6
Auxerre	65	E5
Avallon	65	E5
Avanos	76	F3
Avare	138	G4
Avas	75	H2
Avcilar	76	C2
Avebury	53	F3
Aveiro *Portugal*	66	B2
Aveiro *Portugal*	66	B2
Avellino	69	E5
Avelon Peninsula	121	R8
Aversa	69	E5
Aves, Isla de	133	R7
Avesnes	64	E3
Avesta	63	G6
Aveyron	65	E6
Avezzano	69	D4
Avgo	75	H5
Aviemore	57	E3
Aviemore, Lake	115	C6
Avigliano	69	E5
Avignon	65	F7
Avila	66	D2
Avila, Sierra de	66	D2
Aviles	66	D1
Avisio	68	C2
Aviz	66	C3
Avlum	63	C8
Avoca *Australia*	113	J6
Avoca *Iowa*	124	C6
Avola	69	E7
Avon *Devon, U.K.*	52	D4
Avon *Hampshire, U.K.*	53	F4
Avon *U.K.*	52	E3
Avon *U.K.*	52	E3
Avonmouth	52	E3
Avon Park	129	M7
Avon Water	57	D5
Avranches	64	C4
Avrig	73	H3
Avuavu	114	K6
Awaji-shima	89	E8
Awali	97	K3
Awanui	115	D1
Awarik, Uruq al	96	H7
Awarua Point	115	A6
Awa-shima	89	G6
Awash Wenz	103	H5
Awaso	104	E4
Awatere	115	D4
Awbari	101	H3
Aweil	102	E6
Awe, Loch	57	C4
Awful, Mount	115	B6
Awgu	105	G4
Awjilah	101	K2
Axbridge	52	E3
Axe *Dorset, U.K.*	52	E4
Axe *Somerset, U.K.*	52	E3
Axel-Heiberg Island	120	H2
Axim	104	E5
Axios	75	G2
Ax-les-Thermes	65	D7
Axminster	52	D4
Ayabe	89	E8
Ayacucho *Argentina*	139	E7
Ayacucho *Peru*	136	C6
Ayaguz	86	F2
Ayamonte	66	C4
Ayan *Russia*	84	H5
Ayan *Russia*	85	P5
Ayancik	76	F2
Ayas	76	E3
Ayaviri	136	C6
Ayayei	96	C10
Aya-Yenahin	104	E4
Aybasti	77	G2
Aydarkul, Ozero	86	B3
Aydere	95	N2
Aydin	76	B4
Aydinca	77	G2
Aydincik	76	E4
Aydin Daglari	76	C3
Ayerbe	67	F1
Ayers Rock	112	G4
Ayeshka	84	E6
Ayia Anna	75	G3
Ayia Marina	75	J5
Ayios	75	G4
Ayios Andreas	75	G4
Ayios Evstratios	75	H3
Ayios Kirikos	75	J4
Ayios Nikolaos *Greece*	75	F3
Ayios Nikolaos *Greece*	75	H5
Ayios Petros	75	F3
Aykathonisi	75	J4
Aykhal	84	J3
Aylesbury	53	G3
Ayllon	66	E2
Aylmer, Lake	119	P3
Aylsham	53	J2
Ayn al Bayda	77	G5
Ayni	86	B4
Ayn Tarfawi	77	K5
Ayn, Wadi al	97	M5
Ayod	102	F6
Ayon	85	V3
Ayon, Ostrov	85	V3
Ayora	67	F3
Ayr *U.K.*	57	D5
Ayr *U.K.*	57	D5
Ayranci	76	E4
Ayre, Point of	54	E2
Aysgarth	55	H2
Ayshirak	86	C2
Aytos	73	J4
Ayun	97	L8
Ayutthaya	93	K6
Ayvacik	76	B3
Ayvali	76	D4
Azambuja	66	B3
Azamgarh	92	F3
Azaran	94	H3
Azaz	77	G4
Azazga	67	J4
Azbine	101	G5
Azerbaijan	79	H7
Azezo	96	C10
Azogues	136	B4
Azoum	102	D5
Azov, Sea of	79	F6
Azovskoye More	79	F6
Azpeitia	66	E1
Azraq, Bahr el	103	F5
Azrou	100	D2
Aztec	127	H2
Azuaga	66	D3
Azuari	137	G3
Azuero, Peninsula de	132	G11
Azul *Argentina*	139	E7
Azul *Mexico*	131	Q9
Azul, Cordillera	136	B5
Azur, Cote d'	65	G7
Azvaday	76	E2
Az Zabadani	77	G6
Az Zafir	96	E7
Az Zahran	97	K3
Az Zarqa	97	L4
Az Zawiyah	101	H2
Az Zaydiyah	96	F9
Az Zilfi	96	G3
Az Zubaydiyah	94	G5
Az Zubayr	94	H6
Az Zuhrah	96	F9
Az Zuqur	96	F9

B

Name	Page	Ref
Baaba	114	W16
Baalbek	77	G5
Baamonde	66	C1
Baardheere	107	H2
Babadag	73	K3
Babaeski	76	B2
Babahoyo	136	B4
Babai Gaxun	87	J3
Baba, Koh-i-	92	C2
Babar	91	H7
Babar, Kepulauan	91	H7
Babayevo	78	F4
Babbacombe Bay	52	D4
Babelthuap	91	J4
Babine Lake	118	K5
Babo	114	A2
Babol	95	L3
Babol Sar	95	L3
Baboua	102	B6
Babruysk	79	D5
Babstovo	88	D1
Babushkin	84	H6
Babuyan *Philippines*	91	F4
Babuyan *Philippines*	91	G2
Babuyan Channel	91	G2
Babuyan Islands	91	G2
Bacabal	137	J4
Bacan	91	H6
Bacau	73	J2
Baccegalhaldde	62	J2
Back	119	R2
Backa	63	E6
Backaland	56	F1
Backa Topola	72	E3
Backe	62	G5
Bac Ninh	93	L4
Bacolod	91	G3
Bacup	55	G3
Badagara	92	E6
Badajoz	66	C3
Badalona	67	H2
Badanah	94	E6
Bad Aussee	68	D2
Badby	53	F2
Bad Doberan	70	D1
Bad Ems	70	B3
Baden	68	B2
Baden-Baden	70	C4
Badenoch	57	D4
Badgastein	68	D2
Bad Homburg	70	C3
Badiet esh Sham	94	D5
Bad Ischl	68	D2
Bad Kissingen	70	D3
Bad Kreuznach	70	B4
Bad Lands	123	N4
Bad Mergentheim	70	C4
Badminton	52	E3
Bad Neustadt	70	D3
Bad Oldesloe	70	D2
Ba Don	93	L5
Badong	93	M2
Badrah	94	G5
Badr Hunayn	96	D5
Bad Segeberg	70	D2
Bad Tolz	70	D5
Badulla	92	F7
Bad Wildungen	70	C3
Badzhal	85	N6
Badzhalskiy Khrebet	85	N6
Bae Can	93	L4
Baena	66	D4
Baeza	136	B4
Bafa Golu	76	B4
Bafang	105	H4
Bafata	104	C3
Baffin Bay *Canada*	120	N3
Baffin Bay *U.S.A.*	128	D7
Baffin Island	120	L3
Bafia	105	H5
Bafing Makana	100	C6
Bafoulabe	100	C6
Bafoussam	105	H4
Bafq	95	M6
Bafra	77	F2
Bafra Burun	77	F2
Baft	95	N7
Bafwasende	106	E2
Bagamoya	107	G4
Bagan Datuk	90	C5
Bagansiapiapi	90	C5
Baganyuvam	78	K2
Bagaryak	84	Ad5
Bagdad	126	F3
Bagdere	77	J3
Bage	138	F6
Bagenalstown	59	J7
Baggs	123	L7
Baghdad	77	L6
Bagherhat	93	G4
Bagheria	69	D6
Baghlan	92	C1
Bagh nam Faoileann	56	A3
Bagisli	77	L4
Bagneres-de-Bigorre	65	D7
Bagneres-de-Luchon	65	D7
Bagnoles-de-l'Orne	64	C4
Bagnolo Mella	68	C3
Bagoe	104	D3
Bagrationovsk	71	J1
Bagshot	53	G3
Baguio	91	G2
Bagusa	114	B2
Bahamas	132	J2
Baharampur	93	G4
Bahau	90	C5
Bahaur	90	E6
Bahawalpur	92	D3
Bahce	77	G4
Bahia	137	J6
Bahia Blanca	139	D7
Bahia Bustamante	139	C9
Bahia, Islas de la	132	D6
Bahia Kino	126	G6
Bahia Laura	139	C9
Bahia Negra	138	E4
Bahias, Cabo dos	139	C8
Bahr	96	E7
Bahr, Abu	97	J6
Bahraich	92	F3
Bahrain	97	K3
Bahrain, Gulf of	97	K4
Bahr Sayqal	77	G6
Bahu Kalat	95	Q9
Baia de Maputo	109	F5
Baia Mare	73	G2
Baian, Band-i-	92	C2
Baiao	137	H4
Baiazeh	95	M5
Baibokoum	102	C6
Baicheng *Jilin, China*	87	N2
Baicheng *Xinjiang Uygur Zizhiqu, China*	86	E3
Baie Comeau	125	R2
Baie-du-Poste	121	M7
Baiji	77	K5
Baiju	87	N5
Baikal, Lake	84	H6
Baile Atha Cliath	59	K6
Baile Herculane	73	G3
Bailieborough	58	J5
Baillie Hamilton Island	120	H2
Baillie Island	118	K1
Bailundo	106	C5
Baimuru	114	C3
Bainbridge	129	K5
Bain-de-Bretagne	65	C5
Baing	91	G8
Bains-les-Bains	65	G4
Baird Inlet	118	C3
Baird Mountains	118	C2
Baird Peninsula	120	L4
Bairin Youqi	87	M3
Bairin Zuoqi	87	M3
Bairnsdale	113	K6
Baise	65	D7
Baixingt	87	N3
Baiyanghe	86	F3
Baja	72	E2
Baja, Punta	126	E6
Bajgiran	95	P3
Bajil	96	F9
Bajmok	72	E3
Bakchar	84	C5
Bakel	104	C3
Baker *Chile*	139	B9
Baker *California*	126	E3
Baker *Montana*	123	M4
Baker *Oregon*	122	F5
Baker Foreland	119	S3
Baker Island	111	T1
Baker Lake	119	R3
Baker, Mount	122	D3
Bakersfield	126	C3
Bakewell	55	H3
Bakharden	95	N2
Bakhardok	95	P2
Bakharz	95	P4
Bakhchisaray	79	E7
Bakhmach	79	E5
Bakhta	84	D4
Bakhtaran	94	H4
Bakhtegan, Daryacheh-ye	95	L7
Bakhty	86	F2
Bakinskikh Komissarov	95	M2
Bakir	76	B3
Bakkafjordur	62	X11
Bakkafloi	62	X11
Bakkagerdi	62	Y12
Baklan	76	C4
Bako	103	G6
Bakongan	90	B5
Bakony	72	D2
Bakouma	102	D6
Baku	79	H7
Bakwanga	106	D4
Bala	52	D2
Bala	76	E3
Balabac	91	F4
Balabac Strait	90	F4
Balabio	114	W16
Bala, Cerros de	136	D6
Balacita	73	G3
Balad	77	L6
Baladch	95	K3
Balagannoye	85	R5
Balaghat	92	E5
Balaghat Range	92	E5
Balaguer	67	G2
Balaikarangan	90	E5
Balaka	107	F5
Balakhta	84	E5

Name	Page	Grid
Balakleya	79	F6
Balakovo	79	H5
Bala Lake	52	D2
Balama	109	G2
Balambangan	91	F4
Bala Morghab	95	R4
Balangir	92	F4
Balashov	79	G5
Balassagyarmat	72	E1
Balaton	72	D2
Balatonszentgyorgy	72	D2
Balazote	66	E3
Balbi, Mount	114	E3
Balboa	132	H10
Balbriggan	58	K5
Balcarce	139	E7
Balchik	73	K4
Balchrick	56	C2
Balclutha	115	B7
Bald Knob	128	G3
Baldock	53	G3
Baleares, Islas	67	H3
Balearic Islands	67	H3
Baleia, Ponta da	137	K7
Baleine, Grande Riviere de la	121	L6
Baleine, Riviere a la	121	N6
Baler	91	G2
Balerno	57	E5
Balestrand	63	B6
Baley	85	K6
Balfes Creek	113	K3
Balfour	56	F1
Balguntay	86	F3
Balhaf	97	J10
Bali	90	F7
Baligrod	71	K4
Balikesir	76	B3
Balik Golu	77	K3
Balikpapan	90	F6
Bali, Laut	90	F7
Balimbing	91	F4
Balimo	114	C3
Balinqiao	87	M3
Balintang Channel	91	G2
Balkashino	84	Ae6
Balkh	92	C1
Balkhash	86	C2
Balkhash, Ozero	86	C2
Balladonia	112	E5
Ballaghaderreen	58	E5
Ballandean	113	L4
Ballangen	62	G2
Ballantrae	57	C5
Ballao	69	B6
Ballarat	113	J6
Ballard, Lake	112	E4
Ballasalla	54	E2
Ballash	92	F4
Ballater	57	E3
Balle	100	D5
Ballenas, Bahia de	126	F7
Ballenas, Canal de las	126	F6
Balleny Islands	141	L5
Ballia	92	F3
Ballina	58	D4
Ballinafad	58	F4
Ballinamore	58	G4
Ballinasloe	59	F6
Ballincollig	59	E9
Ballindine	58	E5
Ballineen	59	E9
Ballinhassig	59	E9
Ballinluig	57	E4
Ballinskelligs Bay	59	B9
Ball Peninsula	120	K5
Ballsh	74	E2
Ballybay	58	J4
Ballybofey	58	G3
Ballybunion	59	C7
Ballycastle Ireland	58	D4
Ballycastle U.K.	58	K2
Ballyclare	58	L3
Ballycotton Bay	59	G9
Ballycroy	58	C4
Ballydesmond	59	D8
Ballyduff	59	C8
Ballygalley Head	58	L3
Ballygawley	58	H4
Ballygowan	58	L4
Ballyhaunis	58	E5
Ballyheige	59	C8
Ballyheige Bay	59	C8
Ballyhooly	59	F8
Ballyjamesduff	58	H5
Ballykeel	58	H3
Ballylongford	59	D7
Ballymahon	59	G5
Ballymena	58	K3
Ballymoe	58	F5
Ballymoney	58	J2
Ballymore Eustace	59	J6
Ballymote	58	E4
Ballynahinch	58	L4
Ballyquintin Point	58	M4
Ballyragget	59	H7
Ballyshannon	58	F3
Ballysitteragh	59	B8
Ballyteige Bay	59	J8
Ballyvaghan Bay	59	D6
Ballyvourney	59	D9
Ballywater	58	M3
Balmedie	56	F3
Balonne	113	K4
Balotra	92	D3
Balrampur	92	F3
Balranald	113	J5
Bals	73	H3
Balsas Brazil	137	H5
Balsas Mexico	131	J8
Balsas Peru	136	B5
Balsta	63	G7
Balta	79	D6
Baltanas	66	D2
Baltasound	56	A1
Balti	73	J2
Baltic Sea	63	G9
Baltim	102	F1
Baltimore	125	M7
Baltinglass	59	J7
Baluchistan	92	C3
Balurghat	93	G3
Balvicar	57	C4
Balya	76	B3
Balykshi	79	J6
Bam	95	N3
Bam	95	P7
Bama	105	H3
Bamako	100	D6
Bamba	100	E5
Bambari	102	D6
Bamberg Germany	70	D4
Bamberg U.S.A.	129	M4
Bambesa	106	E2
Bamenda	105	H4
Bami	95	N2
Bamian	92	C2
Bam Posht	95	R8
Bampton	53	F3
Bampur	95	Q8
Banaba	111	Q2
Banadia	133	M11
Banagher	59	G6
Banalia	106	E2
Banam	93	L6
Bananal, Ilha do	137	G6
Ban Aranyaprathet	93	K6
Banas	92	E3
Banas, Ras	96	C5
Bana, Wadi	96	G10
Banaz	76	C3
Banbridge	58	K4
Banbury	53	F2
Banchory	57	F3
Bancroft	125	M4
Banda	92	F3
Banda Aceh	90	B4
Banda Elat	91	J7
Banda, Kepulauan	91	H6
Banda, Laut	91	H7
Bandama Blanc	104	D4
Bandan Kuh	95	Q6
Banda, Punta la	126	D5
Bandar Abbas	95	N8
Bandarbeyla	103	K6
Bandar-e Anzali	94	J3
Bandar-e Deylam	95	K6
Bandar-e Lengeh	95	M8
Bandar e Mashur	94	J6
Bandar-e Moghuyeh	95	M8
Bandar-e Rig	95	K7
Bandar-e Torkeman	95	M3
Bandar Khomeyni	94	J6
Bandar Seri Begawan	90	E5
Bande	66	C1
Band-e-pay	95	L3
Bandiagara	100	E6
Bandirma	76	B2
Bandol	65	F7
Bandon Ireland	59	E9
Bandon Ireland	59	E9
Bandundu	106	C3
Bandung	90	D7
Baneh	94	G4
Banes	133	K4
Banff Canada	122	G2
Banff U.K.	56	F3
Banfora	104	E3
Bangalore	92	E6
Bangangte	105	H4
Bangassou	102	D7
Bangeta, Mount	114	D3
Banggai	91	G6
Banggai, Kepulauan	91	G6
Banggi	91	F4
Banghazi	101	K2
Bangka	90	D6
Bangkalan	90	E7
Bangkaru	90	B5
Bangka, Selat	90	D6
Bangko	90	D6
Bangkok	93	K6
Bangkok, Bight of	93	K6
Bangladesh	93	G4
Bangor Down, U.K.	58	L3
Bangor Gwynedd, U.K.	54	E2
Bangor U.S.A.	125	R4
Bangor Erris	58	C4
Bang Saphan Yai	93	J6
Bangui Central African Rep.	102	C7
Bangui Philippines	91	G2
Bangweulu, Lake	107	E5
Bangweulu Swamps	107	E5
Ban Hat Yai	93	K7
Ban Houei Sai	93	K4
Bani	100	D6
Bani	133	M5
Baniara	114	D3
Banika	114	J6
Bani Khatmah	96	G7
Bani Maarid	96	H7
Bani Walid	101	H2
Baniyas	94	B5
Baniyas	94	B4
Bani Zaynan, Hadh	97	J6
Banja Luka	72	D3
Banjarmasin	90	E6
Banjul	104	B3
Banka Banka	113	G2
Ban Kantang	93	J7
Ban Keng Phao	93	L6
Bankfoot	57	E4
Ban Khemmarat	93	L5
Ban Khok Kloi	93	J7
Banks Island Australia	114	C4
Banks Island British Columbia, Canada	118	J5
Banks Island NW.Territories, Canada	119	L1
Banks Islands	111	Q4
Banks Peninsula	115	D5
Banks, Point	118	E4
Banks Strait	113	K7
Ban Kui Nua	93	J6
Bankura	93	G4
Bankya	73	G4
Ban Mae Sariang	93	J5
Banmauk	93	J4
Ban Me Thuot	93	L6
Bann	58	K3
Ban Nabo	93	L5
Ban Na San	93	J7
Bannockburn	108	E4
Bannu	92	D2
Banolas	67	H1
Banovce	71	H4
Ban Pak Chan	93	J6
Ban Sao	93	K5
Banska Bystrica	71	H4
Banska Stiavnica	71	H4
Bansko	73	G5
Banstead	53	G3
Banswara	92	D4
Bantaeng	91	F7
Ban Takua Pa	93	J7
Ban Tan	93	K6
Banteer	59	E8
Ban Tha Sala	93	J7
Bantry	59	D9
Bantry Bay	59	C9
Banya	73	H4
Banyak, Kepulauan	90	B5
Banyo	105	H4
Banyuls	65	E7
Banyuwangi	90	E7
Banzyville	106	D2
Baoding	87	M4
Baofeng	93	M2
Baoji	93	L2
Baoqing	88	D2
Baoshan	93	J4
Baoting	93	L5
Baotou	87	L3
Baoxing	88	C1
Bapatla	92	F5
Bapaume	64	E3
Baqubah	77	L6
Bar Ukraine	73	J1
Bar Yugoslavia	77	E1
Bara	102	F5
Baraawe	107	H2
Barabai	90	F6
Barabinsk	84	B5
Barabinskaya Step	84	B6
Baracoa	133	K4
Baraganul	73	J3
Barahona	133	M5
Barail Range	93	H3
Baraka	96	C8
Barakkul	84	Ae6
Baram	90	E5
Baran	92	E3
Baranavichy	71	L2
Barang, Dasht-i-	95	Q5
Barankul	84	Ae6
Baranof Island	118	H4
Baraoltului, Muntii	73	H2
Barapasai	114	B2
Barat Daya, Kepulauan	91	H7
Barbacena	138	H4
Barbados	133	T6
Barbas, Cap	100	B4
Barbastro	67	G1
Barberton South Africa	108	F5
Barberton U.S.A.	125	K6
Barbezieux	65	C6
Barbuda	133	S6
Barcaldine	113	K3
Barcelona Spain	67	H2
Barcelona Venezuela	136	E2
Barcelonnette	65	G6
Barcelos Brazil	136	E4
Barcelos Portugal	66	B2
Barcin	71	G2
Barcoo	113	J3
Barcs	72	D3
Barda	79	H7
Bardai	102	C3
Bardas Blancas	139	C7
Barddhaman	93	G4
Bardejov	71	J4
Bardneshorn	62	Y12
Bardney	55	J3
Bardsey Island	52	C2
Bareilly	92	E3
Barentsevo More	78	F2
Barentsoya	80	D2
Barents Sea	78	F2
Barentu	103	G4
Bareo	90	F5
Barfleur, Point de	64	C4
Barford	53	F2
Bargennan	57	D5
Barguzinskiy Khrebet	84	H6
Barh	92	G3
Barhaj	92	F3
Barham	53	J3
Bar Harbor	125	R4
Bari	69	F5
Baridi, Ra's	96	C4
Barika	67	J5
Barinas	136	C2
Baring, Cape	119	M1
Baripada	92	G4
Bari Sadri	92	D4
Barisal	93	H4
Barisan, Pegunungan	90	C6
Barito	90	E6
Barka	97	N5
Barkan, Ra's-e	95	J7
Barking	53	H3
Barkley Sound	122	B3
Barkly East	108	E6
Barkly Tableland	113	H2
Barkol	86	F3
Barkston	53	G2
Barle	52	D3
Bar-le-Duc	64	F4
Barlee, Lake	112	D4
Barlestone	53	F2
Barletta	69	F5
Barmby Moor	55	J3
Barmer	92	D3
Barmouth	52	D2
Barnard Castle	55	H2
Barnaul	84	C6
Barnes Ice Cap	120	M3
Barnet	53	G3
Barnhart	127	M5
Barnoldswick	55	G3
Barnsley	55	H3
Barnstaple	52	C3
Barnstaple Bay	52	C3
Baro	105	G4
Baroda	92	D4
Barony, The	56	E1
Barquila	66	D3
Barquinha	66	B3
Barquisimeto	136	D1
Barra Brazil	137	J6
Barra U.K.	57	A4
Barra do Bugres	138	E3
Barra do Corda	137	H5
Barra Head	57	A4
Barra Mansa	138	H4
Barranca Peru	136	B4
Barranca Venezuela	133	L10
Barrancabermeja	136	C2
Barrancas	133	R10
Barrancos	66	C3
Barranqueras	138	E5
Barranquilla	136	C1
Barra, Sound of	57	A3
Barre	125	P4
Barreiras	137	H6
Barreiro	66	B3
Barren Island, Cape	110	L10
Barren Islands	118	E4
Barren River Lake	124	H8
Barretos	138	G4
Barrhead Canada	119	N5
Barrhead U.K.	57	F4
Barrhill	57	D5
Barrie	125	L4
Barrier, Cape	115	E2
Barriere	122	D2
Barrington Tops	113	L5
Barrocao	138	H3
Barrow Argentina	139	D7
Barrow Ireland	59	H8
Barrow U.S.A.	118	D1
Barrowford	55	G3
Barrow Islands	112	D3
Barrow, Point	118	D1
Barrow Range	112	F4
Barrow Strait	120	G3
Barry	52	D3
Barry's Bay	125	M4
Barsalpur	92	D3
Barsi	92	E5
Barstow	126	D3
Bar-sur-Aube	64	F4
Bar-sur-Seine	64	F4
Barth	70	E1
Bartica	136	F2
Bartin	76	E2
Bartle Frere, Mount	113	K2
Bartlesville	128	D2
Barton Philippines	91	F3
Barton U.S.A.	125	P4
Barton-upon-Humber	55	J3
Bartoszyce	71	J1
Barumun	90	C5
Barus	90	B5

Name	Page	Grid
Baruun Urt	87	L2
Barvas	56	B2
Barwani	92	D4
Barwon	113	K4
Barysaw	63	Q9
Barysh	79	H5
Basaidu	95	M8
Basankusu	106	C2
Basco	91	G1
Bascunan, Cabo	138	B5
Basel	68	A2
Basento	69	F5
Bashakerd, Kuhha-ye	95	P8
Bashi Haixia	87	N7
Basht	95	K6
Basilan *Philippines*	91	G4
Basilan *Philippines*	91	G4
Basildon	53	H3
Basingstoke	53	F3
Baskale	77	L3
Baskatong, Reservoir	125	N3
Baskil	77	H3
Baskoy	77	K2
Basle	68	A2
Basoko	106	D2
Bassano del Grappa	68	C3
Bassar	104	F4
Bassas da India	109	G4
Bassein	93	H5
Bassenthwaite	55	F2
Bassenthwaite Lake	55	F2
Basse Santa Su	104	C3
Basseterre	133	R6
Basse Terre	133	S6
Bassett	123	Q6
Bassila	105	F4
Bass Strait	113	K6
Bastad	63	E8
Bastak	95	M8
Bastam	95	M3
Basti	92	F3
Bastia	69	B4
Bastogne	64	F4
Bastrop *Louisiana*	128	G4
Bastrop *Texas*	128	D5
Basyurt	77	J3
Bata	105	G5
Batabano, Golfo de	132	F3
Batagay	85	N3
Batagay-Alyta	85	N3
Batakan	90	E6
Bataklik Golu	76	E4
Batala	92	E2
Batalha	66	B3
Batamay	85	M4
Batan	91	G1
Batang	93	J2
Batangafo	102	C6
Batangas	91	G3
Batanghari	90	C6
Batan Islands	91	G1
Batatais	138	G4
Batavia	125	L5
Bataysk	79	F6
Batchelor	112	G1
Batesville	128	G3
Bath *U.K.*	52	E3
Bath *U.S.A.*	125	M5
Batha	102	C5
Bathgate	57	E5
Bathurst *Australia*	113	K5
Bathurst *Canada*	125	T3
Bathurst *Gambia*	104	B3
Bathurst Inlet	119	P2
Bathurst Island	112	G1
Bathurst Islands	120	F2
Batie	104	E4
Batiki	114	R8
Batinah, Al	97	N4
Batin, Wadi al	96	H2
Batiscan	125	P3
Batitoroslar	76	D4
Batlaq-e Gavkhuni	95	L5
Batley	55	H3
Batman *Turkey*	77	J4
Batman *Turkey*	77	J4
Batna	101	G1
Baton Rouge	128	G5
Batouri	105	H5
Batroun	77	F5
Batsfjord	62	N1
Battambang	93	K6
Batticaloa	92	F7
Battle *Canada*	119	N5
Battle *U.K.*	53	H4
Battle Creek	124	H5
Battle Harbour	121	Q7
Battle Mountain	122	F7
Batu	103	G6
Batubetumbang	90	D6
Batum	77	J2
Batumi	77	J2
Batu Pahat	90	C5
Batuputih	91	F5
Baturaja	90	D6
Baturite	137	K4
Baubau	91	G7
Bauchi	105	G3
Bauda	92	F4
Baudette	124	C2
Baudo	136	B2
Baudouinville	107	E4
Bauge	65	C5
Bauhinia Downs	113	K3
Baukau	91	H7
Bauld, Cape	121	Q7
Baumann Fjord	120	J2
Baunie	113	L4
Baurtregaum	59	C8
Bauru	138	G4
Baus	138	F3
Bautzen	70	F3
Bawdeswell	53	J2
Bawdsey	53	J2
Bawean	90	E7
Bawiti	102	E2
Bawku	104	E3
Bawtry	55	H3
Baxley	129	L5
Bayamo	132	J4
Bayamon	133	P5
Bayan	88	A2
Bayan-Aul	84	B6
Bayandalay	87	J3
Bayanday	84	H6
Bayan Harshan	93	J2
Bayanhongor	86	J2
Bayan Mod	87	J3
Bayan Obo	87	K3
Bayano, Laguna	132	H10
Bayan-Ondor	86	H3
Bayantsagaan	86	H3
Bayantsogt	87	K2
Bayan-Uul	87	L2
Bayard *Nebraska*	123	N7
Bayard *New Mexico*	127	H4
Bayat *Turkey*	76	D3
Bayat *Turkey*	76	F2
Bayburt	77	J2
Bay City *Michigan*	124	J5
Bay City *Texas*	128	E6
Baydaratskaya Guba	84	Ae3
Baydhabo	107	H2
Baydon	53	F3
Bayerischer Wald	70	E4
Bayeux	64	C4
Bayfield	124	E3
Bayhan al Qasab	96	G9
Bayindir	76	B3
Bayir	94	C6
Baykadam	86	B3
Baykal	84	G6
Baykalovo	84	Ae5
Baykal, Ozero	84	H6
Baykan	77	J3
Bay-Khak	84	E6
Baykit	84	F4
Baynunah	97	L5
Bayombong	91	G2
Bayona	66	B1
Bayonne	65	C7
Bayo Point	91	G3
Bayram-Ali	95	R3
Bayramic	76	B3
Bayramiy	94	J2
Bayramtepe	76	C2
Bayreuth	70	D4
Bayrut	76	F6
Bay Saint Louis	128	H5
Bayt al Faqih	96	F9
Baytown	128	E6
Bayy al Kabir, Wadi	101	H2
Baza	66	E4
Bazaliya	71	M4
Bazar-Dyuzi	79	H7
Bazaruto, Ilha do	109	G4
Bazas	65	C6
Bazman	95	Q8
Bazman, Kuh-e-	95	Q7
Bcharre	77	F5
Beach	123	N4
Beachy Head	53	H4
Beaconsfield	53	G3
Beadnell Bay	55	H1
Beagh, Lough	58	G2
Beagle Gulf	112	G1
Beagle Reef	112	E2
Beal	57	G5
Bealanana	109	J2
Beaminster	52	E4
Beampingaratra	109	J4
Bear	122	J6
Beara Peninsula	59	C9
Beardmore	124	G2
Beardstown	124	E6
Bear Island *Canada*	121	K7
Bear Island *Ireland*	59	C9
Bear Lake	122	J7
Bearley	53	F2
Bearn	65	C7
Bear Paw Mount	122	K3
Bearsden	57	D5
Beartooth Range	123	K5
Beata, Cabo	133	M6
Beata, Isla	133	M6
Beatrice	123	R7
Beatty	126	D2
Beattyville	125	M2
Beau Basin	109	L7
Beaucaire	65	F7
Beaufort *Malaysia*	90	F4
Beaufort *U.S.A.*	129	M4
Beaufort Sea	118	H1
Beaufort West	108	D6
Beaugency	65	D2
Beauly *U.K.*	56	D3
Beauly *U.K.*	56	D3
Beauly Firth	56	D3
Beaumaris	54	E3
Beaumont *France*	64	E4
Beaumont *California*	126	D4
Beaumont *Texas*	128	E5
Beaune	65	F5
Beaurepaire	65	F6
Beauvais	64	E4
Beauvoir-sur-Mer	65	B5
Beaver *Saskatchewan, Canada*	119	P5
Beaver *Yukon, Canada*	118	K3
Beaver Dam *Kentucky*	124	G8
Beaver Dam *Wisconsin*	124	F5
Beaverhill Lake	119	N5
Beawar	92	D3
Beazley	139	C6
Bebedouro	138	G4
Bebington	55	F3
Beccles	53	J2
Becej	72	F3
Becerrea	66	C1
Bechar	100	E2
Becharof Lake	118	D4
Bechet	73	G4
Beckingham	55	J3
Beckley	125	K8
Beclean	73	H2
Bedale	55	H2
Bedarieux	65	E7
Bedford *U.K.*	53	G2
Bedford *U.S.A.*	124	G7
Bedford Level	53	H2
Bedfordshire	53	G2
Bedlington	55	H1
Bedwas	52	D3
Bedworth	53	F2
Beer Sheva	94	B6
Beeston	53	F2
Beeswing	57	E5
Beeville	128	D6
Befale	106	D2
Befandriana	109	J3
Begejska Kanal	72	F3
Begoml	63	N10
Behbehan	95	K6
Behraamkale	76	B3
Behshahr	95	L3
Beian	87	P2
Beibu Wan	93	L4
Beihai	93	L4
Beijing	87	M4
Beila	100	B5
Beinn a' Ghlo	57	E4
Beinn Bheigier	57	B5
Beinn Dearg *Highland, U.K.*	56	D3
Beinn Dearg *Tayside, U.K.*	57	E4
Beinn Dorain	57	D4
Beinn Eighe	56	C3
Beinn Fhada	56	C3
Beinn Ime	57	D4
Beinn Mhor	56	A3
Beinn na Caillich	57	C3
Beinn Resipol	57	C4
Beinn Sgritheall	57	C3
Beipiao	87	N3
Beira	109	F3
Beirut	76	F6
Bei Shan	86	H3
Beit Lahm	94	B6
Beius	73	G2
Beja	66	C3
Beja	101	G1
Bejaia	101	G1
Bejaia, Golfe de	67	J4
Bejar	66	D2
Bejestan	95	P4
Beji	92	C3
Bekdast	79	J7
Bekescsaba	73	F2
Bekily	109	J4
Bekopaka	109	H3
Bekwai	104	E4
Bela *India*	92	F3
Bela *Pakistan*	92	C3
Belabo	105	H5
Belaga	90	E5
Belang	91	G5
Bela Palanka	73	G4
Belarus	71	L2
Bela Vista	109	F5
Belawan	90	B5
Belaya *Russia*	78	K4
Belaya *Russia*	85	W3
Belaya-Kalitva	79	G6
Belaya Kholunitsa	78	J4
Belayan	90	F5
Belcher Channel	120	G2
Belcher Islands	121	L6
Belchiragh	94	S4
Belchite	67	F2
Belcoo	58	G4
Belderg	58	C4
Belebey	78	J5
Beledweyne	103	J7
Belem	137	H4
Belen *Turkey*	76	E4
Belen *U.S.A.*	127	J3
Belep, Iles	114	V15
Belesar, Embalse de	66	C1
Belev	79	F5
Belfast *New Zealand*	115	D5
Belfast *U.K.*	58	L3
Belfast Lough	58	L3
Belfield	123	N4
Belford	57	G5
Belfort	65	G5
Belgaum	92	D5
Belgium	64	E3
Belgorod	79	F5
Belgorod-Dnestrovskiy	79	E6
Belgrade	72	F3
Belgrano	141	X3
Belica	71	L2
Beli Lom	73	J4
Beli Manastir	72	E3
Belimbing	90	C7
Belin	65	C6
Belinskiy	79	G5
Belinyu	90	D6
Belitsa	73	G5
Belitung	90	D6
Belize	132	C6
Belkina, Mys	88	F3
Belknap, Mount	122	H8
Belkovskiy, Ostrov	85	P1
Bella Bella	118	K5
Bellac	65	D5
Bella Coola	118	K5
Bellaire	128	E6
Bellary	92	E5
Bella Vista *Argentina*	138	C5
Bella Vista *Argentina*	138	C5
Belleek	58	F4
Bellefontaine	124	J6
Belle Fourche *South Dakota*	123	N5
Belle Fourche *Wyoming*	123	M5
Belle Glade	129	M7
Belle Ile	65	B5
Belle Isle	121	Q7
Belleme	64	D4
Belleville *Canada*	125	M4
Belleville *Illinois*	124	F7
Belleville *Kansas*	123	R8
Bellevue *Idaho*	122	G6
Bellevue *Washington*	122	C4
Belley	65	F6
Bellingham *U.K.*	57	F5
Bellingham *U.S.A.*	122	C3
Bellinghaussen Sea	141	U5
Bellingshaussen	141	W6
Bellinzona	68	B2
Bello	136	B2
Bellona Island	114	J7
Bellona Reefs	111	N6
Bellpuig	67	G2
Bellshill	57	D5
Belluno	68	D2
Bell Ville	138	D6
Belly	122	H3
Belmont	56	A1
Belmonte *Portugal*	66	C2
Belmonte *Spain*	66	E3
Belmopan	132	C6
Belmullet	58	B4
Belogorsk	79	E6
Belogorye	71	M4
Belogradchik	73	G4
Belo Horizonte	138	K4
Beloit	124	F5
Belokorovichi	79	D5
Belomorsk	78	E3
Belorado	66	E1
Belorechensk	79	F7
Beloren	76	E4
Belorusskaya Gryada	71	L2
Belot, Lac	118	K2
Belo-Tsiribihina	109	H3
Belousovka	84	C6
Belovo	84	D6
Beloye More	78	F2
Beloye Ozero	78	F3
Belozersk	78	F4
Belozerskoye	84	Ae5
Belper	55	H3
Belsay	57	G5
Belterra	137	F4
Belton	55	J3
Belturbet	58	H4
Belukha, Gora	86	F2
Belvedere Marittimo	69	E6
Belvidere	124	F5
Belvoir, Vale of	53	G2
Belyando, River	113	K3
Belyayevka	73	L2
Belyy, Ostrov	85	A2
Belyy Yar	84	D5
Belzyce	71	K3
Bemaraha, Plateau du	109	J3
Bembridge	53	F4
Bemidji	124	C3
Benabarre	67	G1
Ben Alder	57	D4
Benalla	113	K6
Benares	92	F3
Benavente	66	D2
Ben Avon	57	E3
Benbaun	59	C5
Ben Chonzie	57	E4
Bencorr	59	C5
Ben Cruachan	57	C4
Bend	122	D5
Bende	105	G4
Bender Qaasim	103	J5
Bendigo	113	J6
Benesov	70	F4
Benevento	69	E5
Bengbu	87	M5
Benghazi	101	K2

Name	Page	Ref
Bengkalis	90	C5
Bengkulu	90	C6
Bengo, Baia do	106	B4
Bengoi	91	J6
Bengtsfors	63	E7
Benguela	106	B5
Benguerua, Ilha	109	G4
Benha	102	F1
Ben Hope	56	D2
Beni *Bolivia*	136	D6
Beni *Zaire*	107	E2
Beni Abbes	100	E2
Benicarlo	67	G2
Benidorm	67	F3
Beni Mazar	102	F2
Beni Mellal	100	D2
Benin	105	F4
Benin, Bight of	105	F4
Benin City	105	G4
Beni Saf	100	E1
Beni Suef	102	F2
Ben Klibreck	56	D2
Ben Lawers	57	D4
Ben Ledi	57	D4
Ben Lomond	57	D4
Ben Loyal	56	D2
Ben Lui	57	D4
Ben Macdui	57	E3
Ben MorCoigach	56	C3
Ben More *Central, U.K.*	57	D4
Ben More *Strathclyde, U.K.*	56	B4
Ben More Assynt	56	D2
Benmore, Lake	115	C6
Bennachie	56	F3
Benn Cleuch	57	E4
Bennetta, Ostrov	85	R1
Ben Nevis	57	C4
Bennington	125	P5
Benoni	108	E5
Be, Nosy	109	J2
Ben Rinnes	56	E3
Bensheim	70	C4
Benson *U.K.*	53	F3
Benson *U.K.*	126	G5
Ben Starav	57	C4
Bent	95	P8
Bentinck Island	93	J6
Bent Jbail	94	B5
Bentley	55	H3
Benton	128	F3
Benton Harbor	124	G5
Bentung	90	C5
Benue	105	G4
Ben Venue	57	D4
Ben Vorlich	57	D4
Benwee	58	C5
Benwee Head	58	C4
Ben Wyvis	56	D3
Benxi	87	N3
Beo	91	H5
Beograd	72	F3
Beppu	89	C9
Beqa	114	R9
Berat	74	E2
Berau, Teluk	114	A2
Berber	103	F4
Berbera	103	J5
Berberati	102	C7
Berck	64	D3
Berdichev	79	D6
Berdigestyakh	85	M4
Berdyansk	79	F6
Berea	124	H8
Bereeda	103	K5
Beregovo	79	C6
Berens	119	R5
Berens River	119	R5
Bere Regis	52	E4
Berettyo	73	F2
Berettyoujfalu	73	F2
Bereza	71	L2
Berezhany	71	L4
Berezhnykh, Mys	85	Q1
Berezina	78	D5
Berezino	78	D5
Berezna	79	E5
Berezniki	78	K4
Berezno	71	M3
Berezovka *Russia*	78	K3
Berezovka *Russia*	85	K5
Berezovka *Russia*	85	T3
Berezovka *Ukraine*	79	E6
Berezovo *Russia*	84	Ae4
Berezovo *Russia*	85	W4
Berezovskaya	85	K5
Berg	108	C6
Berga	67	G1
Bergama	76	B3
Bergamo	68	B3
Bergeforsen	62	G5
Bergen *Germany*	70	E1
Bergen *Norway*	63	J6
Bergen op Zoom	64	F3
Bergerac	65	D6
Bergfors	62	H2
Bergisch-Gladbach	70	B3
Bergsviken	62	J4
Berhala, Selat	90	C6
Beringa, Ostrov	81	T4
Bering Glacier	118	G3
Beringovskiy	85	X4
Bering Sea	143	H3
Bering Strait	118	B2
Berislav	79	E6

Name	Page	Ref
Beris, Ra's	95	Q9
Berja	66	E4
Berkak	62	C5
Berkakit	85	L5
Berkeley *U.K.*	52	E3
Berkeley *U.S.A.*	126	A2
Berkhamsted	53	G3
Berkner Island	141	W3
Berkovitsa	73	G4
Berkshire	53	F3
Berkshire Downs	53	F3
Berkshire Mountains	125	P5
Berlevag	62	N2
Berlin *Germany*	70	E2
Berlin *U.S.A.*	125	Q4
Bermeja, Sierra	66	D4
Bermejo *Argentina*	138	C6
Bermejo *Argentina*	138	D4
Bermeo	66	E1
Bermillo de Sayago	66	C2
Bermuda	117	N5
Bern	68	A2
Bernau	70	E2
Bernay	64	D4
Bernburg	70	D3
Berne	68	A2
Berner Alpen	68	A2
Berneray *U.K.*	57	A4
Berneray *U.K.*	56	A3
Bernina, Piz	68	B2
Beroroha	109	J4
Berounka	70	E4
Berre, Etang de	65	F7
Berriedale	56	E2
Berriedale Water	56	E2
Berrigan	113	K6
Berringarra	112	D4
Berry *Australia*	113	L5
Berry *France*	65	E5
Berryessa, Lake	122	C8
Berry Head	52	D4
Berry Islands	132	J1
Bershad	73	K1
Berthoud Pass	123	L8
Bertoua	105	H5
Beru	111	S2
Beruri	136	E4
Berwick	125	M6
Berwick-upon-Tweed	57	F5
Berwyn Mountains	52	D2
Berzence	72	D2
Besalampy	109	H3
Besancon	65	G5
Besar, Kai	91	J7
Besbre	65	E5
Beshneh	95	M7
Besiri	77	J4
Beskidy Zachodnie	71	H4
Beslan	79	G7
Besni	77	G4
Bessarabia	73	K2
Bessarabka	73	K2
Bessbrook	58	K4
Bessemer *Alabama*	129	J4
Bessemer *Winconsin*	124	F3
Bestamak *Kazakhstan*	86	D2
Bestamak *Kazakhstan*	79	K6
Bestobe	84	A6
Bestuzhevo	78	G3
Betafo	109	J3
Betanzos	66	B1
Betare Oya	105	H4
Bethal	108	E5
Bethanie	108	C5
Bethany	124	C6
Bethel	118	C3
Bethel Park	125	L6
Bethesda *U.K.*	54	E3
Bethesda *U.S.A.*	125	M7
Bethlehem *Israel*	94	B6
Bethlehem *South Africa*	108	E5
Bethulie	108	E6
Bethune *France*	64	D4
Bethune *France*	64	E3
Betioky	109	H4
Betpak-Dala	86	B2
Bet-Pak-Data	86	B2
Betroka	109	J4
Betsiamites	125	R2
Betsiboka	109	J3
Bettiah	92	F3
Bettyhill	56	D2
Betul	92	E4
Betwa	92	E4
Betws-y-coed	54	F3
Beuvron	65	D5
Beverley *Australia*	112	D5
Beverley *U.K.*	55	J3
Beverly Hills	126	C3
Bexhill	53	H4
Beykoz	76	C2
Beyla	104	D4
Beylul	96	F10
Beyneu	79	K6
Beypazari	76	D2
Beypinar	77	G3
Beysehir	76	D4
Beysehir Golu	76	D4
Beyton	53	H2
Beytussebap	77	K4
Bezhetsk	78	F4
Beziers	65	E7
Bezmein	95	P2

Name	Page	Ref
Bhadgaon	92	G3
Bhadrachalam	92	F5
Bhadrakh	92	G4
Bhadravati	92	E6
Bhagalpur	92	G3
Bhakkar	92	D2
Bhamo	93	J4
Bhandara	92	E4
Bhanrer Range	92	F4
Bharatpur *Pradesh, India*	92	F4
Bharatpur *Rajasthan, India*	92	E3
Bharuch	92	D4
Bhatinda	92	D2
Bhatpara	93	G4
Bhavnagar	92	D4
Bhawanipatna	92	F5
Bhilwara	92	D3
Bhima	92	E5
Bhiwani	92	E3
Bhopal	92	E4
Bhopalpatnam	92	F5
Bhor	92	D5
Bhubaneshwar	92	G4
Bhuj	92	C4
Bhumiphol Dam	93	J5
Bhusawal	92	E4
Bhutan	93	G3
Bia	136	D4
Biaban	95	N8
Biabanak	95	S5
Biak	114	B2
Biala Podlaska	71	K2
Bialobrzegi	71	J3
Bialowieza	71	K2
Bialystok	71	K2
Bianco	69	F6
Biankouma	104	D4
Biaro	91	H5
Biarritz	65	C7
Biasca	68	B2
Biba	102	F2
Bibai	88	H4
Bibala	106	B5
Bibby Island	119	S3
Biberach	70	C4
Bibury	53	F3
Bicester	53	F3
Bicheno	113	K7
Bickle Knob	125	L7
Bida	105	G4
Bidar	92	E5
Biddeford	125	Q5
Biddulph	55	G3
Bidean Nam Bian	57	C4
Bideford	52	C3
Bideford Bay	52	C3
Bidford-on-Avon	53	F2
Bidokht	95	P4
Bidzhan *Russia*	88	C1
Bidzhan *Russia*	88	C2
Biebrza	71	K2
Biel	68	A2
Bielefeld	70	C2
Biella	68	B3
Bielsko-Biala	71	H4
Bielsk Podlaski	71	K2
Bien Hoa	93	L6
Bienne	68	A2
Bienveneu	137	G3
Bienville, Lac	121	M6
Biferno	69	E5
Biga	76	B2
Bigadic	76	C3
Big Bay	114	T11
Big Belt Mountains	122	J4
Big Blue	123	R7
Bigbury Bay	52	D4
Biggar *Canada*	123	K1
Biggar *U.K.*	57	E5
Biggleswade	53	G2
Big Horn	123	K5
Big Horn Mountains	123	L5
Big Island	120	M5
Big Pine	126	C2
Big Piney	123	J6
Big Sheep Mountains	123	L4
Big Sioux	123	R5
Big Snowy Mount	122	K4
Big Spring	127	M4
Big Stone Gap	124	J8
Big Timber	123	J5
Big Trout Lake	119	T4
Bihac	72	C3
Bihar	92	G4
Bihar	92	G3
Biharamulo	107	F3
Bihoro	88	K4
Bihu	87	M6
Bijagos, Arquipelago dos	104	B3
Bijapur	92	E5
Bijar	94	H4
Bijeljina	72	E3
Bijelo Polje	72	E4
Bijie	93	L3
Bijnor	92	E3
Bikaner	92	D3
Bikin *Russia*	88	E2
Bikin *Russia*	88	F2
Bikoro	106	C3
Bilad Bani Bu Ali	97	P5
Bilad Ghamid	96	E6
Bilad Zahran	96	E6
Bilaspur	92	F4
Bila Tserkva	79	E6

Name	Page	Ref
Bilauktaung Range	93	J6
Bilbao	66	E1
Bilchir	85	J6
Bilecik	76	C2
Biled	73	F3
Bile Karpaty	71	G4
Bilesha Plain	107	H2
Bilgoraj	71	K3
Bili	106	E2
Bilin	93	J5
Billabalong	112	D4
Billericay	53	H3
Billingham	55	H2
Billings	123	K5
Billingshurst	53	G3
Bilma	101	H5
Bilma, Grand Erg de	101	H5
Biloela	113	L3
Bilo Gora	72	D3
Biloxi	128	H5
Biltine	102	D5
Bilugyun	93	J5
Binalud, Kuh-e	95	P3
Binatang	90	E5
Binder	87	L2
Bindloe Island	136	A7
Bindura	108	F3
Binefar	67	G2
Binga	108	E3
Bingara	113	L4
Bingerville	104	E4
Bingham	125	R4
Binghamton	125	N5
Bingley	55	H3
Bingol	77	J3
Bingol Daglari	77	J3
Binjai *Indonesia*	90	B5
Binjai *Indonesia*	90	D5
Binongko	91	G7
Bintan	90	C5
Bintuhan	90	C6
Bintulu	90	E5
Bin Xian *Heilongjiang, China*	88	A3
Bin Xian *Shaanxi, China*	93	L2
Binyang	93	L4
Bio	114	K7
Biobio	139	B7
Biograd	72	C4
Bioko	105	G5
Bir	92	E5
Bira *Russia*	88	D1
Bira *Russia*	88	D1
Bira *Russia*	85	P7
Birag, Kuh-e	95	Q8
Birak	101	H3
Bir al Hisw	96	E4
Bir al War	101	H4
Birao	102	D5
Biratnagar	93	G3
Bir Butayman	77	H4
Birca	73	G4
Birch Island	122	D2
Birch Mountains	119	N4
Bird	119	S4
Bird Island	133	R7
Birdlip	53	E2
Birdum	113	G2
Birecik	77	G4
Bireun	90	B4
Bir Fardan	97	J5
Bir Ghabalou	67	H4
Bir Hadi	97	K7
Birhan	103	G5
Birikchul	84	D6
Birjand	95	P5
Birkenhead *New Zealand*	115	E2
Birkenhead *U.K.*	55	F3
Birksgate Range	112	F4
Birlad *Romania*	73	J2
Birlad *Romania*	73	J2
Birlestik	86	B2
Birmingham *U.K.*	53	F2
Birmingham *U.S.A.*	129	J4
Bir Moghrein	100	C3
Birnie Island	111	U2
Birnin Kebbi	105	F3
Birni nKonni	101	G6
Birobidzhan	88	D1
Birofeld	88	D1
Birr	59	G6
Bir, Ras el	103	H5
Birreencorragh	58	C5
Birrimbah	112	G2
Birsk	78	K4
Birtle	123	P2
Birtley	55	H2
Biryusa	84	F5
Birzai	63	L8
Biscay, Bay of	65	B6
Bischofshofen	68	D2
Biscotasi Lake	124	J3
Bisert	78	K4
Bisevo	72	D4
Bisha	96	C9
Bishah, Wadi	96	F6
Bishkek	86	C3
Bishnupur	93	G4
Bishop	126	C2
Bishop Auckland	55	H2
Bishop Burton	55	J3
Bishop's Castle	52	D2
Bishops Falls	121	Q8
Bishop's Stortford	53	H3
Bishri, Jbel	77	H5

Name	Page	Grid
Biskra	101	G2
Biskupiec	71	J2
Bislig	91	H4
Bismarck Archipelago	114	D2
Bismarck Range	114	D3
Bismark	123	P4
Bismil	77	J4
Bismo	63	C6
Bisotun	94	H4
Bispfors	62	G5
Bissau	104	B3
Bissett	123	S2
Bistcho Lake	119	M4
Bistretu	73	G4
Bistrita *Romania*	73	H2
Bistrita *Romania*	73	J2
Bistritei, Muntii	73	H2
Bitburg	70	B3
Bitche	64	G4
Bitik	79	J5
Bitkine	102	C5
Bitlis	77	K3
Bitola	73	F5
Bitonto	69	F5
Bitterfontein	108	C6
Bitterroot	122	G4
Bitterroot Range	122	G4
Bitti	69	B5
Biu	105	H3
Bivolu	73	H2
Biwa-ko	89	E8
Biyad, Al	96	H5
Biyagundi	96	C9
Biysk	84	D6
Bizerta	69	B7
Bizerte	101	G1
Bjargtangar	62	S12
Bjelovar	72	D3
Bjerkvik	62	L2
Bjorklinge	63	G6
Bjorksele	62	H4
Bjorna	62	H5
Bjorneborg *Finland*	63	J6
Bjorneborg *Sweden*	63	F7
Bjornevatn	62	N2
Bjornoya	80	C2
Bjurholm	62	H5
Bjursas	63	F6
Bla Bheinn	56	B3
Black *Alaska*	118	G2
Black *Arizona*	127	H4
Black *Arkansas*	128	G3
Black *New York*	125	N5
Blackadder Water	57	F5
Blackall	113	K3
Black Bay	124	F2
Black Belt	129	J4
Blackburn	55	G3
Black Canyon City	126	F3
Blackdown Hills	52	D4
Blackfoot	122	H6
Blackford	57	E4
Black Head	59	D6
Blackhead Bay	59	D6
Blackhill	55	H3
Black Hills	123	N5
Black Isle	56	D3
Black Mesa	126	G2
Blackmill	52	D3
Black Mountain	52	D3
Black Mountains	52	D3
Blackpool	55	F3
Black Range	127	J4
Black River Falls	124	E4
Blackrock	58	K5
Black Rock Desert	122	E7
Black Sea	51	P7
Blacksod Bay	58	B4
Blackstairs Mount	59	J7
Blackstairs Mountains	59	J7
Blackthorn	53	F3
Black Volta	104	E4
Black Water	57	E4
Blackwater *Australia*	113	K3
Blackwater *Meath, Ireland*	58	J5
Blackwater *Waterford, Ireland*	59	F8
Blackwater *Essex, U.K.*	53	H3
Blackwater *Hampshire, U.K.*	53	G3
Blackwaterfoot	57	C5
Blackwater Lake	119	L3
Blackwater Reservoir *Highland, U.K.*	57	D4
Blackwater Reservoir *Tayside, U.K.*	57	E4
Blackwell	128	D2
Blackwood	112	D5
Blaenavon	52	D3
Blafjall	62	W12
Blagodarnyy	79	G6
Blagoevgrad	73	G4
Blagoveshchensk *Russia*	78	K4
Blagoveshchensk *Russia*	85	M6
Blagoyevo	78	H3
Blair Atholl	57	E4
Blairgowrie	57	E4
Blaka	101	H4
Blakely	129	K5
Blakeney	53	J2
Blakesley	53	F2
Blanca, Bahia	139	D7
Blanca, Costa	67	F3
Blanca Peak	127	K2
Blanca, Punta	126	E6
Blanca, Sierra	127	K4
Blanc, Cap	69	B7
Blanche Channel	114	H6
Blanche, Lake	113	H4
Blanchland	55	G2
Blanc, Mont	65	G6
Blanco	136	E7
Blanco, Cabo	139	C9
Blanco, Cape	122	B6
Blanda	62	V12
Blandford Forum	53	E4
Blanes	67	H2
Blangy	64	D4
Blankenberge	64	E3
Blanquilla, Isla	136	E1
Blantyre	107	G6
Blarney	59	E9
Blasket Islands	59	A8
Blavet	65	B5
Blaydon	55	H2
Blaye	65	C6
Bleadon	52	E3
Bleaklow Hill	55	H3
Bled	72	C2
Blekinge	63	F8
Bletchley	53	G3
Bleus, Monts	107	F2
Blida	101	F1
Bligh Water	114	R8
Blind River	124	J3
Blisworth	53	G2
Block Island	125	Q6
Bloemfontein	108	E5
Blois	65	D5
Blonduos	62	U12
Bloodvein	123	R2
Bloody Foreland	58	F2
Bloomfield	124	D6
Bloomington *Illinois*	124	F6
Bloomington *Indiana*	124	G7
Bloomington *Minnesota*	124	D4
Bloomsbury	113	K3
Blouberg	108	E4
Blubberhouses	55	H3
Bludenz	68	B2
Bluefield	125	K8
Bluefields	132	F9
Blue Mountain Lake	125	N5
Blue Mountain Peak	132	J5
Blue Mountains	122	E5
Bluemull Sound	56	A1
Bluenose Lake	119	M2
Blue Ridge	129	K3
Blue Ridge Mountains	129	L3
Blue Stack	58	F3
Blue Stack Mountains	58	F3
Bluff *New Zealand*	115	B7
Bluff *U.S.A.*	127	H2
Bluff Knoll	112	D5
Bluff Point	112	C4
Bluff, Punta	126	F6
Blumenau	138	G5
Blunt	123	Q5
Blyth *Northumberland, U.K.*	55	H1
Blyth *Nottinghamshire, U.K.*	55	H3
Blyth *Suffolk, U.K.*	53	J2
Blythe	126	E4
Blythe Bridge	53	E2
Blytheville	128	H3
Bo	104	C4
Boac	91	G3
Boa Fe	136	C5
Boa Vista *Cape Verde*	104	L7
Boa Vista *Amazonas, Brazil*	136	D4
Boa Vista *Roraima, Brazil*	136	E3
Bobai	93	M4
Bobaomby, Tanjoni	109	J2
Bobbili	92	F5
Bobbio	68	B3
Bobo Dioulasso	104	E3
Bobolice	71	G2
Bobr	70	F3
Bobrinents	79	E6
Bobrka	71	L4
Bobrov	79	G5
Bobures	133	M10
Boca del Pao	136	E2
Boca do Acre	136	D5
Boca Grande	136	E2
Bocaiuva	138	H3
Boca Mavaca	136	D3
Bocaranga	102	C6
Boca Raton	129	M7
Bochnia	71	J4
Bocholt	70	B3
Bochum	70	B3
Bodalla	113	L6
Bodaybo	85	J5
Boddam	56	A2
Boden	62	J4
Bodensee	70	C5
Bodhan	92	E5
Bodmin	52	C4
Bodmin Moor	52	C4
Bodo	62	F3
Bodrum	76	B4
Bodva	71	J4
Bodza, Pasul	73	J3
Boen	65	F6
Boende	106	D3
Boffa	104	C3
Bogalusa	128	H5
Bogan	113	K5
Bogaz	76	E2
Bogazkale	76	F2
Bogazkaya	77	F2
Bogazkopru	76	F3
Bogazliyan	76	F3
Bogbonga	106	C2
Bogen	62	L2
Boggeragh Mountains	59	E8
Boghar	67	H5
Bogia	114	D2
Bognes	62	G2
Bognor Regis	53	G4
Bogo	91	G3
Bogodukhov	79	F5
Bogong, Mount	113	K6
Bogor	90	D7
Bogorodchany	71	L4
Bogorodskoye *Russia*	78	K4
Bogorodskoye *Russia*	85	Q6
Bogota	136	C3
Bogotol	84	D5
Bogra	93	G4
Boguchany	84	F5
Boguchar	79	G6
Bogue	100	C5
Bogue Chitto	128	G5
Boguslav	79	E6
Bo Hai	87	K4
Bohemia	70	E4
Bohmer Wald	70	E4
Bohol	91	G4
Bohol Sea	91	G4
Boiano	69	E5
Boigul	114	C3
Boipeba, Ilha	137	K6
Bois Blanc Island	124	H4
Boisdale, Loch	57	A3
Boise *U.S.A.*	122	F6
Boise *U.S.A.*	122	F6
Boise City	127	L2
Bois, Lac des	118	K2
Boissevain	123	P3
Boizenburg	70	D2
Bojana	74	E2
Bojnurd	95	N3
Boka	73	F3
Boka Kotorska	72	E4
Boke	104	C3
Bokhara	113	K4
Boknafjord	63	A7
Bokol	107	G2
Bokoro	102	C5
Boksitogorsk	78	E4
Boktor	85	P6
Bokungu	106	D3
Bolama	104	B3
Bolanos	130	H7
Bolan Pass	92	C3
Bolbec	64	D4
Bolchary	84	Ae5
Bole	104	E4
Boleslawiec	70	F3
Bolgatanga	104	E3
Bolgrad	79	D6
Boli	88	C3
Bolia	106	C3
Boliden	62	J4
Bolinao	91	F2
Bol Irgiz	79	H5
Bolivar	139	D7
Bolivar *Missouri*	124	D8
Bolivar *Tennessee*	128	H3
Bolivar, Cerro	133	R11
Bolivar, Pico	133	M10
Bolivia	138	C3
Boljevac	73	F4
Bolkhov	79	F5
Bollington	55	G3
Bollnas	63	G6
Bollon	113	K4
Bollstabruk	62	G5
Bolmen	63	E8
Bolobo	106	C3
Bologna	68	C3
Bologoye	78	E4
Bolotnoye	84	C5
Boloven, Cao Nguyen	93	L5
Bolsena, Lago di	69	C4
Bolsherechye	84	A5
Bolsheretsk	85	T6
Bolshevik	85	R4
Bolshevik, Ostrov	81	M2
Bolshezemelskaya Tundra	78	K2
Bolshoy Anyuy	85	U3
Bolshoy Atlym	84	Ae4
Bolshoy Balkhan, Khrebet	95	M2
Bolshoy Begichev, Ostrov	84	J2
Bolshoy Chernigovka	79	J5
Bolshoy Kavkaz	77	L1
Bolshoy Kunyak	84	A5
Bolshoy Lyakhovskiy, Ostrov	85	Q2
Bolshoy Murta	84	E5
Bolshoy Pit	84	E5
Bolshoy Porog	84	E3
Bolshoy Shantar, Ostrov	85	P5
Bolshoy Usa	78	K4
Bolshoy Yenisey	84	E6
Bolshoy Yugan	84	A5
Bolsover	55	H3
Boltana	67	G1
Bolt Head	52	D4
Bolton *Greater Manchester, U.K.*	55	G3
Bolton *Northumberland, U.K.*	57	G5
Bolu	76	D2
Bolucan	77	G3
Bolus Head	59	B9
Bolvadin	76	D3
Bolyarovo	73	J4
Bolzano	68	C2
Bom	114	D3
Boma	106	B4
Bombala	113	K6
Bombay (Mumbai)	92	D5
Bomili	106	E2
Bom Jesus	137	J5
Bom Jesus da Lapa	137	J6
Bomlafjord	63	A7
Bomlo	63	A7
Bomongo	106	C2
Bonab	94	H3
Bonaire	133	N8
Bonaire Trench	133	N9
Bona, Mount	118	G3
Bonar Bridge	56	D3
Bonavista	121	R8
Bonavista Bay	121	R8
Bon, Cap	101	H1
Bondo	106	D2
Bondokodi	91	F7
Bondoukou	104	E4
Bone	69	A7
Bo'ness	57	E4
Bonete, Cerro	138	C5
Bone, Teluk	91	G6
Bongabong	91	G3
Bongor	102	C5
Bonham	128	D4
Bonifacio	69	B5
Bonifacio, Strait of	69	B5
Bonn	70	B3
Bonners Ferry	122	F3
Bonnetable	64	D4
Bonneval	64	D4
Bonneville	65	G5
Bonneville Salt Flats	122	H7
Bonnie Rock	112	D5
Bonny *France*	65	E5
Bonny *Nigeria*	105	G5
Bonnyrigg	57	E5
Bono	69	B5
Bonobono	91	F4
Bonorva	69	B5
Bonthe	104	C4
Bontoc	91	G2
Booligal	113	J5
Boologooro	112	C3
Boone *Iowa*	124	D5
Boone *N. Carolina*	129	M2
Booneville *Mississippi*	128	H3
Booneville *New York*	125	N5
Booroorban	113	J5
Boosaaso	103	J5
Boothia, Gulf of	120	J4
Boothia Peninsula	120	H3
Bootle	55	F3
Boot Reefs	114	C3
Bopeechee	113	H4
Boquilla, Presa de la	127	K7
Boquillas del Carmen	127	L6
Bor *Sudan*	102	F6
Bor *Turkey*	76	F4
Bor *Yugoslavia*	73	G3
Boraha, Nosy	109	J3
Borah Peak	122	H5
Boras	63	E8
Borasambar	92	F4
Borazjan	95	K7
Borba	136	F4
Borborema, Planalto da	137	K5
Borca	73	H2
Borcka	77	J2
Bordeaux	65	C6
Borden Island	120	D2
Borden Peninsula	120	K3
Borders	57	F5
Bordertown	113	J6
Bordeyri	62	U12
Bordj-Bou-Arreridj	67	J4
Bordj Bounaama	67	G5
Bordj Omar Driss	101	G3
Borensberg	63	F7
Boreray	56	A3
Borga	63	L6
Borgarnes	62	U12
Borgefjellet	62	E4
Borger	127	M3
Borgholm	63	G8
Borgo San Lorenzo	68	C4
Borgosesia	68	B3
Borgo Val di Taro	68	B3
Borgo Valsugana	68	C2
Borislav	71	K4
Borisoglebsk	79	G5
Borispol	79	E5
Borja	67	F2
Borkovskaya	78	H2
Borkum	70	B2
Borlange	63	F6
Borlu	76	C3
Bormida	68	B3
Bormio	68	C2
Borneo	90	E5
Bornholm	70	F1
Bornholmsgattet	63	F9
Bornova	76	B3
Borohoro Shan	86	E3
Boroko	91	G5
Boromo	104	E3
Boronga Islands	93	H5
Borongan	91	H3

Caherciveen 59 B9
Caherconlish 59 F7
Cahir 59 G8
Cahore Point 59 K7
Cahors 65 D6
Caia 109 G3
Caiaponia 138 F3
Caibarien 132 H3
Cai Be 93 L6
Caicos Islands 133 M4
Caicos Passage 133 L3
Cairndow 57 D4
Cairn Gorm 57 E3
Cairngorm Mountains 57 E3
Cairnryan 54 D2
Cairns 113 K2
Cairn Water 57 E5
Cairo *Egypt* 102 F1
Cairo *U.S.A.* 124 F8
Caiundo 106 C6
Caiwarro 113 J4
Cajamarca 136 B5
Cajapio 137 J4
Cajatambo 136 B6
Cajati 138 G4
Cajazeiras 137 K5
Cakiralan 77 F2
Cakirgol Dagi 77 H2
Cal 76 C3
Cal 103 J5
Cala 73 G2
Calabar 105 G5
Calabozo 136 D2
Calafat 73 G4
Calafate 139 B10
Calafell 67 G2
Calagua Islands 91 G3
Calahorra 67 F1
Calais *France* 64 D3
Calais *U.S.A.* 125 S4
Calama 138 C4
Calamar *Colombia* 136 C1
Calamar *Colombia* 136 C3
Calamian Group 91 G3
Calamocha 67 F2
Calandula 106 C4
Calang 90 B5
Calapan 91 G3
Calarasi 73 J3
Calatayud 67 F2
Calatele 73 G2
Calatrava, Campo de 66 E3
Calau 70 F3
Calavite, Cape 91 G3
Calayan 91 G2
Calbayog 91 G3
Calcanhar, Ponta do 137 K5
Calcasieu 128 F5
Calcasieu Lake 128 F6
Calcutta 93 G4
Caldararu 73 H3
Caldas da Rainha 66 B3
Caldbeck 55 F2
Caldeirao, Sierra do 66 B4
Calder 55 H3
Caldera 138 B5
Caldew 55 G2
Caldicot 52 E3
Caldiran 77 K3
Caldwell 122 F6
Caledon 108 E6
Calella de la Costa 67 H2
Caleta Lobos 138 C4
Caleta Olivia 139 C9
Calexico 126 E4
Calf of Man 54 E2
Calfsound 56 F1
Calgary 122 G2
Cali 136 B3
Caliach Point 57 B4
Calicut 92 E6
Calienta 126 E2
California 126 B1
California, Golfo de 126 G7
Calimani, Muntii 73 H2
Calimere, Point 92 E6
Calingasta 139 C6
Calino 75 J4
Calitri 69 E5
Callabonna, Lake 113 J4
Callan 59 H7
Callander 57 D4
Callao 136 B6
Callington 52 C4
Calne 53 E3
Caloosahatchee 129 M7
Calpe 67 G3
Calpulalpan 131 K8
Caltagirone 69 E7
Caltanissetta 69 E7
Caltilbuk 76 C3
Calulo 106 B5
Caluula 103 K5
Caluula, Raas 103 K5
Calvados Chain, The 114 T10
Calvert 113 H2
Calvert Hills 113 H2
Calvert Island 118 K5
Calvi 69 B4
Calvinia 108 C6
Calvo, Monte 69 E6
Cam 53 G2
Camabatela 106 C4
Camacupa 106 C5
Camaguey 132 J4
Camaguey, Archipielago de 132 H3
Camalan 76 F4
Camana 138 B3
Camaqua 138 F6
Camardi 76 F4
Camaron, Cabo 132 E7
Camarones 139 C8
Camaross 59 J8
Camas 122 C5
Camatindi 138 D4
Cambados 66 B1
Camberley 53 G3
Cambodia 93 K6
Cambo-les-Bains 65 C7
Camborne 52 B4
Cambrai 64 E3
Cambrian Mountains 52 D2
Cambridge *New Zealand* 115 E2
Cambridge *U.K.* 52 H2
Cambridge *Maryland* 125 M7
Cambridge *Massachusetts* 125 Q5
Cambridge *Minnesota* 124 D4
Cambridge *Ohio* 125 K6
Cambridge Bay 119 Q2
Cambridge Gulf 112 F1
Cambridgeshire 53 G2
Cambrils 67 G2
Cambundi-Catembo 106 C5
Camden *Arkansas* 128 F4
Camden *New Jersey* 125 N7
Camden *S. Carolina* 129 M3
Cameia 106 D5
Camelford 52 C4
Cameli 76 C4
Camerino 68 D4
Cameron *Arizona* 126 G3
Cameron *Missouri* 124 C7
Cameron *Texas* 128 D5
Cameron Hills 119 M4
Cameron Island 120 F2
Cameron Mountains 115 A7
Cameroon 105 H4
Cameroun, Mont 105 G5
Cameta 137 H4
Camiguin *Philippines* 91 G2
Camiguin *Philippines* 91 G4
Camilla 129 K5
Caminha 66 B2
Camiri 138 D4
Camissombo 106 D4
Camlidere 76 E2
Camlidere 77 H4
Camlihemsin 77 J2
Camliyayla 76 F4
Camocim 137 J4
Camooweal 113 H2
Camorta 93 H7
Campana 139 E6
Campana, Isla 139 A9
Campanario 138 H3
Campanario *Argentina* 139 B7
Campanario *Spain* 66 D3
Campbell 108 D5
Campbell, Cape 115 E4
Campbell Island 141 M8
Campbellpore 92 D2
Campbell River 122 B2
Campbellsville 124 H8
Campbellton 125 S3
Campbelltown 113 L5
Campbeltown 57 C5
Campeche 131 P8
Campeche, Bahia de 131 N8
Camperdown 113 J6
Campillo de Arenas 66 E4
Campillos 66 D4
Campina Grande 137 K5
Campinas 138 G4
Campo 105 G5
Campoalegre 136 B3
Campobasso 69 E5
Campo de Diauarum 137 G6
Campo Grande 138 F4
Campo Maior *Brazil* 137 J4
Campo Maior *Portugal* 66 C3
Campo Mourao 138 F4
Campos *Bahia, Brazil* 137 J6
Campos *Rio de Janeiro, Brazil* 138 H4
Campos del Puerto 67 H3
Campos Sales 137 J5
Campos, Tierra de 66 D1
Campsie Fells 57 D4
Camrose 119 N5
Can 76 B2
Canada 116 F5
Canada de Gomez 138 D6
Canadian 127 M3
Canadian Shield 116 K3
Canakkale 76 B2
Canakkale Bogazi 76 B2
Canala 114 W16
Canal Casiquiare 136 D3
Canal Cockburn 139 B10
Cananea 126 G5
Canarias, Islas 100 B3
Canarreos, Archipielago de los 132 G4
Canary Islands 100 B3
Canastota 125 N5
Canaveral, Cape 129 M6
Canaveras 66 E2
Canberra 113 K6
Cancarli 76 B3
Candarli Korfezi 75 J3
Cande 65 C5
Candelaria 131 P8
Candia 75 H5
Candir 76 E2
Cando 123 Q3
Canea 75 H5
Canelones 139 E6
Canete 67 F2
Caney 128 E2
Cangallo 136 C6
Cangamba 106 C5
Cangas de Narcea 66 C1
Cangas de Onis 66 D1
Canguaretama 137 K5
Cangucu 138 F6
Cangzhou 87 M4
Caniapiscau *Canada* 121 N7
Caniapiscau *Canada* 121 N6
Caniapiscau, Lac 121 N7
Canicatti 69 D7
Canik Daglari 77 G2
Canisp 56 C2
Canjayar 66 E4
Cankaya 76 E3
Cankiri 76 E2
Canna 57 B3
Cannanore 92 E6
Canna, Sound of 57 B3
Cannes 65 G7
Cannich *U.K.* 56 D3
Cannich *U.K.* 56 D3
Canning 118 F2
Canning Basin 112 E2
Cannington 52 D3
Cannock 53 E2
Cann River 113 K6
Canoas 138 F5
Canoas 138 F5
Canoeiros 138 G3
Canoe Lake 119 P4
Canon City 127 K1
Canosa di Puglia 69 F5
Canta 136 B6
Cantabrica, Cordillera 66 D1
Cantabrico, Mar 66 D1
Cantanhede 66 B2
Canterbury 53 J3
Canterbury Bight 115 D6
Canterbury Plains 115 C6
Can Tho 93 L6
Canton *China* 93 M4
Canton *Illinois* 124 E6
Canton *Mississippi* 128 H4
Canton *New York* 125 N4
Canton *Ohio* 125 K6
Canton *S. Dakota* 123 R6
Canudos *Amazonas, Brazil* 136 F5
Canudos *Bahia, Brazil* 137 K5
Canuma 136 F4
Canutama 136 E5
Canvey Island 53 H3
Canyon 127 M3
Cao Bang 93 L4
Caombo 106 C4
Capanaparo 136 D2
Capanema 137 H4
Capao Bonito 138 G4
Capatarida 136 C1
Cap de la Madeleine 125 P3
Cape Breton Island 121 P8
Cape Coast 104 E4
Cape Coral 129 M7
Cape Dorset 120 L5
Cape Dyer 120 P4
Cape Egmont 115 D3
Cape Girardeau 124 F8
Capel 53 G3
Capelinha 138 H3
Capella 114 C2
Cape Town 108 C6
Cape Verde 104 L7
Cape York Peninsula 113 J1
Cap-Haitien 133 L5
Capim 137 H4
Capitan Arturo Prat 141 V6
Capixaba 138 J6
Cappoquin 59 G8
Capraia, Isola di 68 B4
Caprera, Isola 69 B5
Capricorn Channel 113 L3
Capri, Isola di 69 E5
Caprivi Strip 108 D3
Captieux 65 C6
Capua 69 E5
Caqueta 136 C4
Carabinani 136 E4
Caracal 73 H3
Caracarai 136 E3
Caracas 136 D1
Carajari 137 G4
Carajas, Serra dos 137 G5
Carangola 138 H4
Caratasca 132 F7
Caratasca, Laguna 132 F7
Caratinga 138 H3
Carauari 136 D4
Caravaca de la Cruz 67 F3
Caravelas 137 K7
Carballo 66 B1
Carbonara, Capo 69 B6
Carbondale 125 N6
Carbonear 121 R8
Carboneras de Guadazaori 67 F3
Carbonia 69 B6
Carcans, Etang de 65 C6
Carcans-Plage 65 C6
Carcarana 138 D6
Carcassonne 65 E7
Carcross 118 J3
Cardak 76 C4
Cardamon Hills 92 E7
Cardenas 131 N9
Cardiel, Lago 139 B9
Cardiff 52 D3
Cardigan 52 C2
Cardigan Bay 52 C2
Cardona 67 G2
Cardston 122 H3
Carei 73 G2
Carentan 64 C4
Carey, Lake 112 E4
Carhaix-Plougeur 64 B4
Carhue 139 D7
Cariacica 138 H4
Caribbean Sea 132 H7
Cariboa Lake 124 F1
Cariboo Mountains 119 L5
Caribou *Canada* 119 R4
Caribou *U.S.A.* 125 S3
Caribou Mountains 119 M4
Carinena 67 F2
Carinhanha 137 J6
Carinish 56 A3
Caripito 133 R9
Carleton, Mount 125 S3
Carlingford 58 K4
Carlingford Lough 58 K4
Carlisle *U.K.* 55 G2
Carlisle *U.S.A.* 125 M6
Carlos Chagas 138 H3
Carlow *Ireland* 59 J7
Carlow *Ireland* 59 J7
Carloway 56 C2
Carlsbad *Czech Rep.* 70 E3
Carlsbad *California* 126 D4
Carlsbad *New Mexico* 127 K4
Carlton *Nottinghamshire, U.K.* 53 F2
Carlton *N. Yorkshire, U.K.* 55 H2
Carlyle 123 N3
Carmacks 118 H3
Carmagnola 68 A3
Carmarthen 52 C3
Carmarthen Bay 52 C3
Carmaux 65 E6
Carmel Head 54 E3
Carmelo 139 E6
Carmen 136 B2
Carmen Alto 138 C4
Carmen de Patagones 139 D8
Carmen, Isla 126 G8
Carmen, Sierra del 127 L6
Carmi 124 F7
Carmona 66 D4
Carnarvon *Australia* 112 C3
Carnarvon *South Africa* 108 D6
Carn Ban 57 D3
Carnedd Llewelyn 54 F3
Carnegie, Lake 112 E4
Carnew 59 K7
Carney Island 141 R4
Carnforth 55 G2
Carn Glas-choire 56 E3
Carniche, Alpi 68 D2
Car Nicobar 93 H7
Carnlough 58 L3
Carnlough Bay 58 L3
Carnot 102 C7
Carnsore Point 59 K8
Carnwath 118 K2
Carolina 137 H5
Caroline Islands 91 K4
Carondelet Reef 111 U3
Caroni 136 E2
Carora 133 M9
Carpathians 73 F1
Carpatii Meridionali 73 G3
Carpentaria, Gulf of 113 H1
Carpentras 65 F6
Carpi 68 C3
Carpina 137 K5
Carra, Lough 58 D5
Carranza, Cabo 139 B7
Carranza, Presa V. 127 M7
Carrara 68 C3
Carrauntoohil 59 C9
Carriacou 133 S8
Carrick 57 D5
Carrickfergus 58 L3
Carrickmacross 58 J5
Carrick-on-Shannon 58 F5
Carrick-on-Suir 59 H8
Carrigallen 58 G5
Carrigtwohill 59 F9
Carrington 123 Q4
Carrion 66 D1
Carrizal 136 C1
Carrizal Bajo 138 B5
Carrizo Springs 127 N6
Carrizozo 127 K4
Carroll 124 C5
Carrollton *Georgia* 129 K4
Carrollton *Kentucky* 124 H7
Carron 56 D3
Carron, Loch 56 C3
Carrot 119 Q5
Carrowkeel 58 H2
Carrowmore Lough 58 C4

Chugunash 84 D6
Chuguyevka 88 D3
Chukchi Sea 118 B2
Chuken 88 F2
Chukhloma 78 G4
Chukotat 121 L5
Chukotskiy Khrebet 85 W3
Chukotskiy Poluostrov 81 V3
Chulak-Kurgan 86 B3
Chula Vista 126 D4
Chulman 85 L5
Chulmleigh 52 D4
Chulym *Russia* 84 C5
Chulym *Russia* 84 C5
Chum 78 L2
Chumbicha 138 C5
Chumek 86 F2
Chumikan 85 P6
Chumphon 93 J6
Chuna 84 F5
Chunchon 87 P4
Chungju 87 P4
Chunhua 88 C4
Chunoyar 84 F5
Chunya 107 F4
Chunyang 88 B4
Chunyang 89 B7
Chuquibamba 138 B3
Chuquicamata 138 B4
Chur 68 B2
Churan 85 L4
Churapcha 85 N4
Churchill *Canada* 119 S4
Churchill *Canada* 119 S4
Churchill *Newfoundland, Canada* 121 P7
Churchill, Cape 119 S4
Churchill Falls 121 P7
Churchill Peak 118 L4
Church Stretton 52 E2
Churia Ghati Hills 92 G3
Churin 136 B6
Churu 92 D3
Churuguara 136 D1
Chushevitsy 78 G3
Chushul 92 E2
Chusovaya 78 K4
Chusovov 78 K4
Chust 86 C3
Chute des Passes 125 Q2
Chuuronjang 88 B5
Chuxiong 93 K4
Chu Yang Sin 93 L6
Chwarta 94 G4
Chyulu Range 107 G3
Cianjur 90 D7
Cicekdagi 76 F3
Cicia 114 S8
Cide 76 E2
Cidones 66 E2
Ciechanow 71 J2
Ciego de Avila 132 H4
Cienaga 136 C1
Cienfuegos 132 G3
Cieszyn 71 H4
Cieza 67 F3
Ciftehan 76 F4
Cifteler 76 D3
Cifuentes 66 E2
Cihanbeyli 76 E3
Cijara, Embalse de 66 D3
Cilacap 90 D7
Cildir 77 K2
Cildir Golu 77 K2
Cilo Dagi 77 L4
Cimarron 128 A2
Cimone, Monte 68 C3
Cimpeni 73 G2
Cimpina 73 H3
Cimpulung 73 H3
Cimpuri 73 J2
Cinar 77 J4
Cinaruco 136 D2
Cina, Tanjung 90 C7
Cinca 67 G2
Cincer 72 D4
Cincinnati 124 H7
Cinderford 52 E3
Cine 76 C4
Cingus 77 H3
Cinto, Monte 69 B4
Circeo, Capo 69 D5
Circle *Alaska* 118 G2
Circle *Montana* 123 M4
Circular Reef 114 D2
Cirebon 90 D7
Cirencester 53 F3
Ciri 136 E5
Ciria 67 E2
Ciro 69 F6
Cisco 128 C4
Cislau 73 J3
Cisna 71 K4
Cisneros 136 B2
Cistierna 66 D1
Citac, Nevado 136 C6
Citlaltepetl, Volcan 131 L8
Citt a di Castello 68 D4
Cittanova 69 F6
Ciucului, Muntii 73 H2
Ciudad Acuna 127 M6
Ciudad Bolivar 136 E2
Ciudad Camargo 127 K7
Ciudad Cuauhtemoc 131 P10
Ciudad del Carmen 131 P8
Ciudad del Maiz 131 K6
Ciudad de Mexico 131 K8
Ciudadela 67 H3
Ciudad Guayana 136 E2
Ciudad Guzman 130 H8
Ciudad Ixtepec 131 M9
Ciudad Juarez 127 J5
Ciudad Lerdo 127 L8
Ciudad Madero 131 L6
Ciudad Mante 131 K6
Ciudad Mier 128 C7
Ciudad Obregon 127 H7
Ciudad Ojeda 133 M9
Ciudad Piar 133 R11
Ciudad Real 66 E3
Ciudad Rodrigo 66 C2
Ciudad Valles 131 K7
Ciudad Victoria 131 K6
Civa Burun 77 G2
Cividale del Friuli 68 D2
Civita Castellana 69 D4
Civitanova Marche 68 D4
Civitavecchia 69 C4
Civray 65 D5
Civril 76 C3
Cizre 77 K4
Clach Leathad 57 D4
Clacton-on-Sea 53 J3
Cladich 57 C4
Claerwen Reservoir 52 D2
Clain 65 D5
Claire, Lac a lEau 121 M6
Claire, Lake 119 N4
Clamecy 65 E5
Clane 59 J6
Clanton 129 J4
Clanwilliam 108 C6
Claonaig 57 C5
Clare *Australia* 113 H5
Clare *Ireland* 59 D7
Clare Island 58 B5
Claremont 125 P5
Claremorris 58 D5
Clarence *New Zealand* 115 D5
Clarence *New Zealand* 115 D5
Clarence, Cape 120 H3
Clarence Head 120 L2
Clarence Strait *Australia* 112 G1
Clarence Strait *U.S.A.* 118 J4
Clarence Town 133 K3
Clarinda 124 C6
Clarion 125 L6
Clark 123 K5
Clarke River 113 K2
Clark Fork *Montana* 122 H4
Clark Fork *Washington* 122 F3
Clark, Lake 118 E3
Clarksburg 125 K7
Clarksdale 128 G3
Clarks Hill Lake 129 L4
Clarkston 122 F4
Clarksville *Arkansas* 128 F3
Clarksville *Tennessee* 129 J2
Clar, Loch nan 56 D2
Clatteringshaws Loch 57 D5
Claughton 55 G2
Clavering O 120 X3
Claxton 129 M4
Clay Center 123 R8
Clay Cross 55 H3
Claydon 53 J2
Clayton *Georgia* 129 L3
Clayton *New Mexico* 127 L2
Clear, Cape 59 C10
Clearfield *Pennsylvania* 125 L6
Clearfield *Utah* 122 J7
Clear Fork 127 N4
Clear Hills 119 M4
Clear Island 59 D10
Clear Lake *California* 122 C8
Clear Lake *Iowa* 124 D5
Clear Lake Reservoir 122 D7
Clearwater *Canada* 122 G1
Clearwater *Canada* 119 P4
Clearwater *Florida* 129 L7
Clearwater *Idaho* 122 F4
Clearwater Mountains 122 G4
Cleethorpes 55 J3
Clerke Reef 112 D2
Clermont *Australia* 113 K3
Clermont *France* 64 E4
Clermont-Ferrand 65 E6
Clermont-l'Herault 65 E7
Clervaux 64 G3
Cleve 113 H5
Clevedon 52 E3
Cleveland *U.K.* 55 H2
Cleveland *Mississippi* 128 G4
Cleveland *Ohio* 125 K6
Cleveland *Tennessee* 129 K3
Cleveland *Texas* 128 E5
Cleveland, Cape 113 K2
Cleveland Hills 55 H2
Cleveland, Mount 122 H3
Cleveleys 55 F3
Clew Bay 58 C5
Clifden *Ireland* 59 B6
Clifden *New Zealand* 115 A7
Cliffe 53 H3
Cliffs of Moher 59 D7
Clifton 55 G2
Clincha Alta 136 B6
Clinch Mountains 129 L2
Clingmans Dome 129 L3
Clinton *Canada* 122 D2
Clinton *Illinois* 124 F6
Clinton *Iowa* 124 E6
Clinton *Mississippi* 128 G4
Clinton *Missouri* 124 D7
Clinton *N. Carolina* 129 N3
Clinton *Oklahoma* 128 C3
Clinton-Colden Lake 119 P3
Clipperton Island 117 J7
Clisham 56 B3
Clisson 65 C5
Clitheroe 55 G3
Cliza 138 C3
Cloates, Point 112 C3
Clogheen 59 G8
Clogherhead 58 K5
Clogher Head 58 K5
Clogh Mills 58 K3
Clonakilty 59 E9
Clonakilty Bay 59 E9
Cloncurry *Australia* 113 J3
Cloncurry *Australia* 113 J3
Clonmel 59 G8
Clonmult 59 F9
Clophill 53 G2
Cloppenburg 70 C2
Cloquet 124 D3
Cloud Peak 123 L5
Cloudy Bay 115 E4
Clough 58 L4
Cloughton 55 J2
Clovelly 52 C3
Clovis 127 L3
Cloyes 65 D4
Cluanie, Loch 57 C3
Cluj-Napoca 73 G2
Clun 52 E2
Cluny 65 F5
Cluses 65 G5
Clusone 68 B3
Clutha 115 B7
Clwyd *U.K.* 55 F3
Clwyd *U.K.* 55 F3
Clwydian Range 55 F3
Clyde *Canada* 120 N3
Clyde *U.K.* 57 E5
Clydebank 57 D5
Clyde, Firth of 57 D5
Clydesdale 57 E5
Clynnog-fawr 54 E3
Clywedog, Llyn 52 D2
Coa 66 C2
Coachella 126 D4
Coachella Canal 126 E4
Coaldale 126 D2
Coalinga 126 B2
Coalisland 58 J3
Coal River 118 K4
Coalville 53 F2
Coan, Cerro 136 B5
Coari *Brazil* 136 E4
Coari *Brazil* 136 E4
Coast Mountains 122 B2
Coast Range 122 C5
Coatbridge 57 D5
Coaticook 125 Q4
Coats Island 120 K5
Coats Land 141 Y3
Coatzacoalcos *Mexico* 131 M8
Coatzacoalcos *Mexico* 131 M9
Coban 132 B7
Cobar 113 K5
Cobh 59 F9
Cobija 136 D6
Cobourg 125 L5
Cobram 113 K6
Cobue 109 F2
Coburg 70 D3
Coburg Island 120 L2
Cochabamba 138 C3
Cochem 70 B3
Cochin 92 E7
Cochrane *Canada* 122 G2
Cochrane *Chile* 139 B9
Cock Bridge 57 E3
Cockburn 113 J5
Cockburnspath 57 F5
Cockenzie 57 F4
Cockerham 55 G3
Cockermouth 55 F2
Cockfield *Durham, U.K.* 55 H2
Cockfield *Suffolk, U.K.* 53 H2
Coco 132 E7
Cocoa 129 M6
Coco Channel 93 H6
Coco Islands 93 H6
Cocoparra Range 113 K5
Cocos 137 J6
Cocula 130 H7
Codajas 136 E4
Cod, Cape 125 R6
Codera, Cabo 136 D1
Codfish Island 115 A7
Codford 53 E3
Codigoro 68 D3
Cod Island 121 P6
Codo 137 J4
Codogno 68 B3
Cod's Head 59 B9
Coen 113 J1
Coeroeni 137 F3
Coesfeld 70 B3
Coeur d'Alene 122 F4
Coeur d'Alene Lake 122 F4
Coevorden 64 G2
Coffeyville 128 E2
Coffin Bay 113 H5
Coff's Harbour 113 L5
Cogealac 73 K3
Coghinas 69 B5
Cognac 65 C6
Cogo 105 G5
Cogolludo 66 E2
Cohuna 113 J6
Coiba, Isla 132 G11
Coigach 56 C2
Coigeach, Rubha 56 C2
Coihaique 139 B9
Coimbatore 92 E6
Coimbra 66 B2
Coipasa, Salar de 138 C3
Cokak 77 G4
Colac 113 J6
Colap 77 H4
Colatina 138 E3
Colby 123 P8
Colchester 53 H3
Cold Ashton 52 E3
Coldstream 57 F5
Coldwater *Kansas* 127 N2
Coldwater *Michigan* 124 H6
Colebrook 125 Q4
Coleman *Australia* 113 J1
Coleman *U.S.A.* 127 N5
Colemerick 77 K4
Coleraine *Australia* 113 J6
Coleraine *U.K.* 58 J2
Colesberg 108 E6
Coleshill 53 F2
Coles, Punta de 139 B3
Colfax 122 F4
Colgrave Sound 56 B1
Colhue Huapi, Lago 139 C9
Colima 130 H8
Colima, Nevado de 130 H8
Colinas 137 J5
Colintraive 57 C5
Coll 57 C4
Collatto 68 D2
College Park 129 K4
Collie 112 D5
Collier Bay 112 E2
Colliford Lake Reservoir 52 C4
Collingbourne Kingston 53 F3
Collingham 55 J3
Collingwood *Canada* 125 K4
Collingwood *New Zealand* 115 D4
Collins 128 H5
Collin Top 58 K3
Collooney 58 F4
Colmar 64 G4
Colmars 65 G6
Colmenar 66 D4
Colmenar Viejo 66 E2
Colne *Essex, U.K.* 53 H3
Colne *Lancashire, U.K.* 55 G3
Cologne 70 B3
Colombia 136 C3
Colombo 92 E7
Colomoncagua 132 C7
Colon *Cuba* 132 G3
Colon *Panama* 132 H10
Colonia Las Heras 139 C9
Colonna, Capo 69 F6
Colonsay 57 B4
Colorado *Argentina* 139 D7
Colorado *Arizona* 126 E4
Colorado *Texas* 127 M4
Colorado *U.S.A.* 123 L8
Colorado Canal 123 N8
Colorado, Cerro 126 E5
Colorado City 127 M4
Colorado River Aqueduct 126 D4
Colorado Springs 127 K1
Colsterworth 53 G2
Coluene 137 G6
Columbia *Missouri* 124 D7
Columbia *Pennsylvania* 125 M7
Columbia *S. Carolina* 129 M4
Columbia *Tennessee* 129 J3
Columbia *Washington* 122 D5
Columbia, District of 125 M7
Columbia Falls 122 G3
Columbia, Mount 119 M5
Columbine, Cape 108 C6
Columbus *Georgia* 129 K4
Columbus *Indiana* 124 H7
Columbus *Mississippi* 128 H4
Columbus *Montana* 123 K5
Columbus *Nebraska* 123 R7
Columbus *Ohio* 124 J7
Columbus *Texas* 128 D6
Colville *Alaska* 118 D2
Colville *Washington* 122 F3
Colville, Cape 115 E2
Colville Channel 115 E2
Colville Lake 118 K2
Colwyn Bay 54 F3
Comacchio 68 D3
Comana 73 J3
Comandante Ferraz 141 W6
Comandante Fontana 138 E5
Comayagua 132 D7
Combarbala 138 B6
Combe Martin 52 C3
Comber 58 L3
Combermere Bay 93 H5

Combourg 64 C4
Comeragh Mountains 59 G8
Comfort, Cape 120 K4
Comilla 93 H4
Comitan 131 N9
Committee Bay 120 J4
Como 68 B3
Comodoro Rivadavia 139 C9
Como, Lago di 68 B3
Comorin, Cape 92 E7
Comoros 109 H2
Compiegne 64 E4
Comporta 66 B3
Compostela 130 G7
Conakry 104 C4
Conara Junction 113 K7
Concarneau 65 B5
Conceicao do Araguaia 137 H5
Concepcion *Bolivia* 138 D3
Concepcion *Chile* 138 B7
Concepcion *Panama* 132 F10
Concepcion *Paraguay* 138 E4
Concepcion del Oro 130 J5
Concepcion del Uruguay 138 E6
Concepcion, Punta 126 G7
Conception Bay 121 R8
Conception Island 133 K3
Conception, Point 126 B3
Concho 127 M5
Conchos *Mexico* 128 C8
Conchos *Mexico* 127 K6
Concord *California* 126 A2
Concord *N. Carolina* 129 M3
Concord *New Hampshire* 125 Q5
Concordia *Argentina* 138 E6
Concordia *U.S.A.* 123 R8
Condamine 113 L4
Condeuba 138 J6
Condolobin 113 K5
Condom 65 D7
Conecuh 129 J5
Conegliano 68 D3
Conflict Group 114 E4
Confolens 65 D5
Congjiang 93 L3
Congleton 55 G3
Congo 106 B3
Congo 106 D2
Congo Basin 99 E6
Conisbrough 55 H3
Coniston 55 F2
Coniston Water 54 E2
Connah's Quay 55 F3
Connaught 58 D5
Conneaut 125 K6
Connecticut *U.S.A.* 125 P6
Connecticut *U.S.A.* 125 P6
Connellsville 125 L6
Conn, Lough 58 D4
Connors Range 113 K3
Conon 56 D3
Conon Bridge 56 D3
Conrad 122 J3
Conselheiro Lafaiete 138 H4
Conselheiro Pena 138 H3
Consett 55 H2
Con Son 93 L7
Constance, Lake 70 C5
Constancia dos Baetas 136 E5
Constanta 73 K3
Constantina 66 D4
Constantine 101 G1
Constantine Bay 52 B4
Constantine, Cape 118 D4
Constantinople 76 C2
Constitucion 139 B7
Contamana 136 C5
Contas 137 J6
Contratacion 136 C2
Contrexeville 64 F4
Contulmo 139 B7
Contwoyto Lake 119 N2
Conway *Arkansas* 128 F3
Conway *New Hampshire* 125 Q5
Conway *S. Carolina* 129 N4
Conway Bay 54 F3
Conwy 54 F3
Coober Pedy 113 G4
Cook 112 G5
Cook, Cape 122 A2
Cookeville 129 K2
Cook Inlet 118 E3
Cook Islands 143 H5
Cook, Mount 115 C5
Cook, Recif de 114 W15
Cookstown 58 J3
Cook Strait 115 E4
Cooktown 113 K2
Coolibah 112 G2
Coolidge 126 G4
Cooma 113 K6
Coomnadiha 59 C9
Coomscarrea 59 B9
Coonamble 113 K5
Coondapoor 92 D6
Coongan 112 D3
Coopers Creek 113 H4
Cooroy 113 L4
Coosa 129 J4
Coos Bay *U.S.A.* 122 B6
Coos Bay *U.S.A.* 122 B6
Cootamundra 113 K5
Cootehill 58 H4
Copacabana 138 C3
Copa, Cerro 138 C4
Cope 123 N8
Copenhagen 63 E9
Copiapo 138 B5
Copinsay 56 F2
Copkoy 76 B2
Copper 118 G3
Copper Center 118 F3
Coppermine *Canada* 119 M2
Coppermine *Canada* 119 N2
Copper Mount 122 F2
Copplestone 52 D4
Copsa Mica 73 H2
Coquet 57 G5
Coquimbo 138 B5
Coquimbo, Bahia de 138 B5
Corabia 73 H4
Coracora 136 C7
Coral Harbour 120 K5
Coral Sea Plateau 113 K2
Corantijn 136 F3
Corbeil-Essonnes 64 E4
Corbiere 53 M7
Corbieres 65 E7
Corbigny 65 E5
Corbin 124 H8
Corbones 66 D4
Corbridge 55 G2
Corby 53 G2
Corby Glen 53 G2
Corcaigh 59 E9
Corcovado, Golfo 139 B8
Corcubion 66 B1
Cordele 129 L5
Cordoba 131 L8
Cordoba *Argentina* 138 D6
Cordoba *Spain* 66 D4
Cordoba, Sierras de 138 D6
Cordova 136 B6
Cordova 118 F3
Corfe 52 D4
Corfu *Greece* 74 E3
Corfu *Greece* 74 E3
Coria 66 C2
Corigliano Calabro 69 F6
Corinda 113 H2
Corinth *Greece* 75 G4
Corinth *U.S.A.* 128 H3
Corinth, Gulf of 75 G3
Corinto *Brazil* 138 H3
Corinto *Nicaragua* 132 D8
Corixa Grande 138 E3
Cork *Ireland* 59 E9
Cork *Ireland* 59 E9
Corlay 64 B4
Corleone 69 D7
Corlu 76 B2
Cornafulla 59 F6
Corner Brook 121 Q8
Cornhill-on-Tweed 57 F4
Corning 125 M5
Corn Islands 132 F8
Cornudilla 66 E1
Cornwall *U.K.* 52 C4
Cornwall *Canada* 125 N4
Cornwallis Island 120 H2
Cornwall Island 120 H2
Coro 136 D1
Coroata 137 J4
Corocoro 138 C3
Coromandel *Brazil* 138 G3
Coromandel *New Zealand* 115 E2
Coromandel Coast 92 F6
Coromandel Peninsula 115 E2
Corona 127 K3
Coronado, Bahia de 132 E10
Coronation Gulf 119 N2
Coronel 139 B7
Coronel Dorrego 139 D7
Coronel Pringles 139 D7
Coronel Suarez 139 D7
Corovode 75 F2
Corps 65 F6
Corpus Christi 128 D7
Corpus Christi Bay 128 D7
Corpus Christi, Lake 128 D6
Corque 138 C3
Corran 57 C4
Corraun Peninsula 58 C5
Corrib, Lough 59 D6
Corrientes *Argentina* 138 E5
Corrientes *Peru* 136 B4
Corrientes, Cabo *Colombia* 136 B2
Corrientes, Cabo *Cuba* 132 E4
Corrientes, Cabo *Mexico* 130 G7
Corrigan 128 E5
Corrigin 112 D5
Corry 125 L6
Corryvreckan, Gulf of 57 C4
Corse 69 B4
Corse, Cap 68 B4
Corsewall Point 57 C5
Corsica 69 B4
Corsicana 128 D4
Corte 69 B4
Cortegana 66 C4
Cortez 127 H2
Cortina d'Ampezzo 68 D2
Cortland 125 M5
Cortona 68 C4
Corubal 104 C3
Coruche 66 B3
Coruh 77 J2
Corum 76 F2
Corumba 138 E3
Corumba 138 G3
Corunna 66 B1
Corvallis 122 C5
Corve 52 E2
Corwen 52 D2
Cos 75 J4
Cosamaloapan 131 M8
Cosamozza 69 B4
Cosenza 69 F6
Cosiguina, Volcan 132 D8
Cosmoledo Islands 82 C7
Cosne 65 E5
Costa, Cordillera de la 133 N9
Costa Rica 132 E9
Costesti 73 H3
Cotabato 91 G4
Cotacachi 136 B3
Cotagaita 138 C4
Cotahuasi 138 B3
Cotentin 64 C4
Cotiella 67 G1
Cotonou 105 F4
Cotopaxi 136 B4
Cottage Grove 122 C6
Cottbus 70 F3
Cottingham 55 J3
Cottonwood 126 F3
Coubre, Pointe de la 65 C6
Coulommiers 64 E4
Coulonge 125 M3
Council Bluffs 124 C6
Coupar Angus 57 E4
Courantyne 136 F3
Courchevel 65 G6
Couronne, Cap 65 F7
Courtenay 122 B3
Courtmacsherry Bay 59 E9
Coutances 64 C4
Couto Magalhaes 137 H5
Coutras 65 C6
Cove 56 C3
Coventry 53 F2
Covilha 66 C2
Covington *Kentucky* 124 H7
Covington *Virginia* 125 L8
Cowal 57 C4
Cowan, Lake 112 E5
Cowbit 53 G2
Cowbridge 52 D3
Cowdenbeath 57 E4
Cowes 53 F4
Cowfold 53 G4
Cowlitz 122 C4
Cowra 113 K5
Coxim 138 F3
Coxs Bazar 93 H4
Coxwold 55 H2
Cozumel 131 R7
Cozumel, Isla de 131 R7
Cracow 71 H3
Cradock 108 E6
Craig 123 L7
Craigavon 58 K4
Craignure 57 C4
Crail 57 F4
Crailsheim 70 D4
Craiova 73 G3
Cramlington 55 H1
Cranborne 53 F4
Cranbrook 122 G3
Crane 127 L5
Cranleigh 53 G3
Cranstown, Kap 120 Q3
Craponne-sur-Arzon 65 E6
Crasna *Romania* 73 G2
Crasna *Romania* 73 J2
Crater Lake 122 C6
Crateus 137 J5
Crati 69 F6
Crato 137 K5
Cravo Norte 136 C2
Crawford 123 N6
Crawford Point 91 F3
Crawfordville 129 K5
Crawley 53 G3
Crazy Mountains 123 J4
Creach Bheinn 57 C4
Creag Meagaidh 57 D3
Creagorry 56 A3
Crediton 52 D4
Cree *Canada* 119 P4
Cree *U.K.* 57 D5
Cree Lake 119 P4
Creeslough 58 G2
Creetown 54 E2
Creggan 58 H3
Creggs 58 F5
Crema 68 B3
Cremona 68 B3
Crepaja 72 F3
Creran, Loch 57 C4
Cres *Croatia* 72 C3
Cres *Croatia* 72 C3
Crescent 122 D6
Crescent City 122 B7
Crest 65 F6
Creston 124 C6
Crestview 129 J5
Crete 75 H5
Cretin, Cape 114 D3
Creus, Cap 67 H1
Creuse 65 D5
Crevillente 67 F3
Crewe 55 G3
Crewkerne 52 E4
Crianlarich 57 D4
Criccieth 52 C2
Criciuma 138 G5
Crick 53 F2
Crickhowell 52 D3
Cricklade 53 F3
Crieff 57 E4
Criffel 55 F2
Crikvenica 72 C3
Crimea 79 E6
Cristalandia 137 H6
Cristalina 138 G3
Cristobal Colon, Pico 136 C1
Crisu Alb 73 F2
Crisu Negru 73 F2
Crisu Repede 73 G2
Crna Reka 73 F5
Crni Drim 72 F5
Croaghgorm Mountains 58 F3
Croagh Patrick 58 C5
Croatia 72 C3
Crocketford 57 E5
Crockett 128 E5
Croggan 57 C4
Crohy Head 58 F3
Croick 56 D3
Croisette, Cap 65 F7
Croke, Mount 112 D5
Croker Island 112 G1
Cromalt Hills 56 C2
Cromar 57 F3
Cromarty 56 D3
Cromarty Firth 56 D3
Cromdale, Hills of 56 E3
Cromer 53 J2
Cromwell 115 B6
Crook 55 H2
Crooked *Canada* 122 D5
Crooked *U.S.A.* 119 L4
Crooked Island 133 K3
Crooked Island Passage 133 K3
Crookham 57 F4
Crookhaven 59 C10
Crookston 124 B3
Croom 59 E7
Crosby *Isle of Man, U.K.* 54 E2
Crosby *Merseyside, U.K.* 55 F3
Crosby *U.S.A.* 124 D3
Cross 105 G4
Crossett 128 G4
Cross Fell 55 G2
Crossgar 58 L4
Cross Hands 52 C3
Crosshaven 59 F9
Cross Lake 119 R5
Crossmaglen 58 J4
Crossmolina 58 D4
Cross Sound 118 H4
Crossville 129 K3
Crotone 69 F6
Crouch 53 H3
Crowborough 53 H3
Crowle 55 J3
Crowley's Ridge 128 G3
Crowsnest Pass 119 N6
Croxton Kerrial 53 G2
Croydon *Australia* 113 J2
Croydon *U.K.* 53 G2
Crozet, Iles 142 C6
Crozier Channel 120 C2
Cruces, Punta 136 B2
Crudgington 52 E2
Crumlin 58 K3
Cruz Alta 138 F5
Cruz, Cabo 132 J5
Cruz del Eje 138 C6
Cruzeiro do Sul 136 C5
Cruz Grande *Chile* 138 B5
Cruz Grande *Mexico* 131 K9
Crymych 52 C3
Crystal City 127 N6
Crystal Falls 124 F3
Csongrad 72 F2
Csorna 72 D2
Cuamba 109 G2
Cuando 106 D6
Cuangar 106 C6
Cuango 106 C4
Cuanza 106 C4
Cuatro Cienegas 127 L7
Cuauhtemoc 127 J6
Cuautla 131 K8
Cuba 132 G4
Cubango 106 C6
Cubara 133 L11
Cubuk 76 E2
Cuchi 106 C5
Cuchilla Grande 138 E6
Cuchivero 136 D2
Cuchumatanes, Alto 132 B7
Cuckfield 53 G3
Cucuta 136 C2
Cuddalore 92 E6
Cuddapah 92 E6
Cudgwa 113 K6
Cue 112 D4
Cuellar 66 D2
Cuenca 136 B4
Cuencame 130 H5
Cuenca, Serrania de 66 E2
Cuernavaca 131 K8
Cuero 128 D6

El Sahuaro	126	F5
El Salado	139	C9
El Salto	130	G6
El Salvador	132	C8
El Sam'an de Apure	133	N11
El Sauzal	126	D5
Elsham	55	J3
El Socorro	126	F5
Elster	70	E3
Elsterwerda	70	E3
El Sueco	127	J6
El Suweis	103	F2
El Tambo	136	B4
Eltham	115	E3
El Thamad	96	B2
El Tigre	133	Q10
El Tih	96	A2
Eltisley	53	G2
El Tocuyo	133	N10
Elton *U.K.*	53	G2
Elton *Russia*	79	H6
El Tule	131	L9
El Tur	96	A2
Eluru	92	F5
Elvanfoot	57	E5
Elvas	66	C3
Elveden	53	H2
Elverum	63	D6
El Viejo	133	L11
El Vigia	136	C2
Elwy	55	F3
Ely *Cambridgeshire, U.K.*	53	H2
Ely *Mid Glamorgan, U.K.*	52	D3
Ely *Minnesota*	124	E3
Ely *Nevada*	126	E1
Elze	70	C2
Ema	63	M7
Emae	114	U12
Emamrud	95	M3
Emam Taqi	95	P4
Eman	63	G8
Emao	114	U12
Emba	79	K6
Embarcacion	138	D4
Embleton	55	H1
Embona	75	J4
Embrun	65	G6
Embu	107	G3
Emden	70	B2
Emerald	113	K3
Emerald Island	120	D2
Emerson	123	R3
Emet	76	C3
Emeti	114	C3
Emi	84	F6
Emigrant Pass	122	F7
Emin	86	E2
Emine, Nos	73	J4
Emirdag	76	D3
Emir Dagi	76	D3
Emita	113	K7
Emmaboda	63	F8
Emmaste	63	K7
Emmen	64	G2
Emory Peak	127	L6
Empalme	126	G7
Empangeni	109	F5
Empedrado	138	E5
Empingham	53	G2
Empoli	68	C4
Emporia *Kansas*	128	D1
Emporia *Virginia*	125	M8
Ems	70	B2
Emu	88	B4
Enard Bay	56	C2
Encantada, Cerro Del La	126	E5
Encarnacion	138	E5
Enchi	104	E4
Encinal	128	C6
Encontrados	136	C2
Encounter Bay	113	H6
Endau	90	C5
Ende	91	G7
Endeavour Strait	113	J1
Enderbury Island	111	U2
Enderby Land	141	D5
Endicott Mountains	118	C2
Ene	136	C6
Enez	76	B2
Enfield *Ireland*	59	J6
Enfield *U.K.*	53	G3
Engano, Cabo	133	N5
Engano, Cape	91	G2
Engaru	88	J3
Engels	79	H5
Enggano	90	C7
Engger Us	87	J3
Engineer Group	114	E4
Englehart	125	L3
Englewood	123	M8
English Channel	50	G5
Enguera	67	F3
Enguera, Sierra de	67	F3
Enid	128	D2
Enkhuizen	64	F2
Enkoping	63	G7
Enna	69	E7
Ennadai Lake	119	Q3
En Nahud	102	E5
Ennedi	102	D4
Ennell, Lough	59	H6
Ennerdale Water	55	F2
Enning	123	N5
Ennis *Ireland*	59	E7

Ennis *U.S.A.*	128	D4
Enniscorthy	59	J7
Enniskillen	58	G4
Ennistymon	59	D7
Enns	68	E1
Enonkoski	62	N5
Enontekio	62	K2
Enrekang	91	F6
Enschede	64	G2
Ensenada	126	D5
Enshi	93	L2
Enstone	53	F3
Entebbe	107	F2
Enterprise	129	K5
Entinas, Punta de las	66	E4
Entraygues	65	E6
Entrecasteaux, Recifs d'	111	N5
Enugu	105	G4
Enurmino	118	A2
Enz	70	C4
Eo	66	C1
Eolie	69	E6
Epano Fellos	75	H4
Epanomi	75	G2
Ephrata	122	E4
Epi	114	U12
Epinal	64	G4
Epping	53	H3
Eppynt, Mynydd	52	D2
Epsi	77	J4
Epsom	53	G3
Eqlid	95	L6
Equatorial Guinea	105	G5
Equeipa	114	D3
Erap	114	D3
Erbaa	77	G2
Erba, Jebel	96	C6
Ercek	77	K3
Ercis	77	K3
Ercsi	72	E2
Erdek	76	B2
Erdemli	76	F4
Erdenet	87	J2
Erdre	65	C5
Erechim	138	F5
Ereenstav	87	M2
Eregli *Turkey*	76	D2
Eregli *Turkey*	76	F4
Erek Dagi	77	K3
Erenhot	87	L3
Erentepe	77	K3
Eresma	66	D2
Eressos	75	H3
Erfelek	76	F2
Erfurt	70	D3
Ergani	77	H3
Ergene	76	B2
Ergli	63	L8
Ergun He	85	K6
Ergun Zuoqi	87	N1
Eriboll, Loch	56	D2
Ericht, Loch	57	D4
Ericiyas Dagi	76	F3
Erie	125	K5
Erie, Lake	125	K5
Erikousa	74	E3
Erimanthos	75	F4
Erimo-misaki	88	J5
Eriskay	57	A3
Erkelenz	70	B3
Erkilet	76	F3
Erkowit	96	C7
Erlandson Lake	121	N6
Erlangen	70	D4
Erldunda	113	G4
Erme	52	D4
Ermelo	108	F5
Ermenak	76	E4
Ernakulam	92	E7
Erne	58	H5
Erne, Lower Lough	58	G4
Erne, Upper Lough	58	G4
Erode	92	E6
Eromanga	113	J4
Er Rachidia	100	E2
Er Rahad	102	F5
Errego	109	G3
Errigal	58	F2
Erris Head	58	B4
Errochty, Loch	57	D4
Errogie	56	D3
Erromango	114	U13
Erseke	75	F2
Erskine	124	C3
Ertai	86	G2
Eruh	77	K4
Erwigol	86	F3
Eryuan	93	J3
Erzen	74	E2
Erzgebirge	70	E3
Erzin	84	F6
Erzincan	77	H3
Erzurum	77	J3
Esa-Ala	114	E3
Esan-misaki	88	H5
Esashi *Japan*	88	H5
Esashi *Japan*	88	J3
Esbjerg	63	C9
Esbo	63	N6
Escalona	66	D2
Escambia	129	J5
Escanaba	124	G4
Escarpe, Cape	114	X16

Escocesa, Bahia de	133	N5
Escondido *Brazil*	138	J3
Escondido *U.S.A.*	126	D4
Escrick	55	H3
Escuintla	132	B7
Ese-Khayya	85	N3
Esemer	77	K3
Esen	76	C4
Esendere	77	L4
Esfahan	95	K5
Esfarayen, Reshteh ye	95	N3
Eshan	93	K4
Esha Ness	56	A1
Esh Sheikh, Jbel	77	G6
Esino	68	D4
Esk	57	E5
Eskdale	57	E5
Eske, Lough	58	F3
Eskifjordur	62	Y12
Eskilstuna	63	G7
Eskimalatya	77	H3
Eskimo Lakes	118	J2
Eskimo Point	119	S3
Eskipazar	76	E2
Eskishir	76	D3
Esla	66	D1
Eslamabad-e Gharb	94	H4
Eslam Qaleh	95	Q4
Esme	76	C3
Esmeralda, Isla	139	A9
Esmeraldas	136	B3
Espalion	65	E6
Espana *Canada*	125	K3
Espanola *U.S.A.*	127	J3
Espanola, Isla	136	A7
Espenberg, Cape	118	C2
Esperance	112	E5
Esperance Bay	112	E5
Esperanza *Antarctic*	141	W6
Esperanza *Argentina*	139	B10
Esperanza *Argentina*	138	D6
Espiel	66	D3
Espinhaco, Serra da	138	H3
Espinho	66	B2
Espinosa de los Monteros	66	E1
Espirito Santo	138	H3
Espiritu Santo	114	T11
Espiritu Santo, Cape	91	H3
Espiritu Santo, Isla	130	D5
Espiye	77	H2
Espoo	63	N6
Esposende	66	B2
Espot	67	G1
Espungabera	109	F4
Esquel	139	B8
Es Sahra en Nubiya	96	B6
Essaouira	100	D2
Es Semara	100	C3
Essen	70	B3
Essex	53	H3
Essex, Punta	136	A7
Esslingen	70	C4
Esso	85	T5
Estacado, Llanos	127	L4
Estados, Isla de los	139	D10
Estahbanat	95	M7
Estancia	138	K6
Estcourt	108	E5
Este	68	C3
Esteli	132	D8
Estella	67	E1
Estepona	66	D4
Este, Punta del	139	F6
Esterhazy	123	N2
Esternay	64	E4
Estes Park	123	M7
Estevan	123	N3
Estherville	124	C5
Eston	55	H2
Estonia	63	L7
Estrela, Sierra da	66	C2
Estrella, Punta	126	E5
Estremadura	66	B3
Estremoz	66	C3
Estrondo, Serra do	137	H5
Esztergom	72	E2
Etah	92	E3
Etain	64	F4
Etampes	64	E4
Etaples	64	D3
Etawah	92	E3
Ethiopia	103	G6
Etive, Loch	57	C4
Etna, Monte	69	E7
Eton	53	G3
Etosha Pan	108	C3
Etretat	64	D4
Ettington	53	F2
Ettlingen	70	C4
Ettrick	57	E5
Ettrick Forest	57	E5
Etwall	53	F2
Eu	64	D3
Eua	111	U6
Euboea	75	H3
Euclid	125	K6
Euclides da Cunha	137	K5
Eufala	129	K5
Eufaula Lake	128	E3
Eugene	122	C5
Eugenia, Punta	126	E7
Eunice	128	F5
Euphrates	94	G6
Eupora	128	H4

Eure	64	D4
Eureka *California*	122	B7
Eureka *Montana*	122	G3
Eureka *Nevada*	126	D1
Eureka Sound	120	J2
Europa, Ile de l	109	H4
Europa, Picos de	66	D1
Europa Point	66	D4
Eutaw	129	J4
Evans, Lake	121	L7
Evans, Mount	123	M8
Evans Strait	120	K5
Evanston *Illinois*	124	G5
Evanston *Wyoming*	122	J7
Evansville	124	G7
Evaux-les-Bains	65	E5
Evaz	95	L8
Evenlode	53	F3
Everard, Cape	113	K6
Everard, Lake	113	G5
Everest, Mount	92	G3
Everett	122	C4
Everett Mountains	120	N5
Everglades, The	129	M7
Evesham	53	F2
Evesham, Vale of	53	F2
Evigheds Fjord	120	R4
Evisa	69	B4
Evora	66	C3
Evreux	64	D4
Evropos	75	G2
Evros	75	J2
Evrotas	75	G4
Evvoia	75	H3
Evvoikos Kolpos	75	G3
Ewasse	114	E3
Ewe, Loch	56	C3
Ewes	57	E5
Exbourne	52	D4
Exe	52	D4
Exeter	52	D4
Exford	52	D3
Exmoor	52	D3
Exmouth	52	D4
Exmouth Gulf	112	C3
Exo Hora	75	F4
Expedition Range	113	K3
Exploits	121	Q8
Exton	52	D3
Extremadura	66	C3
Exuma Sound	132	J2
Eyakit-Terde	85	J3
Eyam	55	H3
Eyasi, Lake	107	F3
Eyemouth	57	F4
Eye Peninsula	56	B2
Eyjafjallajokull	62	U13
Eyjafjordur	62	V11
Eyl	103	J6
Eynesil	77	H2
Eynsham	53	F3
Eyre	112	F5
Eyre Creek	113	H4
Eyre Mountains	115	B6
Eyre North, Lake	113	H4
Eyre Peninsula	113	H5
Eyre South, Lake	113	H4
Eysturoy	62	Z14
Eyvanaki	95	L4
Ezequil Ramos Mexia, Embalse	139	C7
Ezine	76	B3

F

Faber Lake	119	M3
Faborg	63	D9
Fabriano	68	D4
Facatativa	136	C3
Facundo	139	C9
Fada	102	D4
Fada NGourma	104	F3
Faddeya, Zaliv	84	H2
Faddeyevskiy, Ostrov	85	Q1
Faenza	68	C3
Faeros	62	Z14
Fafen Shet	103	H6
Fagaras	73	H3
Fagersta	63	F6
Faget	73	G3
Fagnano, Lago	139	C10
Fagnes	64	F4
Faguibine, Lac	100	E5
Fagurholsmyri	62	W13
Fahraj	95	P7
Fairbanks	118	F3
Fairborn	124	J7
Fairfield	126	A1
Fair Isle	56	A2
Fairlie	115	C6
Fairlight *Australia*	113	J2
Fairlight *U.K.*	53	H4
Fairmont *Minnesota*	124	C5
Fairmont *W. Virginia*	125	K7
Fair Ness	120	M5
Fairview	128	C2
Fairweather, Mount	118	H4
Faisalabad	92	D2
Faith	123	N5
Faither, The	56	A1
Faizabad	92	F3
Fajr, Wadi	96	D2

168

Name	Page	Ref
Forth, Firth of	57	F4
Fortin Carlos Antonio Lopez	138	E4
Fortin General Mendoza	138	D4
Fortin Gral Eugenio Garay	138	D4
Fortin Infante Rivarola	138	D4
Fortin Juan de Zalazar	138	E4
Fortin Madrejon	138	E4
Fortin Ravelo	138	D3
Fort Jameson	107	F3
Fort Kent	125	R3
Fort Lamy	102	C5
Fort Lauderdale	129	M7
Fort Liard	118	L3
Fort Macleod	122	H3
Fort McMurray	119	N4
Fort McPherson	118	J2
Fort Madison	124	E6
Fort Manning	107	F5
Fort Morgan	123	N7
Fort Myers	129	M7
Fort Nelson	119	L4
Fort Norman	118	K3
Fortore	69	E5
Fort Payne	129	K3
Fort Peck	123	L3
Fort Peck Dam	123	L4
Fort Peck Reservoir	123	L4
Fort Pierce	129	M7
Fort Portal	107	F2
Fort Providence	119	M3
Fort Qu'Appelle	123	N2
Fort Randall	118	Af8
Fort Resolution	119	N3
Fortrose	56	D3
Fort Rosebery	107	E5
Fort Saint James	118	L5
Fort Saint John	119	L4
Fort Scott	124	C8
Fort Severn	120	J6
Fort Shevchenko	79	J7
Fort Simpson	119	L3
Fort Smith U.S.A.	128	E4
Fort Soufflay	106	B2
Fort Stockton	127	L5
Fort Sumner	127	K3
Fort Trinquet	100	D1
Fortuna	122	B7
Fortune Bay	121	Q8
Fort Valley	129	L4
Fort Vermilion	119	M4
Fort Victoria	108	F4
Fort Walton Beach	129	J5
Fort Wayne	124	H6
Fort William	57	C4
Fort Worth	128	D4
Fort Yukon	118	F2
Forur	95	M8
Foshan	93	M4
Fosheim Peninsula	120	K2
Fosna	62	D5
Fossombrone	68	D4
Fossvellir	62	X12
Foster	113	K6
Fougeres	64	C4
Foula	56	A2
Foula Morie	104	C3
Foulden	57	F4
Foulness Island	53	H3
Foulness Point	53	H3
Foulwind, Cape	115	C4
Foumban	105	H4
Foundiougne	104	B3
Fountainhall	57	F5
Four Mountains, Islands of the	118	Ad9
Fournoi	75	J4
Foveaux Strait	115	B7
Fowey U.K.	52	C4
Fowey U.K.	52	C4
Fowler	127	K1
Fowler, Point	112	G5
Fowlers Bay	112	G5
Fowman	94	J3
Fox Canada	118	K4
Fox U.S.A.	124	F6
Foxe Basin	120	L4
Foxe Peninsula	120	L5
Foxford	58	D5
Fox Islands	118	Ae9
Foxton	115	E4
Foyers, Falls of	56	D3
Foyle	58	H3
Foyle, Lough	58	H2
Foynes	59	D7
Foz do Iguacu	138	F5
Fraga	67	G2
Framington	125	Q5
Framlingham	53	J2
Frampol	71	K3
Franca	138	G4
Francais, Recif des	114	V15
France	65	C5
France, Ile de	64	E4
Frances Australia	113	J6
Frances Canada	118	K3
Franceville	106	B3
Franche Comte	65	G5
Francis Case, Lake	123	Q6
Francisco Escarcega	131	P8
Francistown	108	E4
Francois Lake	118	K5
Frangista	75	F3
Frankfort Indiana	124	G6
Frankfort Kentucky	124	H7
Frankfurt	70	F2
Frankfurt am Main	70	C3
Frankischer Alb	70	D4
Franklin Indiana	124	H7
Franklin Louisiana	128	G6
Franklin N. Carolina	129	L3
Franklin Pennsylvania	125	L6
Franklin Tennessee	129	J3
Franklin Bay	118	K2
Franklin D Roosevelt Lake	122	E3
Franklin, Lake	119	R2
Franklin Mountains	118	K3
Franklin, Point	118	D1
Franklin Strait	120	G3
Frank's Peak	123	K6
Fransta	62	G5
Frantsa-Iosifa, Zemlya	80	G2
Frascati	69	D5
Fraserburg	108	D6
Fraserburgh	56	F3
Fraserdale	125	K2
Fraser Island	113	L4
Fraser, Mount	112	D4
Frasertown	115	F3
Frauenfeld	68	B2
Fray Bentos	138	E6
Frazer	122	D2
Freckleton	55	G3
Fredericia	63	C9
Frederick Maryland	125	M7
Frederick Oklahoma	128	C3
Frederick Reef	110	M6
Fredericksburg	125	M7
Fredericton	125	S4
Fredericktown	124	E8
Fredericton	125	S4
Frederikshab	120	S5
Frederikshabs Isblink	120	S5
Frederikshavn	63	D8
Frederiksted	133	Q6
Fredonia	125	L5
Fredrika	62	M4
Fredrikshamn	63	M6
Fredrikstad	63	D7
Freeling, Mount	113	G3
Freeport Illinois	124	F5
Freeport Texas	128	E6
Freeport City	132	H1
Freer	128	C7
Freetown	104	C4
Fregenal de la Sierra	66	C3
Frehel, Cap	64	B4
Freiberg	70	E3
Freiburg	70	B4
Freising	70	D4
Freistadt	68	E1
Frejus	65	G7
Fremantle	112	D5
Fremont California	126	A2
Fremont Nebraska	123	R7
Fremont Utah	122	J8
French	125	K1
French Broad	129	L2
French Guiana	136	G3
Frenchman	123	L3
Frenchpark	58	F5
French Polynesia	143	J5
Frenda	100	F1
Frensham	53	G3
Fresco	137	G5
Freshfield, Mount	122	F2
Freshwater	53	F4
Fresnillo	130	H6
Fresno	126	C2
Freu, Cabo del	67	H3
Frias	138	C5
Fribourg	68	A2
Fridaythorpe	55	J2
Friedrichshafen	70	C5
Friesach	68	E2
Frio	127	N6
Frio, Cabo	138	H4
Friona	127	L3
Frisco	123	L8
Friza, Proliv	85	R7
Frobisher Bay	120	N5
Frobisher Lake	119	P4
Frodsham	55	G3
Frohavet	62	C5
Frolovo	79	G6
Frome Dorset, U.K.	52	E4
Frome Somerset, U.K.	52	E3
Frome, Lake	113	H5
Fronteira	66	C3
Frontera	131	N8
Front Royal	125	L7
Frosinone	69	D5
Froya	62	C5
Frutal	138	G3
Frydek Mistek	71	H4
Fteri	75	F3
Fuan	87	M6
Fudai	88	H5
Fuding	87	N6
Fudzin	88	E3
Fuengirola	66	D4
Fuente el Fresno	66	E3
Fuente Obejuna	66	D3
Fuentesauco	66	D2
Fuentes de Onoro	66	C2
Fuerte	127	H7
Fuerteventura	100	C3
Fufeng	93	L2
Fuga	91	G2
Fuhai	86	F2
Fujian	87	M6
Fu Jiang	93	L2
Fujin	88	D2
Fujinomiya	89	G8
Fuji-san	89	G8
Fujisawa	89	G8
Fukang	86	F3
Fukaura	88	G5
Fukuchiyama	89	E8
Fukue-shima	89	B9
Fukui	89	F7
Fukuoka Japan	89	C9
Fukuoka Japan	88	H5
Fukura	88	G6
Fukushima	89	H7
Fukuyama Japan	89	C10
Fukuyama Japan	89	D8
Fulacunda	104	B3
Fulad Mahalleh	95	L3
Fulaga	114	S9
Fulanga Passage	114	S9
Fulbourn	53	H2
Fulda Germany	70	C3
Fulda Germany	70	C3
Fullerton	126	D4
Fullerton, Cape	119	T3
Fulufjallet	63	E6
Fulwood	55	G3
Fumas, de Represa	138	G4
Fumay	64	F4
Fumel	65	D6
Funabashi	89	H8
Funafuti	111	S3
Funasdalen	62	E5
Funauke	89	F11
Funchal	100	B2
Fundao	66	C2
Fundy, Bay of	121	N8
Funing Jiangsu, China	87	M5
Funing Yunnan, China	93	L4
Funtua	105	G3
Fuqing	87	M6
Furancungo	109	F2
Furano	88	J4
Furg	95	M7
Furmanov	78	G4
Furmanovka	86	C3
Furmanovo	79	H6
Furneaux Group	113	K7
Furstenfeld	68	E2
Furstenwalde	70	F2
Furth	70	D4
Furukawa Japan	89	F7
Furukawa Japan	88	H6
Fury and Hecla Strait	120	K4
Fushun	87	N3
Fusui	93	L4
Futuna	114	U13
Fuwayrit	97	K3
Fu Xian	93	L1
Fuxin	87	N3
Fuyang	93	N2
Fuyu	87	N2
Fuyuan	88	E1
Fuyun	86	F2
Fuzesabony	72	F2
Fuzhou Fujian, China	87	M6
Fuzhou Jiangxi, China	87	M6
Fuzhoucheng	87	N4
Fuzuli	94	H2
Fyfield	53	H3
Fyn	63	D9
Fyne, Loch	57	C4
Fyresdal	63	C7
Fyvie	56	F3

G

Name	Page	Ref
Gaalkacyo	103	J6
Gabas	65	C7
Gabbac, Raas	103	K6
Gabela	106	B5
Gabes	101	H2
Gabes, Golfe de	101	H2
Gabgaba, Wadi	103	F3
Gabin	71	H2
Gabon	106	B3
Gaborone	108	E4
Gabriel, Mount	59	C9
Gabriel Vera	138	C3
Gabrik	95	P9
Gabrovo	73	H4
Gace	64	D4
Gach Sar	95	K3
Gach Saran	95	K6
Gacko	72	E4
Gadag	92	E5
Gaddede	62	F4
Gador, Sierra de	66	E4
Gadsden	129	K3
Gadwal	92	E5
Gadyach	79	E5
Gaesti	73	H3
Gaeta	69	D5
Gaeta, Golfo di	69	D5
Gafsa	101	G2
Gagarin	78	E4
Gagnoa	104	D4
Gagnon	121	N7
Gagra	79	G7
Gagui	102	C6
Gaibanda	93	G3
Gaidhouronisi	75	H5
Gailey	53	E2
Gaillac	65	D7
Gaillimh	59	D6
Gailtaler Alpen	68	D2
Gainesville Florida	129	L6
Gainesville Georgia	129	L3
Gainesville Texas	128	D4
Gainford	55	H2
Gainsborough	55	J3
Gairdner, Lake	113	H5
Gairloch, Loch	56	C3
Gai Xian	87	N3
Gaktsynka	85	P6
Galana	107	G3
Galand	95	M3
Galanino	84	E5
Galapagos, Islas	136	A7
Galashiels	57	F5
Galati	73	K3
Galatz	73	K3
Galax	125	K8
Galela	91	H5
Galena Alaska	118	D3
Galena Illinois	124	E5
Galena Kansas	124	C8
Galeota Point	136	E1
Galera, Punta de la	139	B7
Galesburg	124	E6
Galeton	125	M6
Galgate	55	H3
Galich Russia	78	G4
Galich Ukraine	71	L4
Galicia	66	C1
Galilee, Lake	113	K3
Galimyy	85	T4
Gallabat	103	G5
Gallan Head	56	A2
Gallarate	68	B3
Gallatin	129	J2
Galle	92	F7
Gallegos	139	B10
Galley Head	59	E9
Gallinas Mountains	127	J3
Gallinas, Punta	136	C1
Gallipoli Italy	69	F5
Gallipoli Turkey	76	B2
Gallivare	62	J3
Gallo	67	F2
Gallo	62	F5
Gallo, Capo	69	D6
Galloway	54	E2
Galloway, Mull of	54	E2
Gallup	127	H3
Galmisdale	57	B4
Galtymore Mount	59	F8
Galty Mountains	58	F8
Galveston	128	E6
Galveston Bay	128	E6
Galveston Island	128	E6
Galway Ireland	59	D6
Galway Ireland	59	E6
Galway Bay	59	D6
Gambell	118	A3
Gambia, The	104	B3
Gambier, Iles	143	J5
Gamboma	106	C3
Gamkunoro, Gunung	91	H5
Gamlakarleby	62	K5
Gamleby	63	G8
Gamshadzai Kuh	95	Q7
Gamvik	62	N1
Ganado	127	H3
Gananoque	125	M4
Ganaveh	95	K7
Gand	64	E3
Gandadiwata, Bukit	91	F6
Gandajika	106	D4
Gandak	92	F3
Gander	121	R8
Gander Lake	121	R8
Gandesa	67	G2
Gandhi Sagar	92	E4
Gandia	67	F3
Ganga	93	G3
Ganga, Mouths of the	93	G4
Gangan	139	C8
Ganganagar	92	D3
Gangara	101	G6
Gangdise Shan	92	F2
Ganges	93	G4
Gangew Taungdan	93	J4
Gangtok	93	G3
Gangu	93	L2
Ganjam	92	G5
Gan Jiang	87	M6
Gannat	65	E5
Gannett Peak	123	K6
Gansu	93	K2
Gantheaume, Cape	113	H6
Gantsevichi	71	M2
Ganyushkino	79	H6
Ganzhou	87	L6
Gao	100	E5
Gaoan	93	N3
Gaohe	93	M4
Gaolan	93	K1
Gaoqing	87	M4
Gaoua	104	E3
Gaoual	104	C3
Gaoyou Hu	87	M5
Gap	65	G6
Gar	92	E2
Garachine, Punta	132	H10

Name	Page	Grid
Gara, Lough	58	F5
Garanhuns	137	K5
Garara	114	D3
Garberville	122	C7
Garboldisham	53	H2
Garbosh, Kuh-e	95	K5
Garcas	138	F3
Gard	65	F7
Garda, Lago di	68	C3
Gardelegen	70	D2
Garden City	127	M2
Garden Grove	126	C4
Gardez	92	C2
Gardhiki	75	F3
Gardiner	123	J5
Gardnerville	126	C1
Gardno, Jezioro	71	G1
Garelochhead	57	D4
Gareloi Island	118	Ac9
Garessio	68	B3
Garforth	55	H3
Gargalianoi	75	F4
Gargunnock	57	D4
Garies	108	C6
Garissa	107	G3
Garland	128	D4
Garmish-Partenkirchen	70	D5
Garmsar	95	L4
Garnet Bay	120	L4
Garnett	128	E1
Garonne	65	C6
Garoua	105	H4
Garrison Dam	123	P4
Garron Point	58	L2
Garrovillas	66	C3
Garry Lake	119	R2
Garry, Loch	57	D3
Garstang	55	G3
Gartempe	65	D5
Gartocharn	57	D4
Garton Lough	58	G3
Garton-on-the-Wolds	55	J2
Garut	90	D7
Garvagh	58	J3
Garve	56	D3
Garvie Mountains	115	B6
Garwa	92	F4
Garwolin	71	J3
Gary	124	G6
Gar Zangbo	92	F2
Garze	93	J2
Garzon	136	B3
Gasan Kuli	95	L3
Gascogne	65	D7
Gascogne, Golfe de	65	C7
Gasconade	124	D8
Gascoyne	112	C3
Gascuna, Golfo de	67	F1
Gasht	95	Q8
Gashua	105	H3
Gask	95	P5
Gasmata	114	E3
Gaspar, Selat	90	D6
Gaspe	121	P8
Gaspe, Cape	121	P8
Gaspe Peninsula	121	N8
Gastonia	129	M3
Gaston, Lake	129	N2
Gastouni	75	F4
Gastre	139	C8
Gata, Cabo de	66	E4
Gatas, Akra	76	E5
Gata, Sierra de	66	C2
Gatchina	63	P7
Gatehouse of Fleet	54	E2
Gateshead	55	H2
Gateshead Island	119	Q1
Gatineau	125	N3
Gatooma	108	E3
Gatruyeh	95	M7
Gatun Lake	132	H10
Gatvand	94	J5
Gatwick	53	G3
Gaud-i-Zureh	95	R7
Gauer Lake	119	R4
Gauhati	93	H3
Gauja	63	L8
Gauldalen	62	D5
Gausta	63	C7
Gavater	95	Q9
Gavbus, Kuh-e	95	L8
Gavdhopoula	75	G5
Gavdhos	75	H5
Gaviao	66	C3
Gav Koshi	95	N7
Gavle	63	G6
Gavleborg	63	G6
Gavrilov-Yam	78	F4
Gawler	113	H5
Gawler Ranges	113	H5
Gaxun Nur	86	J3
Gaya	92	G4
Gaya La	92	F3
Gaydon	53	F2
Gayndah	113	L4
Gaysin	73	K1
Gayvoron	79	D6
Gaza	94	B6
Gazelle Peninsula	114	E2
Gazelle, Recif de la	114	W16
Gaziantep	77	G4
Gazimur	85	K6
Gazimurskiy Zavod	85	K6
Gazipasa	76	E4
Gbarnga	104	D4
Gboko	105	G4
Gdansk	71	H1
Gdov	63	M7
Geary	56	B3
Gebeit	96	C7
Gebze	76	C2
Gecitli	77	K4
Gedaref	103	G5
Gediz *Turkey*	76	B3
Gediz *Turkey*	76	C3
Gedney Hill	53	G2
Gedser	70	D1
Gee	64	F3
Geelong	113	J6
Geelvink Channel	112	C4
Geeveston	113	K7
Gegyai	92	F2
Geikie	119	Q4
Geilo	63	C6
Geita	107	F3
Geitlandsjokull	62	U12
Gejiu	93	K4
Geka, Mys	85	X4
Gela	69	E7
Geladi	103	J6
Gelendost	76	D3
Gelendzhik	79	F7
Gelibolu	76	B2
Gelibolu Yarimadasi	75	J2
Gelligaer	52	D3
Gelnhausen	70	C3
Gelsenkirchen	70	B3
Gemena	106	C2
Gemerek	77	G3
Gemlik	76	C2
Gemlik Korfezi	75	K2
Gemona del Friuli	68	D2
Gemund	70	B3
Genale Wenz	103	H6
Genc	77	J3
Geneina	102	D5
General Acha	139	D7
General Alvear	139	C7
General Bernardo O'Higgins	141	W6
General Conesa	139	D8
General La Madrid	139	D7
General Lavalle	139	E7
General Madariaga	139	E7
General Paz	139	E7
General Paz, Lago	139	B8
General Pico	139	D7
General Roca	139	C7
General Sam Martin	141	V5
General Santos	91	H4
General Villegas	139	D7
Geneseo	125	M5
Genessee	125	L5
Geneva *Switzerland*	68	A2
Geneva *U.S.A.*	125	M5
Geneva, Lake of	68	A2
Geneve	68	A2
Gen He	87	N1
Genichesk	79	E6
Genil	66	D4
Gennargentu, Monti del	69	B6
Genoa *Australia*	113	K6
Genoa *Italy*	68	B3
Genova	68	B3
Genova, Golfo di	68	B3
Genovesa, Isla	136	B7
Genriyetty, Ostrov	81	S2
Gent	64	E3
Genteng	90	D7
Genyem	91	L6
Geographe Bay	112	D5
Geographe Channel	112	C3
Geokchay	79	H7
George *Canada*	121	N6
George *South Africa*	108	D6
Georgeham	52	C3
George Island	139	E10
George, Lake	129	M6
George Sound	115	A6
Georgetown *Australia*	113	H5
George Town *Australia*	113	K7
Georgetown *Gambia*	104	C3
Georgetown *Grand Cayman, U.K.*	132	G5
Georgetown *Guyana*	136	F2
George Town *Malaysia*	90	C4
Georgetown *U.S.A.*	129	N4
George V Land	141	X4
George VI Sound	141	V4
Georgia	77	K1
Georgia	129	K4
Georgian Bay	125	K4
Georgia, Strait of	122	C3
Georgina	113	H3
Georgina Bay	121	K8
Georgiyevka	86	E2
Georgiyevsk	79	G7
Georg von Neumayer	141	Z4
Gera	70	E3
Geral de Goias, Serra	137	H6
Geraldine	115	C6
Geraldton *Australia*	112	C4
Geraldton *U.S.A.*	124	G2
Gerardmer	64	G4
Gerasimovka	84	A5
Gercus	77	J4
Gerede *Turkey*	76	E2
Gerede *Turkey*	76	E2
Gereshk	92	B2
Gergal	66	E4
Gerger	77	H4
Gerik	90	C4
Geris	76	D4
Gerlachovsky	71	J4
Germany	70	C3
Germencik	76	B4
Germi	94	J2
Germiston	108	E5
Gerona	67	H2
Gerrards Cross	53	G3
Gerze	76	F2
Geseke	70	C3
Geta	63	G6
Getafe	66	E2
Gettysburg *Pennsylvania*	125	M7
Gettysburg *S. Dakota*	123	Q5
Geumapang	90	B5
Gevan	95	N8
Gevas	77	K3
Geyik Dagi	76	E4
Geyik Daglari	76	E4
Geyve	76	D2
Gezi	77	F3
Ghadamis	101	G2
Ghaghara	92	F3
Ghana	104	E4
Ghanzi	108	D4
Gharah, Wadi	97	L8
Gharbi, Al Hajar al	97	N4
Gharbiya, Es Sahra el	103	E2
Ghardaia	101	F2
Ghardimaou	69	B7
Gharrat, Shatt al	94	H6
Gharyan	101	H2
Ghat	101	H3
Ghatampur	92	F3
Ghatere	114	J5
Ghayl Ba Wazir	97	J9
Ghayl Bin Yumayn	97	J9
Ghazaouet	100	E1
Ghaziabad	92	E3
Ghazipur	92	F3
Ghazni	92	C2
Gheorgheni	73	H2
Ghimes-Faget	73	J2
Ghisonaccia	69	B4
Ghisoni	69	B4
Ghubbah	97	P10
Ghubeish	102	E5
Ghudaf, Wadi al	94	E5
Ghurian	95	Q4
Giant's Causeway Head	58	J2
Giarre	69	E7
Gibostad	62	H2
Gibraltar	66	D4
Gibraltar Point	55	K3
Gibraltar, Strait of	66	D5
Gibson Desert	112	E3
Gichgeniyn Nuruu	86	H2
Gidole	103	G6
Gien	65	E5
Giesseckes Isfjord	120	Q3
Giessen	70	C3
Gifatin	96	A3
Gifford Creek	112	D3
Gifhorn	70	D2
Gifu	89	F8
Giganta, Sierra de la	130	D5
Gigha Island	57	C5
Gigha, Sound of	57	C5
Giglio, Isola di	69	C4
Gijon	66	D1
Gijunabena Islands	114	J5
Gila	126	F4
Gila Bend	126	F4
Gilan Garb	94	G4
Gilbert	113	J2
Gilbert Islands	111	R2
Gilbert, Mount	122	B2
Gilbues	137	H5
Gile	109	G3
Gilford	58	K4
Gilgandra	113	K5
Gilgit	92	D1
Gillam	119	S4
Gillen, Mount	113	G3
Gillesnuole	62	G4
Gillespie Point	115	B5
Gillette	123	M5
Gillian Lake	120	L4
Gillingham	53	H3
Gill, Lough	58	F4
Gilroy	126	B2
Giluwe, Mount	114	C3
Gimli	123	R2
Gimo	63	H6
Gimone	65	D7
Ginda	96	D9
Gingin	112	D5
Ginir	103	H6
Gioia del Colle	69	F5
Gioia, Golfo di	69	E6
Giona	75	G3
Girardot	136	C3
Girdle Ness	57	F3
Giresun	77	H2
Girga	103	F2
Girgir, Cape	114	C2
Giridih	92	G4
Girifalco	69	F6
Gironde	65	C6
Girvan	57	D5
Gisborne	115	G3
Gisenye	107	E3
Gislaved	63	E8
Gisors	64	D4
Gitega	107	E3
Giurgeni	73	J3
Giurgiu	73	H4
Givet	64	F3
Givors	65	F6
Gizhiginskaya Guba	85	T4
Gizol	114	H6
Gizycko	71	J1
Gjesvar	62	L1
Gjirokaster	75	F2
Gjoa Haven	120	G4
Gjovik	63	D6
Gjuhezes, Kep i	74	E2
Glace Bay	121	Q8
Glacier Bay	118	H4
Glacier Peak	122	D3
Gladstone *Australia*	113	L3
Gladstone *U.S.A.*	124	G4
Glama	63	D6
Glamis	57	E4
Glamoc	72	D3
Glarus	68	B2
Glasdrumman	58	L4
Glasgow *U.K.*	57	D5
Glasgow *Kentucky*	124	H8
Glasgow *Montana*	123	L3
Glas Maol	57	E4
Glass	56	D3
Glass, Loch	56	D3
Glastonbury	52	E3
Glatz	71	G3
Glauchau	70	E3
Glazov	78	J4
Glda	71	G2
Gleiwitz	71	H3
Glen Affric	56	D3
Glenan, Iles de	65	B5
Glenavy	115	C6
Glen Cannich	56	D3
Glen Canyon	126	G2
Glen Canyon Dam	126	G2
Glencarse	57	E4
Glen Coe	57	D4
Glencoe	108	F5
Glen Cove	125	N5
Glendale *Arizona*	126	F4
Glendale *California*	126	C3
Glendive	123	M4
Glenelg *Australia*	113	J6
Glenelg *U.K.*	56	C3
Glen Esk	57	F4
Glenfinnan	57	C4
Glengad Head	58	H2
Glen Garry *Highland, U.K.*	57	C3
Glen Garry *Tayside, U.K.*	57	D4
Glen Innes	113	L4
Glen Mor	57	D3
Glen Moriston	57	D3
Glennallen	118	F3
Glen Orrin	56	D3
Glenrothes	57	E4
Glens Falls	125	P5
Glenshee	57	E4
Glentham	55	J3
Glenwood	128	F3
Glenwood Springs	123	L8
Glin	59	D7
Glina	72	D3
Glittertind	63	C6
Gliwice	71	H3
Gllave	74	E2
Globe	126	G4
Glockner, Gross	68	D2
Glogau	70	G3
Glogow	70	G3
Glomach, Falls of	56	C3
Glomfjord	62	E3
Glommerstrask	62	H4
Glossop	55	H3
Glottof, Mount	118	E4
Gloucester *Australia*	113	L5
Gloucester *Papua New Guinea*	114	D3
Gloucester *U.K.*	52	E3
Gloucester *U.S.A.*	125	Q5
Gloucestershire	52	E3
Gloup	56	A1
Glover Reef	132	D6
Glowno	71	H3
Glubczyce	71	G3
Glubinnoye	88	E2
Glubokoye *Belarus*	63	M9
Glubokoye *Kazakhstan*	84	C6
Gluckstadt	70	C2
Glukhov	79	E5
Glyadyanskoye	84	Ae6
Glybokaya	73	H1
Glyder Fawr	54	E3
Gmelinka	79	H5
Gmund	68	D2
Gmunden	68	D2
Gnalta	113	J5
Gnarp	63	G5
Gniezno	71	G2
Gnoien	70	E2
Gnosall	52	E2
Goa	92	D5
Goalpara	93	H3
Goatfell	57	C5
Goba	103	H6
Gobabis	108	C4

Gobi	87	K3
Gobo	89	E9
Gochas	108	C4
Godafoss	62	W12
Godalming	53	G3
Godavari	92	F5
Godbout	125	S2
Goderich	125	K5
Godhavn	120	R4
Godhra	92	D4
Godollo	72	E2
Gods	119	S4
Godshill	53	F4
Gods Lake	119	S5
Godthab	120	R5
Godwin Austen	92	E1
Goeland, Lac au	121	L8
Goes	64	E3
Gogama	125	K3
Goginan	52	D2
Gogland, Ostrov	63	M6
Gogolin	71	H3
Goiana	137	L5
Goiania	138	G3
Goias *Brazil*	138	F3
Goias *Brazil*	137	H6
Gojome	88	H6
Gokceada	76	A2
Gokcekaya Baraji	76	D2
Gokdere	77	G2
Gokirmak	76	F2
Gokova Korfezi	76	B4
Goksu *Turkey*	76	E4
Goksu *Turkey*	77	F4
Goksun	77	G3
Goktas	77	J2
Goktepe	76	E4
Gol	63	C6
Golaghat	93	H3
Golam Head	59	C6
Golashkerd	95	N8
Golbasi *Turkey*	76	E3
Golbasi *Turkey*	77	G4
Golcar	55	H3
Golchikha	84	C2
Golconda	122	F7
Golcuk	76	C2
Golcuk Daglari	76	B3
Goldap	71	K1
Gold Coast	113	L4
Golden	122	F2
Golden Bay	115	D4
Goldendale	122	D5
Golden Hinde	122	B3
Goldsboro	129	P3
Goldsworthy	112	D3
Gole	77	K2
Golebert	77	K2
Goleniow	70	F2
Golfito	132	F10
Golfo Aranci	69	B5
Golgeli Daglari	76	C4
Golhisar	76	C4
Golija Planina	72	F4
Golkoy	77	G2
Golmarmara	76	B3
Golmud	93	H1
Golo	69	B4
Golova	76	D4
Golovanevsk	73	L1
Golovnino	88	K4
Golpayegan	95	K5
Golpazari	76	D2
Goma	107	E3
Gombe	105	H3
Gombi	105	H3
Gomera	100	B3
Gomez Palacio	127	L8
Gomishan	95	M3
Gonaives	133	L5
Gonam *Russia*	85	M5
Gonam *Russia*	85	N5
Gonave, Golfe de la	133	L5
Gonave, Ile de la	133	L5
Gonbad-e Kavus	95	M3
Gonda	92	F3
Gondal	92	D4
Gonder	103	G5
Gondia	92	F4
Gonen *Turkey*	76	B2
Gonen *Turkey*	76	B3
Gongbogyamda	93	H3
Gongolo	105	H3
Gongpoquan	86	H3
Goniadz	71	K2
Gonumillo	139	C8
Gonzales *California*	126	B2
Gonzales *Texas*	128	D6
Gonzales Chaves	139	D7
Goob Weyn	107	H3
Goodenough, Cape	141	J5
Goodenough Island	114	E3
Good Hope, Cape of	108	C6
Gooding	122	G6
Goodland	123	P8
Goole	55	J3
Goolgowi	113	K5
Goomen	113	L4
Goondiwindi	113	L4
Goose Bay	121	P7
Goose Creek	129	M4
Goose Lake	122	D7
Goplo, Jezioro	71	H2
Goppingen	70	C4

Gora Kalwaria	71	J3
Gorakhpur	92	F3
Gorazde	72	E4
Gorda, Punta	138	B3
Gordes	76	C3
Gordonsville	125	L7
Gore	115	B7
Gore	103	G6
Gorele	77	H2
Goresbridge	59	J7
Gorey *Ireland*	59	K7
Gorey *U.K.*	53	M7
Gorgan	95	M3
Gorgan, Rud-e	95	M3
Gorgona, Isola di	68	B4
Gorgoram	105	H3
Gori	77	L1
Gorice	75	F2
Gorinchem	64	F3
Goris	94	H2
Gorizia	68	D3
Gorka	78	H3
Gorkha	92	F3
Gorki *Belarus*	78	E5
Gorki *Russia*	84	Ae3
Gorki *Russia*	78	H4
Gorkovskoye Vodokhranilishche	78	G4
Gorlev	63	D9
Gorlice	71	J4
Gorlitz	70	F3
Gornji Milanovac	72	F3
Gornji Vakuf	72	D4
Gorno-Altaysk	84	D6
Gornozavodsk	88	H2
Gornyak	84	C6
Gornyy *Russia*	79	H5
Gornyy *Russia*	85	P6
Gorodenka	73	H1
Gorodets	78	G4
Gorodok	71	K4
Gorodovikovsk	79	G6
Goroka	114	D3
Gorokhov	71	L3
Gorong, Kepulauan	91	J6
Gorongoza	109	F3
Gorontalo	91	G5
Goroshikha	84	D3
Gorran Haven	52	C4
Gorseinon	52	C3
Gort	59	E6
Gortaclare	58	H3
Gortahork	58	F2
Gorumna Island	59	C6
Goryn	79	D5
Gorzow Wielkopolski	70	F2
Goschen Strait	114	E4
Gosforth	55	H1
Goshogawara	88	H5
Gospic	72	C3
Gosport	53	F4
Gostivar	73	F5
Gota	62	Z14
Gota Kanal	63	G7
Gotaland	63	E8
Goteborg	63	H8
Goteborg Och Bohus	63	D7
Gotene	63	E7
Gotha	70	D3
Gothenburg	63	D8
Gotland	63	H8
Goto-retto	89	B9
Gotse Delchev	73	G5
Gotska Sandon	63	H7
Gotsu	89	D8
Gottingen	70	C3
Gottwaldov	71	G4
Gouda	64	F2
Goudhurst	53	H3
Gough Island	48	F6
Gouin, Reservoir	125	N2
Goulais	124	J3
Goulburn	113	K5
Goulburn Islands	113	G1
Goundam	100	E5
Gourdon	65	D6
Goure	101	H6
Gourma-Rharous	100	E5
Gournay	64	D4
Gourock	57	D5
Govena, Mys	85	V5
Goverla	71	L4
Governador Valadares	138	H3
Governor's Harbour	132	J2
Govind Pant Sagar	92	F4
Govorovo	85	M2
Gowanbridge	115	D4
Gowanda	125	L5
Gower	52	C3
Gowna, Lough	58	G5
Goya	138	E5
Goynucek	77	F2
Goynuk *Turkey*	76	D2
Goynuk *Turkey*	77	J3
Goz Beida	102	D5
Gozne	76	F4
Gozo	74	C4
Goz Regeb	96	B8
Graaff Reinet	108	D6
Gracac	72	C3
Gradaus, Serra dos	137	G5
Grado *Italy*	68	D3
Grado *Spain*	66	C1
Gradoli	69	C4

Gradsko	73	F5
Grafham Water	53	G2
Grafton *Australia*	113	L4
Grafton *N. Dakota*	123	R3
Grafton *W. Virginia*	125	K7
Grafton, Islas	139	B10
Graham	128	C4
Graham Island *British Columbia, Canada*	118	J5
Graham Island *NW. Territories, Canada*	120	H2
Graham Land	141	V5
Grahamstown	108	E6
Graie, Alpi	68	A3
Graiguenamanagh	59	J7
Grain	53	H3
Grajau	137	H4
Grajewo	71	K2
Grampian	56	E3
Grampian Mountains	57	D4
Grampound	52	C4
Gramsh	75	F2
Gran	137	F3
Granada *Nicaragua*	132	E9
Granada *Spain*	66	E4
Granard	58	H5
Gran Bajo	139	C9
Granby *Canada*	125	P4
Granby *U.S.A.*	123	L7
Gran Canaria	100	B3
Gran Chaco	138	D4
Grand *Canada*	125	K5
Grand *Michigan*	124	H5
Grand *Missouri*	124	C6
Grand *S. Dakota*	123	P5
Grand Bahama	132	H1
Grand Bois, Coteau de	124	C3
Grand Canal *China*	87	M5
Grand Canal *Ireland*	59	H6
Grand Canyon *U.S.A.*	126	F2
Grand Canyon *U.S.A.*	126	F2
Grand Cayman	132	G5
Grand Coulee	122	E4
Grand Coulee Dam	122	E4
Grande *Brazil*	138	G4
Grande *Mexico*	131	L9
Grande *Nicaragua*	132	E8
Grande, Bahia	139	C10
Grande Cache	119	M5
Grande, Cienaga	133	K10
Grande Comore	109	H2
Grande Miquelon	121	Q8
Grande O'Guapay	138	D3
Grande Prairie	119	M4
Grande, Punta	137	G3
Grande, Rio	127	M6
Grande Ronde	122	F5
Gran Desierto	126	E5
Grandes Rocques	53	M7
Grand Falls *New Brunswick, Canada*	125	S3
Grand Falls *Newfoundland, Canada*	121	Q8
Grand Forks	123	R4
Grand Island	123	Q7
Grand Isle	128	H6
Grand Junction	127	H1
Grand Lahou	104	E4
Grand Lake *New Brunswick, Canada*	128	G6
Grand Lake *Newfoundland, Canada*	121	Q8
Grand Lake *U.S.A.*	125	S3
Grand Lake O' the Cherokees	128	E2
Grand-Lieu, Lac de	65	C5
Grand Manan Island	125	S4
Grand Marais *Michigan*	124	H3
Grand Marais *Minnesota*	124	E3
Grand-Mere	125	P3
Grandola	66	B3
Grand Popo	105	F4
Grand Prairie	128	D4
Grand Rapids *Canada*	119	R5
Grand Rapids *Michigan*	124	H5
Grand Rapids *Minnesota*	124	D3
Grandrieu	65	E6
Grand Saint Bernard, Col du	68	A3
Grand Santi	137	G3
Graney, Lough	59	E7
Grangemouth	57	E4
Grange-over-Sands	55	G2
Grangesberg	63	F6
Grangeville	122	F5
Granite Peak	123	K5
Granitola, Capo	69	D7
Granna	63	F7
Granollers	67	H2
Gran Pajonal	136	C6
Gran Paradiso	68	A3
Grantham	53	G2
Grant Island	141	R4
Grant, Mount	122	E8
Grantown-on-Spey	56	E3
Grants	127	J3
Grantshouse	57	F4
Grants Pass	122	C6
Granville	64	C4
Granville Lake	119	Q4
Grasby	55	J3
Gras, Lac de	119	N3
Grasmere	55	F2
Graso	63	H6
Grasse	65	G7
Grassrange	123	K4

Grass Valley	122	D8
Grassy	113	J7
Grassy Knob	125	K7
Gratens	65	D7
Graus	67	G1
Gravatai	138	F5
Gravdal	62	E2
Gravelines	64	E3
Grave, Pointe de	65	C6
Gravesend	53	H3
Gravois, Pointe-a-	133	L5
Gray	65	F5
Grayling	124	H4
Grays	53	H3
Grays Harbor	122	B4
Graz	68	E2
Great Abaco	132	J1
Great Artesian Basin	113	J4
Great Astrolabe Reef	114	R9
Great Australian Bight	112	F5
Great Ayton	55	H2
Great Baddow	53	H3
Great Bahama Bank	132	H2
Great Bardfield	53	H3
Great Barrier Island	115	E2
Great Barrier Reef	113	K2
Great Basin	122	F7
Great Bear Lake	119	L2
Great Bend	127	N1
Great Blasket Island	59	A8
Great Budworth	55	G3
Great Cumbrae	57	D5
Great Dividing Range	113	K3
Great Driffield	55	J2
Great Dunmow	53	H3
Greater Antarctica	141	D2
Greater Antilles	132	G4
Greater Khingan Range	87	N2
Greater London	53	G3
Greater Manchester	55	G3
Great Exuma Island	132	K3
Great Falls	122	J4
Great Fish	108	E6
Great Gable	55	F2
Great Guana Cay	132	J2
Great Harwood	55	G3
Great Inagua	133	L4
Great Indian Desert	92	D3
Great Island	59	F9
Great Karas Berg	108	C5
Great Karoo	108	D6
Great Lakes	143	L3
Great Longton	55	H2
Great Malvern	52	E2
Great Mercury Island	115	E2
Great Nicobar	93	H7
Great North East Channel	114	C3
Great Ormes Head	54	F3
Great Ouse	53	H2
Great Papuan Plateau	114	C3
Great Plains	123	J2
Great Ruaha	107	G4
Great Sacandaga Lake	125	N5
Great Salt Lake	122	H7
Great Salt Lake Desert	122	H7
Great Sand Hills	123	K2
Great Sandy Desert	112	E3
Great Sankey	55	G3
Great Sea Reef	114	R8
Great Sitkin Island	118	Ac9
Great Slave Lake	119	N2
Great Smeaton	55	H2
Great Stour	53	J3
Great Sugar Loaf	59	K6
Great Torrington	52	C4
Great Victoria Desert	112	F4
Great Wall of China, The	87	L4
Great Whernside	55	H2
Great Witley	52	E2
Great Yarmouth	53	J2
Great Yeldham	53	H2
Great Zab	94	F3
Gredos, Sierra de	66	D2
Greece	75	F3
Greeley	123	M7
Greely Fjord	120	K1
Green *Kentucky*	124	G8
Green *Wyoming*	123	J6
Green Bay *U.S.A.*	124	G4
Green Bay *U.S.A.*	124	G4
Green Bell, Ostrov	80	H1
Greenbrier	125	K8
Greencastle	58	K4
Greeneville	129	L2
Greenfield	125	P5
Green Hammerton	55	H2
Greenhead	55	G2
Green Island	115	C6
Greenisland	58	L3
Green Islands	114	E2
Greenland	116	Q1
Greenlaw	57	F4
Greenlough	112	D4
Greenlowther	57	D5
Green Mountains	125	P5
Greenock	57	D5
Green River *Papua New Guinea*	114	C2
Green River *Utah*	127	G1
Green River *Wyoming*	123	K7
Greensboro	129	N2
Greensburg	125	L6
Greenstone Point	56	C3
Green Valley	126	G5
Greenville *Alabama*	129	J5

Name	Page	Grid
Jahrom	95	L7
Jaicos	137	J5
Jailolo	91	H5
Jailolo, Selat	91	H5
Jaipur	92	E3
Jaisalmer	92	D3
Jajarm	95	N3
Jajce	72	D3
Jajpur	92	G4
Jakarta	90	D7
Jakhau	92	C4
Jakobstad	62	K5
Jakupica	73	F5
Jalaid Qi	87	N2
Jalalabad	92	D2
Jalalpur Pirwala	92	D3
Jalapa *Mexico*	131	L8
Jalapa *Mexico*	131	N9
Jalasjarvi	62	K5
Jalgaon	92	E4
Jalingo	105	H4
Jalna	92	E5
Jalon	67	F2
Jalor	92	D3
Jalostotitlan	130	H7
Jalpa	130	H7
Jalpaiguri	93	G3
Jalpan	131	K7
Jalu	101	K2
Jam	95	Q4
Jamaica	132	J5
Jamaica Channel	133	K5
Jamalpur *Bangladesh*	93	G4
Jamalpur *India*	92	G3
Jamanxim	137	F5
Jamari	136	E5
Jambi	90	C6
James	123	R6
James Bay	121	K7
James Island	136	A7
James Ross, Cape	120	D3
James Ross Island	141	W6
James Ross Strait	120	G4
Jamestown *South Africa*	108	E6
Jamestown *N. Dakota*	123	Q4
Jamestown *New York*	125	L5
Jamjo	63	F8
Jamkhandi	92	E5
Jamkhed	92	E5
Jammerbugten	63	C8
Jammu	92	D2
Jammu and Kashmir	92	E2
Jamnagar	92	D4
Jampur	92	D3
Jamsa	63	L6
Jamshedpur	92	G4
Jamtland	62	F5
Jamuna	93	G3
Janda, Laguna de la	66	D4
Jandaq	95	M4
Jandiatuba	136	D4
Janesville	124	F5
Janjira	92	D5
Jan Mayen	48	F2
Jannatabad	95	Q4
Janos	127	H5
Januaria	138	H3
Janubiyah, Al Badiyah al	94	H6
Jaora	92	E4
Japan	89	G7
Japan, Sea of	88	D6
Japan Trench	142	F3
Japaratuba	137	K6
Japura	136	D4
Jarabulus	94	D3
Jaragua	138	G3
Jaraguari	138	F4
Jarama	66	E2
Jarandilla	66	D2
Jarash	94	B5
Jardee	112	D5
Jardines de la Reina	132	H4
Jari	137	G3
Jarir, Wadi al	96	F4
Jarna	63	G7
Jarnac	65	C6
Jaromer	70	F3
Jaroslaw	71	K3
Jarpen	62	E5
Jarrow	55	H2
Jarruhi	94	J6
Jartai	87	K4
Jarvso	63	G6
Jashpurnagar	92	F4
Jask	95	N9
Jasper *Canada*	119	M5
Jasper *Alabama*	129	J4
Jasper *Florida*	129	L5
Jasper *Texas*	128	F5
Jassy	73	J2
Jastrebarsko	72	C3
Jastrowie	71	G2
Jastrzebie-Zdroj	71	H4
Jaszbereny	72	E2
Jatai	138	F3
Jatapu	136	F4
Jath	92	E5
Jativa	67	F3
Jatoba	137	G6
Jau	136	E4
Jau	138	G4
Jauaperi	136	E4
Jauja	136	B6
Jaunpur	92	F3
Java	90	E7
Java Trench	142	E5
Javier, Isla	139	B9
Javor	72	E3
Javorniky	71	H4
Jawa	90	D7
Jawa, Laut	90	E7
Jawb, Al	97	K5
Jawhar	107	J2
Jawor	71	G3
Jayanca	136	B5
Jaya, Puncak	91	K6
Jayapura	91	L6
Jayawijaya, Pegunungan	91	K6
Jayena	66	E4
Jaypur	92	F5
Jayrud	94	C5
Jazirah, Al	94	E4
Jaz Murian, Hamun-e	95	P8
Jebal Barez, Kuh-e	95	P7
Jebba	105	F4
Jebel, Bahr el	102	F6
Jech Doab	92	D2
Jedburgh	57	F5
Jedeida	69	B7
Jefferson	122	H5
Jefferson City *Missouri*	124	D7
Jefferson City *Tennessee*	129	L2
Jefferson, Mount *Nevada*	122	F8
Jefferson, Mount *Oregon*	122	D5
Jef Jef el Kebir	102	D3
Jehile Puzak	95	Q6
Jekabpils	63	L8
Jeldesa	103	H6
Jelgava	63	K8
Jelow Gir	94	H5
Jemaja	90	D5
Jember	90	E7
Jeminay	86	F2
Jemnice	70	F4
Jena	70	D3
Jendouba	69	B7
Jenin	94	B5
Jenkins	124	J8
Jennings	128	F5
Jenny Lind Island	119	Q2
Jens Munk Island	120	L4
Jequie	137	J6
Jequitinhonha *Brazil*	138	H3
Jequitinhonha *Brazil*	138	H3
Jerada	100	E2
Jerba, Ile de	101	H2
Jeremie	133	K5
Jeremoabo	137	K6
Jerevan	77	L2
Jerez	130	H6
Jerez de la Frontera	66	C4
Jericho *Australia*	113	K3
Jericho *Israel*	94	B6
Jerome	122	G6
Jersey	53	M7
Jersey City	125	N6
Jerseyville	124	E7
Jerusalem	94	B6
Jervis Inlet	122	C2
Jeseniky	71	G3
Jessheim	63	D6
Jessore	92	G4
Jesup	129	M5
Jevnaker	63	D6
Jezerce	74	E1
Jeziorak, Jezioro	71	H2
Jeznas	71	L1
Jezzine	94	B5
Jhang Maghiana	92	D2
Jhansi	92	E3
Jhelum *Pakistan*	92	D2
Jhelum *Pakistan*	92	D2
Jialing Jiang	93	L2
Jiamusi	88	C2
Jian	93	N3
Jianchuan	93	J3
Jiande	87	M6
Jiange	93	L2
Jiangjin	93	L3
Jiangjunmiao	86	F3
Jiangmen	93	M4
Jiangsu	87	M5
Jiangxi	93	M3
Jianning	87	M6
Jianou	87	M6
Jianquanzi	86	H3
Jianshi	93	L2
Jiaohe	87	P3
Jiaoling	87	M7
Jiaozuo	93	M1
Jia Xian	87	L4
Jiaxing	87	N5
Jiayin	88	C1
Jiayuguan	86	H4
Jiboia	136	D3
Jibou	73	G2
Jibsh, Ra's	97	P6
Jicatuyo	132	C7
Jiddah	96	D6
Jidong	88	C3
Jiekkevarre	62	H2
Jieknaffo	62	G3
Jiesavrre	62	L2
Jihlava *Czech Rep.*	70	F4
Jihlava *Czech Rep.*	71	G4
Jijel	101	G1
Jijia	73	J2
Jijiga	103	H6
Jijihu	86	F3
Jilava	73	J3
Jilin *China*	87	P3
Jilin *China*	87	P3
Jiloca	67	F2
Jilove	70	F4
Jima	103	G6
Jimba Jimba	112	D4
Jimena de la Frontera	66	D4
Jimenez	127	M6
Jimenez *Mexico*	128	C8
Jimenez *Mexico*	127	K7
Jimo	87	N4
Jinan	87	M4
Jincheng	87	K4
Jingchuan	93	L1
Jingdezhen	87	M6
Jinghai	87	M4
Jinghe	86	E3
Jinghong	93	K4
Jingle	87	L4
Jingmen	93	M2
Jingpo	88	B3
Jingpo Hu	88	B4
Jingtai	93	K1
Jingxi	93	L4
Jing Xian	93	L3
Jinhua	87	M6
Jining *Nei Mongol Zizhiqu, China*	87	L3
Jining *Shandong, China*	87	M4
Jinja	107	F2
Jinkou	87	N4
Jinning	93	K4
Jinotepe	132	D9
Jinsha Jiang	93	J3
Jinta	86	H4
Jinxi	87	N3
Jin Xian	87	N4
Jinzhou	87	N3
Jinzhou Wan	87	N4
Jiparana	136	E5
Jipijapa	136	A4
Jiquilpan	130	H8
Jirriban	103	J6
Jirueque	66	E2
Jirwan	97	K5
Jishou	93	L3
Jisr ash Shughur	94	C4
Jiu	73	G3
Jiujiang	93	N3
Jiuling Shan	93	M3
Jiutai	87	P3
Jiwa, Al	97	M5
Jiwani	92	B3
Jiwani, Ras	92	B4
Jixi *Anhui, China*	87	M5
Jixi *Heilongjiang, China*	87	Q2
Jixian	88	C2
Jizan	96	F8
Jizl, Wadi	96	C3
Jiz, Wadi al	97	K8
Joao Pessoa	137	L5
Joaquin V. Gonzalez	138	D5
Joban	89	H7
Jodar	66	E4
Jodhpur	92	D3
Joensuu	62	N5
Joetsu	89	G7
Jofane	109	F4
Joffre, Mount	122	G2
Jogeva	63	M7
Joghatay	95	N3
Johannesburg	108	E5
John Day *U.S.A.*	122	D5
John Day *U.S.A.*	122	E5
John H. Kerr Reservoir	129	N2
John O'Groats	56	E2
Johnshaven	57	F4
Johnson City	129	L2
Johnston *U.K.*	52	B3
Johnston *U.S.A.*	129	M4
Johnstone	57	D5
Johnston Lakes, The	112	E5
Johnstown	125	L6
Johor Baharu	90	C5
Joigny	65	E5
Joinville *Brazil*	138	G5
Joinville *France*	64	F4
Joinville Island	141	W6
Jokkmokk	62	H3
Jokulbunga	62	T11
Jokulsa a Bru	62	X12
Jokulsa-a Fjollum	62	W12
Jolfa	94	G2
Joliet	124	G3
Joliette	125	P3
Jolo *Philippines*	91	G4
Jolo *Philippines*	91	G4
Jonava	63	N9
Jonesboro	128	G3
Jones Sound	120	J2
Jonglei Canal	102	F6
Joniskis	63	K8
Jonkoping *Sweden*	63	F8
Jonkoping *Sweden*	63	F8
Jonquiere	125	Q2
Jonzac	65	C6
Joplin	124	C8
Jordan	94	B6
Jordan	94	B5
Jordan *U.S.A.*	123	L4
Jordanow	71	H4
Jordan Valley	122	F6
Jorhat	93	H3
Jorn	62	J4
Jorong	90	E6
Jorpeland	63	B7
Jos	105	G3
Jose de San Martin	139	B8
Joseph Bonaparte Gulf	112	F1
Joseph, Lac	121	N7
Josselin	65	B5
Jos Sodarso, Pulau	91	K7
Jostedalsbreen	63	B6
Jotunheimen	63	C6
Jounie	94	B5
Joutsa	63	M6
Joyces Country	59	C5
J. Percy Priest Lake	129	J2
Juan Aldama	130	H5
Juan de Fuca Strait	122	B3
Juan de Nova	109	H3
Juan Fernandez, Islas de	135	A6
Juanjui	136	B5
Juarez, Sierra	126	D4
Juazeiro	137	J5
Juazeiro do Norte	137	K5
Juba	103	F7
Jubany	141	W6
Jubba	107	H2
Juby, Cap	100	C3
Jucar	67	F3
Juchitan	131	M9
Judenburg	68	E2
Juigalpa	132	E8
Juist	70	B2
Juiz de Fora	138	H4
Juklegga	63	E6
Julia	136	D4
Juliaca	138	B3
Julia Creek	113	J3
Julianehab	116	Q2
Julijske Alpe	72	B2
Julio de Castilhos	138	F5
Jullundur	92	E2
Jumilla	67	F3
Jumla	92	F3
Junagadh	92	D4
Junction	127	N5
Junction City	123	R8
Jundiai	138	G4
Juneau	118	J4
Junee	113	K5
Jungfrau	68	A2
Junggar Pendi	86	F2
Junin	139	D6
Junin de los Andes	139	B7
Junosuando	62	K3
Junsele	62	G5
Jun Xian	93	M2
Jura *France*	65	G5
Jura *U.K.*	57	C5
Jura, Sound of	57	C5
Juratishki	71	L1
Juriti	137	F4
Jurua *Brazil*	136	D4
Jurua *Brazil*	136	D4
Juruena	136	F6
Jussey	65	F5
Jutai *Brazil*	136	D4
Jutai *Brazil*	136	D5
Juterbog	70	E3
Juticalpa	132	D7
Jutland	63	C8
Juuka	62	N5
Juva	63	M6
Juventud, Isla de la	132	F4
Ju Xian	87	M4
Juymand	95	P4
Juyom	95	M7
Juzna Morava	73	F4
Jylland	63	C8
Jyvaskyla	62	L5

K

Name	Page	Grid
Kaala-Gomen	114	W16
Kaamanen	62	M2
Kaavi	62	N5
Kaba	104	C4
Kabaena	91	G7
Kabala	104	C4
Kabale	107	E3
Kabalega Falls	107	F2
Kabalo	106	E4
Kabambare	107	E3
Kabara	114	S9
Kabba	105	G4
Kabinatagami	124	H1
Kabinda	106	D4
Kabirkuh	94	H5
Kabompo	106	D5
Kabongo	106	E4
Kabud Gonbad	95	P3
Kabul *Afghanistan*	92	C2
Kabuli	114	D2
Kaburuang	91	H5
Kabwe	107	E5
Kabyrdak	84	A5
Kachchh, Gulf of	92	C4
Kachchh, Rann of	92	C4
Kachemak Bay	118	E4
Kachikattsy	85	M4
Kachug	84	H6

178

Name	Page	Ref
Kaributo	88	H4
Karigasniemi	62	L2
Karikari, Cape	115	D1
Karima	103	F4
Karimata, Kepulauan	90	D6
Karimata, Selat	90	D6
Karimganj	93	H4
Karimnagar	92	E5
Karimunjawa, Kepulauan	90	E7
Karin	103	J5
Karistos	75	H3
Kariz	95	Q4
Karkaralinsk	86	D2
Karkaralong, Kepulauan	91	H5
Karkar Island	114	D2
Karkas, Kuh-e	95	L5
Karkkila	63	L6
Karlino	70	F1
Karliova	77	J3
Karl-Marx-Stadt	70	E3
Karlobag	72	C3
Karlovac	72	C3
Karlovo	73	H4
Karlovy Vary	70	E3
Karlsborg	63	F7
Karlskoga	63	F7
Karlskrona	63	F8
Karlsruhe	70	C4
Karlstad *Sweden*	63	E7
Karlstad *U.S.A.*	124	B2
Karlstadt	70	C4
Karmanovka	79	J6
Karmoy	63	A7
Karnafuli Reservoir	93	H4
Karnal	92	E3
Karnali	92	F3
Karnataka	92	E6
Karnobat	73	J4
Karonie	112	E5
Karora	103	G4
Karossa, Tanjung	91	F7
Karousadhes	74	E3
Karoy	86	D2
Karpathos *Greece*	75	J5
Karpathos *Greece*	75	J5
Karpathos Straits	75	J5
Karpathou, Stenon	75	J5
Karpenision	75	F3
Karpinsk	84	Ad5
Karpogory	78	G3
Karratha	112	D3
Karrats Fjord	120	R3
Karree Berge	108	D6
Kars *Turkey*	77	K2
Kars *Turkey*	77	K2
Karsakpay	86	B2
Karsamaki	62	L5
Karsanti	76	F4
Karshi *Kazakhstan*	79	J7
Karshi *Uzbekistan*	80	H6
Karsiyaka	76	B3
Karskoye More	84	A2
Karsun	78	H5
Kartal	76	C2
Kartayel	78	J3
Kartuni	133	T11
Kartuzy	71	H1
Karufa	91	J6
Karun	94	J6
Karvina	71	H4
Karwar	92	D6
Karym	84	Ae4
Karymskoye	85	J6
Kas	76	C4
Kasai	106	C3
Kasaji	106	D5
Kasama	107	F5
Kasane	108	E3
Kasanga	107	F4
Kasangulu	106	C3
Kasaragod	92	D6
Kasar, Ras	96	D7
Kasba Lake	119	Q3
Kasba Tadla	100	D2
Kasempa	106	E5
Kasese	107	F2
Kashaf	95	Q3
Kashan	95	K5
Kashary	79	G6
Kashgar	86	D4
Kashi	86	D4
Kashima	89	C9
Kashin	78	F4
Kashipur	92	E3
Kashira	78	F5
Kashiwazaki	89	G7
Kashkanteniz	86	C2
Kashkarantsy	78	F2
Kashmar	95	P4
Kasimov	78	G5
Kasin	92	D2
Kasiruta	91	H6
Kaskinen	62	J5
Kasko	62	J5
Kas Kong	93	K6
Kasli	84	Ad5
Kasmere Lake	119	Q4
Kasongo	106	E3
Kasongo-Lunda	106	C4
Kasos	75	J5
Kasos, Stenon	75	J5
Kaspiyskiy	79	H6
Kassala	103	G4
Kassandra	75	G2
Kassel	70	C3
Kasserine	101	G1
Kastamonu	76	E2
Kastaneai	75	J2
Kastelli	75	G5
Kastellorizon	76	C4
Kastoria	75	F2
Kastorias, Limni	75	F2
Kastornoye	79	F5
Kastron	75	H3
Kasulu	107	F3
Kasumi	89	E8
Kasumiga-ura	89	H7
Kasungu	107	F5
Kata	84	G5
Kataba	106	E6
Katagum	105	H3
Katahdin, Mount	125	R4
Katako Kombe	106	D3
Katanning	112	D5
Katastari	75	F4
Katav Ivanovsk	78	K5
Katchall	93	H7
Katen	88	F2
Katerini	75	G2
Katha	93	J4
Katherina, Gebel	103	F2
Katherine	112	G1
Kathmandu	92	G3
Kati	100	D6
Katihar	93	G3
Katikati	115	E2
Katiola	104	D4
Katla	62	V13
Katlabukh, Ozero	73	K3
Katmai Volcano	118	E4
Kato Nevrokopion	75	G2
Katoomba	113	L5
Kato Stavros	75	G2
Katowice	71	H3
Katrineholm	63	G7
Katrine, Loch	57	D4
Katsina	105	G3
Katsina Ala	105	G4
Katsuura	89	H8
Katsuyama	89	F7
Kattavia	75	J5
Kattegat	63	D8
Kauai	126	R9
Kauai Channel	126	R10
Kauhajoki	62	K5
Kauiki Head	126	S10
Kaujuitok	120	H3
Kaulakahi Channel	126	Q9
Kaunakakai	126	S10
Kaunas	71	K1
Kaura Namoda	105	G3
Kaushany	73	K2
Kautokeino	62	K2
Kavacha	85	V4
Kavaje	74	E2
Kavak	77	G2
Kavaklidere	76	C4
Kavalerovo	88	E3
Kavali	92	E6
Kavalla	75	H2
Kavar	95	L7
Kavarna	73	K4
Kavgamis	77	H4
Kavieng	114	E2
Kavir, Dasht-e	95	M4
Kavir-e Namak	95	N4
Kavungo	106	D5
Kavusshap Daglari	77	K3
Kaw	137	G3
Kawagoe	89	G8
Kawaguchi	89	G8
Kawaihae	126	T10
Kawakawa	115	E1
Kawambwa	107	E4
Kawardha	92	F4
Kawasaki	89	G8
Kawerau	115	F3
Kawhia	115	E3
Kawhia Harbour	115	E3
Kawimbe	107	F4
Kawkareik	93	J5
Kawthaung	93	J7
Kayak Island	118	G4
Kayan	91	F5
Kaydak, Sor	79	J7
Kaye, Cape	120	H3
Kayenta	127	G2
Kayes	100	C6
Kaymaz	76	D3
Kaynar	86	D2
Kaynarca	76	D2
Kayseri	76	F3
Kayuagung	90	C6
Kazachinskoye	84	H5
Kazachye	85	P2
Kazakh	77	L2
Kazakhskiy Melkosopochnik	86	C2
Kazakhskiy Zaliv	79	J2
Kazakhstan	79	J6
Kazan	78	H4
Kazan *Turkey*	76	E2
Kazan	119	R3
Kazandzhik	95	M2
Kazan Lake	119	R3
Kazanluk	73	H4
Kazan-retto	83	N4
Kazatin	79	D6
Kazbek	77	L1
Kazerun	95	K7
Kazgorodok	84	Ae6
Kazhim	78	J3
Kazi Magomed	94	J1
Kazim Karabekir	76	E4
Kaztalovka	79	H6
Kazumba	106	D4
Kazy	95	N2
Kazym	84	Ae4
Kazymskaya	84	Ae4
Kazymskiy Mys	84	Ae4
Kea *Greece*	75	H4
Kea *Greece*	75	H4
Keady	58	J4
Keal, Loch na	57	B4
Kearny	126	G4
Keaukaha	126	T11
Keban	77	H3
Keban Baraji	77	H3
Kebemer	104	B2
Kebezen	84	D6
Kebnekaise	62	H3
Kebock Head	56	B2
Kebri Dehar	103	H6
Kech a Terara	103	G6
Kechika	118	K4
Keciborlu	76	D4
Kecil, Kai	91	J7
Kecskemet	72	E2
Kedainiai	63	K9
Kedgwick	125	S3
Kediri	90	E7
Kedong	87	P2
Kedougou	104	C3
Kedva	78	J3
Keel	58	B5
Keelby	55	J3
Keele	118	K3
Keele Peak	118	J3
Keeler	126	D2
Keene	125	P5
Keeper Hill	59	F7
Keetmanshoop	108	C5
Keewatin *Ontario, Canada*	124	C2
Kefallinia	75	F3
Kefamenanu	91	G7
Kefken	76	D2
Keflavik	62	T12
Keglo Bay	121	N6
Kegulta	79	G6
Kehsi Mansam	93	J4
Keighley	55	H3
Keila	62	L5
Keitele *Kaskisuomi, Finland*	62	L5
Keitele *Kuopio, Finland*	62	M5
Keith	56	F3
Keith Arm	119	L2
Keiyasi	114	Q8
Kekertaluk Island	120	N4
Keketa	114	C3
Kel	85	M3
Kelang	90	C5
Keld	55	G2
Keles	76	C3
Kelibia	101	H1
Kelkit *Turkey*	77	G2
Kelkit *Turkey*	77	H2
Keller Lake	119	L3
Kellett, Cape	118	K1
Kellog	84	D4
Kellogg	122	F4
Kelloselka	62	N3
Kells	58	J5
Kelme	63	K9
Kelmentsy	73	J1
Kelo	102	C6
Kelolokan	91	F5
Kelowna	122	E3
Kelsey Bay	122	B2
Kelso *New Zealand*	115	B6
Kelso *U.K.*	57	F5
Keluang	90	C5
Kelvedon	53	H3
Kem	78	E3
Kemah	77	H3
Kemaliye	77	H3
Kemalpasa	77	J2
Kemalpasar	76	B3
Kemano	118	K5
Kemer *Turkey*	76	C4
Kemer *Turkey*	76	C4
Kemer *Turkey*	76	D4
Kemerovo	84	D5
Kemi	62	L4
Kemijarvi *Finland*	62	L3
Kemijarvi *Finland*	62	M3
Kemijoki	62	L3
Kemmerer	123	J7
Kempen	64	F3
Kempendyayi	85	K4
Kemp, Lake	127	N4
Kemps Bay	132	H2
Kempsey	113	L5
Kempten	70	D5
Kempt, Lac	125	N3
Kempton	113	K7
Ken	92	F3
Kenadsa	100	E2
Kenai	118	E3
Kenai Mountains	118	E4
Kenai Peninsula	118	F3
Kendal	55	G2
Kendall, Cape	120	J5
Kendari	91	G6
Kendawangan	90	E6
Kendraparha	92	G4
Kendyrliki	86	F2
Kenema	104	C4
Kenete Karavastas	74	E2
Kenge	106	C3
Kengtung	93	J4
Kenhardt	108	D5
Kenilworth	53	F2
Kenitra	100	D2
Keniut	85	X4
Kenli	87	M4
Kenmare *Ireland*	59	C9
Kenmare *Ireland*	59	C9
Kenmore	57	D4
Kennacraig	57	C5
Kennebec	125	R4
Kenner	128	G5
Kennet	53	F3
Kennewick	122	E4
Kenninghall	53	J2
Kenn Reef	113	M3
Kenogami	121	K7
Keno Hill	118	H3
Kenora	124	C2
Kenosha	124	G5
Kent *U.K.*	53	H3
Kent *U.S.A.*	127	K5
Kentau	86	B3
Kentford	53	H2
Kentmere	55	G2
Kent Peninsula	119	P2
Kentucky *U.S.A.*	124	G8
Kentucky *U.S.A.*	124	H8
Kentucky Lake	124	F8
Kentwood	128	G5
Kenya	107	G2
Keokea	126	S10
Keokuk	124	E6
Keos	75	H4
Kepi	91	K7
Kepno	71	G3
Keppel Bay	113	L3
Kepsut	76	C3
Kerala	92	E6
Kerama-retto	89	H10
Keravat	114	E2
Kerch	79	F6
Kerchenskiy Proliv	79	F6
Kerema	114	D3
Keremeos	122	E3
Keren	103	G4
Kerguelen, Ile	142	D6
Keri	75	F4
Kericho	107	G3
Kerinci, Gunung	90	C6
Keriya He	92	F1
Kerki	95	S3
Kerkinitis, Limni	75	G2
Kerkira *Greece*	74	E3
Kerkira *Greece*	74	E3
Kerma	102	F4
Kermadec Islands	111	T8
Kermadec Trench	143	H6
Kerman	95	N6
Kerman Desert	95	P7
Kermen	73	J4
Kermit	127	L5
Kern	126	C2
Keros	78	J3
Kerpineny	73	K2
Kerrera	57	C4
Kerrville	127	N5
Kerry	59	C8
Kerry Head	59	C8
Kerrykeel	58	G2
Keruh	90	C4
Kerulen	87	L2
Kesalahti	63	N6
Kesan	76	B2
Kesap	77	H2
Kesennuma	88	H6
Keshvar	94	J5
Keskin	76	E3
Keski-Suomi	62	K5
Keskozero	78	E3
Keswick	55	F2
Keszthely	72	D2
Ket	84	D5
Keta	104	F4
Keta, Ozero	84	E3
Ketapang	90	D6
Ketchikan	118	J4
Kete	104	E4
Ketmen, Khrebet	86	E3
Ketoy, Ostrov	85	S7
Ketrzyn	71	J1
Kettering	53	G2
Kettle Ness	55	J2
Kettle River Range	122	E3
Kettlewell	55	G2
Kettusoja	62	N3
Keurus-selka	63	L5
Keushki	84	Ae4
Kew	133	M4
Kewanee	124	F6
Kewaunee	124	G3
Keweenaw	124	G3
Keweenaw Bay	124	G3
Keweenaw Point	124	G3
Keyano	121	M7
Keyaygyr	86	D3
Keyi	86	E3
Key Largo	129	M8
Key, Lough	58	F4
Keynsham	52	E3

Name	Page	Grid
Kirtlington	53	F3
Kirton	55	J3
Kiruna	62	J3
Kiryu	89	G7
Kisa	63	F8
Kisamou, Kolpos	75	G5
Kisangani	106	E2
Kisar	91	H7
Kisarazu	89	G8
Kiselevsk	84	D6
Kishanganj	93	G3
Kishangarh	92	D3
Kishb, Harrat	96	E5
Kishika-zaki	89	C10
Kishiwada	89	E8
Kishorganj	93	H4
Kishorn, Loch	56	C3
Kisii	107	F3
Kiska Island	118	Ab9
Kiskunfelegyhaza	72	E2
Kiskunhalas	72	E2
Kislovodsk	79	G7
Kismaayo	107	H3
Kiso-Fukushima	89	F8
Kiso-sammyaku	89	F8
Kispest	72	E2
Kissidougou	104	C4
Kissimmee	129	M7
Kisumu	107	F3
Kita	100	D6
Kitajaur	62	J3
Kitakami *Japan*	88	H6
Kitakami *Japan*	88	H6
Kitakami-sanmyaku	88	J3
Kita-kyushu	89	C9
Kitale	107	G2
Kitami	88	J4
Kitami-sammyaku	88	H6
Kitangari	107	G5
Kitay, Ozero	73	K3
Kit Carson	127	L1
Kitchener	125	K5
Kitee	62	P5
Kitgum	107	F2
Kithira *Greece*	75	G4
Kithira *Greece*	75	G4
Kithnos *Greece*	75	H4
Kithnos *Greece*	75	H4
Kitikmeot	119	Q2
Kitimat	118	K5
Kitinen	62	M3
Kitkiojoki	62	K3
Kitsuki	89	C9
Kittanning	125	L6
Kittila	62	L3
Kitui	107	G3
Kitunda	107	F4
Kitwe	107	E5
Kitzbuhel	68	D2
Kitzbuheler Alpen	68	D2
Kitzingen	70	D4
Kivalliq	119	R3
Kivalo	62	L3
Kivijarvi	62	L5
Kivu, Lake	107	E3
Kiyevka	88	D4
Kiyevskoye Vodokhranilishche	79	E5
Kiyikoy	76	C2
Kizel	78	K4
Kizema	78	H3
Kizilagac	77	J3
Kizilcaboluk	76	C4
Kizilcadag	76	C4
Kizilhisar	76	C4
Kizilirmak	76	E2
Kizil Irmak	77	F2
Kizilkaya	76	D4
Kiziloren	76	E4
Kiziltepe	77	J4
Kizlyar	79	H7
Kizyl-Arvat	95	N2
Kizyl-Atrek	95	M3
Kizyl Ayak	95	S3
Kizyl-Su	95	L2
Kjollefjord	62	M1
Kjopsvick	62	L2
Kladanj	72	E3
Kladno	70	F3
Kladovo	73	G3
Klagenfurt	68	E2
Klaipeda	63	L9
Klamath *U.S.A.*	122	B7
Klamath *U.S.A.*	122	C7
Klamath Falls	122	D6
Klamath Mountains	122	C6
Klamono	91	J6
Klaralven	63	J6
Klatovy	70	E4
Klekovaca	72	D3
Klenak	72	E3
Klerksdorp	108	E5
Klichka	85	K7
Klimovichi	79	E5
Klin	78	F4
Klinovec	70	E3
Klintsovka	79	H5
Klintsy	79	E5
Klisura	73	H4
Kljuc	72	D3
Klobuck	71	H3
Klodzka *Poland*	71	G3
Klodzko *Poland*	71	G3
Klos	75	F2
Klosterneuberg	68	F1
Klosters	68	B2
Klrovskiy	79	H6
Kluane	118	H3
Kluane Lake	118	H3
Kluczbork	71	H3
Klyevka	84	A6
Klyuchevskaya Sopka	85	U5
Klyuchi	85	U5
Klyukvinka	84	D5
Kmagta	114	J6
Kmanjab	108	B3
K2, Mount	92	E1
Knapdale	57	C5
Knaresborough	55	H2
Knife	123	N4
Knight Island	118	F3
Knighton	52	D2
Knin	72	D3
Knjazevac	73	G4
Knockadoon Head	59	G9
Knockalla Mount	58	G2
Knockanaffrin	59	G8
Knockaunapeebra	59	G8
Knocklayd	58	K2
Knockmealdown Mountains	59	G8
Knocknaskagh	59	F8
Knottingley	55	H3
Knox, Cape	118	J5
Knoxville *Iowa*	124	D6
Knoxville *Tennessee*	129	L3
Knoydart	57	C3
Knud Rasmussen Land	120	P2
Knutholstind	63	C6
Knutsford	55	G3
Knyazhaya Guba	62	Q3
Knyazhevo	78	G4
Knysna	108	D6
Knyszyn	71	K2
Koba	90	D6
Kobarid	72	B2
Kobayashi	89	C10
Kobberminebugt	120	R5
Kobelyaki	79	E6
Kobenhavn	63	E9
Koblenz	70	B3
Kobowre, Pegunungan	91	K6
Kobrin	71	L2
Kobroor	91	J7
Kobuk	118	D2
Kobuleti	77	J2
Kobya	85	M4
Koca *Turkey*	76	B3
Koca *Turkey*	76	C3
Koca *Turkey*	76	E2
Kocapinar	77	K3
Kocarli	76	B4
Koceljevo	72	E3
Koch Bihar	93	G3
Kochechum	84	G3
Kochegarovo	85	K5
Kocher	70	C4
Kochi	89	D9
Koch Island	120	L4
Kochkorka	86	D3
Koch Peak	122	J5
Kochumdek	84	E4
Koden	71	K3
Kodiak	118	E4
Kodiak Island	118	E4
Kodima	78	G3
Kodinar	92	D4
Kodok	103	F6
Kodomari	88	H5
Kodyma	73	L2
Kofcaz	76	B2
Koffiefontein	108	D5
Koflach	68	E2
Koforidua	104	E4
Kofu	89	G8
Koge	63	E9
Kogilnik	73	K2
Ko, Gora	88	F2
Kohat	92	D2
Kohima	93	H3
Koh-i Qaisar	95	S5
Kohtla-Jarve	63	M7
Koide	89	G7
Koi Sanjaq	94	G3
Koitere	62	P5
Koivu	62	L3
Koje	89	B8
Kojonup	112	D5
Kokand	86	B3
Kokas	91	J6
Kokchetav	84	Ae6
Kokemaenjoki	63	K6
Kokenau	91	K6
Kokkola	62	K5
Koko	105	G4
Kokoda	114	D3
Kokomo	124	G6
Kokpekty	86	E2
Koksoak	121	N6
Kokstad	108	E6
Koktas	86	C2
Kokubu	89	C10
Kokuora	85	R2
Kokura	89	C9
Kokuy	85	K6
Kok-Yangak	86	C3
Kola	62	Q2
Kolaka	91	G6
Kolar	92	E6
Kolari	62	K3
Kolarovgrad	73	J4
Kolasin	72	E4
Kolay	77	F2
Kolberg	70	F1
Kolbuszowa	71	J3
Kolchugino	78	F4
Kolda	104	C3
Kolding	63	C9
Kole	106	D3
Kolguyev, Ostrov	78	H2
Kolhapur	92	D5
Kolin	70	F3
Kolki	71	L3
Kolkuskull	62	V12
Kollabudur	62	T12
Koln	70	B3
Kolno	71	J2
Koloa	126	R10
Kolobrzeg	70	F1
Kologriv	78	G4
Kolombangara	114	H5
Kolomna	78	F4
Kolono	91	G6
Koloubara	72	F3
Kolozsvar	73	G2
Kolpashevo	84	C5
Kolpino	78	E4
Kolskiy Poluostrov	78	F2
Koltubanovskiy	79	J5
Koluszki	71	H3
Kolva *Russia*	78	K3
Kolva *Russia*	78	K2
Kolwezi	106	E5
Kolyma	85	U3
Kolymskaya Nizmennost	85	T3
Kolymskiy, Khrebet	85	T4
Komadugu Gana	105	H3
Komandorskiye Ostrova	81	T4
Komarno	71	H5
Komarom	72	E2
Komatsu	89	F7
Komering	90	C6
Komodo	91	F7
Kom Ombo	103	F3
Komoe	104	E4
Komoran	91	K7
Komosomolets, Ostrov	81	L1
Komotini	75	H2
Komovi	74	E1
Kompong Cham	93	L6
Kompong Chhnang	93	K6
Kompong Som	93	K6
Kompong Speu	93	K6
Kompong Sralao	93	L6
Kompong Thom	93	K6
Komrat	79	D6
Komsomolets, Zaliv	79	J6
Komsomolsk	79	E6
Komsomolskiy	79	J6
Komsomolsk-na-Amure	85	P6
Konakovo	78	F4
Koncanica	72	D3
Konch	92	E3
Konda *Indonesia*	91	J6
Konda *Russia*	84	Ae4
Kondagaon	92	F5
Kondinin	112	D5
Kondinskoye	84	Ae5
Kondoa	107	G3
Kondon	85	P6
Kondoponga	78	E3
Konduz	92	C1
Kone	114	W16
Konevo	78	F3
Kong	104	E4
Kongan	89	J10
Kong Christian den X Land	120	W3
Kong Karls Land	80	D2
Kongolo	106	E4
Kongsberg	63	C7
Kongsvinger	63	E6
Kong Wilhelms Land	120	X2
Koniecpol	71	H3
Konigsberg	71	J4
Konigs Wusterhausen	70	E2
Konin	71	H2
Konitsa	75	F2
Koniya	89	B11
Konkamaalv	62	J2
Konkoure	104	C3
Konnern	70	D3
Konnevesi	62	M5
Konosha	78	G3
Konotop	79	E5
Konqi He	86	F3
Konskie	71	J3
Konstantinovsk	79	G6
Konstanz	68	B2
Konstyantynivka	79	F6
Kontagora	105	G3
Kontcha	105	H4
Kontiomaki	62	N4
Kontum	93	L6
Kontum, Plateau du	93	L6
Konya	76	E4
Konya Ovasi	76	E3
Konzhakovskiy Kamen, Gora	78	K4
Kootenai	122	G3
Kootenay	122	F3
Kootenay Lake	122	F3
Kopaonik	73	F4
Kopasker	62	W11
Kopavogur	62	U12
Koper	72	B3
Kopervik	63	A7
Kopet Dag, Khrebet	95	N2
Kopeysk	84	Ad5
Koping	63	F7
Kopka	124	F1
Kopmanholmen	62	H5
Koppang	63	D6
Kopparberg *Sweden*	63	F7
Kopparberg *Sweden*	63	F6
Koppi *Russia*	88	G1
Koppi *Russia*	88	H1
Kopru	76	D4
Koprubasi	76	C3
Koprulu	76	E4
Kopruoren	76	C3
Kopychintsy	73	H1
Kor	95	L6
Kora	77	K2
Korab	72	F5
Korahe	103	H6
Koraluk	121	P6
Korana	72	C3
Korba	69	C7
Korbach	70	C3
Korbu, Gunung	90	C5
Korce	75	F2
Korcula	72	D4
Korda	84	F4
Kord Kuv	95	M3
Korea Bay	87	N4
Korea, North	87	P4
Korea, South	87	P4
Korea Strait	89	B8
Korennoye	84	H2
Korenovsk	79	F6
Korf	85	V4
Korforskiy	88	E1
Korgan	77	G2
Korgen	62	E3
Korhogo	104	D4
Korido	91	K6
Korim	91	K6
Korinthiakos Kolpos	75	G3
Korinthos	75	G4
Koriyama	89	H7
Korkinitskiy Zaliv	79	E6
Korkodon	85	T4
Korkuteli	76	D4
Korla	86	F3
Kormakiti, Akra	76	E5
Kornat	72	C4
Koro	114	R8
Korocha	79	F5
Koroglu Daglari	76	E2
Koronia, Limni	75	G2
Koronowo	71	G2
Koros	72	F2
Korosten	79	D5
Korostyshev	79	D5
Korotaikha	78	L2
Korovin Volcano	118	Ad9
Korpilombolo	62	K3
Korsakov	88	J2
Korsnas	62	J5
Korsor	63	D9
Korti	103	F4
Kortrijk	64	E3
Korucu	76	B3
Koryakskaya Sopka	85	U6
Koryanskiy Khrebet	85	Z5
Koryazhma	78	H3
Korzybie	71	G1
Kos *Greece*	75	J4
Kos *Greece*	75	J4
Koschagyl	79	J6
Koscian	71	G2
Koscierzyna	71	G1
Kosciusco, Mount	113	K6
Kosciusko	128	H4
Kose	77	H2
Kos Golu	76	B2
Koshiki-retto	89	B10
Kosice	71	J4
Koski	63	K6
Koslan	78	H3
Koslin	71	G1
Kosma	78	H2
Kosong	88	B6
Kosong-ni	88	B5
Kossou, Lac de	104	D4
Kossovo	71	L2
Kostajnica	72	D3
Kosti	103	F5
Kostino	84	D3
Kostomuksha	62	P4
Kostopol	71	M3
Kostroma *Russia*	78	G4
Kostroma *Russia*	78	G4
Kostrzyn	70	F2
Kosu-dong	89	B8
Kosva	78	K4
Kosyu	78	K2
Kosyuvom	78	K2
Koszalin	71	G1
Kota	92	E3
Kotaagung	90	C7
Kota Baharu	90	C4
Kotabaru *Indonesia*	90	E6
Kotabaru *Indonesia*	90	F6
Kota Belud	90	F4
Kotabumi	90	C5
Kota Kinabalu	90	F4
Kotala	62	N3

Kotamubagu	91	G5	Krasnovodskiy Poluostrov	79	J7	Kuchinotsu	89	C9	Kurashiki	89	D8
Kota Tinggi	90	C5	Krasnoyarsk	84	E5	Kuchurgan	73	K2	Kurayoshi	89	D8
Kotel	73	J4	Krasnoyarskiy Kray	84	E3	Kucuk	76	B3	Kurday	86	D3
Kotelnich	78	H4	Krasnoye	78	G4	Kucukcekmece	76	C2	Kurdzhali	73	H5
Kotelnikovo	79	G6	Krasnstaw	71	K3	Kucuk Kuyu	76	B3	Kure	89	D8
Kotelnyy, Ostrov	85	P1	Krasnyy Chikoy	84	H6	Kudat	90	F4	Kure	76	E2
Kotikovo	88	E2	Krasnyye Okny	73	K2	Kudirkos-Naumiestis	71	K1	Kurecik	77	G3
Kotka	63	M6	Krasnyy Kholm	79	J5	Kudus	90	E7	Kure Daglari	76	F2
Kot Kapura	92	D2	Krasnyy Kut	79	H5	Kudymkar	78	J4	Kuresaare	63	M7
Kotlas	78	H3	Krasnyy Luch	79	F6	Kufi	76	C3	Kureyka	84	D3
Kotli	92	D2	Krasnyy Yar *Russia*	79	G5	Kufstein	68	D2	Kurgan	84	Ae5
Kotlik	118	C3	Krasnyy Yar *Russia*	79	H6	Kugaly	86	D3	Kurganinsk	79	G7
Koto	85	P7	Kratie	93	L6	Kugi	84	Ad4	Kurgan-Tyube	86	B4
Kotor	72	E4	Kraulshavn	120	Q3	Kugmallit Bay	118	J2	Kurikka	62	N4
Kotovo	79	G5	Kravanh, Chuor Phnum	93	K6	Kuhdasht	94	H5	Kurilskiye Ostrova	85	S7
Kotovsk *Russia*	79	G5	Krefeld	70	B3	Kuh-e Bul	95	L6	Kuril Trench	142	G3
Kotovsk *Ukraine*	79	D6	Kremenchugskoye			Kuh-e Garbosh	95	K5	Kurkcu	76	E4
Kotri	92	C3	Vodokhranilishche	79	E6	Kuh Lab, Ra's	95	Q9	Kurlek	84	C5
Kottagudem	92	F5	Kremenchuk	79	E6	Kuhmo	62	N4	Kurmuk	103	F5
Kottayam	92	E7	Kremnets	79	D5	Kuhpayeh *Iran*	95	L5	Kurnool	92	E5
Kotto	102	D6	Krems	68	E1	Kuhpayeh *Iran*	95	N6	Kuroi	89	E8
Kotuy	84	G2	Krenitzin Islands	118	Ae9	Kuhran, Kuh-e	95	P8	Kuroiso	89	G7
Kotyuzhany	73	K2	Kresevo	72	E4	Kuh, Ra's-al-	95	N9	Kurow	71	K3
Kotzebue	118	C2	Kresttsy	78	E4	Kuito	106	C5	Kursk	79	F5
Kotzebue Sound	118	C2	Kresty	84	D2	Kuji	88	H5	Kursumlija	73	F4
Kouango	102	C6	Krestyakh	85	K4	Kuju-san	89	C9	Kursunlu	76	E2
Koudougou	104	E3	Krestyanka	84	C2	Kukalar, Kuh-e	95	K6	Kurtalan	77	J4
Koufonisi	75	J5	Kretinga	63	J9	Kukes	75	F1	Kurtamysh	84	Ad6
Koukajuak, Great Plain			Kribi	105	G5	Kukhomskaya Volya	71	L3	Kurtun	77	H2
of the	120	M4	Krichev	79	E5	Kukmor	78	J4	Kuru	63	K6
Kouki	102	C6	Krichim	73	H4	Kukpowruk	118	C2	Kurucasile	76	E2
Koumac	114	W16	Krieza	75	H3	Kukudu	114	H6	Kuruman *South Africa*	108	D5
Koumenzi	86	F3	Krifovon	75	F3	Kukup	90	C5	Kuruman *South Africa*	108	D5
Koumra	102	C6	Krilon, Mys	88	J3	Kukushka	85	M6	Kurume	89	C9
Koundara	104	C3	Krios, Akra	75	G5	Kula *Turkey*	76	C3	Kurunegala	92	F7
Koungou Mountains	106	B3	Krishna	92	E5	Kula *Yugoslavia*	72	E3	Kurzeme	63	K8
Kounradskiy	86	D2	Krishnagiri	92	E6	Kulagino	79	J6	Kusadasi	76	B4
Kourou	137	G2	Krishnanagar	93	G4	Kulakshi	79	K6	Kusadasi Korfezi	76	B4
Kouroussa	104	D3	Kristdala	63	G8	Kulal, Mont	107	G2	Kusel	70	B4
Kousseri	105	J3	Kristel	67	F5	Kulata	73	G5	Kusey Andolu Daglari	77	H2
Koutiala	100	D6	Kristiansand	63	B7	Kuldiga	63	N8	Kushchevskaya	79	F6
Kouvola	63	M6	Kristianstad *Sweden*	63	E8	Kule	108	D4	Kushima	89	C10
Kova	84	G5	Kristianstad *Sweden*	63	F8	Kulebaki	78	G4	Kushimoto	89	E9
Kovachevo	73	J4	Kristiansund	62	B5	Kulgera	113	G6	Kushiro	88	K4
Kovanlik	77	H2	Kristiinankaupunki	63	J5	Kulikov	71	L4	Kushka *Russia*	85	U4
Kovdor	62	P3	Kristinestad	63	J5	Kulinda *Russia*	84	G4	Kushmurun	84	Ad6
Kovdozero, Ozero	62	Q3	Kristinovka	73	K1	Kulinda *Russia*	84	H4	Kushtia	93	G4
Kovel	71	L3	Kriti	75	H5	Kulmac Daglari	77	G3	Kushva	78	K4
Kovernino	78	G4	Kritikon Pelagos	75	H5	Kulmbach	70	D3	Kuskokwim	118	C3
Kovero	62	P5	Kriulyany	73	K2	Kuloy *Russia*	78	G3	Kuskokwim Bay	118	C4
Kovik Bay	121	L5	Kriva Palanka	73	G4	Kuloy *Russia*	78	G2	Kuskokwim Mountains	118	D3
Kovno	71	K1	Krivoye Ozero	73	L2	Kulp	77	J3	Kusma	92	F3
Kovrov	78	G4	Krk	72	C3	Kulsary	79	J6	Kussharo-ko	88	K4
Kovylkino	78	G5	Krnov	71	G3	Kultay	79	J6	Kustanay	84	Ad6
Kowalewo	71	H2	Krokodil	108	E4	Kultuk	84	G6	Kustrin	70	F2
Kowloon	87	L7	Krokom	62	F5	Kulu	76	E3	Kuta	105	G4
Koycegiz	76	C4	Krokong	90	E5	Kulu Island	118	J4	Kutahya	76	C3
Koyda	78	G2	Krokowa	71	H1	Kulul	96	E9	Kutaisi	77	K1
Koyuk	118	C3	Krolevets	79	E5	Kulunda	84	B6	Kutchan	88	H4
Koyukuk	118	D3	Kromy	79	F5	Kulundinskoye, Ozero	84	B6	Kutima	84	H5
Koyulhisar	77	G2	Kronach	70	D3	Kulyab	86	B4	Kut, Ko	93	K6
Koza	89	E9	Krononberg	63	F8	Kuma	79	H7	Kutna Hora	70	F4
Kozakli	76	F3	Kronshtadt	63	N7	Kumagaya	89	G7	Kutno	71	H2
Kozan	77	F4	Kroonstad	108	E5	Kumakh-Surt	85	M2	Kutu	106	C3
Kozani	75	F2	Kropotkin	79	G6	Kumamoto	89	C9	Kutubdia	93	H4
Kozekovo	71	M1	Krosno	71	J4	Kumano	89	F9	Kutum	102	D5
Kozelsk	78	F5	Krotoszyn	71	G3	Kumanovo	73	F4	Kuujjuaq	121	N6
Kozhevnikovo	84	B5	Krsko	72	C3	Kumara	115	C5	Kuujjuarapik	121	L6
Kozhikode	92	E6	Krugersdorp	108	E5	Kumasi	104	E4	Kuuli-Mayak	79	J7
Kozhim	78	K2	Krui	90	C7	Kumba	105	G5	Kuusamo	62	N4
Kozhposelok	78	F3	Kruje	74	E2	Kumbakonam	92	E6	Kuvango	106	C5
Kozhva	78	K2	Krumbach	70	D4	Kum-Dag	95	M2	Kuvet	85	X3
Kozlu	76	D2	Krumovgrad	73	H5	Kumertau	79	K5	Kuwait	94	H7
Kozludere	77	G4	Krung Thep	93	K6	Kuminki	62	L4	Kuwait	97	J2
Kozluk	77	J3	Krusenstern, Cape	118	C2	Kuminskiy	84	Ae5	Kuwana	89	F8
Kozmodemyansk	78	H4	Krusevac	73	F4	Kumkuduk	86	F3	Kuya	78	G2
Kozu-shima	89	G8	Krusevo	73	F5	Kumluca	76	D4	Kuybyshev *Russia*	84	B5
Kpalime	104	F4	Krustpils	63	M8	Kummerower See	70	E2	Kuybyshevskoye		
Krabi	93	J7	Kruzenshterna, Proliv	85	S7	Kumnyong	87	P5	Vodokhranilishche	78	H4
Kragero	63	C7	Kruzof Island	118	H4	Kumon Bum	93	J3	Kuyeda	78	K4
Kragujevac	73	F3	Krym	79	E6	Kumru	77	G2	Kuygan	86	C2
Krakow	71	H3	Krymsk	79	F7	Kumsong	87	P4	Kuytun	86	F3
Krakowska, Jura	71	H3	Krynki	71	K2	Kumta	92	D6	Kuyucak	76	C4
Kral Chlmec	71	K4	Kryry	70	E3	Kumyr	86	C3	Kuyumba	84	F4
Kralendijk	133	N8	Kryvyy Rih	79	E6	Kunas	86	E3	Kuyus	84	D6
Kraljevo	72	F4	Krzeszowice	71	H3	Kunas Chang	86	E3	Kuzino	78	K4
Kralovvany	71	H4	Ksabi	100	E3	Kunashir, Ostrov	88	L3	Kuzitrin	118	C2
Kralupy	70	F3	Ksar El Boukhari	101	F1	Kundelungu Mountains	107	E5	Kuzmovka	84	E4
Kramatorsk	79	F6	Ksarel Kebir	100	D2	Kunduz	92	C1	Kuznetsk	79	H5
Kramfors	62	G5	Ksar es Souk	100	E2	Kungalv	63	H8	Kuznetsovo	88	G2
Krania	75	F3	Ksenofontova	78	K3	Kungar	78	K4	Kuzomen	78	F2
Kranidhion	75	G4	Ksour Essaf	101	H1	Kunghit Island	118	J5	Kuzucubelen	76	F4
Kranj	72	C2	Kstovo	78	G4	Kungrad	51	U7	Kvaloy	62	H2
Kranskop	108	F5	Kualakapuas	90	E6	Kungsor	63	G7	Kvaloya	62	K1
Krasavino	78	H3	Kuala Kerai	90	C4	Kungu	106	C2	Kvalsund	62	L1
Krasino	84	Ab2	Kuala Lipis	90	C5	Kunlun Shan	92	F1	Kvarner	72	C3
Kraskino	88	C4	Kuala Lumpur	90	C5	Kunmadaras	72	F2	Kvarneric	72	C3
Krasneno	85	X4	Kualapembuang	90	E6	Kunming	93	K4	Kvichak Bay	118	D4
Krasnoarmeyesk	84	Ae6	Kuala Penyu	90	F4	Kunsan	87	P4	Kvidinge	63	E8
Krasnoarmeyskiy	85	W3	Kuala Terengganu	90	C4	Kununurra	112	F2	Kvigtind	62	E4
Krasnoborsk	78	H3	Kuandian	87	N3	Kunu-ri	87	P4	Kvikkjokk	62	G3
Krasnodar	79	F6	Kuantan	90	C5	Kuolayarvi	62	N3	Kvina	63	B7
Krasnogorsk	88	J1	Kuba	89	D8	Kuopio *Sweden*	62	M5	Kvorning	63	C8
Krasnograd	79	F6	Kuban	79	G6	Kuopio *Sweden*	62	M5	Kwa	106	C3
Krasnokamsk	78	K4	Kubenskoye Ozero	78	F4	Kupa	72	C3	Kwale	105	G4
Krasnokutskoye	84	B6	Kubkain	114	C2	Kupang	91	G7	Kwamouth	106	C3
Krasnolesnyy	79	F5	Kubokawa	89	D9	Kuparuk	118	E2	Kwangju	87	P4
Krasnorechenskiy	88	E3	Kubonitu, Mount	114	J6	Kupino	84	B6	Kwango	106	C3
Krasnoselkup	84	C3	Kubor, Mount	114	C3	Kupreanof Island	118	J4	Kwanso-ri	88	B5
Krasnoslobodsk	78	G5	Kubrat	73	J4	Kupreanof Point	118	Ag8	Kwatisore	91	J6
Krasnoturinsk	84	Ad5	Kubuang	90	F5	Kupyansk	79	F6	Kwekwe	108	E3
Krasnoufimsk	78	K4	Kucevo	73	F3	Kuqa	86	E3	Kwidzyn	71	H2
Krasnousolskiy	78	K5	Kuching	90	E5	Kura	77	L2	Kwilu	106	C3
Krasnovishersk	78	K3	Kuchinoerabu-jima	89	C10	Kurashasayskiy	79	K5	Kwoka	91	J6

Kyabe 102 C6
Kyaikto 93 J5
Kyakhta 84 H6
Kyaukpyu 93 H5
Kyaukse 93 J4
Kybartai 71 K1
Kychema 78 G2
Kyeburn 115 C6
Kyelang 92 E2
Kyle 57 D5
Kyleakin 56 C3
Kyle of Lochalsh 56 C3
Kylestrome 56 C2
Kymi 63 M6
Kymijoki 63 M6
Kynuna 113 J3
Kyoga, Lake 107 F2
Kyongju 89 B8
Kyoto 89 E8
Kyrdanyy 85 M3
Kyrgyzstan 86 C3
Kyritz 70 E2
Kyrkheden 63 E6
Kyronjoki 62 K5
Kyrosjarvi 63 K6
Kyrta 78 K3
Kyssa 78 H3
Kystyk, Plato 85 L2
Kyuekh-Bulung 84 J3
Kyurdamir 79 H7
Kyushu 89 C9
Kyushu-sanchi 89 C9
Kyustendil 73 G4
Kyyiv 79 E5
Kyyjarvi 62 L5
Kyyvesi 63 M6
Kyzyk 79 J7
Kyzyl 84 E6
Kyzyldyykan 86 B2
Kyzylkoga 79 J6
Kyzyl-Kommuna 86 B2
Kyzylkum 80 H5
Kzyl-Dzhar 86 B2
Kzyl-Orda 86 B3
Kzyltu 84 A6

L

La Almunia de Dona Godina 67 F2
Laascaanood 103 J6
Laas Dhuure 103 J5
La Asuncion 136 E1
Laayoune 100 C3
La Baie 125 Q2
La Banda 138 D5
La Baneza 66 D1
La Barca 130 H7
Labasa 114 R8
La Baule 65 B5
Labaz, Ozero 84 F2
Labbah, Al 96 E2
Labe 104 C3
Labe 70 F3
Labelle 125 N3
Laberge, Lake 118 H3
Labi 90 E5
Labin 72 C3
Labinsk 79 G7
Labis 90 C5
La Bisbal 67 H2
Labouheyre 65 C6
Laboulaye 139 D6
La Bourboule 65 E6
Labrador 121 P7
Labrador City 121 N7
Labrador Sea 121 Q6
Labrea 136 E5
Labrit 65 C6
Labuha 91 H6
Labuhan 90 D7
Labuhanbajo 91 F7
Labuhanbilik 90 C5
Labytnangi 84 Ae3
Lac 74 E2
La Calzada de Calatrava 66 E3
Lacanau 65 C6
La Carlota 139 D6
La Carolina 66 E3
La Cava 67 G2
Laccadive Islands 92 D6
Laccadive Sea 92 E7
La Ceiba 132 D7
Lacepede Bay 113 H6
La Chaise-Dieu 65 E6
Lacha, Ozero 78 F3
La Charite 65 E5
La Chartre-sur-le-Loir 65 D5
La Chatre 65 D5
La Chaux-de-Fonds 68 A2
Lachin 94 H2
Lachlan 113 K5
La Chorrera 132 H10
Lachute 125 N4
La Cieneguita 126 G6
La Ciotat 65 F7
Lac la Biche 119 N5
Lac Megantic 125 Q4
La Colorada 126 G6
Laconi 69 B6
Laconia 125 Q5
La Coruna 66 B1
La Croix, Lac 124 D2
La Crosse 124 E5

La Cruz Costa Rica 132 E9
La Cruz Mexico 130 F6
Lacul Razelm 73 K3
Ladakh Range 92 E2
Ladder Hills 56 E3
La Desirade 133 S6
Ladik 77 F2
Ladismith 108 D6
Ladiz 95 Q7
Ladozhskoye Ozero 63 P6
Ladybank 57 E4
Ladybower Reservoir 55 H3
Ladybrand 108 E5
Ladysmith Canada 122 C3
Ladysmith South Africa 108 E5
Ladysmith U.S.A. 124 K4
Ladyzhenka 84 Ae6
Ladyzhinka 79 D6
Lae 93 K5
Laem Ngop 93 K6
La Esmeralda Paraguay 138 D4
La Esmeralda Venezuela 136 D3
La Fayette 129 K3
Lafayette Colorado 123 M8
Lafayette Indiana 124 G6
Lafayette Louisiana 128 F5
La Fe 132 E3
La Ferte-Bernard 64 D4
La-Ferte-Saint-Aubin 65 D5
Laffan, Ra's 97 K4
Lafia 105 G4
Lafiagi 105 G4
La Fleche 65 C5
La Follette 129 K2
La Fria 136 C2
Laft 95 M8
La Fuente de San Esteban 66 C2
La Galite 69 B7
Lagan 63 E8
Lagarfljot 62 X12
Lagen Norway 63 C6
Lagen Norway 63 D6
Laggan 57 D3
Laggan Bay 57 B5
Laggan, Loch 57 D4
Laghouat 101 F2
Lagny 64 E4
Lagonegro 69 E5
Lago Posadas 139 B9
Lagos Nigeria 105 F4
Lagos Portugal 66 B4
Lagos de Moreno 130 J7
La Grande Canada 121 M7
La Grande U.S.A. 122 C5
La Grande 2, Reservoir 121 L7
La Grande 3, Reservoir 121 L7
La Grande 4, Reservoir 121 M7
La Grange Georgia 129 K4
La Grange Kentucky 124 H7
La Grange Texas 128 D6
La Granja 66 D2
La Gran Sabana 136 E2
La Guardia 66 B2
Laguardia 66 E1
La Gudina 66 C1
La Guerche-de-Bretagne 65 C5
Laguna 138 G5
Laguna Grande 139 C9
Lagunillas Bolivia 138 D3
Lagunillas Venezuela 133 M9
Laha 87 N2
La Habana 132 F3
Lahad Datu 91 F4
Lahave 121 P9
Lahij 96 G10
Lahijan 95 J3
Lahn Germany 70 C3
Lahn Germany 70 C3
Lahore 92 D2
Lahr 70 B4
Lahti 63 L6
Laibach 72 C2
Laibin 93 L4
Lai Chau 93 K4
L'Aigle 64 D4
Laihia 62 J5
Laingsburg 108 D6
Lainioalven 62 K3
Lair 56 C3
Lairg 56 D2
Lais 90 C6
Laitila 63 J6
Laiwui 91 H6
Laixi 87 N4
Laiyang 87 N4
Laiyuan 87 L4
Laizhou Wan 87 M4
Lajes 138 F5
La Junta 127 L2
Lakatrask 62 J3
Lake Andes 123 Q6
Lakeba 114 S9
Lakeba Passage 114 S9
Lake Cargelligo 113 K5
Lake Charles 128 F5
Lake City Florida 129 L5
Lake City S. Carolina 129 N4
Lake District 55 F2
Lake Grace 112 D5
Lake Harbour 120 N5
Lake Havasu City 126 E3
Lake Jackson 128 E6

Lake King 112 D5
Lake Kopiago 114 C3
Lakeland 129 M6
Lake Louise 122 F2
Lake Murray 114 C3
Lakeport 122 C8
Lake Providence 128 G4
Lakeview 122 D6
Lake Wales 129 M7
Lakewood 124 K6
Lakhdaria 67 H4
Lakhpat 92 C4
Lakki 92 D2
Lakonikos Kolpos 75 G4
Laksefjorden 62 M1
Lakselv 62 L1
Lakshadweep 92 D6
Lakuramau 114 E2
Lala Musa 92 D2
Lalaua 109 G2
Laleh Zar, Kuh-e 95 N7
Lalibela 103 G5
La Libertad 132 B6
La Ligua 139 B6
Lalin 66 B1
Lalin 87 P2
La Linea 66 D4
Lalin He 88 A3
Lalitpur 92 E4
Lalla Khedidja 67 J4
La Loche 119 P4
La Loupe 64 D4
La Louviere 64 F3
La Luz 132 E8
Lalyo 102 F7
Lamag 91 F4
La Mancha 66 E3
La Manza 136 D6
Lama, Ozero 84 D3
Lamar Colorado 127 L1
Lamar Missouri 124 C8
Lamas 136 B5
Lamastre 65 F6
Lamballe 64 B4
Lambarene 106 B3
Lambas 114 R8
Lambay Island 59 K6
Lamberhurst 53 H3
Lambert, Cape 114 E2
Lambert Glacier 141 E4
Lamberts Bay 108 C6
Lamb Head 56 F1
Lambia 75 F4
Lambon 114 E2
Lambourn 53 F3
Lamb's Head 59 B9
Lambton, Cape 118 L1
Lame 102 B6
Lamego 66 C2
Lamenu 114 U12
Lameroo 113 J6
Lamia 75 G3
Lammermuir 57 F5
Lammermuir Hills 57 F5
Lammhult 63 F8
Lammi 63 L6
Lamon Bay 91 G3
Lamont California 126 C3
Lamont Wyoming 123 L6
La Morita 127 K6
La Moure 123 Q4
Lam Pao Reservoir 93 K5
Lampasas 128 C5
Lampazos de Naranjo 128 B7
Lampedusa 74 B5
Lampeter 52 C2
Lampinou 75 G3
Lampione 74 B5
Lamport 53 G2
Lampsa 62 P4
Lamu 107 H3
Lan 71 M2
Lanai 126 S10
Lanai City 126 S10
Lanark 57 D5
La Nava de Ricomalillo 66 D3
Lanbi Kyun 93 J6
Lancang 93 K4
Lancashire 55 G3
Lancaster U.K. 55 G2
Lancaster Ohio 124 J7
Lancaster Pennsylvania 125 M6
Lancaster S. Carolina 129 M3
Lancaster Sound 120 J3
Lanciano 69 E4
Lancut 71 K3
Landau 70 C4
Landeck 68 C2
Lander 123 K6
Landerneau 64 A4
Landes 65 C6
Landi 95 R6
Landor 112 D4
Landrum 129 L3
Landsberg Poland 70 F2
Landsberg Germany 70 D4
Landsborough 113 J3
Land's End 52 B4
Lands End 120 B2
Landshut 70 E4
Landskrona 63 E9
Lanesborough 58 G5
Lanett 129 K4
Langa Co 92 F2

Langadhia 75 F4
Langavat, Loch 56 B2
Langdon 123 Q3
Lange Berg 108 C6
Langebergen 108 D5
Langeland 63 D9
Langelmavesi 63 L6
Langeoog 70 B2
Langesund 63 C7
Langevag 62 B5
Langfang 87 M4
Langfjord 62 B5
Lang Head 56 A1
Langhirano 68 C3
Langholm 57 E5
Langjokull 62 U12
Langkawi 93 J7
Langnau 68 A2
Langness Point 54 E2
Langogne 65 E6
Langon 65 C6
Langoya 62 F2
Langport 52 E3
Langres 65 F5
Langsa 90 B5
Langsele 62 G5
Langsett 55 H3
Lang Son 93 L4
Langtoft 55 J2
Langtrask 62 J4
Languedoc 65 E7
Langwathby 55 G2
Langzhong 93 L2
Lannemezan 65 D7
Lannion 64 B4
Lansing 124 H5
Lansjarv 62 K3
Lanslebourg 65 G6
Lanta, Ko 93 J7
Lanusei 69 B6
Lanvaux, Landes de 65 B5
Lanxi 87 P2
Lanzarote 100 C3
Lanzhou 93 K1
Laoag 91 G2
Laoang 91 H3
Lao Cai 93 K4
Laois 59 H7
Laon 64 E4
La Oroya 136 B6
Laos 90 C2
Laoye Ling 88 B3
Laoyemiao 86 F3
Lapa 138 G5
Lapalisse 65 E5
La Palma Panama 132 H10
La Palma Spain 100 B3
La Palma del Condado 66 C4
La Paragua 136 E2
La Paz Argentina 139 C6
La Paz Argentina 138 E6
La Paz Bolivia 138 C3
La Paz Mexico 130 D5
La Pedrera 136 D4
La Piedad 130 H7
La Place 128 G5
La Plant 123 P5
La Plata 139 E6
La Pocatiere 125 R3
La Pola de Gordon 66 D1
La Porte 124 G6
Lapovo 73 F3
Lappajarvi 62 K5
Lappeenranta 63 N6
Lappi 62 M3
Lapseki 76 B2
Laptev Sea 85 M1
Laptevykh, More 85 M1
Lapua 62 K5
La Puebla 67 H3
La Puntilla 136 A4
La Quiaca 138 C4
L'Aquila 69 D4
Lar 95 M8
Larache 100 D1
Larak 95 N8
La Rambla 66 D4
Laramie 123 M7
Laramie Mountains 123 M6
Laranjal 137 F4
Larantuka 91 G7
Larat Indonesia 114 A3
Larat Indonesia 114 A3
Larba 67 H4
Laredo Spain 66 E1
Laredo U.S.A. 128 C7
La Reole 65 C6
Largo U.S.A. 129 L7
Largo Venezuela 133 R10
Largoward 57 F4
Largs 57 D5
Lari 94 H2
Larino 69 E5
La Rioja 138 C5
Larisa 75 G3
Lark 53 H2
Larkana 92 C3
Larkhall 57 F4
Larlomkiny 84 A5
Larne 58 L3
La Robla 66 D1
La Roche 114 Y16
La Roche-Bernard 65 B5
La Rochelle 65 C5

Lidkoping	63 E7				

Lidkoping 63 E7
Lidzbark Warminski 71 J1
Liebling 73 F3
Liechtenstein 70 C5
Liege 64 F3
Liegnitz 71 G3
Lielope 63 L8
Lienz 68 D2
Liepaja 63 L8
Lier 64 F3
Liestal 68 A2
Liezen 68 E2
Liffey 59 J6
Lifford 58 H3
Lifi Mahuida 139 C8
Lifou 114 X16
Ligger Bay 52 B4
Lighthouse Reef 132 D6
Ligonha 109 G3
Ligui 126 G8
Ligure, Appennino 68 B3
Ligurian Sea 68 B4
Lihir Group 114 E2
Lihou Reefs 113 L2
Lihue 126 R10
Lihula 63 K7
Lijiang 93 K3
Likasi 106 E5
Likhoslavl 78 F4
Liku 90 D5
Likupang 91 H5
L'Ile-Rousse 69 B4
Lille 64 E3
Lille Balt 63 C8
Lillebonne 64 D4
Lillehammer 63 D6
Lillesand 63 C7
Lillestrom 63 H7
Lillhamra 63 F6
Lillhardal 63 F6
Lillholmsjon 62 F5
Lillo 66 E3
Lillviken 62 G3
Lilongwe 107 F5
Liloy 91 G4
Lima *Paraguay* 138 E4
Lima *Peru* 136 B6
Lima *Portugal* 66 B2
Lima *Montana* 122 H5
Lima *Ohio* 124 H6
Limah 97 N4
Limankoy 76 C2
Limavady 58 J2
Limay 139 C7
Limbang 90 E5
Limbani 136 D6
Limbe *Cameroon* 105 G5
Limbe *Malawi* 107 G6
Limburg 70 C3
Limeira 138 G4
Limenaria 75 H2
Limen Vatheos 75 J4
Limerick *Ireland* 59 E8
Limerick *Ireland* 59 E7
Limfjorden 63 C8
Limin 75 H2
Limmen Bight 113 H1
Limni 75 G3
Limnos 75 H3
Limoeiro *Ceara, Brazil* 137 K5
Limoeiro *Pernambuco, Brazil* 137 K5
Limoges 65 D6
Limon 132 F9
Limon 123 N8
Limousin 65 D6
Limoux 65 E7
Limpopo 109 F4
Linaalv 62 J3
Linah 96 F2
Linapacan Strait 91 F3
Linares *Chile* 139 B7
Linares *Mexico* 128 C8
Linares *Spain* 66 E3
Lincang 93 K4
Lincoln *New Zealand* 115 D5
Lincoln *U.K.* 55 J3
Lincoln *Illinois* 124 F6
Lincoln *Maine* 125 R4
Lincoln *Nebraska* 123 R7
Lincoln City 122 B5
Lincoln Sea 140 R2
Lincolnshire 55 J3
Lincolnton 129 M3
Lindau 70 C5
Linde 85 L3
Linden *Guyana* 136 F2
Linden *U.S.A.* 129 J3
Linderodsasen 63 E9
Lindesberg 63 F7
Lindi 107 G4
Lindley 108 E5
Lindos 75 K4
Lindsay *Canada* 125 L4
Lindsay *California* 126 C2
Lindsay *Montana* 123 M4
Lindu Point 114 S8
Linfen 93 M1
Lingao 93 L5
Lingayen 91 G2
Lingen 70 B2
Lingfield 53 G3
Lingga 90 C6
Lingga, Kepulauan 90 C6
Lingle 123 M6

Lingling 93 M3
Lingshi 87 L4
Lingshui 93 M5
Lingsugur 92 E5
Ling Xian 93 M3
Lingyuan 87 M3
Lingyun 93 L4
Linhai 87 N6
Linhares 138 H3
Linhe 87 K3
Linh, Ngoc 93 L5
Linkoping 63 F7
Linkou 88 C3
Linlithgow 57 E5
Linnhe, Loch 57 C4
Linosa 74 B5
Linru 93 M2
Lins 138 G4
Linsell 63 E5
Linslade 53 G3
Lintao 93 K1
Linton *U.K.* 53 H2
Linton *U.S.A.* 123 P4
Linwu 93 M3
Linxi 87 M3
Linxia 93 K1
Linyi *China* 87 M4
Linyi *China* 87 M4
Linz *Austria* 68 E1
Linz *Germany* 70 B3
Linze 86 J4
Lion, Golfe du 65 F7
Liouesso 106 C2
Lipa *Philippines* 91 G3
Lipa *Bos.* 72 D3
Lipari, Isola 69 E6
Lipari, Isole 69 E6
Lipenska nadrz 70 F4
Lipetsk 79 F5
Lipiany 70 F2
Lipin Bor 78 F3
Liping 93 L3
Lipkany 79 D6
Lipljan 73 F4
Lipnishki 71 L2
Lipno 71 H2
Lippe 70 C3
Lipsoi 75 J4
Lipson 75 F3
Lipu 93 M4
Lipusz 71 G1
Lira 107 F2
Lircay 136 C6
Liri 69 D5
Lisabata 91 H6
Lisala 106 D2
Lisboa 66 B3
Lisbon *Portugal* 66 B3
Lisbon *U.S.A.* 123 R4
Lisburn 58 K3
Lisburne, Cape 118 B2
Liscannor Bay 59 D7
Lisdoonvarna 59 D6
Lishi 87 L4
Lishui 87 M6
Lisieux 64 D4
Liskeard 52 C4
Liski 79 F5
L'Isle-Jourdain 65 D7
Lismore *Australia* 113 L4
Lismore *Ireland* 59 G8
Lismore *U.K.* 57 C4
Liss 53 G3
Listowel 59 D8
Lit 62 F5
Litang 93 K3
Litani 137 G3
Litchfield 124 F7
Litherland 55 G3
Lithgow 113 L5
Lithinon, Akra 75 H5
Litos 66 C2
Lithuania 63 K9
Litovko 85 P7
Little 128 E4
Little Abaco 132 J1
Little Aden 96 G10
Little Andaman 93 H6
Little Bahama Bank 132 H1
Little Barrier Island 115 E2
Little Belt Mountains 122 J4
Little Bow 122 H2
Little Cayman 132 G5
Little Colorado 126 G3
Little Falls *Minnesota* 124 C3
Little Falls *New York* 125 N5
Littlefield 127 L4
Littlehampton 53 G4
Little Inagua Island 133 L4
Little Karoo 108 D6
Little Minch, The 56 B3
Little Missouri 123 M5
Little Nicobar 93 H7
Little Ouse 53 H2
Little Pamir 92 D1
Littleport 53 H2
Little Red 128 G3
Little Rock 128 F3
Little Rocky Mountains 123 K3
Little Scarcies 104 C4
Little Sitkin Island 118 Ab9
Little Smoky 119 M5

Little Snake 123 K7
Little South-west Miramichi 125 S3
Little Strickland 55 G2
Littleton *Colorado* 123 M8
Littleton *New Hampshire* 125 Q4
Little Wabash 124 F7
Little Waltham 53 H3
Liulin 87 L4
Liupan Shan 93 L1
Liuyang 93 M3
Liuzhou 93 L4
Livani 63 M8
Live Oak 129 L5
Livermore 126 B2
Livermore, Mount 127 K5
Liverpool *Australia* 113 L5
Liverpool *U.K.* 55 G3
Liverpool Bay *Canada* 118 K1
Liverpool Bay *U.K.* 55 F3
Livingston *Canada* 121 N7
Livingston *U.K.* 57 E5
Livingston *Montana* 123 J5
Livingston *Texas* 128 E5
Livingstone 106 E6
Livingstone, Chutes de 106 B4
Livingstone Falls 106 B4
Livingstone Mountains 107 F4
Livingston Island 141 V6
Livingston, Lake 128 E5
Livno 72 D4
Livny 79 F5
Livojoki 62 M4
Livonia 124 J5
Livorno 68 C4
Liwale 107 G4
Li Xian 93 M3
Liyang 87 M5
Lizard 52 B4
Lizardo 137 H5
Lizard Point 52 B4
Ljosavatn 62 W12
Ljubinje 72 E4
Ljubisnja 72 E4
Ljubljana 72 C4
Ljungan 62 G5
Ljungby 63 E8
Ljusdal 63 G6
Ljusnan 63 F5
Llanarmon Dyffryn Ceiriog 52 D2
Llanbadarn Fynydd 52 D2
Llanbedr 52 C2
Llanberis 54 E3
Llanbrynmair 52 D2
Llandeilo 52 D3
Llandovery 52 D3
Llandrindod Wells 52 D2
Llandudno 54 F3
Llanelli 52 C3
Llanerchymedd 54 E3
Llanes 66 D1
Llanfaethlu 54 E3
Llanfair Caereinion 52 D2
Llanfairfechan 54 F3
Llanfair Talhaiarn 55 F3
Llanfyllin 52 D2
Llangefni 55 E3
Llanglydwen 52 C3
Llangollen 52 D2
Llangranog 52 C2
Llangurig 52 D2
Llanidloes 52 D2
Llanilar 52 C2
Llanos 136 D2
Llanquihue, Lago 139 B8
Llanrhystud 52 C2
Llanrwst 54 F3
Llantrisant 52 D3
Llanwenog 52 C2
Llanwrtyd Wells 52 D2
Llawhaden 52 C3
Llerena 66 C3
Lleyn Peninsula 52 C2
Lliria 67 F3
Llivia 67 G1
Llobregat 67 G2
Lloydminster 119 P5
Lluchmayor 67 H3
Llyswen 52 D2
Loa 138 C4
Loanhead 57 E5
Lobatse 108 E5
Lobau 70 F3
Loberia 139 E7
Lobez 70 F2
Lobito 106 B5
Lobos 139 E7
Lobos, Island 126 G7
Locarno 68 B2
Lochaber 57 D4
Lochan Fada 56 C3
Loch Ard Forest 57 D4
Lochboisdale 57 A3
Lochearnhead 57 D4
Loches 65 D5
Lochgelly 57 E4
Lochgilphead 57 C4
Lochinver 56 C2
Lochmaben 57 E5
Lochmaddy 56 A3
Lochnagar 57 E4
Lochranza 57 C5
Loch Shin 56 D2

Lochy, Loch 57 D4
Lock 113 H5
Lockerbie 57 E5
Lockhart 128 D6
Lock Haven 125 M6
Lockport 125 L5
Locri 69 F6
Loddekopinge 63 E9
Loddon *Australia* 113 J6
Loddon *U.K.* 53 J2
Lodeve 65 E7
Lodeynoye Pole 78 E3
Lodge Grass 123 L5
Lodgepole 123 M7
Lodi *Italy* 68 B3
Lodi *U.S.A.* 126 B1
Lodingen 62 F2
Lodja 106 D3
Lodwar 107 G2
Lodz 71 H3
Loeriesfontein 108 C6
Lofoten 62 E2
Loftus 55 J2
Logan 122 J7
Logan, Mount 118 G3
Logansport *Indiana* 124 G6
Logansport *Louisiana* 128 F5
Loge 106 B4
Logishin 71 M2
Logone 102 C5
Logrono 66 E1
Logrosan 66 D3
Loh 114 T10
Lohardaga 92 F4
Loharu 92 E3
Lohit 93 J3
Lohja 63 L6
Lohtaja 62 K4
Loikaw 93 J5
Loimaa 63 K6
Loimijoki 63 K6
Loing 65 E5
Loir 65 C5
Loi, Phu 93 K4
Loire 65 B5
Loja *Ecuador* 136 B4
Loja *Spain* 66 D4
Lokantekojarvi 62 M3
Lokhpodgort 78 M2
Lokhvitsa 79 E5
Lokichokio 107 F2
Lokilalaki, Gunung 91 G6
Lokka 62 M3
Loknya 78 E4
Lokoja 105 G4
Lokshak 85 N6
Lokuru 114 H6
Lol 102 E6
Lola 104 D4
Lolland 63 D9
Lolo 122 G4
Loloda 91 H5
Lolo Pass 122 G4
Lolvavana, Passage 114 U11
Lom *Bulgaria* 73 G4
Lom *Norway* 63 C6
Lomami 106 D3
Lomas Coloradas 139 C8
Lomazy 71 K3
Lombarda, Serra 137 G3
Lombe 107 G4
Lombez 65 D7
Lomblen 91 G7
Lombok 90 F7
Lome 104 F4
Lomela 106 D3
Lomir 94 J2
Lomond Hills 57 E4
Lomond, Loch 57 D4
Lomonosov Ridge 140 A1
Lompobattang, Gunung 91 F7
Lompoc 126 B3
Lomza 71 K2
London *Canada* 125 K5
London *U.K.* 53 G3
Londonderry *U.K.* 58 H2
Londonderry *U.K.* 58 J3
Londonderry, Cape 112 F1
Londonderry, Isla 139 B11
Londoni 114 R8
Londrina 138 F4
Lone Pine 126 C2
Longa *Angola* 106 C5
Longa *Angola* 106 C6
Longa Island 56 C3
Long Akah 90 E5
Longa, Ostrova de 81 S2
Long Bay 129 N4
Long Beach *California* 126 C4
Long Beach *New York* 125 P6
Long Branch 125 P6
Longchang 93 L3
Longchuan 87 M7
Longde 93 L1
Long Eaton 53 F2
Longford *Ireland* 58 G5
Longford *Ireland* 58 G5
Longformacus 57 F5
Longframlington 57 G5
Longhoughton 55 H5
Longhua 87 M3
Longhui 93 M3
Long Island *Bahamas* 133 K3
Long Island *Canada* 121 L7

Name	Page	Grid
McComb	128	G5
McCook	123	P7
McCreary	123	Q2
McDermitt	122	F7
Macdonnell Ranges	113	G3
Macduff	56	F3
Maceio	137	K5
Maceio, Punta da	137	K4
Macenta	104	D4
Macerata	68	D4
McGehee	128	G4
Macgillycuddy's Reeks	59	C9
Macha	85	K5
Machachi	136	B4
Machakos	107	G3
Machala	136	B4
Machanga	109	G4
Macharioch	57	C5
Machias	125	S4
Machichaco, Cap	66	E1
Machilipatnam	92	F5
Machiques	136	C2
Machir Bay	57	B5
Machynlleth	52	D2
Macin	73	K3
McIntosh	123	P5
Macka	77	H2
Mackay	113	K3
Mackay, Cape	120	D2
Mackay, Lake	112	F3
MacKay Lake	119	N3
McKean Island	111	U2
McKeesport	125	L6
Mackenzie Australia	113	K3
Mackenzie Canada	118	J2
Mackenzie Bay Antarctic	141	E5
Mackenzie Bay Canada	118	H2
Mackenzie King Island	120	D2
Mackenzie Mountains	118	H3
Mackinac, Straits of	124	H4
McKinley, Mount	118	E3
McKinney	128	D4
Macklin	123	K1
McLaughlin	123	P5
Maclean Strait	120	F2
Maclear	108	E6
McLeod, Lake	112	C3
Macmillan	118	J3
McMillan, Lake	127	K4
McMinnville Oregon	122	C5
McMinnville Tennessee	129	K3
McMurdo	141	M3
Macomb	124	E6
Macomer	69	B5
Macon	65	F5
Macon Georgia	129	L4
Macon Missouri	124	D7
Macossa	109	F3
McPherson	128	D1
Macquarie	113	K5
Macquarie Harbour	113	K7
Macquarie Island	141	L8
McRae	129	L4
Macroom	59	E9
McTavish Arm	119	M2
Macuspana	131	N9
Macuzari, Presa	127	H7
McVicar Arm	119	L2
Mad	122	C7
Madaba	94	B6
Madade	109	F4
Madagascar	109	J3
Madang	114	D3
Madaoua	101	G6
Madaripur	93	H4
Madawaska	125	M4
Maddalena, Isola di	69	B5
Maddaloni	69	E5
Maddy, Loch	56	A3
Madeira Brazil	136	E5
Madeira Portugal	100	B2
Madelia	124	C5
Maden Turkey	77	H3
Maden Turkey	77	J2
Madera Mexico	127	H6
Madera U.S.A.	126	B2
Madetkoski	62	M3
Madhubani	92	G3
Madhya Pradesh	92	E4
Madidi	136	D6
Madinat ash Shab	96	G10
Madingo-Kayes	106	B3
Madingou	106	B3
Madin Jadid	77	H5
Madison Indiana	124	H7
Madison Montana	122	J5
Madison Nebraska	123	R7
Madison S. Dakota	123	R5
Madison Wisconsin	124	F5
Madisonville Kentucky	124	G8
Madisonville Texas	128	E5
Madiun	90	E7
Mado Gashi	107	G2
Madoi	93	J2
Madona	63	M8
Madrakah, Ra's	97	N7
Madras (Chennai) India	92	F6
Madras U.S.A.	122	D5
Madre de Dios	136	D6
Madre de Dios, Isla	139	A10
Madre, Laguna Mexico	128	D8
Madre, Laguna U.S.A.	128	D7
Madre Occidental, Sierra	127	H6
Madre Oriental, Sierra	127	L7
Madre, Sierra	91	G2
Madrid	66	E2
Madridejos	66	E3
Madrigalejo	66	D3
Madrona, Sierra	66	D3
Madura Australia	112	F5
Madura Indonesia	90	E7
Madurai	92	E7
Madura, Selat	90	E7
Madzharovo	73	H5
Maebashi	89	G7
Maerus	73	H3
Maesteg	52	D3
Maestra, Sierra	132	J4
Maevatanana	109	J3
Maewo	114	U11
Mafa	91	H5
Mafeteng	108	E5
Mafia Island	107	G4
Mafikeng	108	E5
Mafra	66	B3
Mafraq	94	C5
Maga	114	S8
Magadan	85	S5
Magadan Oblast	85	V3
Magadi	107	G3
Magallanes, Estrecho de	139	B10
Magangue	136	C2
Magara	76	E4
Magarida	114	D4
Magburaka	104	C4
Magdagachi	85	M6
Magdalena Bolivia	136	E6
Magdalena Colombia	136	C2
Magdalena Mexico	126	F7
Magdalena Mexico	126	G5
Magdalena Mexico	130	H7
Magdalena, Isla	130	C5
Magdalena, Llano de la	130	D5
Magdalen Islands	121	P8
Magda Plateau	120	K3
Magdeburg	70	D2
Magdelena	127	J3
Magee, Island	58	L3
Magelang	90	E7
Magellan, Strait of	139	B10
Magenta, Lake	112	D5
Mageroya	62	L1
Maggiore, Lago	68	B3
Maghagha	102	F2
Magharee Islands	59	B8
Maghera	58	J3
Magherafelt	58	J3
Magheramorne	58	L3
Magilligan Point	58	J2
Magina	66	E4
Maglic	72	E4
Maglie	69	G5
Magnolia	128	F4
Magoe	109	F3
Magog	125	P4
Magpie	121	P7
Magro	67	F3
Magude	109	F5
Maguse Lake	119	R3
Maguse Point	119	S3
Magwe	93	H4
Mahabad	94	G3
Mahabe	109	J3
Mahabharat Range	92	G3
Mahabo	109	H4
Mahaddayweyne	107	J2
Mahadeo Hills	92	E4
Mahagi	107	F2
Mahajanga	109	J3
Mahakam	90	F5
Mahalapye	108	E4
Mahallat	95	K5
Mahanadi	92	F4
Mahanoy City	125	M6
Mahao	88	A4
Maharashtra	92	E5
Maharlu, Daryacheh-ye	95	L7
Maha Sarakham	93	K5
Mahavavy	109	J3
Mahbubnagar	92	E5
Mahdah	97	M4
Mahdia Guyana	136	F2
Mahdia Tunisia	101	H1
Mahe	92	E6
Mahebourg	109	L7
Mahenge	107	G4
Mahesana	92	D4
Mahi	92	D4
Mahia Peninsula	115	G3
Mahilyow	78	E5
Mahmudabad India	92	F3
Mahmudabad Iran	95	L3
Mahmudia	73	K3
Mahmudiye	76	D3
Mahnomen	124	B3
Mahon	67	J3
Mahrah, Al	97	K8
Mahukona	126	T10
Mahuva	92	D4
Maicao	136	C1
Maiche	65	G5
Maicuru	137	G4
Maidenhead	53	G3
Maidi	91	H5
Maidstone	53	H3
Maiduguri	105	H3
Maihar	92	F4
Maijdi	93	H4
Maikala Range	92	F4
Main U.K.	58	K3
Main Germany	70	C4
Main Barrier Range	113	J5
Main Channel	125	K4
Mai-Ndombe, Lac	106	C3
Maine France	64	C4
Maine U.S.A.	125	R4
Maine Soroa	101	H6
Maingkwan	93	J3
Mainland Orkney Is., U.K.	56	E2
Mainland Shetland Is., U.K.	56	A1
Maintirano	109	H3
Mainua	62	M4
Mainz	70	C4
Maio	104	L7
Maipu	139	E7
Maiquetia	133	P9
Maira	68	A3
Maisi, Cabo	133	K4
Maiskhal	93	H4
Maitland New South Wales, Australia	113	L5
Maitland S. Australia, Australia	113	H5
Maiz, Islas del	132	F8
Maizuru	89	E8
Majagual	136	C2
Majene	91	F6
Maji	103	G6
Majiang	93	L3
Majin	87	M6
Majorca	67	H3
Maka Senegal	104	C3
Maka Solomon Is.	114	K6
Makale	91	F6
Makambako	107	F4
Makanza	106	C2
Makarikha	78	K2
Makarova	84	D2
Makarska	72	D4
Makaryev	78	G4
Makassar	91	F7
Makassar, Selat	91	F6
Makat	79	J6
Makatini Flats	109	F5
Makay, Massif du	109	J4
Makeni	104	C4
Makenu	126	S10
Makhachkala	79	H7
Makharadze	77	K2
Makhmur	94	F4
Makhyah, Wadi	97	J8
Maki	91	J6
Makinsk	84	A6
Makiyivka	79	F6
Makkah	96	D6
Makkovik	121	Q6
Makkovik, Cape	121	Q6
Makogai	114	R8
Makokou	106	B2
Makondi Plateau	107	G5
Makov	71	H4
Makra	75	H4
Makrai	92	E4
Makran	92	B3
Makri	75	H2
Makronisi	75	H4
Maksatikha	78	F4
Maksim	78	K3
Maksimovka	88	F2
Makteir	100	C4
Makra	75	H4
Makrai	92	E4
Maku	94	G2
Makurazaki	89	C10
Makurdi	105	G4
Makushin Volcano	118	Ae9
Mala	62	M4
Malabang	91	G4
Malabar Coast	92	D6
Malabo	105	G5
Malacca, Strait of	90	C5
Malacky	71	G4
Mala Fatra	71	H4
Malaga Colombia	136	C2
Malaga Spain	66	D4
Malagarasi	107	F3
Malahide	59	K6
Malaita	114	K6
Malakal	103	F6
Malakanagiri	92	F5
Malakand	92	D2
Malakula	114	T12
Malang	90	E7
Malanje	106	C4
Malao	114	T11
Mala, Punta	136	B2
Malaren	63	G7
Malargue	139	C7
Malartic	125	L2
Malaspina	139	C8
Malaspina Glacier	118	G4
Malatya	77	H3
Malatya Daglari	77	H3
Malavate	137	G3
Malavi	94	H5
Malawi	107	F5
Malawi, Lake	107	F5
Malaybalay	91	H4
Malayer	94	J4
Malay Peninsula	90	C5
Malaysia	90	D5
Malazgirt	77	K3
Malbork	71	H1
Malchin Germany	70	E2
Malchin Mongolia	86	G2
Malcolm's Point	57	B4
Malden	124	F8
Maldives	82	F6
Maldon	53	H3
Maldonado	139	F6
Maldonado, Punta	131	K9
Male	82	F6
Malea, Akra	75	G4
Malegaon	92	D4
Male Karpaty	71	G4
Malema	109	G2
Malemba-Nkulu	106	E4
Maleme	75	G5
Maler Kotla	92	E2
Malesherbes	64	E4
Maleta	84	H6
Malevangga	114	H5
Malgobek	79	G7
Malgomaj	62	G4
Malhat	77	K5
Malheur	122	F6
Malheur, Lake	122	E6
Mali	100	E5
Mali Hka	93	J3
Mali Kanal	72	E3
Mali Kyun	93	J6
Malimba, Mont	107	E4
Malin Ireland	58	H2
Malin Ukraine	79	D5
Malin Beg	58	E3
Malindi	107	H3
Malin Head	58	H2
Malin More	58	E3
Malka	85	T6
Malkachan	85	S5
Malkapur	92	E4
Malkara	76	B2
Malkinia	71	K2
Malko Turnovo	73	J5
Mallaig	57	C4
Mallawi	102	F2
Mallorca	67	H3
Mallow	59	E8
Mallwyd	52	D2
Malm	62	D4
Malmberget	62	J3
Malmedy	64	G3
Malmesbury South Africa	108	C6
Malmesbury U.K.	53	E3
Malmo	63	E9
Malmohus	63	E9
Malmyzh	78	J4
Malo	114	T11
Malolo	114	Q8
Malone	125	N4
Malorita	71	L3
Malo Strait	114	T11
Maloy	62	A6
Maloyaroslavets	78	F4
Malozemelskaya Tundra	84	Ab3
Malpartida de Caceras	66	C3
Malpas	55	G3
Malpelo, Isla	134	A2
Malta	74	C5
Malta U.S.A.	123	L3
Malta Channel	74	C4
Maltahohe	108	C4
Maltby	55	H3
Maltepe	76	C2
Malton	55	J2
Malu	73	J3
Maluku	91	H6
Maluku, Laut	91	H5
Malung	63	E6
Maluu	114	K6
Malvan	92	D5
Malvern	128	F3
Malvern Hills	52	E2
Malvinas, Islas	139	E10
Malykay	85	K4
Malyy Anyuy	85	U3
Malyy Lyakhovskiy, Ostrov	85	Q2
Malyy Taymyr, Ostrov	81	M2
Malyy Yenisey	84	F6
Mama	85	J5
Mamankhalinka	79	J6
Mamanuca Group	114	Q8
Mamaru	137	F4
Mambasa	107	E2
Mamberamo	114	B2
Mamburao	91	G3
Mamers	64	D4
Mamfe	105	G4
Mamlyutka	84	Ae6
Mamonovo	71	H1
Mamore	138	D3
Mamore Forest	57	D4
Mamoria	138	D5
Mamou	104	C3
Mampong	104	E4
Mamry, Jezioro	71	J1
Mamuju	91	F6
Man India	92	F3
Man Ivory Coast	104	D4
Mana	63	C7
Mana Fr. Guiana	137	G3
Mana U.S.A.	126	R9
Manacapuru	136	E4
Manacapuru, Lago de	136	E4
Manacor	67	H3
Manadir, Al	97	M5
Manado	91	G5
Managua	132	D8

Managua, Laguna de	132	D8	Manoa Abuna	136	D5	March	53	H2	Marolambo	109	J4
Manakara	109	J4	Manokwari	91	J6	Marche *Belgium*	64	F3	Marondera	109	F3
Manakhah	96	F9	Manolas	75	F3	Marche *France*	65	D5	Maroni	137	G3
Manambolo	109	H3	Manonga	107	F3	Marchena	66	D4	Maros	91	F6
Manam Island	114	D2	Manono	107	E4	Marchena, Isla	136	A7	Marotiri Islands	115	E1
Mananara *Madagascar*	109	J4	Manorbier	52	C3	Mar Chiquita, Lago	138	D6	Maroua	105	H3
Mananara *Madagascar*	109	J3	Manorcunningham	58	G3	Marcigny	65	F5	Marovoay	109	J3
Mananjary	109	J4	Manorhamilton	58	F4	Marcus Baker, Mount	118	F3	Marowyne	137	G3
Manantavadi	92	E6	Manoron	93	J6	Marcus Island	83	P4	Marple	55	G3
Manaoba	114	K6	Manosque	65	F7	Mardan	92	D2	Marquette	124	G3
Manapire	136	D2	Manouane, Reservoir	121	M7	Mar del Plata	139	E7	Marquise	64	D3
Manapouri	115	A6	Mano-wan	89	G7	Mardin	77	J4	Marquises, Iles	143	J5
Manapouri, Lake	115	A6	Manpojin	87	P3	Mare	114	Y16	Marra, Jebel	102	D5
Manas	93	H3	Manra	111	U2	Mareeba	113	K2	Marrakech	100	D2
Manau	114	D3	Manresa	67	G2	Maree, Loch	56	C3	Marrakesh	100	D2
Manaus	136	F4	Mansa	107	E5	Mareeq	103	J7	Marrak Point	120	R5
Manavgat	76	D4	Mansehra	92	D2	Mareuil	65	D6	Marrawah	113	J7
Manbij	94	C3	Mansel Island	120	L5	Margai Caka	92	G1	Marree	113	H4
Mancha Real	66	E4	Mansfield *U.K.*	55	H3	Marganets	79	E6	Marresale	84	Ae3
Manchester *U.K.*	55	G3	Mansfield *Louisiana*	128	F5	Margaret, Cape	120	H3	Marrupa	109	G2
Manchester *Connecticut*	125	P6	Mansfield *Ohio*	124	J6	Margaret River	112	F2	Marsa Alam	96	B4
Manchester *Kentucky*	124	J8	Mansfield *Pennsylvania*	125	M6	Margarita, Isla de	136	E1	Marsabit	107	G2
Manchester *New Hampshire,*	125	Q5	Mansfield Woodhouse	55	H3	Margaritovo	88	E4	Marsala	69	D7
Manchester *Tennessee*	129	J3	Mansle	65	D6	Margate	53	J3	Marsden *Australia*	113	K5
Mancora	136	A4	Manson Creek	118	L4	Margeride, Monts de la	65	E6	Marsden *U.K.*	55	H3
Mand	95	K7	Mansoura	67	J4	Margita	73	F3	Marseille	65	F7
Mandab, Bab el	103	H5	Manston	53	J3	Margo, Dasht-i	95	R6	Mar, Serra do	138	G5
Mandal *Afghanistan*	95	Q5	Mansurlu	77	F4	Marguerite	121	N7	Marsfjallet	62	G3
Mandal *Norway*	63	B7	Manta	136	A4	Marguerite Bay	141	V5	Marshall *Minnesota*	124	C4
Mandala, Puncak	91	L6	Mantalingajan, Mount	91	F4	Mari	114	C3	Marshall *Missouri*	124	D7
Mandalay	93	J4	Mantaro	136	B6	Maria Elena	138	C4	Marshall *Texas*	128	E4
Mandalgovi	87	K2	Mantecal	136	D2	Maria, Golfo de Ana	132	H4	Marshall Bennett Islands	114	E3
Mandali	94	G5	Mantes	64	D4	Maria Madre, Isla	130	F7	Marshall Islands	143	G4
Mandal-Ovoo	87	J3	Mantiqueira, Serra da	138	G4	Maria Magdalena, Isla	130	F7	Marshalltown	124	D5
Mandan	123	P4	Mantova	68	C3	Mariampole	71	K1	Marshchapel	55	K3
Mandaon	91	G3	Mantsala	63	L6	Marianas Islands	83	N5	Marshfield	124	E4
Mandar, Teluk	91	F6	Mantta	63	L5	Marianas Trench	142	F4	Marsh Island	128	G6
Mandasawu, Poco	91	G7	Mantua	68	C3	Marian Lake	119	M3	Marske-by-the-Sea	55	H2
Mandav Hills	92	D4	Mantyharju	63	M6	Marianna *Arkansas*	128	G3	Marsta	63	G7
Mandeville	132	J5	Manua	111	V4	Marianna *Florida*	129	K5	Martaban	93	J5
Mandi	92	E2	Manuel	131	K6	Marianske Lazne	70	E4	Martaban, Gulf of	93	J5
Mandiore, Lago	138	E3	Manui	91	G6	Marias	122	J3	Martapura	90	E6
Mandla	92	F4	Manu Island	114	C2	Marias, Islas	130	F7	Martes, Sierra	67	F3
Mandoudhion	75	G3	Manujan	95	N8	Mariato, Punta	132	G11	Marthaguy	113	K5
Mandurah	112	D5	Manukau	115	E3	Maria van Diemen, Cape	115	D1	Martha's Vineyard	125	Q6
Manduria	69	F5	Manukau Harbour	115	E2	Mariazell	68	E2	Martigny	68	A2
Mandvi	92	C4	Manulla	58	D5	Marib	96	G9	Martigues	65	F7
Mandya	92	E6	Manus Islands	114	D2	Maribor	72	C2	Martin *Poland*	71	H4
Manea	53	H2	Manya	78	L3	Maridi	102	E7	Martin *Spain*	67	F2
Manevichi	71	L3	Manyas	76	B2	Marie Byrd Land	141	S3	Martin *S. Dakota*	123	P6
Manfredonia	69	E5	Manych Gudilo, Ozero	79	G6	Marie Galante	133	S7	Martin *Tennessee*	128	H2
Manfredonia, Golfo di	69	F5	Manyoni	107	F4	Mariehamn	63	H6	Martinavas	53	N6
Manga	138	J6	Manzanares	66	E3	Marienbad	70	E4	Martinborough	115	E4
Mangakino	115	E3	Manzanillo *Cuba*	132	J4	Marienburg	71	H1	Martinique	133	S7
Mangalia	73	K4	Manzanillo *Mexico*	130	G8	Mariental	108	C4	Martinique Passage	133	S7
Mangalore	92	D6	Manzanillo, Punta	136	B2	Marienwerder	71	H2	Martin Lake	129	K4
Mangaon	92	D5	Manzariyeh	95	K4	Mariestad	63	E7	Martin Point	118	G1
Mangapehi	115	E3	Manzhouli	87	M2	Marietta *Georgia*	129	K4	Martinsberg	68	E1
Mangautu	114	J7	Manzini	109	F5	Marietta *Ohio*	125	K7	Martinsville	125	L8
Mangin Range	93	J4	Manzya	84	F5	Marigot	133	S7	Martock	52	E4
Mangkalihat, Tanjung	91	F5	Mao	102	C5	Mariinsk	84	D5	Marton *New Zealand*	115	E4
Manglares, Punta	136	B3	Maoershan	88	A3	Marina di Carrara	68	C3	Marton *U.K.*	55	J3
Mangochi	107	G5	Maoke, Pegunungan	91	K6	Marina di Leuca	69	G6	Martorell	67	G2
Mangoky	109	H4	Maoming	93	M4	Marina di Monasterace	69	F6	Martos	66	E4
Mangole	91	H6	Mapai	109	F4	Marinette	124	G4	Martre, Lac La	119	M3
Mangonui	115	D1	Mapam Yumco	92	F2	Maringa	106	D2	Martuk	79	K5
Mangoro	109	J3	Mapire	133	Q11	Maringa	138	F4	Martuni	79	H7
Mangotsfield	52	E3	Maple Creek	123	K3	Marion *Illinois*	124	F8	Martyn	78	K2
Mangral	92	D4	Mappi *Indonesia*	91	K7	Marion *Indiana*	124	H6	Martze	136	D4
Manguari	136	D4	Mappi *Indonesia*	91	K7	Marion *Ohio*	124	J6	Marudi	90	E5
Mangueira, Lagoa	138	F6	Maprik	114	C2	Marion *S. Carolina*	129	N3	Marugame	89	D8
Mangui	87	N1	Mapuera	136	F4	Marion *Virginia*	125	K8	Marum, Mount	114	U12
Manguinha, Pontal do	137	K6	Maputo	109	F5	Marion, Lake	129	M4	Marunga	114	E2
Mangut	85	J7	Maqdam, Ras	96	C7	Marion Reefs	113	L2	Marungu	107	E4
Mangyshlak	79	J7	Maqna	96	B2	Maripa	136	D2	Marv Dasht	95	L7
Mangyshlak, Poluostrov	79	J7	Maqueda	66	D2	Marisa	91	G5	Marvejols	65	E6
Mangyshlakskiy Zaliv	79	J7	Maquinchao	139	C8	Mariscal Estigarribia	138	D4	Marvine, Mount	122	J8
Manhan	86	G2	Maraba	137	H5	Maritimes, Alpes	65	G6	Marwar	92	D3
Manhattan	123	R8	Maracaibo	136	C1	Maritsa	73	H4	Mary	95	Q3
Manhica	109	F5	Maracaibo, Lago de	136	C2	Mariupol	79	F6	Maryborough	113	L4
Manicore	136	E5	Maraca, Ilha de	137	G3	Marivan	94	H4	Maryevka	84	Ae6
Manicouagan	121	N7	Maracay	136	D1	Marjamaa	63	L7	Maryland	125	M7
Manicouagan, Reservoir	121	N7	Maradah	101	J3	Marjayoun	94	B5	Maryport	55	F2
Manifah	97	J3	Maradi	101	G6	Marka	96	E7	Mary, Puy	65	E6
Manika, Plateau de la	106	E4	Maragheh	94	H3	Marka	107	H2	Marystown	121	Q8
Manila	91	G3	Marajo, Baia de	137	H4	Markam	93	J3	Marysville *California*	126	B1
Manipa, Selat	91	H6	Marajo, Ilha de	137	H4	Market Deeping	53	G2	Marysville *Kansas*	123	R8
Manipur	93	H4	Maralal	107	G2	Market Drayton	52	E2	Maryvale	113	L4
Manisa	76	B3	Maramasike	114	K6	Market Harborough	53	G2	Maryville *Missouri*	124	C6
Man, Isle of	54	E2	Maramba	106	E6	Markethill	58	J4	Maryville *Tennessee*	129	L3
Manistee *U.S.A.*	124	G4	Maran	90	C5	Market Rasen	55	J3	Marzo, Cabo	132	J11
Manistee *U.S.A.*	124	H4	Marand	94	G2	Market Weighton	55	J3	Masagua	132	B7
Manistique	124	G4	Maranguape	137	K4	Markha	85	K4	Masai Steppe	107	G3
Manitoba	119	R4	Maranhao	137	H5	Markham	114	D3	Masaka	107	F3
Manitoba, Lake	123	Q2	Maranhao Grande, Cachoeira	137	F4	Marlborough *Australia*	113	K3	Masally	94	J2
Manitou Falls	123	T2	Maran, Koh-i-	92	C3	Marlborough *Guyana*	136	F2	Masan	89	B8
Manitou Island	124	G4	Maranon	136	C4	Marlborough *U.K.*	53	F3	Masasi	107	G5
Manitoulin	124	J4	Marans	65	C5	Marlin	128	D5	Masaya	132	D8
Manitowoc	124	G4	Marari	136	D5	Marlinton	125	K7	Masbate *Philippines*	91	G3
Maniwaki	125	N3	Marasesti	73	J3	Marlow	53	G3	Masbate *Philippines*	91	G3
Manizales	136	B2	Marassume	137	H4	Marmagao	92	D5	Mascara	100	F1
Manja	109	H4	Marateca	66	B3	Marmande	65	D6	Mascarene Islands	109	L7
Manjra	92	E5	Marathokambos	75	J4	Marmara *Turkey*	76	B2	Masela	91	H7
Mankato	124	C4	Marathon *Canada*	124	G2	Marmara *Turkey*	76	B2	Maseru	108	E5
Mankono	104	D4	Marathon *Florida*	129	M8	Marmara Denizi	76	C2	Mashabih	96	C4
Mankovka	73	L1	Marathon *Texas*	127	L5	Marmaraereglisi	76	B2	Masham	55	H2
Manna	90	C5	Marau	90	E6	Marmara Golu	76	C3	Mashan *Guangxi, China*	93	L4
Mannar	92	E7	Marau Point	115	G3	Marmara, Sea of	76	C2	Mashan *Heilongjiang, China*	88	B3
Mannar, Gulf of	92	E7	Maravovo	114	J6	Marmaris	76	C4	Mashhad	95	P3
Mannheim	70	C4	Marbella	66	D4	Marmblada	68	C2	Mashike	88	H4
Manning, Cape	120	B2	Marble Bar	112	D3	Marmelos	136	E5	Mashiz	95	N7
Manning Strait	114	J5	Marble Canyon	126	G2	Marne	64	E4	Mashkid	95	R8
Manningtree	53	J3	Marburg	70	C3	Maro	102	C3	Masi	62	K2
Mannu	69	B6	Marcelino	136	D4	Maroantsetra	109	J3	Masilah, Wadi al	97	J9

Name	Page	Ref
Masi-Manimba	106	C3
Masindi	107	F2
Masirah	97	P6
Masirah, Khalij	97	N7
Masirah, Khawr al	97	P6
Masiri	95	K6
Masisi	107	E3
Masjed Soleyman	94	J6
Mask, Lough	58	D5
Maskutan	95	P8
Maslen Nos	73	J4
Masoala, Cap	109	K3
Mason Bay	115	A7
Mason City	124	D5
Ma, Song	93	K4
Masqat	97	P5
Massa	68	C3
Massachusetts	125	P5
Massachusetts Bay	125	Q5
Massakori	102	C5
Massa Marittima	68	C4
Massangena	109	F4
Massape	137	J4
Massava	84	Ad4
Massenya	102	C5
Massigui	100	D6
Massillon	124	K6
Massinga	109	G4
Massingir	109	F4
Masteksay	79	H6
Masterton	115	E4
Mastikho, Akra	75	J3
Mastuj	92	D1
Masturah	96	D5
Masuda	89	C8
Masulch	94	J3
Masurai, Bukit	90	C6
Masvingo	108	F4
Masyaf	94	C4
Mat	74	F2
Mataboor	91	K6
Mataca	109	G2
Matachel	66	C3
Matad	87	M2
Matadi	106	B4
Matafome	66	B3
Matagalpa	132	E8
Matagami *Ontario, Canada*	125	M2
Matagami *Quebec, Canada*	125	M2
Matagami, Lac	125	M1
Matagorda Bay	128	D6
Matagorda Island	128	D6
Matakana Island	115	F2
Matakaoa Point	115	G2
Matala	106	C5
Matale	92	F7
Matam	104	C2
Matamata	115	E2
Matamoros *Mexico*	128	D8
Matamoros *Mexico*	127	L8
Matane	125	S2
Mata Negra	136	F2
Matanzas	132	G3
Matapan, Cape	75	G4
Matapedia	125	S2
Matara	92	F7
Mataram	90	F7
Matarani	138	B3
Mataranka	112	G1
Mataro	67	H2
Matata	115	F2
Matatiele	108	E6
Mataura *New Zealand*	115	B6
Mataura *New Zealand*	115	B7
Matawai	115	F3
Matay	86	D2
Matcha	86	B4
Matehuala	131	J6
Matera	69	F5
Mateszalka	73	G2
Mateur	101	G1
Matfors	62	G5
Matheson	125	K2
Mathis	128	D6
Mathry	52	B3
Mathura	92	E3
Mati	91	H4
Matlock	55	H3
Mato, Cerro	133	Q11
Mato Grosso	136	F6
Mato Grosso do Sul	138	E3
Mato Grosso, Planalto do	138	E3
Matra	72	E2
Matrah	97	P5
Matrosovo	71	J1
Matruh	102	E1
Matsubara	89	J10
Matsue	89	D8
Ma-tsu Lieh-tao	87	M6
Matsumae	88	H5
Matsumoto	89	F7
Matsusaka	89	F8
Matsuyama	89	D9
Mattagami	121	K8
Mattancheri	92	E7
Mattawa	125	L3
Matterhorn *Switzerland*	68	A3
Matterhorn *U.S.A.*	122	G7
Matthews Peak	107	G2
Matthew Town	133	L4
Matti, Sabkhat	97	K10
Mattoon	124	F7
Matty Island	120	G3
Matua, Ostrov	85	S7
Matuku	114	R9
Maturin	136	E2
Matyushkinskaya	84	B5
Mau	92	F3
Maua	109	G2
Maubara	91	H7
Maubeuge	64	E3
Maubin	93	J5
Maubourguet	65	D7
Mauchline	57	D5
Maud	56	F3
Maues	136	F4
Mauganj	92	F4
Maui	126	S10
Maula	62	L4
Maule	139	B7
Mauleon-Licharre	65	C7
Maumere	91	G7
Maumtrasna	58	C5
Maumturk Mountains	59	C5
Maun	108	D4
Mauna Kea	126	T11
Mauna Loa	126	T11
Maungmagan Islands	93	J6
Maunoir, Lac	118	L2
Maures	65	G7
Mauriac	65	E6
Maurice, Lake	112	G4
Mauritania	100	C5
Mauritius	109	L7
Mauron	64	B4
Mauston	124	E5
Mautern	68	E2
Mavinga	106	D6
Mawbray	55	F2
Mawhai Point	115	G3
Mawlaik	93	H4
Mawson	141	E5
Maxaila	109	F4
Maxmo	62	K5
Maya	85	N5
Mayaguana Island	133	L3
Mayaguana Passage	133	L3
Mayaguez	133	P5
Mayak *China*	86	F2
Mayak *Russia*	71	H1
Mayak *Russia*	79	K5
Mayamey	95	M3
Mayas, Montanas	132	C6
Maybole	57	D5
May, Cape	125	N7
Maychew	96	D10
Maydh	103	J5
Mayenne *France*	64	C4
Mayenne *France*	65	C5
Mayero	84	G3
Mayfaah	97	H9
Mayfield *U.K.*	53	H3
Mayfield *U.S.A.*	124	F8
May, Isle of	57	F4
Maykop	79	G7
Maykor	78	K4
Maymakan *Russia*	85	N5
Maymakan *Russia*	85	P5
Maymyo	93	J4
Mayn	85	W4
Maynooth	59	J6
Mayo *Argentina*	139	B9
Mayo *Canada*	118	H3
Mayo *Ireland*	58	D5
Mayo *Mexico*	130	E4
Mayor Island	115	F2
Mayor, Pic	67	H3
Mayotte	109	J2
May Pen	132	J6
Mayraira Point	91	G2
Mayrata	75	F3
Maysville	124	J7
Mayumba	106	A3
Mayuram	92	E6
Mayville	123	R4
Mayyun Island	96	F10
Mazalat	73	H4
Mazamari	136	C6
Mazamet	65	E7
Mazar	92	E1
Mazar-e Sharif	92	C1
Mazarete	67	E2
Mazarredo	139	C9
Mazarron	67	F4
Mazarsu	86	C3
Mazaruni	136	F2
Mazatenango	132	B7
Mazatlan	130	F6
Mazdaj	95	K5
Mazeikiai	63	K8
Mazgirt	77	H3
Mazhur, Irq al	96	G3
Mazidagi	77	J4
Mazinan	95	N3
Mazirbe	63	K8
Mazury	71	J2
Mbabane	108	F5
Mbaiki	102	C7
Mbala	107	F4
Mbalavu	114	S8
Mbale	107	F2
Mbalmayo	105	H5
Mbalo	114	K6
Mbandaka	106	C2
MBanza Congo	106	B4
Mbanza-Ngungu	106	B4
Mbarara	107	F3
Mbengwi	105	G4
Mbeya	107	F4
Mbouda	105	H4
Mbour	104	B3
Mbout	100	C5
Mbuji-Mayi	106	D4
Mchinji	107	F5
MClintock	119	S4
Meade *Alaska*	118	D1
Meade *Kansas*	127	M2
Meade, Loch	56	D2
Mead, Lake	126	E2
Meadow Lake	119	P5
Meadville	125	K6
Mealhada	66	B2
Meana	95	Q3
Meath	58	J5
Meaux	64	E4
Mebula	91	G7
Mecca	96	D6
Mechelen	64	F3
Mecheria	100	E2
Mechigmen	118	A2
Mechigmen Zaliv	118	A2
Mecidie	76	B2
Mecitozu	76	F2
Mecklenburger Bucht	70	D1
Mecsek	72	E2
Mecufi	109	H2
Mecula	109	G2
Medak	92	E5
Medan	90	B5
Medanos	139	D7
Medanosa, Punta	139	C9
Medea	101	F1
Medellin	136	B2
Medelpad	62	G5
Medenine	101	H2
Mederdra	100	B5
Medford	122	C6
Medgidia	73	K3
Medicine Bow Mountains	123	L7
Medicine Bow Peak	123	L7
Medicine Hat	123	J3
Medicine Lodge	127	N2
Medina *Saudi Arabia*	96	D4
Medina *N. Dakota*	123	Q4
Medina *New York*	125	L5
Medinaceli	66	E2
Medina del Campo	66	D2
Medina de Rioseco	66	D2
Medina Sidonia	66	D4
Medina Terminal Canal	125	L5
Medinipur	93	G4
Mediterranean Sea	98	D3
Medjerda, Monts de la	69	B7
Medkovets	73	G4
Mednyy, Ostrov	81	T4
Medoc	65	C6
Medole	68	C3
Medvezhl, Ostrova	85	U2
Medvezhyegorsk	78	E3
Medveditsa	78	F4
Medway	53	H3
Medyn	78	F5
Medynskiy Zavorot, Poluostrov	78	K2
Meeberrie	112	D4
Meechkyn, Kosa	85	Y3
Meekatharra	112	D4
Meeker	123	L7
Meerut	92	E3
Meeteetse	123	K5
Mega	91	J6
Megalo Khorio	75	J4
Megalopolis	75	G4
Megara	75	G3
Megeve	65	G6
Megget Reservoir	57	E5
Meghalaya	93	H3
Megion	84	B4
Megisti	76	C4
Megra *Russia*	78	F3
Megra *Russia*	78	G2
Mehamn	62	M1
Mehndawal	92	F3
Mehran	94	H5
Meig	56	D3
Meighen Island	120	G2
Meiktila	93	J4
Meiningen	70	D3
Meira	66	C1
Meissen	70	E3
Mei Xian	87	M7
Mejez El Bab	69	B7
Mejillones	138	B4
Mekambo	106	B2
Mekele	103	G5
Meknes	100	D2
Mekong	93	L6
Mekong, Mouths of the	93	L7
Mela	62	U12
Melaka	90	C5
Melambes	75	H5
Melanesia	142	F4
Melawi	90	E6
Melbourne *Australia*	113	J6
Melbourne *U.S.A.*	129	M6
Melbourne Island	119	Q2
Melbu	62	F2
Melchor Muzquiz	127	M7
Melenki	78	G4
Meleuz	78	K5
Melfi *Chad*	102	C5
Melfi *Italy*	69	E5
Melfort	119	Q5
Melgaco	137	G4
Melhus	62	D4
Melilla	100	E1
Melipilla	139	B6
Melita	123	P3
Melito di Porto Salvo	69	E7
Melitopol	79	F6
Melk	68	E1
Melksham	53	E3
Mellegue, Oued	101	G1
Mellerud	63	E7
Melle-sur-Bretonne	65	C5
Melling	55	G2
Mellish Reef	113	M2
Mellte	52	D3
Melnik	70	F3
Melo	138	F6
Mololo	91	G7
Melozitna	118	E2
Melrhir, Chott	101	G2
Melrose	124	C4
Melsungen	70	C3
Meltaus	62	L3
Melton Mowbray	53	G2
Melun	64	E4
Melut	103	F5
Melvern Lake	124	C7
Melville	123	N2
Melville Bugt	120	P2
Melville, Cape	113	J1
Melville Hills	118	L2
Melville Island *Australia*	112	G1
Melville Island *Canada*	120	D2
Melville, Kap	120	P2
Melville, Lake	121	Q7
Melville Peninsula	120	K4
Melvin, Lough	58	F4
Melykut	72	E2
Melyuveyem	85	W4
Memba	109	H2
Memberamo	91	K6
Memboro	91	F7
Memel	63	L9
Memmingen	70	D4
Mempawah	90	D5
Memphis *Tennessee*	128	H3
Memphis *Texas*	127	M3
Mena	128	E3
Menai Bridge	55	E3
Menaka	101	F5
Mendawai	90	E6
Mende	65	E6
Mendi	114	C3
Mendip Hills	52	E3
Mendocino, Cape	122	B7
Mendoza	138	C6
Menemen	76	B3
Menen	64	E3
Menfi	69	D7
Mengcheng	93	N2
Mengcun	87	M4
Mengen	76	E2
Mengene Dagi	77	L3
Menggala	90	D6
Menghai	93	K4
Mengjiagang	88	C2
Mengjiawan	87	K4
Mengla	93	K4
Mengshan	93	M4
Mengyin	87	M4
Meniet	101	F3
Menihek, Lac	121	N7
Meningie	113	H6
Menkya	78	L3
Menominee *U.S.A.*	124	G4
Menominee *U.S.A.*	124	G4
Menomonee Falls	124	F5
Menongue	106	C5
Menorca	67	J3
Mentawai, Kepulauan	90	B6
Mentawai, Selat	90	B6
Mentok	90	D6
Menton	68	A4
Mentor	125	K6
Menyamya	114	D3
Menzel Bourguiba	69	B7
Meon	53	F4
Meppel	64	G2
Meppen	70	B2
Mequinenza	67	G2
Merabellou, Kolpos	75	H5
Merak	90	D7
Merano	68	C2
Merauke	91	L7
Mercan Dagi	77	H3
Mercato Saraceno	68	D4
Merced	126	B2
Mercedario, Cerro	138	B6
Mercedes *Argentina*	139	C6
Mercedes *Argentina*	139	E6
Mercedes *Argentina*	138	E5
Mercedes *Uruguay*	138	E6
Mercimek	77	F4
Mercimekkale	77	J3
Mercurea	73	G3
Mercury Bay	115	E2
Mercy, Cape	120	P5
Mere	52	E3
Meredith, Cape	139	D10
Meredoua	100	F3
Mere Lava	114	U11
Mereworth	53	H3
Mergenovo	79	J6

Name	Page	Grid
Mergui	93	J6
Mergui Archipelago	93	J6
Meribah	113	J5
Meric	76	B2
Merida *Mexico*	131	Q7
Merida *Spain*	66	C3
Merida *Venezuela*	136	C2
Merida, Cordillera de	136	C2
Meriden	125	P6
Meridian	128	H4
Merig	114	T11
Merir	91	J5
Meriruma	137	G3
Merkys	63	L9
Mermaid Reef	112	D2
Merowe	103	F4
Merredin	112	D5
Merrick	57	D5
Merrill	124	F4
Merrillville	124	G6
Merrimack	125	Q5
Merritt	122	D2
Merritt Island	129	M6
Merriwa	113	L5
Mersa Fatma	96	E9
Mersea Island	53	H3
Merseburg	70	D3
Merse, The	57	F5
Mersey	55	G3
Merseyside	55	G3
Mersin	76	F4
Mersing	90	C5
Mersrags	63	K8
Merthyr Tydfil	52	D3
Mertola	66	C4
Mertvyy Kultuk, Sor	79	J6
Mertz Glacier	141	K5
Merzifon	76	F2
Merzig	70	B4
Mesa	126	G4
Mesaras, Kolpos	75	H5
Meschede	70	C3
Meselefors	62	G4
Meshik	118	D4
Meshraer Req	102	E6
Mesolongion	75	F3
Messina *Italy*	69	E6
Messina *South Africa*	108	F4
Messina, Stretto di	69	E6
Messingham	55	J3
Messini	75	F4
Messiniakos Kolpos	75	F4
Messo	84	B3
Messoyakha	84	B3
Mesta	75	H2
Mestiya	77	K1
Mestre	68	D3
Mesudiye	77	G2
Meta	136	D2
Metan	138	D5
Metapan	132	C7
Metaponto	69	F5
Metema	103	G5
Meteran	114	E2
Methven *New Zealand*	115	C5
Methven *U.K.*	57	E4
Methwin, Mount	112	E4
Metkovic	72	D4
Metlika	72	C3
Metropolis	124	F8
Metsovon	75	F3
Metu	103	G6
Metz	64	G4
Meulaboh	90	B5
Meureudu	90	B4
Meurthe	64	G4
Meuse	64	F3
Mexborough	55	H3
Mexia	128	D5
Mexicali	126	E4
Mexico	130	H6
Mexico *U.S.A.*	124	E7
Mexico City	131	K8
Mexico, Gulf of	117	K6
Meydancik	77	K2
Meydan e Gel	95	M7
Meydani, Ra's e	95	P9
Meymaneh	94	S4
Meymeh	95	K5
Meynypilgyno	85	X4
Meyrueis	65	E6
Mezdra	73	G4
Mezen *Russia*	78	G2
Mezen *Russia*	78	H2
Mezenc, Mont	65	F6
Mezenskaya Guba	78	G2
Mezenskiy	84	F2
Mezhdurechensk	84	D6
Mezhdusharskiy, Ostrov	80	C2
Mezhgorye	71	K4
Mezotur	72	F2
Mezquital	130	G6
Mezzana	68	C2
Mhangura	108	F3
Mhow	92	E4
Miahuatlan	131	L9
Miajadas	66	D3
Miami *Arizona*	126	G4
Miami *Florida*	129	M8
Miami *Ohio*	124	H7
Miami Beach	129	M8
Mianabad	95	N3
Miandowab	94	H3
Mianeh	94	H3
Miang, Pou	93	K5
Mianwali	92	D2
Mianyang	93	K2
Miarinarivo *Madagascar*	109	J3
Miarinarivo *Madagascar*	109	J3
Miass	84	Ad5
Miastko	71	G1
Micang Shan	93	L2
Michalovce	71	J4
Michelson, Mount	118	G2
Michigan	124	H5
Michigan City	124	G6
Michigan, Lake	124	G5
Michipicoten	124	H3
Michipicoten Island	124	H3
Michurinsk	79	G5
Mickle Fell	55	G2
Mickleton	53	F2
Micronesia	142	F4
Micurin	73	J4
Middelburg *Netherlands*	64	E3
Middelburg *South Africa*	108	E5
Middelburg *South Africa*	108	E6
Middle Andaman	93	H6
Middle Barton	53	F3
Middlebury	125	P4
Middlefart	63	C9
Middlemarch	115	C6
Middlesboro	124	J8
Middlesbrough	55	H2
Middleton *Greater Manchester, U.K.*	55	G3
Middleton *Strathclyde, U.K.*	55	B4
Middleton Cheney	53	F2
Middle Tongue	55	G2
Middleton-on-the-Wolds	55	J3
Middleton Reef	113	M4
Middletown *U.K.*	52	D2
Middletown *New York*	125	N6
Middletown *Ohio*	124	H7
Middlewich	55	G3
Mid Glamorgan	52	D3
Midhurst	53	G4
Midi	96	F8
Midland *Canada*	125	L4
Midland *Michigan*	124	H5
Midland *Texas*	127	M5
Midleton	59	F9
Midongy Atsimo	109	J4
Midsomer Norton	52	E3
Midwest	123	L6
Midwest City	128	D3
Midyan	96	B3
Midyat	77	J4
Mid Yell	56	A1
Midzor	73	G4
Miechow	71	J3
Miedwie, Jezioro	70	F2
Miedzyrzecz	70	F2
Mielec	71	J3
Miena	113	K7
Mieres	66	D1
Mieso	103	H6
Mieszkowice	70	F2
Miford Sound	115	A6
Mighan	95	P6
Miguel Aleman, Presa	131	L8
Miguel Alves	137	J4
Miguel Hidalgo, Presa	127	H7
Mihaliccik	76	D3
Mihara	89	D8
Miharu	89	H7
Mihrad, Al	97	L6
Miida	96	E9
Mijares	67	F2
Mikha Tskhakaya	77	J1
Mikhaylova	84	D1
Mikhaylovgrad	73	G4
Mikhaylov Island	141	F6
Mikhaylovka *Russia*	88	C4
Mikhaylovka *Russia*	79	G5
Mikindani	107	G5
Mikkeli *Finland*	63	M6
Mikkeli *Finland*	63	M6
Mikolajki	71	J2
Mikonos	75	H4
Mikri Prespa, Limni	75	F2
Mikulov	71	G4
Mikun	78	J3
Mikuni	89	F7
Mikuni-sammyaku	89	G7
Mikura-jima	89	G9
Milaca	124	D4
Milagro	136	B4
Milan *Italy*	68	B3
Milan *U.S.A.*	128	H3
Milano	68	B3
Milas	76	B4
Milazzo	69	E6
Milbank	123	R5
Mildenhall	53	H2
Mildurra	113	J5
Mile	93	K4
Mileh Tharthar	94	F5
Miles	113	L4
Miles City	123	M4
Milford *U.K.*	58	G2
Milford *U.S.A.*	125	N7
Milford Haven	52	B3
Milford Sound	115	A6
Milgun	112	D4
Milh, Bahr al	94	F5
Miliana	101	F1
Miliane, Oued	69	C7
Milk	123	L3
Millas	65	E7
Millau	65	E6
Milledgeville	129	L4
Mille Lacs, Lac des	124	E2
Mille Lacs Lake	124	D3
Miller	123	Q5
Millerovo	79	G6
Millers Flat	115	B6
Millford	58	F4
Millington	128	H3
Mill Island *Antarctic*	141	G5
Mill Island *Canada*	120	L5
Millisle	58	L3
Millnocket	125	R4
Millom	55	F2
Millport	57	D5
Mills Lake	119	M3
Milltown	58	K2
Milltown Malbay	59	D7
Millville	125	N7
Millwood Lake	128	F4
Milngavie	57	D5
Milogradovo	88	E4
Milolii	126	T11
Milos *Greece*	75	H4
Milos *Greece*	75	H4
Milowka	71	H4
Milparinka	113	J4
Milpillas	131	K9
Milton *New Zealand*	115	B7
Milton *Florida*	129	J5
Milton *Pennsylvania*	125	M6
Milton Abbot	52	C4
Milton Ernest	53	G2
Milton Keynes	53	G2
Miluo	93	M3
Milwaukee	124	G5
Mimizan	65	C6
Mimon	70	F3
Mina Abd Allah	97	J2
Minab	95	N8
Mina de San Domingos	66	C4
Minahassa Peninsula	91	G5
Minamata	89	C9
Minas *Indonesia*	90	C5
Minas *Uruguay*	139	E6
Mina Saud	97	J2
Minas Gerais	138	G3
Minas, Sierra de las	132	C7
Minatitlan	131	M8
Minbu	93	H4
Minch, The	56	C2
Mincio	68	C3
Mindanao	91	G4
Mindelo	104	L7
Minden *U.S.A.*	128	F4
Minden *Germany*	70	C2
Mindoro	91	G3
Mindoro Strait	91	G3
Mindra	73	G3
Minehead	52	D3
Mine Head	59	G9
Mineola	128	E4
Mineral Wells	128	C4
Minerva Reefs	111	T6
Minervino Murge	69	F5
Minfeng	92	F1
Mingechaur	79	H7
Mingela	113	K2
Minglanilla	67	F3
Mingshui *Gansu, China*	86	H3
Mingshui *Heilongjiang, China*	87	P2
Mingulay	57	A4
Minho	66	B1
Minicoy	92	D7
Minigwal	112	E4
Min Jiang	93	K3
Minle	86	J4
Minna	105	G4
Minneapolis	124	D4
Minnedosa	123	Q2
Minnesota *U.S.A.*	124	C3
Minnesota *U.S.A.*	124	C4
Minnitaki Lake	124	E1
Mino	66	B1
Minorca	67	J3
Minot	123	P3
Minsk	78	D5
Minsk Mazowiecki	71	J2
Minsterley	52	E2
Mintlaw	56	F3
Minto	125	S3
Minto Inlet	119	M1
Minto, Lac	121	L6
Minturn	123	L8
Minusinsk	84	E6
Minwakh	97	J8
Min Xian	93	K2
Minyar	78	K4
Miquelon	125	M2
Mira *Italy*	68	D3
Mira *Portugal*	66	B4
Mirabad	95	Q6
Miracema do Norte	137	H5
Miraflores	136	C2
Miraj	92	D5
Miramichi Bay	121	N8
Miramont	65	D6
Miram Shah	92	D2
Miranda *Brazil*	138	E4
Miranda *Brazil*	138	E4
Miranda de Ebro	66	E1
Miranda do Douro	66	C2
Mirande	65	D7
Mirandela	66	C2
Mirandola	68	C3
Mirapinima	136	E4
Miravci	73	G5
Mirbat, Ra's	97	M8
Mirbut	97	M8
Mirear Island	96	B5
Mirebeau	65	D5
Mirgorod	79	E6
Miri	90	E5
Miri Hills	93	H3
Mirimire	136	D1
Mirim, Lagoa	138	F6
Mirjaveh	95	Q7
Mirnyy *Antarctic*	141	G5
Mirnyy *Russia*	85	J4
Mironovo	84	H5
Mirpur Khas	92	C3
Mirriam Vale	113	L3
Mirtoan Sea	75	G4
Mirtoon Pelagos	75	G4
Miryang	89	B8
Mirzapur	92	F3
Misgar	92	D1
Mishan	88	C3
Mi-shima	89	C8
Mishkino	78	K4
Misima Island	114	T10
Miskolc	73	F1
Misool	91	J6
Misratah	101	J2
Missinaibi	121	K7
Mission *Canada*	122	C3
Mission *U.S.A.*	123	P6
Mission Viejo	126	D4
Mississauga	125	L5
Mississippi *U.S.A.*	128	G4
Mississippi *U.S.A.*	128	G5
Mississippi Delta	128	H6
Missoula	122	G4
Missouri *U.S.A.*	124	D7
Missouri *U.S.A.*	124	E7
Missouri, Coteau de	123	P4
Mistassibi	121	M8
Mistassini *Canada*	125	P2
Mistassini *Canada*	125	P2
Mistassini, Lac	121	M7
Mistelbach	68	F1
Mistretta	69	E7
Mitatib	96	C9
Mitchell *Australia*	113	J2
Mitchell *Australia*	113	K4
Mitchell *U.S.A.*	123	Q6
Mitchell, Mount	129	L3
Mitchelstown	59	F8
Mithankot	92	D3
Mithimna	75	J3
Mitilini	75	J3
Mito	89	H7
Mitre	111	R4
Mitrofanovskaya	78	K3
Mitsio, Nosy	109	J2
Mitsiwa	103	G4
Mitsiwa Channel	96	D9
Mittelland Kanal	70	B2
Mittelmark	70	E2
Mitumba, Chaine des	107	E4
Mitwaba	107	E4
Mitzic	106	B2
Mixteco	131	K8
Miyah, Wadi al	77	H5
Miyake-jima	89	G8
Miyake-shoto	89	G11
Miyako	88	H6
Miyako-jima	89	G11
Miyakonojo	89	C10
Miyaly	79	J6
Miyazaki	89	C10
Miyazu	89	E8
Miyoshi	89	D8
Mizdah	101	H2
Mizen Head *Cork, Ireland*	59	C10
Mizen Head *Wicklow, Ireland*	59	K7
Mizhi	87	L4
Mizil	73	J3
Mizoram	93	H4
Mizpe Ramon	94	B6
Mjolby	63	F7
Mjosa	63	D6
Mlada Boleslav	70	F3
Mladenovac	72	F3
Mlawa	71	J2
Mljet	72	D4
Moa *Cuba*	133	K4
Moa *Indonesia*	91	H7
Moab	127	H1
Moa Island	114	C4
Moala	114	R9
Moate	59	G6
Moatize	109	F3
Moba	107	E4
Mobaye	102	D7
Mobayi-Mbongo	106	D2
Moberly	124	D7
Mobile	129	H5
Mobile Bay	129	H5
Mobridge	123	P5
Mobutu Sese Seko, Lake	107	F2
Moca	114	S9
Mocajuba	137	G4
Mocambique	109	H3
Mocamedes	106	B6
Mocha, Isla	139	B7
Mochudi	108	E4

Name	Page	Grid
Mocimboa da Praia	109	H2
Moctexuma	127	H6
Moctezuma	131	K7
Mocuba	109	G3
Modder	108	E5
Modena *Italy*	68	C3
Modena *U.S.A.*	126	F7
Modesto	126	B2
Modica	69	E7
Modigliana	68	C3
Modling	68	F1
Modowi	91	J6
Moe	113	K6
Moelv	63	D6
Moengo	137	G2
Moffat	57	E5
Moffat Peak	115	B6
Mogadishu	107	J2
Mogadouro	66	C2
Mogdy	85	N6
Mogilev-Podolskiy	79	D6
Mogi-Mirim	138	G4
Mogincual	109	H3
Moglice	75	F2
Mogocha	85	L6
Mogoi	91	J6
Mogok	93	J4
Mogollon Plateau	126	G3
Mogotoyevo, Ozero	85	R2
Mogoyn	86	H2
Mogoytuy	85	J6
Moguer	66	C4
Mohacs	72	E2
Mohaka	115	F3
Mohall	123	P3
Mohammadabad	95	Q6
Mohammadia	100	F1
Mohawk	125	N5
Moheli	109	H2
Mohill	58	G5
Mohoro	107	G4
Moi	63	B7
Moidart	57	C4
Moimenta da Beira	66	C2
Moindou	114	W16
Mointy	86	C2
Mo i Rana	62	F3
Moisie	121	N7
Moissac	65	D6
Moissala	102	C6
Mojave	126	C3
Mojave Desert	126	D3
Moji	89	C9
Mojones, Cerro	138	C5
Moju	137	H4
Mokai	115	E3
Mokelumne	122	D8
Moknine	101	H1
Mokohinau Island	115	E1
Mokokchung	93	H3
Mokolo	105	H3
Mokpo	87	P5
Mokra Gora	72	F4
Molaoi	75	G4
Molat	72	C3
Mold	55	F3
Moldavia	73	J2
Molde	62	B5
Moldova	73	J2
Moldova Noua	73	F3
Moldoveanu	73	H3
Moldovita	73	H2
Mole *Devon, U.K.*	52	D4
Mole *Surrey, U.K.*	53	G3
Molepolole	108	E4
Molfetta	69	F5
Molina de Aragon	67	F2
Molina de Segura	67	F3
Moline	124	E6
Molkom	63	E7
Mollakendi	77	H3
Mollaosman	77	K3
Mollendo	138	B3
Molln	70	D2
Molnlycke	63	E8
Molodechno	71	M1
Molodezhnaya	141	D5
Molodo *Russia*	85	L3
Molodo *Russia*	85	L3
Mologa	78	F4
Molokai	126	S10
Moloma	78	H4
Molotov	78	K4
Moloundou	105	J5
Molsheim	64	G4
Molson Lake	119	R5
Moluccas	91	H6
Moma *Mozambique*	109	R3
Moma *Russia*	85	Q3
Mombasa	107	R3
Mombetsu	88	J3
Momboyo	106	C3
Momi, Ra's	97	P9
Momol	71	L2
Mompos	136	C2
Mon	63	E9
Monach Islands	56	A3
Monach, Sound of	56	A3
Monaco	65	G7
Monadhliath Mountains	57	D3
Monaghan	58	J4
Monahans	127	L5
Mona, Isla	133	P5
Mona Passage	133	N5
Monarch Mount	118	K5
Monarch Pass	123	L8
Monar, Loch	56	C3
Monashe Mountains	122	E2
Monasterevin	59	H6
Monastir *Albania*	73	F5
Monastir *Italy*	69	B6
Monastir *Tunisia*	101	H1
Monastyriska	73	H1
Monatele	105	H5
Moncalieri	68	A3
Moncao	66	B1
Monchdorf	68	E1
Monchegorsk	62	Q3
Monchique	66	B4
Monclova	127	M7
Moncontour	64	B4
Moncton	121	P8
Mondego	66	C2
Mondonedo	66	C1
Mondovi	68	A3
Mondragone	69	D5
Mondsee	68	D2
Monemvasia	75	G4
Moneron, Ostrov	88	H2
Monesterio	66	C3
Moneymore	58	J3
Monfalcone	68	D3
Monforte	66	C3
Monforte de Lemos	66	C1
Monga	106	D2
Mongala	106	D2
Mongalla	103	F6
Mong Cai	93	L4
Mongga	114	H5
Mongge	91	J6
Mong Hang	93	J4
Monghyr	92	G3
Mong Lin	93	K4
Mongo	102	C5
Mongolia	86	G2
Mongororo	102	D5
Mongu	106	D6
Monhhaan	87	L2
Moniaive	57	E5
Monifieth	57	F4
Moniquira	136	C2
Monitor Range	122	F8
Monkira	113	J3
Monkland	52	E2
Monkoto	106	D3
Monmouth *U.K.*	52	E3
Monmouth *U.S.A.*	124	E6
Monnow	52	E3
Mono	105	F4
Mono Lake	126	C2
Monolithos	75	J4
Monopoli	69	F5
Monovar	67	F3
Monreal del Campo	67	F2
Monreale	69	D6
Monroe *Georgia*	129	L4
Monroe *Louisiana*	128	F4
Monroe *Michigan*	124	J6
Monroe *N. Carolina*	129	M3
Monroe *Wisconsin*	124	F5
Monrovia	104	C4
Mons	64	E3
Monsaras, Ponta da	138	J3
Monselice	68	C3
Monserrat	67	F3
Montaigu	65	C5
Montalban	67	F2
Montalbo	66	E3
Montalcino	68	C4
Montalto	69	E6
Montalvo	136	B4
Montamarta	66	D2
Montana	122	K4
Montanchez	66	C3
Montanita	136	B3
Montargis	65	E5
Montauban	65	D6
Montauk Point	125	Q6
Montbard	65	F5
Montbeliard	65	G5
Montblanch	67	G2
Montbrison	65	F6
Montceau-les-Mines	65	F5
Montcornet	64	F4
Mont-de-Marsan	65	C7
Montdidier	64	E4
Monte Alegre	137	G4
Monte Azul	138	H3
Monte Bello	136	B5
Montebello	125	N4
Monte Carlo	68	A4
Monte Caseros	139	E6
Montecatini Terme	68	C4
Monte Cristi	133	M5
Montecristo, Isola di	69	C4
Montego Bay	132	J5
Montelimar	65	F6
Montemaggiore Belsito	69	D7
Montemorelos	128	C8
Montemor-o-Novo	66	B3
Montenegro	72	E4
Montepuez	109	G2
Montepulciano	68	C4
Monte Quemado	138	D5
Montereau-faut-Yonne	64	E4
Monterey	126	B2
Monterey Bay	126	B2
Monteria	136	B2
Montero	138	D3
Monterotondo	69	D4
Monterrey	128	B8
Monte Santu, Capo di	69	B5
Montes Claros	138	E3
Montevideo *Uruguay*	139	E6
Montevideo *U.S.A.*	124	C4
Monte Vista	127	J2
Montezuma Peak	127	J2
Montfort-sur-Meu	64	B4
Montgomery *U.K.*	52	D2
Montgomery *U.S.A.*	129	J4
Montguyon	65	C6
Monti	69	B5
Monticello *Arkansas*	128	G4
Monticello *Florida*	129	L5
Monticello *New York*	125	N6
Monticello *Utah*	127	H2
Montiel, Campo de	66	E3
Montilla	66	D4
Mont-Joli	125	R2
Mont Laurier	125	N3
Montlucon	65	E5
Montmagny	125	Q3
Montmedy	64	F4
Montmirail	64	E4
Montmorillon	65	D5
Monto	113	L3
Montoro	66	D4
Montpelier	122	J6
Montpellier *France*	65	E7
Montpellier *U.S.A.*	125	P4
Montraux	68	A2
Montreal	124	H3
Montreal	125	P4
Montreal Lake	119	P5
Montreal River Harbour	124	H3
Montrose *U.K.*	57	F4
Montrose *U.S.A.*	127	J1
Mont Saint-Michel	64	C4
Montseny	67	H2
Montserrat	133	R6
Mont Wright	121	N7
Monywa	93	J4
Monza	68	B3
Monzon	67	G2
Moonie	113	K4
Moopna	112	F5
Moora	112	D5
Mooraberree	113	J4
Moorcroft	123	M5
Moore, Lake	112	D4
Moorfoot Hills	57	E5
Moorhead	124	B3
Moorlands	113	H6
Moorlinch	52	E3
Moose	121	K7
Moosehead Lake	125	R4
Moose Jaw	123	M2
Moose Lake *Canada*	119	Q5
Moose Lake *U.S.A.*	124	D3
Moose Mountain Creek	123	N2
Moosonee	121	K7
Mopeia Velha	109	G3
Mopti	100	E6
Moqor	92	C2
Moquequa	138	B3
Mora *Cameroon*	105	H3
Mora *Portugal*	66	B3
Mora *Sweden*	63	F6
Moradabad	92	E3
Moradal, Sierra do	66	C3
Mora de Rubielos	67	F2
Morafenobe	109	H3
Morag	71	H2
Morales	132	C7
Moramanga	109	J3
Moran	123	J6
Morant Cays	132	K6
Morant Point	132	J6
Moratuwa	92	E7
Morava *Czech Rep.*	71	G4
Morava	73	F3
Moraveh Tappeh	95	M3
Morawa	112	D4
Moray Firth	56	E3
Morbi	92	D4
Mor Budejovice	70	F4
Morbylanga	63	G8
Morden	123	Q3
Mordogan	76	B3
Mordovo	79	G5
Moreau	122	N5
Morebattle	57	F5
Morecambe	55	G2
Morecambe Bay	55	E2
Moreda	66	E4
Moree	113	K4
Morehead *Papua New Guinea*	114	C3
Morehead *U.S.A.*	124	J7
Morehead City	129	P3
Morelia	131	J8
Morella	67	F2
Morena, Sierra	66	D3
Moreno	126	G6
Moreno, Bahia	138	B4
More og Romsdal	62	C2
Moresby Island	118	J5
Mores Island	132	J1
Moreton Bay	113	L4
Moreton-in-Marsh	53	F3
Moreton Island	113	L4
Morez	65	G5
Morgan City	128	G6
Morganton	129	M3
Morgantown	125	L7
Morgongava	63	G7
Mori *China*	86	F3
Mori *Japan*	88	H4
Moriarty	127	K3
Morioka	88	H6
Morlaix	64	B4
Morley	55	H3
Morlunda	63	F8
Mormanno	69	F6
Mornington, Isla	139	A9
Mornington Island	113	H2
Morobe	114	D3
Morocco	100	D2
Morogoro	107	G4
Morokovo	85	W3
Moroleon	131	J7
Morombe	109	H4
Moron	132	H3
Moron *Mongolia*	86	J2
Moron *Mongolia*	87	L2
Moronade, Cerro des	130	G7
Morondava	109	H4
Moron de la Frontera	66	D4
Moroni	109	H2
Moron Us He	93	H2
Morotai	91	H5
Moroto	107	F2
Morozovsk	79	G6
Morpara	137	J6
Morpeth	55	H1
Morrilton	128	F3
Morrinhos	138	G3
Morrinsville	115	E2
Morris *Canada*	123	R3
Morris *U.S.A.*	124	C4
Morris Jesup, Kap	140	Q2
Morris, Mount	112	G4
Morristown	129	L2
Morro Bay	126	B3
Morro do Chapeu	137	J6
Morro, Punta	139	B5
Morros, Punta	131	P8
Morrosquillo, Golfo de	133	K10
Mors	63	C8
Morshansk	79	G5
Mortagne	64	D4
Mortain	64	C4
Mortara	68	B3
Morteau	65	G5
Morte Bay	52	C3
Mortes	137	G6
Morton *U.K.*	53	G2
Morton *U.S.A.*	122	C4
Morundah	113	K5
Morven *Australia*	113	K4
Morven *U.K.*	57	E3
Morvern	57	C4
Morwell	113	K6
Mosakula	63	L7
Mosby	63	B7
Moscow *U.S.A.*	122	F4
Moscow *Russia*	78	F4
Mosedale	55	F2
Mosel	70	B4
Moselle	64	G4
Moses Lake	122	E4
Moseyevo	78	H2
Mosgiel	115	C6
Mosha	78	G3
Moshchnyy, Ostrov	63	M6
Moshi	107	G3
Mosjoen	62	E4
Moskenesoya	62	E3
Moskosel	62	H4
Moskva	78	F4
Mosonmagyarovar	72	D2
Mosquera	136	B3
Mosquitia	132	E7
Mosquito Lake	119	Q3
Mosquitos, Costa de	132	F8
Mosquitos, Golfo de los	132	G10
Moss	63	D7
Mossaka	106	C3
Mossburn	115	B6
Mosselbaai	108	D6
Mossley	58	L3
Mossman	113	K2
Mossoro	137	K5
Most	70	E3
Mosta	74	C5
Mostaganem	100	F1
Mostar	72	D4
Mostiska	71	K4
Mosty	71	L2
Mostyn	55	F3
Mosul	77	K4
Mosulpo	87	P5
Mota	103	G5
Mota	114	T10
Mota del Cuervo	66	E3
Motala	63	F7
Mota Lava	114	T10
Motegi	89	H7
Motherwell	57	E5
Motihari	92	F3
Motilla del Palancar	67	F3
Motovskiy Zaliv	62	G2
Motril	66	E4

Name	Pg	Grid
Motueka *New Zealand*	115	D4
Motueka *New Zealand*	115	D4
Motupiko Blenheim	115	D4
Motykleyka	85	R5
Moudhros	75	H3
Moudjeria	100	C5
Mouka	102	D6
Mould Bay	120	C2
Moulins	65	E5
Moulmein	93	J5
Moulouya, Oued	100	E2
Moulton	55	H2
Moultrie	129	L5
Moultrie, Lake	129	M4
Mounda, Akra	75	F3
Mound City	124	C6
Moundou	102	C6
Moung	93	K6
Mountain	118	K2
Mountain Ash	52	D3
Mountain Home *Arkansas*	128	F2
Mountain Home *Idaho*	122	G6
Mountain Village	118	C3
Mount Airy	129	M2
Mount Ararat	77	L3
Mount Bellew	59	E6
Mount Desert Island	125	R4
Mount Doreen	112	G3
Mount Douglas	113	K3
Mount Elba	113	H5
Mount Gambier	113	J6
Mount Hagen	114	C3
Mount Isa	113	H3
Mount Magnet	112	D4
Mountmellick	59	H6
Mount Pleasant *Iowa*	124	E6
Mount Pleasant *Michigan*	124	H5
Mount Pleasant *Texas*	128	E4
Mount Pleasant *Utah*	126	G1
Mountrath	59	H6
Mount's Bay	52	B4
Mount Shasta	122	C7
Mount Thule	120	L3
Mount Vernon *Alabama*	129	H5
Mount Vernon *Illinois*	124	F7
Mount Vernon *Indiana*	124	G8
Mount Vernon *Ohio*	124	J6
Mount Vernon *Washington*	122	C3
Moura *Brazil*	136	E4
Moura *Portugal*	66	C3
Mourdi, Depression du	102	D4
Mourne Mountains	58	K4
Moussoro	102	C5
Moutong	91	G5
Movas	127	H6
Moville	58	H4
Moy	58	D4
Moyale	107	G2
Moyamba	104	C4
Moyen Atlas	100	E2
Moygashel	58	J4
Moyo *Indonesia*	91	F7
Moyo *Uganda*	106	F2
Moyobamba	136	B5
Moyu	92	E1
Mozambique	109	G3
Mozambique Channel	109	H3
Mozhaysk	78	F4
Mozhga	78	J4
Mozyr	79	D5
Mpanda	107	F4
Mpe	106	B3
Mpika	107	F5
Mporokoso	107	F4
Mpraeso	104	E4
Mrakovo	79	K5
M.R. Gomez, Presa	127	N7
Mrkonjic Grad	72	D3
Msaken	101	H1
MSila	67	J5
Msta	78	E4
Mstislav	78	E5
Mtsensk	79	F5
Mtwara	107	G5
Mualo	109	G2
Muang Chiang Rai	93	J5
Muang Khon Kaen	93	K5
Muang Lampang	93	J5
Muang Lamphun	93	J5
Muang Loei	93	K5
Muang Nan	93	J5
Muang Phayao	93	J5
Muang Phetchabun	93	K5
Muang Phichit	93	K5
Muang Phitsanulok	93	K5
Muang Phrae	93	K5
Muanza	109	F3
Muar	90	C5
Muara	90	E4
Muarabungo	90	D6
Muaraenim	90	D6
Muaralesan	91	F5
Muarasiberut	90	B6
Muarasigep	90	B6
Muarasipongi	90	B5
Muaratebo	90	D6
Muarateweh	90	E6
Mubende	107	F2
Mubi	105	H3
Mubrani	91	J6
Mucajai	136	E3
Muchinga Escarpment	107	F5
Much Wenlock	52	E2
Muck	57	B4
Muckanagh Lough	59	E7
Muckish Mount	58	G2
Muckle Roe	56	A1
Muckross Head	58	E3
Muconda	106	D5
Mucuim	136	E5
Mucur	76	F3
Mudanjiang	88	B3
Mudan Jiang	88	B3
Mudanya	76	C2
Mudayy	97	L8
Muddy Gap Pass	123	L6
Mudgee	113	K5
Mudurnu	76	D2
Mueda	109	G2
Muelas	66	D2
Mueo	114	W16
Mufulira	107	E5
Mufu Shan	93	M3
Muganskaya Step	94	J2
Mughar	95	L5
Mughshin	97	M7
Mugi	89	E9
Mugia	66	B1
Mugila, Monts	107	E4
Mugla	76	C4
Muhammad Qol	103	G3
Muhammad, Ras	103	F2
Muhaywir	77	J6
Muhldorf	70	E4
Muhlhausen	70	D3
Muhu	63	K7
Mui Bai Bung	93	K7
Muick	57	E3
Muirkirk	57	D5
Muite	109	G2
Mukachevo	79	C6
Mukah	90	E5
Mukawa	88	H4
Mukawwar	96	C6
Mukdahan	93	K5
Mukden	87	N3
Mukhen	88	F1
Mukhor-Konduy	85	J6
Mukomuko	90	D6
Mukur	79	J6
Mula	67	F3
Mulaly	86	D2
Mulan	88	B3
Mulanay	91	G3
Mulayit Taung	93	J5
Mulchatna	118	D3
Mulchen	139	B7
Mulde	70	E3
Muleshoe	127	L3
Mulga Downs	112	D3
Mulgrave	121	P8
Mulgrave Island	114	C4
Mulhacen	66	E4
Mulheim	70	B3
Mulhouse	65	G5
Muligort	84	Ad4
Muling *China*	88	C3
Muling *China*	88	C3
Muling He	88	D3
Mull	57	C4
Mullaghanattin	59	C9
Mullaghanish	59	D9
Mullaghareirk Mountains	59	D8
Mullaghcleevaun	59	K6
Mullaghmore	58	J3
Muller, Pegunungan	90	E5
Mullet, The	58	B4
Mullewa	112	D4
Mull Head *U.K.*	56	F2
Mull Head *U.K.*	56	F1
Mullinavat	59	H8
Mullingar	59	H5
Mullsjo	63	E8
Mull, Sound of	57	C4
Mulobezi	106	E6
Mulrany	58	C5
Multan	92	D2
Multanovy	84	A4
Multia	62	L5
Mulymya	84	Ad4
Mumbai (Bombay)	92	D5
Mumbles, The	52	C3
Mumbwa	106	E6
Mumra	79	H6
Muna *Indonesia*	91	G7
Muna *Russia*	85	L3
Munayly	79	J6
Munchberg	70	D3
Munchen	70	D4
Munchengladbach	70	B3
Muncie	124	H6
Munda	114	H6
Mundesley	53	J2
Mundford	53	H2
Mundo	67	F3
Mundo Novo	138	J6
Mungbere	107	E2
Munich	70	D4
Muniesa	67	F2
Munkfors	63	E7
Mun, Mae Nam	93	K5
Munoz Gamero, Peninsula de	139	B10
Munster	70	B3
Munster	59	D8
Munsterland	70	B3
Muntenia	73	J3
Muntinlupa	91	G3
Munzur Daglari	77	H3
Muong Khoua	93	K4
Muong Ou Tay	93	K4
Muong Sing	93	K4
Muonio	62	K3
Muoniojoki	62	K3
Muqdisho	107	J2
Muqshin, Wadi	97	M7
Mur	68	E2
Mura	72	D2
Muradiye *Turkey*	76	B3
Muradiye *Turkey*	77	K3
Murallon, Cerro	139	B9
Muranga	107	G3
Murashi	78	H4
Murat *France*	65	E6
Murat *Turkey*	77	J3
Muratbasi	77	K3
Murat Dagi	76	C3
Muratli	76	B2
Muraysah, Ras al	101	K2
Murban	97	L5
Murcheh Khvort	95	K5
Murchison *Australia*	112	C4
Murchison *Canada*	120	H4
Murchison *New Zealand*	115	D4
Murchison Sund	120	M2
Murcia *Spain*	67	F4
Murcia *Spain*	67	F3
Murdo	123	P6
Murdochville	125	T2
Murefte	76	B2
Mures	73	F2
Muret	65	D7
Murfreesboro *N. Carolina*	129	P2
Murfreesboro *Tennessee,*	129	J3
Murgab *Tajikistan*	86	C4
Murgab *Turkmenistan*	95	R3
Muri	95	N3
Muriae	138	H4
Muriege	106	D4
Muritz See	70	E2
Murmansk	78	E2
Murmanskaya Oblast	62	P2
Murmansk Bereg	78	F2
Murmashi	62	Q2
Murnau	70	D5
Murom	78	G4
Muromtsevo	84	B5
Muroran	88	H4
Muros	66	B1
Muroto-zaki	89	E9
Murphy	129	L3
Murra Murra	113	K4
Murray *Australia*	113	H5
Murray *Kentucky*	124	F8
Murray *Utah*	122	J7
Murray Bridge	110	J9
Murray Harbour	121	P8
Murray, Lake *Papua New Guinea*	114	C3
Murray, Lake *U.S.A.*	129	M3
Murraysburg	108	D6
Murree	92	D2
Murrumbidgee	113	K5
Mursal	77	H3
Mursala	90	B5
Murud	90	F5
Murukta	84	G3
Murupara	115	F3
Murwara	92	F4
Murwillumbah	113	L4
Murz	68	E2
Murzuq	101	H3
Murzuq, Idhan	101	H4
Murzzuschlag	68	E2
Mus	77	J3
Musala	73	G4
Musallam, Wadi	97	N5
Musan	88	B4
Musandam Peninsula	97	N3
Musayid	97	K4
Muscat	97	P5
Musgrave Ranges	112	G4
Mushash al Hadi	97	J3
Musheramore	59	D8
Mushie	106	C3
Musi	90	C6
Musian	94	H5
Muskegon *U.S.A.*	124	G5
Muskegon *U.S.A.*	124	H5
Muskingum	124	K7
Muskogee	128	E3
Musmar	103	G4
Musoma	107	F3
Mussau	114	D2
Musselburgh	57	E5
Musselshell	123	K4
Mussende	106	C5
Musserra	106	B4
Mussidan	65	D6
Mussuma	106	D5
Mussy	65	F5
Mustafakemalpasa	76	C2
Mustang	92	F3
Mustang Draw	127	L4
Musters, Lago	139	C9
Mustvee	63	M7
Musu-dan	88	B5
Muswellbrook	113	L5
Mut *Egypt*	102	E2
Mut *Turkey*	76	E4
Muta Ponta do	137	K6
Mutarara	109	G3
Mutare	109	F3
Mutki	77	J3
Mutnyy Materik	78	K2
Mutoko	109	F3
Mutoray	84	G4
Mutsu-wan	88	H3
Muurame	63	L5
Muurola	62	L3
Muwaffaq	97	M7
Muxima	106	B4
Muya	85	J5
Muyunkum, Peski	86	C3
Muzaffarabad	92	D2
Muzaffargarh	92	D2
Muzaffarnagar	92	E3
Muzaffarpur	92	G3
Muzon, Cape	118	J5
Muz Tagh Ata Range	92	E1
Mvuma	108	F3
Mwaniwowo	114	L7
Mwanza	107	F4
Mwaya	107	F4
Mweelrea	58	C5
Mwene Ditu	106	D4
Mwenezi *Zimbabwe*	108	F4
Mwenezi *Zimbabwe*	108	F4
Mwenga	107	E3
Mweru, Lake	107	E4
Mweru Wantipa, Lake	107	E4
Mwinilunga	106	D5
Myakit	85	S4
Myanaung	93	J5
Myanmar	93	J4
Myaundzha	85	R4
Myaungmya	93	H5
Myeik Kyunzu	93	J6
Myingyan	93	J4
Myinmu	93	J4
Myitkyina	93	J3
Myitnge	93	J4
Myittha	93	J4
Mykolayiv	79	E6
Myla	78	J2
Mymensingh	93	H4
Myre	62	F2
Myri	62	W12
Myrtle Beach	129	N4
Myrviken	62	F5
Mysen	63	H7
Mysliborz	70	F2
Mysore	92	E6
Mys Shmidta	85	Y3
My Tho	93	L6
Mytishchi	78	F4
Mzab	101	F2
Mze	70	E4
Mzuzu	107	F5

N

Name	Pg	Grid
Naalehu	126	T11
Naantali	63	K6
Naas	59	J2
Nabao	66	B3
Nabavatu	114	R8
Naberezhnyye Chelny	78	J4
Nabeul	101	H1
Nabire	91	K6
Nablus	94	B5
Nabouwalu	114	R8
Naburn	55	H3
Nacala-a-Velha	109	H2
Nacaome	132	D8
Nachiki	85	T6
Nachvak Fjord	121	P6
Nacogdoches	128	E5
Nacozari de Garcia	127	H5
Nadachi	89	G7
Nadezhdinskoye	88	D1
Nadezhnyy, Mys	85	S2
Nadi	114	Q8
Nadiad	92	D4
Nadlac	72	F2
Nador	100	E1
Naduri	114	R8
Nadvornaya	71	L4
Nadym	84	A3
Naft-e Safid	94	J6
Nafud, An	96	E2
Nafy	96	F4
Naga	91	G3
Nagagami	124	H2
Nagahama	89	D9
Naga Hills	93	H3
Nagai	89	G6
Nagaland	93	H3
Nagano	89	G7
Nagaoka	89	G7
Nagappattinam	92	E6
Nagarjuna Sagar	92	E5
Nagasaki	89	B9
Nagashima	89	F8
Nagato	89	C8
Nagaur	92	D3
Nagercoil	92	E7
Nagishot	103	F7
Nagles Mountains	59	F8
Nagornyy	85	L5
Nagorsk	78	J4
Nagoya	89	F8
Nagpur	92	E4
Naggu	93	H2
Nags Head	129	Q3
Nagykanizsa	72	D2
Nagykata	72	E2

Nagykoros	72 E2	Nan, Mae Nam	93 K5
Naha	89 H10	Nanning	93 L4
Nahariya	94 B5	Nanortalik	116 Q2
Nahavand	94 J4	Nanpan Jiang	93 K4
Nahe	70 B4	Nanpara	92 F3
Nahoi, Cap	114 T11	Nanpi	87 M4
Nahuel Huapi, Lago	139 B8	Nanping	87 M6
Naikliu	91 G7	Nansei-shoto	89 H10
Nailsea	52 E3	Nansen Sound	120 H1
Nailsworth	52 E3	Nanshan Islands	90 E4
Naiman Qi	87 N3	Nansha Qundao	90 E4
Nain	95 L5	Nantais, Lac	121 M5
Nain	121 P6	Nantes	65 C5
Naini Tal	92 E3	Nantong	87 N5
Nairai	114 R8	Nantua	65 F5
Nairn	56 E3	Nantucket Island	125 Q6
Nairobi	107 G3	Nantucket Sound	125 Q6
Najafabad	95 K5	Nantwich	55 G3
Najd	96 E4	Nant-y-moch Reservoir	52 D2
Najibabad	92 E3	Nanuku Passage	114 S8
Najin	88 C4	Nanuku Reef	114 S8
N Ajjer, Tassili	101 G3	Nanumanga	111 S3
Najran	96 G8	Nanumea	111 S3
Najran, Wadi	96 G8	Nanusa, Kepulauan	91 H5
Nakadori-shima	89 B9	Nanyang	93 M2
Nakajo	89 G6	Nanyuki	107 G2
Nakamura	89 D9	Nao, Cabo de la	67 G3
Nakano	89 G7	Naococane, Lake	121 M7
Nakano-shima	89 B11	Naousa	75 G2
Nakatay	84 Ad5	Napa	126 A1
Nakatsu	89 C9	Napabalana	91 G6
Nakatsugawa	89 F8	Napalkovo	84 A2
Nakfa	103 G4	Napas	84 C5
Nakhichevan	77 L3	Nape	93 L5
Nakhl *Eygpt*	96 A2	Napier	115 F3
Nakhl *Oman*	97 N5	Naples *Italy*	69 E5
Nakhodka *Russia*	84 B3	Naples *U.S.A.*	129 M7
Nakhodka *Russia*	88 D4	Napo	136 C4
Nakhon Pathom	93 J6	Napoleon	124 H6
Nakhon Phanom	93 K5	Napoletano, Appennino	69 E5
Nakhon Ratchasima	93 K6	Napoli	69 E5
Nakhon Sawan	93 K5	Napoli, Golfo di	69 E5
Nakhon Si Thammarat	93 J7	Naqadeh	94 G3
Nakina	121 J7	Nar	53 H2
Nakiri	89 F8	Nara *Japan*	89 E8
Naknek Lake	118 D4	Nara *Mali*	100 D5
Nakskov	63 F9	Nara *Pakistan*	92 C4
Naktong	87 P4	Naracoorte	113 J6
Nakuru	107 G3	Naran	87 L2
Nakusp	122 F2	Narasapur	92 F5
Nalchik	79 G7	Narat	86 E3
Nalgonda	92 E5	Narathiwat	93 K7
Nallamala Hills	92 E5	Narayanganj	93 H4
Nallihan	76 D2	Narberth	52 C3
Nalut	101 H2	Narbonne	65 E7
Namaa, Tanjung	91 H6	Narborough Island	136 A7
Namacunde	106 C6	Narcea	66 C1
Namacurra	109 G3	Nardin	95 M3
Namak, Daryacheh-ye	95 K4	Narew *Poland*	71 J2
Namaki	95 M6	Narew *Poland*	71 K2
Namakzar	95 Q5	Narince	77 H4
Namakzar, Daryacheh-ye	95 Q5	Narken	62 K3
Namangan	86 C3	Narkher	92 E4
Namapa	109 G2	Narli	77 G4
Namaponda	109 G3	Narmada	92 E4
Namarroi	109 G3	Narman	77 J2
Namasagali	107 F2	Narnaul	92 E3
Namatanai	114 E2	Narodnaya, Gora	84 Ad3
Nambour	113 L4	Naro-Fominsk	78 F4
Nam Can	93 K7	Narowal	92 D2
Nam Co	93 H2	Narpes	62 J5
Nam Dinh	93 L4	Narrabri	113 K5
Nametil	109 G3	Narrandera	113 K5
Namib Desert	108 B4	Narrogin	112 D5
Namibe	106 B6	Narromine	113 K5
Namibia	108 C4	Narsimhapur	92 E4
Namlea	91 H6	Narsinghgarh	92 E4
Namoi	113 L5	Nart	87 M3
Namosi Peak	114 R8	Nartabu	91 J6
Nampa	122 F6	Naruko	88 H6
Nampula	109 G3	Narva	63 N7
Namse La	92 F3	Narvik	62 G2
Namsen	62 E4	Naryan Mar	78 J2
Namsos	62 D4	Narymskiy Khrebet	86 E2
Namti	93 J3	Naryn *Russia*	84 F6
Namtok	93 J5	Naryn *Kyrgyzstan*	86 C3
Namuka-i-Lau	114 S9	Naryn *Kyrgyzstan*	86 D3
Namuli	109 G3	Nasarawa	105 G4
Namur	64 F3	Naseby	115 C6
Namutoni	108 C3	Nashua	125 Q5
Namwala	106 E6	Nashville	129 J2
Nana Barya	102 C6	Nasice	72 E3
Nanaimo	122 C3	Nasielsk	71 J2
Nanam	88 B5	Nasijarvi	63 K6
Nanao	89 F7	Nasik	92 D5
Nancha	88 B2	Nasir	103 F6
Nanchang	87 M6	Nasir, Buhayrat	103 F3
Nanchong	93 L2	Nasorolevu	114 R8
Nancowry	93 H7	Nasrabad	95 K4
Nancy	64 G4	Nass	118 K4
Nanda Devi	92 E2	Nassau	129 P8
Nandan	93 L3	Nasser, Lake	103 F3
Nanded	92 E5	Nassjo	63 F8
Nandurbar	92 D4	Nastapoka Islands	121 L6
Nandyal	92 E5	Nastved	63 D9
Nanfeng	87 M6	Nata	108 E4
Nanga Eboko	105 H5	Natagaima	136 B3
Nangahpinoh	90 E6	Natal *Brazil*	137 K5
Nanga Parbat	92 D1	Natal *Indonesia*	90 B5
Nangatayap	90 E6	Natanz	95 K5
Nangong	87 M4	Natara	85 L3
Nan Hai	83 K5	Natashquan	121 P7
Nanjing	87 M5	Natchez	128 G5
Nanking	87 M5	Natchitoches	128 F5

Natewa Bay	114 R8	Nefedovo	84 A5
National City	126 D4	Nefta	101 G2
Natitingou	105 F3	Neftechala	94 J2
Natividade	137 H6	Neftegorsk	79 H5
Natori	89 H6	Neftekamsk	78 J4
Natron, Lake	107 G3	Nefyn	52 C2
Nattavaara	62 J3	Nefza	69 B7
Natuna Besar	90 D5	Negele	103 G6
Natuna, Kepulauan	90 D5	Negev	94 B6
Naturaliste, Cape	112 D5	Negoiu	73 H3
Naturaliste Channel	112 C4	Negombo	92 E7
Nauen	70 E2	Negotin	73 G3
Naueyi Akmyane	63 K8	Negrais, Cape	93 H5
Naujoji Vilnia	71 L1	Negra, Punta	136 A5
Naul	58 K5	Negritos	136 A4
Naumburg	70 D3	Negro *Argentina*	139 C7
Naungpale	93 J5	Negro *Amazonas, Brazil*	136 E4
Nauru	111 Q2	Negro *Santa Catarina, Brazil*	138 F5
Naurzum	84 Ad6	Negro *Uruguay*	138 F6
Nausori	114 R9	Negros	91 G3
Nautanwa	92 F3	Negru Voda	73 K4
Nautla	131 L7	Nehavand	94 J4
Nauzad	95 S5	Nehbandan	95 Q6
Navadwip	93 G4	Nehe	87 N2
Navahermosa	66 D3	Nehoiasu	73 J3
Naval	91 G3	Neijiang	93 K3
Navalcarnero	66 D2	Nei Mongol Zizhiqu	87 L3
Navalmoral de la Mata	66 D3	Neisse *Poland*	70 F3
Navalpino	66 D3	Neisse *Poland*	71 G3
Navan	58 J5	Neiteyugansk	84 A4
Navarin, Mys	85 X4	Neiva	136 B3
Navarino, Isla	139 C11	Neixiang	93 M2
Navarra	67 F1	Nekemte	103 G6
Navars	67 G2	Neksikan	85 R4
Navasota	128 D5	Nekso	63 H9
Navassa Island	133 K5	Nelidovo	78 E4
Navax Point	52 B4	Neligh	123 Q6
Navenby	55 J3	Nelkan	85 P5
Naver, Loch	56 D2	Nellore	92 E6
Navia *Spain*	66 C1	Nelma	88 G2
Navia *Spain*	66 C1	Nelson *Canada*	122 F3
Naviti	114 Q8	Nelson *New Zealand*	115 D4
Navlya	79 E5	Nelson *U.K.*	55 G3
Navojoa	127 H7	Nelson, Cape *Australia*	113 J6
Navolato	130 F5	Nelson, Cape *Papua New Guinea*	114 D3
Navpaktos	75 F3	Nelson Lagoon	118 Af8
Navplion	75 G4	Nelspruit	108 F5
Navrongo	104 E3	Nema	100 D5
Navsari	92 D4	Neman	78 C4
Navua	114 R9	Neman	71 K1
Nawabshah	92 C3	Nemira	73 J2
Nawada	92 G4	Nemirov	73 K1
Nawah	92 C2	Nemiscau	121 L7
Nawasif, Harrat	96 F6	Nemours	64 E4
Naws, Ra's	97 M8	Nemun	63 J9
Nawton	55 J2	Nemuro	88 K4
Naxos *Greece*	75 H4	Nemuro-kaikyo	88 K4
Naxos *Greece*	75 H4	Nemuy	85 P5
Nayagarh	92 G4	Nenagh	59 F7
Nayau	114 S8	Nenana	118 F3
Nay Band	95 L8	Nene	53 G2
Nay Band	95 N5	Nen Jiang	87 P1
Nayoro	88 J3	Nenjiang	87 P2
Nazare	137 K6	Nenthead	55 G2
Nazareth *Israel*	94 B5	Neokhorion	75 F3
Nazareth *Peru*	136 B5	Neon Karlovasi	75 J4
Nazarovo	84 E5	Neosho *Kansas*	124 C7
Nazas	130 G5	Neosho *Missouri*	124 C8
Nazca	136 C6	Nepa *Russia*	84 H5
Naze	89 B11	Nepa *Russia*	84 H5
Nazerat	94 B5	Nepal	92 F3
Naze, The	53 J3	Nephi	126 G1
Nazik	94 G2	Nephin Beg Range	58 C4
Nazik Golu	77 K3	Nera	69 D4
Nazilli	76 C4	Nerac	65 D6
Nazmiye	77 H3	Nerchinsk	85 K6
Nazwa	97 N5	Neretva	72 D4
Nazyvayevsk	84 A5	Neriquinha	106 D6
Ncheu	107 F5	Neris	63 L9
Ndalatando	106 B4	Nermete, Punta	136 A5
Ndele	102 D6	Neryuktey-l-y	85 K4
Ndeni	114 N7	Neryuvom	84 Ad3
Ndjamena	102 C5	Nes	63 C6
Ndjote	106 B3	Nesbyen	63 C6
Ndola	107 E5	Neskaupstadur	62 Y12
Nea	62 D5	Nesna	62 E3
Nea Filippias	75 F3	Nesscliffe	52 E2
Neagh, Lough	58 K3	Ness, Loch	56 D3
Neah Bay	122 B3	Nesterov *Russia*	71 K3
Neale, Lake	112 G3	Nesterov *Ukraine*	71 K1
Nea Moudhania	75 G2	Nesterovo	84 H6
Neapolis *Greece*	75 F2	Neston	55 F3
Neapolis *Greece*	75 H5	Nestos	75 H2
Nea Psara	75 G3	Nesvizh	71 M2
Near Islands	118 Aa9	Netanya	94 B5
Neath	52 D3	Netherlands	64 F2
Nebine	113 K4	Neto	69 F6
Nebit Dag	95 M2	Nettilling Lake	120 M4
Neblina, Pico da	136 D3	Nettleham	55 J3
Nebraska	123 N7	Netzahualcoyotl, Presa	131 N9
Nebraska City	124 C6	Neubrandenburg	70 E2
Nebrodi, Monti	69 E7	Neuchatel	68 A2
Nechako	118 L5	Neuchatel, Lac de	68 A2
Nechi	133 K11	Neufchateau *Belgium*	64 F4
Neckar	70 C4	Neufchateau *France*	64 F4
Necochea	139 E7	Neufchatel	64 D4
Nedong	93 H3	Neufelden	68 D1
Nedstrand	63 A7	Neumunster	70 C1
Needles *Canada*	122 E3	Neunkirchen *Austria*	68 F2
Needles *U.S.A.*	126 E3	Neunkirchen *Germany*	70 B4
Needles Point	115 E2	Neuquen *Argentina*	139 C7
Needles, The	53 F4	Neuquen *Argentina*	139 C7
Neepawa	123 Q2	Neuruppin	70 E2
Neergaard Lake	120 L3		

Norrkoping	63	L7	Nosovshchina	78	F3	Novyy Uzen	79	J7	Nybster	56	E2		
Norrland	62	F5	Nosratabad	95	P7	Nowbaran	95	J4	Nyeri	107	G3		
Norrtalje	63	H7	Nossen	70	E3	Nowe	71	H2	Nyerol	103	F6		
Norseman	112	E5	Noss Head	56	E2	Nowen Hill	59	D9	Nyima	93	G2		
Norsjo	62	M4	Noss, Island of	56	A2	Nowgong	93	H3	Nyirbator	73	G2		
Norsk	85	N6	Nosy-Varika	109	J4	Nowitna	118	E3	Nyiregyhaza	73	F2		
Norsup	114	T12	Notec	71	G2	Nowograd	70	F2	Nyiru, Mont	107	G2		
Norte, Punta *Argentina*	139	D8	Noto	69	E7	Nowogrod	71	J2	Nykarleby	62	N4		
Norte, Punta *Argentina*	139	E7	Notodden	63	C7	Nowra	113	L5	Nykobing *Denmark*	63	C8		
Norte, Serra do	136	F6	Noto-hanto	89	F7	Now Shahr	95	K3	Nykobing *Denmark*	63	D9		
Northallerton	55	H2	Notre Dame Bay	121	Q8	Nowshera	92	D2	Nykoping	63	G7		
Northam	112	D5	Notre Dame Mountains	121	N8	Nowy Sacz	71	J4	Nylstroom	108	E4		
Northampton *U.K.*	53	G2	Nottingham	53	F2	Nowy Targ	71	J4	Nymagee	113	K5		
Northampton *U.S.A.*	125	P5	Nottingham Island	120	L5	Noyon *France*	64	E4	Nymburk	70	F3		
Northamptonshire	53	G2	Nottinghamshire	55	H3	Noyon *Mongolia*	86	J3	Nynashamn	63	G7		
North Andaman	93	H6	Notukeu Creek	123	L3	Nozay	65	C5	Nyngan	113	K5		
North Arm	119	N3	Nouadhibou	100	B4	Nsanje	107	G6	Nyong	105	H5		
North Astrolabe Reef	114	R9	Nouadhibou, Ras	100	B4	Nsukka	105	G4	Nyons	65	F6		
North Battleford	119	P5	Nouakchott	100	B5	Nsuta	104	E4	Nyrany	70	E4		
North Bay *Canada*	125	L3	Noukloof Mountains	108	C4	Ntem	105	H5	Nyrud	62	N2		
North Bay *Ireland*	59	K8	Noumea	114	X17	Ntwetwe Pan	108	E4	Nysa	71	G3		
North Bend	122	B6	Noup Head	56	E1	Nuba, Lake	102	F3	Nysh	85	Q6		
North Berwick	57	F4	Noupoort	108	D6	Nuba Mountains	102	F5	Nyshott	63	N6		
North Canadian	128	C3	Nouvelle-Caledonie	114	W16	Nubian Desert	103	F3	Nystad	63	J6		
North, Cape	121	P8	Nouvelle Caledonie	114	W16	Nubiya	102	E4	Nytva	78	K4		
North Cape *New Zealand*	115	D1	Nouvelle-France, Cap de	120	M5	Nubiya, Es Sahra en	103	F3	Nyuk, Ozero	62	P4		
North Cape *Norway*	62	L1	Novabad	86	C4	Nudo Coropuna	136	C7	Nyuksenitsa	78	G3		
North Cape *U.S.A.*	118	A3	Nova Bana	71	H4	Nueces	128	C6	Nyunzu	107	E4		
North Carolina	129	M3	Nova Cruz	137	K5	Nueltin Lake	119	R3	Nyurba	85	K4		
North Cave	55	J3	Nova Era	138	H3	Nueva Florida	133	N10	Nyurolskiy	84	B5		
North Channel *Canada*	124	J3	Nova Friburgo	138	H4	Nueva Rosita	127	M7	Nyuya	85	J4		
North Channel *U.K.*	58	L2	Nova Iguacu	138	H4	Nueva San Salvador	132	C8	Nyvrovo	85	Q6		
Northchapel	53	G3	Nova Lima	138	H4	Nueve de Julio	139	D7	Nzambi	106	B3		
North Charlton	55	H1	Nova Mambone	109	G4	Nuevitas	132	J4	Nzega	107	F3		
Northcliffe	112	D5	Novara	68	B3	Nuevo, Bajo	132	H7	Nzerekore	104	D4		
North Dakota	123	P4	Nova Remanso	137	J5	Nuevo Casas Grandes	127	J5	Nzeto	106	B4		
North Dorset Downs	52	E4	Nova Scotia	121	P8	Nuevo Churumuco	130	J8	Nzo	104	D4		
North Downs	53	H3	Nova Sento Se	137	J5	Nuevo Laredo	128	C7					
Northeast Cape	118	B3	Nova Sofala	109	F4	Nugaruba Islands	114	E2					
Northeast Providence Channel	132	J2	Nova Vanduzi	109	F3	Nugget Point	115	B7	**O**				
North Elmham	53	H2	Nova Varos	72	E4	Nugrus, Gebel	96	B4					
Northern Ireland	58	H3	Novaya Kakhovka	79	E6	Nuhaka	115	F3	Oadby	53	F2		
Northern Sporades	75	H3	Novaya Katysh	84	Ae5	Nuh, Ra's	95	R9	Oahe Dam	123	P5		
Northern Territory	112	G3	Novaya Kazanka	79	H6	Nui	111	S3	Oahe, Lake	123	P5		
North Esk	57	F4	Novaya Novatka	84	G5	Nuits-Saint-Georges	65	F5	Oahu	126	S10		
Northfield	124	D4	Novaya Odessa	79	E6	Nu Jiang	93	J3	Oakdale	126	B2		
North Flinders Range	113	H5	Novaya Sibir, Ostrov	85	R1	Nukhayb	94	F5	Oakengates	52	E2		
North Foreland	53	J3	Novaya Tevriz	84	B5	Nukiki	114	H5	Oakes	123	Q4		
North Geomagnetic Pole	140	S3	Novaya Vodolaga	79	F6	Nukualofa	111	T6	Oakford	52	D4		
North Henik Lake	119	R3	Novaya Zemlya	84	Ab2	Nukufetau	111	S3	Oakham	53	G2		
North Korea	87	P4	Novayo Ushitsa	73	J1	Nukufuhu	114	D3	Oak Hill	125	K8		
North Kyme	55	J3	Nove Mesto	70	G4	Nukulaelae	111	S3	Oakington	53	H2		
North Lakhimpur	93	H3	Nove Zamky	71	H4	Nukumanu Islands	111	N2	Oakland *California*	126	A2		
Northleach	53	F3	Novgorod	78	E4	Nukunau	111	S2	Oakland *Nebraska*	123	R7		
North Magnetic Pole	140	U3	Novgorod Serverskiy	79	E5	Nukunono	111	U3	Oak Lawn	124	G6		
North Miami Beach	129	M8	Novigrad	72	C3	Nukus	51	U7	Oakley	123	P8		
North Platte *U.S.A.*	123	N7	Novikovo	88	J2	Nullarbor	112	G5	Oakover	112	E3		
North Platte *U.S.A.*	123	P7	Novi Ligure	68	B3	Nullarbor Plain	112	F5	Oakridge	122	C6		
North Point *Canada*	121	P8	Novi Pazar	72	F4	Numan	105	H4	Oak Ridge	129	K2		
North Point *U.S.A.*	124	J4	Novi Sad	72	E3	Numata	89	G7	Oak Valley	125	N7		
North Pole	140	A1	Novo Acre	137	J6	Numazu	89	G8	Oamaru	115	C6		
North River	119	S4	Novoaleksandrovsk	79	G6	Numedal	63	C6	Oa, Mull of	57	B5		
North Roe	56	A1	Novoalekseyevka	79	K5	Numfor	114	B2	Oates Land	141	L4		
North Ronaldsay	56	F1	Novoanninskiy	79	G5	Numto	84	A4	Oa, The	57	B5		
North Ronaldsay Firth	56	F1	Novoarchangelsk	73	L1	Nunavut	119	Q2	Oatlands	113	K7		
North Saskatchewan	119	P5	Novo Aripuana	136	E5	Nuneaton	53	F2	Oaxaca	131	L9		
North Sea	50	H4	Novobogatinskoye	79	J6	Nunivak Islands	116	C2	Ob	84	Ae3		
North Sentinel	93	H6	Novocheboksarsh	78	H4	Nunligran	85	Y4	Oban	57	D4		
North Shields	55	H1	Novocherkassk	79	G6	Nunney	52	E3	Oberammergau	70	D5		
North Shoshone Peak	122	F8	Novodolinka	84	A6	Nuomin He	87	N2	Oberhausen	70	B3		
North Sound	59	C6	Novodvinsk	78	G3	Nuoro	69	B5	Oberlin	123	P8		
North Sound, The	56	F1	Novograd-Volynskiy	79	D5	Nupani	114	M7	Obidos *Brazil*	137	F4		
North Stradbroke Island	113	L4	Novogrudok	71	L2	Nuqdah, Ra's an	97	P6	Obidos *Portugal*	66	B3		
North Taranaki Bight	115	E3	Novo Hamburgo	138	F5	Nuqrah	96	E4	Obihiro	88	J4		
North Tawton	52	D4	Novoilinovka	85	P6	Nur	95	K3	Obi, Kepulauan	91	H6		
North Thoresby	55	J3	Novokazalinsk	86	A2	Nura	86	C2	Obilnoye	79	G6		
North Tolsta	56	B2	Novokhopersk	79	G5	Nurabad	95	K6	Obion	128	H2		
North Tonawanda	125	L5	Novokiyevskiy Uval	85	M6	Nur Daglari	77	G4	Obninsk	78	F4		
North Twin Island	121	K7	Novokocherdyk	84	Ad6	Nure	68	B3	Obo	102	E6		
North Tyne	57	F5	Novokuybyshevsk	79	H5	Nurek	86	B4	Obock	103	H5		
North Uist	56	A3	Novokuznetsk	84	D6	Nurhak	77	G4	Obok-tong	88	B5		
Northumberland	57	F5	Novolazareyskaya	141	A4	Nurhak Dagi	77	G3	Oborniki	71	G2		
Northumberland Islands	113	L3	Novoletovye	84	G2	Nuristan	92	D1	Oboyan	79	F5		
Northumberland O	120	M2	Novo Milosevo	72	F3	Nurmes	62	N5	Obozerskiy	78	G3		
Northumberland Strait	121	P8	Novomitino	84	Ae5	Nurnberg	70	D4	Obregon, Presa	127	H6		
Northwall	56	F1	Novomoskovsk *Russia*	78	F5	Nurri	69	B6	Obruk	76	E3		
North Walsham	53	J2	Novomoskovsk *Ukraine*	79	F6	Nurzec	71	K2	Obryvistoye	85	Q7		
Northway Junction	118	G3	Novopavlovka	84	H6	Nusaybin	77	J4	Observatoire, Caye de l'	111	N6		
Northwest Cape	118	A3	Novopokrovskaya	79	G6	Nusayriyah, Jebel al	77	G5	Obskaya Guba	84	A3		
North West Cape	112	C3	Novopolotsk	63	N9	Nushagak Bay	118	D4	Obuasi	104	E4		
North West Highlands	56	C3	Novo Redondo	106	B5	Nu Shan	93	J3	Ocala	129	L6		
Northwest Providence Channel	132	H1	Novo-Rokrovka	88	E3	Nushki	92	C3	Ocana *Colombia*	136	C2		
Northwest Territories	118	K3	Novoromanovo	84	C6	Nutak	121	P6	Ocana *Spain*	66	E3		
Northwich	55	G3	Novorossiysk	79	F7	Nuugaatsiaq	120	R3	Occidental, Cordillera *Colombia*	136	B3		
North York	125	L5	Novorzhev	63	N8	Nuuk	120	R5	Occidental, Cordillera *Peru*	136	B6		
North Yorkshire	55	H2	Novo Sagres	91	H7	Nuupas	62	M3	Occidental, Grand Erg	100	F2		
Norton *U.K.*	55	J2	Novo Sergeyevka	79	J5	Nuwara	92	F7	Oceanside	126	D4		
Norton *U.S.A.*	123	Q8	Novoshakhtinsk	79	F6	Nuweveldreeks	108	D6	Ocejon, Pic	66	E2		
Norton Bay	118	C3	Novosibirsk	84	C4	Nuyakuk, Lake	118	D4	Ochamchire	77	J1		
Norton Sound	118	C3	Novosibirskiye Ostrova	85	Q1	Nuyts, Point	112	D6	Ochil Hills	57	E4		
Norvegia, Cape	141	Z4	Novospasskoye	79	H5	Nuzayzah	77	H5	Ochiltree	57	D5		
Norwalk	124	J6	Novoukrainka	79	E6	Nyahururu	107	G2	Ock	53	F3		
Norway	63	C6	Novo Uzensk	79	H5	Nyainqentanglha Shan	92	G3	Ockelbo	63	G6		
Norway House	119	R5	Novo-Vyatsk	78	H4	Nyaksimvol	84	Ad4	Ocmulgee	129	L5		
Norwegian Bay	120	H2	Novoyeniseysk	84	E5	Nyala	102	D5	Ocna Mures	73	G2		
Norwegian Sea	62	A3	Novozhilovskaya	78	J3	Nyamboyto	84	C3	Oconee	129	L4		
Norwich *U.K.*	53	J2	Novozybkov	79	E5	Nyandoma	78	G3	Ocotlan	130	H7		
Norwich *U.S.A.*	125	Q6	Novska	72	D3	Nyang	93	H3	Ocracoke Island	129	Q3		
Noshiro	88	G5	Novy Jicin	71	G4	Nyanza	107	E3	Ocreza	66	C3		
Noshul	78	H3	Novyy	84	H2	Nyasa, Lake	107	F5	Ocsa	72	E2		
Nosok	84	C2	Novyy Bor	78	J2	Nyashabozh	78	J2	Oda	89	D8		
Nosop	108	D5	Novyy Bug	79	E6	Nyaungu	93	H4	Oda	104	E4		
			Novyy Oskol	79	F5	Nyayba	85	N2	Odadhraun	62	W12		
			Novyy Port	84	A3	Nyborg	63	D9					

Name	Page	Grid
Ornain	64	F4
Orne	64	C4
Ornskoldsvik	62	H5
Oro	130	G4
Orobi, Alpi	68	B3
Orocue	136	C3
Orofino	122	F4
Oromocto	125	S4
Oron	85	K5
Orona	111	U2
Oronsay	57	B5
Oronsay, Passage of	57	B5
Orontes	77	G5
Oropesa	66	D3
Oroqen Zizhiqi	87	N1
Oroquieta	91	G4
Orosei, Golfo di	69	B5
Oroshaza	72	F2
Orotukan	85	S4
Oroville *California*	122	D8
Oroville *Washington*	122	E3
Oroville, Lake	122	D8
Orrin Reservoir	56	D3
Orsa	63	F6
Orsa *Finnmark*	63	F6
Orsaro, Monte	68	C3
Orsha	78	E5
Orsta	62	B5
Orta	76	E2
Ortabag	77	K4
Ortaca	76	C4
Ortakoy *Turkey*	76	F2
Ortakoy *Turkey*	76	F3
Ortatoroslar	76	F4
Ortega	136	B3
Ortegal, Cabo	66	C1
Ortelsburg	71	J2
Orthez	65	C7
Ortigueira	66	C1
Ortiz	133	P10
Ortles	68	C2
Ortona	69	E4
Orto-Tokoy	86	D3
Orumiyeh	77	L4
Orumiyeh, Daryacheh-ye	94	G3
Oruro	138	C3
Orvieto	69	D4
Orwell	53	J3
Oryakhovo	73	G4
Os	62	D5
Osa	78	K4
Osage	124	D7
Osaka *Japan*	89	E8
Osaka *Japan*	89	F8
Osaka-wan	89	E8
Osa, Peninsula de	132	F10
Osceola *Arkansas*	128	H3
Osceola *Iowa*	124	D6
Osh	86	B3
Oshamambe	88	H4
Oshawa	125	L5
O-shima	89	G8
Oshkosh	124	F4
Oshkurya	84	Ac3
Oshmarino	84	C2
Oshmyanskaya Vozvyshennost	71	M1
Oshmyany	71	L1
Oshnoviyeh	94	G3
Oshogbo	105	F4
Oshtoran Kuh	94	J5
Oshtorinan	94	J4
Oshwe	106	C3
Osijek	72	E3
Osimo	68	D4
Osinniki	84	D6
Osipovichi	79	D5
Oskaloosa	124	D6
Oskamull	57	B4
Oskara, Mys	84	F1
Oskarshamn	63	G8
Oskarstrom	63	E8
Oskoba	84	G4
Oskol	79	F5
Oslo *Norway*	63	D7
Oslo *Norway*	63	D7
Oslob	91	G4
Oslofjorden	63	H7
Osmanabad	92	E5
Osmancik	76	F2
Osmaneli	76	C2
Osmaniye	77	G4
Osmington	52	E4
Osmino	63	N7
Osmo	63	G7
Osnabruck	70	C2
Osogovska Planina	73	G4
Osorno *Chile*	139	B8
Osorno *Spain*	66	D1
Osoyro	63	A6
Osprey Reef	113	K1
Oss	64	F3
Ossa	75	G3
Ossa, Mount	110	L10
Ossett	55	H3
Ossian, Loch	57	D4
Ossokmanuan Lake	121	P7
Ostashkov	78	E4
Ostavall	62	F5
Ostby	63	E6
Oste	70	C2
Osterburken	70	C4
Osterdalalven	63	E6
Osterdalen	63	D5
Ostergotland	63	F7
Osterode	71	H2
Ostersund	62	F5
Ostfold	63	D7
Ost Friesische Inseln	70	B2
Ostfriesland	70	B2
Osthammar	63	H6
Ostiglia	68	C3
Ostra	68	D4
Ostrava	71	H4
Ostroda	71	H2
Ostrog	79	D5
Ostrogozhsk	79	F5
Ostroleka	71	J2
Ostrov	63	N8
Ostrovnoy, Mys	88	D4
Ostrow	71	G3
Ostrowiec	71	J3
Ostrow Mazowiecki	71	J2
Ostuni	69	F5
Osum	75	F2
Osum	73	H4
Osumi-kaikyo	89	C10
Osumi-shoto	89	C10
Osuna	66	D4
OsVan	78	K2
Oswaldtwistle	55	G3
Oswego	125	M5
Oswestry	52	D2
Otaki	115	E4
Otaru	88	H4
Otava	70	E4
Otavi	108	C3
Otawara	89	G7
Otchinjau	106	B6
Otelec	73	F3
Otelu Rosu	73	G3
Otematata	115	C6
Othe, Foret d'	65	E4
Othonoi	74	E3
Othris	75	G3
Oti	104	F4
Otira	115	C5
Otis	123	N7
Otish, Monts	121	M7
Otjiwarongo	108	C4
Otley	55	H3
Otocac	72	C3
Otorohanga	115	E3
Otoskwin	121	H7
Otra	63	B7
Otranto	69	G5
Otranto, Capo d	69	G5
Otranto, Strait of	74	E2
Otsu	89	E8
Otsu	89	H7
Otta *Norway*	63	C6
Otta *Norway*	63	C6
Ottawa *Canada*	125	L3
Ottawa *Canada*	125	N4
Ottawa Islands	121	K6
Otter	52	D4
Otterburn	57	F5
Otter Rapids	125	K1
Otterup	63	D9
Ottery	52	C4
Ottery Saint Mary	52	C4
Ottumwa	124	D6
Oturkpo	105	G4
Otway, Bahia	139	B10
Otway, Cape	113	J6
Otway, Seno	139	B10
Otwock	71	J2
Otynya	71	L4
Otztaler Alpen	68	C2
Ouachita	128	F4
Ouachita, Lake	128	F3
Ouachita Mountains	128	E3
Ouadda	102	D6
Ouagadougou	104	E3
Ouahigouya	104	E3
Oualata	100	D5
Oua-n Ahagar, Tassili	101	G4
Ouanda Djaile	102	D6
Ouarane	100	D4
Ouargla	101	G2
Ouarra	102	E6
Ouarsenis, Massif de l'	67	G5
Ouarzazate	100	D2
Ouatoais	125	M4
Oubangui	106	C3
Oudenaarde	64	E3
Oude Rijn	64	F2
Oudtshoorn	108	D6
Oued Zem	100	D2
Oueme	105	F4
Ouen	114	X17
Ouessant, Ile d'	64	A4
Ouesso	106	C2
Ouezzane	100	D2
Oughterard	59	D6
Oughter, Lough	58	H4
Ouidah	105	F4
Oujda	100	E2
Oulainen	62	L4
Oulmes	100	D2
Oulu *Finland*	62	L4
Oulu *Finland*	62	M4
Oulujarvi	62	M4
Oulujoki	62	M4
Oulx	68	A3
Oum Chalouba	102	D4
Oum El Bouaghi	101	G1
Oum er Rbia, Oued	100	D2
Ou, Nam	93	K4
Ounasjoki	62	L3
Oundle	53	G2
Ouninga Kebir	102	D4
Oupu	87	P1
Ouricuri	137	J5
Ourinhos	138	G4
Ouro Preto	138	H4
Ourthe	64	F3
Ouse *Australia*	113	K7
Ouse *U.K.*	55	H3
Oust	65	B5
Outardes, Reservoir	121	N7
Outer Hebrides	56	A3
Outokumpu	62	N5
Out Skerries	56	B1
Outwell	53	H2
Ouvea	114	X16
Ouyen	113	J6
Ovacik *Turkey*	77	H4
Ovacik *Turkey*	77	J2
Ovada	68	B3
Ovalau Batiki	114	R8
Ovalle	138	B6
Ovau	114	H5
Ovejo	66	D3
Oven	115	X17
Overbister	56	F1
Overbygd	62	H2
Overkalix	62	K3
Overnas	62	G3
Overtornea	62	K3
Oviedo	66	D1
Ovinishche	78	F4
Ovre Ardal	63	B6
Ovruch	79	D5
Owahanga	115	F4
Owaka	115	B7
Owando	106	C3
Owase	89	F8
Owatonna	124	D4
Owbeh	95	R4
Owel, Lough	58	H5
Owenbeg	58	E4
Owenkillew	58	H3
Owenmore	58	C4
Owens	126	C2
Owensboro	124	G8
Owens Lake	126	D2
Owen Sound	125	K4
Owen Stanley Range	114	D3
Owerri	105	G4
Owo	105	G4
Owosso	124	H5
Owyhee *Nevada*	122	F7
Owyhee *Oregon*	122	F6
Oxbow	123	N3
Oxelosund	63	G7
Oxenholme	55	G2
Oxenhope	55	H3
Oxford *New Zealand*	115	D5
Oxford *U.K.*	53	F3
Oxford *U.S.A.*	128	H3
Oxfordshire	53	F3
Ox Mountains	58	E4
Oxnard	126	C3
Oxton	55	H3
Oyaca	76	E3
Oyali	77	J4
Oyapock	137	G3
Oyem	106	B2
Oykel	56	D3
Oykel Bridge	56	D3
Oymyakon	85	Q4
Oyo	105	F4
Ozalp	77	L3
Ozamiz	91	G4
Ozark Plateau	124	D8
Ozarks, Lake of the	124	D7
Ozd	72	F1
Ozernovskiy	85	T6
Ozernoye	84	A5
Ozersk	71	K1
Ozhogina	85	R3
Ozieri	69	B5
Ozinki	79	H5
Ozona	127	M5
Ozora	72	E2
Ozyurt	76	F3

P

Name	Page	Grid
Paama	114	U12
Paarl	108	C6
Pabbay *U.K.*	56	A3
Pabbay *U.K.*	57	A4
Pabellon de Arteaga	130	H6
Pabjanice	71	H3
Pabna	92	G4
Pabrade	63	L9
Pacaas Novos, Serra dos	136	E6
Pacaraima, Sierra	136	E3
Pacasmayo	136	B5
Pachino	69	E7
Pachora	92	E4
Pachuca	131	K7
Pacifica	126	A2
Pacific Ocean	87	P7
Pacific Ocean, North	143	H3
Pacific Ocean, South	143	J5
Pacitan	90	E7
Packwood	122	D4
Padang *Indonesia*	90	C6
Padang *Indonesia*	90	C5
Padangpanjang	90	D6
Padangsidimpuan	90	B5
Padasjoki	63	L6
Padauiri	136	E3
Paderborn	70	C3
Pades	73	G3
Padiham	55	G3
Padilla *Bolivia*	138	D3
Padilla *Mexico*	131	K5
Padina	73	J3
Padje-Ianta	62	G3
Padloping Island	120	P4
Padova	68	C3
Padrao, Pointa do	106	B4
Padron	66	B1
Padstow	52	C4
Padstow Bay	52	C4
Padua	68	C3
Paducah *Kentucky*	124	F8
Paducah *Texas*	127	M4
Padunskoye More	62	P2
Paekariki	115	E4
Paengnyong-do	87	N4
Paeroa	115	E2
Pag *Croatia*	72	C3
Pag *Croatia*	72	C3
Pagadian	91	G4
Pagasitikos Kolpos	75	G3
Pagatan	90	F6
Page	126	G2
Pagosa Springs	127	J2
Pagwa River	124	H2
Pagwi	114	C2
Pahala	126	T11
Pahang	90	C5
Pahia Point	115	A7
Pahiatua	115	E4
Pahlavi Dezh	95	M3
Pahoa	126	T11
Pahokee	129	M7
Pahra Kariz	95	Q4
Paia	126	S10
Paide	63	L7
Paignton	52	D4
Paijanne	63	L6
Pailolo Chan	126	S10
Paimpol	64	B4
Painswick	53	E3
Painted Desert	126	G2
Paisley	57	D5
Paita	136	A5
Paita	114	X17
Paittasjarvi	62	K2
Pajala	62	K3
Pakaraima Mountains	136	E2
Pakistan	92	C3
Pak Lay	93	K5
Pakokku	93	H4
Pakpattan	92	D2
Pakrac	72	D3
Paks	72	E2
Pakse	93	L5
Pala	102	B6
Palabuhanratu	90	D7
Palafrugell	67	H2
Palagruza	72	D4
Palaiokastron	75	J5
Palaiokhora	75	G5
Pala Laharha	92	G4
Palamos	67	H2
Palana	85	T5
Palanan Point	91	G2
Palanga	63	J9
Palangan, Kuh-e-	95	Q6
Palangkaraya	90	E6
Palanpur	92	D4
Palapye	108	E4
Palar	92	E6
Palata	69	E5
Palatka *U.S.A.*	129	M6
Palatka *Russia*	85	S4
Palau	69	B5
Palau Islands	91	J4
Palawan	91	F4
Palawan Passage	91	F4
Palayankottai	92	E7
Palazzola Acreide	69	E7
Paldiski	63	L7
Palembang	90	C6
Palena, Lago	139	B8
Palencia	66	D1
Palermo	69	D6
Palestine	128	E5
Paletwa	93	H4
Palghat	92	E6
Palgrave Point	108	B4
Palhoca	138	G5
Pali	92	D3
Palisade	127	H1
Palit, Kep i	74	E2
Palkane	63	L6
Palk Strait	92	E7
Pallaresa	67	G1
Pallas Green	59	F7
Pallasovka	79	H5
Pallastunturi	62	K2
Palliser Bay	115	E4
Palliser, Cape	115	E4
Palma *Mozambique*	109	H2
Palma *Spain*	67	H3
Palma, Baia de	67	H3

Name	Page	Ref
Palma del Rio	66	D4
Pal Malmal	114	E3
Palmanova	68	D3
Palmares	137	K5
Palmar, Punta del	139	F6
Palmas	138	G5
Palmas, Cape	104	D5
Palmas, Golfo di	69	B6
Palma Soriano	132	J4
Palmatkina	85	V4
Palmeira	138	F5
Palmeiras	137	J6
Palmer *Antarctic*	141	V6
Palmer *U.S.A.*	118	F3
Palmer Land	141	V4
Palmerston	115	C6
Palmerston Island	111	W5
Palmerston North	115	E4
Palm Harbor	129	L6
Palmi	69	E6
Palmira	136	B3
Palm Springs	126	D4
Palmyra	94	D4
Palmyras Point	92	G4
Palo de las Letras	136	B2
Palomar, Mount	126	D4
Palopo	91	G6
Palos, Cabo de	67	F4
Palpetu, Tanjung	91	H6
Palu *Indonesia*	91	F6
Palu *Indonesia*	91	F6
Palu *Turkey*	77	H3
Palyavaam	85	W3
Pama	104	F3
Pamban	92	E7
Pamekasan	90	E7
Pameungpeuk	90	D7
Pamiers	65	D7
Pamisos	75	F4
Pamlico Sound	129	P3
Pampa	127	M3
Pampachiri	136	C6
Pampas *Argentina*	139	D7
Pampas *Peru*	136	C6
Pampilhosa da Serra	66	C2
Pamplona *Colombia*	136	C2
Pamplona *Spain*	67	F1
Pana	124	F7
Panaca	126	E2
Panagyurishte	73	H4
Panaji	92	D5
Panama	132	G10
Panama	132	H10
Panama, Bahia de	132	H10
Panama Canal	136	B2
Panama City	129	K5
Panama, Golfo de	136	B2
Panandak	95	K4
Panaro	68	C3
Panay	91	G3
Pancevo	72	F3
Panda	109	F4
Pandan *Philippines*	91	G3
Pandan *Philippines*	91	G3
Pandany	78	E3
Pandharpur	92	E5
Pando	139	E6
Pandunskoye More	78	E2
Panevezys	63	N9
Panfilov	86	E3
Pangalanes, Canal des	109	J4
Pangani	107	G4
Panggoe	114	H5
Pangi	106	E3
Pangkalanbuun	90	E6
Pangkalpinang	90	D6
Pangnirtung	120	N4
Pangong Tso	92	E2
Pangrango, Gunung	90	D7
Pangtara	93	J4
Pangururar	90	B5
Pangutaran Group	91	G4
Panhandle	127	M3
Paniai, Donau	114	B2
Panie, Mount	114	W16
Panipat	92	E3
Panjim	92	D5
Panna	92	F4
Panovo	84	G5
Pant *Essex, U.K.*	53	H3
Pant *Shropshire, U.K.*	52	D2
Pantar	91	G7
Pantelleria, Isola di	69	D7
Pantones	66	E3
Panuco *Mexico*	131	K6
Panuco *Mexico*	131	K6
Pan Xian	93	K3
Panyam	105	G4
Pao-de-Acucar	137	K5
Paola	69	F6
Paoua	102	C6
Papa	72	D2
Papakura	115	E2
Papantla	131	L7
Paparoa	115	E2
Paparoa Range	115	C5
Papa Stour	56	A1
Papatoetoe	115	E2
Papa Westray	56	F1
Papenburg	70	B2
Papigochic	127	J6
Papisoi, Tanjung	114	A2
Paps of Jura	57	B5
Paps, The	59	D8
Papua, Gulf of	114	C3
Papua New Guinea	114	C2
Papuk	72	D3
Papun	93	J5
Para	137	G4
Paracas, Peninsula	136	B6
Paracatu *Brazil*	138	G3
Paracatu *Brazil*	138	G3
Paracin	73	F4
Paradubice	70	F3
Paragould	128	G2
Paragua	136	E6
Paragua	136	E2
Paraguacu	137	J6
Paraguai	136	F7
Paraguana, Peninsula de	133	M8
Paraguari	138	E5
Paraguay	138	E4
Paraguay	138	E4
Paraiba	138	H4
Paraiba	137	K5
Parajuru	137	K4
Parakou	105	F4
Paralakhemundi	92	F5
Paralkot	92	F5
Paramaribo	137	F2
Paramillo	136	B2
Paramirim	137	J6
Paramonga	136	B6
Paramushir, Ostrov	85	T6
Parana	138	D6
Parana	137	H6
Paranagua	138	G5
Paranaiba *Maranhao, Brazil*	137	J4
Paranaiba *Mato Grosso do Sul, Brazil*	138	F3
Paranaiba *Minas Gerais, Brazil*	138	G3
Paranaidji	137	H5
Paranapanema	138	F4
Paranapiacaba, Serra	138	G4
Paranatinga	137	F6
Parangipettai	92	E6
Paraparaum	115	E4
Parapola	75	G4
Parauna	138	F3
Parbati	92	E4
Parbhani	92	E5
Parcel Islands	93	M5
Parchim	70	D2
Pardo	138	F4
Parecis, Serra dos	136	F6
Pareditas	139	C6
Pare Mountains	107	G3
Parengarenga Harbour	115	D1
Parepare	91	F6
Paria, Golfo de	133	R9
Pariaguan	136	E2
Paria, Peninsula de	133	R9
Paricutin, Volcan el	130	H8
Parigi	91	G6
Parikkala	63	N6
Parima, Serra	136	E3
Parintins	137	F4
Paris *France*	64	E4
Paris *Kentucky*	124	H7
Paris *Tennessee*	129	H2
Paris *Texas*	128	E4
Parkano	63	K5
Parker	126	E3
Parkersburg	125	K7
Parkes	113	K5
Parkgate	57	E5
Park Range	123	L7
Parksville	122	B3
Parma *Italy*	68	C3
Parma *U.S.A.*	125	K6
Parnaiba	137	J4
Parnamirim	137	K5
Parnassos	75	G3
Parnassus	115	D5
Parnis	75	G3
Parnon Oros	75	G4
Parnu	63	L7
Parnu	63	L7
Paro	93	G3
Paropamisus	95	R4
Paros *Greece*	75	H4
Paros *Greece*	75	H4
Parowan	126	F2
Parral	139	B7
Parras	127	L8
Parrett	52	E3
Parrsboro	121	P8
Parry Bay	120	K4
Parry Islands	120	C2
Parry, Kap	120	M2
Parry Peninsula	118	L2
Parry Sound	125	L4
Parseta	71	G2
Parshino	85	J5
Parsons	128	E2
Partabpur	92	F4
Parthenay	65	C5
Partizansk	88	D4
Parton	57	D5
Partry Mountains	58	C5
Paru	137	G4
Parys	108	E5
Pasa Barris	137	K6
Pasadena *California*	126	C3
Pasadena *Texas*	128	E6
Pasado, Cabo	136	A4
Pa Sak, Mae Nam	93	K5
Pasarwajo	91	G7
Pascagoula *U.S.A.*	128	H5
Pascagoula *U.S.A.*	128	H5
Pascani	73	J2
Pasco	122	E4
Pascua, Isla de	143	K5
Pasewalk	70	F2
Pashiya	78	K4
Pashkovo	88	C1
Pasig	91	G3
Pasinler	77	J3
Pasirpangarayan	90	C5
Paslek	71	H1
Pasley, Cape	112	E5
Pasmajarvi	62	L3
Pasman	72	C4
Pasni	92	B3
Paso de los Indios	139	C8
Paso de los Libres	138	E5
Paso de los Toros	138	E6
Paso Real	131	M9
Paso Rio Mayo	139	B9
Paso Robles	126	B3
Pasquia Hills	119	Q5
Passage East	59	J8
Passage West	59	F9
Passamaquoddy Bay	125	S4
Passau	70	E4
Passero, Capo	69	E7
Passo Fundo	138	F5
Passos	138	G4
Pastaza	136	B4
Pas, The	119	Q5
Pasto	136	B3
Pastol Bay	118	C3
Pastos Bons	137	J5
Pastrana	66	E2
Pasuruan	90	E7
Patache, Punta de	138	B4
Patagonia	139	C9
Patan *India*	92	D4
Patan *Nepal*	92	G3
Patani	91	H5
Patea	115	E3
Pateley Bridge	55	H2
Paterno	69	E7
Paterson	125	N6
Pathankot	92	E2
Pathfinder Reservoir	123	L6
Pathhead	57	F4
Patiala	92	E2
Patkai Bum	93	J3
Patman, Lake	128	E4
Patmos	75	J4
Patna	92	G3
Patnagarh	92	F4
Patnos	77	K3
Patomskoye Nagorye	85	J4
Patos	137	K5
Patos de Minas	138	G3
Patos, Lagoa dos	138	F6
Patquia	138	C6
Patrai	75	F3
Patras	75	F3
Patrasuy	78	L3
Patricio Lynch, Isla	139	A9
Patrington	55	J3
Patrocinio	138	G3
Pattani	93	K7
Patterdale	55	G2
Patti	69	E6
Patu	137	K5
Patuca	132	E7
Patuca, Punta	132	E7
Patzcuaro	130	J8
Patzcuaro, Laguna	130	J8
Pau	65	C7
Pau d'Arco	137	H5
Pau dos Ferros	137	K5
Pau, Gave de	65	C7
Pauini *Brazil*	136	D5
Pauini *Brazil*	136	D5
Paulilatino	69	B5
Paulista	137	K5
Paulistana	137	J5
Pauls Valley	128	D3
Paungde	93	J5
Pauni	92	E4
Pauri	92	E2
Pauto	136	C2
Pavarandocito	136	B2
Paveh	94	H4
Pavia	68	B3
Pavilosta	63	J8
Pavlikeni	73	H4
Pavlodar	84	B6
Pavlof Volcano	118	Af8
Pavlohrad	79	F6
Pavlovo	78	G4
Pavlovsk	79	G5
Pavlovskaya	79	F6
Pavullo nel Frigano	68	C3
Pavuvu	114	J6
Pawan	90	E6
Paxoi	75	F3
Paxton	57	F4
Payakumbuh	90	D6
Payette *U.S.A.*	122	F5
Payne, Lake	121	M6
Paynes Find	112	D4
Paysandu	138	E6
Payun, Volcan	139	C7
Pazanan	95	J6
Pazar	77	J2
Pazarbasi Burun	76	D2
Pazarcik	77	G4
Pazardzhik	73	H4
Pazaroren	77	G3
Pazaryeri	76	C2
Paz, Bahia de la	130	D5
Pazin	72	B3
Pcim	71	H4
Peabody Bugt	120	N2
Peace *Canada*	119	N4
Peace *U.S.A.*	129	M7
Peacehaven	53	M4
Peace River	119	M4
Peaima Falls	136	E2
Pea Island	129	Q3
Peak Hill	112	D4
Peale, Mount	123	K8
Pearl	128	H5
Pearl City	126	R10
Pearl Harbor	126	R10
Pearsall	128	C6
Peary Channel	120	F2
Pease	127	N3
Pebane	109	G3
Pec	72	F4
Pechenezhin	71	L4
Pechenga	62	P2
Pechora	78	J2
Pechorskaya Guba	78	J2
Pechorskoye More	78	J2
Pechory	63	M8
Pecos *U.S.A.*	127	L5
Pecos Plains	127	K4
Pecs	72	E2
Pedasi	132	G11
Pededze	63	M8
Pedernales	133	M5
Pedo La	92	F3
Pedorovka	79	J5
Pedra Azul	138	H3
Pedregal	132	F10
Pedreiras	137	J4
Pedro Afonso	137	H5
Pedro Cays	132	J6
Pedro Juan Caballero	138	E4
Pedro Luro	139	D7
Peebles	57	E5
Pee Dee	129	N3
Peel *Canada*	118	J2
Peel *U.K.*	54	E2
Peel Sound	120	G3
Peene	70	E2
Pegasus Bay	115	D5
Pegnitz *Germany*	70	D4
Pegnitz *Germany*	70	D4
Pegu	93	J5
Pegu Yoma	93	J5
Pegwell Bay	53	J3
Pegysh	78	J3
Pehlivankoy	76	B2
Pehuajo	139	D7
Peine	70	D2
Peipus, Lake	63	M7
Peixe	137	H6
Pei Xian	93	N2
Pekalongan	90	D7
Pekan	90	C5
Pekanbaru	90	C5
Pekin	124	F6
Peking	87	M4
Pekkala	62	M3
Pelabuanratu, Teluk	90	D7
Pelabuhan Kelang	90	C5
Pelagie, Isole	74	B5
Pelagos	75	H3
Pelat, Mont	65	G6
Peleaga	73	G3
Peleduy	85	J5
Pelee Island	124	J6
Peleng	91	G6
Peljesac	72	D4
Pelkosenniemi	62	M3
Pella	124	D6
Pellegrini	139	D7
Pello	62	L3
Pellworm	70	C1
Pelly	118	J3
Pelly Bay	120	J4
Pelly Mountains	118	J3
Peloponnisos	75	G4
Pelotas	138	F5
Pelplin	71	H2
Pelym	78	L3
Pemali, Tanjung	91	G6
Pematangsiantar	90	B5
Pemba	109	H2
Pemba Island	107	G4
Pemberton	122	C2
Pembina	119	M5
Pembroke *Canada*	125	M4
Pembroke *U.K.*	52	C3
Pembroke Dock	52	C3
Pena de Francia, Sierra da	66	C2
Penafiel	66	B2
Penafiel	66	D2
Penala	113	J6
Penalara, Pic de	66	E2
Penamacor	66	C2
Penapolis	138	F4
Penaranda de Bracamonte	66	D2
Penarroya	67	C2
Penarroya-Pueblonuevo	66	D3
Penarth	52	D3
Penas, Cabode	66	C1
Penasco, Puerto	126	F5

Name	Page	Grid
Pena, Sierra de la	67	F1
Pencader	52	C3
Pencaitland	57	F5
Pendalofon	75	F2
Pendembu	104	C4
Pendine	52	C3
Pendleton	122	E5
Pend Oreille Lake	122	F3
Pendra	92	F4
Penedo	138	K6
Penfro	52	C3
Penganga	92	E5
Pengkou	87	M6
Pengze	87	M5
Peniche	66	B3
Penicuik	57	E5
Peniscola	67	G2
Penistone	55	H3
Penitentes, Serra do	137	H5
Penmaenmawr	54	F3
Penmarch, Pointe de	65	A5
Penne	69	D4
Penner	92	E6
Penneshaw	113	H6
Pennine, Alpi	68	A2
Pennines	55	G2
Pennsylvania	125	L6
Penny Highlands	120	N4
Peno	78	E4
Penobscot	125	R4
Penobscot Bay	125	R4
Penonome	132	G10
Penrith	55	G2
Penryn	52	B4
Pensacola	129	J5
Pensamiento	136	E6
Pentecost Island	114	U11
Pentire Head	52	C4
Pentland Firth	56	E2
Pentland Hills	57	E5
Pen-y-ghent	55	G2
Penza	79	H5
Penzance	52	B4
Penzhina	85	V4
Penzhinskaya Guba	85	U4
Peoria	124	F6
Peqin	74	E2
Perak	90	C5
Perama	75	F3
Percival Lakes	112	E3
Perdido, Monte	67	G1
Peregrebnoye	84	Ae4
Pereira	136	B3
Perelazovskiy	79	G6
Perello	67	G2
Peremyshlyany	71	L4
Perenjori	112	D4
PereslavlZalesskiy	78	F4
Perevolotskiy	79	J5
Pereyaslavka	88	E2
Pergamino	139	D6
Pergamum	76	B3
Perhojoki	62	K5
Peri	77	J3
Peribonca	121	M8
Peribonca	125	Q2
Perigueux	65	D6
Perija, Sierra de	136	C2
Perim	96	F10
Peris	73	J3
Peristrema	76	F3
Perito Moreno	139	B9
Peritoro	137	J4
Perlas, Punta de	132	F8
Perlez	72	F3
Perm	78	K4
Pernambuca	137	K5
Pernik	73	G4
Peronne	64	E4
Perote	131	L8
Perote, Cofre de	131	L8
Perouse Strait, La	88	J3
Perpignan	65	E7
Perran Bay	52	B4
Perranporth	52	B4
Perros-Guirec	64	B4
Perry *Canada*	119	Q2
Perry *Florida*	129	L5
Perry *Oklahoma*	128	D2
Perryton	127	M2
Perryville *Alaska*	118	D4
Perryville *Missouri*	124	F8
Persembe	77	G2
Perseverancia	136	E6
Persian Gulf	97	K3
Pertek	77	H3
Perth *Australia*	112	D5
Perth *Canada*	125	M4
Perth *U.K.*	57	E4
Perth-Andover	125	S3
Pertominsk	78	F3
Pertugskiy	78	H4
Pertuis Breton	65	C5
Peru	136	B5
Peru *Illinois*	124	F6
Peru *Indiana*	124	G6
Peru-Chile Trench	143	L5
Perugia	68	D4
Perushtitsa	73	H4
Pervari	77	K4
Pervomaskiy	79	K5
Pervomaysk *Russia*	78	G5
Pervomaysk *Ukraine*	79	E6
Pervouralsk	84	Ac5
Pesaro	68	D4
Pescara	69	E4
Peschanyy, Mys	79	J7
Pesha	78	H2
Peshanjan	95	Q5
Peshawar	92	D2
Peshkopi	75	F2
Peski *Belarus*	71	L2
Peski *Kazakhstan*	84	Ae6
Pesqueira *Brazil*	137	K5
Pesqueria *Mexico*	127	N8
Pestovo	78	F4
Petah Tiqwa	94	B5
Petajavesi	62	L5
Petalcalco, Bahia	130	H9
Petalioi	75	H4
Petalion, Kolpos	75	H4
Petaluma	126	A1
Petatlan	131	J9
Petauke	107	F5
Peterborough *Australia*	113	H5
Peterborough *Canada*	125	L4
Peterborough *U.K.*	53	G2
Peterhead	56	G3
Peterlee	55	H2
Petermann Ranges	112	F3
Peter Pond Lake	119	P4
Petersburg *Alaska*	118	J4
Petersburg *Virginia*	125	M8
Petersfield	53	G3
Peterstow	52	E3
Petite Kabylie	67	J4
Petite Miquelon	121	Q8
Petit Mecatina, Riviere du	121	P7
Petitot	119	L4
Petkula	62	M3
Peto	131	Q7
Petoskey	124	H4
Petra Velikogo, Zaliv	88	C4
Petre Bay	115	F6
Petrila	73	G3
Petrodvorets	63	N7
Petrolandia	137	K5
Petrolina *Amazonas, Brazil*	136	D4
Petrolina *Pernambuco, Brazil*	137	J5
Petropavlovsk	84	Ae6
Petropavlovsk-Kamchatskiy	85	T6
Petropolis	138	H4
Petrovac	72	E4
Petrovsk	79	H5
Petrovskoye	78	K5
Petrovsk-Žabaykalskiy	84	H6
Petrozavodsk	78	E3
Petsamo	62	P2
Petteril	55	G2
Petukhovo	84	Ae5
Petworth	53	G4
Peureula	90	B5
Pevek	85	W3
Pewsey, Vale of	52	F3
Peza	78	H2
Pezenas	65	E7
Pezinok	71	G4
Pezmog	78	J3
Pfaffenhofen	70	D4
Pfarrkirchen	70	E4
Pforzheim	70	C4
Phalaborwa	108	F4
Phalodi	92	D3
Phaltan	92	D5
Phangan, Ko	93	K6
Phangnga	93	J7
Phan Rang	93	L6
Phan Thiet	93	L6
Phatthalung	93	K7
Phenix City	129	K4
Phet Buri	93	J6
Phetchabun, Thiu Khao	93	K5
Philadelphia *Mississippi*	128	H4
Philadelphia *Pennsylvania*	125	N6
Philip	123	P5
Philip Island	111	Q7
Philippeville	64	F3
Philippines	91	G2
Philippine Sea	91	G1
Philipstown	108	D6
Phillipsburg	123	Q8
Philpots Island	120	L2
Phnom Penh	93	K6
Phoenix	126	F4
Phoenix Islands	111	U2
Phong Saly	93	K4
Phong Tho	93	K4
Phu Cuong	93	L6
Phu Dien Chau	93	L5
Phuket	93	J7
Phuket, Ko	93	J7
Phulabani	92	F4
Phu Ly	93	L4
Phuoc Le	93	L6
Phu Tho	93	L4
Phyajoki	62	L4
Piacenza	68	B3
Piana	69	B4
Pianosa, Isola	69	C4
Piatra Neamt	73	J2
Piaui	137	J5
Piaui, Serra do	137	J5
Piave	68	D3
Piaya	90	F7
Piazza Armerina	69	E7
Pibor	103	F6
Pibor Post	103	F6
Pic	124	G2
Picardie	64	E4
Picayune	128	H5
Pichilemu	139	B6
Pickering	55	J2
Pickering, Vale of	55	J2
Pickle Lake	121	J7
Pico	69	D5
Picos	137	J5
Pico Truncado	139	C9
Picton	115	E4
Picun-Leufu	139	C7
Pidalion, Akra	76	F5
Pidurutalagala	92	F7
Piedecuesta	136	C2
Piedrabuena	66	D3
Piedrahita	66	D2
Piedralaves	66	D2
Piedras Negras	127	M6
Piedra Sola	138	E6
Pielavesi	62	M5
Pielinen	62	N5
Pierowall	56	F1
Pierre	123	P5
Pietarsaari	62	K5
Pietermaritzburg	108	F5
Pietersburg	108	E4
Pietrosu	73	H2
Pieve di Cadore	68	D2
Pigadhia	75	J5
Piggott	128	G2
Pihtipudas	62	L5
Pijijiapan	131	N10
Pikes Peak	123	M8
Pikeville	124	J8
Pikhtovka	84	C5
Pila	71	G2
Pilar	138	E5
Pilaya	138	D4
Pilcaniyeu	139	B8
Pilcomayo	138	D4
Pili	75	J4
Pilibhit	92	E3
Pilica	71	H3
Pilion	75	G3
Pilos	75	F4
Pilot Point	118	D4
Pilsen	70	E4
Pimenta Bueno	136	E6
Pimentel	137	G4
Pina	67	F2
Pinang *Malaysia*	90	C4
Pinang *Malaysia*	90	C4
Pinarbasi *Turkey*	76	E2
Pinarbasi *Turkey*	77	G3
Pinar del Rio	132	F3
Pinarhisar	76	B2
Pinawa	123	S2
Pincher Creek	122	H3
Pindare	137	H4
Pindhos Oros	75	F3
Pindi Gheb	92	D2
Pine Bluff	128	F3
Pine Bluffs	123	M7
Pine City	124	D4
Pine Creek	112	G1
Pine Creek Lake	128	E3
Pinedale	123	K6
Pine Falls	119	R5
Pinega *Russia*	78	G3
Pinega *Russia*	78	G3
Pine Island Bay	141	T4
Pine Pass	119	L5
Pine Point	119	N3
Pine Ridge	123	N6
Pinerolo	68	A3
Pines, Lake O' the	128	E4
Pinetop-Lakeside	127	H3
Pineville	124	J8
Pingban	93	K4
Pingdingshan	93	M2
Pingelly	112	D5
Pingeyri	62	T12
Pingguo	93	L4
Pingjiang	93	M3
Ping, Mae Nam	93	J5
Pingquan	93	L1
Pingtan Dao	87	M6
Ping-tung	87	N7
Pingwu	93	K2
Pingxiang *Guangxi, China*	93	L4
Pingxiang *Jiangxi, China*	93	M3
Pingyang	87	N6
Pingyao	87	L4
Pingyi	87	M4
Pingyin	87	M4
Pinhao	66	C2
Pinhel	66	C2
Pini	90	B5
Pinios *Greece*	75	F4
Pinios *Greece*	75	F3
Pinnes, Akra	75	H2
Pinos, Point	126	B2
Pinotepa Nacional	131	L9
Pinrang	91	F6
Pins, Ile des	114	X17
Pinsk	71	M2
Pintados	138	C4
Pinta, Isla	136	A7
Pinto	138	D5
Pinyug	78	H3
Pioche	126	E2
Piombino	69	C4
Pioner, Ostrov	81	L2
Pionerskiy *Russia*	84	Ad4
Pionerskiy *Russia*	71	J1
Piotrkow Trybunalski	71	H3
Piove di Sacco	68	D3
Piperi	75	H3
Pipestone	124	B5
Pipmudcan, Reservoir	125	Q2
Piracicaba	138	G4
Piracuruca	137	J4
Piraeus	75	G4
Pirahmet	77	H2
Piraievs	75	G4
Piranhas *Amazonas, Brazil*	136	E5
Piranhas *Sergipe, Brazil*	137	K5
Piranshahr	77	L4
Pirapora	138	H3
Pirara	136	F3
Pirgos *Greece*	75	F4
Pirgos *Greece*	75	H5
Pirimapun	114	B3
Pirineos	67	F1
Pirin Planina	73	G5
Piripiri	137	J4
Pirmasens	70	B4
Pirna	70	E3
Piro do Rio	138	G3
Pirot	73	G4
Pir Panjal Range	92	D2
Piru	91	H6
Piryatin	79	E5
Piryi	75	H3
Pisa	68	C4
Pisco	136	B6
Piscopi	75	J4
Pisek	70	F4
Pishan	92	E1
Pishin	95	Q8
Pishin-Lora	92	C3
Pistayarvi, Ozero	62	P4
Pisticci	69	F5
Pistilfjordur	62	X11
Pistoia	68	C4
Pisuerga	66	D1
Pit	122	D7
Pita	104	C3
Pitanga	138	E4
Pitcairn Island	143	J5
Pitea	62	J4
Pitealven	62	H4
Pitesti	73	H3
Pithiviers	64	E4
Pitkyaranta	78	E3
Pitlochry	57	E4
Pitlyar	84	Ae3
Pitt Island *Canada*	118	K5
Pitt Island *New Zealand*	115	F7
Pittsburg	124	C8
Pittsburgh	125	K6
Pittsfield	124	E7
Pitt Strait	115	F7
Piui	138	G4
Piura	136	A5
Pjorsa	62	N2
Pjorsa	62	V12
Placentia Bay	121	Q8
Placer	91	G3
Placerville	126	B1
Placido do Castro	136	D6
Plackoviea	73	G5
Plainview	127	M3
Plaka	75	H2
Plakenska Planina	73	F5
Plampang	91	F7
Plana	70	E4
Planeta Rica	133	K10
Plankinton	123	Q6
Plant City	129	L7
Plaquemine	128	G5
Plasencia	66	C2
Plastun	88	F3
Platani	69	D7
Plata, Rio de la	139	E6
Plati	75	G2
Plato	136	C2
Platte	123	R7
Platteville	124	E5
Plattling	70	E4
Plattsburgh	125	P4
Plattsmouth	124	C6
Plauen	70	E3
Plav	72	E4
Playa Azul	130	H8
Pleasanton	128	C6
Pleihari	90	E6
Pleiku	93	L6
Plenty, Bay of	115	F2
Plentywood	123	M3
Plesetsk	78	G3
Plessisville	125	Q3
Pleszew	71	G3
Pletipi Lake	121	M7
Pleven	73	H4
Plitra	75	G4
Pljevlja	72	E4
Plock	71	H2
Plockenstein	70	E4
Ploermel	65	B5
Ploiesti	73	J3
Plomb du Cantal	65	E6
Plombieres	65	G5
Ploner See	70	D1
Plonsk	71	J2
Ploty	70	F2
Plovdiv	73	H4
Plumpton	55	G2

Saginaw Bay **124** J5
Sagiz *Kazakhstan* **79** J6
Sagiz *Kazakhstan* **79** J6
Sagiz *Kazakhstan* **79** J6
Sagkaya **77** F4
Saglek Bay **121** P6
Sagone, Golfe de **69** B4
Sagres **66** B4
Saguache **127** J1
Sagua la Grande **132** G3
Saguenay **121** M8
Sagunto **67** F3
Sahagun **66** D1
Sahand, Kuh-e **94** H3
Sahara **98** C4
Saharanpur **92** E3
Sahin **76** B2
Sahiwal *Pakistan* **92** D2
Sahiwal *Pakistan* **92** D2
Sahm **97** N4
Sahra al Hijarah **94** G6
Sahuaripa **127** H6
Sahuayo **130** H7
Sa Huynh **93** L6
Sahy **71** H4
Saibai Island **114** C3
Saicla **94** B5
Saida *Algeria* **100** F2
Saida *Lebanon* **76** F6
Saidabad **95** M7
Saidapet **92** F6
Saidor **114** D3
Saidpur **93** G3
Saigon **93** L6
Saijo **89** D9
Saimaa **63** M6
Saimbeyli **77** G3
Saindak **95** Q7
Saindezh **94** H3
Saint Abb's Head **57** B5
Saint-Affrique **65** E7
Saint-Agathe-des-Monts **125** N3
Saint Agnes *U.K.* **52** B4
Saint Agnes *U.K.* **52** K5
Saint-Agreve **65** F6
Saint Albans *U.K.* **53** G3
Saint Albans *Vermont* **125** P4
Saint Albans *W. Virginia* **124** K7
Saint Alban's Head **53** E4
Saint Aldhelm's **53** E4
Saint-Amand-Montrond **65** E5
Saint-Ambroix **65** F6
Saint Andre, Cap **109** H3
Saint Andrew **53** M7
Saint Andrews *New Zealand* **115** C6
Saint Andrews *U.K.* **57** F4
Saint Andrews Bay **57** F4
Saint-Anne-des-Monts **125** S2
Saint Annes **53** M6
Saint Ann's Bay **132** J5
Saint Ann's Head **52** B3
Saint Anthony *Canada* **121** Q7
Saint Anthony *U.S.A.* **122** J6
Saint Arnaud **115** D4
Saint Asaph **55** F3
Saint Aubin **53** M7
Saint Augustin **121** Q7
Saint Augustine **129** M6
Saint Augustin Saguenay **121** Q7
Saint Austell **52** C4
Saint Austell Bay **52** C4
Saint Bees **55** F2
Saint Bees Head **55** F2
Saint Benoit **109** L7
Saint Blazey **52** C4
Saint Brides **52** B3
Saint Brides Bay **52** B3
Saint-Brieuc **64** B4
Saint-Calais **65** D5
Saint Catherines **125** L5
Saint Catherines Island **129** M5
Saint Catherine's Point **53** F4
Saint-Cere **65** D6
Saint-Chamond **65** F6
Saint Charles **124** E7
Saint Clair, Lake **124** J5
Saint-Claude **65** F5
Saint Clears **52** C3
Saint Cloud *Florida* **129** M6
Saint Cloud *Minnesota* **124** C4
Saint Columb Major **52** C4
Saint Croix *Canada* **125** S4
Saint Croix *Minnesota* **124** D4
Saint Croix *U.S.A.* **133** Q6
Saint Croix Falls **124** D4
Saint David's **52** B3
Saint David's Head **52** B3
Saint-Denis **64** E4
Saint Denis **109** L7
Sainte-Foy-la-Grande **65** D6
Saint Elias, Mount **118** G3
Saint Elias Mountains **118** H3
Sainte-Marie **109** J3
Sainte-Marie-aux-Mines **64** G4
Sainte Marie, Cap **109** J5
Sainte-Maxime **65** G7
Sainte-Menehould **64** F4
Sainte Nazaire **65** B5
Saintes **65** C6
Saintes, Iles des **133** S7
Saintes-Maries-de-la-Mer **65** F7
Saint Etienne **65** F6
Saint Eustatius **133** R6
Saint-Fargeau **65** E5
Saintfield **58** L4
Saint Finan's Bay **59** B9
Saint-Florent, Golfe de **69** B4
Saint-Florentin **65** E4
Saint-Flour **65** E6
Saint Francis *Canada* **125** P4
Saint Francis *Arkansas* **128** G3
Saint Francis *Kansas* **123** P8
Saint Francis, Cape **108** D6
Saint Gallen **68** B2
Saint-Gaudens **65** D7
Saint George *Australia* **113** K4
Saint George *U.S.A.* **126** F2
Saint George, Cape *Canada* **121** Q8
Saint George, Cape *Papua New Guinea* **114** E2
Saint George Head **113** L6
Saint George Island *Alaska* **118** Ae8
Saint George Island *Florida* **129** K6
Saint Georges **125** Q3
Saint George's **133** S8
Saint Georges Bay **121** Q8
Saint George's Channel *Papua New Guinea* **114** E2
Saint George's Channel *U.K.* **52** B3
Saint-Germain **64** D4
Saint-Gildas-de-Rhuys **65** B5
Saint-Gilles-Croix-de-Vie **65** C5
Saint-Girons **65** D7
Saint Gotthard Pass **68** B2
Saint Govan's Head **52** C3
Saint Helena **99** C8
Saint Helena Bay **108** C6
Saint Helens *Australia* **113** K7
Saint Helens *U.K.* **55** G3
Saint Helens, Mount **122** C4
Saint Helens Point **113** K7
Saint Helier **53** M4
Saint Ignace **124** H4
Saint Ignatius **122** G4
Saint Ives *Cambridgeshire, U.K.* **53** G2
Saint Ives *Cornwall, U.K.* **52** B4
Saint Ives Bay **52** B4
Saint James, Cape **118** J5
Saint-Jean-d'Angely **65** C6
Saint-Jean-de-Luz **65** C7
Saint-Jean-de-Maurienne **65** G6
Saint-Jean-de-Monts **65** B5
Saint-Jean, Lac **125** P2
Saint-Jean-Pied-de-Port **65** C7
Saint-Jean-Sur-Richelieu **125** P4
Saint Jerome **125** P4
Saint John *Canada* **121** N8
Saint John *Canada* **121** N8
Saint John *U.K.* **53** M7
Saint John *U.S.A.* **133** Q5
Saint John Bay **121** Q7
Saint John's *Antigua* **133** S6
Saint Johns *Canada* **121** R8
Saint Johns *Arizona* **127** H3
Saint Johns *Florida* **129** M6
Saint Johns *Michigan* **124** H5
Saint Johnsbury **125** Q4
Saint John's Point *Ireland* **58** F3
Saint John's Point *U.K.* **58** L4
Saint Joseph *Arkansas* **128** G5
Saint Joseph *Missouri* **124** C7
Saint Joseph Island **128** D7
Saint-Junien **65** D6
Saint Just **52** B4
Saint Keverne **52** B4
Saint Kitts-Nevis **133** R6
Saint Laurent **137** G2
Saint Lawrence *Australia* **113** K3
Saint Lawrence *Canada* **121** N8
Saint Lawrence *Canada* **121** Q8
Saint Lawrence, Gulf of **121** P8
Saint Lawrence Island **118** B3
Saint Lawrence Seaway **125** N4
Saint Leonard **125** S3
Saint-Leonard-de-Noblat **65** D6
Saint Lewis **121** Q7
Saint Lo **64** C4
Saint Louis *Minnesota* **124** D3
Saint Louis *Missouri* **124** E7
Saint Louis *Senegal* **104** B2
Saint Lucia **133** S8
Saint Lucia, Cape **109** F5
Saint Lucia Channel **133** S7
Saint Lucia, Lake **109** F5
Saint Magnus Bay **56** A1
Saint-Maixent-l'Ecole **65** C5
Saint Malo **64** B4
Saint-Malo, Golfe de **64** C4
Saint Marc **133** L5
Saint-Marcellin **65** F6
Saint Margaret's-at-Cliffe **53** J3
Saint Maries **122** F4
Saint Martin *France* **133** R5
Saint Martin *U.K.* **53** M7
Saint Martin, Lake **123** Q2
Saint Martin's **52** L5
Saint-Martin-Vesubie **65** G6
Saint Mary Peak **113** H5
Saint Marys *Australia* **113** K7
Saint Mary's *Cornwall, U.K.* **52** L5
Saint Mary's *Orkney Islands, U.K.* **56** F2
Saint Marys *Florida* **129** M5
Saint Marys *Pennsylvania* **125** L6
Saint Mary's Loch **57** E5
Saint Matthias Group **114** D2
Saint-Maurice **121** M8
Saint Maurice **125** P3
Saint Mawes **52** B4
Saint-Maximin **65** F7
Saint Michael **118** C3
Saint-Mihiel **64** F4
Saint Monance **57** F4
Saint Moritz **68** B2
Saint Neots **53** G2
Saint Niklaas **64** F3
Saint Ninian's Island **56** A2
Saintogne **65** C6
Saint Omer **64** E3
Saint Pamphile **125** R3
Saint Pascal **125** R3
Saint Paul *Alberta, Canada* **119** N5
Saint Paul *Quebec, Canada* **121** Q7
Saint Paul *Liberia* **104** C4
Saint Paul *U.S.A.* **124** D4
Saint Paul Island **118** Ad8
Saint Peter **124** D4
Saint Peter Port **53** M7
Saint Petersburg *U.S.A.* **129** L7
Saint Petersburg *Russia* **78** E4
Saint Pierre *Canada* **121** Q8
Saint Pierre *France* **109** L7
Saint Pierre Bank **121** Q8
Saint Pol **64** E3
Saint-Pol-de-Leon **64** B4
Saint Polten **68** E1
Saint-Pons **65** E7
Saint-Pourcain **65** E5
Saint Queens Bay **53** M7
Saint-Quentin **64** E4
Saint-Raphael **65** G7
Saint Sampson **53** M7
Saint Sebastian Bay **108** D6
Saint-Seine-l'Abbaye **65** F5
Saint-Sever **65** C7
Saint Simeon **125** R3
Saint Stephen *Canada* **125** S4
Saint Stephen *U.S.A.* **129** N4
Saint Thomas *Canada* **125** K5
Saint Thomas *U.S.A.* **133** Q5
Saint-Tropez **65** G7
Saint-Valery-en-Caux **64** D4
Saint Veit **68** E2
Saint Vincent **133** S6
Saint Vincent, Gulf of **113** H6
Saint Vincent Island **129** K6
Saint Vincent Passage **133** S8
Saint Vith **64** G3
Saint-Yrieix **65** D6
Sajama **138** C3
Sajama, Nevado de **138** C3
Saji-dong **88** B5
Sajir, Ra's **97** L8
Sak **108** D6
Sakai **89** E8
Sakai-Minato **89** D8
Sakakah **96** E2
Sakakawea, Lake **123** P4
Sakami **121** L7
Sakami, Lake **121** L7
Sakania **107** E5
Sakarya *Turkey* **76** D2
Sakarya *Turkey* **76** D2
Sakata **88** G6
Sakete **105** F4
Sakhalin **85** Q6
Sakht-Sar **95** K3
Sakiai **71** K1
Sakmara **79** K5
Sakon Nakhon **93** K5
Sak-shima-shoto **89** G11
Sakti **92** F4
Sal *Cape Verde* **104** L7
Sal *Russia* **79** G6
Sala **63** G7
Salaberry-De-Valleyfield **125** N4
Salaca **63** L8
Salacgriva **63** L8
Sala Consilina **69** E5
Saladillo **139** E7
Salado *Argentina* **139** C6
Salado *Argentina* **138** D5
Salaga **104** E4
Salalah **97** M8
Salama **132** B7
Salamanca *Mexico* **131** J7
Salamanca *Spain* **66** D2
Salamanca *U.S.A.* **125** L5
Salamina **136** B2
Salamis **75** G4
Salamiyah **77** G5
Salard **73** G2
Salas **73** G3
Salas de los Infantes **66** E1
Salat **77** J4
Salavat **78** K5
Salawati **91** J6
Salba **84** E6
Salbris **65** E5
Salcha **118** F3
Salcia **73** H4
Salcombe **52** D4
Salda Golu **76** C4
Saldana **66** D1
Saldanha **108** C6
Saldus **63** K8
Sale **100** D2
Sale *Australia* **113** K6
Sale *U.K.* **55** G3
Salebabu **91** H5
Salekhard **84** Ae3
Salem *India* **92** E6
Salem *Illinois* **124** F7
Salem *Oregon* **122** C5
Salemi **69** D7
Salen *Highland, U.K.* **57** C4
Salen *Strathclyde, U.K.* **57** C4
Salernes **65** G7
Salerno **69** E5
Salerno, Golfo di **69** E5
Salford **55** G3
Salgotarjan **72** E1
Salgueiro **137** K5
Salida **127** J1
Salies-de-Bearn **65** C7
Salihli **76** C3
Salima **107** F5
Salina *Kansas* **123** R8
Salina *Utah* **126** G1
Salina, Isola **69** E6
Salinas *Ecuador* **136** A4
Salinas *U.S.A.* **126** B2
Salinas, Cabo de **67** H3
Salinas Grandes **138** C4
Salinas O'Lachay, Punta de **136** B6
Salinas, Pampa de la **138** C6
Saline **123** Q8
Salinopolis **137** H4
Salins **65** F5
Salisbury *Maryland* **125** N7
Salisbury *N. Carolina* **129** M3
Salisbury *U.K.* **53** F3
Salisbury *Zimbabwe* **108** F3
Salisbury Island **120** L5
Salisbury Plain **52** F3
Saliste **73** G3
Salkhad **94** C5
Salla **62** N3
Sallisaw **128** E3
Sallvit **120** L5
Sallybrook **59** F9
Salmas **77** L3
Salmi **78** E3
Salmon *Canada* **119** L5
Salmon *U.S.A.* **122** F5
Salmon *U.S.A.* **122** H5
Salmon Arm **122** E2
Salmon Falls Creek **122** G6
Salmon River Mountains **122** G5
Salo **68** C3
Salo **63** K6
Salon-de-Provence **65** F7
Saloniki **75** G2
Salonta **73** F2
Salor **66** C3
Sal, Punta **132** D7
Salsacate **139** C6
Salsbruket **62** H4
Salsipuedes, Punta **126** D4
Salsk **79** G6
Salso **69** D7
Salsomaggiore Terme **68** B3
Salt *Jordan* **94** B5
Salt *Kentucky* **124** H8
Salt *Missouri* **124** D7
Salt *Oklahoma* **128** D2
Salta **138** C4
Saltash **52** C4
Saltburn-by-the-Sea **55** J2
Salt Cay **133** M4
Saltcoats **57** D5
Saltfjellet **62** F3
Saltfjord **62** F3
Saltfleet **55** K3
Saltillo **127** M8
Salt Lake City **122** J7
Salto *Italy* **69** D4
Salto *Uruguay* **138** E6
Salto da Divisa **138** G3
Salton Sea **126** E4
Saltpond **104** E4
Saluda *U.S.A.* **129** L3
Saluda *U.S.A.* **129** M3
Salumbar **92** D4
Saluzzo **68** A3
Salvador **137** K6
Salvatierra **131** J7
Salwah **97** K4
Salween **93** J5
Salyany **94** J2
Salyersville **124** J8
Salzach **68** D2
Salzburg **68** D2
Salzgitter **70** D2
Salzwedel **70** D2
Samah **96** G2
Samaipata **138** D3
Samak, Tanjung **90** D6
Samales Group **91** G4
Samana, Bahia de **133** N5
Samana, Cabo **133** N5
Samana Cay **133** L3
Samandag **77** F4
Samani **88** J4
Samanli Daglari **76** D2
Samanskoye **86** C2
Samar **91** H3
Samara **79** J5
Samarga *Russia* **88** G2
Samarga *Russia* **88** G2
Samariapo **136** D2
Samarina **75** F2
Samarinda **91** F6
Samarka **88** E3
Samarkand **86** B4
Samarra **77** K5
Samarskoye **86** F2

Sambah 97 N10
Sambaliung 91 F5
Sambalpur 92 F4
Sambar, Tanjung 90 E6
Sambas 90 D5
Sambava 109 K2
Sambhal 92 E3
Sambhar 92 E3
Sambhar Lake 92 D3
Samboja 91 F6
Sambor 79 C6
Samborombon, Bahia 139 E7
Sambre 64 F3
Samchok 89 B7
Samhan, Jabal 97 M8
Sami 75 F3
Samirah 96 F3
Sam Neua 93 K4
Samoded 78 G3
Samos 75 J4
Samosomo Strait 114 R8
Samothraki *Greece* 74 E3
Samothraki *Greece* 75 H2
Samothraki *Greece* 75 H2
Samoylovka 79 G5
Sampit *Indonesia* 90 E6
Sampit *Indonesia* 90 E6
Sam Rayburn Lake 128 E5
Samre 96 D10
Samrong 93 K6
Samso 63 D9
Samsu 88 A5
Samsun 77 G2
Samtredia 77 K1
Samui, Ko 93 K6
Samut Prakan 93 K6
San *Mali* 100 E6
San *Poland* 71 K3
Sana 72 D3
Sana 96 G9
Sanae 141 Z4
Sanaga 105 H5
San Agustin 136 B3
San Agustin, Cape 91 H4
Sanaigmore 57 B5
Sanak Island 118 Af9
Sanam, As 97 K6
San Ambrosio, Isla 135 B5
Sanana 91 H6
Sanandaj 94 H4
San Andreas 126 B1
San Andres, Isla de 132 G8
San Andres Mountains 127 J4
San Andres Tuxtla 131 M8
San Angelo 127 M5
San Antonio *Chile* 139 B6
San Antonio *New Mexico* 127 J4
San Antonio *Texas* 128 C6
San Antonio *Texas* 128 D6
San Antonio Abad 67 G3
San Antonio, Cabo 132 E4
San Antonio de Caparo 136 C2
San Antonio de los Cobres 138 C4
San Antonio Nuevo 132 C6
San Antonio, Punta 126 E6
Sanaw 97 K8
San Bartolomeo in Galdo 69 E5
San Benedetto del Tronto 69 D4
San Benedicto, Isla 130 D8
San Benito 128 D7
San Bernardino *Paraguay* 138 E5
San Bernardino *U.S.A.* 126 D3
San Bernardino Mountains 126 D3
San Bernardino Pass 68 B2
San Bernardo *Chile* 139 B6
San Bernardo *Mexico* 127 K7
San Bernardo do Campo 138 G4
San Blas 127 H7
San Blas, Cape 129 K6
San Blas, Punta 136 B2
San Borja 136 D6
San Borjas, Sierra de 126 F6
Sancak 77 J3
San Carlos *Argentina* 139 C6
San Carlos *Chile* 139 B7
San Carlos *Colombia* 136 D3
San Carlos *Nicaragua* 132 E9
San Carlos *Philippines* 91 G3
San Carlos *Philippines* 91 G2
San Carlos *Uruguay* 139 F6
San Carlos *U.S.A.* 126 G4
San Carlos *Venezuela* 136 D2
San Carlos de Bariloche 139 B8
San Carlos de la Rapita 67 G2
San Carlos del Zulia 136 C2
San Carlos Lake 126 G4
Sancerre 65 E5
Sanchakou 86 D4
Sanchor 92 D4
San Clemente 66 E3
San Clemente Island 126 C4
San Cristobal *Argentina* 138 D6
San Cristobal *Bolivia* 138 C4
San Cristobal *Solomon Is.* 114 L7
San Cristobal *Venezuela* 136 C2
San Cristobal, Bahia de 126 E7
San Cristobal de las Casas 131 N9
San Cristobal, Isla 136 A7
Sancti Spiritus 132 H4
Sancy, Puy de 65 E4
Sandagou 88 E4
Sanda Island 57 C5
Sandakan 91 F4
Sandanski 73 G5

Sandaohumiao 87 J4
Sandaotong 88 B3
Sandarne 63 G6
Sandasel 62 V13
Sanday 56 F1
Sanday Sound 56 F1
Sandbach 55 G3
Sandefjord 63 D7
Sanderson 127 L5
Sandhead 54 E2
Sand Hills 123 N6
San Diego 126 D4
San Diego, Cabo 139 C10
Sandikli 76 D3
Sandila 92 F3
Sandnes 63 A7
Sandness 56 A1
Sandnessjoen 62 E3
Sandoa 106 D4
Sandomierz 71 J3
Sandon 53 E2
San Dona di Piave 68 D3
Sandoway 93 H5
Sandown 53 F4
Sandoy 62 Z14
Sandpoint 122 F3
Sandray 57 A4
Sandsele 62 G4
Sandstone *Australia* 112 D4
Sandstone *U.S.A.* 124 D3
Sandusky *U.S.A.* 124 J6
Sandvig 70 F1
Sandvika 62 E5
Sandviken 63 G6
Sandwich 53 J3
Sandy 53 G2
Sandy Cape 113 L3
Sandy Lake 119 S5
Sandy Point 93 H6
San Esteban, Isla de 126 F6
San Felipe *Chile* 139 B6
San Felipe *Mexico* 126 E5
San Felipe *Mexico* 131 J7
San Felipe *Venezuela* 136 D1
San Felix, Isla 135 A5
San Fermin, Punta 126 E5
San Fernando *Chile* 139 B6
San Fernando *Mexico* 128 C8
San Fernando *Mexico* 128 C8
San Fernando *Philippines* 91 G2
San Fernando *Spain* 66 C4
San Fernando *Trinidad and Tobago* 133 S9
San Fernando de Apure 136 D2
San Fernando de Atabapo 136 D3
Sanford *Florida* 129 M6
Sanford *Maine* 125 Q5
Sanford *N. Carolina* 129 N3
Sanford, Mount 118 G3
San Francisco *Argentina* 138 D6
San Francisco *California* 126 A2
San Francisco *New Mexico* 127 H4
San Francisco, Cabo de 136 A3
San Francisco de Assis 138 E5
San Francisco del Oro 127 K7
San Francisco de Macoris 133 M5
San Francisco de Paula, Cabo 139 C9
San Francisco Javier 67 G3
San Francisco, Paso de 138 C5
San Gabriel, Punta 126 F6
Sangan 95 P4
Sangar 85 M4
Sang Bast 95 P3
Sangeang 91 F7
Sanggau 90 E5
Sangha 106 C2
Sangihe 91 H5
Sangihe, Kepulauan 91 H5
San Gil 136 C2
San Giovanni in Fiore 69 F6
Sangkhla Buri 93 J6
Sangli 92 D5
Sangmelima 105 H5
Sangonera 67 F4
San Gorgonio Peak 126 D3
Sangowo 91 H5
Sangre de Cristo Range 127 K1
Sangro 69 E4
Sangue 137 F6
Sanguesa 67 F1
San Guiseppe Iato 69 D7
San Hipolito, Punta 126 F7
Sanibel Island 129 L7
San Ignacio *Bolivia* 138 D3
San Ignacio *Bolivia* 136 D6
San Ignacio *Mexico* 126 F7
San Ignacio *Paraguay* 138 E5
Sanikiluaq 121 L6
San Ildefonso, Cape 91 G2
San Javier 138 D3
Sanjbod 94 J3
Sanjo 89 G7
San Joaquin *Bolivia* 136 E6
San Joaquin *U.S.A.* 126 B2
San Joaquin Valley 126 B2
San Jorge *Colombia* 133 K10
San Jorge *Solomon Is.* 114 J6
San Jorge, Bahia de 126 F5
San Jorge, Golfo de *Argentina* 139 C9
San Jorge, Golfo de *Spain* 67 G2
San Jose *Costa Rica* 132 E10
San Jose *Philippines* 91 G3
San Jose *Spain* 67 E4
San Jose *California* 126 B2

San Jose *New Mexico* 127 J3
San Jose de Amacuro 136 E2
San Jose de Buenavista 91 G3
San Jose de Chiquitos 138 D3
San Jose de Gracia 126 F7
San Jose de Jachal 139 C6
San Jose del Cabo 130 E6
San Jose de Mayo 139 E6
San Jose, Isla 130 D5
San Juan 131 M8
San Juan *Argentina* 138 C6
San Juan *Argentina* 138 C6
San Juan *Dominican Republic* 133 M5
San Juan *Mexico* 127 N8
San Juan *Nicaragua* 132 E8
San Juan *Peru* 136 B7
San Juan *Puerto Rico* 133 P5
San Juan *Utah* 127 H2
San Juan Bautista 67 G3
San Juan Bautista, Cabo 126 F6
San Juan del Norte 132 F9
San Juan del Norte, Bahia de 132 F9
San Juan de los Morros 136 D2
San Juan del Rio 131 K7
San Juanico, Punta 126 F7
San Juan Islands 122 C3
San Juan Mountains 127 J2
San Julian 139 C9
Sankt Blasjon 62 F4
Sankuru 106 D3
San Lazaro, Cabo 130 C5
San Lazaro, Sierra de 130 E6
San Lorenzo 136 D6
San Lorenzo, Cabo 136 A4
San Lorenzo, Cerro 139 B9
San Lorenzo de El Escorial 66 D2
San Lorenzo de la Parrilla 66 E3
San Lorenzo, Isla 126 F6
Sanlucar de Barrameda 66 C4
Sanlucar la Mayor 66 C4
San Lucas *Bolivia* 138 C4
San Lucas *Mexico* 130 E6
San Lucas, Cabo 130 E6
San Luis 132 C6
San Luis *Argentina* 139 C6
San Luis *Venezuela* 133 N9
San Luis Obispo 126 B3
San Luis Potosi 131 J6
San Luis Rio Colorado 126 E4
Sanluri 69 B6
San Manuel 126 G4
San Marco, Capo 69 B6
San Marcos *Mexico* 131 K9
San Marcos *U.S.A.* 128 D6
San Marcos, Island 126 F7
San Marino 68 D4
San Marino 68 D4
San Martin *Bolivia* 136 E6
San Martin *Colombia* 136 C3
San Martin de Valdeiglesias 66 D2
San Martin, Lago 139 B9
San Mateo 136 E2
San Matias 138 E3
San Matias, Golfo 139 D8
Sanmenxia 93 M2
San Miguel *Bolivia* 138 D3
San Miguel *Bolivia* 138 D3
San Miguel *El Salvador* 132 C8
San Miguel de Allende 131 J7
San Miguel de Tucuman 138 C5
San Miguel do Araguaia 137 G6
San Miguel Island 126 B3
San Miguelito 132 H10
Sanming 87 M6
Sannicandro Garganico 69 E5
San Nicolas 138 D6
San Nicolas, Bahia de 136 B7
San Nicolas Island 126 C4
Sannikova, Proliv 85 Q2
Sanok 71 K4
San Pablo 91 G3
San Pablo, Cabo 139 C10
San Pablo de Loreto 136 C4
San Pablo, Punta 126 E7
San Pedro 104 D5
San Pedro *Argentina* 139 E6
San Pedro *Mexico* 130 D6
San Pedro *Paraguay* 138 E4
San Pedro *U.S.A.* 126 G4
San Pedro Channel 126 C4
San Pedro de las Colonias 127 L8
San Pedro de Lloc 136 B5
San Pedro Martir, Sierra 126 E5
San Pedro, Punta 138 B5
San Pedros 130 G6
San Pedros de Macoris 133 N5
San Pedro, Sierra de 66 C3
San Pedro Sula 132 C7
San Pietro, Isola di 69 B6
Sanquhar 57 E5
San Quintin, Bahia de 126 E5
San Rafael *Argentina* 139 C6
San Rafael *Colombia* 136 C1
San Rafael *U.S.A.* 126 A2
San Remo 68 A4
San Salvador *Bahamas* 133 K2
San Salvador *El Salvador* 132 C8
San Salvador de Jujuy 138 C4
San Salvador, Isla 136 A7
San Sebastian 67 F1
San Sebastian Bahia de 139 C10
San Sebastiao, Ponta 109 G4
Sansepolcro 68 D4
San Severo 69 E5

San Silvestre 133 M10
Santa Ana *Bolivia* 136 D6
Santa Ana *El Salvador* 132 C7
Santa Ana *Mexico* 126 G5
Santa Ana *U.S.A.* 126 D4
Santa Ana Island 114 L7
Santa Barbara 126 C3
Santa Barbara *Honduras* 132 C7
Santa Barbara *Mexico* 127 K7
Santa Barbara Channel 126 B3
Santa Catalina, Gulf of 126 D4
Santa Catalina, Isla 130 D5
Santa Catalina Island 126 C4
Santa Catarina 138 F5
Santa Catarina, Ilha 138 G5
Santa Clara 132 H3
Santa Coloma de Farnes 67 H2
Santa Coloma de Gramanet 67 H2
Santa Comba Dao 66 B2
Santa Comba de Rossas 66 C2
Santa Cruz *Argentina* 139 B10
Santa Cruz *Bolivia* 138 D3
Santa Cruz *U.S.A.* 126 A2
Santa Cruz de la Palma 100 B3
Santa Cruz de Moya 67 F3
Santa Cruz de Tenerife 100 B3
Santa Cruz do Sul 138 F5
Santa Cruz, Isla *Ecuador* 136 A7
Santa Cruz, Isla *Mexico* 130 D5
Santa Cruz Island 126 C3
Santa Cruz Islands 114 N7
Santa Elena 136 E3
Santa Elena, Cabo 132 E9
Santa Eulalia del Rio 67 G3
Santafe 66 E4
Santa Fe *Argentina* 138 D6
Santa Fe *Panama* 132 G10
Santa Fe *U.S.A.* 127 K3
Sant Agata di Militello 69 E6
Santai *Sichuan, China* 93 L2
Santai *Xinjiang Uygur Zizhiqu, China* 86 E3
Santa Ines, Isla 139 B10
Santa Isabel *Argentina* 139 C7
Santa Isabel *Equatorial Guinea* 105 G5
Santa Isabel *Solomon Is.* 114 J5
Santa Lucia 139 E6
Santa Lucia Range 126 B2
Santa Luzia 137 K5
Santa Margarita, Isla 130 D5
Santa Maria *Brazil* 138 F5
Santa Maria *Mexico* 127 J6
Santa Maria *Mexico* 127 K8
Santa Maria *U.S.A.* 126 B3
Santa Maria *Vanuatu* 114 T11
Santa Maria *Venezuela* 133 P11
Santa Maria, Cabo de *Mozambique* 109 F5
Santa Maria, Cabo de *Portugal* 66 C4
Santa Maria di Leuca, Capo 69 G6
Santa Maria, Isla 136 A7
Santa Maria, Laguna de 127 J5
Santa Marta 136 C1
Santa Marta, Cabo de 106 B5
Santa Marta Grande, Cabo de 138 G5
Santa Maura 75 F3
Santa Monica 126 C3
Santan 91 F6
Santana 137 J6
Santana do Ipanema 137 K5
Santana do Livramento 138 E6
Santander *Colombia* 136 B3
Santander *Spain* 66 E1
Sant Antioco 69 B6
Santarem *Brazil* 137 G4
Santarem *Spain* 66 B3
Santaren Channel 132 H3
Santa Rita 136 C1
Santa Rosa *Argentina* 139 C6
Santa Rosa *Argentina* 139 D7
Santa Rosa *Bolivia* 136 D6
Santa Rosa *Brazil* 138 F5
Santa Rosa *California* 126 A1
Santa Rosa *New Mexico* 127 K3
Santa Rosa de Cabal 136 B3
Santa Rosa de Copan 132 C7
Santa Rosa Island 126 B4
Santa Rosalia 126 F7
Santa Rosa Range 122 F7
Santa Teresa Gallura 69 B5
Santa Vitoria do Palmar 139 F6
Santa Ynez 126 B3
Santee 129 M4
Santerno 68 C3
Sant Eufemia, Golfo di 69 F6
Santhia 68 B3
Santiago *Brazil* 138 F5
Santiago *Chile* 139 B6
Santiago *Dominican Republic* 133 M5
Santiago *Panama* 132 G10
Santiago *Peru* 136 B4
Santiago, Cerro 132 G10
Santiago de Chuco 136 B5
Santiago de Compostela 66 B1
Santiago de Cuba 133 K4
Santiago del Estero 138 D5
Santiago do Cacem 66 B3
Santiago Ixcuintla 130 G7
Santiago Papasquiaro 130 G5
San Tiburcio 130 J5
Santo Amaro 137 K6
Santo Andre 138 G4
Santo Angelo 138 F5

Name	Page	Grid
Shibotsu-jima	88	L4
Shibushi	89	C10
Shickshock Mountains	125	S2
Shiel Bridge	56	C3
Shieldaig	56	C3
Shiel, Loch	57	C4
Shihan, Wadi	97	L8
Shihezi	86	F3
Shiikh	103	J6
Shijiazhuang	87	L4
Shikarpur	92	C3
Shikoku	89	D9
Shikoku-sanchi	89	D9
Shikong	87	K4
Shikotan-to	88	L4
Shikotsu-ko	88	H4
Shildon	55	H2
Shilega	78	G3
Shiliguri	93	G3
Shilka *Russia*	85	K6
Shilka *Russia*	85	L6
Shillingstone	52	E4
Shillong	93	H3
Shilovo	78	G5
Shimabara	89	C9
Shimada	89	G8
Shimanovsk	85	M6
Shimian	93	K3
Shimizu	89	G8
Shimoda	89	G8
Shimoga	92	E6
Shimonoseki	89	C9
Shinano	89	G7
Shinas	97	N4
Shindand	95	R5
Shin Falls	56	D3
Shingu	89	E9
Shinjo	88	H6
Shinness	56	D2
Shinshar	77	G5
Shinyanga	107	F3
Shiogama	89	H6
Shiono-misaki	89	E9
Shiosawa	89	G7
Shiping	93	K4
Shipley	55	H3
Shippensburg	125	M6
Shippigan Island	121	P8
Shipston-on-Stour	53	F2
Shipton	55	H2
Shipton-under-Wychwood	53	F3
Shipunovo	84	C6
Shirakawa	89	H7
Shirane-san *Japan*	89	G8
Shirane-san *Japan*	89	G7
Shiraz	95	L7
Shire	107	F6
Shirebrook	55	H3
Shiretoko-misaki	88	K3
Shiriya-saki	88	H5
Shir Kuh	95	M6
Shirten Holoy Gobi	86	H3
Shirvan	95	N3
Shishaldin Volcano	118	Af9
Shivpuri	92	E3
Shivwits Plateau	126	F2
Shiwan Dashan	93	L4
Shiyan	93	M2
Shizhu	93	L3
Shizugawa	88	H6
Shizuishan	87	K4
Shizuoka	89	G8
Shkoder	74	E1
Shkumbin	74	E2
Shmidta, Ostrov	81	L1
Shobara	89	D8
Shokalskogo, Ostrov	84	A2
Shorapur	92	E5
Shorawak	95	S6
Shoreham-by-Sea	53	G4
Shorkot	92	D2
Shoshone	122	G6
Shoshone Mountains	122	F8
Shoshoni	123	K6
Shostka	79	E5
Shouguang	87	M4
Shouning	87	M6
Showa	141	C5
Showak	96	B9
Shozhma	78	G3
Shpikov	73	K1
Shpola	79	E6
Shrankogl	68	C2
Shreveport	128	F4
Shrewsbury	52	E2
Shrewton	53	F3
Shrigonda	92	D5
Shropshire	52	E2
Shrule	59	D5
Shuab, Ra's	97	P9
Shuanghezhen	87	P3
Shuangliao	87	N3
Shuangyashan	87	Q2
Shubar-Kuduk	79	K6
Shubra el-Khema	102	F1
Shucheng	87	M5
Shuga	84	B6
Shuicheng	93	K3
Shuikou	87	M6
Shujaabad	92	D3
Shulan	87	P3
Shumagin Islands	118	Af9
Shumen	73	J4
Shumerlya	78	H4
Shungnak	118	D2
Shuqrah	96	G10
Shura	77	K4
Shurab	95	K5
Shurab	95	N5
Shusf	95	Q6
Shush	94	J5
Shushenskoye	84	E6
Shushtar	94	J5
Shuswap Lake	122	E2
Shuya	78	G4
Shuya	89	G7
Shwebo	93	J4
Shwegyin	93	J5
Shweli	93	J4
Shyok	92	E2
Siahan Range	92	B3
Siah Koh	95	S5
Sialkot	92	D2
Siargao	91	H4
Siau	91	H5
Siauliai	63	K9
Sibenik	72	C4
Siberut	90	B6
Siberut, Selat	90	B6
Sibi	92	C3
Sibirskaya Nizmennost	84	G2
Sibirtsevo	88	D3
Sibiryakovo, Ostrov	84	B2
Sibiti	106	B3
Sibiu	73	H3
Sibolga	90	B5
Sibsagar	93	H3
Sibsey	55	K3
Sibu	90	E5
Sibut	102	C6
Sibutu	91	F5
Sibutu Passage	91	F5
Sibuyan	91	G3
Sibuyan Sea	91	G3
Sicasica	138	C3
Sichuan	93	K2
Sichuan Pendi	93	L3
Sicie, Cap	65	F7
Sicilia	69	D7
Sicilian Channel	69	C7
Sicily	69	D7
Sicuani	136	C6
Sidatun	88	E3
Sideby	63	J5
Sidheros, Akra	75	J5
Sidhirokastron	75	G2
Sidi Akacha	67	G4
Sidi Barram	102	E1
Sidi Bel Abbes	100	E1
Sidi Ifni	100	C3
Sidi Kacem	100	D2
Sidima	88	E1
Sidlaw Hills	57	E4
Sidmouth	52	D4
Sidmouth, Cape	113	J1
Sidney *Canada*	122	C3
Sidney *Montana*	123	M4
Sidney *Ohio*	124	H6
Sidon	94	B5
Sidorovsk	84	C3
Siedlce	71	K2
Siegen	70	C3
Siemiatycze	71	K2
Siem Reap	93	K6
Siena	68	C4
Sieniawa	71	K3
Sierpc	71	H2
Sierra Colorada	139	C8
Sierra Leone	104	C4
Sierra Vista	127	G5
Sierre	68	A2
Sifnos	75	H4
Sifton Pass	118	K4
Sigatoka *Fiji*	114	Q8
Sigatoka *Fiji*	114	Q9
Sigean	65	E7
Sighetu Marmatiei	73	G2
Sighisoara	73	H2
Sigli	90	B4
Siglufjordur	62	V11
Sigmaringen	70	C4
Signy	141	W6
Sigovo	84	D4
Sigtuna	63	G7
Siguenza	66	E2
Siguiri	104	D3
Sigulda	63	L8
Siikajoki	62	L4
Siikavuopio	62	J2
Siilinjarvi	62	M5
Siin	88	E2
Siipyy	63	J5
Siirt	77	J4
Sikar	92	E3
Sikasso	100	D6
Sikeston	124	F8
Sikhote Alin	88	E3
Sikinos	75	H4
Sikkim	93	G3
Sil	66	C1
Sila	97	K4
Silchar	93	H4
Sile	76	C2
Silesia	71	G3
Silgarhi	92	F3
Silifke	76	E4
Siligir	84	J3
Siling Co	93	G2
Silistra	73	J3
Silivri	76	C2
Siljan	63	F6
Silkeborg	63	C8
Sillajhuay	138	C3
Sillan, Lough	58	J4
Sillon de Talbert	64	B4
Siloam Springs	128	E2
Silom	114	E2
Silopi	77	K4
Silovayakha	78	L2
Silsbee	128	E5
Silute	63	J9
Silvan	77	J3
Silver Bay	124	E3
Silver City	127	H4
Silvermines Mountains	59	F7
Silver Spring	125	M7
Silverstone	53	F2
Silverton *U.K.*	52	D4
Silverton *U.S.A.*	127	J2
Simanggang	90	E5
Simard, Lac	125	L3
Simareh Karkheh	94	H5
Simav *Turkey*	76	C3
Simav *Turkey*	76	C2
Simayr	96	E8
Simcoe	125	K5
Simcoe, Lake	125	L4
Simeonovgrad	73	H4
Simeulue	90	B5
Simferopol	79	E7
Simi	75	J4
Simiti	136	C2
Simitli	73	G5
Simla	92	E2
Simleu Silvaniei	73	G2
Simmern	70	B3
Simojarvi	62	M3
Simojoki	62	L4
Simonka	71	J4
Simplicio Mendes	137	J5
Simplon Pass	68	B2
Simpson Bay	119	N2
Simpson Desert	113	H3
Simpson Peninsula	120	J4
Simrishamn	63	F9
Simsor	77	J3
Simushir, Ostrov	85	S7
Sinabang	90	B5
Sinabung	90	B5
Sinac	72	C3
Sinafir	96	B3
Sinaia	73	H3
Sinai Peninsula	103	F2
Sinaloa	130	F4
Sinanaj	74	E2
Sinaxtla	131	L9
Sincan *Turkey*	76	E3
Sincan *Turkey*	77	G3
Since	133	K10
Sincelejo	136	B2
Sinclair's Bay	56	E2
Sind	92	E3
Sinda	88	F1
Sindal	63	D8
Sindangbarang	90	D7
Sindel	73	J4
Sindhuli Garhi	92	G3
Sindirgi	76	C3
Sindominic	73	H2
Sindor	78	J3
Sind Sagar Doab	92	D2
Sinegorye	78	J4
Sinelnikovo	79	F6
Sines	66	B4
Sines, Cabo de	66	B4
Sinetta	62	L3
Sinfra	104	D4
Singa	103	F5
Singapore	90	C5
Singaraja	90	F7
Sing Buri	93	K6
Singida	107	F3
Singitikos, Kolpos	75	G2
Singkang	91	G6
Singkawang	90	D5
Singkep	90	C6
Singleton	53	G4
Singleton, Mount	112	G3
Singosan	87	P4
Siniatsikon	75	F2
Siniscola	69	B5
Sinj	72	D4
Sinjai	91	G7
Sinjajevina	72	E4
Sinjar	77	J4
Sinkat	103	G4
Sinnamary	137	G2
Sinnes	63	B7
Sinni	69	F5
Sinnicolau Mare	72	F2
Sinoe	104	D4
Sinoe, Lacul	73	K3
Sinop	76	F2
Sinpo	88	B5
Sinpung-dong	88	B5
Sintang	90	E5
Sint Maarten	133	R5
Sinton	128	D6
Sintra	66	B3
Sinu	136	B2
Sinuiju	87	N4
Sinyavka	71	M2
Sinyaya	63	N8
Siocon	91	G4
Siofok	72	E2
Sion	68	A2
Sionascaig, Loch	56	C2
Sion Mills	58	H3
Sioule	65	E5
Sioux City	124	B5
Sioux Falls	123	R6
Sioux Lookout	119	S5
Sipalay	91	G4
Siping	87	N3
Sip Song Chau Thai	93	K4
Sipul	114	D3
Sipura	90	B6
Siquia	132	E8
Siquijor	91	G4
Sira *India*	92	E6
Sira *Norway*	63	B7
Sir Abu Nuayr	97	M4
Siracusa	69	E7
Sirajganj	93	G4
Sir Alexander, Mount	119	M5
Siran	77	H2
Sir Bani Yas	97	L4
Sir Edward Pellew Group	113	H2
Siret *Romania*	73	J2
Siret *Romania*	73	J2
Sirhan, Wadi	94	D6
Siri Kit Dam	93	K5
Sirik, Tanjung	90	E5
Sir James McBrien, Mount	118	R3
Sirjan, Kavir-e	95	L6
Sirk	95	N8
Sirna	75	J4
Sirnal	77	K4
Sirohi	92	D4
Siros *Greece*	75	H4
Siros *Greece*	75	H4
Sirri	95	M9
Sirr, Nafud as	96	G4
Sirsa	92	D3
Sir Sanford, Mount	122	F2
Sirsi	92	D6
Sirte	101	J2
Sirte, Gulf of	101	J2
Sirvan	77	K3
Sisak	72	D3
Sisaket	93	K5
Sisophon	93	K6
Sisseton	123	R5
Sissonne	64	E4
Sistan	95	P8
Sistan, Daryacheh-ye-	95	Q6
Sisteron	65	F6
Sistig-Khem	84	F6
Sistranda	62	C5
Sitamau	92	E4
Sitapur	92	F3
Sitges	67	G2
Sithonia	75	G2
Sitia	75	J5
Sitian	86	F3
Sitidgi Lake	118	J2
Sitio da Abadia	138	H6
Sitka	118	H4
Sittang	93	J5
Sittingbourne	53	H3
Sittwe	93	H4
Situbondo	90	E7
Siuri	93	G4
Siuruanjoki	62	M4
Sivas	77	G3
Sivasli	76	C3
Siverek	77	H4
Siverskiy	63	P7
Sivrice	77	H3
Sivrihisar	76	D3
Sivrihisar Daglari	76	D3
Sivuk	85	Q6
Siwa	102	E2
Siwalik Range	92	F3
Siwan	92	F3
Si Xian	87	M5
Sixmilebridge	59	E7
Sixpenny Handley	53	E4
Siya	78	G3
Siyal Islands	96	C5
Sizin	84	F6
Sjælland	63	D9
Sjorup	63	C8
Skadarsko Jezero	74	E1
Skadovsk	79	E6
Skafta	62	V13
Skagafjordur	62	V12
Skagaflos	62	T12
Skagen	63	D8
Skagerrak	63	C8
Skagit	122	D3
Skagway	118	H4
Skaill	56	F2
Skala-Podolskaya	73	J1
Skanderborg	63	C8
Skanor	63	E9
Skansholm	62	G4
Skantzoura	75	H3
Skara	63	E7
Skaraborg	63	E7
Skarbak	63	C9
Skard	62	V12
Skardu	92	E1
Skarnes	63	D6
Skattkarr	63	E7
Skaudvile	63	K9

Skaulo	62 J3	Slobodskoy	78 J4	Soderala	63 G6	Sonipat	92 E3

Skaulo 62 J3 — Slobodskoy 78 J4 — Soderala 63 G6 — Sonipat 92 E3
Skawina 71 H4 — Slobodzeya 73 K2 — Soderhamn 63 G6 — Sonkajarvi 62 M5
Skeena 118 K5 — Slobozia *Romania* 73 H3 — Soderkoping 63 G7 — Sonkovo 78 F4
Skeena Mountains 118 K4 — Slobozia *Romania* 73 J3 — Sodermanland 63 G7 — Son La 93 K4
Skegness 55 K1 — Slonim 71 L2 — Sodertalje 63 G7 — Sonmiani 92 C3
Skeidararsandur 62 W13 — Slot, The 114 J6 — Sodra Ratansbyn 62 F5 — Sonmiani Bay 92 C3
Skelda Ness 56 A2 — Slough 53 G3 — Soe 91 G7 — Sonoita 126 F5
Skelleftea 62 J4 — Slovak Republic 70 H4 — Soest 70 C3 — Sonora 126 G6
Skelleftealven 62 H4 — Slovenia 72 C2 — Sofia *Bulgaria* 73 G4 — Sonoran Desert 126 F4
Skelmersdale 55 G3 — Slovyansk 79 F6 — Sofia *Madagascar* 109 J3 — Sonsonate 132 C8
Skelton 55 J2 — Sluch 79 D5 — Sofiya 73 G4 — Sonsorol Island 91 J4
Skerpioenpunt 108 D5 — Slunj 72 C3 — Sofiysk 85 P6 — Son Tay 93 L4
Skerries 58 K5 — Slupsk 71 G1 — Sogamoso *Colombia* 136 C2 — Sooghemeghat 118 B3
Skerries, The 54 E3 — Slussfors 62 G4 — Sogamoso *Colombia* 136 C2 — Sopi, Tanjung 91 H5
Skhiza 75 F4 — Slutsk 79 D5 — Sogndalsfjora 63 B6 — Sopot 71 H1
Ski 63 D7 — Slyne Head 59 B6 — Sognefjorden 63 A6 — Sopron 72 D2
Skiathos 75 G3 — Slyudyanka 84 G6 — Sogn og Fjordan 63 B6 — Sopur 92 D2
Skibbereen 59 D9 — Smaland 63 F8 — Sogod 91 G3 — Sor 66 B3
Skiddaw 55 F2 — Smallwood Reservoir 121 P7 — Sogut *Turkey* 76 C4 — Sora 69 D5
Skidegate 118 J5 — Smcanli 76 D3 — Sogut *Turkey* 76 D2 — Sorada 92 F5
Skidel 71 L2 — Smederevo 73 F3 — Sogutlu 76 D2 — Soraker 62 G5
Skien 63 C7 — Smela 79 E6 — Sog Xian 93 H2 — Sorata 138 C3
Skierniewice 71 J3 — Smethwick 53 E2 — Sohag 103 F2 — Sorbas 67 E4
Skiftet Kihti 63 J6 — Smidovich 88 D1 — Sohano 114 E3 — Sore 65 C6
Skikda 101 G1 — Smiltene 63 M8 — Sohela 92 F4 — Sorel 125 P3
Skipton 55 G3 — Smirnykh 85 Q7 — Sohuksan 87 P5 — Sorgun 76 F3
Skiropoula 75 H3 — Smith Arm 118 L2 — Soissons 64 E4 — Soria 66 E2
Skiros *Greece* 75 H3 — Smith Bay *Canada* 120 L2 — Sojat 92 D3 — Sorisdale 57 B4
Skiros *Greece* 75 H3 — Smith Bay *U.S.A.* 118 E1 — Sojotan Point 91 G4 — Sorka 78 F4
Skive 63 C8 — Smithfield *N. Carolina* 129 N3 — Sokal 71 L3 — Sorkh, Kuh-e 95 M5
Skjakerhatten 62 E4 — Smithfield *Utah* 122 J7 — Soke 76 B4 — Sormjole 62 J5
Skjalfandafljot 62 W12 — Smith Island 121 L5 — Sokhumi 79 G7 — Sorocaba 138 G4
Skjalfandi 62 W11 — Smith Mount Lake 125 L8 — Soko Banja 73 F4 — Sorochinsk 79 J3
Skjern 63 C9 — Smiths Falls 125 N4 — Sokode 104 F4 — Soroki 79 D6
Skjervoy 62 J1 — Smith Sound 120 M2 — Sokol 78 G4 — Sorong 91 J6
Sklad 85 L2 — Smithton 113 K7 — Sokolo 100 D6 — Sorot 63 N7
Skoghall 63 E7 — Smjorfjoll 62 X12 — Sokolovka 88 D4 — Soroti 107 F2
Skole 71 K4 — Smoky 119 M4 — Sokolow Podlaski 71 K2 — Soroya 62 K1
Skomer Island 53 B3 — Smoky Cape 113 L5 — Sokoto *Nigeria* 105 F3 — Soroysundet 62 K1
Skopelos *Greece* 75 G3 — Smoky Falls 121 K7 — Sokoto *Nigeria* 105 G3 — Sorraia 66 B3
Skopelos *Greece* 75 G3 — Smoky Hill 123 R8 — Sola 71 H4 — Sorrento 69 E5
Skopelos Kaloyeroi 75 H3 — Smoky Hills 123 Q8 — Solander Island 115 A7 — Sorsele 62 G4
Skopin 79 F5 — Smola 62 C5 — Solapur 92 E5 — Sorso 69 B5
Skopje 73 F4 — Smolenka 79 H5 — Sol, Costa del 66 D4 — Sorsogon 91 G3
Skopun 62 Z14 — Smolensk 78 E5 — Soledad 133 K9 — Sortavala 63 P6
Skorodum 84 A5 — Smolikas 75 F2 — Soledade 136 D5 — Sortland 62 F2
Skorovatn 62 E4 — Smolyan 73 H5 — Solen 63 D6 — Sor-Trondelag 62 D6
Skoruvik 62 X11 — Smolyaninovo 88 D4 — Solent, The 52 F4 — Sorvagsvatn 62 Z14
Skovde 63 E7 — Smooth Rock Falls 125 K2 — Solhan 77 J3 — Sorvagur 62 Z14
Skovorodino 85 L6 — Smorgon 71 M1 — Soligorsk 79 D5 — Sorvar 62 K1
Skowhegan 125 R4 — Smotrich 73 J1 — Solihull 53 F2 — Sorvattnet 63 E5
Skreia 63 D6 — Smyrna 76 B3 — Solikamsk 78 K4 — Sos del Rey-Catolico 67 F1
Skudenshavn 63 D6 — Snaefell 54 E2 — SolIletsk 79 J5 — Sosnogorsk 78 J3
Skulgam 62 H2 — Snafell 62 X12 — Solimoes 136 E4 — Sosnovka 84 H6
Skull 59 C9 — Snafellsjokull 62 T12 — Solingen 70 B3 — Sosnovo 63 P6
Skulyany 73 J2 — Snaith 55 H3 — Solleftea 62 G5 — Sosnovo-Ozerskoye 85 J6
Skuodas 63 J8 — Snake 122 E4 — Soller 67 H3 — Sosnowiec 71 H3
Skutec 70 F4 — Snake Range 122 G8 — Solnechnogorsk 78 F4 — Sosunova, Mys 88 G2
Skutskar 63 G6 — Snake River Plain 122 H6 — Solo 90 E7 — Sosva 84 Ad5
Skvira 79 D6 — Snap Point 132 J3 — Solobkovtsy 73 J1 — Sotik 107 G3
Skwierzyna 70 F2 — Snap, The 56 B1 — Solok 90 D6 — Sotra 63 A6
Skye 56 B3 — Snares Islands 111 Q11 — Solomon 123 Q8 — Sotuelamos 66 E3
Skyring, Peninsula 139 B9 — Snasa 62 E4 — Solomon Islands 114 J5 — Soubre 104 D4
Skyring, Seno 139 B10 — Snasavatn 62 E4 — Solon Springs 124 E3 — Soudan 113 H3
Slagelse 63 D9 — Sndre Isortoq 120 R4 — Solontsovo 85 K6 — Souflion 75 J2
Slagnas 62 H4 — Sndre Strmfjord 120 R4 — Solor, Kepulauan 91 G7 — Souk Ahras 101 G1
Slamannan 57 E5 — Sndre Sund 120 Q3 — Solothurn 68 A2 — Soumntam 67 J4
Slamet, Gunung 90 D7 — Sneek 64 F2 — Solotobe 86 B3 — Sour 94 B5
Slane 58 J5 — Sneem 59 C9 — Solovyevsk 85 L6 — Sour al Ghozlane 67 H4
Slaney 59 J8 — Snettisham 53 H2 — Solta 72 D4 — Soure 137 H4
Slany 70 F3 — Snezka 70 F3 — Soltanabad 95 P3 — Souris *Manitoba, Canada* 123 P3
Slapin, Loch 57 B3 — Sneznik 72 C3 — Soltaniyeh 94 J3 — Souris *Prince Edward Island, Canada* 121 P8
Slatina 73 H3 — Sniardwy, Jezioro 71 J2 — Soltau 70 C2 — Sousse 101 H1
Slave 119 N4 — Snina 71 K4 — Soltsy 78 E4 — South Africa, Republic of 108 D6
Slave Lake 119 N4 — Snizort, Loch 56 B3 — Solvesborg 63 F8 — Southampton *U.K.* 53 F4
Slavgorod *Russia* 84 B6 — Snodland 53 H3 — Solway Firth 55 F2 — Southampton *U.S.A.* 125 P6
Slavgorod *Ukraine* 79 F6 — Snohetta 62 C5 — Solwezi 106 E5 — Southampton Island 120 K5
Slavo 85 Q6 — Snoqualmie Pass 122 D4 — Soma 76 B3 — Southampton Water 53 F4
Slavyanka 88 C4 — Snoul 93 L6 — Soma 89 H7 — South Andaman 93 H6
Slavyansk-na-Kubani 79 F6 — Snowdon 54 E3 — Somalia 103 J6 — South Baldy 127 J4
Slawno 71 G1 — Snowtown 113 H5 — Sombor 72 E3 — South Baymouth 124 J4
Slawoborze 70 F2 — Snowville 122 H7 — Sombrerete 130 H6 — South Bend *Indiana* 124 G6
Slea 55 J3 — Snowy, Mount 122 G3 — Sombrero Channel 93 H7 — South Bend *Washington* 122 C4
Sleaford 53 G2 — Snug Corner 133 L3 — Somerset *Kentucky* 124 H8 — South Benfleet 53 H3
Sleat, Sound of 57 C3 — Snyatyn 73 H1 — Somerset *Pennsylvania* 125 L6 — Southborough 53 H3
Sleetmute 118 D3 — Snyder 127 M4 — Somerset *U.K.* 52 D3 — South Boston 125 L8
Sleights 55 J2 — Soalala 109 J3 — Somerset East 108 E6 — South Canadian 128 D3
Slidell 128 H5 — Soalara 109 H4 — Somerset Island 120 H3 — South Cape *Fiji* 114 R8
Slieve Anieren 58 G4 — Soan Kundo 87 P5 — Somerton 52 E3 — South Cape *U.S.A.* 126 T11
Slieveanorra 58 K2 — Soa Pan 108 E4 — Somerville Reservoir 128 D5 — South Carolina 129 M3
Slieveardagh Hills 59 G7 — Soar 53 F2 — Somes 73 G2 — South China Sea 87 L7
Slieve Aughty Mountains 59 E6 — Soa-Siu 91 H5 — Somes Point 115 F6 — South Creake 53 H2
Slieve Beagh 58 H4 — Soavinandriana 109 J3 — Somme 64 D3 — South Dakota 123 N5
Slieve Bloom Mountains 59 G6 — Soay 57 B3 — Sommerda 70 D3 — South Dorset Downs 52 E4
Slieve Callan 59 D7 — Soay Sound 57 B3 — Somosomo 114 S8 — South Downs 53 G4
Slieve Car 58 C4 — Sobat 103 F6 — Sompolno 71 H2 — Southeast Cape 118 B3
Slieve Donard 58 L4 — Sobinka 78 F4 — Somport, Puerto de 67 F1 — South East Cape 113 K6
Slieve Elva 59 D6 — Sobopol 85 M3 — Somuncura, Meseta de 139 C8 — Southend 119 Q4
Slieve Gamph 58 E4 — Sobradinho, Barragem de 137 J5 — Son 92 F4 — Southend-on-Sea 53 H3
Slieve Kimalta 59 F7 — Sobrado 137 G5 — Sonakh 85 P6 — Southern Alps 115 C5
Slieve League 58 E3 — Sobral *Acre, Brazil* 136 C5 — Sonapur 92 F4 — Southern Cross 112 D5
Slieve Mish Mountains 59 C8 — Sobral *Ceara, Brazil* 137 J4 — Sonara 127 M5 — Southern Indian Lake 119 R4
Slieve Miskish 58 C9 — Sobv'yevsk 85 K7 — Sonderborg 63 C9 — Southern Pine Hills 128 H5
Slieve Na Calliagh 58 H5 — Soca 72 B2 — Sondre Strmfjord 120 R4 — Southern Pines 129 N3
Slieve Rushen 58 G4 — Socha 136 C2 — Sondrio 68 B2 — Southern Uplands 57 E5
Slieve Snaght 58 H2 — Sochi 79 F7 — Songea 107 G5 — Southery 53 H2
Sligo *Ireland* 58 E4 — Societe, Iles de la 143 H5 — Songhua 88 B2 — South Esk 57 E4
Sligo *Ireland* 58 F4 — Socorro *Colombia* 136 C2 — Songhua Jiang 87 P2 — South Foreland 53 J3
Sligo Bay 58 E4 — Socorro *U.S.A.* 127 J4 — Songjin 88 B5 — South Forty Foot Drain 53 G2
Slioch 56 C3 — Socorro, Isla 130 D8 — Songkhla 93 K7 — South Geomagnetic Pole 141 H3
Slipper Island 115 E2 — Socotra 97 P10 — Songololo 106 B4 — South Georgia 139 J10
Sliven 73 J4 — Soda Lake 126 D3 — Sonhat 92 F4 — South Glamorgan 52 D3
Slobodchikovo 78 H3 — Sodankyla 62 M3 — Sonid Youqi 87 L3 — South Harbour 56 A2
Slobodka 73 K2 — Soda Springs 122 J6 — Sonid Zuoqi 87 L3 — |

Name	Page	Grid
Taganrog	79	F6
Taganrogskiy Zaliv	79	F6
Tagbilaran	91	G4
Taghmon	59	J8
Tagliamento	68	D3
Tagolo Point	91	G4
Tagounite	100	D3
Tagu	73	H2
Taguatinga	138	H6
Tagudin	91	G2
Tagula	114	E4
Tagula Island	114	E4
Tagum	91	H4
Tagus	66	C3
Tahan, Gunung	90	C5
Tahat, Mont	101	G4
Ta He	87	N1
Tahe	87	N1
Taheri	95	L8
Tahiryuak Lake	119	N1
Tahiti	143	J5
Tahlab, Dasht-i-	92	B3
Tahlequah	128	E3
Tahoe Lake *Canada*	119	P1
Tahoe, Lake *U.S.A.*	122	E8
Tahoka	127	M4
Tahoua	101	G6
Tahrud	95	N7
Tahta	102	F2
Tahtali Daglari	77	G3
Tahuamanu	136	D6
Tahulandang	91	H5
Taian	87	M4
Taibai Shan	93	L2
Taibus Qi	87	M3
Tai-chung	87	N7
Taier	115	C6
Taieri	115	C6
Taigu	87	L4
Taihape	115	E3
Taihe *Anhui, China*	93	N2
Taihe *Jiangxi, China*	93	M3
Tai Hu	87	N5
Taimba	84	F4
Tain	56	D3
Tai-nan	87	N7
Tainaron, Akra	75	G4
Taining	87	M6
Taipale	62	N5
Tai-pei	87	N6
Taiping	90	C5
Taipingbao	86	J4
Taipinggou	88	C1
Taira	89	H7
Taisei	88	G4
Taisha	89	D8
Taitao, Peninsula de	139	B9
Tai-tung	87	N7
Taivalkoski	62	N4
Taiwan	87	N7
Taiwan Haixia	87	M7
Taiyetos Oros	75	G4
Taiyuan	87	L4
Taiza	89	E8
Taizhou	87	M5
Taizz	96	G10
Tajabad	95	M6
Tajikistan	86	B4
Tajima	89	G7
Tajin-dong	88	B5
Tajito	126	F5
Tajo	66	D3
Tajrish	95	K4
Tajumuclo, Volcan de	132	B7
Tajuna	66	E2
Tak	93	J5
Takab	94	H3
Takada	89	G7
Takaka	115	D4
Takamatsu	89	E8
Takanabe	89	C9
Takaoka	89	F7
Takapuna	115	E2
Takasaki	89	G7
Takatshwane	108	D4
Takaungu	107	G3
Takayama	89	F7
Takefu	89	F8
Takengon	90	B5
Takeo	93	K6
Takestan	95	J3
Takhadid	94	G7
Takhi-i-Suleiman	95	K3
Takhta Bazar	95	R4
Takhtabrod	84	Ae6
Takikawa	88	H4
Takinoue	88	J3
Taklimakan Shamo	92	F1
Taku	118	J4
Takum	105	G4
Takwa	114	K6
Talagang	92	D2
Talamanca, Cordillera de	132	F10
Talangbetutu	90	C6
Talara	136	A4
Talar-i-Band	92	B3
Talas	86	C3
Talasea	114	E3
Talaton	52	D4
Talaud, Kepulauan	91	H5
Talavera de la Reina	66	D3
Talayuelas	67	F3
Talbot Inlet	120	L2
Talca	139	B7
Talcahuano	139	B7
Talcher	92	G4
Taldy-Kurgan	86	D2
Talgarth	52	D3
Taliabu	91	G6
Talihina	128	E3
Tali Post	102	F6
Talisay	91	G3
Talitsa	84	Ad5
Taliwang	91	F7
Talkeetna	118	E3
Talkeetna Mountains	118	F3
Talladega	129	J4
Tall Afar	77	K4
Tallahassee	129	K5
Tallinn	63	L7
Tall Kalakh	77	G5
Tall Kayf	77	K4
Tall Kujik	77	K4
Tallow	59	F8
Tall Tamir	77	J4
Talmenka	84	C6
Talnoye	79	E6
Taloda	92	D4
Talodi	102	F5
Talok	91	F5
Talovka	84	E5
Taloye	85	M4
Talsi	63	K8
Taltal	138	B5
Taltson	119	N3
Talu	114	F3
Taluma	85	L5
Talvik	62	K1
Tama	124	D6
Tamabo Range	90	F5
Tamale	104	E4
Tamames	66	C2
Tamana	111	S2
Tamano	89	D8
Tamanrasset *Algeria*	100	F4
Tamanrasset *Algeria*	101	G4
Tamar *Australia*	113	K7
Tamar *U.K.*	52	C4
Tamar, Alto de	133	K11
Tamarite de Litera	67	G2
Tamatave	109	J3
Tamaulipas, Llanos de	128	C8
Tamazunchale	131	K7
Tambacounda	104	C3
Tambangsawah	90	C6
Tambelan, Kepulauan	90	D5
Tambey	84	A2
Tambo	113	K3
Tambora, Gunung	91	F7
Tamboril	137	J4
Tambov	79	G5
Tambre	66	B1
Tambura	102	E6
Tamchaket	100	C5
Tame	136	C2
Tamega	66	C2
Tamiahua, Laguna de	131	L7
Tamil Nadu	92	E6
Tamis	72	F3
Tamit, Wadi	101	J2
Tammerfors	63	M6
Tammisaari	63	K6
Tampa	129	L7
Tampa Bay	129	L7
Tampere	63	M6
Tampico	131	L6
Tamsagbulag	87	M2
Tamuin	131	K7
Tamworth *Australia*	113	L5
Tamworth *U.K.*	53	F2
Tana *Chile*	138	C3
Tana *Kenya*	107	H3
Tana *Norway*	62	M1
Tanabe	89	E9
Tana bru	62	N2
Tanafjorden	62	N1
Tana Hayk	103	G5
Tanahbala	90	B6
Tanahgrogot	90	F6
Tanahjampea	91	G7
Tanahmasa	90	B6
Tanahmerah	114	C3
Tanah Merah	90	C4
Tanami	112	F3
Tanana	118	E2
Tananarive	109	J3
Tanchon	88	B5
Tandag	91	H4
Tandek	91	F4
Tandil	139	E7
Tando Adam	92	C3
Tandragee	58	K4
Taneatua	115	F3
Tanega-shima	89	C10
Tan Emellel	101	G3
Tanen Tong Dan	93	J5
Tanew	71	K3
Tanezrouft	100	E4
Tanf, Jbel al	77	H6
Tanga *Tanzania*	107	G4
Tanga *Russia*	85	J6
Tanga Islands	114	E2
Tanganyika, Lake	107	F4
Tangarare	114	J6
Tanger	100	D1
Tanggula Shan	93	G2
Tanggula Shankou	93	H2
Tangra Yumco	92	G2
Tangshan	87	M4
Tangwang He	88	B2
Tangwanghe	88	B1
Tangyuan	88	B2
Tan Hill	53	F3
Tanhua	62	M3
Taniantaweng Shan	93	J2
Tanimbar, Kepulauan	114	A3
Tanjung	90	F6
Tanjungbalai	90	B5
Tanjungkarang Telukbetung	90	D7
Tanjungpandan	90	D6
Tanjungpura	90	B5
Tanjungredeb	91	F5
Tanjungselor	91	F5
Tankapirtti	62	M2
Tankovo	84	D4
Tankse	92	E2
Tanlovo	84	A3
Tanna	114	U13
Tannu Ola	84	E6
Tannurah, Ra's	97	K3
Tanout	101	G6
Tan-shui	87	N6
Tanta	102	F1
Tan-Tan	100	C3
Tantoyuca	131	K7
Tanumshede	63	D7
Tanzania	107	G4
Tao He	93	K2
Tao, Ko	93	J6
Taolanaro	109	J5
Taormina	69	E7
Taos	127	K2
Taoudenni	100	E4
Taourirt	100	E2
Tapa	63	L7
Tapachula	131	N10
Tapah	90	C5
Tapajos	137	F4
Tapaktuan	90	B5
Tapan	90	D6
Tapanahoni	137	F3
Tapaua	136	D5
Taperoa	137	K6
Tappahannock	125	M8
Tappi-saki	88	H5
Tapsuy	78	L3
Tapti	92	D4
Tapuaenuku	115	D4
Tapul Group	91	G4
Taqah	97	M8
Taqtaq	94	G4
Taquari	138	E3
Taquari, Pantanal do	138	E3
Tara	84	A5
Tarabulus	101	H2
Taradale	115	F3
Tara, Hill of	58	J5
Tarakan	91	F5
Tarakli	76	D2
Tarakliya	73	K3
Taramana	91	G7
Taramo-jima	89	G11
Taran	84	A2
Tarancon	66	E2
Taransay	56	A3
Taransay, Sound of	56	A3
Taranto	69	F5
Taranto, Golfo di	69	F5
Tarapoto	136	B5
Tararua Range	115	E4
Tarascon	65	F7
Tarasovo	78	H2
Tarauaca *Brazil*	136	C5
Tarauaca *Brazil*	136	C5
Taravo	69	B5
Tarazona	67	F2
Tarazona de la Mancha	67	F3
Tarbagatay, Khrebet	86	E2
Tarbert *Ireland*	59	D7
Tarbert *Strathclyde, U.K.*	57	C5
Tarbert *Western Isles, U.K.*	56	B3
Tarbes	65	D7
Tarbet	57	D4
Tarbolton	57	D5
Tarboro	129	P3
Tarcaului, Muntii	73	J2
Tarcoola	113	G5
Tardienta	67	F2
Tardoki-yani, Gora	88	F1
Taree	113	L5
Tarendo	62	K3
Tareya	84	E2
Tarfa, Ra's at	96	F8
Tarfa, Wadi el	103	F2
Tarfaya	100	C3
Tarfside	57	F4
Targhee Pass	122	J5
Tarhunah	101	H2
Tarif	97	L4
Tarifa	66	D4
Tarija	138	D4
Tariku	114	B2
Tarim	97	J8
Tarim Basin	86	E3
Tarim He	86	E3
Tarim Pendi	86	E3
Taritatu	114	B2
Tarkasale	84	A3
Tarkastad	108	E6
Tarkhankut, Mys	79	E6
Tarkio	124	C6
Tarkwa	104	E4
Tarlac	91	G2
Tarlak	86	E3
Tarleton	55	G3
Tarma	136	B6
Tarn	65	D7
Tarna	72	F2
Tarnaby	62	F4
Tarnobrzeg	71	J3
Tarnow	71	J4
Tarnsjo	63	G6
Taro	68	B3
Taron	114	E2
Taroom	113	K4
Taroudannt	100	D2
Tarporley	55	G3
Tarragona	67	G2
Tarrasa	67	H2
Tarrega	67	G2
Tarsus	76	F4
Tartagal	138	D4
Tartas	65	C7
Tartu	63	P7
Tartung	90	B5
Tartus	94	B4
Tartus	77	F5
Tarutino	73	K2
Tarzout	67	G4
Tasci	77	F3
Tashakta	86	F2
Tashigang	93	H3
Tashk, Daryacheh-ye	95	L7
Tashkent	86	B3
Tashkepri	95	R3
Tashla	79	J5
Tashtagol	84	D6
Tasikmalaya	90	D7
Tasiujaq	121	N6
Taskesken	86	E2
Taskopru	76	F2
Tas-Kumsa	85	N3
Taslicay	77	K3
Tasman Bay	115	D4
Tasmania	113	K7
Tasman Mountains	115	D4
Tasnad	73	G2
Tasova	77	G2
Tas-Tumus	85	N2
Tasty	86	B3
Tasucu	76	E4
Tasuj	77	L3
Tataba	91	G6
Tatabanya	72	E2
Tatarbunary	73	K3
Tatarka	84	B5
Tatarsk	84	B5
Tataurovo	85	J6
Tateyama	89	G8
Tathlina Lake	119	M3
Tathlith	96	F7
Tathlith, Wadi	96	F6
Tatnam, Cape	119	S4
Tatry	71	H4
Tatsinskiy	79	G6
Tatsuno	89	E8
Tatta	92	C4
Tatum	127	L4
Tatvan	77	K3
Tau	111	V4
Tauari	137	F4
Taubate	138	G4
Tauchik	79	J7
Taumarunui	115	E3
Taung-gyi	93	J4
Taungnyo Range	93	J5
Taunton *U.K.*	52	D3
Taunton *U.S.A.*	125	Q6
Taunus	70	C3
Taupo	115	F3
Taupo, Lake	115	E3
Tauq	94	G4
Tauq	77	L5
Tauranga	115	F2
Tauroa Point	115	D1
Taurus	76	E4
Tauste	67	F2
Tau Islands	114	F2
Tavalesh, Kuhha-ye	94	J3
Tavana-i-Tholo	111	T6
Tavas	76	C4
Tavda *Russia*	84	Ad5
Tavda *Russia*	84	Ae5
Taverner Bay	120	M4
Taveuni	114	S8
Tavira	66	C4
Tavistock	52	C4
Tavolara, Isola di	69	B5
Tavoy	93	J6
Tavrichanka	88	C4
Tavsanli	76	C3
Tavua	114	Q8
Tavuna-i-Ra	111	T6
Tavy	52	D4
Taw	52	D4
Tawakoni, Lake	128	E4
Tawau	91	F5
Tawe	52	D3
Taweisha	102	E5
Tawila	96	A3
Tawil, At	96	D2
Tawitawi Group	91	G4
Ta-wu	87	N7
Tawurgha, Sabkhat	101	J2

Taxco	131	K8
Taxkorgan	92	E1
Tay	57	E4
Tayandu, Kepulauan	91	J7
Tayastehus	63	L6
Tayeeglow	107	H2
Tay, Firth of	57	E4
Tayga	84	D5
Tayinloan	57	C5
Tay, Loch	57	D4
Taylor	123	Q7
Taylor Island	119	Q2
Taylor, Mount	127	J3
Taylorville	124	F7
Tayma	96	D3
Taymura	84	F4
Taymyr	84	E3
Taymyr, Ozero	84	G2
Taymyr, Poluostrov	84	F2
Tay Ninh	93	L6
Taynuilt	57	C4
Tayport	57	F4
Tayshet	84	F5
Tayshir	86	H2
Tayside	57	E4
Taysiyah, At	96	F2
Taytay	91	F3
Tayyebad	95	Q4
Taz Russia	84	B3
Taz Russia	84	C3
Taza	100	E2
Tazin Lake	119	P4
Tazirbu	101	K3
Tbilisi	77	L2
Tchad, Lac	102	B5
Tchibanga	106	B3
Tczew	71	H1
Teaca	73	H2
Te Anau	115	A6
Te Anau, Lake	115	A6
Te Anga	115	E3
Te Aroha	115	E2
Te Awamutu	115	E2
Tebesjuak Lake	119	R3
Tebessa	101	G1
Tebingtinggi Indonesia	90	B5
Tebingtinggi Indonesia	90	C6
Teboursouk	69	B7
Tecate	126	D4
Techirghiol	73	K3
Tecirli	77	G4
Tecoman	130	H8
Tecuci	73	J3
Tedelkynak	84	C4
Tedzhen	95	Q3
Teeapo, Lake	115	C5
Tees	55	H2
Tees Bay	55	H2
Teesdale	55	H2
Tefe Brazil	136	D4
Tefe Brazil	136	E4
Tefenni	76	C4
Tegal	90	D7
Tegid, Llyn	52	D2
Tegua	114	T10
Tegucigalpa	132	D7
Tehachapi Mountains	126	C3
Tehachapi Pass	126	C3
Te Haroto	115	F3
Tehek Lake	119	R2
Tehert	119	R2
Tehoru	91	H6
Tehran	95	K4
Tehuacan	131	L8
Tehuantepec Mexico	131	M9
Tehuantepec Mexico	131	M9
Tehuantepec, Golfo de	131	M10
Teign	52	D4
Teignmouth	52	D4
Tejo	66	C3
Te Karaka	115	F3
Tekeze	96	C9
Tekin	88	D1
Tekirdag	76	B2
Tekman	77	J3
Te Kopuru	115	D2
Te Kuiti	115	E3
Tela	132	D7
Tel Ali	77	K5
Telavi	77	L2
Tel Aviv-Yafo	94	B5
Telegraph Creek	118	J4
Telekhany	71	L2
Telemark	63	C7
Telemba	85	J6
Telen	139	C7
Telen	90	F5
Teleorman	73	H3
Telescope Peak	126	D2
Teles Pires	136	F5
Telford	52	E2
Teli	84	E6
Telimele	104	C3
Tell City	124	G8
Tellicherry	92	E6
Telposiz, Gora	78	K3
Telsen	139	C8
Telsiai	63	K9
Teluk Anson	90	C5
Telukbatang	90	D6
Telukdalam	90	B5
Tem	84	G5
Tema	104	E4

Temagami, Lake	125	K3
Temascaltepec	131	K8
Tembenchi	84	F4
Tembleque	66	E3
Tembo Aluma	106	C4
Teme	52	E2
Temerin	72	E3
Temerloh	90	C5
Temirtau	86	C2
Temiscamingve, Lac	125	L3
Temnikov	78	G5
Temnyy	85	K6
Tempe	126	G4
Tempio Pausania	69	B5
Temple	128	D5
Templemore	59	G7
Tempoal	131	K7
Tempue	106	C5
Temryuk	79	F6
Temuco	139	B7
Temuka	115	C6
Tena	136	B4
Tenali	92	F5
Tenasserim	93	J6
Tenbury Wells	52	E2
Tenby	52	C3
Tende	68	A3
Ten Degree Channel	93	H7
Tendelti	103	F5
Tendrovskaya Kosa	79	E6
Tenduruk Dagi	77	K3
Tenerife	100	B3
Tenes	100	F1
Tenevo	73	J4
Tengahdai	91	G7
Tengchong	93	J3
Tenggarong	90	F6
Tengiz, Ozero	84	Ae6
Teng, Nam	93	J4
Teng Xian	87	M4
Teniente Rodolfo Marsh	141	W6
Tenkasi	92	E7
Tenke	106	E5
Tenkodogo	104	E3
Tennant Creek	113	G2
Tennessee U.S.A.	129	H2
Tennessee U.S.A.	129	J2
Tennessee Pass	123	L8
Tenniojoki	62	N3
Tenosique	131	P9
Tenquehuen, Isla	139	B9
Tensift, Oued	100	D2
Tenterden	53	H3
Tenterfield	113	L4
Teofilo Otoni	138	E3
Teouta	114	X16
Tepasto	62	L2
Tepatitlan	130	H7
Tepebasi	76	E4
Tepecikoren	77	F4
Tepeji	131	K8
Tepelene	74	F2
Tepic	130	G7
Teplice	70	E3
Teplik	73	K1
Tepoca, Cabo	126	F5
Te Puke	115	F2
Ter	67	H2
Tera	66	C2
Teramo	69	D4
Terasa	93	H7
Tercan	77	J3
Teren-Uzyak	86	A2
Teresina	137	J5
Teresita	136	D3
Teresopolis	138	H4
Teriberka	78	F2
Terme	77	G2
Termez	80	H6
Termini Imerese	69	D7
Terminillo	69	D4
Terminos, Laguna de	131	P8
Termoli	69	E4
Ternate	91	H5
Terneuzen	64	E3
Terney	88	F3
Terni	69	D4
Ternopil	79	D6
Terpeniya, Mys	85	Q7
Terpeniya, Zaliv	85	Q7
Terrace	118	K5
Terrace Bay	124	G2
Terracina	69	D5
Terrak	62	E4
Terralba	69	B6
Terre Adelie	141	K7
Terre Haute	124	G7
Terrell	128	D4
Terschelling	64	F2
Terskiy Bereg	78	F2
Teruel	67	F2
Terutao	93	J7
Tervel	73	J4
Tervo	62	M5
Teseney	103	G4
Teshekpuk Lake	118	E1
Teshio	88	H3
Teshio-sammyaku	88	H4
Tesica	73	F4
Tesiyn Gol	86	H2
Teslin Canada	118	J3
Teslin Canada	118	J3
Tesouro	138	F3
Tessalit	100	F4

Tessaoua	101	G6
Test	53	F3
Testa, Capo	69	B5
Testa del Gargano	69	F5
Tet	65	E7
Tetbury	53	E3
Tete	109	F3
Tetepare	114	H6
Tetere	84	G4
Teterow	70	E2
Tetouan	100	D1
Tetovo	73	F4
Te Tungano	114	K7
Teulada	69	B6
Teulada, Capo	69	B6
Teun	91	H7
Tevere	69	D4
Teverya	94	B5
Teviot	57	F5
Tevriz	84	A5
Te Waewae Bay	115	A7
Te Whanga Lagoon	115	F6
Tewkesbury	53	E3
Tewo	93	K2
Texada Islands	122	B3
Texarkana	128	E4
Texas	127	M5
Texas City	128	E6
Texcoco	131	K8
Texel	64	F2
Texoma, Lake	128	D4
Teykovo	78	G4
Teziutlan	131	L8
Tezpur	93	H3
Tha-anne	119	R3
Thabana Ntlenyana	108	E5
Thabazimbi	108	E4
Thadiq	96	G4
Thai Binh	93	L4
Thailand	93	K5
Thailand, Gulf of	93	K7
Thai Nguyen	93	L4
Thakhek	93	K5
Thal	92	D2
Thalab, Dasht-i	95	Q7
Thal Desert	92	D2
Thale Luang	93	K7
Thamarit	97	M8
Thame	53	G3
Thames Canada	124	J5
Thames New Zealand	115	E2
Thames U.K.	53	H3
Thamud	97	J8
Thane	92	D5
Thanet, Isle of	53	J3
Thanh Hoa	93	L5
Thanjavur	92	E6
Thankerton	57	E5
Thann	65	G5
Thano Bula Khan	92	C3
Tharabwin	93	J6
Tharad	92	D4
Thar Desert	92	D3
Thargomindah	113	J4
Tharrawaddy	93	J5
Tharthar	77	K5
Tharthar, Wadi ath	77	K5
Thasos Greece	75	H2
Thasos Greece	75	H2
Thatcham	53	F3
Thaton	93	J5
Thaungdut	93	H4
Thayetmyo	93	J5
Thazi	93	J4
Thebes	75	G3
Thedford	123	P7
Thelon	119	Q3
Thenia	67	H4
Theniet El Had	67	H5
Theodore Roosevelt Reservoir	126	G4
Thermaikos Kolpos	75	G2
Thermia	75	H4
Thermon	75	F3
Thermopolis	123	K6
Thessalon	124	J3
Thessaloniki	75	G2
Thetford	53	H2
Thetford Mines	125	Q3
Thiamis	75	F3
Thibodaux	128	G6
Thief River Falls	124	B2
Thiel Mountains	141	U1
Thierache	64	F4
Thiers	65	E6
Thies	104	B3
Thiladummathi Atoll	92	D7
Thimbu	93	G3
Thimphu	93	G3
Thio	114	X16
Thionville	64	G4
Thira Greece	75	H4
Thira Greece	75	H4
Thirasia	75	H4
Thirsk	55	H2
Thisted	63	C8
Thivai	75	G3
Thiviers	65	D6
Thlewiaza	119	R3
Thohoyandou	108	F4
Thomaston	129	K4
Thomastown	59	H7
Thomasville Alabama	129	J5
Thomasville Georgia	129	L5

Thompson British Columbia, Canada	119	L5
Thompson Manitoba, Canada	119	R4
Thompson U.S.A.	124	C6
Thompson Sound	115	A6
Thomson Australia	113	J3
Thomson U.S.A.	129	L4
Thonon-les-Bains	65	G5
Thornaby	55	H2
Thornbury	52	E3
Thornby	53	F2
Thorndon	53	J2
Thorne	55	J3
Thorney	53	G2
Thornhill	57	E5
Thornley	55	H2
Thornton	55	F3
Thouars	65	C5
Thouet	65	C5
Thrakikon Pelagos	75	H2
Thrapston	53	G2
Three Forks	122	J5
Three Kings Islands	111	R8
Three Points, Cape	104	E5
Three Rivers Michigan	124	H6
Three Rivers Texas	128	C6
Three Sisters Islands	114	K7
Threshfield	55	G2
Throsell Range	112	E3
Thueyts	65	F6
Thuin	64	F3
Thule	120	N2
Thun	68	A2
Thunder Bay	124	F2
Thunder Mount	118	C2
Thung Song	93	J7
Thuringer Wald	70	D3
Thurles	59	G7
Thurloo Downs	113	J4
Thurnscoe	55	H3
Thursby	55	F2
Thurso U.K.	56	E2
Thurso U.K.	56	E2
Thurston Island	141	T4
Thusis	68	B2
Thwaites Glacier	141	S3
Tiancang	86	H3
Tianchang	87	M5
Tiandong	93	L4
Tiane	93	L3
Tiangua	137	J4
Tianjin	87	M4
Tianjun	93	J1
Tianqiaoling	88	B4
Tianshui	93	L2
Tianyang	93	L4
Tianzhen	87	L3
Tianzhu	93	K1
Tiaret	100	F1
Tibati	105	H4
Tiber	69	D4
Tiberias	94	B5
Tibesti	102	C3
Tibet	92	F2
Tibet, Plateau of	92	F2
Tiboku Falls	136	F2
Tiburon, Isla	126	F6
Tichitt	100	D5
Ticino	68	B3
Ticul	131	Q7
Tidaholm	63	E7
Tidjikdja	100	C5
Tieli	88	B2
Tieling	87	N3
Tien Shan	86	D3
Tien Yen	93	L4
Tierp	63	G6
Tierra Amarilla	127	J2
Tierra Blanca	131	L8
Tierra del Fuego, Isla Grande de	139	C10
Tietar	66	D2
Tiete	138	F4
Tifton	129	L5
Tifu	91	H6
Tiger	122	F3
Tigharry	56	A3
Tighina	79	D6
Tigil Russia	85	T5
Tigil Russia	85	T5
Tignish	121	P8
Tigre Peru	136	B4
Tigre Venezuela	136	E2
Tigres, Baia dos	106	B6
Tigris	94	H6
Tigzerte, Oued	100	D3
Tigzirt	67	J4
Tihamat ash Sham	96	E7
Tihamat Asir	96	F8
Tihsimir	77	J3
Tijoca	137	H4
Tijuana	126	D4
Tikal	132	C6
Tikamgarh	92	E4
Tikanlik	86	F3
Tikhoretsk	79	G6
Tikhvin	78	E4
Tikitiki	115	G2
Tikopica	111	Q4
Tikrit	77	K5
Tiksi	85	M2
Tilburg	64	F3
Tilbury	53	H3
Tilemsi, Vallee du	100	F5

Name	Page	Ref
Till	57	F5
Tillaberi	100	F6
Tillanchang	93	H7
Tillicoultry	57	E4
Tilomar	91	H7
Tilos	75	J4
Tilsit	71	J1
Tilt	57	E4
Timanskiy Kryazh	78	H3
Timar	77	K3
Timaru	115	C6
Timashevsk	79	F6
Timbakion	75	H5
Timbedra	100	D5
Timbo *Guinea*	104	C3
Timbo *Liberia*	104	D4
Timbuktu	100	E5
Timfristos	75	F3
Timimoun	100	F3
Timiris, Cap	100	B5
Timis	73	G3
Timisoara	73	F3
Timkapaul	84	Ad4
Timmernabben	63	G8
Timmins	125	K2
Timok	73	G3
Timolin	59	J7
Timor	91	H7
Timor, Laut	91	H7
Timoshino	78	F3
Timsher	78	J3
Tinaca Point	91	H4
Tinaco	133	N10
Tinahely	59	K7
Tinakula	114	M7
Tindivanam	92	E6
Tindouf	100	D3
Tineo	66	C1
Tinglev	63	C9
Tingo Maria	136	B5
Tingsryd	63	F8
Tingvoll	62	C5
Tinhare, Ilha de	137	K6
Tinogasta	138	C5
Tinompo	91	G5
Tinos *Greece*	75	H4
Tinos *Greece*	75	H4
Tintinara	113	J6
Tinto *Spain*	66	C4
Tinto *U.K.*	57	E5
Tinto Hills	57	E5
Tinwald	115	C5
Tiomilaskogen	63	E6
Tipaza	67	H4
Tipitapa	132	D8
Tippecanoe	124	G6
Tipperary *Ireland*	59	F8
Tipperary *Ireland*	59	G7
Tipton	124	H6
Tiptree	53	H3
Tiquicheo	131	J8
Tiracambu, Serra do	137	H4
Tiran	96	B3
Tirana	74	E2
Tirane	74	E2
Tirano	68	C2
Tiraspol	79	D6
Tire	76	B3
Tirebolu	77	H2
Tiree	57	C4
Tirga Mor	56	B3
Tirgoviste	73	H3
Tirgu Bujor	73	J3
Tirgu Carbunesti	73	G3
Tirgu Frumos	73	J2
Tirgu Jiu	73	G3
Tirgu Mures	73	H2
Tirgu Neamt	73	J2
Tirgu Ocna	73	J2
Tirich Mir	92	D1
Tirnava Mare	73	H2
Tirnava Mica	73	H2
Tirnavos	75	G3
Tirol	68	C2
Tirpul	95	Q4
Tirso	69	B6
Tirua Point	115	E3
Tiruchchirappalli	92	E6
Tirumangalam	92	E7
Tirunelveli	92	E7
Tirupati	92	E6
Tiruppur	92	E6
Tiruvannamalai	92	E6
Tisa	72	F3
Tisisat Falls	103	G5
Tissa	71	K4
Tissington	55	H3
Tista	93	G3
Tisza	72	F2
Tit-Ary	85	M2
Titchfield	53	F4
Titicaca, Lago	138	C3
Titograd	72	E4
Titova Mitrovica	73	F4
Titovo Uzice	72	E4
Titovo Velenje	72	C2
Titov Veles	73	F5
Titran	62	C5
Tittmoning	70	E4
Titu	73	H3
Titusville	129	M6
Tiumpan Head	56	B2
Tivaouane	104	B2
Tiveden	63	F7
Tiverton	52	D4
Tivoli	69	D5
Tiwi	97	P5
Tiyas	77	G5
Tizimin	131	Q7
Tizi Ouzou	101	F1
Tiznit	100	D3
Tjamotis	62	H3
Tjornuvik	62	Z14
Tjotta	62	E4
Tlaltenango	130	H7
Tlapa	131	K9
Tlapehuala	131	J8
Tlaxiaco	131	L9
Tlemcen	100	E2
Toad River	118	K4
Toamasina	109	J3
Tobago	133	S9
Toba Kakar Ranges	92	C2
Tobercurry	58	E4
Tobermory *Canada*	125	K4
Tobermory *U.K.*	57	B4
Toberonochy	57	C4
Tobi	91	J5
Tobin Lake	112	F3
Tobi-shima	88	G6
Toboali	90	D6
Tobol	84	Ae5
Tobolsk	84	Ae5
Tobseda	78	J2
Tobysh	78	J3
Tocache Nuevo	136	B5
Tocantins	137	H4
Toccoa	129	L3
Toco	133	S9
Toconao	138	C4
Tocopilla	138	B4
Tocuyo	133	N9
Todeli	91	G6
Todi	68	B2
Todi	69	D4
Todmorden	55	G3
Todog	86	E3
Todos os Santos, Baia de	137	K6
Todos Santos *Bolivia*	138	C3
Todos Santos *Mexico*	130	D6
Todos Santos, Bahia de	126	D5
Toe Head *Ireland*	59	D10
Toe Head *U.K.*	56	A3
Toetoes Bay	115	B7
Tofino	122	B3
Toft	56	A1
Tofte	63	D7
Tofua	111	T5
Toga	114	T10
Togi	89	F7
Togian, Kepulauan	91	G6
Togni	96	B7
Togo	104	F4
Togtoh	87	L3
Toguchi	89	H10
Togur	84	C5
Tohamiyam	103	G4
Tohatchi	127	H3
Tohma	77	G3
Toi-misaki	89	C10
Tojo	89	D8
Tok	118	G3
Tokachi	88	J4
Tokachi-Dake	88	J4
Tokaj	73	F1
Tokanui	115	B7
Tokar	103	G4
Tokara-kaikyo	89	C10
Tokara-retto	89	B11
Tokat	77	G2
Tokelau	111	U3
Tokiwa	88	J3
Tokke	63	C7
Toklar	77	G3
Tokmak	86	D3
Tokolon	84	H5
Tokoro	88	K3
Tokoroa	115	E3
Toksun	86	F3
Tok-to	89	C7
Toktogul	86	C3
Tokuno-shima	89	J10
Tokushima	89	E8
Tokuyama	89	C8
Tokyo	89	G8
Tolar, Cerro	138	C5
Tolbonuur	86	G2
Tolbukhin	73	J4
Toledo *Spain*	66	D3
Toledo *U.S.A.*	124	J6
Toledo Bend Reservoir	128	F5
Toledo, Montes de	66	D3
Tolentino	68	D4
Toliara	109	H4
Tolitoli	91	G5
Tolka	84	C4
Tolmezzo	68	D2
Tolmin	72	B2
Tolochin	78	D5
Tolosa	67	E1
Tolo, Teluk	91	G6
Tolsta Head	56	B2
Tolstoye	73	H1
Tolstoy, Mys	85	T5
Toluca	131	K8
Toluca, Nevado de	131	K8
Tolyatti	79	H5
Tomah	124	E4
Tomahawk	124	F4
Tomakomai	88	H4
Tomani	90	F5
Tomaniivi	114	R8
Tomar *Portugal*	66	B3
Tomar *Kazakhstan*	86	D2
Tomari	88	J2
Tomarza	77	F3
Tomasevo	72	E4
Tomashevka	71	K3
Tomaszow Lubelski	71	K3
Tomaszow Mazowiecka	71	J3
Tombador, Serra do	136	F6
Tombe	103	F6
Tombigbee	129	H5
Tomboco	106	B4
Tombouctou	100	E5
Tombua	106	B6
Tomelilla	63	E9
Tomelloso	66	E3
Tomini, Teluk	91	G6
Tomioka	89	H7
Tomkinson Ranges	112	F4
Tomma	62	E3
Tommot	85	M5
Tomo	136	D2
Tomochic	127	J6
Tompa	84	H5
Tompo	85	P4
Tomsk	84	D5
Tonbridge	53	H3
Tondano	91	G5
Tonder	70	C1
Tone	52	E3
Tonelagee	59	K6
Tonga	111	U6
Tonga *Sudan*	102	F6
Tongariro	115	E3
Tongatapu	111	U6
Tongatapu Group	111	T6
Tonga Trench	143	H5
Tongcheng	93	M3
Tongchuan	93	L1
Tongdao	93	L3
Tonggu	93	M3
Tongguan	93	M2
Tonghai	93	K4
Tonghe	88	B2
Tonghua	87	P3
Tongjiang	88	D2
Tongking, Gulf of	93	L5
Tongliao	87	N3
Tongling	87	M5
Tonglu	87	M6
Tongnae	89	B8
Tongoa	114	U12
Tongren	93	L3
Tongtianheyan	93	H2
Tongue *U.K.*	56	D2
Tongue *U.S.A.*	123	L5
Tongue, Kyle of	56	D2
Tongue of the Ocean	132	J2
Tong Xian	87	M4
Tongxin	93	L1
Tongyu	87	N3
Tongzi	93	L3
Tonichi	127	H6
Tonk	92	E3
Tonkabon	95	K3
Tonle Sap	93	K6
Tonneins	65	D6
Tonnerre	65	E5
Tono	88	H6
Tonopah	126	D2
Tonosi	132	G11
Tonsberg	63	D7
Tonstad	63	B7
Tonya	77	H2
Tooele	122	H7
Toowoomba	113	L4
Topeka	124	C7
Toplane	74	E1
Toplica	73	F4
Toplita	73	H2
Topocalma, Punta	138	B6
Topola	72	F3
Topolcani	73	F5
Topoli	79	J6
Topolkki	63	N6
Topolovgrad	73	J4
Topozero, Ozero	62	P4
Toppenish	122	D4
Toprakli	76	F3
Toraka Vestale	109	H3
Tora-Khem	84	F6
Torbali	76	B3
Torbat-e Heydariyeh	95	P4
Torbat-e Jam	95	Q4
Tor Bay *Australia*	112	D5
Tor Bay *U.K.*	52	D4
Tordesillas	66	D2
Tore	56	D3
Tore	62	K4
Torfastadir	62	U12
Torgau	70	E3
Torgo	85	K5
Torhout	64	E3
Torino	68	A3
Torkaman	94	H2
Tormes	66	D2
Tornealven	62	K3
Tor Ness	56	E2
Torne-trask	62	H2
Torngat Mountains	121	P6
Tornio	62	L4
Toro, Cerro de	138	C5
Toroiaga	73	H2
Torokina	114	F3
Torokszentmiklos	72	F2
Toronaios, Kolpos	75	G2
Toronto	125	L5
Toropets	78	E4
Tororo	107	F2
Toros Dagi	76	F4
Toros Daglari	76	E4
Torpoint	52	C4
Torquay	52	D4
Torrance	126	C4
Torrao	66	B3
Torre Annunziata	69	E5
Torre Baja	67	F2
Torreblanca	67	G2
Torrecilla en Cameros	66	E1
Torre del Greco	69	E5
Torrelaguna	66	E2
Torrelavega	66	D1
Torremolinos	66	D4
Torrens Creek	113	K3
Torrens, Lake	113	H5
Torrente	67	F3
Torreon	127	L8
Torres Island	114	T10
Torres Novas	66	B3
Torres Strait	114	C4
Torres Vedras	66	B3
Torrevieja	67	F4
Torr Head	58	K2
Torridge	52	C4
Torridon, Loch	56	C3
Torrijos	66	D3
Torrington *Connecticut*	125	P6
Torrington *Wyoming*	123	M6
Torrox	66	E4
Torsas	63	F8
Torsby	63	E6
Torshavn	62	Z14
Torsken	62	L2
Tortkuduk	84	A6
Tortola	133	Q5
Tortona	68	B3
Tortosa	67	G2
Tortosa, Cabo de	67	G2
Tortue, Ile de la	133	L4
Tortuga, Isla	126	G7
Tortuga, Isla la	136	D1
Tortum	77	J2
Torul	77	H2
Torun	71	H2
Tory Island	58	F2
Torysa	71	J4
Tory Sound	58	F2
Torzhok	78	F4
Torzym	70	F2
Tosa-shimizu	89	D9
Tosa-wan	89	D9
Toscaig	56	C3
Tosco-Emiliano, Appennino	68	C3
Tostado	138	D5
Tosya	76	F2
Totana	67	F4
Totes	64	D4
Totma	78	G4
Totnes	52	D4
Totness	137	F2
Totora	138	C3
Totota	104	C4
Totoya	114	S9
Totton	53	F4
Tottori	89	E8
Touba	104	D4
Toubkal, Jebel	100	D2
Tougan	104	E3
Touggourt	101	G2
Touho Ouegoa	114	W16
Toul	64	F4
Toulon	65	F7
Toulouse	65	D7
Toummo	101	H4
Toumodi	104	D4
Toungoo	93	J5
Touraine	65	D5
Tourcoing	64	E3
Tournai	64	E3
Tournon *France*	65	D5
Tournon *France*	65	F6
Tournus	65	F5
Touros	137	K5
Tours	65	D5
Tousside, Pic	102	C3
Touws River	108	D6
Tovarkovskiy	79	F5
Towada	88	H5
Towanda	125	M6
Towcester	53	G2
Tower Island	136	B7
Towie	56	F3
Townsend	122	J4
Townshend Island	113	L3
Townsville	113	K2
Towson	125	M7
Toxkan He	86	D3
Toya-ko	88	H4
Toyama	89	F7
Toyama-wan	89	F7
Toyohashi	89	F8
Toyonaka	89	E8
Toyooka	89	E8

V

Name	Page	Grid
Vaajakoski	62	L5
Vaal	108	E5
Vaala	62	M4
Vaal Dam	108	E5
Vaasa *Finland*	62	J5
Vaasa *Finland*	62	K5
Vacaria	138	F5
Vacha	70	D3
Vache, Ile-a-	133	L5
Vadodara	92	D4
Vadso	62	N1
Vadu	73	K3
Vaduz	68	B2
Vaga	78	G3
Vagar	62	Z14
Vagay *Russia*	84	Ae5
Vagay *Russia*	84	Ae5
Vage	63	A6
Vaghena	114	H5
Vagnharad	63	G7
Vah	71	G5
Vaich, Loch	56	D3
Vainikkala	63	N6
Vaitupu	111	S3
Vakarel	73	G4
Vakfikebir	77	H2
Valaam, Ostrov	63	P6
Valandovo	73	G5
Valcheta	139	C8
Valday *Russia*	78	E4
Valday *Russia*	78	F3
Valdayskaya Vozvyshennost	78	E4
Valdemarsvik	63	G7
Valdepenas	66	E3
Valderaduey	66	D2
Valderrobres	67	G2
Valdes, Peninsula	139	D8
Valdez	118	F3
Valdivia	139	B7
Val-d'Or	125	M2
Valdosta	129	L5
Valdres	63	C6
Valea Lui Mihai	73	G2
Valenca	66	B2
Valenca	138	K6
Valenca do Piaui	137	J5
Valencay	65	D5
Valence	65	F6
Valencia *Spain*	67	F3
Valencia *Venezuela*	136	D1
Valencia de Alcantara	66	C3
Valencia de Don Juan	66	D1
Valencia, Golfo de	67	G3
Valencia Island	59	B9
Valencia, Lago de	133	P9
Valenciennes	64	E3
Valentim, Serra do	137	J5
Valentin	88	E4
Valentine	123	P6
Valenzuela	91	G3
Valera	136	C2
Valga	63	M8
Valiente, Peninsula	132	G10
Valjevo	72	E3
Valkininkay	71	L1
Valladolid *Mexico*	131	Q7
Valladolid *Spain*	66	D2
Vallasana de Mena	66	E1
Vallay	56	A3
Valle de la Pascua	136	D2
Valle de Santiago	131	J7
Valledupar	136	C1
Valle Grande	138	D3
Valle Hermosa	128	D8
Vallejo	126	A1
Vallenar	138	B5
Valletta	74	C5
Valley Falls	122	D6
Valleyview	119	M4
Vallgrund	62	J5
Vallimanca	139	D7
Vallo di Lucania	69	E5
Valls	67	G2
Valmiera	63	L8
Valognes	64	C4
Val-Paradis	125	L2
Valparaiso	129	J5
Valparaiso *Chile*	139	B6
Valparaiso *Mexico*	130	H6
Valpovo	72	E3
Valsjobyn	62	F4
Vals, Tanjung	114	B3
Valtos	56	B2
Valurfossen	63	B6
Valuyki	79	F5
Valverde	100	B3
Valverde de Jucar	66	E3
Valverde del Camino	66	C4
Van	77	K3
Vanadzor	77	L2
Vanajanselka	63	L6
Vanavona	114	H6
Van Buren *Arkansas*	128	E3
Van Buren *Maine*	125	S3
Van Canh	93	L6
Vancouver *Canada*	122	C3
Vancouver *U.S.A.*	122	C5
Vancouver Island	122	A2
Vanda	63	N6
Vandalia	124	F7
Vanderhoof	118	L5
Van Diemen, Cape	112	G1
Van Diemen Gulf	112	G1
Vanern	63	E7
Vanersborg	63	E7
Vanga	107	G3
Vangaindrano	109	J4
Van Golu	77	K3
Vangou	88	D4
Vangunu	114	J6
Van Horn	127	K5
Vanikoro Islands	114	N7
Vanimo	114	C2
Vanna	62	H1
Vannas	62	H5
Vannes	65	B5
Van Rees, Pegunungan	114	B2
Vanrock	113	J2
Vansbro	63	F6
Vanset	77	K4
Vansittart Island	120	K4
Vantaa	63	N6
Vanua Balavu	114	S8
Vanua Lava	114	T10
Vanua Levu	114	R8
Vanua Levu Barrier Reef	114	R8
Vanuatu	114	T12
Vanwyksvlei	108	D6
Vanzevat	84	Ae4
Vapnyarka	73	K1
Varallo	68	B3
Varamin	95	K4
Varanasi	92	F3
Varandey	78	K2
Varangerfjorden	62	P1
Varangerhalvoya	62	N1
Varazdin	72	D2
Varazze	68	B3
Varberg	63	E8
Vardar	73	F5
Varde	63	C9
Vardo	62	P1
Varena	71	L1
Varennes	65	E5
Varese	68	B3
Varfolomeyevka	88	D3
Vargarda	63	E7
Vargas Guerra	136	B4
Varginha	138	G4
Varilla	138	B4
Varkaus	63	L5
Varmland	63	E7
Varmlands-nas	63	E7
Varna	73	J4
Varnamo	63	F8
Varnek	84	Ad3
Varnya	84	A3
Varoy	62	E3
Varto	77	J3
Vartry Reservoir	59	K6
Varzea Grande	137	J5
Varzino	78	F2
Varzuga	78	F2
Varzy	65	E5
Vasa	62	J5
Vascao	66	C4
Vascongadas	66	E1
Vashkovtsy	73	H1
Vasilishki	71	L2
Vasilkov	79	E5
Vasilyevka	79	F6
Vaskha	78	H3
Vaslui	73	J2
Vassdalsegga	63	B7
Vasteras	63	G7
Vasterbotten	62	G4
Vasterdalalven	63	E6
Vastergotland	63	E7
Vasterhaninge	63	H7
Vasternorrland	62	G5
Vastervik	63	G8
Vastmanland	63	G7
Vasto	69	E4
Vasyugan	84	B5
Vatersay	57	A4
Vathi *Greece*	75	F3
Vathi *Greece*	75	J4
Vaticano, Capo	69	E6
Vatilau	114	J6
Vatnajokull	62	W12
Vatneyri	62	A2
Vatoa	111	T5
Vatomandry	109	J3
Vatra Dornei	73	H2
Vattern	63	F7
Vatu-i-Ra Channel	114	R8
Vatulele	114	Q9
Vaughn	127	K3
Vaupes	136	C3
Vavatenina	109	J3
Vavau Group	111	U5
Vavuniya	92	F7
Vaxholm	63	H7
Vaxjo	63	F8
Vayalpad	92	G6
Vaygach	84	Ac2
Vaygach, Ostrov	84	Ac2
Veberod	63	E9
Vebomark	62	J4
Vecht	64	G2
Vechta	70	C2
Vechte	70	B2
Veddige	63	E8
Vega *Norway*	62	D4
Vega *U.S.A.*	127	L3
Vegorritis, Limni	75	F2
Vegreville	119	N5
Veidholmen	62	B5
Veinge	63	E8
Vejen	63	C9
Vejer de la Frontera	66	D4
Vejle	63	C9
Velanidhia	75	G4
Velas, Cabo	132	E9
Velasco, Sierra de	138	C5
Velay, Monts du	65	E6
Velebit Planina	72	C3
Velestinon	75	G3
Velez Malaga	66	D4
Velez Rubio	67	E4
Velhas	138	H3
Velichayevskoye	79	H7
Velika Gorica	72	D3
Velika Kapela	72	C3
Velikaya *Russia*	78	H2
Velikaya *Russia*	85	W4
Velikaya Kema	88	F3
Veliki Kanal	72	E3
Velikiy Bereznyy	71	K4
Velikiye Luki	78	E4
Velikonda Range	92	E6
Veliko Turnovo	73	H4
Veliky Ustyug	78	H3
Velingara	104	C3
Velingrad	73	H4
Velizh	78	E4
Vella Gulf	114	H5
Vella Lavella	114	H5
Velletri	69	D5
Vellore	92	E6
Velsk	78	G3
Velt	78	J2
Velvestad	62	E4
Venado Tuerto	139	D6
Venafro	69	E5
Venaria	68	A3
Venda Nova	66	C2
Vendas Novas	66	B3
Vendome	65	D5
Vendsyssel	63	D8
Venecia	136	D6
Venezia	68	D3
Venezia, Golfo di	68	D3
Venezuela	136	D2
Venezuela Basin	134	C1
Venezuela, Golfo de	136	C1
Vengurla	92	D5
Veniaminof Volcano	118	Ag8
Venice *Italy*	68	D3
Venice *U.S.A.*	128	H6
Venkatapuram	92	F5
Venlo	64	G3
Vennesla	63	C7
Venta	63	J8
Ventimiglia	68	A4
Ventnor	53	F4
Ventry	59	B8
Ventspils	63	N8
Ventuari	136	D3
Ventura	126	C3
Venus Bay	113	K6
Venustiano Carranza *Mexico*	130	G5
Venustiano Carranza *Mexico*	131	N9
Vera *Argentina*	138	D5
Vera *Spain*	67	F4
Veracruz	131	L8
Veranopolis	138	F5
Veraval	92	D4
Verbania	68	B3
Vercelli	68	B3
Verdalsora	62	D5
Verde *Mexico*	131	L9
Verde *U.S.A.*	126	G3
Verden	70	C2
Verdigris	124	C8
Verdinho, Serra do	138	F3
Verdon	65	G7
Verdun	64	F4
Vereeniging	108	E5
Vereshchagino	78	J4
Verga, Cap	104	C3
Verin	66	C2
Verin Talin	77	K2
Verkhne-Avzyar	78	K5
Verkhnedvinsk	63	M9
Verkhne-Imanskiy	88	E3
Verkhneimbatskoye	84	D4
Verkhne Matur	84	D6
Verkhne Nildino	84	Ad4
Verkhne Skoblino	84	D5
Verkhnetulomskiy	62	P2
Verkhne Tura	78	K4
Verkhnevilyuysk	85	L4
Verkhniy Baskunchak	79	H6
Verkhniy Shar	78	J2
Verkhnyaya Amga	85	M5
Verkhnyaya Inta	78	L2
Verkhnyaya Toyma	78	H3
Verkhoturye	84	Ad5
Verkhovye	79	F5
Verkhoyansk	85	N3
Verkhoyanskiy Khrebet	85	M3
Verkhyaya Nildino	78	L3
Vermilion	119	N5
Vermilion Bay	128	G6
Vermilion Lake	124	D3
Vermillion	123	R6
Vermillion Bay	124	D2
Vermont	125	P5
Vernal	123	K7
Vernon *Canada*	122	E2
Vernon *France*	64	D4
Vernon *U.S.A.*	127	N3
Veroia	75	G2
Verona	68	C3
Versailles	64	E4
Vert, Cape	104	B3
Verviers	64	F3
Vervins	64	E4
Veryan Bay	52	C4
Veryuvom	78	L2
Veshenskaya	79	G6
Vesoul	65	G5
Vest-Agder	63	B7
Vesteralen	62	F2
Vestfjorden	62	F2
Vest-Fold	63	D7
Vestre Jakobselv	62	N1
Vestvagoy	62	E2
Vesuvio	69	E5
Vesyegonsk	78	F4
Veszprem	72	D2
Vetekhtina	85	K5
Vetlanda	63	F8
Vetluga *Russia*	78	H4
Vetluga *Russia*	78	H4
Vetluzskiy	78	H4
Vettore, Monte	69	D4
Veun Kham	93	L6
Veurne	64	E3
Vevey	68	A2
Veyatie, Loch	56	C2
Vezelay	65	E5
Vezere	65	D6
Vezirkopru	76	F2
Viacha	138	C3
Viamao	138	F6
Viana	137	J4
Viana do Castelo	66	B2
Viangchan	93	K5
Viareggio	68	C4
Viaur	65	E6
Viborg	63	C8
Vibo Valentia	69	F6
Vicecomodoro Marambio	141	W6
Vicente Guerrero	130	H6
Vicenza	68	C3
Vich	67	H2
Vichada	136	D3
Vichuga	78	G4
Vichy	65	E5
Vicksburg	128	G4
Vico	69	B4
Vicosa	137	K5
Victor Emanuel Range	114	C3
Victor Harbor	113	H6
Victoria *Argentina*	138	D6
Victoria *Northern Territory, Australia*	112	G2
Victoria *Victoria, Australia*	113	J6
Victoria *Cameroon*	105	G5
Victoria *Canada*	122	C3
Victoria *Chile*	139	B7
Victoria *Hong Kong*	90	E1
Victoria *Malaysia*	90	F4
Victoria *Seychelles*	82	D7
Victoria *U.S.A.*	128	D6
Victoria de las Tunas	132	J4
Victoria Falls	108	E3
Victoria Island	119	P1
Victoria, Lake	107	F3
Victoria Land	141	L4
Victoria, Mount *Myanmar*	93	H4
Victoria, Mount *Papua New Guinea*	114	D3
Victoria Nile	107	F2
Victoria Peak	118	K5
Victoria Strait	119	Q2
Victoriaville	125	Q3
Victoria West	108	D6
Victorica	139	C7
Victorville	126	D3
Vicuna	138	B6
Vidago	66	C2
Vidalia	129	L4
Vidareidi	62	Z14
Vididalur	62	X12
Vidim	84	G5
Vidimyri	62	V12
Vidin	73	G4
Vidisha	92	E4
Vidivellir	62	X12
Vidomlya	71	K2
Vidsel	62	J4
Viedma	139	D8
Viedma, Lago	139	B9
Viella	67	G1
Vienna *Austria*	68	F1
Vienna *Illinois*	124	F8
Vienna *Ohio*	125	K7
Vienne *France*	65	D5
Vienne *France*	65	F6
Vientiane	93	K5
Vieques	133	Q5
Vierwaldstatter See	68	B2
Vierzon	65	E5
Vieste	69	F5
Vietnam	93	L5
Vif	65	F6

Vigan	91	G2
Vigevano	68	B3
Viggiano	69	E5
Vigia	137	G4
Viglio, Monte	69	D5
Vigo	66	B1
Vigrestad	63	A7
Viiala	63	K6
Vijayawada	92	F5
Vijose	74	E2
Vik	62	E4
Vik	62	V13
Vikajarvi	62	M3
Vikersund	63	D7
Vikhorevka	84	G5
Vikna	62	D4
Viksoyri	63	B6
Vila	114	U12
Viladikars	77	K2
Vila Franca	66	B3
Vilaine	65	C5
Vilaller	67	G1
Vilanculos	109	G4
Vila Nova	137	F4
Vila Nova de Famalicao	66	B2
Vila Pouca de Aguiar	66	C2
Vila Real	66	C2
Vila Real de Santo Antonio	66	C4
Vila Velha	138	H4
Vila Velha de Rodao	66	C3
Vila Vicosa	66	C3
Vilcheka, Zemlya	80	H1
Viled	78	H3
Vileyka	71	M1
Vilhelmina	62	G4
Vilhena	136	E6
Viliga-Kushka	85	T4
Viljandi	63	L7
Vilkitskogo, Proliv	81	M2
Vilkovo	73	K3
Villa Abecia	138	C4
Villa Angela	138	D5
Villa Aroma	138	C3
Villa Bella	136	D6
Villa Bens	100	C3
Villablino	66	C1
Villacarrillo	66	E3
Villacastin	66	D2
Villach	68	D2
Villa Cisneros	100	B4
Villa Constitucion	138	D6
Villa de Cura	136	D2
Villadiego	66	D1
Villa Dolores	139	C6
Villafranca del Bierzo	66	C1
Villafranca de los Barros	66	C3
Villafranca del Penedes	67	G2
Villafranca di Verona	68	C3
Villaguay	138	E6
Villa Hayes	138	E5
Villahermosa	131	N9
Villa Huidobro	139	D6
Villa Iris	139	D7
Villajoyosa	67	F3
Villalba	66	C1
Villalon de Campos	66	D1
Villalpando	66	D2
Villa Maria	138	D6
Villamayor de Santiago	66	E3
Villa Montes	138	D4
Villanueva	130	H6
Villanueva de Cordoba	66	D3
Villanueva del Fresno	66	C3
Villanueva de los Castillejos	66	C4
Villanueva de los Infantes	66	E3
Villanueva y Geltru	67	G2
Villaputzu	69	B6
Villarcayo	66	E1
Villarejo	66	E2
Villarrica	138	E5
Villarrobledo	66	E3
Villasandino	66	D1
Villa Union *Argentina*	138	C5
Villa Union *Mexico*	127	M6
Villavicencio	136	C3
Villaviciosa	66	D1
Villazon	138	C4
Villedieu	64	C4
Villefort	65	E6
Villefranche-de-Rouergue	65	E6
Villefranche-sur-Saone	65	F6
Villena	67	F3
Villeneuve-sur-Lot	65	D6
Villeneuve-sur-Yonne	65	E4
Ville Platte	128	F5
Villers-Bocage	64	C4
Villers-Cotterets	64	E4
Villeurbanne	65	F6
Villodrigo	66	D1
Vilna	71	L1
Vilnius	71	L1
Vilnya	71	L1
Vilshofen	70	E4
Vilyuy	85	M4
Vilyuysk	85	L4
Vilyuyskoye Plato	84	H3
Vimmerby	63	F8
Vimperk	70	E4
Vina del Mar	139	B6
Vinaroz	67	G2
Vinas	63	F6
Vincennes	124	G7
Vincennes Bay	141	H5
Vinchina	138	C5
Vindelalven	62	J4
Vindeln	62	H4
Vindhya Range	92	E4
Vineland	125	N7
Vinga	73	F3
Vinh	93	L5
Vinh Loi	93	L7
Vinh Long	93	L6
Vinh Yen	93	L4
Vinica	73	G5
Vinkovci	72	E3
Vinnytsya	79	D6
Vinogradov	71	K4
Vipiteno	68	C2
Vir	72	C3
Virac	91	G3
Viramgam	92	D4
Virandozero	78	F3
Viransehir	77	H4
Virden	123	P3
Vire *France*	64	C4
Vire *France*	64	C4
Virfurile	73	G2
Virgenes, Cabo	139	C10
Virgin	126	E2
Virgin Gorda	133	Q5
Virginia *Ireland*	58	H5
Virginia *Minnesota*	124	D3
Virginia *U.S.A.*	125	L8
Virginia Beach	125	N8
Virginia Falls	118	L3
Virgin Islands	133	Q5
Virovitica	72	D3
Virrat	63	K5
Virudunagar	92	E7
Vis	72	D4
Visalia	126	C2
Visayan Sea	91	G3
Visby	63	H8
Viscount Melville Sound	120	E3
Visegrad	72	E4
Viseu *Brazil*	137	H4
Viseu *Portugal*	66	C2
Vishakhapatnam	92	F5
Vishera	78	K3
Vishnevets	71	L4
Vislanda	63	F8
Visoko	72	E4
Viso, Monte	68	A3
Vista	126	D4
Vistonis, Limni	75	H2
Vit	73	H4
Vitava	70	F4
Viterbo	69	D4
Viterog Planina	72	D3
Vitiaz Strait	114	C3
Vitichi	138	C4
Vitigudino	66	C2
Viti Levu	114	Q9
Vitim *Russia*	85	J5
Vitim *Russia*	85	J5
Vitina	75	G4
Vitoria	66	E1
Vitoria	138	H4
Vitoria da Conquista	137	J6
Vitoria de Santa Antao	137	K5
Vitre	64	C4
Vitry-le-Francois	64	F4
Vitsyebsk	78	E4
Vittangi	62	J3
Vittel	64	F4
Vittoria	69	E7
Vittorio Veneto	68	D3
Vivarais, Monts du	65	F6
Viver	67	F3
Vivero	66	C1
Vivi *Russia*	84	F4
Vivi *Russia*	84	F4
Vizcaino, Desierto de	126	F7
Vizcaino, Sierra	126	E7
Vize	76	B2
Vizhas	78	H2
Vizianagaram	92	F5
Vizinga	78	J3
Vizzavona	69	B4
Vladicin Han	73	G4
Vladikavkaz	77	L1
Vladimir	78	G4
Vladimirets	71	M3
Vladimirovka	79	J5
Vladimir Volynskiy	71	L3
Vladivostok	88	C4
Vlakherna	75	G4
Vlasenica	72	E3
Vlieland	64	F2
Vlissingen	64	E3
Vlore	74	E2
Vodice	72	C4
Vodlozero, Ozero	78	F3
Vogan	105	F4
Voghera	68	B3
Voh	114	W16
Vohemar	109	J2
Vohilava	109	J4
Vohimarina	109	J2
Vohipeno	109	J4
Voi	107	G3
Voiron	65	F6
Vojens	63	C9
Vojmsjon	62	G4
Vojnic	72	C3
Volary	70	E4
Volborg	123	M5
Volchansk	79	F5
Volda	62	B5
Volga	79	H6
Volga	73	F3
Volgodonsk	79	G6
Volgograd	79	G6
Volgogradskoye Vodokhranilishche	79	H6
Volgsele	62	G4
Volissos	75	H3
Volkhov *Russia*	78	E4
Volkhov *Russia*	78	E4
Volklingen	70	B4
Volkovysk	71	L2
Volksrust	108	E5
Volnovakha	79	F6
Volochankao	84	E2
Volochayevka	88	E1
Volochisk	71	M4
Volodskaya	78	G3
Vologda	78	F4
Volokon	84	H5
Volonga	78	H2
Volos	75	G3
Voloshka	78	F3
Volovets	71	K4
Volozhin	71	M1
Volpa	71	L2
Volsk	79	H5
Volta	104	F4
Volta, Lake	104	E4
Volta Redonda	138	H4
Volterra	68	C4
Volteva	78	G3
Volturno	69	E5
Volvi, Limni	75	G2
Volynskaya Vozvyshennost	71	L3
Volynskoje Polesje	71	L3
Volzhskiy	79	G6
Von Martius, Cachoeira	137	G6
Vopnafjordur	62	X12
Voras Oros	75	F2
Vordingborg	63	D9
Voriai Sporadhes	75	H3
Vorkuta	78	L2
Vormsi	62	K7
Voronezh	79	F5
Voronovo	71	L1
Vorontsovo	63	N8
Voronya	78	F2
Voroshno	78	H4
Vortsjarv	63	M7
Voru	63	M8
Vosges	64	G4
Voskresensk	78	F4
Voss *Norway*	63	B6
Voss *Norway*	63	B6
Vostochno-Sibirskoye More	85	T2
Vostochnyy *Russia*	88	D4
Vostochnyy *Russia*	88	J1
Vostock	141	H3
Vostretsovo	88	E3
Votice	70	F4
Votkinsk	78	J4
Votkinskoye Vodokhranilishche	78	K4
Vot Tande	114	T10
Vouga	66	C2
Vouziers	64	F4
Vowchurch	52	E2
Voxnan *Sweden*	63	F6
Voxnan *Sweden*	63	F6
Voynitsa	62	P4
Voy Vozh	78	J3
Voyvozh	78	K3
Voza	114	H5
Vozhayel	78	H3
Vozhega	78	G3
Vozhe, Ozero	78	F3
Voznesensk	79	E6
Voznesenye	78	F3
Vozvyshennost Karabil	95	R3
Vrancei, Muntii	73	J3
Vrangelya, Mys	85	P6
Vrangelya, Ostrov	81	U2
Vranje	73	G4
Vranov	71	J4
Vratsa	73	G4
Vrbas	72	D3
Vrbovsko	72	C3
Vrede	108	E5
Vrhnika	72	C3
Vrindavan	92	E3
Vrlika	72	D4
Vrondadhes	75	J3
Vrsac	73	F3
Vrsacki Kanal	73	F3
Vryburg	108	D5
Vryheid	108	F5
Vucitrn	73	F4
Vukovar	72	E3
Vulcan	73	G3
Vulcano, Isola	69	E6
Vung Tau	93	L6
Vunisea	114	R9
Vuokatti	62	N4
Vuollerim	62	J3
Vyartsilya	62	P5
Vyatka	78	J4
Vyatskiye Polyany	78	J4
Vyazemskiy	88	E2
Vyazma	78	E4
Vyazniki	78	G4
Vyborg	63	N6
Vychegda	78	H3
Vydrino	84	F5
Vygoda	73	L2
Vygozero, Ozero	78	F3
Vyhorlat	71	K4
Vyksa	78	G4
Vym	78	J3
Vyrnwy	52	D2
Vyshniy-Volochek	78	E4
Vysokoye	71	K2
Vytegra	78	F3
Vyzhva	71	L3

W

Wa	104	E3
Waal	64	F3
Waat	103	F6
Wabana	121	R8
Wabasca	119	N4
Wabash	124	G7
Wabe Gestro Wenz	103	H6
Wabe Shabele Wenz	103	H6
Wabigoon Lake	124	D2
Wabowden	119	R4
Wabush	121	N7
Waccasassa Bay	129	L6
Waco	128	D5
Wad Banda	102	E5
Waddan	101	J3
Waddeneilanden	64	F2
Waddenzee	64	F2
Waddesdon	53	G3
Waddington, Mount	118	K5
Wadebridge	52	C4
Wadena	124	C3
Wadi Gimal	96	B4
Wadi Halfa	102	F3
Wad Medani	103	F5
Wadomari	89	J10
Wad Rawa	103	F4
Wafra	97	H2
Wager Bay	120	J4
Wagga Wagga	113	K6
Wagin	112	D5
Wahai	91	H6
Waharoa	115	E2
Wahiawa	126	R10
Wahibah, Ramlat ahl	97	P6
Wahidi	96	H9
Wahoo	123	R7
Wahpeton	123	R4
Waialua	126	R10
Waianae	126	R10
Waiau *New Zealand*	115	A6
Waiau *New zealand*	115	D5
Waiau *New Zealand*	115	D5
Waibeem	91	J6
Waidhofen *Austria*	68	E2
Waidhofen *Austria*	68	E1
Waigeo	91	J6
Waiheke Island	115	E2
Waihi	115	E2
Waikabubak	91	F7
Waikato	115	E3
Waikerie	113	H5
Waikouaiti	115	C6
Wailuku	126	S10
Waimakariri	115	D5
Waimamaku	115	D1
Waimate	115	C6
Wainganga	92	E4
Waingapu	91	G7
Waini Point	136	F2
Wainwright	118	D1
Waiotapu	115	F3
Waiouru	115	E3
Waipa	115	E2
Waipahi	115	B7
Waipara	115	D5
Waipawa	115	F3
Waipiro	115	G3
Waipu	115	E1
Waipukurau	115	F3
Wairau	115	D4
Wairau Valley	115	D4
Wairio	115	B7
Wairoa	115	F3
Waitaki	115	C6
Waitangi	115	F6
Waitara	115	E3
Waitoa	115	E2
Waiuku	115	E2
Wajima	89	F7
Wajir	107	H2
Wakasa-wan	89	E8
Waka, Tanjung	91	H6
Wakatipu, Lake	115	B6
Wakaya	114	R8
Wakayama	89	E8
Wake	89	E8
Wakeeny	123	Q8
Wakefield	55	H3
Wakkanai	88	H3
Wakool *Australia*	113	J6
Wakool *Australia*	113	J6
Waku Kungo	106	C5
Walachia	73	H3
Walade	114	K6
Walagan	87	N1
Walbrzych	71	G3
Walcha	113	L5

220

Name	Page	Ref
Yagan	86	J3
Yagodnoye	85	R4
Yagodnyy	84	Ae5
Yahuma	106	D2
Yahyali	76	F3
Yaizu	89	G8
Yakacik	77	G4
Yakapinar	77	F4
Yako	104	E3
Yakoruda	73	G4
Yakovlevka	88	D3
Yakrik	86	E3
Yaksha	78	K3
Yakumo	88	H4
Yaku-shima	89	C10
Yakutat	118	H4
Yakutsk	85	M4
Yala	93	K7
Yalak	77	G3
Yalcizcam	77	K2
Yalinca	77	K4
Yalinga	102	D6
Yalkubul, Punta	131	Q7
Yallourn	113	K6
Yalong Jiang	93	K3
Yalova	76	C2
Yalpug	73	K2
Yalpug, Ozero	73	K3
Yalta	79	E7
Yaltushkov	73	J1
Yalu	87	P3
Yalu He	87	N2
Yalutorovsk	84	Ae5
Yalvac	76	D3
Yamagata	89	H6
Yamaguchi	89	C8
Yamal, Poluostrov	84	Ae2
Yaman Dagi	77	G3
Yambering	104	C3
Yambio	102	E7
Yambol	73	J4
Yamdena	91	J7
Yamethin	93	J4
Yamgort	78	L3
Yamin, Puncak	91	K6
Yamma Yamma, Lake	113	J4
Yamoussoukro	104	D4
Yampa	123	L7
Yamparaez	138	D3
Yampol	73	K1
Yam, Ramlat	96	G8
Yamsk	85	S5
Yamuna	92	E3
Yamunanagar	92	E2
Yamyshevo	84	B6
Yamzho Yumco	93	H3
Yana	85	P2
Yanam	92	F5
Yanan	93	L1
Yanaul	78	J4
Yanbual Bahr	96	D4
Yancheng	87	N5
Yanchi	87	K4
Yanchuan	87	L4
Yande	114	V16
Yandrakinot	118	A3
Yandun	86	F3
Yangarey	78	L2
Yangchun	93	M4
Yanghe	87	M5
Yangjiang	93	M4
Yangon (Rangoon)	93	J5
Yangquan	87	L4
Yangshan	93	M4
Yangshuo	93	M4
Yangtze	93	L2
Yangyang	88	B6
Yangzhou	87	M5
Yanina	75	F3
Yanisyarvi, Ozero	62	P6
Yanji	88	B4
Yankton	123	R6
Yanqi	86	F3
Yanshou	88	B3
Yantai	87	N4
Yantra	73	H4
Yanxing	88	C2
Yanzhou	87	M4
Yao	102	C5
Yaoquanzi	86	H4
Yaounde	105	H5
Yaoxiaolong	88	A1
Yapen	91	K6
Yapen, Selat	91	K6
Yap Islands	91	K4
Yaprakali	76	E2
Yaqui	127	H6
Yar *U.K.*	53	F4
Yar *Russia*	78	J4
Yaraka	113	J3
Yaransk	78	H4
Yarashev	73	J1
Yardley Hastings	53	G2
Yare	53	J2
Yarenga	78	H3
Yarensk	78	H3
Yariga-take	89	F7
Yarim	96	G9
Yarimca	76	C2
Yaritagua	136	D2
Yarkant He	92	E1
Yarkovo	84	Ae5
Yarlung Zangbo Jiang	93	H3
Yarma	76	E4
Yarmolintsy	73	J1
Yarmouth	121	N9
Yarongo	84	Ae3
Yaroslavl	78	F4
Yarraloola	112	D3
Yarra Yarra Lakes	112	D4
Yarroto	84	A3
Yarrow	57	E5
Yar Sale	84	A3
Yarsomovy	84	A4
Yartsevo *Russia*	84	D4
Yartsevo *Russia*	78	E4
Yarty	52	D4
Yarumal	136	B2
Yary	84	Ae3
Yasawa	114	Q8
Yasawa Group	114	Q8
Yaselda	71	L2
Yashbum	96	H9
Yashiro-jima	89	D9
Yashkul	79	H6
Yasin	92	D1
Yasinya	71	L4
Yasnaya Polyana	88	F3
Yass	113	K5
Yasuj	95	K6
Yasun Burun	77	G2
Yata	136	D6
Yatagan	76	C4
Yate	114	X17
Yates Center	128	E2
Yates Point	115	A6
Yathkyed Lake	119	R3
Yatsushiro	89	C9
Yatta Plateau	107	G3
Yatton	52	E3
Yauri Espinar	136	C6
Yavatmal	92	E4
Yavi, Cerro	136	D2
Yavlenka	84	Ae6
Yavorov	71	K4
Yavr	62	N2
Yavu	77	G3
Yavuzeli	77	G4
Yawatahama	89	D9
Yawng-hwe	93	J4
Yawri Bay	104	C4
Ya Xian	93	L5
Yaxley	53	G2
Yaya	84	D5
Yaygin	77	J3
Yayla	77	J3
Yayladagi	77	G5
Yazd	95	M6
Yazd-e Khvast	95	L6
Yazihan	77	H3
Yazoo City	128	G4
Yazovir Dimitrov	73	H4
Ybbs	68	E1
Ydseram	105	H3
Ye	93	J5
Yealmpton	52	C4
Yecheng	92	E1
Yecla	67	F3
Yedinka	88	G2
Yedinsty	79	D6
Yedoma *Russia*	78	G3
Yedoma *Russia*	78	J2
Yedondin	85	J6
Yeeda River	112	E2
Yefira	75	G3
Yefremov	79	F5
Yegorova, Mys	88	F3
Yegoryevsk	78	F4
Yei	102	F7
Yeijo, Cerro	136	B4
Yekaterinburg	84	Ad5
Yekaterininka	78	L3
Yekaterinoslavka	85	M6
Yekhegnadzor	77	L3
Yelabuga	78	J4
Yelantsy	84	H6
Yelets	79	F5
Yeletskiy	78	L2
Yelizarovo	84	Ae4
Yelizavety, Mys	85	Q6
Yelkenli	77	K3
Yell	56	A1
Yellandu	92	F5
Yellel	67	G5
Yellowhead Pass	119	M5
Yellowknife *Canada*	119	N3
Yellowknife *Canada*	119	N3
Yellow River	87	M4
Yellow Sea	87	N4
Yellowstone	123	M4
Yellowstone Lake	123	J5
Yell Sound	56	A1
Yelnya	78	E5
Yemen, Republic of	96	G9
Yemetsk	78	G3
Yemtsa	78	G3
Yen Bai	93	K4
Yendi	104	E4
Yengisar *China*	86	D4
Yengisar *China*	86	E3
Yengue	105	G5
Yenice *Turkey*	76	B3
Yenice *Turkey*	77	F3
Yenice *Turkey*	76	F4
Yeniceoba	76	E3
Yenikem	76	E3
Yenikoy *Turkey*	77	G4
Yenikoy *Turkey*	77	K2
Yenipazar	76	C4
Yenisarbademli	76	D4
Yenisehir	76	C2
Yenisey	84	D3
Yeniseysk	84	E5
Yeniseyskiy Zaliv	84	C2
Yenotayevka	79	H6
Yeoryios	75	G4
Yeovil	52	E4
Yeraliyev	79	J7
Yerbent	95	P2
Yerbogachen	84	H4
Yerema	84	H4
Yerevan	77	L2
Yergeni	79	G6
Yerkoy	76	F3
Yermak	84	B6
Yermaki	84	H5
Yermakovo	84	D3
Yermitsa	78	J2
Yermolayevo	79	K5
Yerofey-Pavlovich	85	L6
Yerolimin	75	G4
Yershov	79	H5
Yerupaja, Cerro	136	B6
Yerushalayim	94	B6
Yesil	77	G2
Yesilcay	76	C3
Yesilgolcuk	76	F3
Yesilhisar	76	F3
Yesilkent	77	G4
Yesilova	76	C4
Yesilova	76	E3
Yesilyurt	77	G3
Yessey	84	G3
Yeste	66	E3
Yeu, Ile d'	65	B5
Yevlakh	79	H7
Yevpatoriya	79	E6
Yevreyskaya Ao	88	D1
Ye Xian	87	M4
Yeysk	79	F6
Y-Fenni	52	D3
Yhu	138	E5
Yian	87	P2
Yiannitsa	75	G2
Yibin	93	K3
Yichang	93	M2
Yicheng	93	M2
Yichun	87	P2
Yidu	93	M2
Yidun	93	J2
Yigilca	76	D2
Yilan	88	B2
Yildizeli	77	G3
Yimianpo	88	A3
Yimuhe	87	N1
Yinchuan	87	K4
Yindarlgooda, Lake	112	E5
Yingde	93	M4
Ying He	93	M2
Yingkou	87	N3
Yining	86	E3
Yin Shan	87	K3
Yinxian	87	N6
Yioura *Greece*	75	H4
Yioura *Greece*	75	H3
Yirga Alem	103	G6
Yirol	102	F6
Yishui	87	M4
Yithion	75	G4
Yitong	87	P3
Yi Xian	87	N3
Yixing	87	M5
Yiyang	93	M3
Yliharma	62	N4
Yli-kitka	62	N3
Yli-li	62	L4
Ylitornio	62	K3
Ylivieska	62	L4
Y Llethr	52	C2
Yntaly	86	C2
Yoakum	128	D6
Yogope Yaveo	131	M9
Yogyakarta	90	E7
Yojoa, Laguna de	132	D7
Yokadouma	105	J5
Yokkaichi	89	F8
Yokohama *Japan*	89	G8
Yokohama *Japan*	88	H5
Yokosuka	89	G8
Yokote	88	H6
Yola	105	H4
Yolaina, Cordillera de	132	E9
Yom, Mae Nam	93	J5
Yonabaru	89	H10
Yonago	89	D8
Yon dok	89	B7
Yonezawa	89	H7
Yong-an	88	B5
Yongan	87	M6
Yongchang	86	J4
Yongchuan	93	L3
Yongdeng	93	K1
Yongfeng	87	M6
Yongfu	93	L4
Yonghe	87	L4
Yonghung	87	P4
Yongju	89	B7
Yongkang	87	N6
Yongren	93	K3
Yongsanpo	87	P4
Yongsheng	93	K3
Yonkers	125	P6
Yonne	65	E5
York *U.K.*	55	H3
York *Nebraska*	123	R7
York *Pennsylvania*	125	M7
York, Cape *Australia*	113	J1
York, Cape *Papua New Guinea*	114	C4
Yorke Peninsula	113	H6
Yorketown	113	H6
York Factory	119	S4
York, Kap	120	N2
Yorkshire Moors	55	J2
Yorkshire Wolds	55	J3
Yorkton	123	N2
York, Vale of	55	H2
Yoro	132	D7
Yosemite Valley	126	C2
Yosemite Village	126	C2
Yoshioka	88	H6
Yoshkar-Ola	78	H4
Yosu	87	P5
Yotsukura	89	H7
Youghal	59	G9
Youghal Bay	59	G9
Youhao	88	B2
You Jiang	93	L4
Youkounkoun	104	C3
Young	113	K5
Young, Cape	115	F6
Youngstown	125	K6
Youssoufia	100	D2
You Xian	93	M3
Youyang	93	L3
Yozgat	76	F3
Ypres	64	E3
Yreka	122	C7
Ysabel Channel	114	E2
Ysbyty Ifan	54	F3
Ysgubor-y-coed	52	D2
Yssingeaux	65	F6
Ystad	63	E9
Ythan	56	F3
Ytterbyn	62	K4
Ytterhogdal	63	F5
Yuanjiang	93	K4
Yuan Jiang	93	M3
Yuanling	93	M3
Yuanmou	93	K3
Yuanping	87	L4
Yuba City	126	B1
Yubari	88	H4
Yucatan Channel	132	E4
Yucebag	77	J3
Yuci	87	L4
Yudaokou	87	M3
Yudoma	85	P5
Yudu	87	M6
Yuendumu	112	G3
Yueqing	87	N6
Yuexi	93	N2
Yuexi He	93	K3
Yueyang	93	M3
Yug	78	H3
Yugorskiy Poluostrov	84	Ad3
Yugoslavia	72	F3
Yuhebu	87	K4
Yuhuan	87	N6
Yuilsk	84	Ae4
Yu Jiang	93	L4
Yukon	118	H3
Yukon Delta	118	C3
Yuksekova	77	L4
Yukta	84	H4
Yukutat Bay	118	H4
Yula	78	G3
Yuli	86	F3
Yulin *Guangxi, China*	93	M4
Yulin *Shaanxi, China*	87	K4
Yuma	126	E4
Yumen	86	H4
Yumenzhen	86	H3
Yumurtalik	77	F4
Yuna	133	N5
Yunak	76	D3
Yunaska Island	118	Ad9
Yuncheng	93	M2
Yungay	136	B5
Yunnan	93	K4
Yunotsu	89	D8
Yunta	113	H5
Yunxiao	87	M7
Yurga	84	C5
Yurgamysh	84	Ad5
Yuribey *Russia*	84	A3
Yuribey *Russia*	84	B2
Yurimaguas	136	B5
Yurla	78	J4
Yurya	78	H4
Yuryevets	78	G4
Yuryev Polskiy	78	F4
Yusef, Bahr	102	F2
Yushan	87	M6
Yushino	78	J2
Yushkozero	62	Q4
Yushu *Jilin, China*	87	P3
Yushu *Qinghai, China*	93	J2
Yushugou	86	F3
Yusta	79	H6
Yusufeli	77	J2
Yutian	92	F1
Yuty	138	E5
Yuxi	93	K4

Yu Xian	87	L4
Yuzha	78	G4
Yuzhno Kamyshovyy Khrebet	88	J2
Yuzhno-Sakhalinsk	88	J2
Yuzhnoye	88	J2
Yuzhnyy Bug	79	E6
Yverdon	68	A2
Yvetot	64	D4

Z

Zaandam	64	F2
Zabal Saghir, Nahr al	77	K5
Zabaykalsk	85	K7
Zab-e Kuchek	94	G3
Zabid	96	F9
Zabok	72	C2
Zabol	95	Q6
Zaboli	95	Q8
Zabren	71	G4
Zabrze	71	H3
Zaburunye	79	J6
Zacapa	132	C7
Zacapu	130	J8
Zacatecas	130	H6
Zacatecoluca	132	C8
Zacoalco	130	H7
Zadar	72	C3
Zadetkyi Kyun	93	J7
Zafora	75	J4
Zafra	66	C3
Zagan	70	F3
Zagazig	102	F1
Zagreb	72	C3
Zagros, Kuhha-ye	95	K6
Zagubica	73	F3
Zagyva	72	F2
Zahedan	95	Q7
Zahle	77	F6
Zahran	96	F8
Zahrat al Batin	94	F6
Zaindeh	95	L5
Zajecar	73	G4
Zakamensk	84	G6
Zakatly	79	H7
Zakharovka	86	C2
Zakhmet	95	R3
Zakho	94	F3
Zakho	77	K4
Zakinthos *Greece*	75	F4
Zakinthos *Greece*	75	F4
Zakros	75	J5
Zala	72	D2
Zalaegerszeg	72	D2
Zalalovo	72	D2
Zalau	73	G2
Zaleshchiki	73	H1
Zalim	96	F5
Zalingei	102	D5
Zamakh	97	H8
Zambales Mountains	91	G2
Zambeze	109	F3
Zambezi	106	D5
Zambia	107	E5
Zamboanga	91	G4
Zambrow	71	K2
Zamora *Ecuador*	136	B4
Zamora *Spain*	66	D2
Zamora de Hidalgo	130	H7
Zamosc	71	K3
Zancara	66	E3
Zanesville	124	K8
Zangezurskiy Khrebet	94	G2
Zanjan	94	J3
Zanjon	138	C6
Zante	75	F4
Zanthus	112	E5
Zanule	78	H3
Zanzibar	107	G4
Zanzibar Island	107	G4
Zaoyang	93	M2
Zaozernyy	84	E5
Zaozhuang	87	M5
Zapadna Morava	72	F3
Zapadnaya Dvina	78	E4
Zapadno Sibirskaya Ravnina	84	Ae4

Zapadnyy Chink Ustyurta	79	J7
Zapadnyy Sayan	84	E6
Zapata	128	C7
Zapata, Peninsula de	132	G3
Zapatosa	136	C2
Zapatoza, Cienaga de	133	L10
Zapiga	138	C3
Zapolyarnyy	62	P2
Zaporizhzhya	79	F6
Zapotlanejo	130	H7
Zap Suyu	77	K4
Zara *Turkey*	77	G3
Zara *Croatia*	72	C3
Zaragoza *Colombia*	136	C2
Zaragoza *Spain*	67	F2
Zarand *Iran*	95	K4
Zarand *Iran*	95	N6
Zarandului, Muntii	73	G2
Zaranj	95	Q6
Zarasai	63	M9
Zarate	139	E6
Zaraysk	78	F5
Zaraza	136	D2
Zardak	95	P4
Zard Kuh	95	K5
Zaria	105	G3
Zarnesti	73	H3
Zarqa	94	C5
Zarqan	95	L7
Zary	70	F3
Zarzaitine	101	G3
Zarzis	101	H2
Zashchita	84	C6
Zaskar Mountains	92	E2
Zaslavl	71	M1
Zastron	108	E6
Zatec	70	E3
Zatishye	73	K2
Zator	71	H4
Zavitinsk	85	M6
Zavodskoy	84	C6
Zawiercie	71	H3
Zawr, Ra's az	97	J3
Zaysan	86	E2
Zaysan, Ozero	86	E2
Zbarazh	71	L4
Zbaszyn	70	F2
Zborov	71	L4
Zbruch	71	M4
Zdolbunov	71	M3
Zdunska Wola	71	H3
Zebak	92	D1
Zebirget	96	C5
Zeebrugge	64	E3
Zeerust	108	E5
Zefat	94	B5
Zehdernick	70	E2
Zei Badinan	94	F3
Zei Koya	94	F4
Zeitz	70	E3
Zelenoborskiy	62	Q3
Zelenodolsk	78	H4
Zelenogorsk	63	N6
Zelenogradsk	71	J1
Zelenokumsk	79	G7
Zelina	72	D3
Zella Mehlis	70	D3
Zell am See	68	D2
Zelva	71	L2
Zemaitija	63	K9
Zemetchino	79	G5
Zemgale	63	L8
Zemio	102	E6
Zemlya Bunge	85	Q1
Zemmora	67	G5
Zempoala	131	K8
Zempoaltepec	131	M9
Zemun	72	F3
Zenica	72	D3
Zepce	72	E3
Zerbst	70	E3
Zerkow	71	G2
Zermatt	68	A2
Zernograd	79	G6
Zerqan	75	F2
Zestafoni	77	K1
Zetouji	87	N4

Zeya *Russia*	85	M6
Zeya *Russia*	85	M6
Zeysk	85	M6
Zeytinbagi	76	C2
Zeytinlik	77	J2
Zezere	66	C2
Zgierz	71	H3
Zgorzelec	70	F3
Zhabe	71	L4
Zhalanash	84	Ae6
Zhamansor	79	J6
Zhamshi	86	C2
Zhanabas	86	B2
Zhanatas	86	B3
Zhangbei	87	L3
Zhangdian	87	M4
Zhangguangcai Ling	88	B3
Zhangiz-Tobe	86	E2
Zhangjiakou	87	L3
Zhangping	87	M6
Zhangpu	87	M7
Zhangzhou	87	M7
Zhanjiang	93	M4
Zhaoan	87	M7
Zhaoguang	88	A1
Zhaoqing	93	M4
Zhaotong	93	K3
Zhaoxing	88	C2
Zhaoyuan	87	P2
Zharbulak	86	F2
Zharma	86	E2
Zharyk	86	C2
Zhashkov	79	E6
Zhatay	85	M4
Zhaxigang	92	E2
Zhejiang	87	M6
Zhelaniya, Mys	80	H2
Zheldyadyr	84	Ae7
Zheleznodorozhnyy *Russia*	84	G5
Zheleznodorozhnyy *Russia*	71	J1
Zheleznodorozhnyy *Russia*	78	J3
Zheleznogorsk	79	F5
Zhenan	93	L2
Zhengan	93	L3
Zhenglan Qi	87	M3
Zhengzhou	93	M2
Zhenjiang	87	M5
Zhenyuan	93	L3
Zherdevka	79	G5
Zhigalovo	84	H6
Zhigansk	85	L3
Zhijiang	93	L3
Zhilaya Kosa	79	J6
Zhiloy, Ostrov	79	J7
Zhitkovichi	79	D5
Zhlobin	79	E5
Zhmerinka	79	D6
Zhob *Pakistan*	92	C2
Zhob *Pakistan*	92	C2
Zhodino	78	D5
Zhokhova, Ostrov	85	S1
Zholymbet	84	A6
Zhongba	92	F3
Zhongdian	93	J3
Zhongwei	93	L1
Zhong Xian	93	L2
Zhongyaozhan	87	P1
Zhoushan Dao	87	M6
Zhovten	73	L2
Zhucheng	87	M4
Zhukovka	79	E5
Zhulong	87	M4
Zhuozi	87	L3
Zhuxi	93	L2
Zhuzhou	93	M3
Zhytomyr	79	D5
Ziama-Mansouria	67	J4
Zibo	87	M4
Zicavo	69	B5
Zidani Most	72	C2
Zidarovo	73	J4
Ziel, Mount	112	G3
Zielona Gora	70	F3
Ziesar	70	E2
Zigazinskiy	78	K5
Zigong	93	K3
Ziguinchor	104	B3

Zihuatanejo	131	J9
Zilair	79	K5
Zile	77	F2
Zilina	71	H4
Zima	84	G6
Zimapan	131	K7
Zimbabwe	108	E3
Zimkan	94	H4
Zimnicea	73	H4
Zimniy Bereg	78	G2
Zimovniki	79	G6
Zinapecuaro	131	J8
Zindajan	95	Q4
Zinder	101	G6
Zinjibar	96	G10
Zipaquira	136	C2
Zirje	72	C4
Zi Shui	93	M3
Zitacuaro	131	J8
Ziyun	93	L3
Zizhong	93	K3
Zlatibor	72	E4
Zlitan	101	H2
Zloczew	71	H3
Zlutice	70	E3
Zmigrod	71	G3
Zmiyevka	79	F5
Znamenka *Russia*	84	B6
Znamenka *Ukraine*	79	E6
Znamenskoye	84	A5
Znin	71	G2
Znojmo	70	G4
Zohreh	95	K6
Zoige	93	K2
Zolochev *Ukraine*	79	F5
Zolochev *Ukraine*	71	L4
Zolotinka	85	L5
Zolotonosha	79	E6
Zolotoy, Mys	88	G2
Zomba	107	G6
Zongo	106	C2
Zonguldak	76	D2
Zongyang	87	M5
Zonza	69	B5
Zorleni	73	J2
Zouar	102	C3
Zouerate	100	C4
Zrenjanin	72	F3
Zubayr, Jazair az	96	F9
Zuenoula	104	D4
Zufaf	96	E8
Zufar	97	M8
Zug	68	B2
Zugdidi	77	J1
Zugspitze	70	D5
Zujar	66	D3
Zula	96	D9
Zulia	133	L10
Zumbo	108	F3
Zumpango	131	K8
Zungeru	105	G4
Zuni	127	H3
Zuni Mountains	127	H3
Zunyi	93	L3
Zuo Jiang	93	L4
Zupanja	72	E3
Zuqaq	96	E7
Zurich	68	B2
Zurichsee	68	B2
Zuru	105	G3
Zut	72	C4
Zutphen	64	G2
Zuwarah	101	H2
Zuyevka	78	J4
Zvishavane	108	F4
Zvornik	72	E3
Zwedru	104	D4
Zweibrucken	70	B4
Zwettl	68	E1
Zwickau	70	E3
Zwiesel	70	E4
Zwolen	71	J3
Zwolle	64	G2
Zyrardow	71	J2
Zyryanka *Russia*	84	C2
Zyryanka *Russia*	85	S3
Zyryanovsk	86	E2